Honda
Civic & CR-V
Automotive
Repair
Manual

**by Robert Maddox
and John H Haynes**

Member of the Guild of Motoring Writers

Models covered:
Honda Civic - 2001 through 2010
Honda CR-V - 2002 through 2009
Does not include information specific to CNG or hybrid models

(42026-1S10-2)

ABCDE
FGHIJ
KLMNO
PQR
2

Haynes Publishing Group
Sparkford Nr Yeovil
Somerset BA22 7JJ England

Haynes North America, Inc
861 Lawrence Drive
Newbury Park
California 91320 USA

Acknowledgements

Wiring diagrams provided exclusively for Haynes North America, Inc. by Valley Forge Technical Information Services. Technical writers who contributed to this project include Mike Stubblefield, John Wegmann and Jeff Killingsworth.

© **Haynes North America, Inc. 2004, 2008, 2010**

With permission from J.H. Haynes & Co. Ltd.

A book in the Haynes Automotive Repair Manual Series

Printed in the U.S.A.

ISBN-13: 978-1-56392-849-9
ISBN-10: 1-56392-849-3

Library of Congress Control Number: 2010933666

While every attempt is made to ensure that the information in this manual is correct, no liability can be accepted by the authors or publishers for loss, damage or injury caused by any errors in, or omissions from, the information given.

Contents

Introductory pages

About this manual   0-5
Introduction to the Honda Civic and CR-V   0-5
Vehicle identification numbers   0-6
Recall information   0-7
Buying parts   0-11
Maintenance techniques, tools and working facilities   0-11
Booster battery (jump) starting   0-17
Jacking and towing   0-18
Fraction/decimal/millimeter equivalents   0-19
Conversion factors   0-20
Safety first!   0-21
Automotive chemicals and lubricants   0-22
Troubleshooting   0-23

Chapter 1
Tune-up and routine maintenance   1-1

Chapter 2   Part A
Single overhead camshaft (SOHC) engines   2A-1

Chapter 2   Part B
Double overhead camshaft (DOHC) engines   2B-1

Chapter 2   Part C
General engine overhaul procedures   2C-1

Chapter 3
Cooling, heating and air conditioning systems   3-1

Chapter 4
Fuel and exhaust systems   4-1

Chapter 5
Engine electrical systems   5-1

Chapter 6
Emissions and engine control systems   6-1

Chapter 7   Part A
Manual transaxle   7A-1

Chapter 7   Part B
Automatic transaxle   7B-1

Chapter 8
Clutch and driveline   8-1

Chapter 9
Brakes   9-1

Chapter 10
Suspension and steering systems   10-1

Chapter 11
Body   11-1

Chapter 12
Chassis electrical system   12-1

Wiring diagrams   12-25

Index   IND-1

Haynes mechanic and photographer with a 2003 Honda Civic

About this manual

Its purpose

The purpose of this manual is to help you get the best value from your vehicle. It can do so in several ways. It can help you decide what work must be done, even if you choose to have it done by a dealer service department or a repair shop; it provides information and procedures for routine maintenance and servicing; and it offers diagnostic and repair procedures to follow when trouble occurs.

We hope you use the manual to tackle the work yourself. For many simpler jobs, doing it yourself may be quicker than arranging an appointment to get the vehicle into a shop and making the trips to leave it and pick it up. More importantly, a lot of money can be saved by avoiding the expense the shop must pass on to you to cover its labor and overhead costs. An added benefit is the sense of satisfaction and accomplishment that you feel after doing the job yourself.

Using the manual

The manual is divided into Chapters. Each Chapter is divided into numbered Sections, which are headed in bold type between horizontal lines. Each Section consists of consecutively numbered paragraphs.

At the beginning of each numbered Section you will be referred to any illustrations which apply to the procedures in that Section. The reference numbers used in illustration captions pinpoint the pertinent Section and the Step within that Section. That is, illustration 3.2 means the illustration refers to Section 3 and Step (or paragraph) 2 within that Section.

Procedures, once described in the text, are not normally repeated. When it's necessary to refer to another Chapter, the reference will be given as Chapter and Section number. Cross references given without use of the word "Chapter" apply to Sections and/or paragraphs in the same Chapter. For example, "see Section 8" means in the same Chapter.

References to the left or right side of the vehicle assume you are sitting in the driver's seat, facing forward.

Even though we have prepared this manual with extreme care, neither the publisher nor the author can accept responsibility for any errors in, or omissions from, the information given.

NOTE

A **Note** provides information necessary to properly complete a procedure or information which will make the procedure easier to understand.

CAUTION

A **Caution** provides a special procedure or special steps which must be taken while completing the procedure where the Caution is found. Not heeding a Caution can result in damage to the assembly being worked on.

WARNING

A **Warning** provides a special procedure or special steps which must be taken while completing the procedure where the Warning is found. Not heeding a Warning can result in personal injury.

Introduction to the Honda Civic and CR-V

Civic models are available in two-door coupe, hatchback and four-door sedan body styles. CR-V models are available in a four-door SUV body style only.

The transversely mounted inline four-cylinder engine used in these models is equipped with electronic fuel injection.

The engine drives the front wheels through either a five-speed manual transaxle, six-speed manual transaxle, four-speed automatic transaxle, five-speed automatic transaxle or a Continuously Variable Transaxle (CVT) via independent driveaxles. On 4WD CR-V models, power is transmitted to the rear wheels (automatically) through a transfer case, driveshaft, differential and independent driveaxles, when the front wheels begin to lose traction.

The suspension is independent at all four corners, featuring front coil sping/shock absorber units, and either rear coil spring/shock absorber units or shock absorbers with independently mounted rear coil springs.

The power-assisted rack-and-pinion steering unit is mounted behind the engine.

The brakes are disc at the front and either discs or drums at the rear, with power assist standard. An Anti-lock Braking System (ABS) is available on most models.

Vehicle identification numbers

Modifications are a continuing and unpublicized process in vehicle manufacturing. Since spare parts manuals and lists are compiled on a numerical basis, the individual vehicle numbers are essential to correctly identify the component required.

Vehicle Identification Number (VIN)

This very important identification number is stamped on a plate attached to the dashboard inside the windshield on the driver's side of the vehicle (see illustration). It can also be found on the certification label located on the driver's side door post. The VIN also appears on the Vehicle Certificate of Title and Registration. It contains information such as where and when the vehicle was manufactured, the model year and the body style.

On the models covered by this manual the model year codes* are:

```
1 ..........................2001
2 ..........................2002
3 ..........................2003
4 ..........................2004
5 ..........................2005
6 ..........................2006
7 ..........................2007
8 ..........................2008
9 ..........................2009
A ..........................2010
```

* The model year code is the tenth character in the VIN.

Certification label

The certification label is attached to the driver's door post (see illustration). The plate contains the name of the manufacturer, the month and year of production, the Gross Vehicle Weight Rating (GVWR), the Gross Axle Weight Rating (GAWR) and the certification statement.

Engine identification numbers

The engine serial number can be found on the front side of the engine (see illustration).

The vehicle certification label is located on the end of the driver's door

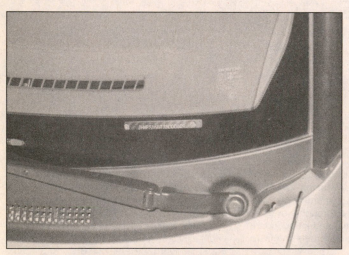

The Vehicle Identification Number (VIN) is located on a plate on top of the dash (visible through the windshield)

The engine number can be found stamped on the side of the engine block

Recall information

Vehicle recalls are carried out by the manufacturer in the rare event of a possible safety-related defect. The vehicle's registered owner is contacted at the address on file at the Department of Motor Vehicles and given the details of the recall. Remedial work is carried out free of charge at a dealer service department.

If you are the new owner of a used vehicle which was subject to a recall and you want to be sure that the work has been carried out, it's best to contact a dealer service department and ask about your individual vehicle - you'll need to furnish them your Vehicle Identification Number (VIN).

The table below is based on information provided by the National Highway Traffic Safety Administration (NHTSA), the body which oversees vehicle recalls in the United States. The recall database is updated constantly. For the latest information on vehicle recalls, check the NHTSA website at www.nhtsa.gov, www.safercar.gov, or call the NHTSA hotline at 1-888-327-4236.

Note: *This a partial list containing only the Honda dealer recalls. There are additional aftermarket recalls available; check the NHTSA website at www.nhtsa.gov or call the NHTSA hotline at 1-888-327-4236.*

Recall date	Recall campaign number	Model(s) affected	Concern
Jun 06, 2001	01V182000	2001 Civic	On certain models, the hose clamps on the filler neck tube have insufficient clamping force. The tube could disconnect from the fuel tank, resulting in fuel leakage. Fuel leakage, in the presence of an ignition source, could result in a fire.
Jun 06, 2001	01V183000	2001 Civic	On certain sedans, a small amount of water may have been left in the fuel pump electrical connector after testing. This residual water could cause the fuel pump to fail due to corrosion. If the pump stops working, the engine will stall without warning, increasing the risk of a crash.
Oct 17, 2001	01V329000	2001, 2002 Civic	On certain models, during the assembly process, the air cleaner box cover may have been damaged, and a broken plastic piece could travel into the intake chamber. If the plastic piece lodges in the throttle body, the throttle could stick in a partially open position. Although the driver can always stop the car by applying additional brake force, or by taking other actions (shift into neutral, turn off the ignition key, etc.), if the car continues to maintain speed when the driver is expecting it to slow, a crash could occur.

Recall information

Recall date	Recall campaign number	Model(s) affected	Concern
Nov 26, 2001	01V351000	2002 CR-V	On certain sport utility vehicles equipped with automatic seat belt pre-tensioners (the CR-V is equipped with two seat belt pre-tensioners - retractor and buckle - in both the driver and front passenger seating positions), some buckle pre-tensioners use a part that restricts the full motion of the mechanism. If these pretensioners activate in a crash, the seat belt could unlatch, leaving the front seat occupants unrestrained.
Dec 13, 2001	01V380000	2001 Civic	Certain models fail to comply with the requirements of Federal Motor Vehicle Safety Standard no. 209, "seat belt assemblies." Certain rear seat belt buckles were improperly manufactured. The rear seat belts will work properly and provide protection in a crash, but the occupants may experience difficulty unfastening the belt after the crash.
Feb 08, 2002	02V051000	2001 Civic	Certain sedans and coupes fail to comply with the requirements of Federal Motor Vehicle Safety Standard no. 209, "seat belt assemblies" Certain rear seat belt buckles were improperly manufactured. The rear seat belts will work properly and provide protection in a crash, but the occupants may experience difficulty unfastening the belt after the crash.
Sep 13, 2002	02V251000	2002 CR-V	On certain sport utility vehicles, the front seat anchorage nut strength is insufficient because the nuts were installed improperly.
Jul 28, 2003	03V274000	2002, 2003 CR-V	On certain sport utility vehicles equipped with automatic transmissions, excessive corrosion of the shift cable linkage could prevent the driver from shifting the automatic transmission into park. If the vehicle operator fails to engage the parking brake, the vehicle could roll and a crash could occur. Dealers will inspect the shift cable linkage for corrosion. If corrosion causes binding, they will replace the shift cable.
Oct 24, 2003	03V422000	2002 CR-V	On certain sport utility vehicles, metal particles in the key cylinder body could interfere with the interlock lever operation, making it possible to remove the ignition key without shifting the transmission to "park." If the vehicle operator does not shift to "park" before removing the key and fails to engage the parking brake, the vehicle could roll and a crash could occur.
Feb 24, 2004	04V086000	2001, 2002 Civic	On certain passenger vehicles, the low-beam terminal on the headlight wire harness can overheat and could cause the low beams to fail without warning. An unexpected loss of low beams could result in a crash.

Recall date	Recall campaign number	Model(s) affected	Concern
Jun 02, 2004	04V255000	2002, 2003, 2004 CR-V	On certain sport utility vehicles, the wire harness of the driver's front air bag was incorrectly wired.
Nov 04, 2004	04V526000	2005 CR-V	On certain passenger vehicles, the occupant position detection system's side sensor is not installed in the correct position and may fail to shut off the passenger's side impact airbag if the occupant is out-of-position. In the event of a crash, such an out-of position occupant may be injured by a deploying side airbag.
Nov 17, 2004	04V550000	2004, 2005 Civic SI	On certain passenger vehicles, some front seat belt anchors may have been installed with an incorrect washer, which could restrict anchor movement. As a result, the seat belt may be improperly positioned for certain occupants. An improperly positioned belt could increase the risk of injury in the event of a crash.
Nov 02, 2005	05V509000	2006 Civic	On certain passenger vehicles, the pedals were not properly installed and may come loose at the floor mounting. If the accelerator pedal is not inserted properly, the pedal can come loose from the pedal stopper, causing the throttle to become stuck, increasing the risk of a crash.
Jul 25, 2006	06V270000	2006 Civic, 2006 CR-V	On certain passenger vehicles, the owner's manuals contain incorrect contact information for the National Highway Traffic Safety Administration's (NHTSA) vehicle safety hotline. The language in the owner's manuals is not in accordance with the current mandatory requirements.
Aug 28, 2006	06V326000	2006 Civic	On certain 2-door passenger vehicles, the rear windshield or rear quarter glass panels do not properly adhere to the body of the car due to improper window opening preparation. The rear windshield or rear quarter glass panels may become loose, rattle or lift from the window opening or separate from the window while driving, increasing the safety hazard to traffic.
Aug 30, 2007	07V399000	2006, 2007 Civic 2006, 2007 Civic GX	On certain vehicles, the wheel speed sensor housing uses an O-ring seal to prevent leakage to or from the wheel bearing. If assembled improperly, the O-ring may not seal properly, allowing water to enter the wheel bearing and eventually cause damage to the bearing, especially in areas where use of road salt is prevalent. If the driver continues to drive with this condition, it is possible for the wheel bearing to become loose, which could cause the bearing to fail. This could cause a wheel to fall off of the vehicle, possibly resulting in a crash.

Recall date	Recall campaign number	Model(s) affected	Concern
Oct 13, 2008	08V535000	2008, 2009 Civic	On some Civic sedans, a bracket that covers the fuel hose connector is secured with a bolt and nut, but during assembly the nut was not installed. In the event of a crash, the bracket may become loose, which could result in damage to the fuel hose connector. A damaged connector could lead to a fuel leak and increases the risk of a fire.
Nov 11, 2008	08V593000	2001 Civic	On some Civic models, the driver's airbag inflator could produce excessive internal pressure. If an affected airbag deploys, the increased internal pressure may cause the inflator to rupture. Metal fragments could pass through the airbag cushion material, possibly causing injury to vehicle occupants.
Jun 30, 2009	09V259000	2001, 2002 Civic	On some Civic models, the driver's airbag inflator could produce excessive internal pressure. If an affected airbag deploys, the increased internal pressure may cause the inflator to rupture. Metal fragments could pass through the airbag cushion material, possibly causing injury to vehicle occupants.

Buying parts

Replacement parts are available from many sources, which generally fall into one of two categories - authorized dealer parts departments and independent retail auto parts stores. Our advice concerning these parts is as follows:

Retail auto parts stores: Good auto parts stores will stock frequently needed components which wear out relatively fast, such as clutch components, exhaust systems, brake parts, tune-up parts, etc. These stores often supply new or reconditioned parts on an exchange basis, which can save a considerable amount of money. Discount auto parts stores are often very good places to buy materials and parts needed for general vehicle maintenance such as oil, grease, filters, spark plugs, belts, touch-up paint, bulbs, etc. They also usually sell tools and general accessories, have convenient hours, charge lower prices and can often be found not far from home.

Authorized dealer parts department: This is the best source for parts which are unique to the vehicle and not generally available elsewhere (such as major engine parts, transmission parts, trim pieces, etc.).

Warranty information: If the vehicle is still covered under warranty, be sure that any replacement parts purchased - regardless of the source - do not invalidate the warranty!

To be sure of obtaining the correct parts, have engine and chassis numbers available and, if possible, take the old parts along for positive identification.

Maintenance techniques, tools and working facilities

Maintenance techniques

There are a number of techniques involved in maintenance and repair that will be referred to throughout this manual. Application of these techniques will enable the home mechanic to be more efficient, better organized and capable of performing the various tasks properly, which will ensure that the repair job is thorough and complete.

Fasteners

Fasteners are nuts, bolts, studs and screws used to hold two or more parts together. There are a few things to keep in mind when working with fasteners. Almost all of them use a locking device of some type, either a lockwasher, locknut, locking tab or thread adhesive. All threaded fasteners should be clean and straight, with undamaged threads and undamaged corners on the hex head where the wrench fits. Develop the habit of replacing all damaged nuts and bolts with new ones. Special locknuts with nylon or fiber inserts can only be used once. If they are removed, they lose their locking ability and must be replaced with new ones.

Rusted nuts and bolts should be treated with a penetrating fluid to ease removal and prevent breakage. Some mechanics use turpentine in a spout-type oil can, which works quite well. After applying the rust penetrant, let it work for a few minutes before trying to loosen the nut or bolt. Badly rusted fasteners may have to be chiseled or sawed off or removed with a special nut breaker, available at tool stores.

If a bolt or stud breaks off in an assembly, it can be drilled and removed with a special tool commonly available for this purpose.

Most automotive machine shops can perform this task, as well as other repair procedures, such as the repair of threaded holes that have been stripped out.

Flat washers and lockwashers, when removed from an assembly, should always be replaced exactly as removed. Replace any damaged washers with new ones. Never use a lockwasher on any soft metal surface (such as aluminum), thin sheet metal or plastic.

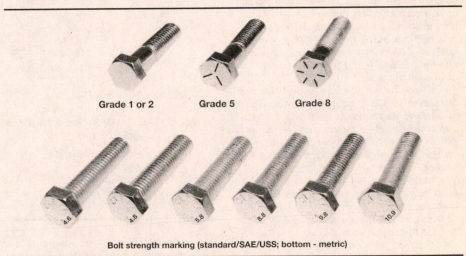

Grade 1 or 2   Grade 5   Grade 8

Bolt strength marking (standard/SAE/USS; bottom - metric)

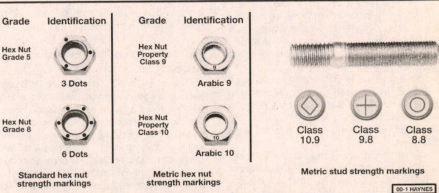

Grade	Identification	Grade	Identification
Hex Nut Grade 5	3 Dots	Hex Nut Property Class 9	Arabic 9
Hex Nut Grade 8	6 Dots	Hex Nut Property Class 10	Arabic 10

Standard hex nut strength markings

Metric hex nut strength markings

Class 10.9   Class 9.8   Class 8.8

Metric stud strength markings

00-1 HAYNES

Fastener sizes

For a number of reasons, automobile manufacturers are making wider and wider use of metric fasteners. Therefore, it is important to be able to tell the difference between standard (sometimes called U.S. or SAE) and metric hardware, since they cannot be interchanged.

All bolts, whether standard or metric, are sized according to diameter, thread pitch and length. For example, a standard 1/2 - 13 x 1 bolt is 1/2 inch in diameter, has 13 threads per inch and is 1 inch long. An M12 - 1.75 x 25 metric bolt is 12 mm in diameter, has a thread pitch of 1.75 mm (the distance between threads) and is 25 mm long. The two bolts are nearly identical, and easily confused, but they are not interchangeable.

In addition to the differences in diameter, thread pitch and length, metric and standard bolts can also be distinguished by examining the bolt heads. To begin with, the distance across the flats on a standard bolt head is measured in inches, while the same dimension on a metric bolt is sized in millimeters (the same is true for nuts). As a result, a standard wrench should not be used on a metric bolt and a metric wrench should not be used on a standard bolt. Also, most standard bolts have slashes radiating out from the center of the head to denote the grade or strength of the bolt, which is an indication of the amount of torque that can be applied to it. The greater the number of slashes, the greater the strength of the bolt. Grades 0 through 5 are commonly used on automobiles. Metric bolts have a property class (grade) number, rather than a slash, molded into their heads to indicate bolt strength. In this case, the higher the number, the stronger the bolt. Property class numbers 8.8, 9.8 and 10.9 are commonly used on automobiles.

Strength markings can also be used to distinguish standard hex nuts from metric hex nuts. Many standard nuts have dots stamped into one side, while metric nuts are marked with a number. The greater the number of dots, or the higher the number, the greater the strength of the nut.

Metric studs are also marked on their ends according to property class (grade). Larger studs are numbered (the same as metric bolts), while smaller studs carry a geometric code to denote grade.

It should be noted that many fasteners, especially Grades 0 through 2, have no distinguishing marks on them. When such is the case, the only way to determine whether it is standard or metric is to measure the thread pitch or compare it to a known fastener of the same size.

Standard fasteners are often referred to as SAE, as opposed to metric. However, it should be noted that SAE technically refers to a non-metric fine thread fastener only. Coarse thread non-metric fasteners are referred to as USS sizes.

Since fasteners of the same size (both standard and metric) may have different strength ratings, be sure to reinstall any bolts, studs or nuts removed from your vehicle in their original locations. Also, when replacing a fastener with a new one, make sure that the new one has a strength rating equal to or greater than the original.

Metric thread sizes	Ft-lbs	Nm
M-6	6 to 9	9 to 12
M-8	14 to 21	19 to 28
M-10	28 to 40	38 to 54
M-12	50 to 71	68 to 96
M-14	80 to 140	109 to 154

Pipe thread sizes		
1/8	5 to 8	7 to 10
1/4	12 to 18	17 to 24
3/8	22 to 33	30 to 44
1/2	25 to 35	34 to 47

U.S. thread sizes		
1/4 - 20	6 to 9	9 to 12
5/16 - 18	12 to 18	17 to 24
5/16 - 24	14 to 20	19 to 27
3/8 - 16	22 to 32	30 to 43
3/8 - 24	27 to 38	37 to 51
7/16 - 14	40 to 55	55 to 74
7/16 - 20	40 to 60	55 to 81
1/2 - 13	55 to 80	75 to 108

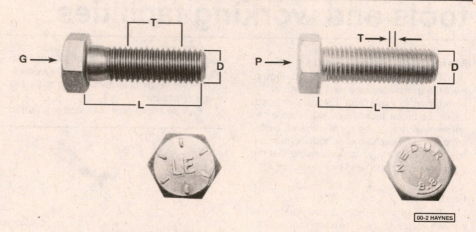

Standard (SAE and USS) bolt dimensions/ grade marks

G　Grade marks (bolt strength)
L　Length (in inches)
T　Thread pitch (number of threads per inch)
D　Nominal diameter (in inches)

Metric bolt dimensions/grade marks

P　Property class (bolt strength)
L　Length (in millimeters)
T　Thread pitch (distance between threads in millimeters)
D　Diameter

Tightening sequences and procedures

Most threaded fasteners should be tightened to a specific torque value (torque is the twisting force applied to a threaded component such as a nut or bolt). Overtightening the fastener can weaken it and cause it to break, while undertightening can cause it to eventually come loose. Bolts, screws and studs, depending on the material they are made of and their thread diameters, have specific torque values, many of which are noted in the Specifications at the beginning of each Chapter. Be sure to follow the torque recommendations closely. For fasteners not assigned a specific torque, a general torque value chart is presented here as a guide. These torque values are for dry (unlubricated) fasteners threaded into steel or cast iron (not aluminum). As was previously mentioned, the size and grade of a fastener determine the amount of torque that can safely be applied to it. The figures listed here are approximate for Grade 2 and Grade 3 fasteners. Higher grades can tolerate higher torque values.

Fasteners laid out in a pattern, such as cylinder head bolts, oil pan bolts, differential cover bolts, etc., must be loosened or tightened in sequence to avoid warping the com-

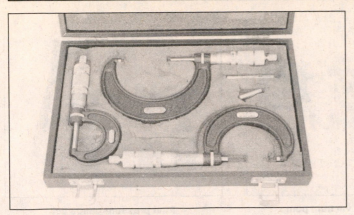

Micrometer set

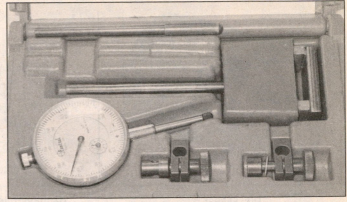

Dial indicator set

ponent. This sequence will normally be shown in the appropriate Chapter. If a specific pattern is not given, the following procedures can be used to prevent warping.

Initially, the bolts or nuts should be assembled finger-tight only. Next, they should be tightened one full turn each, in a criss-cross or diagonal pattern. After each one has been tightened one full turn, return to the first one and tighten them all one-half turn, following the same pattern. Finally, tighten each of them one-quarter turn at a time until each fastener has been tightened to the proper torque. To loosen and remove the fasteners, the procedure would be reversed.

Component disassembly

Component disassembly should be done with care and purpose to help ensure that the parts go back together properly. Always keep track of the sequence in which parts are removed. Make note of special characteristics or marks on parts that can be installed more than one way, such as a grooved thrust washer on a shaft. It is a good idea to lay the disassembled parts out on a clean surface in the order that they were removed. It may also be helpful to make sketches or take instant photos of components before removal.

When removing fasteners from a component, keep track of their locations. Sometimes threading a bolt back in a part, or putting the washers and nut back on a stud, can prevent mix-ups later. If nuts and bolts cannot be returned to their original locations, they should be kept in a compartmented box or a series of small boxes. A cupcake or muffin tin is ideal for this purpose, since each cavity can hold the bolts and nuts from a particular area (i.e. oil pan bolts, valve cover bolts, engine mount bolts, etc.). A pan of this type is especially helpful when working on assemblies with very small parts, such as the carburetor, alternator, valve train or interior dash and trim pieces. The cavities can be marked with paint or tape to identify the contents.

Whenever wiring looms, harnesses or connectors are separated, it is a good idea to identify the two halves with numbered pieces of masking tape so they can be easily reconnected.

Gasket sealing surfaces

Throughout any vehicle, gaskets are used to seal the mating surfaces between two parts and keep lubricants, fluids, vacuum or pressure contained in an assembly.

Many times these gaskets are coated with a liquid or paste-type gasket sealing compound before assembly. Age, heat and pressure can sometimes cause the two parts to stick together so tightly that they are very difficult to separate. Often, the assembly can be loosened by striking it with a soft-face hammer near the mating surfaces. A regular hammer can be used if a block of wood is placed between the hammer and the part. Do not hammer on cast parts or parts that could be easily damaged. With any particularly stubborn part, always recheck to make sure that every fastener has been removed.

Avoid using a screwdriver or bar to pry apart an assembly, as they can easily mar the gasket sealing surfaces of the parts, which must remain smooth. If prying is absolutely necessary, use an old broom handle, but keep in mind that extra clean up will be necessary if the wood splinters.

After the parts are separated, the old gasket must be carefully removed and the gasket surfaces cleaned. If you're working on cast iron or aluminum parts, stubborn gasket material can be soaked with rust penetrant or treated with a special chemical to soften it so it can be easily scraped off. **Caution:** *Never use gasket removal solutions or caustic chemicals on plastic or other composite components.* A scraper can be fashioned from a piece of copper tubing by flattening and sharpening one end. Copper is recommended because it is usually softer than the surfaces to be scraped, which reduces the chance of gouging the part. Some gaskets can be removed with a wire brush, but regardless of the method used, the mating surfaces must be left clean and smooth. If for some reason the gasket surface is gouged, then a gasket sealer thick enough to fill scratches will have to be used during reassembly of the components. For most applications, a non-drying (or semi-drying) gasket sealer should be used.

Hose removal tips

Warning: *If the vehicle is equipped with air conditioning, do not disconnect any of the A/C hoses without first having the system depressurized by a dealer service department or a service station.*

Hose removal precautions closely parallel gasket removal precautions. Avoid scratching or gouging the surface that the hose mates against or the connection may leak. This is especially true for radiator hoses. Because of various chemical reactions, the rubber in hoses can bond itself to the metal spigot that the hose fits over. To remove a hose, first loosen the hose clamps that secure it to the spigot. Then, with slip-joint pliers, grab the hose at the clamp and rotate it around the spigot. Work it back and forth until it is completely free, then pull it off. Silicone or other lubricants will ease removal if they can be applied between the hose and the outside of the spigot. Apply the same lubricant to the inside of the hose and the outside of the spigot to simplify installation.

As a last resort (and if the hose is to be replaced with a new one anyway), the rubber can be slit with a knife and the hose peeled from the spigot. If this must be done, be careful that the metal connection is not damaged.

If a hose clamp is broken or damaged, do not reuse it. Wire-type clamps usually weaken with age, so it is a good idea to replace them with screw-type clamps whenever a hose is removed.

Tools

A selection of good tools is a basic requirement for anyone who plans to maintain and repair his or her own vehicle. For the owner who has few tools, the initial investment might seem high, but when compared to the spiraling costs of professional auto maintenance and repair, it is a wise one.

To help the owner decide which tools are needed to perform the tasks detailed in this manual, the following tool lists are offered: *Maintenance and minor repair, Repair/overhaul* and *Special.*

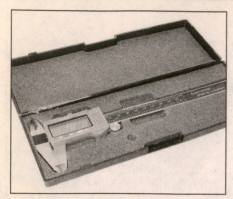

Dial caliper

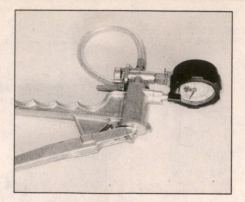

Hand-operated vacuum pump

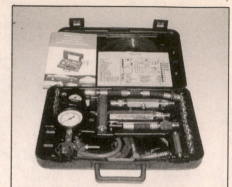

Fuel pressure gauge set

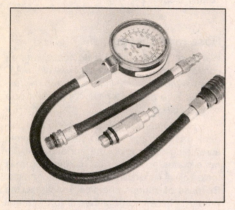

Compression gauge with spark plug hole adapter

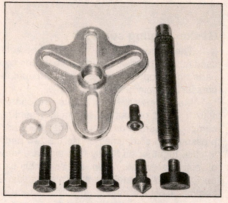

Damper/steering wheel puller

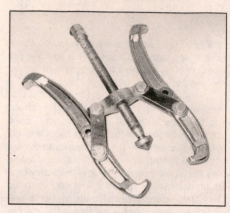

General purpose puller

Hydraulic lifter removal tool

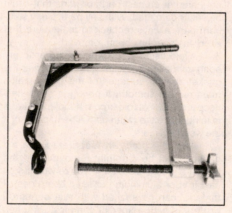

Valve spring compressor

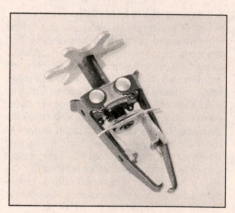

Valve spring compressor

Ridge reamer

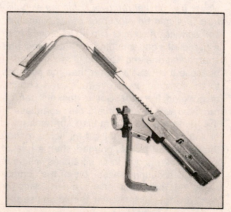

Piston ring groove cleaning tool

Ring removal/installation tool

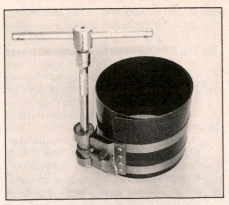

Ring compressor

Cylinder hone

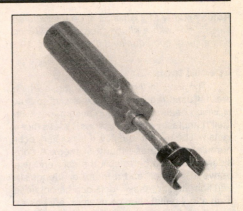

Brake hold-down spring tool

Torque angle gauge

Clutch plate alignment tool

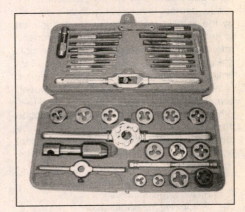

Tap and die set

The newcomer to practical mechanics should start off with the *maintenance and minor repair* tool kit, which is adequate for the simpler jobs performed on a vehicle. Then, as confidence and experience grow, the owner can tackle more difficult tasks, buying additional tools as they are needed. Eventually the basic kit will be expanded into the *repair and overhaul* tool set. Over a period of time, the experienced do-it-yourselfer will assemble a tool set complete enough for most repair and overhaul procedures and will add tools from the special category when it is felt that the expense is justified by the frequency of use.

Maintenance and minor repair tool kit

The tools in this list should be considered the minimum required for performance of routine maintenance, servicing and minor repair work. We recommend the purchase of combination wrenches (box-end and open-end combined in one wrench). While more expensive than open end wrenches, they offer the advantages of both types of wrench.

Combination wrench set (1/4-inch to 1 inch or 6 mm to 19 mm)
Adjustable wrench, 8 inch
Spark plug wrench with rubber insert
Spark plug gap adjusting tool
Feeler gauge set
Brake bleeder wrench
Standard screwdriver (5/16-inch x 6 inch)

Phillips screwdriver (No. 2 x 6 inch)
Combination pliers - 6 inch
Hacksaw and assortment of blades
Tire pressure gauge
Grease gun
Oil can
Fine emery cloth
Wire brush
Battery post and cable cleaning tool
Oil filter wrench
Funnel (medium size)
Safety goggles
Jackstands (2)
Drain pan

Note: *If basic tune-ups are going to be part of routine maintenance, it will be necessary to purchase a good quality stroboscopic timing light and combination tachometer/dwell meter. Although they are included in the list of special tools, it is mentioned here because they are absolutely necessary for tuning most vehicles properly.*

Repair and overhaul tool set

These tools are essential for anyone who plans to perform major repairs and are in addition to those in the maintenance and minor repair tool kit. Included is a comprehensive set of sockets which, though expensive, are invaluable because of their versatility, especially when various extensions and drives are available. We recommend the 1/2-inch drive over the 3/8-inch drive. Although the larger drive is bulky and more expensive, it has the

capacity of accepting a very wide range of large sockets. Ideally, however, the mechanic should have a 3/8-inch drive set and a 1/2-inch drive set.

Socket set(s)
Reversible ratchet
Extension - 10 inch
Universal joint
Torque wrench (same size drive as sockets)
Ball peen hammer - 8 ounce
Soft-face hammer (plastic/rubber)
Standard screwdriver (1/4-inch x 6 inch)
Standard screwdriver (stubby - 5/16-inch)
Phillips screwdriver (No. 3 x 8 inch)
Phillips screwdriver (stubby - No. 2)
Pliers - vise grip
Pliers - lineman's
Pliers - needle nose
Pliers - snap-ring (internal and external)
Cold chisel - 1/2-inch
Scribe
Scraper (made from flattened copper tubing)
Centerpunch
Pin punches (1/16, 1/8, 3/16-inch)
Steel rule/straightedge - 12 inch
Allen wrench set (1/8 to 3/8-inch or 4 mm to 10 mm)
A selection of files
Wire brush (large)
Jackstands (second set)
Jack (scissor or hydraulic type)

Note: *Another tool which is often useful is an electric drill with a chuck capacity of 3/8-inch and a set of good quality drill bits.*

Special tools

The tools in this list include those which are not used regularly, are expensive to buy, or which need to be used in accordance with their manufacturer's instructions. Unless these tools will be used frequently, it is not very economical to purchase many of them. A consideration would be to split the cost and use between yourself and a friend or friends. In addition, most of these tools can be obtained from a tool rental shop on a temporary basis.

This list primarily contains only those tools and instruments widely available to the public, and not those special tools produced by the vehicle manufacturer for distribution to dealer service departments. Occasionally, references to the manufacturer's special tools are included in the text of this manual. Generally, an alternative method of doing the job without the special tool is offered. However, sometimes there is no alternative to their use. Where this is the case, and the tool cannot be purchased or borrowed, the work should be turned over to the dealer service department or an automotive repair shop.

> *Valve spring compressor*
> *Piston ring groove cleaning tool*
> *Piston ring compressor*
> *Piston ring installation tool*
> *Cylinder compression gauge*
> *Cylinder ridge reamer*
> *Cylinder surfacing hone*
> *Cylinder bore gauge*
> *Micrometers and/or dial calipers*
> *Hydraulic lifter removal tool*
> *Balljoint separator*
> *Universal-type puller*
> *Impact screwdriver*
> *Dial indicator set*
> *Stroboscopic timing light (inductive pick-up)*
> *Hand operated vacuum/pressure pump*
> *Tachometer/dwell meter*
> *Universal electrical multimeter*
> *Cable hoist*
> *Brake spring removal and installation tools*
> *Floor jack*

Buying tools

For the do-it-yourselfer who is just starting to get involved in vehicle maintenance and repair, there are a number of options available when purchasing tools. If maintenance and minor repair is the extent of the work to be done, the purchase of individual tools is satisfactory. If, on the other hand, extensive work is planned, it would be a good idea to purchase a modest tool set from one of the large retail chain stores. A set can usually be bought at a substantial savings over the individual tool prices, and they often come with a tool box. As additional tools are needed, add-on sets,

individual tools and a larger tool box can be purchased to expand the tool selection. Building a tool set gradually allows the cost of the tools to be spread over a longer period of time and gives the mechanic the freedom to choose only those tools that will actually be used.

Tool stores will often be the only source of some of the special tools that are needed, but regardless of where tools are bought, try to avoid cheap ones, especially when buying screwdrivers and sockets, because they won't last very long. The expense involved in replacing cheap tools will eventually be greater than the initial cost of quality tools.

Care and maintenance of tools

Good tools are expensive, so it makes sense to treat them with respect. Keep them clean and in usable condition and store them properly when not in use. Always wipe off any dirt, grease or metal chips before putting them away. Never leave tools lying around in the work area. Upon completion of a job, always check closely under the hood for tools that may have been left there so they won't get lost during a test drive.

Some tools, such as screwdrivers, pliers, wrenches and sockets, can be hung on a panel mounted on the garage or workshop wall, while others should be kept in a tool box or tray. Measuring instruments, gauges, meters, etc. must be carefully stored where they cannot be damaged by weather or impact from other tools.

When tools are used with care and stored properly, they will last a very long time. Even with the best of care, though, tools will wear out if used frequently. When a tool is damaged or worn out, replace it. Subsequent jobs will be safer and more enjoyable if you do.

How to repair damaged threads

Sometimes, the internal threads of a nut or bolt hole can become stripped, usually from overtightening. Stripping threads is an all-too-common occurrence, especially when working with aluminum parts, because aluminum is so soft that it easily strips out.

Usually, external or internal threads are only partially stripped. After they've been cleaned up with a tap or die, they'll still work. Sometimes, however, threads are badly damaged. When this happens, you've got three choices:

1) *Drill and tap the hole to the next suitable oversize and install a larger diameter bolt, screw or stud.*
2) *Drill and tap the hole to accept a threaded plug, then drill and tap the plug to the original screw size. You can also buy a plug already threaded to the original size. Then you simply drill a hole to the specified size, then run the threaded*

plug into the hole with a bolt and jam nut. Once the plug is fully seated, remove the jam nut and bolt.
3) *The third method uses a patented thread repair kit like Heli-Coil or Slimsert. These easy-to-use kits are designed to repair damaged threads in straight-through holes and blind holes. Both are available as kits which can handle a variety of sizes and thread patterns. Drill the hole, then tap it with the special included tap. Install the Heli-Coil and the hole is back to its original diameter and thread pitch.*

Regardless of which method you use, be sure to proceed calmly and carefully. A little impatience or carelessness during one of these relatively simple procedures can ruin your whole day's work and cost you a bundle if you wreck an expensive part.

Working facilities

Not to be overlooked when discussing tools is the workshop. If anything more than routine maintenance is to be carried out, some sort of suitable work area is essential.

It is understood, and appreciated, that many home mechanics do not have a good workshop or garage available, and end up removing an engine or doing major repairs outside. It is recommended, however, that the overhaul or repair be completed under the cover of a roof.

A clean, flat workbench or table of comfortable working height is an absolute necessity. The workbench should be equipped with a vise that has a jaw opening of at least four inches.

As mentioned previously, some clean, dry storage space is also required for tools, as well as the lubricants, fluids, cleaning solvents, etc. which soon become necessary.

Sometimes waste oil and fluids, drained from the engine or cooling system during normal maintenance or repairs, present a disposal problem. To avoid pouring them on the ground or into a sewage system, pour the used fluids into large containers, seal them with caps and take them to an authorized disposal site or recycling center. Plastic jugs, such as old antifreeze containers, are ideal for this purpose.

Always keep a supply of old newspapers and clean rags available. Old towels are excellent for mopping up spills. Many mechanics use rolls of paper towels for most work because they are readily available and disposable. To help keep the area under the vehicle clean, a large cardboard box can be cut open and flattened to protect the garage or shop floor.

Whenever working over a painted surface, such as when leaning over a fender to service something under the hood, always cover it with an old blanket or bedspread to protect the finish. Vinyl covered pads, made especially for this purpose, are available at auto parts stores.

Booster battery (jump) starting

Observe the following precautions when using a booster battery to start a vehicle:

a) *Before connecting the booster battery, make sure the ignition switch is in the Off position.*
b) *Turn off the lights, heater and other electrical loads.*
c) *Your eyes should be shielded. Safety goggles are a good idea.*
d) *Make sure the booster battery is the same voltage as the dead one in the vehicle.*
e) *The two vehicles MUST NOT TOUCH each other.*
f) *Make sure the transmission is in Park.*
g) *If the booster battery is not a maintenance-free type, remove the vent caps and lay a cloth over the vent holes.*

Connect the red jumper cable to the positive (+) terminals of each battery.

Connect one end of the black cable to the negative (-) terminal of the booster battery. The other end of this cable should be connected to a good ground on the engine block **(see illustration)**. Make sure the cable will not come into contact with the fan, drivebelts or other moving parts of the engine.

Start the engine using the booster battery, then, with the engine running at idle speed, disconnect the jumper cables in the reverse order of connection

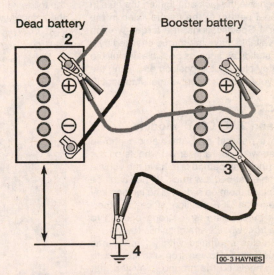

Make the booster battery cable connections in the numerical order shown (note that the negative cable of the booster battery is NOT attached to the negative terminal of the dead battery)

Jacking and towing

Jacking

The jack supplied with the vehicle should only be used for raising the vehicle for changing a tire or placing jackstands under the frame. **Warning:** *Never crawl under the vehicle or start the engine when the jack is being used as the only means of support.*

All vehicles are supplied with a scissors-type jack. When jacking the vehicle, it should be engaged with the notch in the rocker panel flange **(see illustration).**

The vehicle should be on level ground with the wheels blocked and the transmission in Park. Pry off the hub cap (if equipped) using the tapered end of the lug wrench. Loosen the lug nuts one-half turn and leave them in place until the wheel is raised off the ground.

Place the jack under the side of the vehicle in the indicated position. Use the supplied wrench to turn the jackscrew clockwise until the wheel is raised off the ground. Remove the lug nuts, pull off the wheel and install the spare.

With the beveled side in, install the lug nuts and tighten them until snug. Lower the vehicle by turning the jackscrew counterclockwise. Remove the jack and tighten the nuts in a diagonal pattern to the torque listed in the Chapter 1 Specifications. If a torque wrench is not available, have the torque checked by a service station as soon as possible. Install the hubcap by placing it in position and using the heel of your hand or a rubber mallet to seat it.

Towing
Civic and 2WD CR-V models

As a general rule, the vehicle should be towed with the front (drive) wheels off the ground (the best method is to have the vehicle placed on a flat-bed tow truck). If they can't be raised, place them on a dolly. The ignition key must be in the OFF position, since the steering lock mechanism isn't strong enough to hold the front wheels straight while towing.

Vehicles equipped with an automatic transaxle can be towed from the front with all four wheels on the ground, provided that speeds don't exceed 35 mph and the distance is not over 50 miles. Before towing, check the transmission fluid level (see Chapter 1). If the

level is below the HOT line on the dipstick, add fluid or use a towing dolly. Additionally, perform the following steps:

a) Release the parking brake
b) Start the engine
c) Move the transaxle gear selector into D4, then to Neutral
d) Turn off the engine
e) Place the ignition key in the OFF (not the LOCK position).

Caution: *Never tow a vehicle with an automatic transaxle from the rear with the front wheels on the ground.*

4WD CR-V models

The preferred method for towing these models is on a flat-bed tow truck. Tow trucks that use wheel-lift or sling-type equipment cannot be used. These models *can* be towed with all four wheels on the ground, provided that the proper towing equipment is used, towing speed does not exceed 65 miles per hour, and the ignition key is turned to the accessory position (with all accessories turned off so the battery doesn't go dead). Additionally, before towing, the following procedure must be performed, or the transaxle will be severely damaged:

a) Start the engine
b) Depress the brake pedal and move the shift lever through all of the gear positions

c) Move the shift lever to the D position, then to the Neutral position
d) Release the parking brake
e) Turn the engine off, but leave the ignition key in the accessory position (with all accessories turned off)

This procedure must be performed at the beginning of each towing day, and every 300 miles, or damage to the transaxle will occur. **Caution:** *Towing a 4WD CR-V with one end of the vehicle raised will cause damage to the 4WD system.*

All models

When towing a vehicle equipped with a manual transaxle or Continuously Variable Transaxle with all four wheels on the ground, be sure to place the shift lever in neutral and release the parking brake.

Equipment specifically designed for towing should be used. It should be attached to the main structural members of the vehicle, not the bumpers or brackets.

Safety is a major consideration when towing and all applicable state and local laws must be obeyed. A safety chain system must be used at all times. Remember that power steering and power brakes will not work with the engine off.

The jack fits over the rocker panel flange (there are two jacking points on each side of the vehicle)

DECIMALS to MILLIMETERS

Decimal	mm	Decimal	mm
0.001	0.0254	0.500	12.7000
0.002	0.0508	0.510	12.9540
0.003	0.0762	0.520	13.2080
0.004	0.1016	0.530	13.4620
0.005	0.1270	0.540	13.7160
0.006	0.1524	0.550	13.9700
0.007	0.1778	0.560	14.2240
0.008	0.2032	0.570	14.4780
0.009	0.2286	0.580	14.7320
		0.590	14.9860
0.010	0.2540		
0.020	0.5080		
0.030	0.7620		
0.040	1.0160	0.600	15.2400
0.050	1.2700	0.610	15.4940
0.060	1.5240	0.620	15.7480
0.070	1.7780	0.630	16.0020
0.080	2.0320	0.640	16.2560
0.090	2.2860	0.650	16.5100
		0.660	16.7640
0.100	2.5400	0.670	17.0180
0.110	2.7940	0.680	17.2720
0.120	3.0480	0.690	17.5260
0.130	3.3020		
0.140	3.5560		
0.150	3.8100		
0.160	4.0640	0.700	17.7800
0.170	4.3180	0.710	18.0340
0.180	4.5720	0.720	18.2880
0.190	4.8260	0.730	18.5420
		0.740	18.7960
0.200	5.0800	0.750	19.0500
0.210	5.3340	0.760	19.3040
0.220	5.5880	0.770	19.5580
0.230	5.8420	0.780	19.8120
0.240	6.0960	0.790	20.0660
0.250	6.3500		
0.260	6.6040		
0.270	6.8580	0.800	20.3200
0.280	7.1120	0.810	20.5740
0.290	7.3660	0.820	21.8280
		0.830	21.0820
0.300	7.6200	0.840	21.3360
0.310	7.8740	0.850	21.5900
0.320	8.1280	0.860	21.8440
0.330	8.3820	0.870	22.0980
0.340	8.6360	0.880	22.3520
0.350	8.8900	0.890	22.6060
0.360	9.1440		
0.370	9.3980		
0.380	9.6520		
0.390	9.9060	0.900	22.8600
0.400	10.1600	0.910	23.1140
0.410	10.4140	0.920	23.3680
0.420	10.6680	0.930	23.6220
0.430	10.9220	0.940	23.8760
0.440	11.1760	0.950	24.1300
0.450	11.4300	0.960	24.3840
0.460	11.6840	0.970	24.6380
0.470	11.9380	0.980	24.8920
0.480	12.1920	0.990	25.1460
0.490	12.4460	1.000	25.4000

FRACTIONS to DECIMALS to MILLIMETERS

Fraction	Decimal	mm	Fraction	Decimal	mm
1/64	0.0156	0.3969	33/64	0.5156	13.0969
1/32	0.0312	0.7938	17/32	0.5312	13.4938
3/64	0.0469	1.1906	35/64	0.5469	13.8906
1/16	0.0625	1.5875	9/16	0.5625	14.2875
5/64	0.0781	1.9844	37/64	0.5781	14.6844
3/32	0.0938	2.3812	19/32	0.5938	15.0812
7/64	0.1094	2.7781	39/64	0.6094	15.4781
1/8	0.1250	3.1750	5/8	0.6250	15.8750
9/64	0.1406	3.5719	41/64	0.6406	16.2719
5/32	0.1562	3.9688	21/32	0.6562	16.6688
11/64	0.1719	4.3656	43/64	0.6719	17.0656
3/16	0.1875	4.7625	11/16	0.6875	17.4625
13/64	0.2031	5.1594	45/64	0.7031	17.8594
7/32	0.2188	5.5562	23/32	0.7188	18.2562
15/64	0.2344	5.9531	47/64	0.7344	18.6531
1/4	0.2500	6.3500	3/4	0.7500	19.0500
17/64	0.2656	6.7469	49/64	0.7656	19.4469
9/32	0.2812	7.1438	25/32	0.7812	19.8438
19/64	0.2969	7.5406	51/64	0.7969	20.2406
5/16	0.3125	7.9375	13/16	0.8125	20.6375
21/64	0.3281	8.3344	53/64	0.8281	21.0344
11/32	0.3438	8.7312	27/32	0.8438	21.4312
23/64	0.3594	9.1281	55/64	0.8594	21.8281
3/8	0.3750	9.5250	7/8	0.8750	22.2250
25/64	0.3906	9.9219	57/64	0.8906	22.6219
13/32	0.4062	10.3188	29/32	0.9062	23.0188
27/64	0.4219	10.7156	59/64	0.9219	23.4156
7/16	0.4375	11.1125	15/16	0.9375	23.8125
29/64	0.4531	11.5094	61/64	0.9531	24.2094
15/32	0.4688	11.9062	31/32	0.9688	24.6062
31/64	0.4844	12.3031	63/64	0.9844	25.0031
1/2	0.5000	12.7000	1	1.0000	25.4000

Conversion factors

Length (distance)

Inches (in)	X 25.4	= Millimeters (mm)	X 0.0394	= Inches (in)
Feet (ft)	X 0.305	= Meters (m)	X 3.281	= Feet (ft)
Miles	X 1.609	= Kilometers (km)	X 0.621	= Miles

Volume (capacity)

Cubic inches (cu in; in^3)	X 16.387	= Cubic centimeters (cc; cm^3)	X 0.061	= Cubic inches (cu in; in^3)
Imperial pints (Imp pt)	X 0.568	= Liters (l)	X 1.76	= Imperial pints (Imp pt)
Imperial quarts (Imp qt)	X 1.137	= Liters (l)	X 0.88	= Imperial quarts (Imp qt)
Imperial quarts (Imp qt)	X 1.201	= US quarts (US qt)	X 0.833	= Imperial quarts (Imp qt)
US quarts (US qt)	X 0.946	= Liters (l)	X 1.057	= US quarts (US qt)
Imperial gallons (Imp gal)	X 4.546	= Liters (l)	X 0.22	= Imperial gallons (Imp gal)
Imperial gallons (Imp gal)	X 1.201	= US gallons (US gal)	X 0.833	= Imperial gallons (Imp gal)
US gallons (US gal)	X 3.785	= Liters (l)	X 0.264	= US gallons (US gal)

Mass (weight)

Ounces (oz)	X 28.35	= Grams (g)	X 0.035	= Ounces (oz)
Pounds (lb)	X 0.454	= Kilograms (kg)	X 2.205	= Pounds (lb)

Force

Ounces-force (ozf; oz)	X 0.278	= Newtons (N)	X 3.6	= Ounces-force (ozf; oz)
Pounds-force (lbf; lb)	X 4.448	= Newtons (N)	X 0.225	= Pounds-force (lbf; lb)
Newtons (N)	X 0.1	= Kilograms-force (kgf; kg)	X 9.81	= Newtons (N)

Pressure

Pounds-force per square inch (psi; lbf/in^2; lb/in^2)	X 0.070	= Kilograms-force per square centimeter (kgf/cm^2; kg/cm^2)	X 14.223	= Pounds-force per square inch (psi; lbf/in^2; lb/in^2)
Pounds-force per square inch (psi; lbf/in^2; lb/in^2)	X 0.068	= Atmospheres (atm)	X 14.696	= Pounds-force per square inch (psi; lbf/in^2; lb/in^2)
Pounds-force per square inch (psi; lbf/in^2; lb/in^2)	X 0.069	= Bars	X 14.5	= Pounds-force per square inch (psi; lbf/in^2; lb/in^2)
Pounds-force per square inch (psi; lbf/in^2; lb/in^2)	X 6.895	= Kilopascals (kPa)	X 0.145	= Pounds-force per square inch (psi; lbf/in^2; lb/in^2)
Kilopascals (kPa)	X 0.01	= Kilograms-force per square centimeter (kgf/cm^2; kg/cm^2)	X 98.1	= Kilopascals (kPa)

Torque (moment of force)

Pounds-force inches (lbf in; lb in)	X 1.152	= Kilograms-force centimeter (kgf cm; kg cm)	X 0.868	= Pounds-force inches (lbf in; lb in)
Pounds-force inches (lbf in; lb in)	X 0.113	= Newton meters (Nm)	X 8.85	= Pounds-force inches (lbf in; lb in)
Pounds-force inches (lbf in; lb in)	X 0.083	= Pounds-force feet (lbf ft; lb ft)	X 12	= Pounds-force inches (lbf in; lb in)
Pounds-force feet (lbf ft; lb ft)	X 0.138	= Kilograms-force meters (kgf m; kg m)	X 7.233	= Pounds-force feet (lbf ft; lb ft)
Pounds-force feet (lbf ft; lb ft)	X 1.356	= Newton meters (Nm)	X 0.738	= Pounds-force feet (lbf ft; lb ft)
Newton meters (Nm)	X 0.102	= Kilograms-force meters (kgf m; kg m)	X 9.804	= Newton meters (Nm)

Vacuum

Inches mercury (in. Hg)	X 3.377	= Kilopascals (kPa)	X 0.2961	= Inches mercury
Inches mercury (in. Hg)	X 25.4	= Millimeters mercury (mm Hg)	X 0.0394	= Inches mercury

Power

Horsepower (hp)	X 745.7	= Watts (W)	X 0.0013	= Horsepower (hp)

Velocity (speed)

Miles per hour (miles/hr; mph)	X 1.609	= Kilometers per hour (km/hr; kph)	X 0.621	= Miles per hour (miles/hr; mph)

*Fuel consumption**

Miles per gallon, Imperial (mpg)	X 0.354	= Kilometers per liter (km/l)	X 2.825	= Miles per gallon, Imperial (mpg)
Miles per gallon, US (mpg)	X 0.425	= Kilometers per liter (km/l)	X 2.352	= Miles per gallon, US (mpg)

Temperature

Degrees Fahrenheit = (°C x 1.8) + 32   Degrees Celsius (Degrees Centigrade; °C) = (°F - 32) x 0.56

*It is common practice to convert from miles per gallon (mpg) to liters/100 kilometers (l/100km),
where mpg (Imperial) x l/100 km = 282 and mpg (US) x l/100 km = 235*

Safety first!

Regardless of how enthusiastic you may be about getting on with the job at hand, take the time to ensure that your safety is not jeopardized. A moment's lack of attention can result in an accident, as can failure to observe certain simple safety precautions. The possibility of an accident will always exist, and the following points should not be considered a comprehensive list of all dangers. Rather, they are intended to make you aware of the risks and to encourage a safety conscious approach to all work you carry out on your vehicle.

Essential DOs and DON'Ts

DON'T rely on a jack when working under the vehicle. Always use approved jackstands to support the weight of the vehicle and place them under the recommended lift or support points.

DON'T attempt to loosen extremely tight fasteners (i.e. wheel lug nuts) while the vehicle is on a jack - it may fall.

DON'T start the engine without first making sure that the transmission is in Neutral (or Park where applicable) and the parking brake is set.

DON'T remove the radiator cap from a hot cooling system - let it cool or cover it with a cloth and release the pressure gradually.

DON'T attempt to drain the engine oil until you are sure it has cooled to the point that it will not burn you.

DON'T touch any part of the engine or exhaust system until it has cooled sufficiently to avoid burns.

DON'T siphon toxic liquids such as gasoline, antifreeze and brake fluid by mouth, or allow them to remain on your skin.

DON'T inhale brake lining dust - it is potentially hazardous (see *Asbestos* below).

DON'T allow spilled oil or grease to remain on the floor - wipe it up before someone slips on it.

DON'T use loose fitting wrenches or other tools which may slip and cause injury.

DON'T push on wrenches when loosening or tightening nuts or bolts. Always try to pull the wrench toward you. If the situation calls for pushing the wrench away, push with an open hand to avoid scraped knuckles if the wrench should slip.

DON'T attempt to lift a heavy component alone - get someone to help you.

DON'T *rush or take unsafe shortcuts to finish a job.*

DON'T allow children or animals in or around the vehicle while you are working on it.

DO wear eye protection when using power tools such as a drill, sander, bench grinder, etc. and when working under a vehicle.

DO keep loose clothing and long hair well out of the way of moving parts.

DO make sure that any hoist used has a safe working load rating adequate for the job.

DO get someone to check on you periodically when working alone on a vehicle.

DO carry out work in a logical sequence and make sure that everything is correctly assembled and tightened.

DO keep chemicals and fluids tightly capped and out of the reach of children and pets.

DO remember that your vehicle's safety affects that of yourself and others. If in doubt on any point, get professional advice.

Steering, suspension and brakes

These systems are essential to driving safety, so make sure you have a qualified shop or individual check your work. Also, compressed suspension springs can cause injury if released suddenly - be sure to use a spring compressor.

Airbags

Airbags are explosive devices that can **CAUSE** injury if they deploy while you're working on the vehicle. Follow the manufacturer's instructions to disable the airbag whenever you're working in the vicinity of airbag components.

Asbestos

Certain friction, insulating, sealing, and other products - such as brake linings, brake bands, clutch linings, torque converters, gaskets, etc. - may contain asbestos or other hazardous friction material. Extreme care must be taken to avoid inhalation of dust from such products, since it is hazardous to health. If in doubt, assume that they do contain asbestos.

Fire

Remember at all times that gasoline is highly flammable. Never smoke or have any kind of open flame around when working on a vehicle. But the risk does not end there. A spark caused by an electrical short circuit, by two metal surfaces contacting each other, or even by static electricity built up in your body under certain conditions, can ignite gasoline vapors, which in a confined space are highly explosive. Do not, under any circumstances, use gasoline for cleaning parts. Use an approved safety solvent.

Always disconnect the battery ground (-) cable at the battery before working on any part of the fuel system or electrical system. Never risk spilling fuel on a hot engine or exhaust component. It is strongly recommended that a fire extinguisher suitable for use on fuel and electrical fires be kept handy in the garage or workshop at all times. Never try to extinguish a fuel or electrical fire with water.

Fumes

Certain fumes are highly toxic and can quickly cause unconsciousness and even death if inhaled to any extent. Gasoline vapor falls into this category, as do the vapors from some cleaning solvents. Any draining or pouring of such volatile fluids should be done in a well ventilated area.

When using cleaning fluids and solvents, read the instructions on the container carefully. Never use materials from unmarked containers.

Never run the engine in an enclosed space, such as a garage. Exhaust fumes contain carbon monoxide, which is extremely poisonous. If you need to run the engine, always do so in the open air, or at least have the rear of the vehicle outside the work area.

The battery

Never create a spark or allow a bare light bulb near a battery. They normally give off a certain amount of hydrogen gas, which is highly explosive.

Always disconnect the battery ground (-) cable at the battery before working on the fuel or electrical systems.

If possible, loosen the filler caps or cover when charging the battery from an external source (this does not apply to sealed or maintenance-free batteries). Do not charge at an excessive rate or the battery may burst.

Take care when adding water to a non maintenance-free battery and when carrying a battery. The electrolyte, even when diluted, is very corrosive and should not be allowed to contact clothing or skin.

Always wear eye protection when cleaning the battery to prevent the caustic deposits from entering your eyes.

Household current

When using an electric power tool, inspection light, etc., which operates on household current, always make sure that the tool is correctly connected to its plug and that, where necessary, it is properly grounded. Do not use such items in damp conditions and, again, do not create a spark or apply excessive heat in the vicinity of fuel or fuel vapor.

Secondary ignition system voltage

A severe electric shock can result from touching certain parts of the ignition system (such as the spark plug wires) when the engine is running or being cranked, particularly if components are damp or the insulation is defective. In the case of an electronic ignition system, the secondary system voltage is much higher and could prove fatal.

Hydrofluoric acid

This extremely corrosive acid is formed when certain types of synthetic rubber, found in some O-rings, oil seals, fuel hoses, etc. are exposed to temperatures above 750-degrees F (400-degrees C). The rubber changes into a charred or sticky substance containing the acid. *Once formed, the acid remains dangerous for years. If it gets onto the skin, it may be necessary to amputate the limb concerned.*

When dealing with a vehicle which has suffered a fire, or with components salvaged from such a vehicle, wear protective gloves and discard them after use.

Automotive chemicals and lubricants

A number of automotive chemicals and lubricants are available for use during vehicle maintenance and repair. They include a wide variety of products ranging from cleaning solvents and degreasers to lubricants and protective sprays for rubber, plastic and vinyl.

Cleaners

Carburetor cleaner and choke cleaner is a strong solvent for gum, varnish and carbon. Most carburetor cleaners leave a dry-type lubricant film which will not harden or gum up. Because of this film it is not recommended for use on electrical components.

Brake system cleaner is used to remove brake dust, grease and brake fluid from the brake system, where clean surfaces are absolutely necessary. It leaves no residue and often eliminates brake squeal caused by contaminants.

Electrical cleaner removes oxidation, corrosion and carbon deposits from electrical contacts, restoring full current flow. It can also be used to clean spark plugs, carburetor jets, voltage regulators and other parts where an oil-free surface is desired.

Demoisturants remove water and moisture from electrical components such as alternators, voltage regulators, electrical connectors and fuse blocks. They are non-conductive and non-corrosive.

Degreasers are heavy-duty solvents used to remove grease from the outside of the engine and from chassis components. They can be sprayed or brushed on and, depending on the type, are rinsed off either with water or solvent.

Lubricants

Motor oil is the lubricant formulated for use in engines. It normally contains a wide variety of additives to prevent corrosion and reduce foaming and wear. Motor oil comes in various weights (viscosity ratings) from 0 to 50. The recommended weight of the oil depends on the season, temperature and the demands on the engine. Light oil is used in cold climates and under light load conditions. Heavy oil is used in hot climates and where high loads are encountered. Multi-viscosity oils are designed to have characteristics of both light and heavy oils and are available in a number of weights from 0W-20 to 20W-50.

Gear oil is designed to be used in differentials, manual transmissions and other areas where high-temperature lubrication is required.

Chassis and wheel bearing grease is a heavy grease used where increased loads and friction are encountered, such as for wheel bearings, balljoints, tie-rod ends and universal joints.

High-temperature wheel bearing grease is designed to withstand the extreme temperatures encountered by wheel bearings in disc brake equipped vehicles. It usually contains molybdenum disulfide (moly), which is a dry-type lubricant.

White grease is a heavy grease for metal-to-metal applications where water is a problem. White grease stays soft under both low and high temperatures (usually from -100 to +190-degrees F), and will not wash off or dilute in the presence of water.

Assembly lube is a special extreme pressure lubricant, usually containing moly, used to lubricate high-load parts (such as main and rod bearings and cam lobes) for initial start-up of a new engine. The assembly lube lubricates the parts without being squeezed out or washed away until the engine oiling system begins to function.

Silicone lubricants are used to protect rubber, plastic, vinyl and nylon parts.

Graphite lubricants are used where oils cannot be used due to contamination problems, such as in locks. The dry graphite will lubricate metal parts while remaining uncontaminated by dirt, water, oil or acids. It is electrically conductive and will not foul electrical contacts in locks such as the ignition switch.

Moly penetrants loosen and lubricate frozen, rusted and corroded fasteners and prevent future rusting or freezing.

Heat-sink grease is a special electrically non-conductive grease that is used for mounting electronic ignition modules where it is essential that heat is transferred away from the module.

Sealants

RTV sealant is one of the most widely used gasket compounds. Made from silicone, RTV is air curing, it seals, bonds, waterproofs, fills surface irregularities, remains flexible, doesn't shrink, is relatively easy to remove, and is used as a supplementary sealer with almost all low and medium temperature gaskets.

Anaerobic sealant is much like RTV in that it can be used either to seal gaskets or to form gaskets by itself. It remains flexible, is solvent resistant and fills surface imperfections. The difference between an anaerobic sealant and an RTV-type sealant is in the curing. RTV cures when exposed to air, while an anaerobic sealant cures only in the absence of air. This means that an anaerobic sealant cures only after the assembly of parts, sealing them together.

Thread and pipe sealant is used for sealing hydraulic and pneumatic fittings and vacuum lines. It is usually made from a Teflon compound, and comes in a spray, a paint-on liquid and as a wrap-around tape.

Chemicals

Anti-seize compound prevents seizing, galling, cold welding, rust and corrosion in fasteners. High-temperature ant-seize, usually made with copper and graphite lubricants, is used for exhaust system and exhaust manifold bolts.

Anaerobic locking compounds are used to keep fasteners from vibrating or working loose and cure only after installation, in the absence of air. Medium strength locking compound is used for small nuts, bolts and screws that may be removed later. High-strength locking compound is for large nuts, bolts and studs which aren't removed on a regular basis.

Oil additives range from viscosity index improvers to chemical treatments that claim to reduce internal engine friction. It should be noted that most oil manufacturers caution against using additives with their oils.

Gas additives perform several functions, depending on their chemical makeup. They usually contain solvents that help dissolve gum and varnish that build up on carburetor, fuel injection and intake parts. They also serve to break down carbon deposits that form on the inside surfaces of the combustion chambers. Some additives contain upper cylinder lubricants for valves and piston rings, and others contain chemicals to remove condensation from the gas tank.

Miscellaneous

Brake fluid is specially formulated hydraulic fluid that can withstand the heat and pressure encountered in brake systems. Care must be taken so this fluid does not come in contact with painted surfaces or plastics. An opened container should always be resealed to prevent contamination by water or dirt.

Weatherstrip adhesive is used to bond weatherstripping around doors, windows and trunk lids. It is sometimes used to attach trim pieces.

Undercoating is a petroleum-based, tar-like substance that is designed to protect metal surfaces on the underside of the vehicle from corrosion. It also acts as a sound-deadening agent by insulating the bottom of the vehicle.

Waxes and polishes are used to help protect painted and plated surfaces from the weather. Different types of paint may require the use of different types of wax and polish. Some polishes utilize a chemical or abrasive cleaner to help remove the top layer of oxidized (dull) paint on older vehicles. In recent years many non-wax polishes that contain a wide variety of chemicals such as polymers and silicones have been introduced. These non-wax polishes are usually easier to apply and last longer than conventional waxes and polishes.

Troubleshooting

Contents

Symptom	Section

Engine

Engine backfires 15
Engine continues to run after switching off................... 18
Engine hard to start when cold 3
Engine hard to start when hot....................................... 4
Engine lacks power 14
Engine lopes while idling or idles erratically 8
Engine misses at idle speed... 9
Engine misses throughout driving speed range 10
Engine rotates but will not start 2
Engine runs with oil pressure light on.......................... 17
Engine stalls 13
Engine starts but stops immediately............................ 6
Engine stumbles on acceleration................................. 11
Engine surges while holding accelerator steady 12
Engine will not rotate when attempting to start............ 1
Oil puddle under engine 7
Pinging or knocking engine sounds during
   acceleration or uphill 16
Starter motor noisy or excessively rough in engagement............. 5

Engine electrical system

Alternator light fails to go out..................................... 20
Battery will not hold a charge 19
Alternator light fails to come on when key is turned on 21

Fuel system

Excessive fuel consumption 22
Fuel leakage and/or fuel odor...................................... 23

Cooling system

Coolant loss 28
External coolant leakage 26
Internal coolant leakage 27
Overcooling 25
Overheating 24
Poor coolant circulation 29

Clutch

Clutch pedal stays on floor 36
Clutch slips (engine speed increases with no increase
   in vehicle speed 32
Grabbing (chattering) as clutch is engaged................. 33
High pedal effort 37
Noise in clutch area 35
Pedal travels to floor - no pressure
   or very little resistance 30
Transaxle rattling (clicking)... 34
Unable to select gears.. 31

Manual transaxle

Clicking noise in turns.. 41
Clunk on acceleration or deceleration 40
Knocking noise at low speeds 38
Leaks lubricant 47

Symptom	Section

Locked in gear... 48
Noise most pronounced when turning 39
Noisy in all gears 45
Noisy in neutral with engine running............................ 43
Noisy in one particular gear 44
Slips out of gear... 46
Vibration 42

Automatic transaxle/
Continuously Variable Transaxle (CVT)

Engine will start in gears other than Park or Neutral 52
Fluid leakage 49
General shift mechanism problems 51
Transaxle fluid brown or has burned smell 50
Transaxle slips, shifts roughly, is noisy or has no drive
   in forward or reverse gears 53

Driveaxles

Knock or clunk when accelerating after coasting 54
Clicking noise in turns.. 55
Shudder or vibration during acceleration..................... 56
Vibration at highway speeds... 57

Brakes

Brake pedal feels spongy when depressed................... 65
Brake pedal travels to the floor with little resistance.................... 66
Brake roughness or chatter (pedal pulsates).............. 60
Dragging brakes 63
Excessive brake pedal travel.. 62
Excessive pedal effort required to stop vehicle 61
Grabbing or uneven braking action 64
Noise (high-pitched squeal when the brakes are applied)............. 59
Parking brake does not hold... 67
Vehicle pulls to one side during braking 58

Suspension and steering systems

Abnormal or excessive tire wear 69
Abnormal noise at the front end 74
Cupped tires 79
Erratic steering when braking....................................... 76
Excessive pitching and/or rolling around corners or
   during braking 77
Excessive play or looseness in steering system 83
Excessive tire wear on inside edge 81
Excessive tire wear on outside edge 80
Hard steering 72
Poor returnability of steering to center........................ 73
Rattling or clicking noise in steering gear 84
Shimmy, shake or vibration 71
Suspension bottoms 78
Tire tread worn in one place... 82
Vehicle pulls to one side.. 68
Wander or poor steering stability................................. 75
Wheel makes a thumping noise 70

This section provides an easy reference guide to the more common problems which may occur during the operation of your vehicle. These problems and their possible causes are grouped under headings denoting various components or systems, such as Engine, Cooling system, etc. They also refer you to the chapter and/or section which deals with the problem.

Remember that successful troubleshooting is not a mysterious art practiced only by professional mechanics. It is simply the result of the right knowledge combined with an intelligent, systematic approach to the problem. Always work by a process of elimination, starting with the simplest solution and working through to the most complex - and never overlook the obvious. Anyone can run the gas tank dry or leave the lights on overnight, so don't assume that you are exempt from such oversights.

Finally, always establish a clear idea of why a problem has occurred and take steps to ensure that it doesn't happen again. If the electrical system fails because of a poor connection, check the other connections in the system to make sure that they don't fail as well. If a particular fuse continues to blow, find out why - don't just replace one fuse after another. Remember, failure of a small component can often be indicative of potential failure or incorrect functioning of a more important component or system.

Engine

1 Engine will not rotate when attempting to start

1 Battery terminal connections loose or corroded (Chapter 1).
2 Battery discharged or faulty (Chapter 1).
3 Automatic transaxle/Continuously Variable Transaxle (CVT) not completely engaged in Park (Chapter 7) or clutch not completely depressed (Chapter 8).
4 Broken, loose or disconnected wiring in the starting circuit (Chapters 5 and 12).
5 Starter motor pinion jammed in flywheel ring gear (Chapter 5).
6 Starter solenoid faulty (Chapter 5).
7 Starter motor faulty (Chapter 5).
8 Ignition switch faulty (Chapter 12).
9 Starter pinion or flywheel teeth worn or broken (Chapter 5).

2 Engine rotates but will not start

1 Fuel tank empty.
2 Battery discharged (engine rotates slowly) (Chapter 5).
3 Battery terminal connections loose or corroded (Chapter 1).
4 Leaking fuel injector(s), faulty fuel pump, pressure regulator, etc. (Chapter 4).

5 Fuel not reaching fuel rail (Chapter 4).
6 Ignition components damp or damaged (Chapter 5).
7 Worn, faulty or incorrectly gapped spark plugs (Chapter 1).
8 Broken, loose or disconnected wires at the ignition coil or faulty coil (Chapter 5).

3 Engine hard to start when cold

1 Battery discharged or low (Chapter 1).
2 Fault in the fuel injection or engine control system (Chapters 4 and 6).
3 Injector(s) leaking (Chapter 4).

4 Engine hard to start when hot

1 Air filter clogged (Chapter 1).
2 Fuel not reaching the fuel injection system (Chapter 4).
3 Corroded battery connections (Chapter 1).

5 Starter motor noisy or excessively rough in engagement

1 Pinion or flywheel gear teeth worn or broken (Chapter 5).
2 Starter motor mounting bolts loose or missing (Chapter 5).

6 Engine starts but stops immediately

1 Loose or faulty electrical connections at coil or alternator (Chapter 5).
2 Insufficient fuel reaching the fuel injector(s) (Chapter 4).
3 Vacuum leak at the gasket between the intake manifold and throttle body (Chapter 4).

7 Oil puddle under engine

1 Oil pan gasket and/or oil pan drain bolt washer leaking (Chapter 2).
2 Oil pressure sending unit leaking (Chapter 2).
3 Valve cover leaking (Chapter 2).
4 Engine oil seals leaking (Chapter 2).

8 Engine lopes while idling or idles erratically

1 Vacuum leakage (Chapters 2 and 4).
2 Air filter clogged (Chapter 1).
3 Fuel pump not delivering sufficient fuel to the fuel injection system (Chapter 4).
4 Leaking head gasket (Chapter 2).
5 Timing belt worn (Chapter 2).
6 Camshaft lobes worn (Chapter 2).

9 Engine misses at idle speed

1 Spark plugs worn or not gapped properly (Chapter 1).
2 Vacuum leaks (Chapter 1).
3 Uneven or low compression (Chapter 2).
4 Fault in the fuel injection or engine control system (Chapters 4 and 6).

10 Engine misses throughout driving speed range

1 Fuel filter clogged and/or impurities in the fuel system (Chapter 1).
2 Low fuel pressure (Chapter 4).
3 Faulty or incorrectly gapped spark plugs (Chapter 1).
4 Faulty emission system components (Chapter 6).
5 Low or uneven cylinder compression pressures (Chapter 2).
6 Weak or faulty ignition system (Chapter 5).
7 Vacuum leak in fuel injection system, intake manifold, air control valve or vacuum hoses (Chapter 4).

11 Engine stumbles on acceleration

1 Spark plugs fouled (Chapter 1).
2 Fuel injection system faulty (Chapter 4).
3 Fuel filter clogged (Chapters 1 and 4).
4 Intake manifold air leak (Chapters 2 and 4).

12 Engine surges while holding accelerator steady

1 Intake air leak (Chapter 4).
2 Fuel pump faulty (Chapter 4).
3 Loose fuel injector wire harness connectors (Chapter 4).
4 Defective PCM or information sensor (Chapter 6).

13 Engine stalls

1 Fuel filter clogged and/or water and impurities in the fuel system (Chapters 1 and 4).
2 Faulty emissions system components (Chapter 6).
3 Faulty or incorrectly gapped spark plugs (Chapter 1).
4 Vacuum leak in the fuel injection system, intake manifold or vacuum hoses (Chapters 2 and 4).
5 Valve clearances incorrectly set (Chapter 1).

14 Engine lacks power

1   Faulty or incorrectly gapped spark plugs (Chapter 1).
2   Fault in the fuel injection or engine control system (Chapters 4 and 6).
3   Faulty coils (Chapter 5).
4   Brakes binding (Chapter 9).
5   Automatic transaxle/Continuously Variable Transaxle (CVT) fluid level incorrect (Chapter 1).
6   Clutch slipping (Chapter 8).
7   Fuel filter clogged and/or impurities in the fuel system (Chapters 1 and 4).
8   Emission control system not functioning properly (Chapter 6).
9   Catalytic converter plugged (Chapter 6).
10 Low or uneven cylinder compression pressures (Chapter 2).
11 Obstructed exhaust system (Chapter 4).

15 Engine backfires

1   Emission control system not functioning properly (Chapter 6).
2   Faulty secondary ignition system (cracked spark plug insulator, faulty coil(s), (Chapters 1 and 5).
3   Fuel injection system malfunctioning (Chapter 4).
4   Vacuum leak at fuel injector(s), intake manifold, air control valve or vacuum hoses (Chapters 2 and 4).
5   Valve clearances incorrectly set and/or valves sticking (Chapter 1).

16 Pinging or knocking engine sounds during acceleration or uphill

1   Incorrect grade of fuel.
2   Fuel injection system faulty (Chapter 4).
3   Improper or damaged spark plugs (Chapter 1).
4   Vacuum leak (Chapters 2 and 4).
5   Knock sensor malfunctioning (Chapter 6).

17 Engine runs with oil pressure light on

1   Low oil level (Chapter 1).
2   Short in wiring circuit (Chapter 12).
3   Faulty oil pressure sender (Chapter 2).
4   Worn engine bearings and/or oil pump (Chapter 2).

18 Engine continues to run after switching off

1   Idle speed too high (Chapter 6)
2   Excessive engine operating temperature (Chapter 3).

Engine electrical system

19 Battery will not hold a charge

1   Alternator drivebelt defective or not adjusted properly (Chapter 1).
2   Battery electrolyte level low (Chapter 1).
3   Battery terminals loose or corroded (Chapter 1).
4   Alternator not charging properly (Chapter 5).
5   Loose, broken or faulty wiring in the charging circuit (Chapter 5).
6   Internally defective battery (Chapters 1 and 5).

20 Alternator light fails to go out

1   Faulty alternator or charging circuit (Chapter 5).
2   Alternator drivebelt defective or out of adjustment (Chapter 1).
3   Alternator voltage regulator inoperative (Chapter 5).

21 Alternator light fails to come on when key is turned on

1   Warning light bulb defective (Chapter 12).
2   Fault in the printed circuit, dash wiring or bulb holder (Chapter 12).

Fuel system

22 Excessive fuel consumption

1   Dirty or clogged air filter element (Chapter 1).
2   Emissions system not functioning properly (Chapter 6).
3   Faulty fuel injection system (Chapter 4).
4   Low tire pressure or incorrect tire size (Chapter 1).

23 Fuel leakage and/or fuel odor

1   Leaking fuel line (Chapters 1 and 4).
2   Tank overfilled.
3   Evaporative canister defective (Chapters 1 and 6).
4   Faulty fuel injection system (Chapter 4).

Cooling system

24 Overheating

1   Insufficient coolant in system (Chapter 1).

2   Radiator core blocked or grille restricted (Chapter 3).
3   Thermostat faulty (Chapter 3).
4   Cooling fan switch faulty (Chapter 3).
5   Electric coolant fan blades broken or cracked (Chapter 3).
6   Radiator cap not maintaining proper pressure (Chapter 3).

25 Overcooling

1   Faulty thermostat (Chapter 3).
2   Inaccurate temperature gauge sending unit (Chapter 3)

26 External coolant leakage

1   Deteriorated/damaged hoses; loose clamps (Chapters 1 and 3).
2   Water pump defective (Chapter 3).
3   Leakage from radiator core or coolant reservoir bottle (Chapter 3).
4   Engine drain or water jacket core plugs leaking (Chapter 2).

27 Internal coolant leakage

1   Leaking cylinder head gasket (Chapter 2).
2   Cracked cylinder bore or cylinder head (Chapter 2).

28 Coolant loss

1   Too much coolant in system (Chapter 1).
2   Coolant boiling away because of overheating (Chapter 3).
3   Internal or external leakage (Chapter 3).
4   Faulty radiator cap (Chapter 3).

29 Poor coolant circulation

1   Inoperative water pump (Chapter 3).
2   Restriction in cooling system (Chapters 1 and 3).
3   Thermostat sticking (Chapter 3).

Clutch

30 Pedal travels to floor - no pressure or very little resistance

1   No fluid in reservoir (Chapter 1)
2   Faulty clutch master cylinder, release cylinder or hydraulic line (Chapter 8).
3   Broken release bearing or fork (Chapter 8).

31 Unable to select gears

1   Faulty transaxle (Chapter 7).
2   Faulty clutch disc (Chapter 8).
3   Release lever and bearing not assembled properly (Chapter 8).
4   Faulty pressure plate (Chapter 8).
5   Pressure plate-to-flywheel bolts loose (Chapter 8).

32 Clutch slips (engine speed increases with no increase in vehicle speed)

1   Clutch plate worn (Chapter 8).
2   Clutch plate is oil soaked by leaking rear main seal (Chapter 8).
3   Clutch plate not seated. It may take 30 or 40 normal starts for a new one to seat.
4   Warped pressure plate or flywheel (Chapter 8).
5   Weak diaphragm spring (Chapter 8).
6   Clutch plate overheated. Allow to cool.

33 Grabbing (chattering) as clutch is engaged

1   Oil on clutch plate lining, burned or glazed facings (Chapter 8).
2   Worn or loose engine or transaxle mounts (Chapters 2 and 7).
3   Worn splines on clutch plate hub (Chapter 8).
4   Warped pressure plate or flywheel (Chapter 8).
5   Burned or smeared resin on flywheel or pressure plate (Chapter 8).

34 Transaxle rattling (clicking)

1   Release lever loose (Chapter 8).
2   Clutch plate damper spring failure (Chapter 8).
3   Low engine idle speed (Chapter 1).

35 Noise in clutch area

1   Fork shaft improperly installed (Chapter 8).
2   Faulty bearing (Chapter 8).

36 Clutch pedal stays on floor

1   Faulty clutch master or release cylinder (Chapter 8).
2   Broken release bearing or fork (Chapter 8).

37 High pedal effort

1   Piston binding in bore of clutch master or

release cylinder (Chapter 8).
2   Pressure plate faulty (Chapter 8).

Manual transaxle

38 Knocking noise at low speeds

1   Worn driveaxle constant velocity (CV) joints (Chapter 8).
2   Worn driveaxle bore in differential case (Chapter 7A).*

39 Noise most pronounced when turning

Differential gear noise (Chapter 7A).*

40 Clunk on acceleration or deceleration

1   Loose engine or transaxle mounts (Chapters 2 and 7A).
2   Worn differential pinion shaft in case.*
3   Worn driveaxle bore in differential case (Chapter 7A).*
4   Worn or damaged driveaxle inboard CV joints (Chapter 8).

41 Clicking noise in turns

Worn or damaged outboard CV joint (Chapter 8).

42 Vibration

1   Rough wheel bearing (Chapters 1 and 10).
2   Damaged driveaxle (Chapter 8).
3   Out of round tires (Chapter 1).
4   Tire out of balance (Chapters 1 and 10).
5   Worn CV joint (Chapter 8).

43 Noisy in neutral with engine running

1   Damaged input gear bearing (Chapter 7A).*
2   Damaged clutch release bearing (Chapter 8).

44 Noisy in one particular gear

1   Damaged or worn constant mesh gears (Chapter 7A).*
2   Damaged or worn synchronizers (Chapter 7A).*
3   Bent reverse fork (Chapter 7A).*
4   Damaged fourth speed gear or output gear (Chapter 7A).*

5   Worn or damaged reverse idler gear or idler bushing (Chapter 7A).*

45 Noisy in all gears

1   Insufficient lubricant (Chapter 7A).
2   Damaged or worn bearings (Chapter 7A).*
3   Worn or damaged input gear shaft and/or output gear shaft (Chapter 7A).*

46 Slips out of gear

1   Worn or improperly adjusted linkage (Chapter 7A).
2   Transaxle loose on engine (Chapter 7A).
3   Shift linkage does not work freely, binds (Chapter 7A).
4   Input gear bearing retainer broken or loose (Chapter 7A).*
5   Worn shift fork (Chapter 7A).*

47 Leaks lubricant

1   Driveaxle oil seals worn (Chapter 7).
2   Excessive amount of lubricant in transaxle (Chapters 1 and 7A).
3   Loose or broken input gear shaft bearing retainer (Chapter 7A).*
4   Input gear bearing retainer O-ring and/or lip seal damaged (Chapter 7A).*

48 Locked in gear

Lock pin or interlock pin missing (Chapter 7A).*

Although the corrective action necessary to remedy the symptoms described is beyond the scope of the home mechanic, the above information should be helpful in isolating the cause of the condition so that the owner can communicate clearly with a professional mechanic.

Automatic transaxle/Continuously Variable Transaxle (CVT)

Note: *Due to the complexity of the automatic transaxle/Continuously Variable Transaxle (CVT), it is difficult for the home mechanic to properly diagnose and service this component. For problems other than the following, the vehicle should be taken to a dealer or transmission shop.*

49 Fluid leakage

1   Automatic transmission fluid is a deep red color. Fluid leaks should not be confused with engine oil, which can easily be blown onto the transaxle by air flow.

2   To pinpoint a leak, first remove all built-up dirt and grime from the transaxle housing with degreasing agents and/or steam cleaning. Then drive the vehicle at low speeds so air flow will not blow the leak far from its source. Raise the vehicle and determine where the leak is coming from. Common areas of leakage are:

a) Pan (Chapters 1 and 7)
b) Dipstick tube (Chapters 1 and 7)
c) Transaxle oil lines (Chapter 7)
d) Speed sensor (Chapter 7)

50 Transaxle fluid brown or has a burned smell

Transaxle fluid burned (Chapter 1).

51 General shift mechanism problems

1   Chapter 7 deals with checking and adjusting the shift linkage on automatic transaxles. Common problems which may be attributed to poorly adjusted linkage are:

a) Engine starting in gears other than Park or Neutral.
b) Indicator on shifter pointing to a gear other than the one actually being used.
c) Vehicle moves when in Park.

2   Refer to Chapter 7B for the shift linkage adjustment procedure.

52 Engine will start in gears other than Park or Neutral

Transmission range switch malfunctioning (Chapter 6).

53 Transaxle slips, shifts roughly, is noisy or has no drive in forward or reverse gears

There are many probable causes for the above problems, but the home mechanic should be concerned with only one possibility - fluid level. Before taking the vehicle to a repair shop, check the level and condition of the fluid as described in Chapter 1. Correct the fluid level as necessary or change the fluid and filter if needed. If the problem persists, have a professional diagnose the cause.

Driveaxles

54 Knock or clunk when accelerating after coasting

Worn or damaged CV joint. Check for cut or damaged boots (Chapter 1). Repair as necessary (Chapter 8).

55 Clicking noise in turns

Worn or damaged outer CV joint. Check for cut or damaged boots (Chapter 1).

56 Shudder or vibration during acceleration

1   Worn or damaged CV joints (Chapter 8).
2   Sticking inboard CV joint assembly (Chapter 8).

57 Vibration at highway speeds

1   Out-of-balance front wheels and/or tires (Chapters 1 and 10).
2   Out-of-round front tires (Chapters 1 and 10).
3   Worn CV joint(s) (Chapter 8).

Brakes

Note: *Before assuming that a brake problem exists, make sure that:*

a) *The tires are in good condition and properly inflated (Chapter 1).*
b) *The front end alignment is correct (Chapter 10).*
c) *The vehicle is not loaded with weight in an unequal manner.*

58 Vehicle pulls to one side during braking

1   Incorrect tire pressures (Chapter 1).
2   Front end out of alignment (have the front end aligned).
3   Front, or rear, tires not matched to one another.
4   Restricted brake lines or hoses (Chapter 9).
5   Malfunctioning drum brake or caliper assembly (Chapter 9).
6   Loose suspension parts (Chapter 10).
7   Excessive wear of brake shoe or pad material or disc/drum on one side.

59 Noise (squeal or grinding when the brakes are applied)

1   Disc brake pads worn out. Replace pads with new ones immediately (Chapter 9).
2   Drum brake shoes worn out. Replace the shoes immediately (Chapter 9).

60 Brake roughness or chatter (pedal pulsates)

1   Excessive brake disc lateral runout or brake drum out-of-round (Chapter 9).
2   Parallelism of disc not within specifica-

tions (Chapter 9).
32   Defective brake disc (Chapter 9).

61 Excessive brake pedal effort required to stop vehicle

1   Malfunctioning power brake booster (Chapter 9).
2   Partial system failure (Chapter 9).
3   Excessively worn pads or shoes (Chapter 9).
4   Piston in caliper or wheel cylinder stuck or sluggish (Chapter 9).
5   Brake pads or shoes contaminated with oil or grease (Chapter 9).
6   New pads or shoes installed and not yet seated. It will take a while for the new material to seat against the disc or drum.

62 Excessive brake pedal travel

1   Partial brake system failure (Chapter 9).
2   Insufficient fluid in master cylinder (Chapters 1 and 9).
3   Air trapped in system (Chapters 1 and 9).

63 Dragging brakes

1   Incorrect adjustment of brake light switch (Chapter 9).
2   Master cylinder pistons not returning correctly (Chapter 9).
3   Restricted brakes lines or hoses (Chapters 1 and 9).
4   Incorrect parking brake adjustment (Chapter 9).

64 Grabbing or uneven braking action

1   Malfunction of proportioning valve (Chapter 9).
2   Malfunction of power brake booster unit (Chapter 9).
3   Binding brake pedal mechanism (Chapter 9).

65 Brake pedal feels spongy when depressed

1   Air in hydraulic lines (Chapter 9).
2   Master cylinder mounting bolts loose (Chapter 9).
3   Master cylinder defective (Chapter 9).

66 Brake pedal travels to the floor with little resistance

1   Little or no fluid in the master cylinder reservoir caused by leaking caliper piston(s) (Chapter 9).

2   Loose, damaged or disconnected brake lines (Chapter 9).

67   Parking brake does not hold

Parking brake improperly adjusted (Chapter 9).

Suspension and steering systems

Note: *Before attempting to diagnose the suspension and steering systems, perform the following preliminary checks:*

a) *Tires for wrong pressure and uneven wear.*
b) *Steering universal joints from the column to the steering gear for loose connectors or wear.*
c) *Front and rear suspension and the steering gear assembly for loose or damaged parts.*
d) *Out-of-round or out-of-balance tires, bent rims and loose and/or rough wheel bearings.*

68   Vehicle pulls to one side

1   Mismatched or uneven tires (Chapter 10).
2   Broken or sagging springs (Chapter 10).
3   Wheels out of alignment (Chapter 10).
4   Front brakes dragging (Chapter 9).

69   Abnormal or excessive tire wear

1   Wheels out of alignment (Chapter 10).
2   Sagging or broken springs (Chapter 10).
3   Tire out of balance (Chapter 10).
4   Worn shock absorber (Chapter 10).
5   Overloaded vehicle.
6   Tires not rotated regularly.

70   Wheel makes a thumping noise

1   Blister or bump on tire (Chapter 10).
2   Improper shock absorber/coil spring action (Chapter 10).

71   Shimmy, shake or vibration

1   Tire or wheel out-of-balance or out-of-round (Chapter 10).
2   Loose or worn wheel bearings (Chapter 10).
3   Worn tie-rod ends (Chapter 10).
4   Worn balljoints (Chapter 10).
5   Excessive wheel runout (Chapter 10).
6   Blister or bump on tire (Chapter 10).

72   Hard steering

1   Lack of lubrication at balljoints and tie-rod ends (Chapter 1).

2   Front wheels out of alignment (Chapter 10).
3   Low tire pressure(s) (Chapters 10).

73   Poor returnability of steering to center

1   Lack of lubrication at balljoints and tie-rod ends (Chapter 1).
2   Binding in balljoints (Chapter 10).
3   Binding in steering column (Chapter 10).
4   Front wheels out of alignment (Chapter 10).

74   Abnormal noise at the front end

1   Lack of lubrication at balljoints and tie-rod ends (Chapter 1).
2   Damaged shock absorber/coil spring mount (Chapter 10).
3   Worn control arm bushings or tie-rod ends (Chapter 10).
4   Loose stabilizer bar (Chapter 10).
5   Loose wheel nuts (Chapter 1).
6   Loose suspension bolts (Chapter 10)

75   Wander or poor steering stability

1   Mismatched or uneven tires (Chapter 10).
2   Lack of lubrication at balljoints and tie-rod ends (Chapter 1).
3   Worn shock absorber/coil spring assemblies (Chapter 10).
4   Loose stabilizer bar (Chapter 10).
5   Broken or sagging springs (Chapter 10).
6   Wheels out of alignment (Chapter 10).

76   Erratic steering when braking

1   Front hub bearings worn (Chapter 10).
2   Broken or sagging springs (Chapter 10).
3   Leaking wheel cylinder or caliper (Chapter 10).
4   Warped discs or drums (Chapter 10).

77   Excessive pitching and/or rolling around corners or during braking

1   Loose stabilizer bar (Chapter 10).
2   Worn shock absorbers or mounts (Chapter 10).
3   Broken or sagging springs (Chapter 10).
4   Overloaded vehicle.

78   Suspension bottoms

1   Overloaded vehicle.
2   Worn shock absorbers (Chapter 10).
3   Incorrect, broken or sagging springs (Chapter 10).

79   Cupped tires

1   Front wheel or rear wheel alignment (Chapter 10).
2   Worn shock absorbers (Chapter 10).
3   Wheel bearings worn (Chapter 10).
4   Excessive tire or wheel runout (Chapter 10).
5   Worn balljoints (Chapter 10).

80   Excessive tire wear on outside edge

1   Inflation pressures incorrect (Chapter 1).
2   Excessive speed in turns.
3   Front end alignment incorrect (excessive toe-in). Have professionally aligned.
4   Suspension arm bent or twisted (Chapter 10).

81   Excessive tire wear on inside edge

1   Inflation pressures incorrect (Chapter 1).
2   Front end alignment incorrect (toe-out). Have professionally aligned.
3   Loose or damaged steering or suspension components (Chapter 10).

82   Tire tread worn in one place

1   Tires out of balance.
2   Damaged or buckled wheel. Inspect and replace if necessary.
3   Defective tire (Chapter 1).

83   Excessive play or looseness in steering system

1   Front hub bearing(s) worn (Chapter 10).
2   Tie-rod end loose (Chapter 10).
3   Steering gear loose or worn (Chapter 10).
4   Worn or loose steering intermediate shaft (Chapter 10).

84   Rattling or clicking noise in steering gear

1   Steering gear loose (Chapter 10).
2   Steering gear defective (Chapter 10).

Chapter 1
Tune-up and routine maintenance

Contents

	Section		Section
Air filter replacement	15	Introduction	2
Automatic transaxle fluid change	25	Maintenance schedule	1
Battery check, maintenance and charging	8	Manual transaxle fluid change	26
Brake fluid change	20	Rear differential lubricant change (CR-V)	22
Brake system check	12	Seat belt check	11
CHECK ENGINE light on	See Chapter 6	Spark plug check and replacement	24
Cooling system check	9	Steering, suspension and driveaxle boot check	13
Cooling system servicing (draining, flushing and refilling)	21	Tire and tire pressure checks	5
Drivebelt check, adjustment and replacement	19	Tire rotation	10
Engine oil and oil filter change	6	Tune-up general information	3
Exhaust system check	18	Underhood hose check and replacement	14
Fluid level checks	4	Valve clearance check and adjustment	23
Fuel system check	17	Windshield wiper blade inspection and replacement	7
Interior ventilation filter replacement	16		

Specifications

Recommended lubricants and fluids

Note: *The fluids and lubricants listed here are those recommended by the manufacturer at the time this manual was written. Vehicle manufacturers occasionally upgrade their fluid and lubricant specifications, so check with your local auto parts store for the most current recommendations.*

Engine oil	
Type	API "Certified for gasoline engines"
Viscosity	SAE 5W-20
Automatic transaxle fluid	Honda ATF-Z1
Manual transaxle fluid	Honda manual transmission fluid (MTF or equivalent)
Rear differential fluid (CR-V)	Honda Dual Pump System Fluid or equivalent
Brake fluid type	DOT 3 brake fluid
Clutch fluid type	DOT 3 brake fluid
Power steering system fluid	Honda power steering fluid
Fuel type	Unleaded gasoline, 86 octane or higher
Engine coolant	50/50 mixture of Honda All Season Antifreeze/Coolant Type 2 or equivalent

Capacities*

Engine oil (including oil filter)
  Civic
      D17A2, D17A6 engines .... 3.7 quarts (3.5 liters)
      D17A1 engine .... 3.4 quarts (3.2 liters)
      1.8L engine .... 3.9 quarts (3.7 liters)
      2.0L engine .... 4.6 quarts (4.4 liters)
  CR-V and hatchback .... 4.4 quarts (4.2 liters)

Automatic transaxle fluid (drain and refill)**
  Civic
    2005 and earlier models .... 2.9 quarts (2.7 liters)
    2006 and later models .... 2.5 quarts (2.4 liters)
  CR-V
    2006 and earlier 2WD models .... 3.1 quarts (2.9 liters)
    2007 and later 2WD models .... 2.7 quarts (2.6 liters)
    2006 and earlier 4WD models .... 3.3 quarts (3.1 liters)
    2007 and later 4WD models .... 2.6 quarts (2.5 liters)

Manual transaxle (drain and refill)
  Civic .... 1.6 quarts (1.5 liters)
  CR-V (2006 and earlier models only) .... 2.0 quarts (1.9 liters)

Rear differential (CR-V)
  2002 through 2004 .... 1.1 quarts (1.0 liters)
  2005 and later .... 1.5 quarts (1.4 liters)

Cooling system
  Civic
    2005 and earlier manual transaxle models .... 4.2 quarts (4.0 liters)
    2006 and later manual transaxle models (1.8L engine) .... 5.5 quarts (5.2 liters)
    2005 and earlier automatic transaxle models .... 4.1 quarts (3.9 liters)
    2006 and later automatic transaxle models (1.8L engine) .... 5.6 quarts (5.3 liters)
    2006 and earlier models with 2.0L engine .... 5.3 quarts (5.0 liters)
    2006 and later models with 2.0L engine .... 4.7 quarts (4.5 liters)
  CR-V
    Manual transaxle models .... 5.8 quarts (5.5 liters)
    Automatic transaxle models .... 5.7 quarts (5.4 liters)

Front

42026-1-specs HAYNES

**Cylinder locations
(1.7L SOHC engine)**

Front

42026-1-specs HAYNES

**Cylinder locations (1.8L SOHC
engine and DOHC engines)**

All capacities approximate. Add as necessary to bring to appropriate level.
** *If you want to flush the converter during a fluid change, purchase twice the amount of fluid listed here.*

Valve clearances (cold engine)

2001 models
  Civic
    Intake valve .... 0.007 to 0.009 inch (0.18 to 0.23 mm)
    Exhaust valve .... 0.009 to 0.011 inch (0.23 to 0.28 mm)
  CR-V
    Intake valve .... 0.003 to 0.005 inch (0.08 to 0.13 mm)
    Exhaust valve .... 0.006 to 0.008 inch (0.15 to 0.20 mm)

2002 and later models
  Civic
    DOHC
      Intake valve .... 0.008 to 0.010 inch (0.20 to 0.25 mm)
      Exhaust valve
        2002 to 2005 models .... 0.011 to 0.013 inch (0.28 to 0.33 mm)
        2006 and later models .... 0.010 to 0.011 inch (0.25 to 0.28 mm)
    SOHC
      Intake valve .... 0.007 to 0.009 inch (0.18 to 0.23 mm)
      Exhaust valve .... 0.009 to 0.011 inch (0.23 to 0.28 mm)
  CR-V
    Intake valve .... 0.008 to 0.010 inch (0.20 to 0.25 mm)
    Exhaust valve .... 0.011 to 0.013 inch (0.28 to 0.33 mm)

Ignition system

Spark plug type and gap
  Type
    2005 and earlier 1.7L engines .... NGK: PZFR6F-11 or DENSO: PKJ20CR-M11
    2006 and later 1.8L engines .... NGK: IZFR6K-11S or DENSO: SKJ20DR-M11S
    2006 and later 2.0L engines .... DENSO: SK22PR-M11S
    CR-V and 2005 and earlier 2.0L engines .... NGK: IZFR6K-11 or DENSO: SKJ20DR-M11
  Gap .... 0.039 to 0.043 inch (1.0 to 1.1 mm)
Engine firing order 1-3-4-2

Cooling system

Thermostat rating
    Starts to open.. 169 to 176 degrees F (76 to 80 degrees C)
    Fully open.. 194 degrees F (90 degrees C)

Accessory drivebelt deflection (1.7L engine only)

Alternator/air conditioning compressor
    New belt .... 0.20 to 0.26 inch (5.0 to 6.5 mm)
    Old belt... 0.33 to 0.43 inch (8.5 to 11.0 mm)
Power steering pump
    New belt .... 0.35 to 0.43 inch (9.0 to 11.0 mm)
    Old belt... 0.51 to 0.65 inch (13.0 to 16.5 mm)

Brakes

Disc brake pad lining thickness (minimum) .... 1/8 inch
Drum brake shoe lining thickness (minimum)..................................... 1/16 inch
Parking brake adjustment
    2005 and earlier models with 1.7L engines..................................... 6 to 7 clicks
    2005 and earlier models with 2.0L engines..................................... 7 to 8 clicks
    2006 and later (all models).. 8 to 10 clicks
    2006 and earlier CR-V models... 5 to 9 clicks
    2007 and later CR-V models.. 6 to 7 clicks

Torque specifications

Note: *One foot-pound (ft-lb) of torque is equivalent to 12 inch-pounds (in-lbs) of torque. Torque values below approximately 15 ft-lbs are expressed in inch-pounds, since most foot-pound torque wrenches are not accurate at these smaller values.*

	Ft-lbs (unless otherwise indicated)	**Nm**
Engine oil drain plug		
Civic		
All except hatchback and Si models	29	39
Hatchback and Si models	33	45
CR-V		
2002 through 2006 models	33	45
2007 and later models	29	39
Automatic transaxle drain plug	36	49
Drivebelt tensioner mounting bolts		
1.8L engines		
8 mm bolt	17	23
10 mm bolt	40	54
2.0L and 2.4L engines	16	22
Manual transaxle		
Check/fill plug	33	45
Drain plug	29	39
Spark plugs	156 in-lbs	17.5
Wheel lug nuts	80	108

1 Maintenance schedule

The maintenance intervals in this manual are provided with the assumption that you, not the dealer, will be doing the work. These are the minimum maintenance intervals recommended by the factory for vehicles that are driven daily. If you wish to keep your vehicle in peak condition at all times, you may wish to perform some of these procedures even more often. Because frequent maintenance enhances the efficiency, performance and resale value of your car, we encourage you to do so. If you drive in dusty areas, tow a trailer, idle or drive at low speeds for extended periods or drive for short distances (less than four miles) in below freezing temperatures, shorter intervals are also recommended.

When your vehicle is new, follow the maintenance schedule to the letter, record the maintenance performed in your owners manual and keep all receipts to protect the new vehicle warranty. In many cases, the initial maintenance check is done at no cost to the owner.

Every 250 miles (400 km) or weekly, whichever comes first

Check the engine oil level (Section 4)
Check the engine coolant level (Section 4)
Check the windshield washer fluid level (Section 4)
Check the brake fluid level (Section 4)
Check the power steering fluid level (Section 4)
Check the automatic transaxle fluid level (Section 4)
Check the tires and tire pressures (Section 5)
Check the operation of all lights
Check the horn operation

Every 3000 miles (4800 km) or 3 months, whichever comes first

All items listed above plus:
Change the engine oil and oil filter (Section 6)

Every 7500 miles (12,000 km) or 6 months, whichever comes first

All items listed above plus:
Inspect (and replace, if necessary) the windshield wiper blades (Section 7)
Check and service the battery (Section 8)
Check the cooling system (Section 9)
Rotate the tires (Section 10)
Check the seat belts (Section 11)
Inspect the brake system (Section 12)

Every 15,000 miles (24,000 km) or 12 months, whichever comes first

All items listed above plus:
Check the manual transaxle lubricant (Section 4)
Check the rear differential lubricant (4WD CR-V models) (Section 4)
Inspect the suspension, steering components and driveaxle boots (Section 13)*
Inspect and replace, if necessary, all underhood hoses (Section 14)
Replace the air filter (Section 15)*
Replace the interior ventilation filter (Section 16)
Inspect the fuel system (Section 17)
Check the exhaust system (Section 18)

Every 30,000 (48,000 km) miles or 24 months, whichever comes first

All items listed above plus:
Check and adjust, if necessary, the engine drivebelts (Section 19)
Replace the brake fluid (Section 20)
Check (and replace, if necessary) the spark plugs (conventional, non-platinum or iridium type) (Section 24)

Every 60,000 miles (96,000 km) or 36 months

Service the cooling system (drain, flush and refill) (Section 21)

Every 90,000 miles (145,000 km) or 60 months

Change the rear differential lubricant (Section 22)

Every 110,000 miles (176,000 km) or 36 months, whichever comes first

Valve clearance check and adjustment (only if noisy) (see Section 23)
Replace the spark plugs (platinum or iridium type) (Section 24)
Replace the timing belt, and inspect the auto tensioner and water pump (see Chapter 2A and Chapter 3)

Cooling system

Thermostat rating
  Starts to open.. 169 to 176 degrees F (76 to 80 degrees C)
  Fully open.. 194 degrees F (90 degrees C)

Accessory drivebelt deflection (1.7L engine only)

Alternator/air conditioning compressor
  New belt.. 0.20 to 0.26 inch (5.0 to 6.5 mm)
  Old belt... 0.33 to 0.43 inch (8.5 to 11.0 mm)
Power steering pump
  New belt.. 0.35 to 0.43 inch (9.0 to 11.0 mm)
  Old belt... 0.51 to 0.65 inch (13.0 to 16.5 mm)

Brakes

Disc brake pad lining thickness (minimum)............................. 1/8 inch
Drum brake shoe lining thickness (minimum)......................... 1/16 inch
Parking brake adjustment
  2005 and earlier models with 1.7L engines........................ 6 to 7 clicks
  2005 and earlier models with 2.0L engines........................ 7 to 8 clicks
  2006 and later (all models).. 8 to 10 clicks
  2006 and earlier CR-V models.. 5 to 9 clicks
  2007 and later CR-V models.. 6 to 7 clicks

Torque specifications

Note: *One foot-pound (ft-lb) of torque is equivalent to 12 inch-pounds (in-lbs) of torque. Torque values below approximately 15 ft-lbs are expressed in inch-pounds, since most foot-pound torque wrenches are not accurate at these smaller values.*

	Ft-lbs (unless otherwise indicated)	Nm
Engine oil drain plug		
Civic		
All except hatchback and Si models	29	39
Hatchback and Si models	33	45
CR-V		
2002 through 2006 models	33	45
2007 and later models	29	39
Automatic transaxle drain plug	36	49
Drivebelt tensioner mounting bolts		
1.8L engines		
8 mm bolt	17	23
10 mm bolt	40	54
2.0L and 2.4L engines	16	22
Manual transaxle		
Check/fill plug	33	45
Drain plug	29	39
Spark plugs	156 in-lbs	17.5
Wheel lug nuts	80	108

1 Maintenance schedule

The maintenance intervals in this manual are provided with the assumption that you, not the dealer, will be doing the work. These are the minimum maintenance intervals recommended by the factory for vehicles that are driven daily. If you wish to keep your vehicle in peak condition at all times, you may wish to perform some of these procedures even more often. Because frequent maintenance enhances the efficiency, performance and resale value of your car, we encourage you to do so. If you drive in dusty areas, tow a trailer, idle or drive at low speeds for extended periods or drive for short distances (less than four miles) in below freezing temperatures, shorter intervals are also recommended.

When your vehicle is new, follow the maintenance schedule to the letter, record the maintenance performed in your owners manual and keep all receipts to protect the new vehicle warranty. In many cases, the initial maintenance check is done at no cost to the owner.

Every 250 miles (400 km) or weekly, whichever comes first

Check the engine oil level (Section 4)
Check the engine coolant level (Section 4)
Check the windshield washer fluid level (Section 4)
Check the brake fluid level (Section 4)
Check the power steering fluid level (Section 4)
Check the automatic transaxle fluid level (Section 4)
Check the tires and tire pressures (Section 5)
Check the operation of all lights
Check the horn operation

Every 3000 miles (4800 km) or 3 months, whichever comes first

All items listed above plus:
Change the engine oil and oil filter (Section 6)

Every 7500 miles (12,000 km) or 6 months, whichever comes first

All items listed above plus:
Inspect (and replace, if necessary) the windshield wiper blades (Section 7)
Check and service the battery (Section 8)
Check the cooling system (Section 9)
Rotate the tires (Section 10)
Check the seat belts (Section 11)
Inspect the brake system (Section 12)

Every 15,000 miles (24,000 km) or 12 months, whichever comes first

All items listed above plus:
Check the manual transaxle lubricant (Section 4)
Check the rear differential lubricant (4WD CR-V models) (Section 4)
Inspect the suspension, steering components and driveaxle boots (Section 13)*
Inspect and replace, if necessary, all underhood hoses (Section 14)
Replace the air filter (Section 15)*
Replace the interior ventilation filter (Section 16)
Inspect the fuel system (Section 17)
Check the exhaust system (Section 18)

Every 30,000 (48,000 km) miles or 24 months, whichever comes first

All items listed above plus:
Check and adjust, if necessary, the engine drivebelts (Section 19)
Replace the brake fluid (Section 20)
Check (and replace, if necessary) the spark plugs (conventional, non-platinum or iridium type) (Section 24)

Every 60,000 miles (96,000 km) or 36 months

Service the cooling system (drain, flush and refill) (Section 21)

Every 90,000 miles (145,000 km) or 60 months

Change the rear differential lubricant (Section 22)

Every 110,000 miles (176,000 km) or 36 months, whichever comes first

Valve clearance check and adjustment (only if noisy) (see Section 23)
Replace the spark plugs (platinum or iridium type) (Section 24)
Replace the timing belt, and inspect the auto tensioner and water pump (see Chapter 2A and Chapter 3)

Every 120,000 miles (192,000 km) or 72 months, whichever comes first

Change the automatic transaxle fluid (Section 25)**
Change the manual transaxle lubricant (Section 26)***

*This item is affected by "severe" operating conditions as described below. If your vehicle is operated under "severe" conditions, perform all maintenance indicated with a * at 5000 mile/6 month intervals. Severe conditions are indicated if you mainly operate your vehicle under one or more of the following conditions:*

Operating in dusty areas
Towing a trailer
Idling for extended periods and/or low speed operation
Operating when outside temperatures remain below freezing and when most trips are less than five miles

**If operated under one or more of the following conditions, change the automatic transaxle fluid every 30,000 miles.*

***If operated under one or more of the following conditions, change the manual transaxle fluid every 60,000 miles.*

In heavy city traffic where the outside temperature regularly reaches 90-degrees F (32-degrees C) or higher
In hilly or mountainous terrain

2   Introduction

This Chapter is designed to help the home mechanic maintain the Civic and CR-V with the goals of maximum performance, economy, safety and reliability in mind.

Included is a master maintenance schedule, followed by procedures dealing specifically with each item on the schedule. Visual checks, adjustments, component replacement and other helpful items are included. Refer to the accompanying illustrations of the engine compartment for the locations of various components.

Servicing the vehicle, in accordance with the mileage/time maintenance schedule and the step-by-step procedures will result in a planned maintenance program that should produce a long and reliable service life. Keep in mind that it is a comprehensive plan, so maintaining some items but not others at the specified intervals will not produce the same results.

As you service the vehicle, you will discover that many of the procedures can - and should - be grouped together because of the nature of the particular procedure you're performing or because of the close proximity of two otherwise unrelated components to one another.

For example, if the vehicle is raised for chassis lubrication, you should inspect the exhaust, suspension, steering and fuel systems while you're under the vehicle. When you're rotating the tires, it makes good sense

to check the brakes since the wheels are already removed. Finally, let's suppose you have to borrow or rent a torque wrench. Even if you only need it to tighten the spark plugs, you might as well check the torque of as many critical fasteners as time allows.

The first step in this maintenance program is to prepare yourself before the actual work begins. Read through all the procedures you're planning to do, then gather up all the parts and tools needed. If it looks like you might run into problems during a particular job, seek advice from a mechanic or an experienced do-it-yourselfer.

Owner's Manual and VECI label information

Your vehicle owner's manual was written for your year and model and contains very specific information on component locations, specifications, fuse ratings, part numbers, etc. The Owner's Manual is an important resource for the do-it-yourselfer to have; if one was not supplied with your vehicle, it can generally be ordered from a dealer parts department.

Among other important information, the Vehicle Emissions Control Information (VECI) label contains specifications and procedures for applicable tune-up adjustments and, in some instances, spark plugs (see Chapter 6 for more information on the VECI label). The information on this label is the exact maintenance data recommended by the manufacturer. This data often varies by intended oper-

ating altitude, local emissions regulations, month of manufacture, etc.

This Chapter contains procedural details, safety information and more ambitious maintenance intervals than you might find in manufacturer's literature. However, you may also find procedures or specifications in your Owner's Manual or VECI label that differ with what's printed here. In these cases, the Owner's Manual or VECI label can be considered correct, since it is specific to your particular vehicle.

3   Tune-up general information

The term tune-up is used in this manual to represent a combination of individual operations rather than one specific procedure.

If, from the time the vehicle is new, the routine maintenance schedule is followed closely and frequent checks are made of fluid levels and high wear items, as suggested throughout this manual, the engine will be kept in relatively good running condition and the need for additional work will be minimized.

More likely than not, however, there will be times when the engine is running poorly due to lack of regular maintenance. This is even more likely if a used vehicle, which has not received regular and frequent maintenance checks, is purchased. In such cases, an engine tune-up will be needed outside of the regular routine maintenance intervals.

1.7L SOHC engine compartment layout

1	Air filter housing	5	Windshield washer fluid reservoir	8	Coolant reservoir
2	Brake fluid reservoir	6	Power steering fluid reservoir	9	Battery
3	Engine oil dipstick	7	Radiator cap	10	Underhood fuse/relay block
4	Engine oil filler cap				

1.8L SOHC engine compartment layout

1	Air filter housing	5	Windshield washer fluid reservoir	9	Battery
2	Brake fluid reservoir	6	Power steering fluid reservoir	10	Underhood fuse/relay block
3	Engine oil dipstick	7	Radiator cap	11	Drivebelt
4	Engine oil filler cap	8	Coolant reservoir		

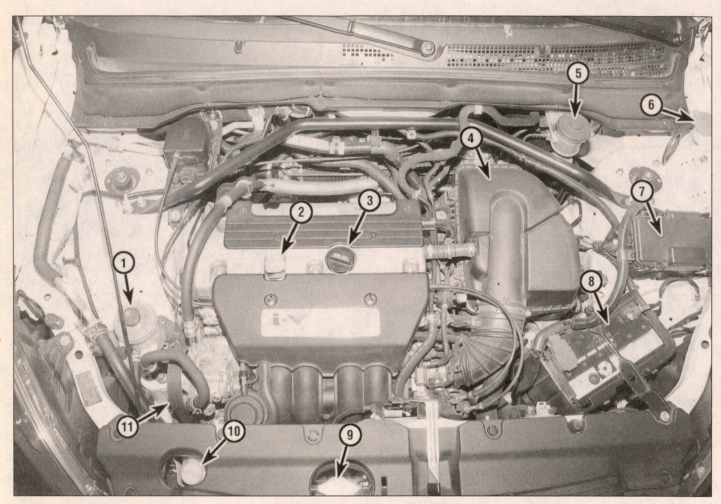

2.4L DOHC engine compartment layout

1	Power steering fluid reservoir	5	Brake fluid reservoir	9 Radiator cap
2	Engine oil dipstick	6	Windshield washer fluid reservoir	10 Coolant reservoir
3	Engine oil filler cap	7	Underhood fuse/relay block	11 Drivebelt
4	Air filter housing	8	Battery	

The first step in any tune-up or diagnostic procedure to help correct a poor running engine is a cylinder compression check. A compression check (see Chapter 2C) will help determine the condition of internal engine components and should be used as a guide for tune-up and repair procedures. If, for instance, a compression check indicates serious internal engine wear, a conventional tune-up will not improve the performance of the engine and would be a waste of time and money. Because of its importance, the compression check should be done by someone with the right equipment and the knowledge to use it properly.

The following procedures are those most often needed to bring a generally poor running engine back into a proper state of tune.

Minor tune-up

Check all engine related fluids (Section 4)
Clean, inspect and test the battery (Section 8)
Check the cooling system (Section 9)
Check all underhood hoses (Section 14)
Check the air filter (Section 15)
Check and adjust the drivebelts (Section 19)

Major tune-up

All items listed under minor tune-up, plus . . .
Replace the air filter (Section 15)
Check the fuel system (Section 17)
Replace the spark plugs (Section 24)

4   Fluid level checks (every 250 miles [400 km] or weekly)

1   Fluids are an essential part of the lubrication, cooling, brake, clutch and other systems. Because these fluids gradually become depleted and/or contaminated during normal operation of the vehicle, they must be periodically replenished. See *Recommended lubricants and fluids* and *Capacities* in this Chapter's Specifications before adding fluid to

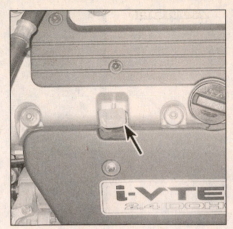
4.2a On DOHC engines, the oil dipstick is located on the front side of the engine

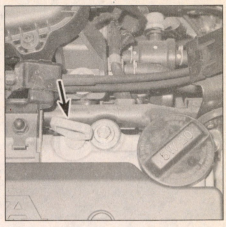
4.2b On SOHC engines, the oil dipstick is located on the left side of the engine

any of the following components. **Note:** *The vehicle must be on level ground before fluid levels can be checked.*

Engine oil

Refer to illustrations 4.2a, 4.2b, 4.4 and 4.6
2   The engine oil level is checked with a dipstick located on top of the valve cover **(see illustrations)**. The dipstick extends through a metal tube from which it protrudes down into the engine oil pan.
3   The oil level should be checked before the vehicle has been driven, or about 5 minutes after the engine has been shut off. If the oil is checked immediately after driving the vehicle, some of the oil will remain in the upper engine components, producing an inaccurate reading on the dipstick.
4   Pull the dipstick from the tube and wipe all the oil from the end with a clean rag or paper towel. Insert the clean dipstick all the way back into its metal tube and pull it out again. Observe the oil at the end of the dipstick. At its highest point, the level should be between the upper and lower holes **(see illustration)**.
5   It takes one quart of oil to raise the level

from the lower hole to the upper hole on the dipstick. Do not allow the level to drop below the lower hole or oil starvation may cause engine damage. Conversely, overfilling the engine (adding oil above the upper hole) may cause oil fouled spark plugs, oil leaks or oil seal failures.
6   Remove the threaded cap from the valve cover to add oil **(see illustration)**. Use a funnel to prevent spills. After adding the oil, install the filler cap hand tight. Start the engine and look carefully for any small leaks around the oil filter or drain plug. Stop the engine and check the oil level again after it has had sufficient time to drain from the upper block and cylinder head galleys.
7   Checking the oil level is an important preventive maintenance step. A continually dropping oil level indicates oil leakage through damaged seals, from loose connections, or past worn rings or valve guides. If the oil looks milky in color or has water droplets in it, a cylinder head gasket may be blown or the oil cooler could be leaking. The engine should be checked immediately. The condition of the oil should also be checked. Each time you check

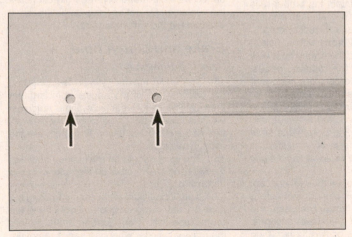
4.4 The oil level should be between the two holes in the dipstick

4.6 The oil filler cap is located on the valve cover - always make sure the area around the opening is clean before unscrewing the cap to prevent dirt from contaminating the engine (DOHC engine shown)

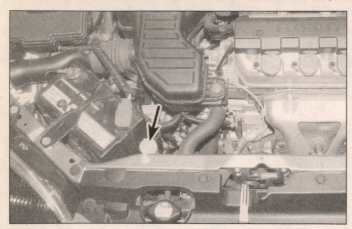

4.9 The cooling system reservoir is located on the right side of the engine compartment on 2005 and earlier models, and on the left side on 2006 and later models

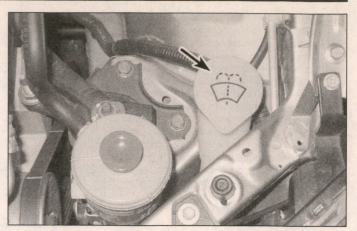

4.14 Fluid for the windshield washer system is stored in this plastic reservoir (1.7L SOHC model shown; consult the engine compartment photos at the beginning of this Chapter for the location on other models)

the oil level, slide your thumb and index finger up the dipstick before wiping off the oil. If you see small dirt or metal particles clinging to the dipstick, the oil should be changed (see Section 6).

Engine coolant

Refer to illustration 4.9

Warning: *Do not allow antifreeze to come in contact with your skin or painted surfaces of the vehicle. Flush contaminated areas immediately with plenty of water. Don't store new coolant or leave old coolant lying around where it's accessible to children or pets - they're attracted by its sweet smell. Ingestion of even a small amount of coolant can be fatal! Wipe up garage floor and drip pan spills immediately. Keep antifreeze containers covered and repair cooling system leaks as soon as they're noticed.*

8   All vehicles covered by this manual are equipped with a pressurized coolant recovery system. A coolant reservoir is connected by a hose to the base of the radiator filler neck. If the coolant overheats, it can escape through the pressurized filler cap, then through the

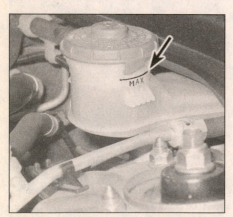

4.16 The brake fluid level should be kept at the MAX mark on the translucent plastic reservoir

connecting hose into the reservoir. As the engine cools, the coolant is automatically drawn back into the cooling system to maintain the correct level.

9   The coolant level in the reservoir should be checked regularly. It must be between the MAX and MIN lines on the tank. The level will vary with the temperature of the engine. When the engine is cold, the coolant level should be at or slightly above the MIN mark on the tank. Once the engine has warmed up, the level should be at or near the MAX mark. If it isn't, allow the fluid in the tank to cool, then remove the cap from the reservoir **(see illustration)** and add coolant to bring the level up to the MAX line. **Warning:** *Do not remove the radiator cap to check the coolant level when the engine is warm!* Use only the recommended coolant and water in the mixture ratio listed in this Chapter's Specifications. Do not use supplemental inhibitors or additives. If only a small amount of coolant is required to bring the system up to the proper level, water can be used. However, repeated additions of water will dilute the recommended antifreeze and water solution. In order to maintain the proper ratio of antifreeze and water, it is advisable to top up the coolant level with the correct mixture.

10   If the coolant level drops within a short time after replenishment, there may be a leak in the system. Inspect the radiator, hoses, engine coolant filler cap, drain plugs and water pump. If no leak is evident, have the radiator cap pressure tested. **Warning:** *Never remove the radiator cap or the coolant reservoir cap when the engine is running or has just been shut down, because the cooling system is hot. Escaping steam and scalding liquid could cause serious injury.*

11   If it is necessary to open the radiator cap, wait until the system has cooled completely, then wrap a thick cloth around the cap and turn it to the first stop. If any steam escapes, wait until the system has cooled further, then remove the cap.

12   When checking the coolant level, always note its condition. It should be relatively clear.

If it is brown or rust colored, the system should be drained, flushed and refilled. Even if the coolant appears to be normal, the corrosion inhibitors wear out with use, so it must be replaced at the specified intervals.

13   Do not allow antifreeze to come in contact with your skin or painted surfaces of the vehicle. Flush contacted areas immediately with plenty of water.

Windshield washer fluid

Refer to illustration 4.14

14   Fluid for the windshield washer system is stored in a plastic reservoir which is located in various locations depending on model and year **(see illustration)**. In milder climates, plain water can be used to top up the reservoir, but the reservoir should be kept no more than 2/3 full to allow for expansion should the water freeze. In colder climates, the use of a specially designed windshield washer fluid, available at your dealer and any auto parts store, will help lower the freezing point of the fluid. Mix the solution with water in accordance with the manufacturer's directions on the container. Do not use regular antifreeze. It will damage the vehicle's paint.

Brake and clutch fluid

Refer to illustration 4.16

15   The brake master cylinder is located on the driver's side of the engine compartment firewall. The clutch master cylinder fluid reservoir is located right next to it on the firewall, behind the left shock tower. They both use the same type of fluid.

16   The level should be maintained between the MIN and MAX marks on the reservoir **(see illustration)**.

17   If additional fluid is necessary to bring the level up, use a rag to clean all dirt off the top of the reservoir. If any foreign matter enters the master cylinder when the cap is removed, blockage in the brake or clutch release system lines can occur. Also, make sure all painted surfaces around the master cylinder are cov-

4.26 The power steering fluid reservoir is translucent so the fluid level can be checked without removing the cap - keep the fluid between the two lines

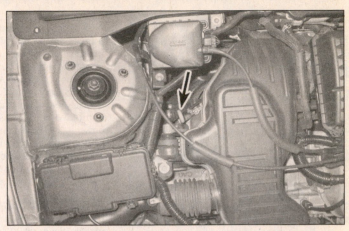

4.32a The automatic transaxle dipstick is located on the right side of the engine compartment on 2005 and earlier Civic models . . .

ered, since brake fluid will ruin paint. Carefully pour new, clean brake fluid into the master cylinder. Be careful not to spill the fluid on painted surfaces. Be sure the specified fluid is used; mixing different types of brake fluid can cause damage to the system. See *Recommended lubricants and fluids* at the beginning of this Chapter or your owner's manual.

18   At this time the fluid and the master cylinder can be inspected for contamination. If deposits, dirt particles or water droplets are seen in the fluid, the system should be drained and refilled with fresh fluid (see Section 20).

19   Reinstall the master cylinder cap.

20   The brake fluid in the master cylinder will drop slightly as the brake shoes or pads at each wheel wear down during normal operation. If the master cylinder requires repeated replenishing to keep the level up, it's an indication of leaks in the brake system, which should be corrected immediately. Check all brake lines and connections, along with the wheel cylinders, if equipped, and booster (see Chapter 9 for more information). As the clutch wears, the fluid level in the clutch master cyl-

inder reservoir will rise. Unless there is a leak in either system, fluid additions shouldn't be necessary.

21   If you discover that the reservoir is empty or nearly empty, the brake (or clutch) system should be filled, bled (see Chapter 9) and checked for leaks.

Power steering fluid

Refer to illustration 4.26

22   Check the power steering fluid level periodically to avoid steering system problems, such as damage to the pump. **Caution:** *DO NOT hold the steering wheel against either stop (extreme left or right turn) for more than five seconds. If you do, the power steering pump could be damaged.*

23   The power steering reservoir is located at the right side of the engine compartment on CR-V models, and on the left side of the engine compartment on Coupe and Sedan models. The reservoir has LOWER LEVEL and UPPER LEVEL fluid level marks on the side. The fluid level can be seen without removing the reservoir cap.

24   Park the vehicle on level ground and apply the parking brake.

25   Run the engine until it has reached normal operating temperature. With the engine at idle, turn the steering wheel back and forth about 10 times to get any air out of the steering system. Shut the engine off with the wheels in the straight-ahead position.

26   Note the fluid level on the side of the reservoir. It should be between the two marks **(see illustration).**

27   Add small amounts of fluid until the level is correct. **Caution:** *Do not overfill the reservoir. If too much fluid is added, remove the excess with a clean syringe or suction pump.*

28   Check the power steering hoses and connections for leaks and wear.

Automatic transaxle fluid

Refer to illustrations 4.32a, 4.32b and 4.32c

29   The level of the automatic transaxle fluid should be carefully maintained. Low fluid level can lead to slipping or loss of drive, while overfilling can cause foaming, loss of fluid and transaxle damage.

30   The transaxle fluid level should only be checked when the transaxle is hot (at its normal operating temperature). If the vehicle has just been driven over 10 miles (15 miles in a frigid climate), and the fluid temperature is 160 to 175-degrees F, the transaxle is hot. **Caution:** *If the vehicle has just been driven for a long time at high speed or in city traffic in hot weather, or if it has been pulling a trailer, an accurate fluid level reading cannot be obtained. Allow the fluid to cool down for about 30 minutes.*

31   If the vehicle has not just been driven, park the vehicle on level ground, set the parking brake and start the engine. While the engine is idling, depress the brake pedal and move the selector lever through all the gear ranges, beginning and ending in Park.

32   With the engine still idling, remove the dipstick from its tube. Check the level of the fluid on the dipstick and note its condition **(see illustrations).**

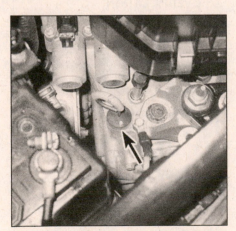

4.32b . . . and on the left side on 2006 and later Civics and all CR-V models

4.32c The automatic transaxle fluid level should be in the cross-hatched area on the dipstick

5.2 A tire tread depth indicator should be used to monitor tire wear - they are available at auto parts stores and service stations and cost very little

33   Wipe the fluid from the dipstick with a clean rag and reinsert it back into the filler tube until the cap seats.

34   Pull the dipstick out again and note the fluid level. The fluid level should be in the operating temperature range (between the upper and lower mark). If the level is at the low side of either range, add the specified automatic transmission fluid through the dip-stick tube with a funnel.

35   Add just enough of the recommended fluid to fill the transaxle to the proper level. It takes about one pint to raise the level from the low mark to the high mark when the fluid is hot, so add the fluid a little at a time and keep checking the level until it is correct.

36   The condition of the fluid should also be checked along with the level. If the fluid at the end of the dipstick is black or a dark reddish brown color, or if it emits a burned smell, the fluid should be changed (see Section 25). If you are in doubt about the condition of the fluid, purchase some new fluid and compare the two for color and smell.

Manual transaxle lubricant

Note: *It isn't necessary to check this lubricant weekly; every 15,000 miles (24,000 km) or 12 months will be adequate.*

37   The manual transaxle does not have a dipstick. To check the fluid level, raise the vehicle and support it securely on jackstands. On the transaxle housing, remove the fluid fill plug. If the lubricant level is correct, it should be up to the lower edge of the hole.

38   If the transaxle needs more lubricant (if the level is not up to the hole), use a syringe or a gear oil pump to add more. Stop filling the transaxle when the lubricant begins to run out the hole.

39   Install the plug and tighten it securely. Drive the vehicle a short distance, then check for leaks.

Rear differential lubricant (CR-V)

Note: *It isn't necessary to check this lubricant weekly; every 15,000 miles (24,000 km) or 12 months will be adequate.*

40   To check the fluid level, raise the vehicle and support it securely on jackstands. On the axle housing, remove the check/fill plug. If the lubricant level is correct, it should be up to the lower edge of the hole.

41   If the differential needs more lubricant (if the level is not up to the hole), use a syringe or a gear oil pump to add more. Stop filling the differential when the lubricant begins to run out the hole.

42   Install the plug and tighten it securely. Drive the vehicle a short distance, then check for leaks.

---

5   Tire and tire pressure checks (every 250 miles [400 km] or weekly)

Refer to illustrations 5.2, 5.3, 5.4a, 5.4b and 5.8

1   Periodic inspection of the tires may spare you from the inconvenience of being stranded with a flat tire. It can also provide you with vital information regarding possible problems in the steering and suspension systems before major damage occurs.

UNDERINFLATION

CUPPING

Cupping may be caused by:
- Underinflation and/or mechanical irregularities such as out-of-balance condition of wheel and/or tire, and bent or damaged wheel.
- Loose or worn steering tie-rod or steering idler arm.
- Loose, damaged or worn front suspension parts.

OVERINFLATION

INCORRECT TOE-IN OR EXTREME CAMBER

FEATHERING DUE TO MISALIGNMENT

5.3 This chart will help you determine the condition of your tires, the probable cause(s) of abnormal wear and the corrective action necessary

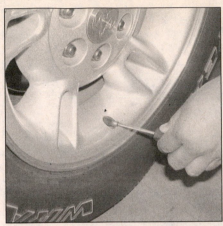

5.4a If a tire loses air on a steady basis, check the valve core first to make sure it's snug (special inexpensive wrenches are commonly available at auto parts stores

5.4b If the valve core is tight, raise the corner of the vehicle with the low tire and spray a soapy water solution onto the tread as the tire is turned slowly - slow leaks will cause small bubbles to appear

5.8 To extend the life of your tires, check the air pressure at least once a week with an accurate gauge (don't forget the spare!)

2   Tires are equipped with 1/2-inch wide bands that will appear when tread depth reaches 1/16-inch, at which point they can be considered worn out. Tread wear can be monitored with a simple, inexpensive device known as a tread depth indicator **(see illustration).**

3   Note any abnormal tread wear **(see illustration).** Tread pattern irregularities such as cupping, flat spots and more wear on one side than the other are indications of front end alignment and/or balance problems. If any of these conditions are noted, take the vehicle to a tire shop or service station to correct the problem.

4   Look closely for cuts, punctures and embedded nails or tacks. Sometimes a tire will hold its air pressure for a short time or leak down very slowly even after a nail has embedded itself into the tread. If a slow leak persists, check the valve core to make sure it is tight **(see illustration).** Examine the tread for an object that may have embedded itself into the tire or for a plug that may have begun to leak (radial tire punctures are repaired with a plug that is installed in a puncture). If a puncture is suspected, it can be easily verified by spraying a solution of soapy water onto the puncture area **(see illustration).** The soapy solution will bubble if there is a leak. Unless the puncture is inordinately large, a tire shop or gas station can usually repair the punctured tire.

5   Carefully inspect the inner side of each tire for evidence of brake fluid leakage. If you see any, inspect the brakes immediately.

6   Correct tire air pressure adds miles to the lifespan of the tires, improves mileage and enhances overall ride quality. Tire pressure cannot be accurately estimated by looking at a tire, particularly if it is a radial. A tire pressure gauge is therefore essential. Keep an accurate gauge in the glove box. The pressure gauges fitted to the nozzles of air hoses at gas stations are often inaccurate.

7   Always check tire pressure when the

tires are cold. "Cold," in this case, means the vehicle has not been driven over a mile in the three hours preceding a tire pressure check. A pressure rise of four to eight pounds is not uncommon once the tires are warm.

8   Unscrew the valve cap protruding from the wheel or hubcap and push the gauge firmly onto the valve **(see illustration).** Note the reading on the gauge and compare this figure to the recommended tire pressure shown on the tire placard on the left door jamb or in your owner's manual. Be sure to reinstall the valve cap to keep dirt and moisture out of the valve stem mechanism. Check all four tires and, if necessary, add enough air to bring them up to the recommended pressure levels.

9   Don't forget to keep the spare tire inflated to the specified pressure (consult your owner's manual). Note that the air pressure specified for the compact spare is significantly higher than the pressure of the regular tires.

6   Engine oil and oil filter change (every 3000 miles [4800 km] or 3 months)

Refer to illustrations 6.2, 6.7, 6.12 and 6.14

Note: *While the vehicle is raised, be sure to check the manual transaxle fluid level (if equipped) and if you have a 4WD CR-V model, the rear differential fluid level.*

1   Frequent oil changes are the best preventive maintenance the home mechanic can give the engine, because aging oil becomes diluted and contaminated, which leads to premature engine wear.

2   Make sure you have all the necessary tools before you begin this procedure **(see illustration).** You should also have plenty of rags or newspapers handy for mopping up any spills.

3   Access to the underside of the vehicle is greatly improved if the vehicle can be lifted

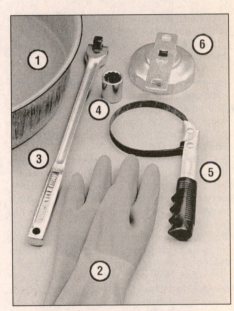

6.2 These tools are required when changing the engine oil and filter

1   *Drain pan - It should be fairly shallow in depth, but wide in order to prevent spills*

2   *Rubber gloves - When removing the drain plug and filter, it is inevitable that you will get oil on your hands (the gloves will prevent burns)*

3   *Breaker bar - Sometimes the oil drain plug is pretty tight and a long breaker bar is needed to loosen it*

4   *Socket - To be used with the breaker bar or a ratchet (must be the correct size to fit the drain plug)*

5   *Filter wrench - This is a metal band-type wrench, which requires clearance around the filter to be effective*

6   *Filter wrench - This type fits on the bottom of the filter and can be turned with a ratchet or beaker bar (different size wrenches are available for different types of filters)*

6.7 Use the proper size box-end wrench or socket to remove the oil drain plug and avoid rounding it off

6.12 Use an oil filter wrench to remove the filter

on a hoist, driven onto ramps or supported by jackstands. **Warning:** *Do not work under a vehicle which is supported only by a bumper, hydraulic or scissors-type jack.*

4   If this is your first oil change, get under the vehicle and familiarize yourself with the locations of the oil drain plug and the oil filter. The engine and exhaust components will be warm during the actual work, so try to anticipate any potential problems before the engine and accessories are hot.

5   Park the vehicle on a level spot. Start the engine and allow it to reach its normal operating temperature. Warm oil and sludge will flow out more easily. Turn off the engine when it's warmed up. Remove the filler cap from the valve cover.

6   Raise the vehicle and support it securely on jackstands. **Warning:** *Never get beneath the vehicle when it is supported only by a jack. The jack provided with your vehicle is designed solely for raising the vehicle to remove and replace the wheels. Always use jackstands to support the vehicle when it becomes necessary to place your body underneath the vehicle.*

7   Being careful not to touch the hot exhaust components, place the drain pan under the drain plug in the bottom of the pan and remove the plug **(see illustration)**. You may want to wear gloves while unscrewing the plug the final few turns if the engine is hot.

8   Allow the old oil to drain into the pan. It may be necessary to move the pan farther under the engine as the oil flow slows to a trickle. Inspect the old oil for the presence of metal shavings and chips.

9   After all the oil has drained, wipe off the drain plug with a clean rag. Even minute metal particles clinging to the plug would immediately contaminate the new oil.

10   Clean the area around the drain plug opening, reinstall the plug and tighten it to the torque listed in this Chapter's Specifications.

11   Move the drain pan into position under the oil filter.

12   Loosen the oil filter **(see illustration)** by turning it counterclockwise with an oil filter wrench. Once the filter is loose, use your hands to unscrew it from the block. Keep the open end pointing up to prevent the oil inside the filter from spilling out. **Warning:** *The exhaust system may still be hot, so be careful.*

13   With a clean rag, wipe off the mounting surface on the block. If a residue of old oil is allowed to remain, it will smoke when the block is heated up. Also make sure that none of the old gasket remains stuck to the mounting surface. It can be removed with a scraper if necessary.

14   Compare the old filter with the new one to make sure they are the same type. Smear some clean engine oil on the rubber gasket of the new filter **(see illustration)**.

15   Attach the new filter to the engine, following the tightening directions printed on the filter canister or packing box. Most filter manufacturers recommend against using a filter wrench due to the possibility of overtightening and damaging the seal.

16   Remove all tools, rags, etc. from under the vehicle, being careful not to spill the oil in the drain pan, then lower the vehicle.

17   Add new oil to the engine through the oil filler cap in the valve cover. Use a funnel, if necessary, to prevent oil from spilling onto the top of the engine. Pour three quarts of fresh oil into the engine. Wait a few minutes to allow the oil to drain into the pan, then check the level on the oil dipstick (see Section 4). If the oil level is at or near the upper hole on the dipstick, install the filler cap hand tight, start the engine and allow the new oil to circulate.

18   Allow the engine to run for about a minute, then turn it off. Look under the vehicle and check for leaks at the oil pan drain plug and around the oil filter. If either is leaking, tighten the plug or filter.

19   Wait a few minutes to allow the oil to trickle down into the pan, then recheck the level on the dipstick and, if necessary, add enough oil to bring the level to the upper hole.

20   During the first few trips after an oil change, make it a point to check frequently for leaks and proper oil level.

21   The old oil drained from the engine cannot be reused in its present state and should be disposed of. Check with your local auto parts store, disposal facility or environmental agency to see if they will accept the oil for recycling. After the oil has cooled it can be drained into a container (capped plastic jugs, topped bottles, milk cartons, etc.) for transport to one of these disposal sites. Don't dispose of the oil by pouring it on the ground or down a drain!

Oil life indicator - resetting

2006 and earlier models

22   With the ignition key Off, press the select/reset button and hold it in the depressed position, then turn the ignition key to the On position.

23   Continue to hold the button for approximately 10 more seconds until the indicator turns off.

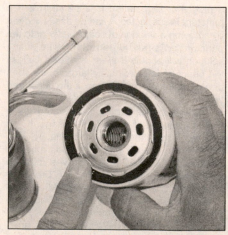

6.14 Lubricate the oil filter gasket with clean engine oil before installing the filter on the engine

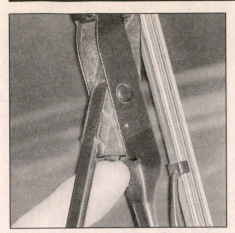

7.5a To release the blade holder, pull up on the release tab . . .

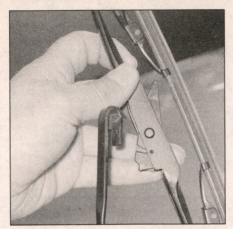

7.5b . . . and pull the wiper blade in the direction of the windshield to separate it from the arm

8.1 Tools and materials required for battery maintenance

1   *Face shield/safety goggles - When removing corrosion with a brush, the acidic particles can easily fly up into your eyes*
2   *Baking soda - A solution of baking soda and water can be used to neutralize corrosion*
3   *Petroleum jelly - A layer of this on the battery posts will help prevent corrosion*
4   *Battery post/cable cleaner - This wire brush cleaning tool will remove all traces of corrosion from the battery posts and cable clamps*
5   *Treated felt washers - Placing one of these on each post, directly under the cable clamps, will help prevent corrosion*
6   *Puller - Sometimes the cable clamps are very difficult to pull off the posts, even after the nut/bolt has been completely loosened. This tool pulls the clamp straight up and off the post without damage*
7   *Battery post/cable cleaner - Here is another cleaning tool which is a slightly different version of number 4 above, but it does the same thing*
8   *Rubber gloves - Another safety item to consider when servicing the battery; remember that's acid inside the battery*

2007 and later Civic models

24   Turn the ignition to the "ON" position but do not start the vehicle.
25   Push the select/reset button repeatedly until the engine oil life indicator comes on.
26   Once the display is on, press and hold the select/reset button for 10 seconds. The display should go to the reset display mode (start blinking).
27   Press and hold the select/reset button again for more than 5 seconds. The display reset mode will disappear and the engine oil life display will reset to 100 percent.

2007 and later CR-V models

28   Turn the ignition to the "ON" position but do not start the vehicle.
29   Push the select/reset knob repeatedly until the engine oil life appears on the screen.
30   Press and hold the select/reset knob for 10 seconds.
31   Turn the select/reset knob until "oil life" is displayed. When the display starts blinking, push the select/reset knob.
32   When the engine oil life and maintenance item code begins to blink, push the select/reset knob; the engine oil life should reset to "100" and the maintenance item code should disappear.

7   Windshield wiper blade inspection and replacement (every 7500 miles [12,000 km] or 6 months)

Refer to illustrations 7.5a and 7.5b

1   The windshield wiper and blade assembly should be inspected periodically for damage, loose components and cracked or worn blade elements.
2   Road film can build up on the wiper blades and affect their efficiency, so they should be washed regularly with a mild detergent solution.
3   The action of the wiping mechanism can loosen bolts, nuts and fasteners, so they should be checked and tightened, as necessary, at the same time the wiper blades are checked.
4   If the wiper blade elements are cracked, worn or warped, or no longer clean adequately, they should be replaced with new ones.
5   Lift the arm assembly away from the glass for clearance, press on the release lever, then slide the wiper blade assembly out of the hook at the end of the arm (see illustrations).
6   Attach the new wiper to the arm. Connection can be confirmed by an audible click.

8   Battery check, maintenance and charging (every 7500 miles [12,000 km] or 6 months)

Refer to illustrations 8.1, 8.6a, 8.6b, 8.7a and 8.7b

Warning: *Certain precautions must be followed when checking and servicing the battery. Hydrogen gas, which is highly flammable, is always present in the battery cells, so keep lighted tobacco and all other open flames and sparks away from the battery. The electrolyte inside the battery is actually diluted sulfuric acid, which will cause injury if splashed on your skin or in your eyes. It will also ruin clothes and painted surfaces. When removing the battery cables, always detach the negative cable first and hook it up last!*

1   A routine preventive maintenance program for the battery in your vehicle is the only way to ensure quick and reliable starts. But before performing any battery maintenance, make sure that you have the proper equipment necessary to work safely around the battery (see illustration).
2   There are also several precautions that should be taken whenever battery maintenance is performed. Before servicing the battery, always turn the engine and all accessories off and disconnect the cable from the negative terminal of the battery (see Chapter 5, Section 1).
3   The battery produces hydrogen gas, which is both flammable and explosive. Never create a spark, smoke or light a match around the battery. Always charge the battery in a ventilated area.
4   Electrolyte contains poisonous and corrosive sulfuric acid. Do not allow it to get in your eyes, on your skin on your clothes. Never ingest it. Wear protective safety glasses when

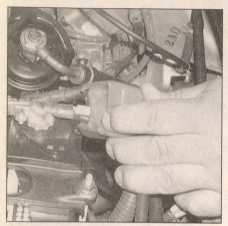

8.6a Battery terminal corrosion usually appears as light, fluffy powder

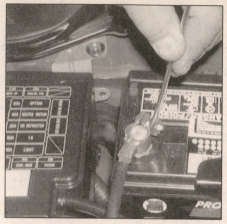

8.6b Removing a cable from the battery post with a wrench - sometimes a pair of special battery pliers are required for this procedure if corrosion has caused deterioration of the nut hex (always remove the ground (-) cable first and hook it up last!)

working near the battery. Keep children away from the battery.

5   Note the external condition of the battery. If the positive terminal and cable clamp on your vehicle's battery is equipped with a rubber protector, make sure that it's not torn or damaged. It should completely cover the terminal. Look for any corroded or loose connections, cracks in the case or cover or loose hold-down clamps. Also check the entire length of each cable for cracks and frayed conductors.

6   If corrosion, which looks like white, fluffy deposits **(see illustration)** is evident, particularly around the terminals, the battery should be removed for cleaning. Loosen the cable clamp bolts with a wrench, being careful to remove the ground cable first, and slide them off the terminals **(see illustration)**. Then disconnect the hold-down clamp bolt and nut, remove the clamp and lift the battery from the engine compartment.

7   Clean the cable clamps thoroughly with a battery brush or a terminal cleaner and a solution of warm water and baking soda **(see illustration)**. Wash the terminals and the top of the battery case with the same solution but make sure that the solution doesn't get into the battery. When cleaning the cables, terminals and battery top, wear safety goggles and rubber gloves to prevent any solution from coming in contact with your eyes or hands. Wear old clothes too - even diluted, sulfuric acid splashed onto clothes will burn holes in them. If the terminals have been extensively corroded, clean them up with a terminal cleaner **(see illustration)**. Thoroughly wash all cleaned areas with plain water.

8   Make sure that the battery tray is in good condition and the hold-down clamp fasteners are tight. If the battery is removed from the tray, make sure no parts remain in the bottom of the tray when the battery is reinstalled. When reinstalling the hold-down clamp bolts, do not overtighten them.

9   Information on removing and installing the battery can be found in Chapter 5. If you disconnected the cable(s) from the negative and/or positive battery terminals, see Chapter 5, Section 1. Information on jump starting

can be found at the front of this manual. For more detailed battery checking procedures, refer to the *Haynes Automotive Electrical Manual.*

10   Corrosion on the hold-down components, battery case and surrounding areas can be removed with a solution of water and baking soda. Thoroughly rinse all cleaned areas with plain water.

11   Any metal parts of the vehicle damaged by corrosion should be covered with a zinc-based primer, then painted.

Charging

Warning: *When batteries are being charged, hydrogen gas, which is very explosive and flammable, is produced. Do not smoke or allow open flames near a charging or a recently charged battery. Wear eye protection when near the battery during charging. Also,*

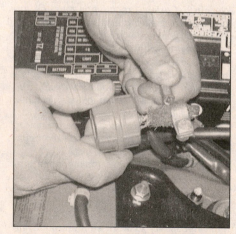

8.7a When cleaning the cable clamps, all corrosion must be removed (the inside of the clamp is tapered to match the taper on the post, so don't remove too much material)

make sure the charger is unplugged before connecting or disconnecting the battery from the charger.

12   Slow-rate charging is the best way to restore a battery that's discharged to the point where it will not start the engine. It's also a good way to maintain the battery charge in a vehicle that's only driven a few miles between starts. Maintaining the battery charge is particularly important in the winter when the battery must work harder to start the engine and electrical accessories that drain the battery are in greater use.

13   It's best to use a one or two-amp battery charger (sometimes called a "trickle" charger). They are the safest and put the least strain on the battery. They are also the least expensive. For a faster charge, you can use a higher amperage charger, but don't use one rated more than 1/10th the amp/hour rating of the battery. Rapid boost charges that claim to restore the power of the battery in one to two hours are hardest on the battery and can damage batteries not in good condition. This type of charging should only be used in emergency situations.

14   The average time necessary to charge a battery should be listed in the instructions that come with the charger. As a general rule, a trickle charger will charge a battery in 12 to 16 hours.

9   Cooling system check (every 7500 miles [12,000 km] or 6 months)

Refer to illustration 9.4

Warning: *Wait until the engine is completely cool before beginning this procedure.*

1   Many major engine failures can be attributed to a faulty cooling system. The cooling system also cools the transaxle fluid and thus plays an important role in prolonging transaxle life.

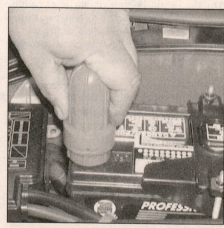

8.7b Regardless of the type of tool used to clean the battery posts, a clean, shiny surface should be the result

Check for a chafed area that could fail prematurely.

Check for a soft area indicating the hose has deteriorated inside.

Overtightening the clamp on a hardened hose will damage the hose and cause a leak.

Check each hose for swelling and oil-soaked ends. Cracks and breaks can be located by squeezing the hose.

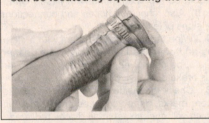

9.4 Hoses, like drivebelts, have a habit of failing at the worst possible time - to prevent the inconvenience of a blown radiator or heater hose, inspect them carefully as shown here

2   The cooling system should be checked with the engine cold. Do this before the vehicle is driven for the day or after the engine has been shut off for at least three hours.

3   Remove the radiator cap by turning it to the left until it reaches a stop. If you hear a hissing sound (indicating there is still pressure in the system), wait until it stops. Now press down on the cap with the palm of your hand and continue turning to the left until the cap can be removed. Thoroughly clean the cap, inside and out, with clean water. Also clean the filler neck on the radiator. All traces of corrosion should be removed. The coolant inside the radiator should be relatively transparent. If it's rust colored, the system should be drained and refilled (see Section 21). If the coolant level isn't up to the top, add additional antifreeze/coolant mixture (see Section 4).

4   Carefully check the large upper and lower radiator hoses along with the smaller diameter heater hoses which run from the

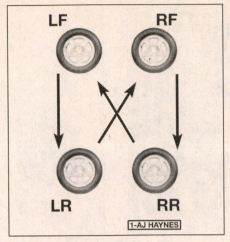

10.2a The recommended rotation pattern for *non-directional* radial tires

engine to the firewall. Inspect each hose along its entire length, replacing any hose which is cracked, swollen or shows signs of deterioration. Cracks may become more apparent if the hose is squeezed **(see illustration)**. Regardless of condition, it's a good idea to replace hoses with new ones every two years.

5   Make sure that all hose connections are tight. A leak in the cooling system will usually show up as white or rust colored deposits on the areas adjoining the leak. If wire-type clamps are used at the ends of the hoses, it may be a good idea to replace them with more secure screw-type clamps.

6   Use compressed air or a soft brush to remove bugs, leaves, etc. from the front of the radiator or air conditioning condenser. Be careful not to damage the delicate cooling fins or cut yourself on them.

7   Every other inspection, or at the first indication of cooling system problems, have the cap and system pressure tested. If you don't have a pressure tester, most gas stations and repair shops will do this for a minimal charge.

10   Tire rotation (every 7500 miles [12,000 km] or 6 months)

Refer to illustrations 10.2a and 10.2b

1   The tires should be rotated at the specified intervals and whenever uneven wear is noticed. Since the vehicle will be raised and the tires removed anyway, check the brakes (see Section 12) at this time.

2   Radial tires must be rotated in a specific pattern **(see illustrations)**. Most models are equipped with non-directional tires, but some models may have directional tires, which have a different rotation pattern. When rotating tires, examine the sidewalls. Directional tires have arrows on the sidewall that indicate the direction they must turn, and a set of these tires includes two left-side tires and two right-side tires. The left and right side tires must not

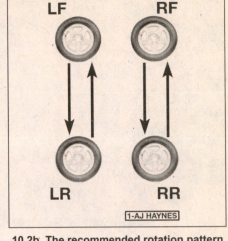

10.2b The recommended rotation pattern for *directional* radial tires

be rotated to the other side.

3   Refer to the information in *Jacking and towing* at the front of this manual for the proper procedures to follow when raising the vehicle and changing a tire. If the brakes are to be checked, do not apply the parking brake as stated. Make sure the tires are blocked to prevent the vehicle from rolling.

4   Preferably, the entire vehicle should be raised at the same time. This can be done on a hoist or by jacking up each corner and then lowering the vehicle onto jackstands placed under the frame rails. Always use four jackstands and make sure the vehicle is firmly supported.

5   After rotation, check and adjust the tire pressures as necessary and be sure to check the lug nut tightness. Ideally, lug nuts should be tightened to the torque listed in this Chapter's Specifications with a torque wrench, and rechecked after 25 miles of driving.

6   For further information on the wheels and tires, refer to Chapter 10.

11   Seat belt check (every 7500 miles [12,000 km] or 6 months)

1   Check seat belts, buckles, latch plates and guide loops for obvious damage and signs of wear.

2   See if the seat belt reminder light comes on when the key is turned to the Run or Start position. A chime should also sound. On passive restraint systems, the shoulder belt should move into position in the A-pillar.

3   The seat belts are designed to lock up during a sudden stop or impact, yet allow free movement during normal driving. Make sure the retractors return the belt against your chest while driving and rewind the belt fully when the buckle is unlatched.

4   If any of the above checks reveal problems with the seat belt system, replace parts as necessary.

12.6 You will find an inspection window in each caliper - the inner brake pad lining thickness can be determined by looking through this window

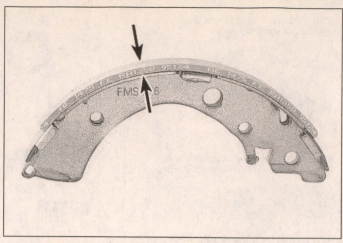

12.14 If the lining is bonded to the brake shoe, measure the lining thickness from the outer surface to the metal shoe; if the lining is riveted to the shoe, measure from the lining outer surface to the rivet head

12   Brake system check (every 7500 miles [12,000 km] or 6 months)

Warning: *The dust created by the brake system is harmful to your health. Never blow it out with compressed air and don't inhale any of it. An approved filtering mask should be worn when working on the brakes. Do not, under any circumstances, use petroleum-based solvents to clean brake parts. Use brake system cleaner only!*

Note: *For detailed photographs of the brake system, refer to Chapter 9.*

1   In addition to the specified intervals, the brakes should be inspected every time the wheels are removed or whenever a defect is suspected.

2   Any of the following symptoms could indicate a potential brake system defect: The vehicle pulls to one side when the brake pedal is depressed; the brakes make squealing or dragging noises when applied; brake pedal travel is excessive; the pedal pulsates; or brake fluid leaks, usually onto the inside of the tire or wheel.

Disc brakes

Refer to illustration 12.6

3   Disc brakes can be visually checked without removing any parts except the wheels. Remove the hub caps (if applicable) and loosen the wheel lug nuts a quarter turn each.

4   Raise the vehicle and place it securely on jackstands. **Warning:** *Never work under a vehicle that is supported only by a jack!*

5   Remove the wheels. Now visible is the disc brake caliper which contains the pads. There is an outer brake pad and an inner pad. Both must be checked for wear.

6   Measure the thickness of the outer pad at each end of the caliper and the inner pad through the inspection hole in the caliper body **(see illustration)**. Compare the measurement with the limit given in this Chapter's

Specifications; if any brake pad thickness is less than specified, then all brake pads must be replaced (see Chapter 9).

7   If you're in doubt as to the exact pad thickness or quality, remove them for measurement and further inspection (see Chapter 9).

8   Check the disc for score marks, wear and burned spots. If any of these conditions exist, the disc should be removed for servicing or replacement (see Chapter 9).

9   Before installing the wheels, check all the brake lines and hoses for damage, wear, deformation, cracks, corrosion, leakage, bends and twists, particularly in the vicinity of the rubber hoses and calipers.

10   Install the wheels, lower the vehicle and tighten the wheel lug nuts to the torque given in this Chapter's Specifications.

Drum brakes

Refer to illustrations 12.14 and 12.16

11   Loosen the rear wheel lug nuts, then raise the vehicle and support it securely on jackstands. Make sure the parking brake is off, then tap on the outside of the drum with a rubber mallet to loosen it.

12   Remove the brake drums. If the drum still won't come off, refer to Chapter 9

13   With the drums removed, carefully clean the brake assembly with brake system cleaner. **Warning:** *Don't blow the dust out with compressed air and don't inhale any of it (it is harmful to your health).*

14   Note the thickness of the lining material on both front and rear brake shoes **(see illustration)**. Compare the measurement with the limit given in this Chapter's Specifications; if any lining thickness is less than specified, then all of the brake shoes must be replaced (see Chapter 9). The shoes should also be replaced if they're cracked, glazed (shiny areas), or covered with brake fluid.

15   Make sure all the brake assembly springs are connected and in good condition.

16   Check the brake components for signs of fluid leakage. With your finger or a small screwdriver, carefully pry back the rubber cups on the wheel cylinder located at the top of the brake shoes **(see illustration)**. Any leakage here is an indication that the wheel cylinders should be replaced immediately (see Chapter 9). Also, check all hoses and connections for signs of leakage.

17   Wipe the inside of the drum with a clean rag and denatured alcohol or brake cleaner. Again, be careful not to breathe the dangerous brake dust.

18   Check the inside of the drum for cracks, score marks, deep scratches and hard spots which will appear as small discolored areas. If imperfections cannot be removed with fine emery cloth, the drum must be taken to an automotive machine shop for resurfacing.

19   Repeat the procedure for the remaining wheel. If the inspection reveals that all parts are in good condition, reinstall the brake drums, install the wheels and lower the vehicle to the ground.

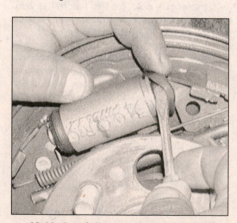

12.16 Carefully peel back the wheel cylinder boot and check for leaking fluid, indicating that the cylinder must be replaced

13.4 Check the shocks for leakage at the indicated area

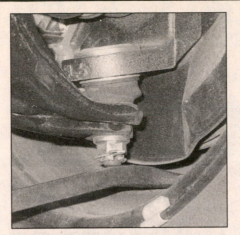

13.10 To check the balljoint for wear, try to pry the control arm up and down to make sure there is no play in the balljoint (if there is, replace it)

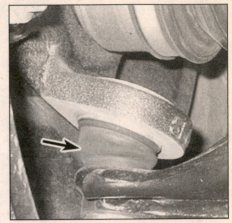

13.11 Check the balljoint boot for damage

Brake booster check

20   Sit in the driver's seat and perform the following sequence of tests.
21   With the brake fully depressed, start the engine - the pedal should move down a little when the engine starts.
22   With the engine running, depress the brake pedal several times - the travel distance should not change.
23   Depress the brake, stop the engine and hold the pedal in for about 30 seconds - the pedal should neither sink nor rise.
24   Restart the engine, run it for about a minute and turn it off. Then firmly depress the brake several times - the pedal travel should decrease with each application.
25   If your brakes do not operate as described, the brake booster has failed. Refer to Chapter 9 for the replacement procedure.

Parking brake

26   Slowly pull up on the parking brake and count the number of clicks you hear until the handle is up as far as it will go. The adjustment is correct if you hear the specified number of clicks (see this Chapter's Specifications). If you hear more or fewer clicks, it's time to adjust the parking brake (see Chapter 9).
27   An alternative method of checking the parking brake is to park the vehicle on a steep hill with the parking brake set and the transmission in Neutral. If the parking brake cannot prevent the vehicle from rolling, it is in need of adjustment (see Chapter 9).

13   Steering, suspension and driveaxle boot check (every 15,000 miles [24,000 km] or 12 months)

Note: For detailed illustrations of the steering and suspension components, refer to Chapter 10.

With the wheels on the ground

Refer to illustration 13.4

1   With the vehicle stopped and the front wheels pointed straight ahead, rock the steering wheel gently back and forth. If freeplay is excessive, a front wheel bearing, steering shaft universal joint or lower arm balljoint is worn or the steering gear is out of adjustment or broken. Refer to Chapter 10 for the appropriate repair procedure.
2   Other symptoms, such as excessive vehicle body movement over rough roads, swaying (leaning) around corners and binding as the steering wheel is turned, may indicate faulty steering and/or suspension components.
3   Check the shock absorbers by pushing down and releasing the vehicle several times at each corner. If the vehicle does not come back to a level position within one or two bounces, the shocks/struts are worn and must be replaced. When bouncing the vehicle up and down, listen for squeaks and noises from the suspension components.
4   Check the struts and shock absorbers for evidence of fluid leakage (see illustration). A light film of fluid is no cause for concern. Make sure that any fluid noted is from the shocks and not from some other source. If leakage is noted, replace the shocks as a set.
5   Check the shocks to be sure they are securely mounted and undamaged. Check the upper mounts for damage and wear. If damage or wear is noted, replace the shocks as a set (front and rear).
6   If the shocks must be replaced, refer to Chapter 10 for the procedure.

Under the vehicle

Refer to illustrations 13.10 and 13.11

7   Raise the vehicle with a floor jack and support it securely on jackstands. See Jacking and towing at the front of this book for the proper jacking points.
8   Check the tires for irregular wear patterns and proper inflation. See Section 5 in this Chapter for information regarding tire wear and Chapter 10 for information on hub bearing replacement.
9   Inspect the universal joint between the steering shaft and the steering gear housing. Check the steering gear housing for lubricant leakage. Make sure that the dust seals and boots are not damaged and that the boot clamps are not loose. Check the steering linkage for looseness or damage. Check the tie-rod ends for excessive play. Look for loose bolts, broken or disconnected parts and deteriorated rubber bushings on all suspension and steering components. While an assistant turns the steering wheel from side to side, check the steering components for free movement, chafing and binding. If the steering components do not seem to be reacting with the movement of the steering wheel, try to determine where the slack is located.
10   Check the balljoints for wear by trying to move each control arm up and down with a pry bar (see illustration) to ensure that its balljoint has no play. If any balljoint does have play, replace it. See Chapter 10 for the balljoint replacement procedure.
11   Inspect the balljoint boots for damage and leaking grease (see illustration). Replace the balljoints with new ones if they are damaged (see Chapter 10).
12   At the rear of the vehicle, inspect the suspension arm bushings for deterioration. Additional information on suspension components can be found in Chapter 10.

Driveaxle boot check

Refer to illustration 13.14

Note: For detailed illustrations of the driveaxles, refer to Chapter 8.

13   The driveaxle boots are very important because they prevent dirt, water and foreign

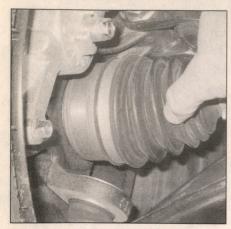

13.14 Flex the driveaxle boots by hand to check for cracks and/or leaking grease

material from entering and damaging the constant velocity (CV) joints. Oil and grease can cause the boot material to deteriorate prematurely, so it's a good idea to wash the boots with soap and water. Because it constantly pivots back and forth following the steering action of the front hub, the outer CV boot wears out sooner and should be inspected regularly.

14   Inspect the boots for tears and cracks as well as loose clamps **(see illustration)**. If there is any evidence of cracks or leaking lubricant, they must be replaced as described in Chapter 8.

14   Underhood hose check and replacement (every 15,000 miles [24,000 km] or 12 months)

Warning: *Replacement of air conditioning hoses must be left to a dealer service department or air conditioning shop that has the equipment to depressurize the system safely. Never remove air conditioning components or hoses until the system has been depressurized.*

General

1   High temperatures under the hood can cause deterioration of the rubber and plastic hoses used for engine, accessory and emission systems operation. Periodic inspection should be made for cracks, loose clamps, material hardening and leaks.

2   Information specific to the cooling system hoses can be found in Section 9.

3   Most (but not all) hoses are secured to the fittings with clamps. Where clamps are used, check to be sure they haven't lost their tension, allowing the hose to leak. If clamps aren't used, make sure the hose has not expanded and/or hardened where it slips over the fitting, allowing it to leak.

PCV system hose

4   To reduce hydrocarbon emissions, crankcase blow-by gas is vented through the PCV

valve in the rocker arm cover to the intake manifold via a rubber hose on most models. The blow-by gases mix with incoming air in the intake manifold before being burned in the combustion chambers.

5   Check the PCV hose for cracks, leaks and other damage. Disconnect it from the valve cover and the intake manifold and check the inside for obstructions. If it's clogged, clean it out with solvent. See Chapter 6 for check and replacement.

Vacuum hoses

6   It's quite common for vacuum hoses, especially those in the emissions system, to be color coded or identified by colored stripes molded into them. Various systems require hoses with different wall thickness, collapse resistance and temperature resistance. When replacing hoses, be sure the new ones are made of the same material.

7   Often the only effective way to check a hose is to remove it completely from the vehicle. If more than one hose is removed, be sure to label the hoses and fittings to ensure correct installation.

8   When checking vacuum hoses, be sure to include any plastic T-fittings in the check. Inspect the fittings for cracks and the hose where it fits over each fitting for distortion, which could cause leakage.

9   A small piece of vacuum hose (1/4-inch inside diameter) can be used as a stethoscope to detect vacuum leaks. Hold one end of the hose to your ear and probe around vacuum hoses and fittings, listening for the hissing sound characteristic of a vacuum leak. **Warning:** *When probing with the vacuum hose stethoscope, be careful not to come into contact with moving engine components such as drivebelts, the cooling fan, etc.*

Fuel hose

Warning: *Gasoline is flammable, so take extra precautions when you work on any part of the fuel system. Don't smoke or allow open flames or bare light bulbs near the work area, and don't work in a garage where a gas-type appliance (such as a water heater or clothes dryer) is present. Since fuel is carcinogenic, wear fuel-resistant gloves when there's a possibility of being exposed to fuel, and, if you spill any fuel on your skin, rinse it off immediately with soap and water. Mop up any spills immediately and do not store fuel-soaked rags where they could ignite. The fuel system is under constant pressure, so, if any fuel lines are to be disconnected, the fuel pressure in the system must be relieved first (see Chapter 4 for more information). When you perform any kind of work on the fuel system, wear safety glasses and have a Class B type fire extinguisher on hand.*

10   The fuel lines are usually under pressure, so if any fuel lines are to be disconnected be prepared to catch spilled fuel. **Warning:** *Your vehicle is equipped with fuel injection and you must relieve the fuel system pressure before servicing the fuel lines.* Refer to Chapter 4 for the fuel system pressure relief procedure.

11   Check all flexible fuel lines for deterioration and chafing. Check especially for cracks in areas where the hose bends and just before fittings, such as where a hose attaches to the fuel pump, fuel filter and fuel injection unit.

12   When replacing a hose, use only hose that is specifically designed for your fuel injection system.

13   Spring-type clamps are sometimes used on fuel return or vapor lines. These clamps often lose their tension over a period of time, and can be sprung during removal. Replace all spring-type clamps with screw clamps whenever a hose is replaced. Some fuel lines use spring-lock type couplings, which require a special tool to disconnect. See Chapter 4 for more information on this type of coupling.

Metal lines

14   Sections of metal line are often used for fuel line between the fuel pump and the fuel injection unit. Check carefully to make sure the line isn't bent, crimped or cracked.

15   If a section of metal fuel line must be replaced, use seamless steel tubing only, since copper and aluminum tubing do not have the strength necessary to withstand vibration caused by the engine.

16   Check the metal brake lines where they enter the master cylinder and brake proportioning unit (if used) for cracks in the lines and loose fittings. Any sign of brake fluid leakage calls for an immediate thorough inspection of the brake system.

15   Air filter replacement (every 15,000 miles [24,000 km] or 12 months)

Refer to illustration 15.1

1   The air filter is located inside a housing inside of the engine compartment. To remove the air filter, loosen the clamp securing the inlet tube to the air filter cover. On 2005 and earlier models, remove the screws securing the two halves of the air filter housing together. On 2006 and later models, release the spring clips, then separate the cover halves and remove the air filter element **(see illustration). Note:** *On some models it may also be necessary to disconnect a PCV hose from the housing cover.*

2   Inspect the outer surface of the filter element. If it is dirty, replace it. If it is only moderately dusty, it can be reused by blowing it clean from the back to the front surface with compressed air. Because it is a pleated paper type filter, it cannot be washed or oiled. If it cannot be cleaned satisfactorily with compressed air, discard and replace it. While the cover is off, be careful not to drop anything down into the housing.

3   Wipe out the inside of the air cleaner housing.

4   Place the new filter into the air cleaner housing, making sure it seats properly.

5   Installation of the housing is the reverse of removal.

15.1 Lift the cover up and out of the way and remove the element

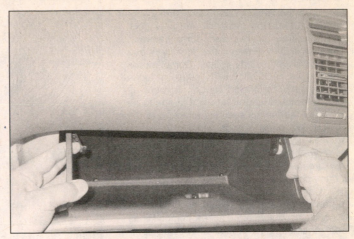

16.2 Release the glove box stops and lower the box

16   Interior ventilation filter replacement (every 15,000 miles [24,000 km] or 12 months)

Refer to illustrations 16.2, 16.3 and 16.4

1   These models are equipped with an air filtering element in the air conditioning system, located in a housing next to the evaporator, under the right side of the instrument panel.

2   Release the glove box stops, then lower the glove box and let it hang **(see illustration)**.

3   On 2005 and earlier Civic models and 2006 and earlier CR-V models, release the tab and remove the filter door **(see illustration)**.

4   On 2006 and later Civic models and 2007 and later CR-V models, release the tabs and remove the filter from the housing **(see illustration)**.

5   Remove the filter element from the frame and install the new one. Make sure the arrows on the filter element point in the same direction as the arrows on the frame (down).

6   Installation is the reverse of the removal procedure.

17   Fuel system check (every 15,000 miles [24,000 km] or 12 months)

Warning: *Gasoline is flammable, so take extra precautions when you work on any part of the fuel system. Don't smoke or allow open flames or bare light bulbs near the work area, and don't work in a garage where a gas-type appliance (such as a water heater or clothes dryer) is present. Since fuel is carcinogenic, wear fuel-resistant gloves when there's a possibility of being exposed to fuel, and, if you spill any fuel on your skin, rinse it off immediately with soap and water. Mop up any spills immediately and do not store fuel-soaked rags where they could ignite. When you perform any kind of work on the fuel system, wear safety glasses and have a Class B type fire extinguisher on hand. The fuel system is under constant pressure, so, before any lines are disconnected, the fuel system pressure must be relieved (see Chapter 4).*

1   If you smell gasoline while driving or after the vehicle has been sitting in the sun, inspect the fuel system immediately.

2   Remove the fuel filler cap and inspect if for damage and corrosion. The gasket should have an unbroken sealing imprint. If the gasket is damaged or corroded, install a new cap.

3   Inspect the fuel feed line for cracks. Make sure that the connections between the fuel lines and the fuel injection system are secure and dry. **Warning:** *Your vehicle is fuel injected, so you must relieve the fuel system pressure before servicing fuel system components. The fuel system pressure relief procedure is outlined in Chapter 4.*

4   Since some components of the fuel system - the fuel tank and the fuel lines, for example - are underneath the vehicle, they can be inspected more easily with the vehicle raised on a hoist. If that's not possible, raise the vehicle and support it on jackstands.

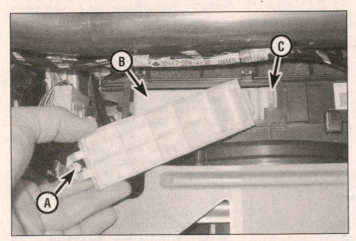

16.3 Release the tab (A) and remove the filter door, remove the first filter (B), then slide the second filter (C) to the left and remove it (2005 and earlier Civic/2006 and earlier CR-V)

16.4 Release the tabs and pull the filter element from the housing (2006 and later Civic/2007 and later CR-V)

5   With the vehicle raised and safely supported, inspect the gas tank and filler neck for punctures, cracks and other damage. The connection between the filler neck and the tank is particularly critical. Sometimes a rubber filler neck will leak because of loose clamps or deteriorated rubber. Inspect all fuel tank mounting brackets and straps to be sure that the tank is securely attached to the vehicle. **Warning:** *Do not, under any circumstances, try to repair a fuel tank (except rubber components); the fuel tanks in these vehicles are made of plastic and must be replaced if damaged,*

6   Carefully check all hoses and lines leading away from the fuel tank. Check for loose connections, deteriorated hoses, crimped lines and other damage. Repair or replace damaged sections as necessary (see Chapter 4).

18.2 Be sure to check each exhaust system rubber hanger for damage

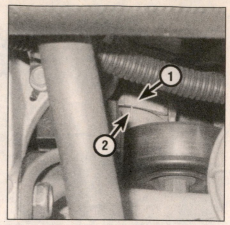

19.1 Details of the automatic drivebelt tensioner (1.8L, 2.0L and 2.4L engines)

1   *Maximum length (belt worn out)*
2   *Belt length indicator*

18   Exhaust system check (every 15,000 miles [24,000 km] or 12 months)

Refer to illustration 18.2

1   With the engine cold (at least three hours after the vehicle has been driven), check the complete exhaust system from the engine to the end of the tailpipe. Ideally, the inspection should be done with the vehicle on a hoist to permit unrestricted access. If a hoist isn't available, raise the vehicle and support it securely on jackstands.

2   Check the exhaust pipes and connections for evidence of leaks, severe corrosion and damage. Make sure that all brackets and hangers are in good condition and tight **(see illustration)**.

3   At the same time, inspect the underside of the body for holes, corrosion, open seams, etc. which may allow exhaust gases to enter the passenger compartment. Seal all body openings with silicone or body putty.

4   Rattles and other noises can often be traced to the exhaust system, especially the mounts and hangers. Try to move the pipes, muffler and catalytic converter. If the components can come in contact with the body or suspension parts, secure the exhaust system with new mounts.

5   Check the running condition of the engine by inspecting inside the end of the tailpipe. The exhaust deposits here are an indication of engine state-of-tune. If the pipe is black and sooty or coated with white deposits, the engine may need a tune-up, including a thorough fuel system inspection and adjustment.

19   Drivebelt check, adjustment and replacement (every 30,000 miles [48,000 km] or 24 months)

Warning: *The electric cooling fan(s) on these models can activate at any time the ignition switch is in the ON position. Make sure the ignition is OFF when working in the vicinity of the fan(s).*

Check

Refer to illustrations 19.1, 19.3 and 19.4

1   The drivebelts are located at the front of the engine and play an important role in the operation of the vehicle and its components. Due to their function and material makeup, the belts are prone to failure after a period of time and should be inspected and adjusted periodically to prevent major damage. On 1.8L, 2.0L and 2.4L engines, no adjustment is necessary because they are equipped with an automatic drivebelt tensioner. If the wear indicator has moved beyond the specified range, replace the drivebelt **(see illustration)**.

2   The number of belts used on a particular vehicle depends on the accessories installed. Drivebelts are used to turn the alternator, power steering pump, water pump (all except 1.7L engines), and air conditioning compressor. Depending on the pulley arrangement, more than one of these components may be driven by a single belt.

3   With the engine turned off, open the hood and locate the drivebelts at the front of the engine. Use a flashlight to carefully check each belt. Check for a severed core, separation of the adhesive rubber on both sides of the core and for core separation from the belt side. Inspect the ribs for separation from the adhesive rubber and for cracking or separation of the ribs, torn or worn ribs or cracks in the inner ridges of the ribs **(see illustration)**. Also check for fraying and glazing, which gives the belt a shiny appearance. Inspect both sides of

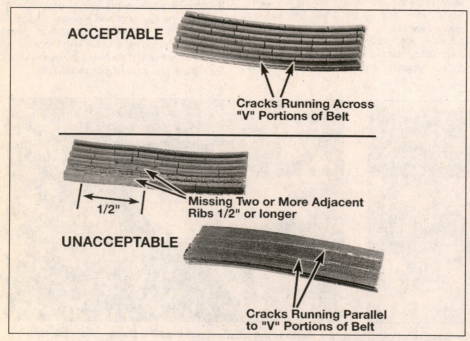

ACCEPTABLE

Cracks Running Across "V" Portions of Belt

1/2"

Missing Two or More Adjacent Ribs 1/2" or longer

UNACCEPTABLE

Cracks Running Parallel to "V" Portions of Belt

19.3 Here are some of the more common problems associated with drivebelts (check the belts very carefully to prevent an untimely breakdown)

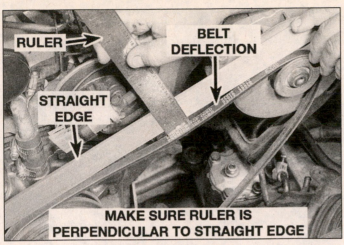

19.4 Measure the drivebelt deflection with a straightedge and ruler - make sure the ruler is perpendicular to the straightedge

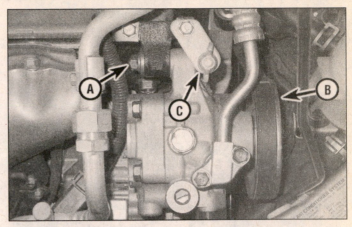

19.5 Power steering pump drivebelt adjustment details

A   *Pump locknut*
B   *Pump mounting bolt/nut (not visible in this photo)*
C   *Adjusting bolt*

the belt by twisting the belt to check the underside. Use your fingers to feel the belt where you can't see it. If any of the above conditions are evident, replace the belt(s).

4   On 1.7L engine models, the tension of each belt is checked by pushing on it at a distance halfway between the pulleys. Apply about 20 pounds of force with your thumb and see how much the belt moves down (deflects). Measure the deflection with a ruler **(see illustration)** and compare your results to the deflection limits listed in this Chapter's Specifications.

Adjustment (1.7L engines)

Power steering belt

Refer to illustration 19.5

5   Loosen the power steering pump mounting bolt nut and locknut, then turn the adjuster bolt to set the belt tension **(see illustration).**

When you have obtained the desired tension, tighten the pump fasteners securely.

Alternator/air conditioning compressor belt

Refer to illustration 19.6

6   Loosen the alternator upper mounting bolt and nut, then loosen the adjuster bracket lock bolt and lower mounting bolt. Turn the adjuster bolt to set the belt tension **(see illustration).** When you have obtained the desired tension, tighten the fasteners securely.

Replacement

1.7L engines

Power steering belt

7   Follow Step 5 for drivebelt adjustment, but slip the belt off the pulleys and remove it.
8   When installing the belt, make sure the

belt is centered on the pulleys.
9   Adjust the drivebelt as described in Step 5.

Alternator/air conditioning compressor belt

10   Remove the power steering pump drivebelt (see Step 5).
11   Follow Step 6 for drivebelt adjustment, but slip the belt off the pulleys and remove it.
12   When installing the belt, make sure the belt is centered on the pulleys.
13   Adjust the drivebelt as described in Step 6.
14   Install the power steering pump drivebelt.

1.8L, 2.0L and 2.4L engines

Refer to illustration 19.16

15   If you're working on a 2.0L or 2.4L engine, apply the parking brake, loosen the

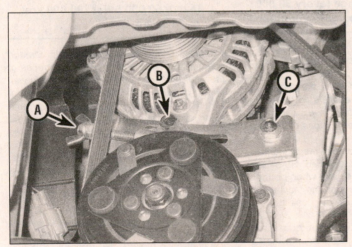

19.6 Alternator/air conditioning compressor belt adjustment details

A   *Adjusting bolt*   C   *Bracket mounting bolt*
B   *Lock bolt*

19.16 Place a wrench or a socket on the tensioner pulley bolt and rotate it clockwise

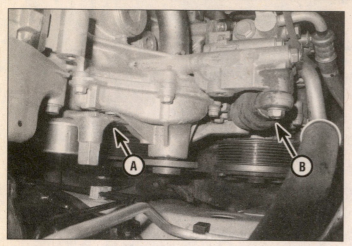

19.23 1.8L engine automatic tensioner mounting bolts

A   *10 mm mounting bolt*   B   *8 mm mounting bolt*

21.3 Location of the radiator drain fitting - before opening the valve, push a short length of rubber hose onto the plastic fitting to prevent the coolant from splashing

right (passenger's side) front wheel lug nuts, raise the front of the vehicle and support it securely on jackstands. Remove the wheel, then remove the splash shield.

16   The automatic tensioner must be rotated to allow drivebelt replacement. Place a wrench or a socket on the tensioner pulley bolt and slowly rotate it **(see illustration)** until the belt can be removed. Remove the belt and slowly release the tensioner. **Note:** *Depending upon design, the automatic tensioner may be rotated away from the belt in either a clockwise or counterclockwise direction. Slow, moderate pressure should enable it to move. If it doesn't move in one direction, use the other.* Install the new belt then rotate the tensioner to allow the belt to slip over it, then release the tensioner slowly until it contacts the drivebelt.

17   When installing the belt, make sure the belt is centered on the pulleys.

18   Install the splash shield, wheel and lug nuts. Lower the vehicle and tighten the lug nuts to the torque listed in this Chapter's Specifications.

Automatic tensioner replacement (1.8L, 2.0L and 2.4L engines)

19   Remove the drivebelt (see Steps 15 and 16).

1.8L engines

Refer to illustration 19.23

20   Remove the alternator (see Chapter 5).

21   Remove the water pump pulley mounting fasteners (see Chapter 3).

22   Remove the automatic tensioner fasteners and tensioner assembly.

23   Install the tensioner and fasteners **(see illustration)** and tighten to the torque listed in this Chapter's Specifications.

24   Place a wrench or a socket on the tensioner **(see illustration 19.16)**. Slowly

compress the tensioner downwards, holding it for three seconds. Push the tensioner slowly upwards and hold for three seconds.

25   Repeat this procedure three times to bleed the tensioner assembly.

26   The remaining installation is the reverse of removal.

2.0L and 2.4L engines

27   If you're working on a 2.4L engine, remove the power steering pump (see Chapter 10).

28   If you're working on a 2.0L engine, remove the idler pulley mounting bolts, then remove the pulley.

29   Unscrew the tensioner pulley bolt, then unscrew the mounting bolts and remove the tensioner.

30   Installation is the reverse of removal.

20   Brake fluid change (every 30,000 miles [48,000 km] or 24 months)

Warning: *Brake fluid can harm your eyes and damage painted surfaces, so use extreme caution when handling or pouring it. Do not use brake fluid that has been standing open or is more than one year old. Brake fluid absorbs moisture from the air. Excess moisture can cause a dangerous loss of braking effectiveness.*

1   At the specified intervals, the brake fluid should be drained and replaced. Since the brake fluid may drip or splash when pouring it, place plenty of rags around the master cylinder to protect any surrounding painted surfaces.

2   Before beginning work, purchase the specified brake fluid (see *Recommended lubricants and fluids* in this Chapter's Specifications).

3   Remove the cap from the master cylinder reservoir.

4   Using a hand suction pump or similar

device, withdraw the fluid from the master cylinder reservoir.

5   Add new fluid to the master cylinder until it rises to the base of the filler neck.

6   Bleed the brake system as described in Chapter 9 at all four brakes until new and uncontaminated fluid is expelled from the bleeder screw. Be sure to maintain the fluid level in the master cylinder as you perform the bleeding process. If you allow the master cylinder to run dry, air will enter the system.

7   Refill the master cylinder with fluid and check the operation of the brakes. The pedal should feel solid when depressed, with no sponginess. **Warning:** *Do not operate the vehicle if you are in doubt about the effectiveness of the brake system.*

21   Cooling system servicing (draining, flushing and refilling) (every 60,000 miles [96,000 km] or 36 months)

Warning: *Do not allow antifreeze to come in contact with your·skin or painted surfaces of the vehicle. Rinse off spills immediately with plenty of water. Antifreeze is highly toxic if ingested. Never leave antifreeze lying around in an open container or in puddles on the floor; children and pets are attracted by its sweet smell and may drink it. Check with local authorities about disposing of used antifreeze. Many communities have collection centers which will see that antifreeze is disposed of safely. Never dump used antifreeze on the ground or pour it into drains.*

1   Periodically, the cooling system should be drained, flushed and refilled to replenish the antifreeze mixture and prevent formation of rust and corrosion, which can impair the performance of the cooling system and cause engine damage. When the cooling system is serviced, all hoses and the radiator cap should be checked and replaced if necessary.

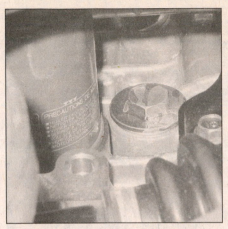

21.4 On SOHC engines, unscrew the engine block drain plug

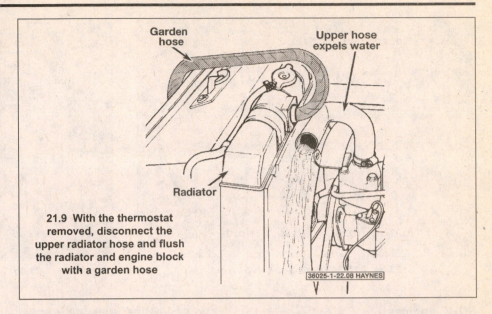

21.9 With the thermostat removed, disconnect the upper radiator hose and flush the radiator and engine block with a garden hose

Draining

Refer to illustrations 21.3 and 21.4

Warning: *If the vehicle has just been driven, wait several hours to allow the engine to cool down before beginning this procedure.*

2   Apply the parking brake and block the wheels. Turn the heater control to maximum heat.

3   Move a large container under the radiator drain to catch the coolant. Open the drain fitting until coolant starts flowing from the drain hole (a pair of pliers may be required to turn it) **(see illustration)**.

4   Remove the radiator cap and allow the radiator to drain, then move the container under the engine. If you're working on an SOHC engine, loosen the engine block drain plug and allow the coolant in the block to drain **(see illustration)**.

5   While the coolant is draining, check the condition of the radiator hoses, heater hoses and clamps (refer to Section 9 if necessary).

6   Replace any damaged clamps or hoses. Close the drain plugs.

Flushing

Refer to illustration 21.9

7   Once the system is completely drained, remove the thermostat from the engine (see Chapter 3), then reinstall the thermostat housing without the thermostat. This will allow the system to be thoroughly flushed.

8   Turn the heating system controls to Hot, so that the heater core will be flushed at the same time as the rest of the cooling system.

9   Disconnect the upper radiator hose from the radiator, then place a garden hose in the upper radiator inlet and flush the system until the water runs clear at the upper radiator hose **(see illustration)**.

10   In severe cases of contamination or clogging of the radiator, remove the radiator (see Chapter 3) and have a radiator repair facility clean and repair it if necessary.

11   Many deposits can be removed by the chemical action of a cleaner available at auto parts stores. Follow the procedure outlined in the manufacturer's instructions. **Note:** *When the coolant is regularly drained and the system refilled with the correct antifreeze/water mixture, there should be no need to use chemical cleaners or descalers.*

12   Remove the overflow hose from the coolant recovery reservoir. Drain the reservoir and flush it with clean water, then reconnect the hose.

Refilling

13   Reconnect the upper radiator hose and reinstall the thermostat.

14   Fill the cooling system with the proper type and mixture of antifreeze (see this Chapter's Specifications), up to the base of the radiator cap filler neck. Loosely install the radiator cap.

15   Start the engine and run it at approximately 1500 rpm until the radiator fan comes on two times. Feel the upper radiator hose - it should be warm, indicating the thermostat has opened.

16   Turn off the engine and let it cool down. Slowly remove the radiator cap and check the coolant level, adding as necessary. **Warning:** *If you hear a hissing sound as you unscrew the cap, STOP. Let the engine cool down longer.* Fill the coolant reservoir up to the MIN mark, if necessary.

17   Start the engine, allow it to reach normal operating temperature once again and check for leaks.

---

22   Rear differential lubricant change (CR-V) (every 90,000 miles [145,000 km] or 60 months)

---

1   This procedure should be performed after the vehicle has been driven, so the lubricant will be warm and therefore will flow out of the differential more easily.

2   Raise the vehicle and support it securely on jackstands. You'll be draining the lubricant by removing the drain plug, so move a drain pan, rags, newspapers and wrench under the vehicle. Remove the check/fill plug.

3   Remove the drain plug and allow the lubricant to drain into the pan, then clean and reinstall the drain plug. Tighten the plug securely.

4   Using a hand pump, syringe or squeeze bottle, fill the differential housing with the specified lubricant until it's level with the bottom of the fill plug hole.

5   Install the plug and tighten it securely. Drive the vehicle a short distance, then check for leaks.

6   The old oil drained from the differential cannot be reused in its present state and should be disposed of. Check with your local auto parts store, disposal facility or environmental agency to see if they will accept the oil for recycling. After the oil has cooled it can be drained into a container (capped plastic jugs, topped bottles, milk cartons, etc.) for transport to one of these disposal sites. Don't dispose of the oil by pouring it on the ground or down a drain!

---

23   Valve clearance check and adjustment (see *Maintenance schedule* for service intervals)

Check

1   Valve clearances generally do not need adjustment unless valvetrain components have been replaced, or a valve job has been performed.

2   The simplest check for proper valve adjustment is to listen carefully to the engine running with the hood open. If the valvetrain is noisy, adjustment is necessary.

Adjustment

3   The valve clearance must be checked and adjusted with the engine cold.

4   Remove the valve cover (see Chapter 2A or 2B).

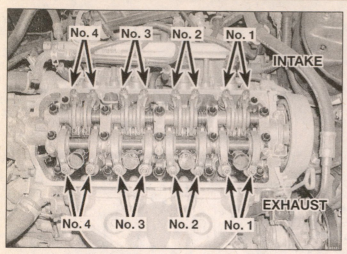

23.6a 1.7L SOHC engine valve layout

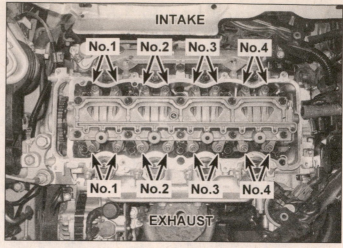

23.6b 1.8L SOHC engine valve layout

SOHC engines

Refer to illustrations 23.6a, 23.6b and 23.7

5   Place the number one piston (closest to the drivebelt end of the engine) at Top Dead Center (TDC) on the compression stroke. This is accomplished by rotating the crankshaft in the normal direction of rotation (which is counterclockwise) until the white TDC mark on the crankshaft pulley aligns with the timing pointer on the lower timing belt cover and the UP mark on the camshaft sprocket is at the twelve o'clock position (see Chapter 2A).

6   With the engine in this position, the number one cylinder valve adjustment can be checked and adjusted **(see illustrations)**.

7   Start with the intake valve clearance. Insert a feeler gauge of the correct thickness (see this Chapter's Specifications) between the valve stem and the rocker arm **(see illustration)**. Withdraw it; you should feel a slight drag. If there's no drag or a heavy drag, loosen the adjuster nut and back off the adjuster screw. Carefully tighten the adjuster screw until you can feel a slight drag on the feeler gauge as you withdraw it.

23.7   To make sure the adjusting screw doesn't move when the locknut is tightened, use a box-end wrench and have a good grip on the screwdriver

8   Hold the adjuster screw with a screwdriver (to keep it from turning) and tighten the locknut. Recheck the clearance to make sure it hasn't changed. Repeat the procedure in this Step and the previous Step on the other intake valve, then on the two exhaust valves.

9   'Rotate the crankshaft pulley 180-degrees counterclockwise (the camshaft pulley will turn 90-degrees) until the number three cylinder is at TDC. With the number three cylinder at TDC, the UP mark on the camshaft sprocket will be at the nine o'clock position. Check and adjust the number three cylinder valves.

10   Rotate the crankshaft pulley 180-degrees counterclockwise until the number four cylinder is at TDC. With the number four cylinder at TDC, the UP mark on the camshaft sprocket will be pointed straight down. Check and adjust the number four cylinder valves.

11   Rotate the crankshaft pulley 180-degrees counterclockwise to bring the number two cylinder to TDC. The UP mark on the camshaft sprocket should be at the three o'clock position. Check and adjust the number two cylinder valves.

12   Install the valve cover (see Chapter 2A).

DOHC engines

Refer to illustration 23.14

13   Place the number one piston (closest to the drivebelt end of the engine) at Top Dead Center (TDC) on the compression stroke. This is accomplished by rotating the crankshaft in the normal direction of rotation (which is clockwise) until the white TDC mark on the crankshaft pulley aligns with the timing pointer on the lower timing belt cover, the punch marks on the camshaft sprockets should be at the twelve o'clock position and the TDC marks are aligned on both sprockets (see Chapter 2B, Section 8).

14   With the engine in this position, the number one cylinder valve adjustment can be checked and adjusted **(see illustration)**.

15   Start with the intake valve clearance. Insert a feeler gauge of the correct thickness

(see this Chapter's Specifications) between an intake valve stem and the rocker arm. Withdraw it; you should feel a slight drag. If there's no drag or a heavy drag, loosen the adjuster nut and back off the adjuster screw. Carefully tighten the adjuster screw until you can feel a slight drag on the feeler gauge as you withdraw it.

16   Hold the adjuster screw with a screwdriver (to keep it from turning) and tighten the locknut **(see illustration 23.7)**. Recheck the clearance to make sure it hasn't changed. Repeat the procedure in this Step and the previous Step on the other intake valve, then on the two exhaust valves.

17   Rotate the crankshaft pulley 180-degrees clockwise (the camshaft pulley will turn 90-degrees) until the number three cylinder is at TDC. With the number three cylinder at TDC, the punch marks on the camshaft sprocket will be at the three o'clock position. Check and adjust the number three cylinder valves.

18   Rotate the crankshaft pulley 180-degrees clockwise until the number four cylinder is at TDC. With the number four cylinder at TDC, the punch marks on the camshaft sprockets will be pointed straight down. Check and adjust the number four cylinder valves.

19   Rotate the crankshaft pulley 180-degrees clockwise to bring the number two cylinder to TDC. The punch marks on the camshaft sprockets should be at the nine o'clock position. Check and adjust the number two cylinder valves.

20   Install the valve cover (see Chapter 2A).

24   Spark plug check and replacement (see *Maintenance schedule* for service intervals)

Refer to illustrations 24.2, 24.5a, 24.5b, 24.9, 24.11a and 24.11b

1   The spark plugs are located in the center of the cylinder head.

2   In most cases the tools necessary for

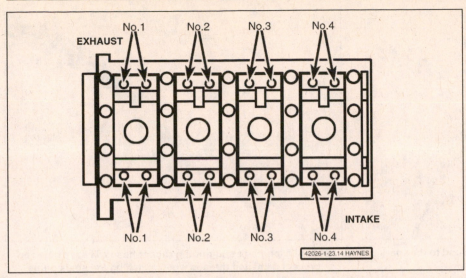

23.14 DOHC valve layout

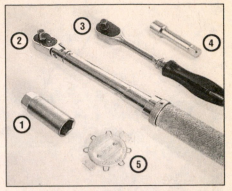

24.2 Tools required for changing spark plugs

1   **Spark plug socket** - *This will have special padding inside to protect the spark plug porcelain insulator*
2   **Torque wrench** - *Although not mandatory, use of this tool is the best way to ensure that the plugs are tightened properly*
3   **Ratchet** - *Standard hand tool to fit the plug socket*
4   **Extension** - *Depending on model and accessories, you may need special extensions and universal joints to reach one or more of the plugs*
5   **Spark plug gap gauge** - *This gauge for checking the gap comes in a variety of styles. Make sure the gap for your engine is included*

spark plug replacement include a spark plug socket which fits onto a ratchet (this special socket is padded inside to protect the porcelain insulators on the new plugs and hold them in place), various extensions and a feeler gauge to check and adjust the spark plug gap **(see illustration)**. Since these engines are equipped with an aluminum cylinder head, a torque wrench should be used when tightening the spark plugs.

3   The best approach when replacing the spark plugs is to purchase the new spark plugs beforehand, adjust them to the proper gap and then replace each plug one at a time. When buying the new spark plugs, be sure to obtain the correct plug for your specific engine. This information can be found in this Chapter's Specifications or in your owner's manual.

4   Allow the engine to cool completely before attempting to remove any of the plugs. During this cooling off time, each of the new

spark plugs can be inspected for defects and the gaps can be checked.

5   The gap is checked by inserting the proper thickness gauge between the electrodes at the tip of the plug **(see illustrations)**. The gap between the electrodes should be as listed in this Chapter's Specifications or in your owner's manual. **Caution:** *The manufacturer recommends against adjusting the gap on platinum- or iridium-tipped spark plugs; if the gap is out of specification, replace the plug.* Also check for cracks in the spark plug body (if any are found, the plug must not be used).

6   Cover the fender to prevent damage to the paint. Fender covers are available from auto parts stores but an old blanket will work just fine.

7   Remove the ignition coils (see Chapter 5).

8   If compressed air is available, use it to blow any dirt or foreign material away from

the spark plug area. **Warning:** *Wear eye protection!* The idea here is to eliminate the possibility of material falling into the cylinder through the spark plug hole as the spark plug is removed.

9   Place the spark plug socket over the plug and remove it from the engine by turning it in a counterclockwise direction **(see illustration)**.

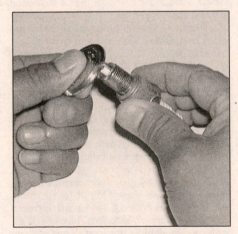

24.5a Slide the thin side of the gauge into the gap and turn it until the gauge just fills the gap, then read the thickness on the gauge - do not force the tool into the gap or use the tapered portion to widen a gap

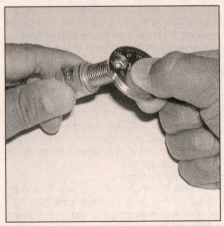

24.5b To change the gap, bend the side electrode only, using the adjuster hole in the tool, and be very careful not to crack or chip the porcelain insulator surrounding the center electrode

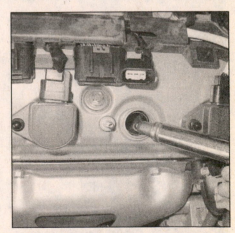

24.9 Use a ratchet and extension to remove the spark plugs

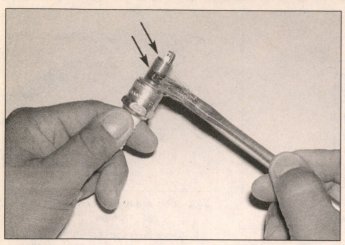

24.11a Apply a thin coat of anti-seize compound to the spark plug threads

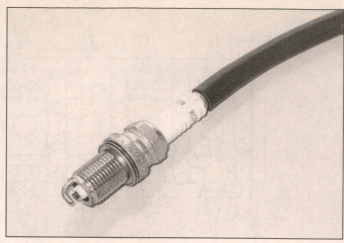

24.11b A length of snug-fitting rubber hose will save time and prevent damaged threads when installing the spark plugs

10   Compare the spark plug with the chart on the inside back cover of this manual to get an indication of the overall running condition of the engine.

11   Apply a small amount of anti-seize compound to the spark plug threads **(see illustration)**. Install one of the new plugs into the hole until you can no longer turn it with your fingers, then tighten it with a torque wrench (if available) or the ratchet. It is a good idea to slip a short length of rubber hose over the end of the plug to use as a tool to thread it into place **(see illustration)**. The hose will grip the plug well enough to turn it, but will start to slip if the plug begins to cross-thread in the hole - this will prevent damaged threads and the accompanying repair costs.

12   Attach the coil to the new spark plug using a twisting motion until it is firmly seated on the end of the spark plug. Tighten the mounting bolts securely.

13   Repeat the procedure for the remaining spark plugs.

25.6 Location of the automatic transaxle fluid drain plug

25   Automatic transaxle fluid change (every 120,000 miles [72,400 km] or 72 months)

Refer to illustration 25.6

1   The automatic transaxle fluid should be changed at the recommended intervals.

2   Before beginning work, purchase the specified transmission fluid (see *Recommended lubricants and fluids* in this Chapter's Specifications).

3   Other tools necessary for this job include jackstands to support the vehicle in a raised position, wrenches, drain pan capable of holding at least four quarts, newspapers and clean rags.

4   The fluid should be drained immediately after the vehicle has been driven. Hot fluid is more effective than cold fluid at removing built up sediment. **Warning:** *Fluid temperature can exceed 350-degrees F in a hot transaxle. Wear protective gloves.*

5   After the vehicle has been driven to warm up the fluid, raise the front of the vehicle and support it securely on jackstands. **Warning:** *Never work under a vehicle that is supported only by a jack!*

6   Place the drain pan under the drain plug in the transaxle pan and remove the drain plug **(see illustration)**. Be sure the drain pan is in position, as fluid will come out with some force. Once the fluid is drained, reinstall the drain plug securely. Measure the amount of fluid drained and write down this figure for reference when refilling.

7   Lower the vehicle.

8   With the engine off, add new fluid to the transaxle through the dipstick tube (see *Recommended lubricants and fluids* for the recommended fluid type). Begin the refill procedure by initially adding 1/3 of the amount drained. Then, with the engine running, add 1/2-pint at a time (cycling the shifter through each gear position between additions) until the level is

correct on the dipstick.

9   If desired, repeat Steps 5 through 8 once to flush any contaminated fluid from the torque converter.

10   The old oil drained from the transaxle cannot be reused in its present state and should be disposed of. Check with your local auto parts store, disposal facility or environmental agency to see if they will accept the oil for recycling. After the oil has cooled it can be drained into a container (capped plastic jugs, topped bottles, milk cartons, etc.) for transport to one of these disposal sites. Don't dispose of the oil by pouring it on the ground or down a drain!

26   Manual transaxle fluid change (every 120,000 miles [72,400 km] or 72 months)

1   Raise the vehicle and support it securely on jackstands in a level position. **Warning:** *Never work under a vehicle that is supported only by a jack!*

2   Remove the fill plug, followed by the drain plug. Drain the fluid into a suitable container capable of holding at least four quarts.

3   After the fluid has completely drained, install the drain plug and tighten it to the torque given in this Chapter's Specifications.

4   Fill the transaxle with the recommended lubricant (see *Recommended lubricants and fluids* in this Chapter's Specifications).

5   The old oil drained from the transaxle cannot be reused in its present state and should be disposed of. Check with your local auto parts store, disposal facility or environmental agency to see if they will accept the oil for recycling. After the oil has cooled it can be drained into a container (capped plastic jugs, topped bottles, milk cartons, etc.) for transport to one of these disposal sites. Don't dispose of the oil by pouring it on the ground or down a drain!

Chapter 2 Part A
Single overhead camshaft (SOHC) engines

Contents

	Section
Camshaft - removal, inspection and installation	13
CHECK ENGINE light on	See Chapter 6
Crankshaft pulley and front oil seal - replacement	12
Cylinder head - removal and installation	14
Engine mounts - check and replacement	19
Exhaust manifold - removal and installation	6
Flywheel/driveplate - removal and installation	17
General information	1
Intake manifold - removal and installation	5
Oil pan - removal and installation	15
Oil pump - removal, inspection and installation	16
Rear main oil seal - replacement	18

	Section
Repair operations possible with the engine in the vehicle	2
Rocker arm assembly - removal, inspection and installation	8
Timing belt and sprockets (1.7L engines) - removal, inspection and installation	9
Timing chain and sprockets (1.8L engines) - removal, inspections and installation	11
Timing chain cover/oil pump housing (1.8L engine) - removal and installation	10
Top Dead Center (TDC) for number one piston - locating	3
Valve cover - removal and installation	4
VTEC system - description and component checks	7

Specifications

General

Firing order	1-3-4-2
1.7L engines	
Bore	2.95 inches (74.98 mm)
Stroke	3.72 inches (94.40 mm)
1.8L engines	
Bore	3.19 inches (81.0 mm)
Stroke	3.44 inches (87.3 mm)
Displacement	
1.7L engines	101.7 cubic inches
1.8L engines	110 cubic inches
Oil pressure	See Chapter 2C

Valve adjustment

Valve adjustment	See Chapter 1

Cylinder locations for the 1.7L
SOHC engine

Cylinder locations for the
1.8L SOHC engine

Camshaft

1.7L engines	
Endplay	
Standard	0.002 to 0.006 inch (0.05 to 0.15 mm)
Maximum	0.020 inch (0.5 mm)
Lobe height	
D17A1	
Intake	1.3897 inches (35.299 mm)
Exhaust	1.4678 inches (37.281 mm)
D17A2	
Intake	
Primary	1.5198 inches (38.604 mm)
Secondary	1.2932 inches (32.848 mm)
Exhaust	1.5269 inches (38.784 mm)
D17A6	
Intake	
Primary	1.5129 inches (38.427 mm)
Secondary	1.2674 inches (32.193 mm)
Exhaust	1.5289 inches (38.784 mm)
Runout	
Standard	0.001 inch (0.03 mm)
Service limit	0.002 inch maximum (0.05 mm)
Journal oil clearance	
Standard	0.002 to 0.004 inch (0.05 to 0.10 mm)
Service limit	0.006 inch maximum (0.15 mm)
1.8L engines	
Endplay	
Standard	0.002 to 0.010 inch (0.05 to 0.25 mm)
Maximum	0.020 inch (0.5 mm)
Lobe height	
Intake (primary)...	1.4076 inches (35.754 mm)
Intake (secondary A)...	1.3920 inches (35.358 mm)
Intake (secondary B)...	1.4184 inches (36.027 mm)
Exhaust	1.4100 inches (35.813 mm)
Runout	
Standard	0.001 inch (0.03 mm)
Service limit	0.002 inch maximum (0.05 mm)
Journal oil clearance	
Standard	0.0018 to 0.0033 inch (0.046 to 0.084 mm)
Service limit	0.006 inch maximum (0.15 mm)

Oil pump

Rotor-to-cover clearance	
Standard..	0.001 to 0.003 inch (0.03 to 0.08 mm)
Service limit..	0.005 inch maximum (0.13 mm)
Tooth tip clearance	
Standard..	0.002 to 0.006 inch (0.05 to 0.15 mm)
Service limit..	0.008 inch maximum (0.20 mm)
Outer rotor-to-pump body clearance	
Standard..	0.004 to 0.0069 inch (0.10 to 0.175 mm)
Service limit..	0.008 inch maximum (0.20 mm)

Torque specifications

Ft-lbs (unless otherwise indicated) **Nm**

Note: *One foot-pound (ft-lb) of torque is equivalent to 12 inch-pounds (in-lbs) of torque. Torque values below approximately 15 ft-lbs are expressed in inch-pounds, since most foot-pound torque wrenches are not accurate at these smaller values.*

	Ft-lbs	Nm
Camshaft bearing cap bolts (1.7L engines)		
6 mm bolts	104 in-lbs	11.5
8 mm bolts	168 in-lbs	19
Camshaft sprocket bolt		
1.7L engines..	27	37
1.8L engines..	41	56
Camshaft thrust cover bolts (1.8L engine)........................	88 in-lbs	10
Crankshaft pulley bolt		
1.7L engines..	181	245
1.8L engines		
Original bolt		
Step 1...	51	69
Step 2...	Tighten an additional 90-degrees	

New bolt		
Step 1	130	176
Step 2	Loosen bolt 2 full turns	
Step 3	51	69
Step 4	Tighten an additional 90-degrees	
Cylinder head bolts		
1.7L engines		
Step 1	168 in-lbs	19
Step 2	36	49
Step 3	49	66
1.8L engines		
Step 1	29	39
Step 2	Tighten an additional 90-degrees	
Step 3	Tighten an additional 90-degrees	
New bolts	Tighten an additional 60-degrees	
Driveplate-to-crankshaft bolts	54	73
Intake manifold bolts/nuts		
1.7L engines	16	22
1.8L engines	17	23
Intake manifold brace bolts (1.7L engines)	104 in-lbs	11.5
Intake manifold bracket bolts (1.8L engines)		
Lower	86 in-lbs	9.5
upper	17	23
Exhaust manifold-to-cylinder head nuts/bolts		
1.7L engines	23	31
1.8L engines	33	45
Exhaust manifold heat shield upper bolts (manifold bolts)		
1.7L engines	23	31
1.8L engines	16	22
Exhaust pipe-to-manifold bolts	16	22
Flywheel-to-crankshaft bolts		
1.7L engines	87	118
1.8L engines	76	103
Oil baffle plate	86 in-lbs	9.5
Oil pan drain plug		
D17A1 engines	33	45
D17A2, D17A6 and 1.8L engines	29	39
Oil pan-to-engine bolts		
1.7L engines	104 in-lbs	11.5
1.8L engines	156 in-lbs	17.5
Oil pump pick-up tube to pump housing nuts (1.7L engines)	96 in-lbs	11
Oil pump pick-up screen-to-main bearing cap fasteners	104 in-lbs	11.5
Oil pump housing-to-block bolts (1.7L engines)	96 in-lbs	11
Oil pump cover-to-housing screws (1.7L engines)		
Aisin	86 in-lbs	9.5
Yamada	42 in-lbs	4.5
Oil pump cover-to-housing screws (1.8L engines)	72 in-lbs	8
Rear main oil seal housing bolts (1.7L engines)	104 in-lbs	11.5
Rocker arm assembly bolts (1.8L engines)	132 in-lbs	15
Timing chain cover bolts (1.8L engines)		
8 mm bolts	23	31
6 mm bolts	86 in-lbs	9.5
Dowel bolts	104 in-lbs	11.5
Timing chain guide bolts (1.8L engines)	104 in-lbs	11.5
Timing chain guide pivot bolt (1.8L engines)	16	22
Timing chain tensioner bolts (1.8L engines)	86 in-lbs	9.5
Timing belt cover bolts (1.7L engines)	86 in-lbs	9.5
Timing belt tensioner mounting bolt (1.7L engines)	33	45
Valve cover bolts		
1.7L engines	86 in-lbs	9.5
1.8L engines	104 in-lbs	11.5

1   General information

This Part of Chapter 2 is devoted to in-vehicle repair procedures for the 1.7L and 1.8L four-cylinder engines. Three different versions of the 1.7L engine and one version of the 1.8L engine have been produced by Honda for the Civic product line, all of which are covered in this Part of Chapter 2. All versions of these engines utilize a Single Overhead Camshaft (SOHC), with 4 valves per cylinder (16V). The 1.8L engine and two versions of the 1.7L engine incorporate the VTEC (Variable valve Timing and lift Electronic Control) system, which electronically alters valve timing to enhance engine performance. For more information on the VTEC system, see Section 7 of this Chapter.

Engine designations include:

D17A1 - 1.7L 16 valve SOHC non-VTEC 115 horsepower engine

D17A2 - 1.7L 16 valve SOHC VTEC 117 horsepower engine (lean burn)

D17A6 - 1.7L 16 valve SOHC VTEC 127 horsepower engine

R18A1 - 1.8L 16 valve SOHC i-VTEC engine

The SOHC engines are lightweight in design with an aluminum alloy block (with steel cylinder liners) and an aluminum alloy cylinder head. The crankshaft rides in a single carriage unit that houses the renewable insert-type main bearings, with separate thrust bearings at the number four position on 1.8L engines and the number five position on 1.7L engines, to control crankshaft endplay.

The pistons have two compression rings and one oil control ring. The semi-floating piston pins are press fitted into the small end of the connecting rod. The connecting rod big ends are also equipped with renewable insert-type plain bearings.

The engine is liquid-cooled, utilizing a centrifugal impeller-type pump (driven by the timing belt on 1.7L engines and the drivebelt on 1.8L engines) to circulate coolant around the cylinders and combustion chambers and through the intake manifold.

Lubrication is handled by a rotor-type oil pump mounted on the front of the engine (under the timing belt cover on 1.7L engines and in the timing chain cover on 1.8L engines). It is driven directly by the crankshaft. The oil is filtered continuously by a cartridge-type filter mounted on the rear of the engine on 1.7L engines and the oil pan on 1.8L engines.

Information concerning engine removal and installation can be found in Part C of this Chapter.

The following repair procedures are based on the assumption that the engine is installed in the vehicle. If the engine has been removed from the vehicle and mounted on a stand, many of the steps outlined in this Part of Chapter 2 will not apply.

The Specifications included in this Part of Chapter 2 apply only to the procedures contained in this Chapter. Chapter 2C contains the Specifications necessary for certain engine block assembly procedures.

2   Repair operations possible with the engine in the vehicle

Clean the engine compartment and the exterior of the engine with some type of degreaser before any work is done. It will make the job easier and help keep dirt out of the internal areas of the engine.

Depending on the components involved, it may be helpful to remove the hood to improve access to the engine as repairs are performed (refer to Chapter 11 if necessary). Cover the fenders to prevent damage to the paint. Special pads are available, but an old bedspread or blanket will also work.

If vacuum, exhaust, oil or coolant leaks develop, indicating a need for gasket or seal replacement, the repairs can generally be made with the engine in the vehicle. The intake and exhaust manifold gaskets, oil pan gasket, crankshaft oil seals and cylinder head gasket are all accessible with the engine in place.

Exterior engine components, such as the intake and exhaust manifolds, the oil pan, the water pump, the starter motor, the alternator, and the fuel system components can be removed for repair with the engine in place.

Since the cylinder head can be removed without pulling the engine, camshaft and valve component servicing can also be accomplished with the engine in the vehicle. Replacement of the timing chain, timing belt and sprockets is also possible with the engine in the vehicle.

In extreme cases caused by a lack of necessary equipment, repair or replacement of piston rings, pistons, connecting rods and rod bearings is possible with the engine in vehicle. However, this practice is not recommended because of the cleaning and preparation work that must be done to the components involved.

3   Top Dead Center (TDC) for number one piston - locating

Refer to illustration 3.5

Note: *These engines are not equipped with a distributor. Piston position must be determined by feeling for compression at the number one spark plug hole, then aligning the ignition timing marks as described in Step 5.*

1   Top Dead Center (TDC) is the highest point in the cylinder that each piston reaches as it travels up-and-down during crankshaft rotation. Each piston reaches TDC on the compression stroke and again on the exhaust stroke, but TDC generally refers to piston position on the compression stroke.

2   Positioning the piston(s) at TDC is an essential part of many other repair procedures discussed in this manual.

3   Before beginning this procedure, be sure to place the transmission in Neutral and apply the parking brake or block the rear wheels. Remove the spark plugs (see Chapter 1) and disable the fuel system (see Chapter 4, Section 3). Install a compression gauge in the spark plug hole for cylinder no. 1.

4   In order to bring any piston to TDC, the crankshaft must be turned using one of the methods outlined below. When looking at the front (timing belt or timing chain end) of the engine, normal crankshaft rotation is:

1.7L engine: counterclockwise

1.8L engine: clockwise

a) *The preferred method is to turn the crankshaft with a socket and ratchet attached to the bolt threaded into the front of the crankshaft.*

b) *A remote starter switch, which may save some time, can also be used. Follow the instructions included with the switch. Once the piston is close to TDC, use a socket and ratchet as described in the previous paragraph.*

c) *If an assistant is available to turn the ignition switch to the Start position in short bursts, you can get the piston close to TDC without a remote starter switch. Make sure your assistant is out of the vehicle, away from the ignition switch, then use a socket and ratchet as described in Paragraph a) to complete the procedure.*

5   Turn the crankshaft until compression registers on the gauge, then turn it slowly until the TDC notch is aligned with the pointer on the timing belt cover **(see illustration)**. **Note:** *There are two marks on the pulley. The white mark is for TDC, the red mark is only for checking ignition timing with a timing light.* The number one piston is now at TDC on the compression stroke.

6   After the number one piston has been positioned at TDC on the compression stroke, TDC for any of the remaining pistons can be located by turning the crankshaft in its normal direction of rotation, in 180-degree (1/2-turn) increments, and following the firing order. Divide the crankshaft pulley into two equal sections with chalk marks at each point, each indicating 180-degrees of crankshaft rotation. Rotating the engine past TDC no. 1 to the next mark will place the engine at TDC for cylinder no. 3.

4   Valve cover - removal and installation

Removal

1   Disconnect the cable from the negative terminal of the battery (see Chapter 5).

2   Remove the harness cover, the injection cover (if equipped) and the ignition coils (see Chapter 5).

3   Mark and detach any hoses or wires from the throttle body, alternator or valve

5.9a Remove the fasteners from the center of the splash shield

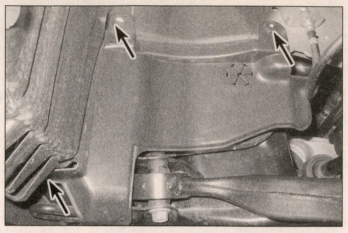

5.9b Remove the fasteners from the right side of the splash shield . . .

5   Disconnect any electrical connectors from the throttle body.
6   Clamp off and disconnect the coolant hoses at the throttle body.
7   Relieve the fuel system pressure and disconnect the fuel feed line at the fuel rail (see Chapter 4).
8   Raise the vehicle and support it securely on jackstands.
9   Remove the splash shield from under the engine (see illustrations).
10   Working from underneath the engine compartment, remove the braces that support the intake manifold (see illustrations).
11   Disconnect the heater hoses from the intake manifold bracket.
12   Remove the intake manifold nuts and bolts and remove the manifold from the engine (see illustration).
13   Remove the injector base and the intake manifold gasket from the cylinder head.

Installation

14   Check the mating surfaces of the manifold for flatness with a precision straightedge

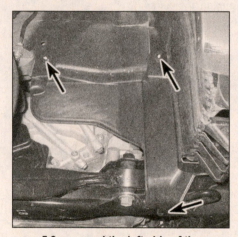

5.9c . . . and the left side of the splash shield

and feeler gauges.
15   Inspect the manifold for cracks and distortion. If the manifold is cracked or warped, replace it or see if it can be resurfaced at an

5.10a Remove the right side intake manifold brace . . .

automotive machine shop.
16   Check carefully for any stripped or broken intake manifold bolts/studs. Replace any defective fasteners with new parts.

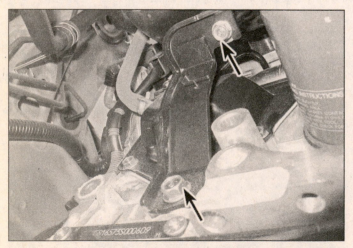

5.10b . . . and the left side intake manifold brace - 1.7L engine shown, 1.8L engine similar

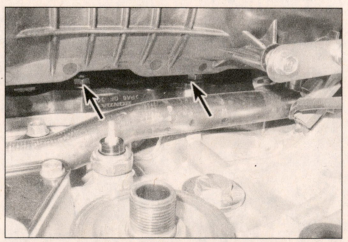

5.12 Location of two of the intake manifold mounting nuts on the underside of the intake manifold - 1.7L engine shown, 1.8L engine similar

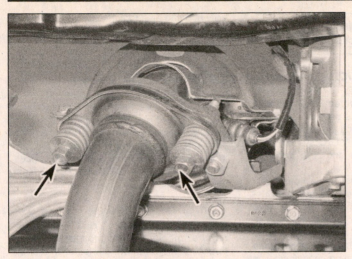

6.5 Remove the exhaust pipe flange bolts

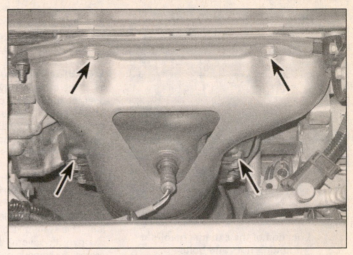

6.6 Remove the bolts retaining the heat shield to the exhaust manifold

17 Remove all traces of old gasket material from the cylinder head and manifold mating surfaces.

18 Install the injector base and intake manifold with a new gasket and O-rings, then install the fasteners and tighten them to the torque listed in this Chapter's Specifications.

19 Reconnect the battery (see Chapter 5).

20 The remainder of installation is the reverse of removal. Refer to Chapter 1 and check the coolant level, adding as necessary.

6 Exhaust manifold - removal and installation

Removal

1 Disconnect the cable from the negative terminal of the battery (see Chapter 5).

2 Raise the front of the vehicle and support it securely on jackstands.

3 Remove the splash shield from under the engine **(see illustrations 5.9a, 5.9b and 5.9c)**.

1.7L engines

Refer to illustrations 6.5, 6.6 and 6.8

4 Disconnect the oxygen sensor electrical connectors on D17A1 and D17A6 engines (see Chapter 6).

5 Detach the exhaust pipe from the exhaust manifold **(see illustration)**. Apply penetrating oil to the fastener threads if they are difficult to remove.

6 Remove the heat shield from the exhaust manifold **(see illustration)**. Be sure to soak the bolts and nuts with penetrating oil before attempting to remove them from the manifold.

7 Remove the exhaust manifold bracket, if equipped.

8 Remove the exhaust manifold nuts **(see illustration)** and detach the exhaust manifold from the cylinder head.

1.8L engines

Refer to illustrations 6.12 and 6.14

Note: *On 1.8L engines, the exhaust manifold and the catalytic converter are one unit.*

9 Disconnect the oxygen sensor electrical connectors and remove the sensors (see Chapter 6).

10 Remove the EGR pipe mounting bolts and EGR pipe (see Chapter 6)

11 Detach the exhaust pipe from the catalytic converter/exhaust manifold. Apply penetrating oil to the fastener threads if they are difficult to remove.

12 Remove the heat shield mounting bolts and shields **(see illustration)**. Be sure to soak the bolts and nuts with penetrating oil before attempting to remove them from the manifold.

13 Remove the lower support bracket mounting bolts, if equipped.

14 Remove the converter nuts and bolts

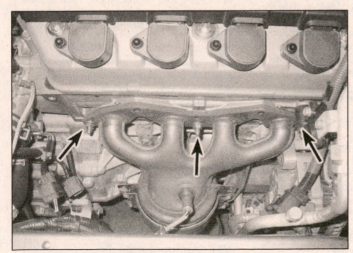

6.8 Location of the exhaust manifold mounting nuts - 1.7L non-VTEC engine shown

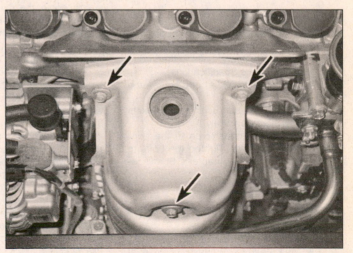

6.12 Heat shield mounting bolts - 1.8L engine shown

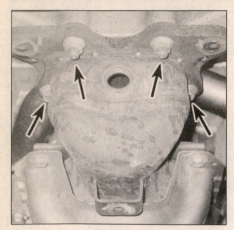

**6.14 Location of the exhaust manifold
mounting nuts and bolts -
1.8L engine shown**

(see illustration) and detach the converter from the cylinder head.

Installation

15   Discard the old gaskets and use a scraper to clean the gasket mating surfaces on the exhaust manifold or catalytic converter and cylinder head, then clean the surfaces with a rag soaked in brake system cleaner.

1.7L engines

16   Place the exhaust manifold in position on the cylinder head and install new nuts. Starting at the center and working out to the ends, tighten the nuts to the torque listed in this Chapter's Specifications.

17   Install the heat shield, using new upper bolts (the two upper bolts are the exhaust manifold upper mounting bolts). Tighten the two upper bolts to the torque listed in this Chapter's Specifications. Tighten the other heat shield bolts securely.

18   Connect the exhaust pipe to the exhaust manifold, using new bolts. Tighten the bolts to the torque listed in this Chapter's Specifications.

1.8L engines

19   Place the catalytic converter in position on the cylinder head and install the nuts and bolts. Tighten the nuts and bolts to the torque listed in this Chapter's Specifications.

20   Install the heat shield(s) and tighten the bolts securely.

21   Install the EGR tube using new gaskets and tighten the bolts securely.

22   Connect the exhaust pipe to the converter, using new bolts. Tighten the bolts to the torque listed in this Chapter's Specifications.

All engines

23   The remainder of installation is the reverse of removal.

24   Reconnect the battery (see Chapter 5).

25   Start the engine and check for exhaust leaks at the cylinder head and the exhaust pipe.

7   VTEC system - description and component checks

General description

1   There are two types of VTEC systems used on the models covered in this manual. The first VTEC system is used on 2005 and earlier Civics and 2006 and earlier CR-V models. The second is an i-VTEC system used on 2006 and later Civics and 2007 and later CR-V models.

2   The VTEC system is Honda's design for Variable Valve Timing and Lift Electronic Control. The VTEC lettering cast into the valve cover identifies models equipped with this system. This system incorporates camshaft technology with several different camshaft lobe profiles for various operating conditions. The rocker arms, along with the various camshaft lobe profiles, are switched during this process by a computer, a VTEC solenoid and VTEC valve. VTEC also incorporates the engine's oil system to hydraulically operate the pistons inside the rocker arm assemblies.

3   The differences between conventional engines and the VTEC system are strictly in the components and operation of the valve train.

4   The engine management computer has the ability to physically change which camshaft intake lobes are being used to operate the intake valves. The computer turns the system ON or OFF, depending on sensor input.

5   The PGM-FI engine management system relies on information from the vehicle speed sensor (vehicle speed), CKP sensor (engine speed), throttle position sensor (throttle angle), coolant temperature sensor (coolant temperature) and the MAP sensor (engine load).

6   The camshaft has two different intake valve lobe profiles (lift and duration specifications).

7   At low speeds, the secondary intake valve operates on its own camshaft lobe, which has lift and duration profiles designed specifically for the low end torque and responsiveness. The opening (valve duration) is intended to be just enough to keep atomized fuel from puddling at the valve head. This limited valve operation is designed to provide good low end torque and responsiveness, by inducing swirl in the combustion chamber from the primary intake valve, which operates with a normal profile.

8   When performance is needed, the primary and secondary rocker arms are locked together through the use of an electrically controlled hydraulic system. Hydraulically operated synchronizing pistons lock two rocker arms together. When activated, the intake valves open to the higher lift and duration of the rocker arm, which has its own camshaft lobe designed with the higher lift profile. **Note:** *Refer to this Chapter's Specifications for the exact camshaft lobe lift profiles.*

9   The i-VTEC system on later models is similar to the VTEC system, but with the capability of being able to *continuously* change the valve lift and timing - not just above a certain engine speed. The main difference is, the i-VTEC uses three different intake cam lobe profiles (instead of two) and two exhaust cam lobes for each cylinder. It is also equipped with a rocker arm control valve (or solenoid), and a rocker arm oil pressure sensor that works with the ECM/PCM and EGR valve, which alters the phasing of the secondary rocker arms to yield maximum potential power output and proper emissions for any given engine speed. For more information on the i-VTEC system, see Chapter 6.

Component checks

Note: *The VTEC and i-VTEC systems will require specialized diagnostic equipment to access the on-board computer to test the electrical circuits, actuators and sensors. However, there are some mechanical tests of the VTEC system that the home mechanic can perform to check for obvious and simple problems within the system. Have the VTEC system diagnosed by a dealer service department or other qualified automotive repair facility. Also, some checks and inspections of the VTEC components require removal of the rocker arm assembly (see Section 8).*

VTEC solenoid valve

Note: *Most common problems in the VTEC system are associated with the solenoid valve and its filter. Regular engine oil and filter changes are necessary for trouble-free operation of the valve.*

10   The VTEC solenoid valve is located on the rear end of the cylinder head on 1.7L engines and on the front of the cylinder head on 1.8L engines. The VTEC oil pressure switch is located in the cylinder head next to the EGR valve on 1.7L engines. The oil pressure sensor for the 1.8L engine is located just below the solenoid valve.

11   Remove the VTEC solenoid valve (see Chapter 6) and check the filter O-ring for clogging. Clean and reinstall with a new O-ring. A clogged filter screen is often the cause of system problems. **Note:** *On 1.8L engines, the filter is part of the solenoid housing gasket.*

Rocker arms

12   Position the number one piston at Top Dead Center (see Section 3). Remove the valve cover (see Section 4).

13   Press on the secondary intake rocker arm(s) for cylinder number 1 to see that it moves independently of the primary intake rocker arm. Check the rockers for the other cylinders at their own TDC positions.

Synchronizing assembly

14   Once the rocker arm assemblies have been removed and disassembled (see Section 8), separate the rocker arms and synchronizing components.

VTEC components:

  a) *Primary rocker arm*

8.4 Remove the camshaft bearing caps, bolts and rocker arm assembly

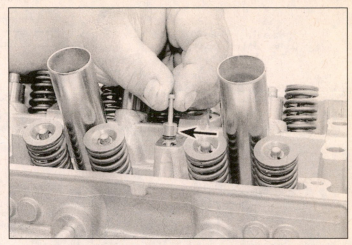

8.8 To remove the oil control orifice for cleaning, thread a machine screw into the top and pull up on the orifice

b) *Secondary rocker arm.* **Note:** *The i-VTEC engines have two secondary rocker arms for each cylinder.*
c) *Synchronizing pistons*

15   Inspect the timing spring, making sure it's not broken or collapsed. Replace it if necessary.
16   Inspect all other parts (rocker arms and rocker arm pistons) for wear, galling, scoring or signs of overheating (bluish in color) **(see illustration 8.12a, 8.12b and 8.12c)**. Use your finger to push on the rocker arm pistons to check for smooth movement. Replace any parts, if necessary.
17   Reassemble each cylinder's components and wrap a rubber band around the rocker arms before trying to assemble them on the rocker shaft (see Section 8).

8   Rocker arm assembly - removal, inspection and installation

Removal

1   Remove the valve cover (see Section 4).
2   Position the number one piston at Top Dead Center (see Section 3).

1.7L engines

Refer to illustration 8.4

Note: *The camshaft bearing caps are removed together with the rocker arm assembly. To prevent the transaxle end of the camshaft from popping up from timing belt tension after the assembly is removed, have an assistant hold the camshaft down, then reinstall the bearing cap on that end to hold it in place until reassembly (assuming the timing belt remains installed).*
Note: *While the camshaft bearing caps are off, inspect them, as well as the camshaft bearing journals, as described in Section 13.*
3   Have an assistant hold down the

transaxle end of the camshaft, then loosen the camshaft bearing cap bolts 1/4-turn at a time, in the correct order, until the spring pressure is relieved. Follow the reverse of the tightening sequence **(see illustration 8.16)**.
4   Lift the rocker arm and shaft assembly from the cylinder head **(see illustration)**.

1.8L engines

5   Loosen the rocker arm/lost motion holder bolts 1/4-turn at a time, in the correct order, until the spring pressure is relieved. Follow the reverse of the tightening sequence **(see illustration 8.19)**.
6   Lift the lost motion holder and lost motion assemblies off of the rocker arm assembly.
7   Lift the rocker arms and shaft assembly from the cylinder head.

Oil control orifice

Refer to illustration 8.8

8   Pull the orifice from the cylinder head **(see illustration)**. **Note:** *VTEC engines are equipped with an O-ring on the lower section of the oil control orifice. Non-VTEC engines are not equipped with an O-ring on the oil control orifice.*

Inspection

Refer to illustration 8.10

9   If you wish to disassemble and inspect the rocker arm assembly (a good idea as long as you have them off), remove the retaining bolts and slip the rocker arms, springs, collars and bearing caps off the shafts. **Caution:** *On 1.8L engines, the rocker arm pistons, located between the secondary intake rocker arms, are spring loaded and can come apart once they are removed from the rocker arm shaft. Mark the relationship of the shaft(s) to the bearing caps or rocker shaft holders and keep the components in order. They must be reassembled in the same positions they were removed from. **Caution:** On all VTEC engines, it is a good idea to bundle the rocker arms together with rubber bands*
10   Thoroughly clean the components and inspect them for wear and damage. Check the rocker arm faces that contact the camshaft and the rocker arm tips **(see illustration)**. Check the surfaces of the shafts that the rocker arms ride on, as well as the bearing surfaces inside the rocker arms, for scoring and excessive wear. Replace any parts that are damaged or excessively worn. **Note:** *On 1.8L engines,*

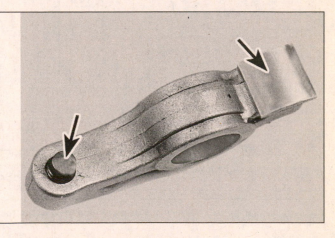

8.10 Check the contact face (A) and adjuster tip (B) for damage or wear - non-VTEC rocker arm shown

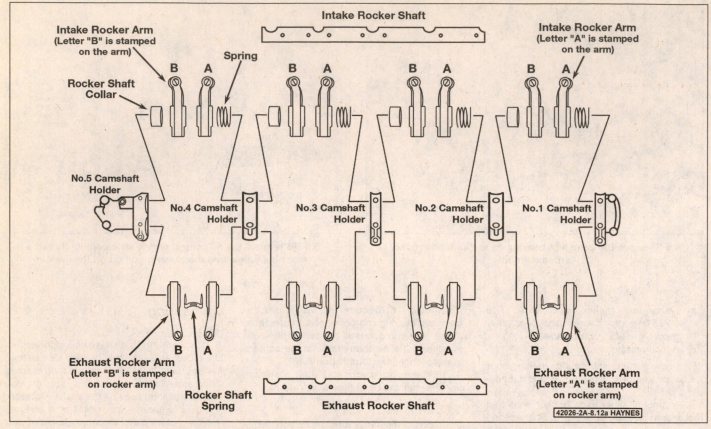

8.12a Exploded view of the rocker arms and shafts on a non-VTEC engine

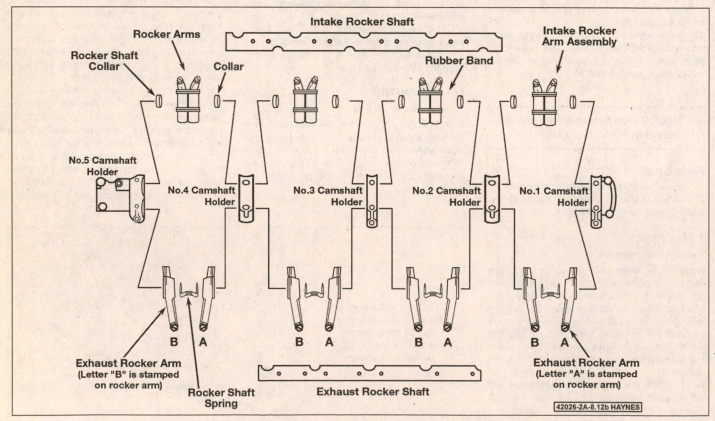

8.12b Exploded view of the rocker arms and shafts on a 1.7L VTEC engine

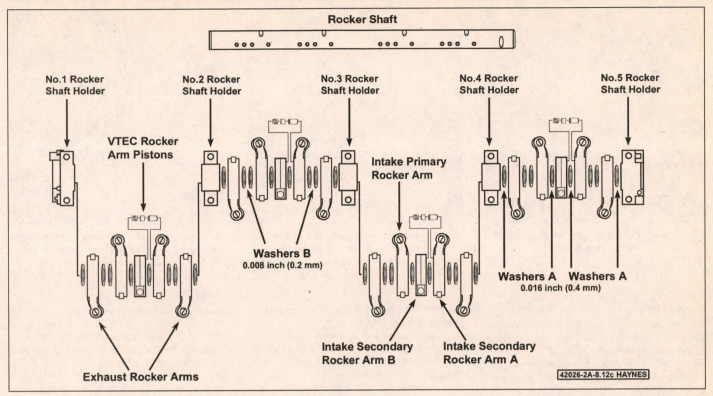

8.12c Exploded view of the rocker arms and shafts on a 1.8L VTEC engine

if any one of the secondary rocker arms are damaged, they must be replaced as an assembly. Make sure the oil holes in the shafts are not plugged.

11   Clean the orifice so there are no obstructions and oil flows freely through the orifice.

Installation

Refer to illustrations 8.12a, 8.12b, 8.12c, 8.16 and 8.19

12   Lubricate all components with engine assembly lubricant or engine oil and reassemble rocker arms on to the shafts. When installing the rocker arms, shafts and springs, note the markings and the difference between the left and right side components **(see illustrations)**.

13   Replace the O-ring on the oil control orifice, then install the orifice in the cylinder head.

1.7L engines

14   Coat the camshaft lobes and journals with camshaft installation lubricant.

15   Apply anaerobic-type sealant to the cylinder head contact surfaces of bearing caps 1 and 5 and install the rocker arm assembly.

16   Tighten the camshaft bearing cap bolts a little at a time, in the proper sequence **(see illustration)** to the torque listed in this Chapter's Specifications.

1.8L engines

17   Install the rocker arm assembly on the cylinder head.

18   Place the lost motion control assemblies into the holder and install the lost motion holder on the rocker assemblies.

19   Tighten the rocker arm/lost motion holder mounting bolts a little at a time, in the proper sequence **(see illustration)** to the torque listed in this Chapter's Specifications.

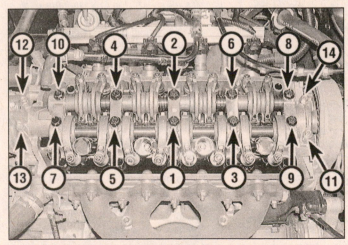

8.16 Rocker arm assembly bolt TIGHTENING sequence - 1.7L engine

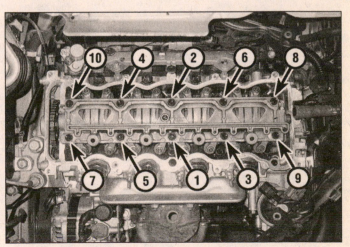

8.19 Rocker arm and lost motion holder assembly bolt TIGHTENING sequence - 1.8L engine

9.13 Timing belt upper cover mounting bolts

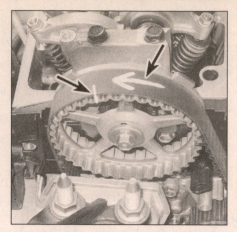

9.17 If you intend to reuse the belt, make an arrow to indicate the direction of rotation, and match marks to align the sprockets with the belt

9.19 Location of the timing belt tensioner bolt (upper arrow) and crankshaft position sensor (lower arrow)

All models

20   Make sure the alignment marks on the cylinder head plug are even with the top edge of the cylinder head.

21   The remainder of installation is the reverse of removal. Adjust the valve clearance, if necessary (see Chapter 1).

22   Run the engine and check for oil leaks and proper operation.

9   Timing belt and sprockets (1.7L engines) - removal, inspection and installation

Removal

Refer to illustrations 9.13, 9.17 and 9.19

1   Disconnect the cable from the negative terminal of the battery (see Chapter 5).

2   Place blocks behind the rear wheels and set the parking brake.

3   Loosen the lug nuts on the left front wheel and raise the front of the vehicle.

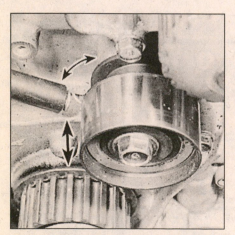

9.21 Check the belt tensioner pulley for rough operation, bearing play and freedom of movement

Support the front of the vehicle securely on jackstands (see Chapter 1).

4   Remove the left front wheel and remove the splash shield from under the engine **(see illustrations 5.9a, 5.9b and 5.9c)**. Remove the drivebelts (see Chapter 1).

5   Remove the power steering pump and position it aside, but don't disconnect the hoses (see Chapter 10).

6   Remove the alternator (see Chapter 5).

7   Remove the valve cover (see Section 4).

8   Support the engine with a floor jack. Place a wood block between the jack pad and the oil pan to avoid damaging the pan.

9   Remove the upper left engine mount bracket (see Section 19).

10   Position the number one piston at Top Dead Center (see Section 3). **Caution:** *Always rotate the crankshaft counterclockwise (viewed from the pulley end of the engine).*

11   Disconnect the Camshaft Position (CMP) sensor/Top Dead Center (TDC) sensor (see Chapter 6).

12   Remove the side engine mount bracket (see Section 19).

13   Remove the upper timing belt cover **(see illustration)**.

14   Unscrew the crankshaft pulley bolt. A special tool that engages with the recessed hex in the pulley opening is available to prevent the crankshaft from turning while unscrewing the bolt. If you can't obtain one of these tools, remove the flywheel/driveplate inspection cover and wedge a screwdriver into the starter ring gear teeth.

15   Slip the pulley off the crankshaft.

16   Remove the lower timing belt cover.

17   If you intend to reuse the timing belt, use white paint or chalk to make match marks to align the sprockets with the belt and an arrow to indicate the direction of rotation **(see illustration)**.

18   Remove the Crankshaft Position (CKP) sensor (see Chapter 6).

19   Loosen the timing belt tensioner bolt **(see illustration)**. Push on the tensioner to

release the tension on the belt, then retighten the bolt. Remove the CKP sensor and slip the belt off. If you're replacing the crankshaft oil seal, slip the sprocket and inner belt guide off the crankshaft (see Section 12).

20   If you're replacing the camshaft or camshaft oil seal, slip a large screwdriver through the camshaft sprocket to keep it from rotating and remove the bolt, then pull off the sprocket. Also remove the Woodruff key.

Inspection

Refer to illustrations 9.21 and 9.22

21   Rotate the belt tensioner pulley by hand and move it from side-to-side, checking for play and rough rotation **(see illustration)**. Replace it if roughness or play is detected.

22   Check the timing belt for wear (especially on the thrust side of the teeth), cracks, splits, fraying and oil contamination **(see illustration)**. Replace the belt if any of these conditions are noted. **Note:** *Unless the engine has very low mileage, it's common practice to replace the timing belt with a new one every time it's removed. Don't reinstall the original belt unless it's in like-new condition. Never reinstall a belt in questionable condition.*

Installation

Refer to illustrations 9.24, 9.25 and 9.26

23   If you removed the sprockets, reinstall them. Don't forget the Woodruff key for the camshaft sprocket and the inner belt guide for the crankshaft sprocket. Tighten the camshaft sprocket bolt to the torque listed in this Chapter's Specifications.

24   Before installing the timing belt, make sure the dot or "UP" mark on the camshaft sprocket is at the top and the two index marks are in line with the cylinder head surface **(see illustration)**.

25   Make sure the timing mark on the crankshaft sprocket and the pointer on the oil pump are aligned **(see illustration)**.

26   Align the holes on the tensioner pulley

and the tensioner base and insert a 0.12 inch (3 mm) diameter pin or drill bit into the holes (**see illustration**).

27 Install the timing belt tightly around the crankshaft sprocket, then around the tensioner pulley, water pump pulley and camshaft sprocket in that order.

28 Loosen the tensioner mounting bolt 1/2-turn (180-degrees), allowing the tensioner to tension the belt slightly.

29 Slowly turn the crankshaft counterclockwise two revolutions and recheck the timing marks and camshaft sprocket index marks for proper alignment. **Caution:** *If the crankshaft binds or seems to hit something, do not force it, as the valves may be hitting the pistons. If this happens, valve timing is incorrect. Remove the belt and repeat the installation procedure, then verify that the installation is correct.*

30 Tighten the tensioner mounting bolt to the torque listed in this Chapter's Specifications and remove the pin (**see illustration 9.26**).

31 Reinstall the remaining parts in the reverse order of removal.

32 Refer to Chapter 1 and adjust the drivebelts.

33 Reconnect the battery (see Chapter 5).

34 Run the engine and check for proper operation.

10 Timing chain cover/oil pump housing (1.8L engine) - removal and installation

Removal

1 Disconnect the cable from the negative battery terminal (see Chapter 5).

2 Loosen the right front wheel lug nuts.

3 Raise the front of the vehicle and support it securely on jackstands. Remove the right front wheel.

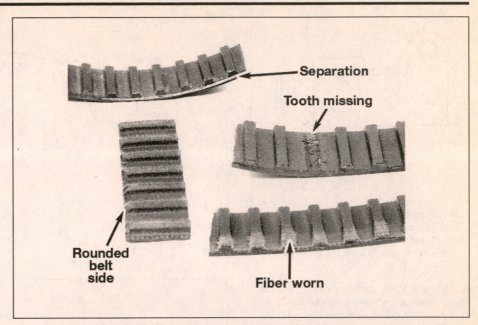

9.22 Carefully inspect the timing belt for cracked or missing teeth - wear on one side of the belt indicates sprocket misalignment problems

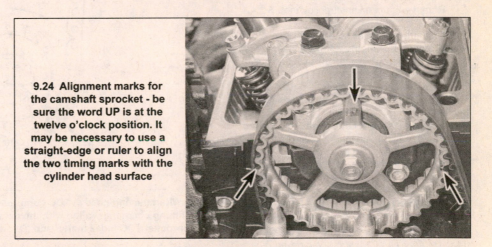

9.24 Alignment marks for the camshaft sprocket - be sure the word UP is at the twelve o'clock position. It may be necessary to use a straight-edge or ruler to align the two timing marks with the cylinder head surface

9.25 Make sure the mark on the crankshaft sprocket is aligned with the pointer on the oil pump

9.26 Align the holes on the tensioner pulley (C) and tensioner base (B), then insert a 0.12 inch (3.0 mm) diameter pin (C) into the holes - after the belt has been installed and rotated, tighten the tensioner mounting bolt (A)

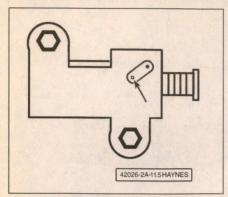

11.5 Align the hole on the lock with the hole in the tensioner, then insert a 0.040 inch (1.0 mm) pin or drill bit through both components to lock the tensioner

4   Remove the splash shield from below the engine compartment (see Section 5).
5   Remove the drivebelt (see Chapter 1).
6   Remove the mounting bolts and detach the drivebelt tensioner from the timing chain cover.
7   Remove the crankshaft pulley (see Section 12).
8   Drain the engine oil (see Chapter 1).
9   Support the engine with a floor jack. Place a wood block between the jack pad and the oil pan to avoid damaging the pan.
10   Remove the ground cable, the right side engine mount and bracket assembly (see Section 19).
11   Remove the valve cover (see Section 4).
12   Remove the mounting bolts and the timing chain cover.
13   Remove the engine cover-to-block silicone gasket.

Installation

14   Inspect and clean all sealing surfaces of the timing chain cover and the block. **Caution:** *Be very careful when scraping on aluminum engine parts. Aluminum is soft and gouges easily. Severely gouged parts may require replacement.*
15   If necessary, replace the crankshaft seal in the timing chain cover (see Section 12).
16   Apply RTV sealant to the cylinder block mating surfaces on the timing chain cover, the upper surface contact areas and to the oil pan mating surfaces. Also, apply a small amount of RTV sealant to the inner thread holes.
17   Install a new timing chain cover O-ring.
18   Install the timing chain cover and fasteners. Make sure the fasteners are in their original locations. Tighten the fasteners by hand until the cover is contacting the block around its entire periphery.
19   Tighten the bolts to the torque listed in this Chapter's Specifications.
20   Install the drivebelt tensioner, tightening the bolts to the torque listed in this Chapter's Specifications.
21   Install the crankshaft pulley (see Section 12).

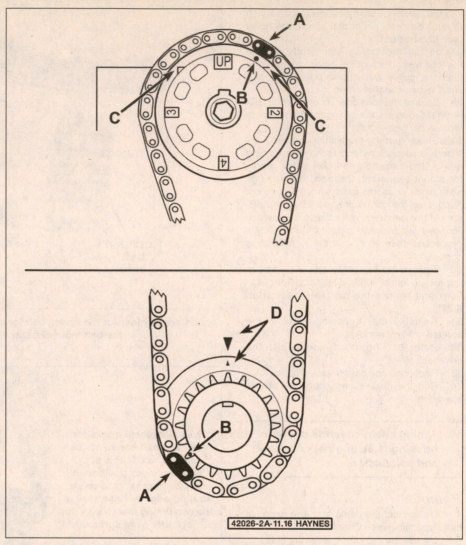

11.16 When the engine is at TDC compression for cylinder no. 1, the plated links (A) on the timing chain must align with the dots (B) on the sprockets. (C) are the camshaft sprocket TDC index marks and (D) are the crankshaft sprocket TDC marks

22   Reinstall the remaining parts in the reverse order of removal.
23   Fill the crankcase with the recommended oil (see Chapter 1).
24   Reconnect the battery (see Chapter 5).
25   Start the engine and check for leaks. Check all fluid levels.

11   Timing chain and sprockets (1.8L engines) - removal, inspection and installation

Removal

Refer to illustration 11.5

1   Disconnect the cable from the negative battery terminal (see Chapter 5).
2   Set the engine to TDC number 1 (see Section 3).
3   Remove the valve cover (see Section 4).
4   Remove the timing chain cover (see Section 10).

5   Rotate the crankshaft counterclockwise slightly to compress the chain tensioner. Install a 0.040 inch (1.0 mm) pin into the alignment holes **(see illustration)**, then rotate the crankshaft slightly clockwise to secure the pin. The timing mark (triangle) on the crankshaft sprocket must align with the pointer on the engine block.
6   Remove the mounting bolts and the timing chain tensioner.
7   Remove the right side cam chain guide.
8   Remove the camshaft chain tensioner arm (chain guide).
9   Remove the timing chain. **Caution:** *Do not turn the crankshaft or camshaft once the timing chain has been removed.*

Inspection

10   Clean all parts with clean solvent. Dry with compressed air.
11   Inspect the chain tensioner for excessive wear or other damage. Be sure to drain

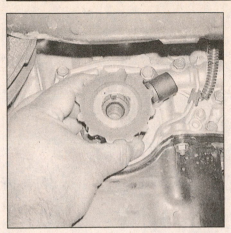

12.3a Remove the crankshaft sprocket . . .

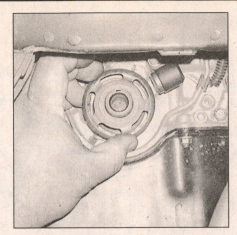

12.3b . . . and the inner belt guide - note that the concave side faces toward the engine (away from the timing belt)

12.4 Carefully pry the oil seal out with a removal tool or a screwdriver - don't nick or scratch the crankshaft or oil pump housing or the new seal will leak

all the oil out of the chain tensioner if it is to be reused.

12   Inspect the timing chain guides for deep grooves, excessive wear, or other damage.

13   Inspect the timing chain for excessive wear or damage.

14   Inspect the crankshaft and camshaft sprocket for chipped or broken teeth, excessive wear, or damage. Replace any component that is in questionable condition.

Installation

Refer to illustration 11.16

15   Make sure the timing mark (triangle) on the crankshaft sprocket is still aligned with the pointer on the engine block.

16   Make sure the "UP" mark on the camshaft sprocket is at the top and the two index marks are in line with the top edge of the cylinder head **(see illustration)**.

17   Install the timing chain around the crankshaft sprocket with the plated link on the chain aligned with the dot (indentation) on the

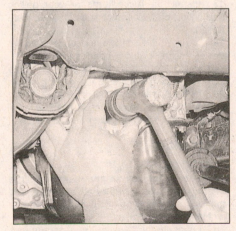

12.5 Drive in a new seal with a seal driver or a socket with an outside diameter slightly smaller than the outside diameter of the seal

crankshaft sprocket **(see illustration 11.16)**.

18   Install the timing chain over the camshaft sprocket with the dot (circular indentations) aligned with the colored chain link.

19   Install the camshaft timing chain guide and the tensioner arm. Tighten the bolts to the torque listed in this Chapter's Specifications.

20   Install the timing chain tensioner. Tighten the bolts to the torque listed in this Chapter's Specifications.

21   Install the timing chain guide. Tighten the bolts to the torque listed in this Chapter's Specifications.

22   Remove the pin from the timing chain tensioner.

23   Slowly turn the crankshaft clockwise two revolutions and recheck the timing marks and camshaft sprocket index marks for proper alignment. **Caution:** *If the crankshaft binds or seems to hit something, do not force it, as the valves may be hitting the pistons. If this happens, valve timing is incorrect. Remove the chain and repeat the installation procedure and verify that the installation is correct.*

24   Install the valve cover (see Section 4).

25   Install the timing chain cover (see Section 10).

26   The remainder of installation is the reverse of the removal Steps.

27   Reconnect the battery (see Chapter 5).

28   Run the engine and check for leaks.

12   Crankshaft pulley and front oil seal - replacement

Refer to illustrations 12.3a, 12.3b, 12.4 and 12.5

1   Disconnect the cable from the negative battery terminal (see Chapter 5). Loosen the left front wheel lug nuts (1.7L engine) or the right front wheel lug nuts (1.8L engine). Raise the vehicle and support it securely on jackstands. Remove the wheel and the splash

shield from below the engine compartment.

2   Unscrew the crankshaft pulley bolt. A special tool that engages with the recessed hex in the pulley opening is available to prevent the crankshaft from turning while unscrewing the bolt. If you can't obtain one of these tools, remove the flywheel/driveplate inspection cover and wedge a screwdriver into the starter ring gear teeth. Slip the pulley off the crankshaft.

3   On 1.7L engines, remove the timing belt (see Section 9). Remove the crankshaft sprocket from the crankshaft, then remove the inner belt guide **(see illustrations)**.

4   Carefully pry the seal out of the housing with a seal removal tool or a screwdriver **(see illustration)**. Don't scratch the seal bore or damage the crankshaft in the process (if the crankshaft is damaged, the new seal will end up leaking).

5   Clean the bore in the seal housing and coat the outer edge of the new seal with engine oil or multi-purpose grease. Using a seal driver or a socket with an outside diameter slightly smaller than the outside diameter of the seal, carefully drive the seal into place with a hammer **(see illustration)**. If a socket is not available, a short section of a large diameter pipe will work. Check the seal after installation to be sure the spring did not pop out.

6   Install the inner belt guide (if equipped) and the crankshaft sprocket. **Note:** *Install the inner belt guide with the concave surface facing in toward the front seal.*

7   On 1.7L engines, install the timing belt (see Section 9).

8   Lubricate the lip of the seal with a thin film of engine oil or multi-purpose grease, then install the crankshaft pulley. **Note:** *On 1.8L engines, the crankshaft pulley has flats on the sleeve that must be aligned with the inner oil pump gear.* The remainder of installation is the reverse of removal.

9   Run the engine and check for leaks.

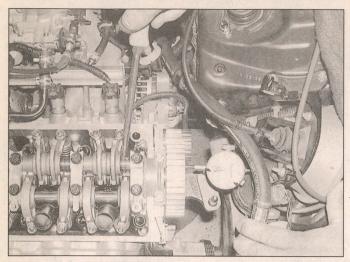

13.1 To check camshaft endplay, set a dial indicator like this, with the gauge plunger touching the nose of the camshaft

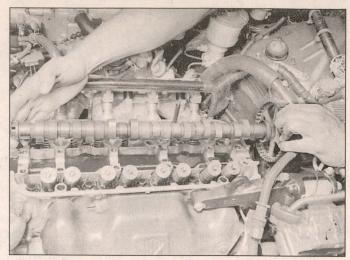

13.8 Lift the camshaft from the cylinder head (1.7L engine)

13   Camshaft - removal, inspection and installation

Endplay and runout check

Refer to illustration 13.1

1   To check camshaft endplay:
a) *With the camshaft installed, reinstall the camshaft bearing caps (1.7L engine) or the rocker arm assembly (with the rocker arms removed from it; 1.8L engine).*
b) *Mount a dial indicator on the cylinder head with the pointer resting on the camshaft nose* **(see illustration)**.
c) *Using a large screwdriver as a lever at the opposite end, move the camshaft forward-and-backward and note the dial indicator reading.*
d) *Compare the reading with the endplay listed in this Chapter's Specifications.*
e) *If the indicated reading is excessive:*

1.7L engine: Either the camshaft or the cylinder head is worn. Replace parts as necessary.

1.8L engine: Replace the thrust cover with a new one and recheck the endplay. If it's still excessive, either the camshaft or the cylinder head is worn. Replace parts as necessary.

2   To check camshaft runout:
a) *Support the camshaft with a pair of V-blocks and set up a dial indicator with the plunger resting against the center bearing journal on the camshaft.*
b) *Rotate the camshaft and note the indicated runout.*
c) *Compare the results to the camshaft runout listed in this Chapter's Specifications.*
d) *If the indicated runout exceeds the specified runout limit, replace the camshaft.*

Removal

Refer to illustration 13.8

Note: *On 1.8L engines, the cylinder head must be removed (see Section 14) from the vehicle before the camshaft can be removed from the cylinder head.*

3   Remove the ignition coils (see Chapter 5).
4   Remove the valve cover (see Section 4).
5   Set the engine at TDC for cylinder number one (see Section 3) and remove the timing belt (see Section 9) or timing chain (see Section 11).
6   **1.7L engine:** If necessary, separate the sprocket from the camshaft by removing the camshaft sprocket bolt. **Note:** *Prevent the camshaft from turning by inserting a screwdriver through one of the holes in the sprocket.*
7   Remove the rocker arm assembly (see Section 8). On 1.7L engines, if the camshaft bearing caps must be removed from the assembly and they don't have numbers on them, number them before removal. Be sure to put the marks on the same ends of all the caps to prevent incorrect orientation of the caps during installation.
8   **1.7L engine:** Lift out the camshaft **(see illustration)**, wipe it off with a clean shop towel, remove the camshaft seal and set the camshaft aside. Remove the oil seal.
9   **1.8L engine:** Hold the camshaft from turning by placing an open-end wrench on the hex at the end of the camshaft opposite that of the sprocket, then unscrew the sprocket bolt and separate the sprocket from the camshaft.
10   **1.8L engine:** Remove the camshaft position sensor (see Chapter 6), then remove the camshaft thrust cover from the end of the cylinder head. Slide the camshaft out of the head.

Inspection

Refer to illustration 13.12

11   Check the camshaft bearing journals and caps for scoring and signs of wear. If they are worn, replace the cylinder head with a new or rebuilt assembly.
12   Check the cam lobes for wear:
a) *Check the toe and ramp areas of each cam lobe for score marks and uneven wear. Also check for flaking and pitting.*
b) *If there's wear on the toe or the ramp, replace the camshaft, but first try to find the cause of the wear. Look for abrasive substances in the oil and inspect the oil pump and oil passages for blockage. Lobe wear is usually caused by inadequate lubrication or dirty oil.*
c) *Using a micrometer, measure the cam lobe height* **(see illustration)**. *If lobe wear is indicated, replace the camshaft.*

13   Inspect the rocker arms for wear, galling and pitting of the contact surfaces (see Section 8).
14   If any of the conditions described above are noted, the cylinder head is probably getting insufficient lubrication or dirty oil. Make sure you track down the cause of this problem (low oil level, low oil pump capacity, clogged oil passage, etc.) before installing a new cylinder head, camshaft or rocker arm assembly.

Installation

Refer to illustration 13.16

15   Thoroughly clean the camshaft, the bearing surfaces in the head and caps and the rocker arms. Wipe off all components with a clean, lint-free cloth.
16   Lubricate the camshaft bearing surfaces in the head and the bearing journals and lobes on the camshaft with camshaft assembly lubricant **(see illustration)**. **Caution:** *Fail-*

13.12 Measure the camshaft lobe heights with a micrometer

13.16 Be sure to apply camshaft assembly lubricant to the lobes and bearing journals before installing the camshaft

ure to adequately lubricate the camshaft and related components can cause serious damage to bearing and friction surfaces during the first few seconds after engine start-up, when the oil pressure is low or nonexistent.

17 Install the camshaft.

18 On 1.7L engines, using an appropriate sized driver or deep socket, install a new camshaft seal with the open (spring) side facing in.

19 On 1.8L engines, install the camshaft thrust cover and camshaft position sensor, then install the camshaft sprocket, tightening the bolt to the torque listed in this Chapter's Specifications. Install the cylinder head (see Section 14).

20 Rotate the camshaft as necessary and position the camshaft sprocket with the "UP" mark stamped on the sprocket at the twelve o'clock position.

21 Make sure the camshaft and crankshaft marks are still set to TDC for cylinder number 1, then install the rocker arm assembly (see Section 8).

22 **1.7L engine:** Install the timing belt and related components as described in Section 9.

23 **1.8L engine:** Install the timing chain and related components as described in Section 11.

24 Rotate the crankshaft counterclockwise (1.7L engine) or clockwise (1.8L engine) slowly by hand through two complete revolutions and recheck the alignment marks on the sprockets. The timing marks should still be aligned. If they're not, reset all the timing marks again. **Caution:** *If you feel resistance while rotating the crankshaft, stop immediately!*

25 The remainder of installation is the reverse of removal.

14 Cylinder head - removal and installation

Warning: *Allow the engine to cool completely before beginning this procedure.*

exhaust manifold (see Section 6).

16 Remove the valve cover (see Section 4).

17 On 1.7L engines, remove the timing belt (see Section 9), rocker arm assembly (see Section 8) and the camshaft (see Section 13). On 1.8L engines, remove the timing chain (see Section 11) and rocker arm assembly (see Section 8).

18 Loosen the cylinder head bolts in 1/4-turn increments until they can be removed by hand. Work in a pattern that's the reverse of the tightening sequence to avoid warping the cylinder head **(see illustrations 14.26a and 14.26b). Caution:** *Discard the old bolts and obtain new ones (re-using the old bolts is not recommended, and, on the 1.8L engine, the final tightening stage assumes that new bolts are being installed).*

19 Lift the cylinder head off the engine. If resistance is felt, don't pry between the head and block gasket mating surfaces - damage to the mating surfaces will result. Instead, pry between the power steering pump bracket and the engine block. Set the head on blocks of wood to prevent damage to the gasket sealing surfaces.

20 Have an automotive machine shop check the cylinder head for warpage.

Installation

Refer to illustration 14.26a and 14.26b

21 The mating surfaces of the cylinder head and block must be perfectly clean when the head is installed.

22 Use a gasket scraper to remove all traces of carbon and old gasket material, then clean the mating surfaces with brake system cleaner. If there's oil on the mating surfaces when the cylinder head is installed, the gasket may not seal correctly and leaks may develop. When working on the engine block, stuff the cylinders with clean shop rags to keep out debris. Use a vacuum cleaner to remove material that falls into the cylinders. Since the cylinder head and engine block are made of aluminum, aggressive scraping can cause damage. Be extra careful not to nick or gouge the mating surfaces with the scraper.

23 Check the block and cylinder head mating surfaces for nicks, deep scratches and other damage. If damage is slight, it can be removed with a file; if it's excessive, machining may be the only alternative.

24 Use a tap of the correct size to chase the threads in the cylinder head bolt holes. Use a wire brush to remove corrosion and clean the bolt threads. Dirt, corrosion, sealant and damaged threads will affect torque readings.

25 Place a new gasket on the engine block. **Note:** *On 1.8L engines, always install a new coolant separator (the hollow dowel pin at the transaxle end of the engine) into the block before installing a new head gasket.* Check to see if there are any markings (such as "TOP") on the gasket to indicate how it is to be installed. Those identification marks must face UP. Set the cylinder head in position.

26 Lubricate the threads and the seats of the NEW cylinder head bolts with clean

Removal

1 Relieve the fuel system pressure (see Chapter 4), then disconnect the cable from the negative terminal of the battery (see Chapter 5).

2 Position the number one piston at Top Dead Center (see Section 3).

3 Drain the cooling system and remove the spark plugs (see Chapter 1).

4 Disconnect the heater hoses, the upper and lower radiator hoses and the bypass hose (see Chapter 3).

5 Remove the air filter housing and intake resonator (see Chapter 4).

6 Remove the drivebelts (see Chapter 1). Unbolt the power steering pump and set it aside without disconnecting any hoses, then remove the power steering pump bracket (see Chapter 10).

7 Disconnect the accelerator cable and cruise control cable (if equipped) from the throttle body (see Chapter 4).

8 Disconnect the EVAP canister hose, the brake booster vacuum hose, the PCV hose and intake breather hose (Chapters 4 and 6).

9 Disconnect the injector harness, the ECT sensor, the TP sensor, the MAP sensor, oxygen sensor, EGR sensor, the CKP sensor, the CMP sensor, the VTEC solenoid (if equipped) and the IAC control valve connectors. Label each connector to prevent incorrect reassembly.

10 Remove the coolant connector hose from the coolant housing.

11 Remove the power steering pump without disconnecting the hoses (see Chapter 10).

12 Remove the alternator (see Chapter 5).

13 Remove the power steering bracket and the alternator bracket from the cylinder head.

14 Support the engine with a floor jack. Place a wood block between the jack pad and the oil pan to avoid damaging the pan. Remove the left engine mount bracket (see Section 19).

15 Remove the intake manifold brace, the intake manifold (see Section 5) and the

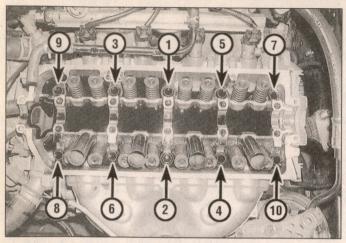

14.26a 1.7L engine cylinder head bolt TIGHTENING sequence

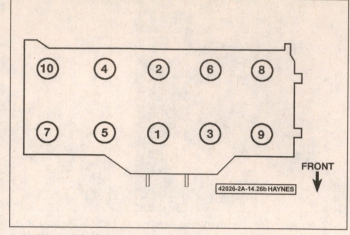

42026-2A-14.26b HAYNES

14.26b 1.8L engine cylinder head bolt TIGHTENING sequence

engine oil, then install them. Tighten the bolts in the recommended sequence, in stages, to the torque listed in this Chapter's Specifications **(see illustrations)**. Because of the critical function of cylinder head bolts, the manufacturer specifies the following conditions for tightening them:

a) *A beam-type or dial-type torque wrench is preferable to a pre-set (click-stop) torque wrench. If you use a pre-set torque wrench, tighten slowly and be careful not to overtighten the bolts.*

b) *If a bolt makes any sound while you're tightening it (squeaking, clicking, etc.), loosen it completely and tighten it again in the specified stages.*

27   On 1.7L engines, install the timing belt (see Section 9), camshaft assembly (see Section 8) and the rocker arm (see Section 13). On 1.8L engines, install the timing chain (see Section 11) and rocker arm assembly (see Section 8).

28   Rotate the crankshaft counterclockwise (1.7L engine) or clockwise (1.8L engine) slowly by hand through two complete revolutions and recheck the alignment marks on the sprockets. **Caution:** *If you feel any resistance while turning the engine over, stop and recheck the camshaft timing. The valves might be hitting the pistons.*

29   Reinstall the remaining parts in the reverse order of removal.

30   Refill the cooling system and change the engine oil and filter (see Chapter 1).

31   Reconnect the battery (see Chapter 5).

32   Run the engine until normal operating temperature is reached. Check for leaks and proper operation.

15 Oil pan - removal and installation

Removal

1   Drain the engine oil and replace the oil filter (see Chapter 1).

2   Disconnect the cable from the negative terminal of the battery.

3   Raise the vehicle and support it securely on jackstands. Remove the splash shield from under the engine.

1.7L engine

Refer to illustration 15.6

4   Disconnect the oxygen sensor connectors (see Chapter 6).

5   Remove the front section of the exhaust pipe (see Chapter 4).

6   Remove the bolts securing the oil pan to the engine block **(see illustration)**.

7   Tap on the pan with a soft-face hammer to break the gasket seal and detach the oil pan from the engine. Don't pry between the block and oil pan mating surfaces.

1.8L engine

8   Remove the front section of the exhaust pipe (see Chapter 4).

9   Remove the lower torque rod (see Section 19).

10   Remove the lower torque rod bracket.

11   Remove the air conditioning compressor bracket (see Chapter 3).

12   On models equipped with an automatic transmission, remove the shift cable cover bolts, torque converter cover bolts and remove the covers.

13   On models equipped with a manual transmission, remove the clutch cover bolts and cover.

14   Remove the bottom two transmission mounting bolts.

15   Remove the bolts securing the oil pan to the engine block.

16   Tap on the pan with a soft-face hammer to break the gasket seal and detach the oil pan from the engine. **Note:** *Pull the dowel pins out from the block once the pan has been removed.*

Installation

17   Using a gasket scraper, remove all traces of old gasket and/or sealant from the engine block and the oil pan. Also make sure the threaded bolt holes in the block are clean.

18   Clean the oil pan with solvent and dry it thoroughly. Check the gasket flanges for distortion, particularly around the bolt holes. If necessary, place the pan on a wood block and use a hammer to flatten and restore the gasket surface.

19   Clean the mating surfaces on the engine block and the oil pan with brake system cleaner to remove any oil residue which will prevent the new gasket from sealing properly.

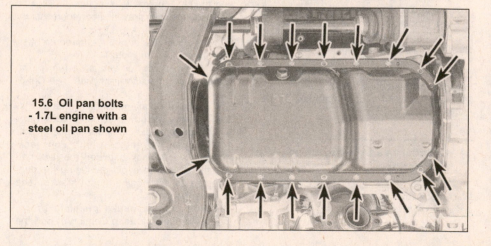

15.6 Oil pan bolts - 1.7L engine with a steel oil pan shown

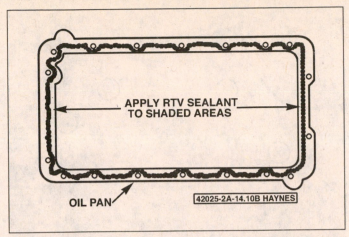

15.20 On aluminum oil pans, apply a bead of RTV sealant to the perimeter of the oil pan flange, inboard of the bolt holes

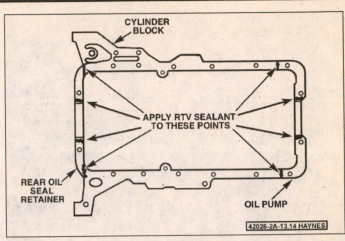

15.23 On LX and DX models, apply a small amount of RTV sealant to the specified points

Aluminum oil pan - 1.7L engine (EX, HX models)

Refer to illustration 15.20

20   Apply a 1/8-inch wide bead of RTV sealant to the perimeter of the oil pan along the inside of the bolt holes **(see illustration)**, then install the gasket onto the oil pan.

21   Carefully place the oil pan in position and install the bolts finger tight.

22   Tighten the oil pan bolts a little at a time, in a criss-cross pattern, to the torque listed in this Chapter's Specifications.

Steel oil pan - 1.7L engine (LX/DX models)

Refer to illustrations 15.23, 15.24 and 15.25

23   Apply a 1/8-inch wide bead of RTV sealant to the oil pump cover and rear main seal housing corners where they meet the engine block **(see illustration)**.

24   Apply RTV sealant to the four corners of the recesses on the oil pan gasket **(see illus-**

tration), then install the gasket onto the oil pan. Carefully place the oil pan in position and install the bolts finger tight.

25   Tighten the oil pan nuts in the correct sequence **(see illustration)** and to the torque listed in this Chapter's Specifications, then tighten all of the fasteners, a little at a time and in a criss-cross pattern, to the torque listed in this Chapter's Specifications. Don't overtighten them or the pan could be distorted.

Aluminum oil pan - 1.8L engine

Refer to illustration 15.28

26   Replace the O-rings and apply a 1/8-inch wide bead of RTV sealant to the perimeter of the oil pan and along the inside of the bolt holes then the oil pan.

27   Carefully place the oil pan in position and install the bolts finger tight.

28   Tighten the oil pan bolts in the correct sequence **(see illustration)** and to the torque listed in this Chapter's Specifications.

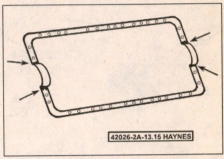

15.24 Apply a small amount of RTV sealant to the oil pan gasket at these points

All models

29   The remainder of installation is the reverse of removal.

30   Reconnect the battery (see Chapter 5).

31   Wait at least one hour before adding oil (see Chapter 1), then run the engine and check for oil leaks.

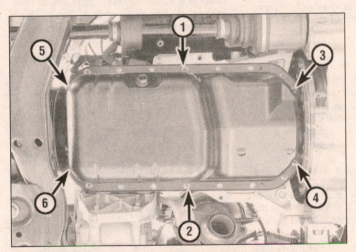

15.25 First tighten the six oil pan nuts finger tight and in sequence to position the oil pan evenly against the engine block - next, tighten all the oil pan bolts and nuts, a little at a time, to the torque listed in this Chapter's Specifications

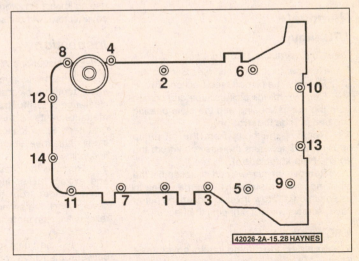

15.28 1.8L engine oil pan bolt tightening sequence

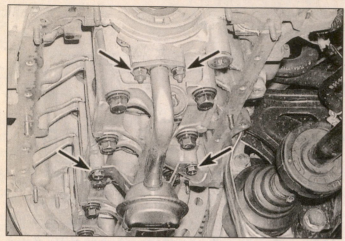

16.3 Remove the oil pick-up tube bolts from the oil pump and main bearing cap bridge

16.4 Remove the oil pump-to-block bolts (circled) and remove the oil pump

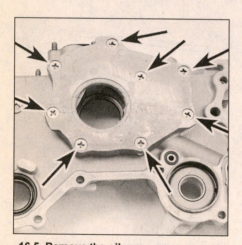

16.5 Remove the oil pump cover screws

16.8a Use a feeler gauge and straight-edge to check the clearance between the rotors and the cover

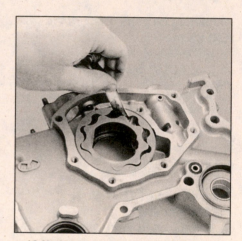

16.8b Use a feeler gauge to check the tooth-tip clearance between the inner and outer rotors

16 Oil pump - removal, inspection and installation

Removal

1.7L engine

Refer to illustrations 16.3, 16.4 and 16.5

1   Remove the timing belt (see Section 9).
2   Remove the oil pan (see Section 15).
3   Remove the oil pick-up tube and screen from the pump housing and the main bearing cap bridge **(see illustration)**.
4   Remove the bolts from the oil pump housing and separate the assembly from the engine **(see illustration)**.
5   Remove the screws and disassemble the oil pump **(see illustration)**. You may need to use an impact screwdriver to loosen the pump cover screws without stripping the heads.

1.8L engine

6   Remove the timing chain cover (see Section 10).
7   Remove the screws from the oil pump cover-to-timing chain cover and separate the oil pump cover from the timing chain cover and disassemble the oil pump. You may need to use an impact screwdriver to loosen the pump cover screws without stripping the heads.

Inspection

Refer to illustrations 16.8a, 16.8b and 16.8c

8   Check the oil pump rotor-to-cover clearance, tooth tip clearance and rotor-to-body clearance **(see illustrations)**. Compare your measurements to the values listed in this Chapter's Specifications. Replace the pump if any of the measurements exceed the specified limits.
9   Remove the pressure relief valve plug and extract the spring and pressure relief valve plunger from the pump housing or cover. Check the spring for distortion and the relief valve plunger for scoring. Replace parts as necessary.
10   Install the pump rotors. Pack the spaces between the rotors with petroleum jelly (this will prime the pump).
11   Apply thread-locking compound to the pump cover screws, install the cover and

tighten the screws to the torque listed in this Chapter's Specifications. Install the oil pressure relief valve and spring assembly. Use a new sealing washer on the plug and tighten the plug securely.

16.8c Use a feeler gauge to check the outer rotor-to-pump body clearance

17.3 Remove the flywheel/driveplate bolts from the crankshaft

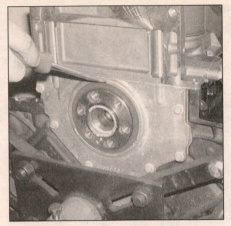

18.4 Carefully pry the oil seal out with a seal removal tool or a screwdriver (don't nick or scratch the crankshaft, or the new seal will be damaged and leaks will develop)

18.5 Lubricate the journal and the seal lip with multi-purpose grease and carefully work the seal over the journal with a smooth, blunt object

Installation

1.7L engine

12 Apply a thin coat of anaerobic sealant to the pump housing-to-block sealing surface and a new O-ring in the pump housing.

13 Install the pump housing to the engine block and tighten the bolts to the torque listed in this Chapter's Specifications.

14 Install the oil pick-up tube and screen, using a new gasket. Tighten the bolts to the torque listed in this Chapter's Specifications. Install the oil pan (see Section 15).

15 The remainder of installation is the reverse of removal. Add the specified type and quantity of oil and coolant (see Chapter 1), run the engine and check for leaks.

1.8L engine

16 Apply a thin coat of anaerobic sealant to the timing chain cover-to-block sealing surface and new O-rings in the engine cover. Install the timing chain cover (see Section 10) to the engine block and tighten the bolts to the torque listed in this Chapter's Specifications.

17 The remainder of installation is the reverse of removal. Add the specified type and quantity of oil and coolant (see Chapter 1), run the engine and check for leaks.

17 Flywheel/driveplate - removal and installation

Removal

Refer to illustration 17.3

1 Raise the vehicle and support it securely on jackstands, then refer to Chapter 7 and remove the transaxle.

2 If the vehicle is equipped with a manual transaxle, remove the pressure plate and clutch disc (see Chapter 8). Now is a good time to check/replace the clutch components and pilot bearing.

3 Remove the bolts that secure the fly-

wheel/driveplate to the crankshaft **(see illustration)**. If the crankshaft turns, wedge a screwdriver in the ring gear teeth (manual transaxle models), or insert a long punch through one of the holes in the driveplate and allow it to rest against a projection on the engine block (automatic transaxle models).

4 Remove the flywheel/driveplate from the crankshaft. Since the flywheel is fairly heavy, be sure to support it while removing the last bolt.

5 Clean the flywheel to remove grease and oil. Inspect the surface for cracks, rivet grooves, burned areas and score marks. Light scoring can be removed with emery cloth. Check for cracked and broken ring gear teeth. Lay the flywheel on a flat surface and use a straightedge to check for warpage.

6 Clean and inspect the mating surfaces of the flywheel/driveplate and the crankshaft. If the rear main oil seal is leaking, replace it before reinstalling the flywheel/driveplate (see Section 18).

Installation

7 Position the flywheel/driveplate against the crankshaft. Note that some engines have an alignment dowel or staggered bolt holes to ensure correct installation. Before installing the bolts, apply thread-locking compound to the threads.

8 Prevent the flywheel/driveplate from turning by using one of the methods described in Step 3. Using a criss-cross pattern, tighten the bolts to the torque listed in this Chapter's Specifications.

9 The remainder of installation is the reverse of the removal procedure.

18 Rear main oil seal - replacement

Refer to illustrations 18.4 and 18.5

1 The transaxle must be removed from the vehicle for this procedure (see Chapter 7).

2 Remove the flywheel/driveplate (see Section 17).

3 Before removing the seal, it is very important that the clearance between the seal and the outside edge of the retainer or block is checked. Use a small ruler or caliper and record the distance. The new seal must not be driven in past this measurement.

4 The seal can be replaced without removing the oil pan or seal retainer (if equipped). Use a screwdriver to carefully pry the seal out **(see illustration)**. **Note:** *On 1.8L engines, 2006 and later 2.0L engines, and 2007 and later 2.4L engines, the oil seal is installed into the block and a seal retainer is not used.*

5 Apply a film of clean oil to the crankshaft seal journal and the lip of the new seal and carefully tap the seal into place. The lip is stiff, so carefully work it onto the seal journal of the crankshaft with a smooth object like the end of a socket extension **(see illustration)**. Tap the seal into the retainer with a seal driver.

6 The remaining steps are the reverse of removal.

7 Run the engine and check for oil leaks.

19 Engine mounts - check and replacement

1 Engine mounts seldom require attention, but broken or deteriorated mounts should be replaced immediately or the added strain placed on the driveline components may cause damage or wear.

Check

2 During the check, the engine must be raised slightly to remove the weight from the mounts.

3 Raise the vehicle and support it securely on jackstands, then position a jack under

19.8a Typical timing-belt end engine mount bracket fasteners

19.8b Typical transaxle-end mount through-bolt location

19.8c Typical rear engine mount bolt locations

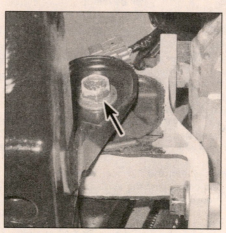

19.8d Typical front transaxle mount through-bolt

19.8e Typical rear transaxle mount bolt locations

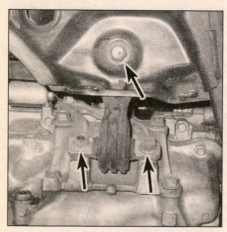

19.8f Lower torque rod mounting bolt location - 1.8L shown

the engine oil pan. Place a large wood block between the jack head and the oil pan, then carefully raise the engine just enough to take the weight off the mounts. **Warning:** *DO NOT place any part of your body under the engine when it's supported only by a jack!*

4   Check the mount insulators to see if the rubber is cracked, hardened or separated from the metal in the center of the mount.

5   Check for relative movement between the mount plates and the engine or frame (use a large screwdriver or pry bar to attempt to move the mounts). If movement is noted, lower the engine and tighten the mount fasteners.

Replacement

Refer to illustrations 19.8a, 19.8b, 19.8c, 19.8d, 19.8e and 19.8f

6   Disconnect the cable from the negative terminal of the battery (see Chapter 5). Raise the vehicle and support it securely on jackstands (if not already done). Support the engine as described in Step 3.

7   Remove the fasteners, raise the engine with the jack and detach the mount from the frame bracket and engine.

8   Install the new mount, making sure it is correctly positioned in its bracket **(see illustrations)**. Install the fasteners and tighten them securely.

Chapter 2 Part B
Double overhead camshaft (DOHC) engines

Contents

Section

Balance shaft assembly and balance shafts - removal,
   inspection and installation 15
Camshafts and rocker arms - removal, inspection
   and installation 11
CHECK ENGINE light on.. See Chapter 6
Compression check.. See Chapter 2C
Crankshaft pulley and front oil seal - removal and installation 9
Cylinder head - removal and installation 12
Drivebelt check, adjustment and replacement................ See Chapter 1
Engine - removal and installation .... See Chapter 2C
Engine mounts - check and replacement 18
Engine oil and filter change .... See Chapter 1
Engine overhaul - general information........................ See Chapter 2C
Exhaust manifold - removal and installation 6
Flywheel/driveplate - removal and installation............................. 16

Section

General information.. 1
Intake manifold - removal and installation 5
i-VTEC system - description and component checks.................. 10
Oil pan - removal and installation 13
Oil pump - removal, inspection and installation 14
Rear main oil seal - replacement... 17
Repair operations possible with the engine in the vehicle............ 2
Spark plug replacement..................................... See Chapter 1
Timing chain and sprockets - removal, inspection
   and installation 8
Timing chain cover - removal and installation 7
Top Dead Center (TDC) for number one piston - locating............ 3
Valve cover - removal and installation 4
Water pump - removal and installation .... See Chapter 3

Specifications

General

Firing order	1-3-4-2
Bore	
CR-V models...	3.43 inches (87 mm)
Civic models...	3.39 inches (86 mm)
Stroke	
CR-V models...	3.90 inches (99 mm)
Civic models...	3.39 inches (86 mm)
Displacement	
CR-V models...	144 cubic inches (2.4 liters)
Civic models...	122 cubic inches (2.0 liters)
Oil pressure	See Chapter 2C

Valve adjustment .... See Chapter 1

Front

Cylinder locations for the
DOHC engines

Camshafts

Lobe height	
Intake	
Primary	
2006 and earlier models	1.3356 inches (33.925 mm)
2007 and later models	1.3489 inches (34.263 mm)
Secondary	1.1668 inches (29.638 mm)
Exhaust	1.3422 inches (34.092 mm)
Endplay	0.002 to 0.008 inch (0.050 to 0.20 mm)
Runout	0.001 inch (0.030 mm)
Journal-to-bearing (oil) clearance	
Journal number 1	0.001 to 0.003 inch (0.030 to 0.076 mm)
Journal number 2, 3, 4, 5	0.002 to 0.004 inch (0.050 to 0.10 mm)

Oil pump

Rotor-to-cover clearance	
2002 and 2003 models	
Standard	0.001 to 0.003 inch (0.030 to 0.076 mm)
Service limit	0.005 inch maximum (0.12 mm)
2004 and later models	
Standard	0.0014 to 0.0028 inch (0.035 to 0.070 mm)
Service limit	0.005 inch maximum (0.12 mm)
Tooth tip clearance	
Standard	0.002 to 0.006 inch (0.05 to 0.15 mm)
Service limit	0.008 inch maximum (0.20 mm)
Outer rotor-to-pump body clearance	
Standard	0.006 to 0.008 inch (0.15 to 0.20 mm)
Service limit	0.009 inch maximum (0.23 mm)

Torque specifications

Note: *One foot-pound (ft-lb) of torque is equivalent to 12 inch-pounds (in-lbs) of torque. Torque values below approximately 15 ft-lbs are expressed in inch-pounds, since most foot-pound torque wrenches are not accurate at these smaller values.*

	Ft-lbs (unless otherwise indicated)	Nm
Balance shaft sprocket bolt	33	45
Balance shaft case bolts		
Short bolts	104 in-lbs	11.5
Long bolts	20	27
Balance shaft assembly-to-engine block bolts		
Short bolts	16	22
Long bolts	33	45
Camshaft sprocket bolts		
Intake camshaft sprocket (VTC actuator)	83	113
Exhaust camshaft sprocket	53	72
Camshaft holder bolts		
6 mm bolts	104 in-lbs	11.5
8 mm bolts	16	22
Crankshaft pulley bolt		
Step 1	36	49
Step 2	Tighten an additional 90-degrees	
Cylinder head bolts*		
Step 1	29	39
Step 2	Tighten an additional 90-degrees	
Step 3	Tighten an additional 90-degrees	
Step 4	Tighten an additional 90-degrees	
Drivebelt tensioner bolts	16	22
Driveplate bolts	54	73
Flywheel bolts		
2002 through 2005	90	122
2006 and later models	76	103

* Bolt(s) must be replaced.

Torque specifications

	Ft-lbs (unless otherwise indicated)	Nm
Exhaust manifold bolts/nuts	33	45
Exhaust manifold heat shield bolts	16	22
Exhaust pipe-to-manifold bolts	16	22
Timing chain cover bolts	104 in-lbs	11.5
Intake manifold bolts	16	22
Oil cooler hose joint pipe mounting bolt	104 in-lbs	11.5
Oil pump housing bolts	104 in-lbs	11.5
Oil pump pressure relief valve plug	29	39
Oil pan bolts	104 in-lbs	11.5
Timing chain tensioner bolts	104 in-lbs	11.5
Timing chain guides		
Camshaft chain guide bolts	104 in-lbs	11.5
Tensioner arm bolt	16	22
Upper timing chain guide bolts	16	22
Valve cover nuts	104 in-lbs	11.5
Intake manifold cover bolts	104 in-lbs	11.5

1 General information

This Part of Chapter 2 is devoted to in-vehicle repair procedures for the 2.0L and 2.4L DOHC (Double Overhead Camshaft), engine as well as procedures such as timing chain and sprocket(s), balance shaft chain and balance shafts and oil pan removal. All information concerning engine removal and installation can be found in Part C of this Chapter.

Two different versions of this engine have been produced by Honda for the CR-V and Civic models, both of which are covered in this Part of Chapter 2. All versions of this engine utilize a Double Overhead Camshaft (DOHC), with 4 valves per cylinder (16V). This engine incorporates the i-VTEC (intelligent Variable Valve Timing and lift Electronic Control) system, which electronically alters valve timing to enhance engine performance. For more information on the i-VTEC system, see Section 10 of this Chapter.

Engine designations include:

K20A3 - 2.0L 16 valve DOHC i-VTEC 160 horsepower engine (2005 and earlier models)

K20Z3 - 2.0L 16 valve DOHC i-VTEC engine (2006 and later models)

K24A1 - 2.4L 16 valve DOHC i-VTEC 160 horsepower engine (2006 and earlier models)

K24Z1 - 2.4L 16 valve DOHC i-VTEC engine (2007 and later models)

The Specifications included in this Part of Chapter 2 apply only to the procedures contained in this Part. Part C of Chapter 2 contains the Specifications necessary for certain procedures concerning engine rebuilding.

2 Repair operations possible with the engine in the vehicle

Many major repair operations can be accomplished without removing the engine from the vehicle.

Clean the engine compartment and the exterior of the engine with some type of degreaser before any work is done. It will make the job easier and help keep dirt out of the internal areas of the engine.

Depending on the components involved, it may be helpful to remove the hood to improve access to the engine as repairs are performed (refer to Chapter 11 if necessary). Cover the fenders to prevent damage to the paint. Special pads are available, but an old bedspread or blanket will also work.

If vacuum, exhaust, oil or coolant leaks develop, indicating a need for gasket or seal replacement, the repairs can generally be made with the engine in the vehicle. The intake and exhaust manifold gaskets, oil pan gasket, crankshaft oil seals and cylinder head gasket are all accessible with the engine in place.

Exterior engine components, such as the intake and exhaust manifolds, the oil pan, the oil pump, the water pump, the starter motor, the alternator and the fuel system components can be removed for repair with the engine in place.

Since the cylinder head can be removed without pulling the engine, camshaft and valve component servicing can also be accomplished with the engine in the vehicle. Replacement of the timing chain and sprockets is also possible with the engine in the vehicle.

In extreme cases caused by a lack of necessary equipment, repair or replacement of piston rings, pistons, connecting rods and rod bearings is possible with the engine in the vehicle. However, this practice is not recommended because of the cleaning and preparation work that must be done to the components involved.

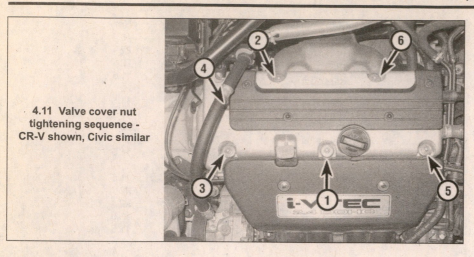

4.11 Valve cover nut tightening sequence - CR-V shown, Civic similar

3   Top Dead Center (TDC) for number one piston - locating

1   Remove the spark plugs (see Chapter 1) and install a compression gauge in the number one cylinder. Turn the crankshaft clockwise with a socket and breaker bar.

2   When the piston approaches TDC, compression will be noted on the compression gauge. Continue turning the crankshaft until the notch in the crankshaft pulley is aligned with the TDC mark on the timing chain cover. At this point, number one cylinder is at TDC on the compression stroke.

3   After the number one piston has been positioned at TDC on the compression stroke, TDC for any of the remaining pistons can be located by turning the crankshaft clockwise, 180-degrees at a time, and following the firing order.

4   Valve cover - removal and installation

Removal

1   Disconnect the cable from the negative battery terminal (see Chapter 5).

2   Remove the intake manifold cover.

3   Remove the ignition coils (see Chapter 5).

4   Remove the bolt attaching the power steering hose bracket to the valve cover.

5   Remove the dipstick and the valve cover breather hose.

6   Remove the valve cover nuts **(see illustration 4.11)**. Lift the valve cover off. Tap gently with a soft-face hammer if necessary to break the gasket seal.

Installation

Refer to illustration 4.11

7   Clean the gasket surfaces on the intake manifold, cylinder head and valve cover. Use a shop rag and brake system cleaner to wipe off all residue and gasket material from the sealing surfaces.

8   Insert a new valve cover gasket into the grooved recess in the valve cover. Make sure the gasket is positioned properly inside the valve cover groove.

9   Install new seals on the spark plug tubes.

10   Apply a slight amount of RTV sealant to the timing chain cover grooves and the number 5 rocker shaft holder mating areas.

11   Tighten the valve cover nuts in the correct sequence to the torque listed in this Chapter's Specifications **(see illustration)**.

12   The remainder of installation is the reverse of removal.

13   Reconnect the battery (see Chapter 5).

5   Intake manifold - removal and installation

Warning: *Wait until the engine is completely cool before beginning this procedure.*

Removal

1   If you're working on a Civic model, relieve the fuel system pressure (see Chapter 4).

2   Disconnect the cable from the negative battery terminal (see Chapter 5).

3   Remove the intake manifold cover, then disconnect the breather hose from the valve cover and the intake manifold.

4   Remove the intake duct and the air filter housing (see Chapter 4).

5   On models so equipped, disconnect the accelerator cable and the cruise control cable from the throttle valve (see Chapter 4). Position the cables off to the side.

6   Clamp off the coolant hoses attached to the throttle body, then loosen the clamps and detach the hoses from the throttle body. Be prepared for a little coolant spillage.

CR-V models

7   Disconnect the Intake Manifold Runner Control (IMRC) actuator solenoid connector (see Chapter 6).

8   Disconnect the PCV hose from the intake manifold (see Chapter 1).

9   Remove the IMRC solenoid mounting

bolts and remove the actuator solenoid from the intake manifold.

10   Remove the radiator support cover (see Chapter 3).

11   Remove the wiring harness clamps along the radiator support.

12   Remove the mounting brackets and lift the radiator support from the engine compartment.

13   Disconnect the vacuum hoses from the intake manifold. Mark each hose with tape to insure correct reassembly.

14   Disconnect the IAC valve, the TPS, the knock sensor and any other electrical connectors that may interfere with manifold removal.

15   Remove the intake manifold mounting bolts and nuts.

16   Lift the intake manifold from the engine compartment.

Civic models

17   Disconnect the inlet line from the fuel rail (see Chapter 4).

18   Remove the intake manifold bracket from below the intake manifold.

19   Disconnect the vacuum hoses from the intake manifold. Mark each hose with tape to insure correct reassembly.

20   Disconnect the IAC valve, the TPS, the knock sensor and any other electrical connectors that may interfere with manifold removal.

21   Disconnect the purge solenoid vacuum hose and the EVAP purge solenoid (see Chapter 6).

22   Remove the intake manifold mounting bolts and nuts.

23   Lift the intake manifold from the engine compartment.

Installation

24   Clean away all traces of old gasket material. Remove oil and dirt.

25   Install a new gasket.

26   Install the manifold and mounting fasteners. Tighten the fasteners to the torque listed in this Chapter's Specifications, starting with the center bolts and working towards the ends.

27   The remainder of installation is the reverse of the removal steps.

28   Check the coolant level and add some, if necessary, to bring it to the appropriate level (see Chapter 1).

29   Reconnect the battery (see Chapter 5).

30   Run the engine and check for oil, coolant and vacuum leaks.

6   Exhaust manifold - removal and installation

Warning: *The engine must be completely cool before beginning this procedure.*

Removal

1   Disconnect the cable from the negative battery terminal (see Chapter 5).

2   Remove the VTEC solenoid valve (see Chapter 6).

3   Remove the exhaust manifold heat shield.
4   Raise the vehicle and support it securely on jackstands.
5   Remove the intermediate shaft heat shield.
6   Detach the exhaust pipe from the manifold.
7   Unbolt the exhaust manifold from the cylinder head.

Installation

8   Using a scraper, thoroughly clean the mating surfaces on the cylinder head, manifold and exhaust pipe. Remove the residue with a solvent such as brake system cleaner.
9   Check that the mating surfaces are perfectly flat and not damaged in any way. Warped or damaged manifolds may require machining. Install the new gasket to the cylinder head studs and place the manifold on the cylinder head. Tighten the bolts evenly to the torque listed in this Chapter's Specifications.
10   Connect the exhaust pipe to the manifold and tighten the nuts evenly to the torque listed in this Chapter's Specifications.
11   The remainder of installation is the reverse of the removal steps.
12   Reconnect the battery (see Chapter 5).
13   Run the engine and check for exhaust leaks.

7   Timing chain cover - removal and installation

Removal

1   Disconnect the cable from the negative battery terminal (see Chapter 5).
2   Remove the VTC oil control solenoid valve from the timing chain cover.
3   Loosen the right front wheel lug nuts. Raise the front of the vehicle and support it securely on jackstands. Remove the right front wheel.
4   Remove the splash shield from below the engine compartment (see Chapter 2A, Section 5).
5   Drain the engine oil (see Chapter 1) and remove the drivebelt (see Chapter 1).
6   Remove the mounting bolts and detach the drivebelt tensioner from the timing chain cover.
7   Remove the crankshaft pulley (see Section 9).
8   Disconnect the crankshaft position sensor harness and other electrical connectors that may interfere with timing chain cover removal.
9   Drain the coolant (see Chapter 1). Remove the oil cooler joint pipe mounting bolt from the water pump (if equipped). Pull the joint pipe back and out, then remove the O-ring.
10   Support the engine with a floor jack. Place a wood block between the jack head and the oil pan to avoid damaging the pan.
11   Remove the ground cable, the right side

engine mount and bracket assembly (see Section 18).
12   Remove the valve cover (see Section 4).
13   Remove the mounting bolts and the timing chain cover.
14   Remove the cover-to-block gasket.

Installation

15   Inspect and clean all sealing surfaces of the timing chain cover and the block. **Caution:** *Be very careful when scraping on aluminum engine parts. Aluminum is soft and gouges easily. Severely gouged parts may require replacement.*
16   If necessary, replace the crankshaft seal (see Section 9).
17   Apply RTV sealant to the cylinder block mating surfaces on the cover, the upper surface contact areas and to the oil pan mating surfaces. Also, apply a small amount of RTV sealant to the inner thread holes.
18   Install a new timing chain cover O-ring.
19   Install the timing chain cover and fasteners. Make sure the fasteners are in their original locations. Tighten the fasteners by hand until the cover is contacting the block around its entire periphery.
20   Tighten the bolts to the torque listed in this Chapter's Specifications.
21   Install a new O-ring onto the oil cooler joint pipe and insert the pipe into the water pump. Tighten the bolt to the torque listed in this Chapter's Specifications.
22   Install the drivebelt tensioner, tightening the bolts to the torque listed in this Chapter's Specifications.
23   Install the crankshaft pulley (see Section 9).
24   Connect the wiring harness connectors. Secure the wiring harnesses with the clamps.
25   Reinstall the remaining parts in the reverse order of removal.
26   Fill the crankcase with the recommended oil (see Chapter 1).
27   Reconnect the battery (see Chapter 5).
28   Start the engine and check for leaks. Check all fluid levels.

8   Timing chain and sprockets - removal, inspection and installation

Removal

Refer to illustration 8.5
Caution: *The timing system is complex. Severe engine damage will occur if you make any mistakes. Do not attempt this procedure unless you are highly experienced with this type of repair. If you are at all unsure of your abilities, consult an expert. Double-check all your work and be sure everything is correct before you attempt to start the engine.*
1   Disconnect the cable from the negative battery terminal (see Chapter 5).
2   Set the engine to TDC number 1 (see Section 3).
3   Remove the valve cover (see Section 4).

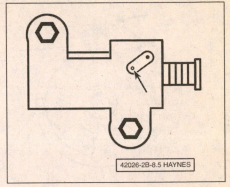

8.5 Align the hole on the lock with the hole in the tensioner, then insert a 0.06 inch (1.5 mm) pin or drill bit through both components to lock the tensioner

4   Remove the timing chain cover (see Section 7).
5   Rotate the crankshaft counterclockwise slightly to compress the chain tensioner. Install a 0.06 inch (1.5 mm) pin into the alignment holes **(see illustration)** and rotate the crankshaft slightly clockwise, returning it to TDC, to secure the pin.
6   Remove the mounting bolts and the timing chain tensioner.
7   Remove the upper timing chain guide from between the camshaft sprockets.
8   Remove the camshaft timing chain guide and the tensioner arm (chain guide).
9   Remove the timing chain.

Inspection

10   Clean all parts with clean solvent. Dry with compressed air.
11   Inspect the chain tensioner for excessive wear or other damage. Be sure to drain all the oil out of the chain tensioner if it is to be reused.
12   Inspect the timing chain guides for deep grooves, excessive wear, or other damage.
13   Inspect the timing chain for excessive wear or damage.
14   Inspect the crankshaft and camshaft sprockets for chipped or broken teeth, excessive wear, or damage. Replace any component that is in questionable condition.

Installation

Refer to illustration 8.16
Caution: *Before starting the engine, carefully rotate the crankshaft by hand through at least two full revolutions (use a socket and breaker bar on the crankshaft pulley center bolt). If you feel any resistance, STOP! There is something wrong - most likely, valves are contacting the pistons. You must find the problem before proceeding. Check your work and see if any updated repair information is available.*
15   Make sure the timing mark (triangle) on the crankshaft sprocket is aligned with the pointer.
16   Make sure the chain alignment dots (circular indentation) on the Variable valve Tim-

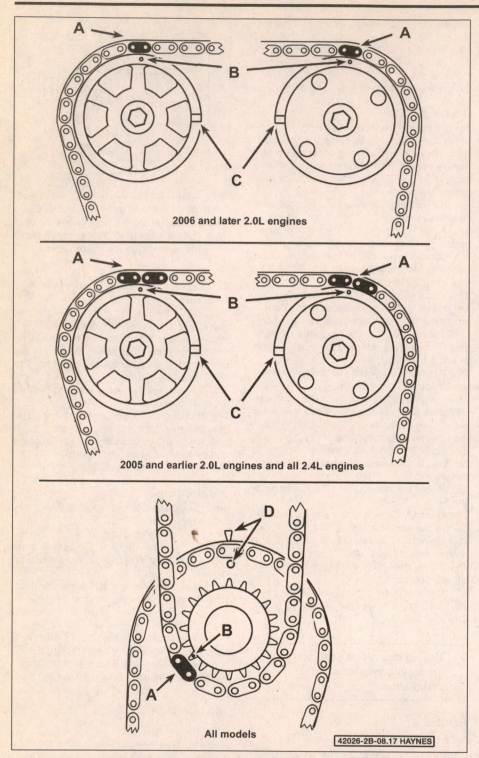

2006 and later 2.0L engines

2005 and earlier 2.0L engines and all 2.4L engines

All models

42026-2B-08.17 HAYNES

8.16 When the engine is at TDC compression for cylinder no. 1, the bright links (A) on the timing chain must align with the marks (B) on the sprockets. (C) are the camshaft sprocket TDC marks and (D) are the crankshaft sprocket TDC marks

Note: *On 2006 and later 2.0L engines, there is only one colored link for each camshaft sprocket; center the timing mark with center of each link.*

19   Install the camshaft timing chain guide and the tensioner arm. Tighten the bolts to the torque listed in this Chapter's Specifications.

20   Install the timing chain tensioner. Tighten the bolts to the torque listed in this Chapter's Specifications.

21   Install the upper timing chain guide. Tighten the bolts to the torque listed in this Chapter's Specifications.

22   Remove the pin from the timing chain tensioner.

23   Slowly turn the crankshaft clockwise two revolutions and recheck the timing marks and camshaft sprocket index marks for proper alignment. **Caution:** *If the crankshaft binds or seems to hit something, do not force it, as the valves may be hitting the pistons. If this happens, valve timing is incorrect. Remove the chain and repeat the installation procedure and verify that the installation is correct.*

24   Install the valve cover (see Section 4).

25   Install the timing chain cover (see Section 7).

26   The remainder of installation is the reverse of the removal Steps.

27   Reconnect the battery (see Chapter 5).

28   Run the engine and check for leaks.

9   Crankshaft pulley and front oil seal - removal and installation

Removal

1   Disconnect the cable from the negative battery terminal (see Chapter 5). Loosen the right-front wheel lug nuts.

2   Raise the vehicle and support it securely on jackstands. Remove the right front wheel.

3   Remove the splash shield from below the engine compartment.

4   Remove the drivebelt (see Chapter 1).

5   Unscrew the crankshaft pulley bolt. A special tool that engages with the recessed hex in the pulley opening is available to prevent the crankshaft from turning while unscrewing the bolt. If you can't obtain one of these tools, remove the flywheel/driveplate inspection cover and wedge a screwdriver into the starter ring gear teeth.

6   Slide the pulley off the crankshaft.

7   Use a seal puller to remove the crankshaft front oil seal. A screwdriver may be used instead, if the tip is wrapped with tape to avoid scratching the crankshaft.

8   Clean the seal bore and check it for nicks or gouges. Also examine the area of the hub that rides in the seal for signs of abnormal wear or scoring. If necessary, replace it.

Installation

9   Coat the lip of the new seal with clean engine oil and drive it into the bore with a seal driver or a socket slightly smaller in diameter than the seal. The open side of the seal faces into the engine.

ing Control (VTC) actuator and the exhaust camshaft sprocket are approximately at the 12 o'clock position. The TDC alignment marks on the sprockets should be opposite each other at the 9 and 3 o'clock positions **(see illustration)**.

17   Install the timing chain around the crankshaft sprocket with the colored link on the chain aligned with the dot (circular indentation) on the crankshaft sprocket **(see illustration 8.16)**.

18   Install the timing chain over the exhaust camshaft sprocket and the VTC actuator (intake camshaft sprocket) with the marks aligned with each pair of colored chain links.

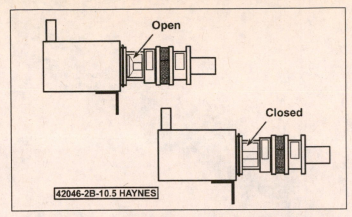

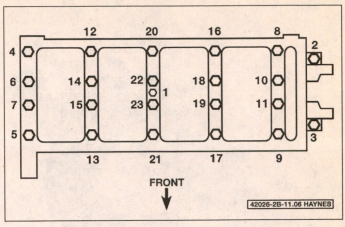

10.5 Check the position of the VTC solenoid valve - if it's stuck open, replace the valve. Be sure to check the condition of the O-ring, too. Note: *Some models have three strainer screens, while others only have one*

11.6 Camshaft holder bolt loosening sequence

10   Using clean engine oil, lubricate the sealing surface of the hub. Install the crankshaft pulley and tighten the bolt to the torque listed in this Chapter's Specifications.

11   The remainder of installation is the reverse of the removal procedure.

12   Reconnect the battery (see Chapter 5).

10   i-VTEC system - description and component checks

General description

1   The i-VTEC system on the DOHC engines is similar to the VTEC system used on the SOHC engine, but with the capability of being able to *continuously* change the intake cam timing - not just above a certain engine speed. Not only does the intake camshaft have two different lobe profiles like on the VTEC system, it is equipped with a Variable valve Timing Control (VTC) actuator, which alters the phasing of the camshaft to yield maximum potential power output for any given engine speed. For more information on the i-VTEC system, see Chapter 6.

Component checks

Note: *The VTEC and VTC systems will require specialized diagnostic equipment to access the on-board computer to test the electrical circuits, actuators and sensors. However, there are some mechanical tests of the VTEC and VTC systems that the home mechanic can perform to check for obvious and simple problems within the system. Have the VTEC and VTC systems diagnosed by a dealer service department or other qualified automotive repair facility. Also, some checks and inspections of the VTEC components require removal of the rocker arm assembly (see Section 11).*

VTEC solenoid valve

Note: *Most common problems in the VTEC system are associated with the solenoid valve*

and its filter. Regular engine oil and filter changes are necessary for trouble-free operation of the valve.

2   The VTEC solenoid valve is located on the rear of the cylinder head. The VTEC solenoid valve filter is mounted directly behind the VTEC solenoid valve (see Chapter 6).

3   Remove the VTEC solenoid valve (see Chapter 6) and check the filter for clogging. Clean and reinstall. A clogged filter screen is often the cause of system problems.

VTC oil control solenoid valve and strainer

Refer to illustration 10.5

Note: *Most common problems in the VTC system are associated with the oil control solenoid valve and its strainer. Regular engine oil and filter changes are necessary for trouble-free operation of the valve.*

4   The VTC oil control solenoid valve is located in the cylinder head on the timing chain end of the engine. The VTC oil strainer is located on the right front corner of the cylinder head, near the intake manifold. The strainer cover is retained by two bolts; remove the bolts and cover and check the strainer for clogging, cleaning it as necessary.

5   Remove the VTC oil control solenoid valve (see Chapter 6) and check the strainer for clogging, cleaning it as necessary (if it's too dirty to clean, replace the valve). Look at the position of the valve through the drain port (the port closest to the solenoid portion of the valve); it should be closed. If it's open **(see illustration)**, the solenoid valve must be replaced.

Rocker arms

6   Position the number one piston at Top Dead Center (see Section 3). Remove the valve cover (see Section 4).

7   Press on the primary intake rocker arm for cylinder number 1 to see that it moves independently of the secondary intake rockers. Check the rockers for the other cylinders at their own TDC positions.

VTEC synchronizing assembly

8   Once the rocker arm assemblies have been removed and disassembled (see Section 11), separate the rocker arms and synchronizing components.

VTEC components:

a) *Primary rocker arm*
b) *Secondary rocker arm*
c) *Synchronizing pistons*

9   Inspect the timing spring, making sure it's not broken or collapsed. Replace it if necessary.

10   Inspect all other parts (rocker arms and synchronizing pistons) for wear, galling, scoring or signs of overheating (bluish in color). Use your finger to push on the rocker arm pistons to check for smooth movement. Replace any parts, if necessary.

11   Reassemble each cylinder's components and wrap a rubber band around the rocker arms before trying to assemble them on the rocker shaft (see Section 11).

11   Camshafts and rocker arms - removal, inspection and installation

Note: *The camshaft holders, the camshafts and the rocker arm assembly are bolted to the cylinder head as one complete assembly. After the assembly is removed from the cylinder head, the different components can be separated on the workbench.*

Removal

Refer to illustration 11.6

1   Disconnect the cable from the negative battery terminal (see Chapter 5).

2   Position the number one piston at Top Dead Center (see Section 3).

3   Remove the valve cover (see Section 4).

4   Remove the timing chain (see Section 8).

11.14 Measure the camshaft lobe height with a micrometer

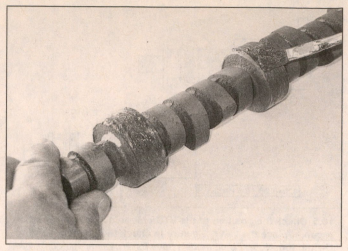

11.18 Be sure to apply camshaft installation lubricant to the lobes and bearing journals before installing the camshaft

5   Loosen all the rocker arm adjusting screws.

6   Remove the camshaft holder bolts. Follow the correct sequence (see illustration).

7   Remove the upper timing chain guide.

8   Lift the camshaft holders and camshafts off the rocker arm assembly. Remove the rocker arm assembly. Install each bolt into the original camshaft holder for correct reassembly. **Caution:** *If the intake camshaft sprocket (VTC actuator) is removed from the camshaft and reused later, be sure to store the intake sprocket properly. First, seal the advance holes and the retard hole on the number 1 camshaft journal with tape. Next, punch a hole in the tape over one of the advance holes and blow compressed air through the opening to release the lock. Double-check that the sprocket moves freely in the advance and retard positions.*

Inspection

Rocker arm assembly

9   If you wish to disassemble and inspect the rocker arm assembly (a good idea as long as you have them off), remove the retaining bolts and slip the rocker arms, springs, collars and bearing caps off the shafts. Mark the relationship of the shafts to the bearing caps and keep the components in order. They must be reassembled in the same positions they were removed from. **Caution:** *It is a good idea to bundle the intake rocker arms together with rubber bands.*

10   Thoroughly clean the components and inspect them for wear and damage. Check the rocker arm faces that contact the camshaft and the rocker arm tips. Check the surfaces of the shafts that the rocker arms ride on, as well as the bearing surfaces inside the rocker arms, for scoring and excessive wear. Replace any parts that are damaged or excessively worn. Also, make sure the oil holes in the shafts are not plugged.

Camshaft endplay and runout

11   To check camshaft endplay:

a) *Install the rocker shaft holders, the camshafts and the camshaft holders and follow the correct torque sequence (see Step 20).*

b) *Mount a dial indicator on the cylinder head with the pointer resting on the camshaft nose.*

c) *Using a large screwdriver as a lever at the opposite end, move the camshaft forward-and-backward and note the dial indicator reading.*

d) *Compare the reading with the endplay listed in this Chapter's Specifications.*

e) *If the indicated reading is excessive, either the camshaft or the cylinder head is worn. Replace parts as necessary.*

12   To check camshaft runout:

a) *With the camshafts on the workbench, support the camshaft with a pair of V-blocks and set up a dial indicator with the plunger resting against the center bearing journal on the camshaft.*

b) *Rotate the camshaft and note the indicated runout.*

c) *Compare the results to the camshaft runout listed in this Chapter's Specifications.*

d) *If the indicated runout exceeds the specified runout limit, replace the camshaft.*

Camshaft lobe height

Refer to illustration 11.14

13   Check the camshaft bearing journals and caps for scoring and signs of wear. If they are worn, replace the camshaft holders and rocker arm assembly with a new or rebuilt assembly.

14   Check the cam lobes for wear:

a) *Check the toe and ramp areas of each cam lobe for score marks and uneven wear. Also check for flaking and pitting.*

b) *If there's wear on the toe or the ramp, replace the camshaft, but first try to find the cause of the wear. Look for abrasive substances in the oil and inspect the oil pump and oil passages for blockage. Lobe wear is usually caused by inadequate lubrication or dirty oil.*

c) *Using a micrometer, measure the cam lobe height (see illustration). If lobe wear is indicated, replace the camshaft.*

15   If any of the conditions described above are noted, the cylinder head is probably getting insufficient lubrication or dirty oil. Make sure you track down the cause of this problem (low oil level, low oil pump capacity, clogged oil passage, etc.) before installing a new cylinder head, camshaft or rocker arm assembly.

Installation

Refer to illustrations 11.18 and 11.20

16   Lubricate all components with engine assembly lubricant or engine oil and reassemble rocker arms onto the shafts.

17   When installing the rocker arms, shafts and springs, note the markings and the difference between the left and right side components.

18   Coat the camshaft lobes and journals with camshaft installation lubricant (see illustration).

19   Make sure the camshaft sprocket timing marks face up and set the camshafts in the rocker shaft holders.

20   Tighten the camshaft holder bolts a little at a time, in the proper sequence (see illustration), to the torque listed in this Chapter's Specifications.

21   The remainder of installation is the reverse of removal. Adjust the valve clearances (see Chapter 1).

22   Run the engine and check for oil leaks and proper operation.

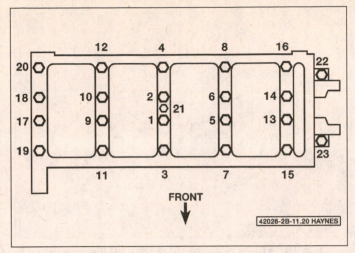

11.20 Camshaft holder bolt tightening sequence

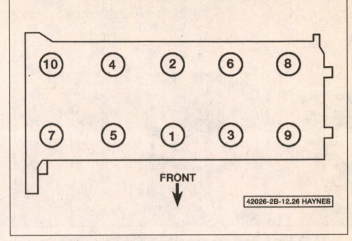

12.16 Cylinder head bolt tightening sequence

12 Cylinder head - removal and installation

Warning: *Wait until the engine is completely cool before beginning this procedure.*

Removal

1   Relieve the fuel system pressure (see Chapter 4). Disconnect the cable from the negative battery terminal (see Chapter 5).

2   Drain the cooling system (see Chapter 1).

3   Remove the drivebelt (see Chapter 1) and the drivebelt tensioner.

4   Remove the exhaust manifold (see Section 6).

5   Remove the intake manifold (see Section 5).

6   Remove the timing chain (see Section 8), camshafts and rocker arm assembly (see Section 11).

7   Label and disconnect the electrical connectors from the cylinder head that will interfere with removal. Use tape and mark each connector to insure correct reassembly. Also detach any coolant hoses that would interfere with removal.

8   Remove the cylinder head bolts, following the reverse of the tightening sequence **(see illustration 12.16)**. Loosen the bolts in sequence 1/4-turn at a time. Discard the bolts; new ones should be used upon installation.

9   Lift the cylinder head off the engine. If resistance is felt, place a wood block against the end and strike the wood block with a hammer. If the cylinder head is still stuck, carefully pry on a casting protrusion to break the gasket seal. **Caution:** *Do not pry between the cylinder head and block mating surfaces!*

10   Store the cylinder head on wood blocks to prevent damage to the gasket sealing surfaces.

11   Remove the old cylinder head gasket.

Installation

Refer to illustration 12.16

12   The mating surfaces of the cylinder head and block must be perfectly clean when the head is installed. Use a gasket scraper to remove all traces of carbon and old gasket material, then clean the mating surfaces with brake system cleaner. If there's oil on the mating surfaces when the cylinder head is installed, the gasket may not seal correctly and leaks may develop. When working on the engine block, cover the open areas of the engine with shop rags to keep debris out during repair and reassembly. Use a vacuum cleaner to remove any debris that falls into the cylinders.

13   Check the engine block and cylinder head mating surfaces for nicks, deep scratches and other damage. Have an automotive machine shop check the cylinder head for warpage.

14   Use a tap of the correct size to chase the threads in the cylinder head bolt holes. Dirt, corrosion, sealant and damaged threads will affect torque readings.

15   Make sure the new gasket is located on the dowels in the block.

16   Carefully position the cylinder head on the engine block without disturbing the gasket. Install new cylinder head bolts, and following the recommended sequence **(see illustration)**, tighten the bolts to the torque listed in this Chapter's Specifications. **Note:** *The method used for the head bolt tightening procedure is referred to as "torque-angle" or "torque-to-yield" method. A special torque angle gauge (available at most auto parts stores) is available to attach to a breaker bar and socket for better accuracy during the tightening procedure.*

17   Install the rocker arm assembly and camshafts (see Section 11).

18   Install the timing chain (see Section 8).

19   Install the exhaust manifold (see Section 6).

20   Install the intake manifold (see Section 5).

21   The remaining installation steps are the reverse of removal.

22   Reconnect the battery (see Chapter 5).

23   Change the engine oil and filter (see Chapter 1), refill the cooling system, then start the engine and check carefully for oil and coolant leaks.

13 Oil pan - removal and installation

Removal

1   Remove the subframe (see Chapter 10).

2   Drain the engine oil (see Chapter 1).

3   On manual transaxles, remove the bellhousing brace from the transaxle and the engine block (see Chapter 7A).

4   Remove the oil pan bolts, loosening them a little at a time in a criss-cross pattern.

5   Carefully remove the oil pan from the lower crankcase. **Caution:** *If the oil pan is difficult to separate from the lower crankcase, use a rubber mallet or a block of wood and a hammer to jar it loose. If that doesn't work, an oil pan gasket cutter may be available from your local auto parts store.*

Installation

6   Using a gasket scraper, thoroughly clean all old gasket material from the lower crankcase and oil pan. Remove residue and oil film with a solvent such as acetone or lacquer thinner.

7   Apply a 2 mm bead of RTV sealant to the perimeter of the oil pan, inboard of the bolt holes.

8   Install the oil pan and bolts. Tighten the bolts a little at a time, in a criss-cross pattern beginning with the center bolts and working outward, to the torque listed in this Chapter's Specifications.

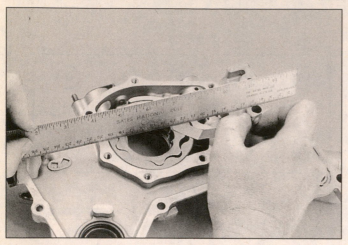

14.6a Use a feeler gauge and straight-edge to check the clearance between the rotors and the housing (typical)

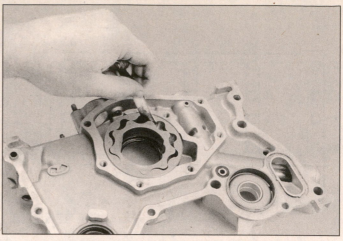

14.6b Use a feeler gauge to check the tooth-tip clearance between the inner and outer rotors (typical)

9   The remaining installation is the reverse of removal.
10   Change the oil filter and fill the crankcase with the specified engine oil (see Chapter 1).

14 Oil pump - removal, inspection and installation

Removal

1   Set the engine to TDC number 1 (see Section 3).
2   Remove the oil pan (see Section 13).
3   Remove the balance shaft assembly (see Section 15).
4   Remove the oil pump housing mounting bolts. Loosen the oil pump mounting bolts one turn. Then, gradually and evenly, loosen each bolt in several steps.
5   When all bolts are loose, remove the bolts and oil pump.

Inspection

Refer to illustrations 14.6a, 14.6b and 14.6c

6   Check the oil pump rotor-to-housing clearance, tooth tip clearance and rotor-to-body clearance **(see illustrations)**. Compare your measurements to the figures listed in this Chapter's Specifications. Replace the pump if any of the measurements exceed the specified limits.
7   Remove the pressure relief valve plug and extract the spring and pressure relief valve plunger from the pump housing. Check the spring for distortion and the relief valve plunger for scoring. Replace parts as necessary.
8   Install the pump rotors. Pack the spaces between the rotors with petroleum jelly (this will prime the pump).
9   Apply clean engine oil to the pump housing bolts, install the housing and tighten the bolts to the torque listed in this Chapter's Specifications. Install the oil pressure relief valve and spring assembly. Use a new sealing

washer on the plug and tighten the plug to the torque listed in this Chapter's Specifications.

Installation

10   Install the oil pump housing bolts and tighten by hand until snug. Tighten the bolts gradually and evenly to the torque listed in this Chapter's Specifications.
11   Make sure the engine is still set to TDC number 1 (see Section 3).
12   Install the balance shaft assembly (see Section 15).
13   Refer to Chapter 1 and fill the engine with fresh engine oil. Install a new oil filter.
14   Reconnect the battery (see Chapter 5).
15   Run the engine and make sure oil pressure comes up to normal quickly. If it doesn't, stop the engine and find out the cause. Severe engine damage can result from running an engine with insufficient oil pressure!

15 Balance shaft assembly and balance shafts - removal, inspection and installation

Removal

1   Remove the oil pan (see Section 13).
2   Remove and discard the oil pump chain tensioner.
3   Remove the oil pump sprocket bolt. To prevent the sprocket from turning, insert a 6 mm guide pin into the maintenance hole directly behind the oil pump housing, below the balance shaft assembly.
4   Remove the oil pump sprocket.
5   Remove the balance shaft assembly mounting bolts and separate the assembly from the lower engine block.

Inspection

6   Remove the balance shaft assembly mounting bolts and separate the upper and lower cases.

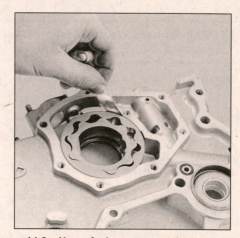

14.6c Use a feeler gauge to check the outer rotor-to-pump body clearance (typical)

7   Clean all parts with clean solvent. Dry with compressed air.
8   Inspect the balance shaft chain for excessive wear or damage.
9   Inspect the balance shaft chain sprocket for chipped or broken teeth, excessive wear, or damage.
10   Inspect the balance shaft gears for chipping, scoring or missing teeth. Replace the assembly if necessary.

Installation

Refer to illustrations 15.11 and 15.14

11   Working on the two balance shafts, align the center punch mark on the rear (drive) balance shaft with the two marks on the front balance shaft (driven) **(see illustration)**.
12   Apply engine oil to the threads and install the balance shaft case mounting bolts. Torque the bolts to the Specifications listed in this Chapter.
13   Install the oil pump housing (see Section 14).

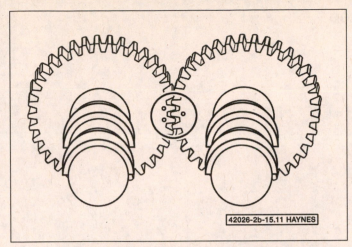

15.11 Align the center punch mark on the rear (drive) balance shaft with the two marks on the front balance shaft (driven)

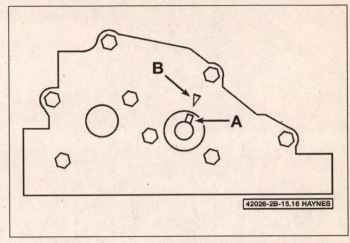

15.14 Align the dowel pin on the rear balance shaft (A) with the mark on the oil pump housing (B)

14   Align the dowel pin on the rear balance shaft with the mark on the oil pump housing **(see illustration)**.

15   Install the balance shaft assembly onto the lower engine block and install the bolts finger tight

16   Insert a 6 mm guide pin into the maintenance hole directly behind the oil pump housing (see Step 3).

17   Engage the oil pump sprocket with the chain, then with the balance shaft. Install the oil pump sprocket bolt. Tighten the bolt to the torque listed in this Chapter's Specifications.

18   Remove the guide pin.

19   Tighten the balancer assembly mounting bolts to the torque listed in this Chapter's Specifications.

20   Working with a new balance shaft chain tensioner, make sure the tensioner holder clip is installed onto the tensioner and install the tensioner onto the lower engine block.

21   Tighten the balance shaft chain tensioner bolts to the torque listed in this Chapter's Specifications.

22   Remove the holder clip from the tensioner to apply tension to the chain.

23   Install the oil pan (see Section 13).

24   Reconnect the battery (see Chapter 5).

25   Run the engine and make sure oil pressure comes up to normal quickly. If it doesn't, stop the engine and find out the cause. Severe engine damage can result from running an engine with insufficient oil pressure!

16   Flywheel/driveplate - removal and installation

This procedure is essentially the same as for the SOHC engine. Refer to Part A and follow the procedure outlined there. However,

use the bolt torque listed in this Chapter's Specifications.

17   Rear main oil seal - replacement

This procedure is essentially the same as for the SOHC engine. Refer to Part A and follow the procedure outlined there.

18   Engine mounts - check and replacement

This procedure is essentially the same as for the SOHC engine. Refer to Part A and follow the procedure outlined there.

Notes

Chapter 2 Part C
General engine overhaul procedures

Contents

	Section
CHECK ENGINE light on	See Chapter 6
Crankshaft - removal and installation	10
Cylinder compression check	3
Engine - removal and installation	7
Engine overhaul - disassembly sequence	8
Engine overhaul - reassembly sequence	11
Engine rebuilding alternatives	5

	Section
Engine removal - methods and precautions	6
General information - engine overhaul	1
Initial start-up and break-in after overhaul	12
Oil pressure check	2
Pistons and connecting rods - removal and installation	9
Vacuum gauge diagnostic checks	4

Specifications

General

Displacement
  SOHC models
    2005 and earlier models .... 101.7 cubic inches (1.7 liters)
    2006 and later models .... 110 cubic inches (1.8 liters)
  DOHC models
    CR-V .... 144 cubic inches (2.4 liters)
    Hatchback and 2006 and later Civics .... 122 cubic inches (2.0 liters)
Bore and stroke
  SOHC models
    2005 and earlier models .... 2.95 x 3.72 inches (75.0 x 94.4 mm)
    2006 and later models .... 3.19 x 3.44 inches (81.0 x 87.3 mm)
  DOHC models
    CR-V .... 3.43 x 3.90 inches (87.0 x 99.0 mm)
    Hatchback and 2006 and later Civics .... 3.39 x 3.39 inches (86.0 x 86.0 mm)
Cylinder compression
  SOHC models
    Minimum .... 128 psi (930 kPa)
    Maximum variation between cylinders .... 28 psi (200 kPa)
  DOHC models
    Minimum .... 135 psi (930 kPa)
    Maximum variation between cylinders .... 28 psi (200 kPa)
Oil pressure (engine at operating temperature)
  Idle speed .... 10 psi (70 kPa)
  3,000 rpm .... 44 psi (300 kPa)

Torque specifications

	Ft-lbs (unless otherwise indicated)	**Nm**

Note: *One foot-pound (ft-lb) of torque is equivalent to 12 inch-pounds (in-lbs) of torque. Torque values below approximately 15 foot-pounds are expressed in inch-pounds, because most foot-pound torque wrenches are not accurate at these smaller values.*

	Ft-lbs (unless otherwise indicated)	Nm
Subframe mounting bolts...	See Chapter 10	
Connecting rod bearing cap bolts*		
SOHC models		
2005 and earlier 1.7L engines	24	32
2006 and later 1.8L engines		
Step 1...	168 in-lbs	19
Step 2...	Tighten an additional 90 degrees	
DOHC models		
2005 and earlier 2.0L engines		
Step 1...	168 in-lbs	19
Step 2...	Tighten an additional 90 degrees	
2006 and later 2.0L engines		
Step 1...	22	30
Step 2...	Tighten an additional 90 degrees	
2.4L engines		
Step 1...	168 in-lbs	19
Step 2...	Tighten an additional 90 degrees	
Crankshaft Position Sensor (CKP) pulse plate bolts	84 in-lbs	9.5
Main bearing bridge bolts (SOHC engine) **(see illustration 10.19a)**		
1.7L engines		
Step 1	18	24
Step 2	38	52
1.8L engines		
Main bridge bolts (inner bolts) **(see illustration 10.19b)**		
Step 1...	18	24
Step 2...	Tighten an additional 57 degrees	
Perimeter bolts (outer bolts) **(see illustration 10.19c)**.................	17	23
Main bearing bridge bolts (DOHC engine)		
Main bridge bolts (inner bolts) **(see illustration 10.19b)**		
Step 1	22	30
Step 2	Tighten an additional 56 degrees	
Perimeter bolts (outer bolts) **(see illustration 10.19d)**....................	16	22

* Bolt(s) must be replaced.

1   General information - engine overhaul

Refer to illustrations 1.1, 1.2, 1.3, 1.4, 1.5 and 1.6

Included in this portion of Chapter 2 are general information and diagnostic testing procedures for determining the overall mechanical condition of your engine.

The information ranges from advice concerning preparation for an overhaul and the purchase of replacement parts and/or components to detailed, step-by-step procedures covering removal and installation.

The following Sections have been written to help you determine whether your engine needs to be overhauled and how to remove and install it once you've determined it needs to be rebuilt. For information concerning in-vehicle engine repair, see Chapter 2A or 2B.

The Specifications included in this Part are general in nature and include only those necessary for testing the oil pressure and checking the engine compression. Refer to Chapter 2A or 2B for additional engine Specifications.

It's not always easy to determine when, or if, an engine should be completely overhauled, because a number of factors must be considered.

High mileage is not necessarily an indication that an overhaul is needed, while low mileage doesn't preclude the need for an overhaul. Frequency of servicing is probably the most important consideration. An engine that's had regular and frequent oil and filter changes, as well as other required maintenance, will most likely give many thousands of miles of reliable service. Conversely, a neglected engine may require an overhaul very early in its service life.

Excessive oil consumption is an indication that piston rings, valve seals and/or valve guides are in need of attention. Make sure that oil leaks aren't responsible before decid-

1.1 An engine block being bored. An engine rebuilder will use special machinery to recondition the cylinder bores

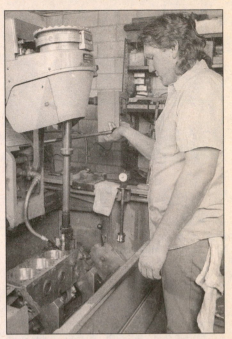

1.2 If the cylinders are bored, the machine shop will normally hone the engine on a machine like this

ing that the rings and/or guides are bad. Perform a cylinder compression check to determine the extent of the work required (see Section 3). Also check the vacuum readings under various conditions (see Section 4).

Check the oil pressure with a gauge installed in place of the oil pressure sending unit and compare it to this Chapter's Specifications (see Section 2). If it's extremely low, the bearings and/or oil pump are probably worn out.

Loss of power, rough running, knocking or metallic engine noises, excessive valve train noise and high fuel consumption rates may also point to the need for an overhaul, especially if they're all present at the same time. If a complete tune-up doesn't remedy

the situation, major mechanical work is the only solution.

An engine overhaul involves restoring the internal parts to the specifications of a new engine. During an overhaul, the piston rings are replaced and the cylinder walls are reconditioned (rebored and/or honed) **(see illustrations 1.1 and 1.2)**. If a rebore is done by an automotive machine shop, new oversize pistons will also be installed. The main bearings, connecting rod bearings and camshaft bearings are generally replaced with new ones and, if necessary, the crankshaft may be reground to restore the journals **(see illustration 1.3)**. Generally, the valves are serviced as well, since they're usually in less-than-perfect condition at this point. While the engine is being overhauled, other components, such as the starter and alternator, can be rebuilt as well. The end result should be similar to a new engine that will give many trouble free miles. **Note:** *Critical cooling system components such as the hoses, drivebelts, thermostat and water pump should be replaced with new parts when an engine is overhauled. The radiator should be checked carefully to ensure that it isn't clogged or leaking (see Chapter 3). If you purchase a rebuilt engine or short block, some rebuilders will not warranty their engines unless the radiator has been professionally flushed. Also, we don't recommend overhauling the oil pump - always install a new one when an engine is rebuilt.*

Overhauling the internal components on today's engines is a difficult and time-consuming task which requires a significant amount of specialty tools and is best left to a professional engine rebuilder **(see illustrations 1.4,**

1.3 A crankshaft having a main bearing journal ground

1.4 A machinist checks for a bent connecting rod, using specialized equipment

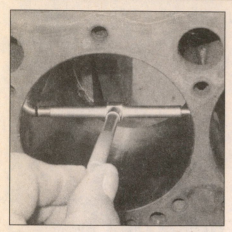

1.5 A bore gauge being used to check the main bearing bore

1.6 Uneven piston wear like this indicates a bent connecting rod

2.2 Location of the oil pressure sending unit on 2005 and earlier SOHC models

1.5 and 1.6). A competent engine rebuilder will handle the inspection of your old parts and offer advice concerning the reconditioning or replacement of the original engine; never purchase parts or have machine work done on other components until the block has been thoroughly inspected by a professional machine shop. As a general rule, time is the primary cost of an overhaul, especially since the vehicle may be tied up for a minimum of two weeks or more. Be aware that some engine builders only have the capability to rebuild the engine you bring them while other rebuilders have a large inventory of rebuilt exchange engines in stock. Also be aware that many machine shops could take as much as two weeks time to completely rebuild your engine depending on shop workload. Sometimes it makes more sense to simply exchange your engine for another engine that's already rebuilt to save time.

2   Oil pressure check

Refer to illustrations 2.2 and 2.3

1   Low engine oil pressure can be a sign of an engine in need of rebuilding. A low oil pressure indicator (often called an "idiot light") is not a test of the oiling system. Such indicators only come on when the oil pressure is dangerously low. Even a factory oil pressure gauge in the instrument panel is only a relative indication, although much better for driver information than a warning light. A better test is with a mechanical (not electrical) oil pressure gauge.
2   Locate the oil pressure sending unit on the engine block:

  a) *On 2005 and earlier Single Overhead Camshaft (SOHC) engines, the oil pressure sending unit is located above the oil filter on the rear of the engine block* **(see illustration)**. *On 2006 and later Single Overhead Camshaft (SOHC) engines, the oil pressure sending unit is located to the rear of the engine block on the side facing the radiator.*

  b) *On all 2.0L and 2006 and earlier 2.4L Double Overhead Camshaft (DOHC) engines, the oil pressure sending unit is located above the oil filter on the front of the engine block. On 2007 and later 2.4L engines, the oil pressure sending unit is located to the front of the engine block, just below the cylinder head on the side facing the firewall.*

3   Unscrew and remove the oil pressure sending unit and screw in the hose for your oil pressure gauge **(see illustration)**. If necessary, install an adapter fitting. Use Teflon tape or thread sealant on the threads of the adapter and/or the fitting on the end of your gauge's hose.
4   Connect an accurate tachometer to the engine, according to the tachometer manufacturer's instructions.
5   Check the oil pressure with the engine running (normal operating temperature) at the specified engine speed, and compare it to this Chapter's Specifications. If it's extremely low, the bearings and/or oil pump are probably worn out.

3   Cylinder compression check

Refer to illustration 3.6

1   A compression check will tell you what mechanical condition the upper end of your engine (pistons, rings, valves, head gaskets) is in. Specifically, it can tell you if the compression is down due to leakage caused by worn piston rings, defective valves and seats or a blown head gasket. **Note:** *The engine must be at normal operating temperature and the battery must be fully charged for this check.*
2   Begin by cleaning the area around the ignition coils and spark plugs before you remove them (compressed air should be used, if available). The idea is to prevent dirt from getting into the cylinders as the compression check is being done.
3   Remove the ignition coil cover (if equipped), remove all the individual coils (see Chapter 5) and remove all of the spark plugs

from the engine (see Chapter 1).
4   Block the throttle wide open.
5   Disable the fuel system by removing the PGM-FI main relay number 2 (see Chapter 4, Section 3).
6   Install a compression gauge in the spark plug hole **(see illustration)**.
7   Crank the engine over at least seven compression strokes and watch the gauge. The compression should build up quickly in a healthy engine. Low compression on the first stroke, followed by gradually increasing pressure on successive strokes, indicates worn piston rings. A low compression reading on the first stroke, which doesn't build up during successive strokes, indicates leaking valves or a blown head gasket (a cracked head could also be the cause). Deposits on the undersides of the valve heads can also cause low compression. Record the highest gauge reading obtained.
8   Repeat the procedure for the remaining cylinders and compare the results to this Chapter's Specifications.
9   Add some engine oil (about three squirts from a plunger-type oil can) to each cylinder, through the spark plug hole, and repeat the test.

2.3 Remove the oil pressure sending unit and install an oil pressure gauge

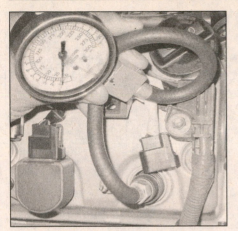

3.6 Use a compression gauge with a threaded fitting for the spark plug hole, not the type that requires hand pressure to maintain the seal

4.4 A simple vacuum gauge can be handy in diagnosing engine condition and performance

the test or false readings will result.

5   Before you begin the test, allow the engine to warm up completely. Block the wheels and set the parking brake. With the transaxle in Park, start the engine and allow it to run at normal idle speed. **Warning:** *Keep your hands and the vacuum gauge clear of the fans.*

6   Read the vacuum gauge; an average, healthy engine should normally produce about 17 to 22 in-Hg with a fairly steady needle **(see illustration)**. Refer to the following vacuum gauge readings and what they indicate about the engine's condition:

7   A low steady reading usually indicates a leaking gasket between the intake manifold and cylinder head(s) or throttle body, a leaky vacuum hose, late ignition timing or incorrect camshaft timing. Check ignition timing with a timing light and eliminate all other possible causes, utilizing the tests provided in this Chapter before you remove the timing chain cover to check the timing marks.

8   If the reading is three to eight inches below normal and it fluctuates at that low reading, suspect an intake manifold gasket leak at an intake port or a faulty fuel injector.

9   If the needle has regular drops of about two-to-four inches at a steady rate, the valves are probably leaking. Perform a compression check or leak-down test to confirm this.

10   An irregular drop or down-flick of the needle can be caused by a sticking valve or an ignition misfire. Perform a compression check or leak-down test and read the spark plugs.

10   If the compression increases after the oil is added, the piston rings are definitely worn. If the compression doesn't increase significantly, the leakage is occurring at the valves or head gasket. Leakage past the valves may be caused by burned valve seats and/or faces or warped, cracked or bent valves.

11   If two adjacent cylinders have equally low compression, there's a strong possibility that the head gasket between them is blown. The appearance of coolant in the combustion chambers or the crankcase would verify this condition.

12   If one cylinder is slightly lower than the others, and the engine has a slightly rough idle, a worn lobe on the camshaft could be the cause.

13   If the compression is unusually high, the combustion chambers are probably coated with carbon deposits. If that's the case, the cylinder head(s) should be removed and decarbonized.

14   If compression is way down or varies greatly between cylinders, it would be a good idea to have a leak-down test performed by an automotive repair shop. This test will pinpoint exactly where the leakage is occurring and how severe it is.

---

4   Vacuum gauge diagnostic checks

Refer to illustrations 4.4 and 4.6

1   A vacuum gauge provides inexpensive but valuable information about what is going on in the engine. You can check for worn rings or cylinder walls, leaking head or intake manifold gaskets, restricted exhaust, stuck or burned valves, weak valve springs, improper ignition or valve timing and ignition problems.

2   Unfortunately, vacuum gauge readings are easy to misinterpret, so they should be used in conjunction with other tests to confirm the diagnosis.

3   Both the absolute readings and the rate of needle movement are important for accurate interpretation. Most gauges measure

vacuum in inches of mercury (in-Hg). The following references to vacuum assume the diagnosis is being performed at sea level. As elevation increases (or atmospheric pressure decreases), the reading will decrease. For every 1,000 foot increase in elevation above approximately 2,000 feet, the gauge readings will decrease about one inch of mercury.

4   Connect the vacuum gauge directly to the intake manifold vacuum, not to ported (throttle body) vacuum **(see illustration)**. Be sure no hoses are left disconnected during

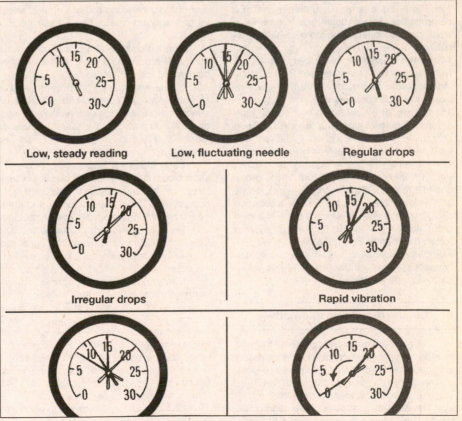

4.6 Typical vacuum gauge readings

6.1 After tightly wrapping water-vulnerable components, use a spray cleaner on everything, with particular concentration on the greasiest areas, usually around the valve cover and lower edges of the block. If one section dries out, apply more cleaner

6.2 Depending on how dirty the engine is, let the cleaner soak in according to the directions and hose off the grime and cleaner. Get the rinse water down into every area you can get at; then dry important components with a hair dryer or paper towels

11   A rapid vibration of about four in-Hg vibration at idle combined with exhaust smoke indicates worn valve guides. Perform a leak-down test to confirm this. If the rapid vibration occurs with an increase in engine speed, check for a leaking intake manifold gasket or head gasket, weak valve springs, burned valves or ignition misfire.

12   A slight fluctuation, say one inch up and down, may mean ignition problems. Check all the usual tune-up items and, if necessary, run the engine on an ignition analyzer.

13   If there is a large fluctuation, perform a compression or leak-down test to look for a weak or dead cylinder or a blown head gasket.

14   If the needle moves slowly through a wide range, check for a clogged PCV system, incorrect idle fuel mixture, throttle body or intake manifold gasket leaks.

15   Check for a slow return after revving the engine by quickly snapping the throttle open until the engine reaches about 2,500 rpm and let it shut. Normally the reading should drop to near zero, rise above normal idle reading (about 5 in-Hg over) and return to the previous idle reading. If the vacuum returns slowly and doesn't peak when the throttle is snapped shut, the rings may be worn. If there is a long delay, look for a restricted exhaust system (often the muffler or catalytic converter). An easy way to check this is to temporarily disconnect the exhaust ahead of the suspected part and redo the test.

5   Engine rebuilding alternatives

The do-it-yourselfer is faced with a number of options when purchasing a rebuilt engine. The major considerations are cost, warranty, parts availability and the time required for the rebuilder to complete the project. The decision to replace the engine block, piston/connecting rod assemblies and crankshaft depends on the final inspection results

of your engine. Only then can you make a cost effective decision whether to have your engine overhauled or simply purchase an exchange engine for your vehicle.

Some of the rebuilding alternatives include:

Individual parts - If the inspection procedures reveal that the engine block and most engine components are in reusable condition, purchasing individual parts and having a rebuilder rebuild your engine may be the most economical alternative. The block, crankshaft and piston/connecting rod assemblies should all be inspected carefully by a machine shop first.

Short block - A short block consists of an engine block with a crankshaft and piston/connecting rod assemblies already installed. All new bearings are incorporated and all clearances will be correct. The existing camshafts, valve train components, cylinder head and external parts can be bolted to the short block with little or no machine shop work necessary.

Long block - A long block consists of a short block plus an oil pump, oil pan, cylinder head, valve cover, camshaft and valve train components, timing sprockets and chain or gears and timing cover. All components are installed with new bearings, seals and gaskets incorporated throughout. The installation of manifolds and external parts is all that's necessary.

Low mileage used engines - Some companies now offer low mileage used engines which is a very cost effective way to get your vehicle up and running again. These engines often come from vehicles which have been in totaled in accidents or come from other countries which have a higher vehicle turn over rate. A low mileage used engine also usually has a similar warranty like the newly remanufactured engines.

Give careful thought to which alternative is best for you and discuss the situation with local automotive machine shops, auto parts

dealers and experienced rebuilders before ordering or purchasing replacement parts.

6   Engine removal - methods and precautions

Refer to illustrations 6.1, 6.2, 6.3 and 6.4

If you've decided that an engine must be removed for overhaul or major repair work, several preliminary steps should be taken. Read all removal and installation procedures carefully prior to committing to this job.

Locating a suitable place to work is extremely important. Adequate work space, along with storage space for the vehicle, will be needed. If a shop or garage isn't available, at the very least a flat, level, clean work surface made of concrete or asphalt is required.

Cleaning the engine compartment and engine before beginning the removal procedure will help keep tools clean and organized **(see illustrations 6.1 and 6.2)**.

An engine hoist will also be necessary. Make sure the hoist is rated in excess of the combined weight of the engine and transaxle. Safety is of primary importance, considering the potential hazards involved in removing the engine from the vehicle.

A vehicle hoist will be necessary for engine removal, since on these models the subframe must be removed and the engine/transaxle assembly must be lowered from the engine compartment, then the vehicle is raised and the powertrain unit is removed from under the vehicle. If the necessary equipment is not available, the engine will have to be removed by a qualified automotive repair facility.

If you're a novice at engine removal, get at least one helper. One person cannot easily do all the things you need to do to remove a big heavy engine and transaxle assembly from the engine compartment. Also helpful is to seek advice and assistance from someone who's experienced in engine removal.

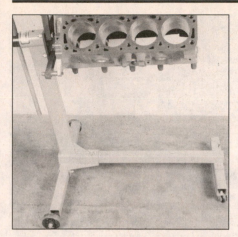

6.3 Get an engine stand sturdy enough to firmly support the engine while you're working on it. Stay away from three-wheeled models; they have a tendency to tip over more easily, so get a four-wheeled unit

Plan the operation ahead of time. Arrange for or obtain all of the tools and equipment you'll need prior to beginning the job **(see illustrations 6.3 and 6.4)**. Some of the equipment necessary to perform engine removal and installation safely and with relative ease are (in addition to a vehicle hoist and an engine hoist) a heavy duty floor jack (preferably fitted with a transaxle jack head adapter), complete sets of wrenches and sockets as described in the front of this manual, wooden blocks, plenty of rags and cleaning solvent for mopping up spilled oil, coolant and gasoline.

Plan for the vehicle to be out of use for quite a while. A machine shop can do the work that is beyond the scope of the home mechanic. Machine shops often have a busy schedule, so before removing the engine, consult the shop for an estimate of how long it will take to rebuild or repair the components that may need work.

7 Engine - removal and installation

Refer to illustrations 7.10, 7.35 and 7.40

Warning: *Gasoline is extremely flammable, so take extra precautions when you work on any part of the fuel system. Don't smoke or allow open flames or bare light bulbs near the work area, and don't work in a garage where a gas-type appliance (such as a water heater or clothes dryer) is present. Since gasoline is carcinogenic, wear fuel-resistant gloves when there's a possibility of being exposed to fuel, and, if you spill any fuel on your skin, rinse it off immediately with soap and water. Mop up any spills immediately and do not store fuel-soaked rags where they could ignite. The fuel system is under constant pressure, so, if any fuel lines are to be disconnected, the fuel pressure in the system must be relieved first (see Chapter 4 for more information). When you perform any kind of work on the fuel sys-*

6.4 A clutch alignment tool is necessary if you plan to install a rebuilt engine mated to a manual transaxle

tem, wear safety glasses and have a Class B type fire extinguisher on hand.

Warning: *The engine must be completely cool before beginning this procedure.*

Note: *Engine removal on these models is a difficult job, especially for the do-it-yourself mechanic working at home. Because of the vehicle's design, the manufacturer states that the engine and transaxle have to be removed as a unit from the bottom of the vehicle, not the top. With a floor jack and jackstands, the vehicle can't be raised high enough or supported safely enough for the engine/transaxle assembly to slide out from underneath. The manufacturer recommends that removal of the engine transaxle assembly only be performed with the use of a frame-contact type vehicle hoist.*

Note: *Read through the entire Section before beginning this procedure. The engine and transaxle are removed as a unit from below, then separated outside the vehicle.*

Note: *Keep in mind that during this procedure you'll have to adjust the height of the vehicle with the vehicle hoist to perform certain operations.*

Removal

1   Park the vehicle on a frame-contact type vehicle hoist, then engage the arms of the hoist with the jacking points of the vehicle. Raise the hoist arms until they contact the vehicle, but not so much that the wheels come off the ground.
2   Relieve the fuel system pressure (see Chapter 4).
3   Disconnect the cable from the negative battery terminal (see Chapter 5).
4   Disconnect the fuel lines from the fuel rail (see Chapter 4).
5   Remove the engine splash shield (see Chapter 2A) and fender splash shields and the hood (see Chapter 11). Cover the fenders and cowl using special pads. An old bedspread or blanket will also work.
6   Remove the accessory drivebelt(s) (see Chapter 1).
7   Remove the intake resonator and the air filter housing (see Chapter 4).
8   Disconnect the accelerator cable, the cruise control cable, if equipped, and bracket from the engine and position them aside (see Chapter 4).

9   Remove the battery and the battery tray (see Chapter 5).
10   Clearly label and disconnect all vacuum lines, emissions hoses, wiring harness connectors and fuel lines. Masking tape and/or a touch up paint applicator work well for marking items **(see illustration)**. Take photos or sketch the locations of components and brackets.
11   Disconnect the electrical connectors from the PCM (see Chapter 6). Remove the retaining clip on the engine compartment firewall and remove the wiring harness.
12   Detach the positive cables and the electrical connectors from the engine compartment fuse/relay box (see Chapter 5) and the ground cable from the vehicle.
13   Detach any other electrical connectors between the engine and the vehicle.
14   Loosen the front wheel lug nuts, then raise the vehicle. Remove the front wheels.
15   Detach the heat shields, exhaust brackets and the exhaust pipes from the exhaust manifold(s) (see Chapter 4).
16   Remove the alternator (see Chapter 5).
17   Remove the power steering pump without disconnecting the power steering hoses (see Chapter 10). Position it off to the side.
18   Remove the exhaust pipe from the exhaust manifold to the catalytic converter (see Chapter 6).
19   Drain the cooling system (see Chapter 1).
20   Drain the engine oil (see Chapter 1).
21   Detach the lower radiator hose from the engine (see Chapter 3).

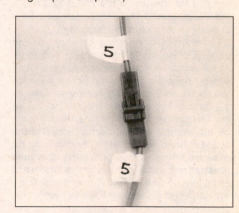

7.10 Label both ends of each wire and hose before disconnecting it

7.35 Attach the chain to the cylinder head using the engine lifting bracket on the front of the cylinder head and the other end of the chain to a transaxle mounting bolt

7.40 The engine/transaxle assembly can be lowered onto the floor using the engine hoist

22   Lower the vehicle and detach the heater hoses at the firewall (see Chapter 3).

23   Remove the upper radiator hose (see Chapter 3).

24   Remove the cooling fan(s) and shroud(s) (see Chapter 3).

25   Remove the radiator (see Chapter 3).

26   Remove the clutch release cylinder and hydraulic line (see Chapter 8).

27   Remove the starter (see Chapter 5).

28   On manual transaxle models, disconnect the shift cables and the select cable from the transaxle (see Chapter 7A). Also disconnect any wiring harness connectors from the transaxle.

29   On automatic transaxle models, disconnect the shift control cable from the transaxle (see Chapter 7B).

30   Disconnect the stabilizer bar links (see Chapter 10).

31   Disconnect the balljoints from the lower control arms (see Chapter 10).

32   Remove the driveaxles (see Chapter 8).

33   Unplug the downstream oxygen sensor electrical connectors.

34   Remove the air conditioning compressor without disconnecting the hoses (see Chapter 3). Use wire to tie the compressor to a bracket or other components mounted on the unibody structure (not the subframe).

35   Attach a lifting sling or chain to the engine, using the lifting brackets provided. At the transaxle end there should be a lifting eye built into the plate sandwiched between the transaxle and the engine (or secured to the transaxle by two of the mounting bolts). At the drivebelt end of the engine there should be a lifting eye in a bracket attached to the cylinder head. If not, lifting hooks may be available from your local auto parts store **(see illustration)**. Take up the slack until there is slight tension on the hoist. Remember that the transaxle end of the engine will be heavier, so position the chain on the hoist so it balances the engine and the transaxle level with the vehicle. **Note:** *Depending on the design of*

the engine hoist, it may be helpful to position the hoist from the side of the vehicle, so that when the engine/transaxle assembly is lowered, it will fit between the legs of the hoist. **Note:** *The sling or chain must be long enough to allow the engine hoist to lower the engine/transaxle assembly to the ground, without letting the hoist arm contact the vehicle.*

36   Remove the front and rear engine/transaxle mount through-bolts (see Chapter 2A or 2B).

37   Remove the engine mount and the transaxle mount (see Chapter 2A or 2B).

38   Recheck to be sure nothing is still connecting the engine or transaxle to the vehicle. Disconnect and label anything still remaining.

39   Remove the subframe mounting bolts (see Chapter 10). Separate the subframe from the chassis and the engine/transaxle assembly.

40   Lower the engine/transaxle assembly **(see illustration)**. Once the engine/transaxle assembly is on the floor, disconnect the engine lifting hoist and raise the vehicle until it clears the engine/transaxle assembly.

41   Reconnect the chain or sling to support the engine and transaxle.

42   Raise the engine/transaxle assembly, then support the engine with blocks of wood or another floor jack, while leaving the sling or chain attached. Support the transaxle with another floor jack, preferably one with a transaxle jack head adapter. At this point the transaxle can be unbolted and removed from the engine. Be very careful to ensure that the components are supported securely so they won't topple off their supports during disconnection.

43   Reconnect the lifting chain to the engine, then raise the engine and attach it to an engine stand.

Installation

44   Installation is the reverse of removal, noting the following points:

a) *Check the engine/transaxle mounts. If they're worn or damaged, replace them.*

b) *Attach the transaxle to the engine following the procedure described in Chapter 7.*

c) *When installing the subframe, tighten the subframe mounting bolts to the torque listed in Chapter 10 Specifications. Note the locations of the various size bolts.*

d) *Add coolant, oil, power steering and transaxle fluids as needed (see Chapter 1).*

e) *Reconnect the battery (see Chapter 5).*

f) *Run the engine and check for proper operation and leaks. Shut off the engine and recheck fluid levels.*

8   Engine overhaul - disassembly sequence

1   It's much easier to remove the external components if the engine is mounted on a portable engine stand. A stand can often be rented quite cheaply from an equipment rental yard. Before the engine is mounted on a stand, the flywheel/driveplate should be removed from the engine.

2   If a stand isn't available, it's possible to remove the external engine components with it blocked up on the floor. Be extra careful not to tip or drop the engine when working without a stand.

3   If you're going to obtain a rebuilt engine, all external components must come off first, to be transferred to the replacement engine. These components include:

Clutch and flywheel (models with manual transaxle)

Driveplate (models with automatic transaxle)

Ignition system components

Emissions-related components

Engine mounts and mount brackets

Engine rear cover (spacer plate between flywheel/driveplate and engine block)

Intake/exhaust manifolds

9.1 Before you try to remove the pistons, use a ridge reamer to remove the raised material (ridge) from the top of the cylinders

9.3 Checking the connecting rod endplay (side clearance) (typical)

9.4 If the connecting rods and caps are not marked, use paint to mark the caps to the rods by cylinder number (for example, this would be the No. 4 connecting rod)

Fuel injection components
Oil filter
Ignition coils and spark plugs
Thermostat and housing assembly
Water pump

Note: *When removing the external components from the engine, pay close attention to details that may be helpful or important during installation. Note the installed position of gaskets, seals, spacers, pins, brackets, washers, bolts and other small items.*

4   If you're going to obtain a short block (assembled engine block, crankshaft, pistons and connecting rods), then remove the timing chain or belt, cylinder head(s), oil pan, oil pump pick-up tube, oil pump, oil jets and water pump from your engine so that you can turn in your old short block to the rebuilder as a core. See *Engine rebuilding alternatives* for additional information regarding the different possibilities to be considered.

9   Pistons and connecting rods - removal and installation

Removal

Refer to illustrations 9.1, 9.3 and 9.4

Note: *Prior to removing the piston/connecting rod assemblies, remove the cylinder head and oil pan (see Chapter 2A).*

1   Use your fingernail to feel if a ridge has formed at the upper limit of ring travel (about 1/4-inch down from the top of each cylinder). If carbon deposits or cylinder wear have produced ridges, they must be completely removed with a special tool **(see illustration)**. Follow the manufacturer's instructions provided with the tool. Failure to remove the ridges before attempting to remove the piston/connecting rod assemblies may result in piston breakage.

2   After the cylinder ridges have been removed, turn the engine so the crankshaft is facing up.

3   Before the connecting rods are removed, check the connecting rod endplay with feeler

gauges. Slide them between the first connecting rod and the crankshaft throw until the play is removed **(see illustration)**. Repeat this procedure for each connecting rod. The endplay is equal to the thickness of the feeler gauge(s). Check with an automotive machine shop for the endplay service limit (a typical endplay limit should measure between 0.004 to 0.014 inch [0.10 to 0.35 mm]). If the play exceeds the service limit, new connecting rods will be required. If new rods (or a new crankshaft) are installed, the endplay may fall under the minimum allowable. If it does, the rods will have to be machined to restore it. If necessary, consult an automotive machine shop for advice.

4   Check the connecting rods and caps for identification marks. If they aren't plainly marked, use paint or marker to clearly identify each rod and cap (1, 2, 3, etc., depending on the cylinder they're associated with) **(see illustration)**.

5   Remove the connecting rod cap bolts from the number one connecting rod. **Note:** *New connecting rod cap bolts must be used when reassembling the engine, but save the old bolts - they'll be required for the bearing oil clearance check during reassembly.* **Note:** *It will be necessary to remove the main bearing bridge to access the connecting rod bearing caps. Refer to Section 10 and remove the main bearing bridge.*

6   Remove the number one connecting rod cap and bearing insert. Don't drop the bearing insert out of the cap.

7   Remove the bearing insert and push the connecting rod/piston assembly out through the top of the engine. Use a wooden dowel to push on the connecting rod. If resistance is felt, double-check to make sure that all of the ridge was removed from the cylinder.

8   Repeat the procedure for the remaining cylinders.

9   After removal, reassemble the connecting rod caps and bearing inserts in their respective connecting rods and install the cap bolts finger tight. Leaving the old bearing

inserts in place until reassembly will help prevent the connecting rod bearing surfaces from being accidentally nicked or gouged.

10   The pistons and connecting rods are now ready for inspection and overhaul at an automotive machine shop.

Piston ring installation

Refer to illustrations 9.13, 9.14, 9.15, 9.19a, 9.19b and 9.22

11   Before installing the new piston rings, the ring end gaps must be checked. It's assumed that the piston ring side clearance has been checked and verified correct.

12   Lay out the piston/connecting rod assemblies and the new ring sets so the ring sets will be matched with the same piston and cylinder during the end gap measurement and engine assembly.

13   Insert the top (number one) ring into the first cylinder and square it up with the cylinder walls by pushing it in with the top of the piston **(see illustration)**. The ring should be near the bottom of the cylinder, at the lower limit of ring travel.

9.13 Install the piston ring into the cylinder then push it down into position using a piston so the ring will be square in the cylinder

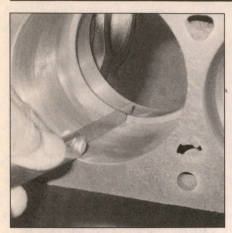

9.14 With the ring square in the cylinder, measure the ring end gap with a feeler gauge

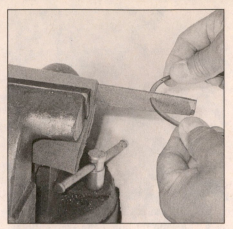

9.15 If the ring end gap is too small, clamp a file in a vise as shown and file the piston ring ends - be sure to remove all raised material

14   To measure the end gap, slip feeler gauges between the ends of the ring until a gauge equal to the gap width is found **(see illustration)**. The feeler gauge should slide between the ring ends with a slight amount of drag. A typical ring gap should fall between 0.008 and 0.020 inch (0.20 to 0.50 mm) for compression rings and up to 0.028 inch (0.70 mm) for the oil ring steel rails. If the gap is larger or smaller than specified, double-check to make sure you have the correct rings before proceeding.

15   If the gap is too small, it must be enlarged or the ring ends may come in contact with each other during engine operation, which can cause serious damage to the engine. If necessary, increase the end gaps by filing the ring ends very carefully with a fine file. Mount the file in a vise equipped with soft jaws, slip the ring over the file with the ends contacting the file face and slowly move the ring to remove material from the ends. When performing this operation, file only by pushing the

ring from the outside end of the file towards the vise **(see illustration)**.

16   Excess end gap isn't critical unless it's greater than 0.031 inch (0.80 mm). Again, double-check to make sure you have the correct ring type.

17   Repeat the procedure for each ring that will be installed in the first cylinder and for each ring in the remaining cylinders. Remember to keep rings, pistons and cylinders matched up.

18   Once the ring end gaps have been checked/corrected, the rings can be installed on the pistons.

19   The oil control ring (lowest one on the piston) is usually installed first. It's composed of three separate components. Slip the spacer/expander into the groove **(see illustration)**. If an anti-rotation tang is used, make sure it's inserted into the drilled hole in the ring groove. Next, install the upper side rail in the same manner **(see illustration)**. Don't use a piston

ring installation tool on the oil ring side rails, as they may be damaged. Instead, place one end of the side rail into the groove between the spacer/expander and the ring land, hold it firmly in place and slide a finger around the piston while pushing the rail into the groove. Finally, install the lower side rail.

20   After the three oil ring components have been installed, check to make sure that both the upper and lower side rails can be rotated smoothly inside the ring grooves.

21   The number two (middle) ring is installed next. It's usually stamped with a mark which must face up, toward the top of the piston. Do not mix up the top and middle rings, as they have different cross-sections. **Note:** *Always follow the instructions printed on the ring package or box - different manufacturers may require different approaches.*

22   Use a piston ring installation tool and make sure the identification mark is facing the top of the piston, then slip the ring into the middle groove on the piston **(see illustration)**. Don't expand the ring any more than necessary to slide it over the piston.

23   Install the number one (top) ring in the same manner. Make sure the mark is facing up. Be careful not to confuse the number one and number two rings.

24   Repeat the procedure for the remaining pistons and rings.

Installation

25   Before installing the piston/connecting rod assemblies, the cylinder walls must be perfectly clean, the top edge of each cylinder bore must be chamfered, and the oil jets and crankshaft must be in place.

26   Remove the cap from the end of the number one connecting rod (refer to the marks made during removal). Remove the original bearing inserts and wipe the bearing surfaces of the connecting rod and cap with a clean, lint-free cloth. They must be kept spotlessly clean.

9.19a Installing the spacer/expander in the oil ring groove

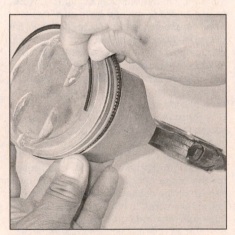

9.19b DO NOT use a piston ring installation tool when installing the oil control side rails

9.22 Use a piston ring installation tool to install the number 2 and the number 1 (top) rings - be sure the directional mark on the piston ring(s) is facing toward the top of the piston

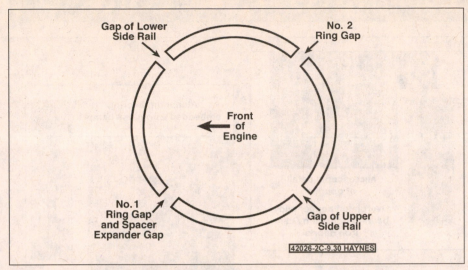

9.30 Position the piston ring end gaps as shown

9.35 Use a plastic or wooden hammer handle to push the piston into the cylinder

Connecting rod bearing oil clearance check

Refer to illustrations 9.30, 9.35, 9.37 and 9.41

27   Clean the back side of the new upper bearing insert, then lay it in place in the connecting rod.

28   Make sure the tab on the bearing fits into the recess in the rod. Don't hammer the bearing insert into place and be very careful not to nick or gouge the bearing face. Don't lubricate the bearing at this time.

29   Clean the back side of the other bearing insert and install it in the rod cap. Again, make sure the tab on the bearing fits into the recess in the cap, and don't apply any lubricant. It's critically important that the mating surfaces of the bearing and connecting rod are perfectly clean and oil free when they're assembled.

30   Position the piston ring gaps at the specified intervals around the piston as shown (see illustration).

31   Lubricate the piston and rings with clean engine oil and attach a piston ring compressor to the piston. Leave the skirt protruding about 1/4-inch to guide the piston into the cylinder. The rings must be compressed until they're flush with the piston.

32   Rotate the crankshaft until the number one connecting rod journal is at BDC (bottom dead center) and apply a liberal coat of engine oil to the cylinder walls.

33   With the arrow on top of the piston facing the front (timing belt end or timing chain) of the engine, gently insert the piston/connecting rod assembly into the number one cylinder bore and rest the bottom edge of the ring compressor on the engine block. Install the pistons with the cavity mark(s) or arrow facing toward the timing belt or timing chain end of the engine.

34   Tap the top edge of the ring compressor to make sure it's contacting the block around its entire circumference.

35   Gently tap on the top of the piston with the end of a wooden or plastic hammer handle (see illustration) while guiding the end of

the connecting rod into place on the crankshaft journal (a pair of wooden dowels would be helpful for this). The piston rings may try to pop out of the ring compressor just before entering the cylinder bore, so keep some downward pressure on the ring compressor. Work slowly, and if any resistance is felt as the piston enters the cylinder, stop immediately. Find out what's hanging up and fix it before proceeding. Do not, for any reason, force the piston into the cylinder - you might break a ring and/or the piston.

36   Once the piston/connecting rod assembly is installed, the connecting rod bearing oil clearance must be checked before the rod cap is permanently installed.

37   Cut a piece of the appropriate size Plastigage slightly shorter than the width of the connecting rod bearing and lay it in place on the number one connecting rod journal, parallel with the journal axis (see illustration).

38   Clean the connecting rod cap bearing face and install the rod cap. Make sure the mating mark on the cap is on the same side as the mark on the connecting rod (see illustration 9.4).

39   Install the old rod bolts at this time, and tighten them to the torque listed in this Chapter's Specifications. **Note:** *Use a thin-wall socket to avoid erroneous torque readings that can result if the socket is wedged between the rod cap and the bolt. If the socket tends to wedge itself between the fastener and the cap, lift up on it slightly until it no longer contacts the cap. DO NOT rotate the crankshaft at any time during this operation.*

40   Remove the fasteners and detach the rod cap, being very careful not to disturb the Plastigage. Install the cap bolts. **Note:** *You MUST use new connecting rod bolts if the clearance is not as specified (see Step 5).*

41   Compare the width of the crushed Plastigage to the scale printed on the Plastigage envelope to obtain the oil clearance (see illustration). The connecting rod oil clearance

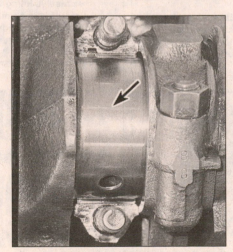

9.37 Place Plastigage on each connecting rod bearing journal parallel to the crankshaft centerline

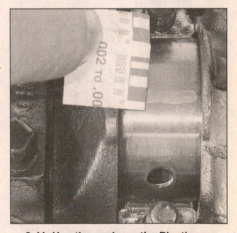

9.41 Use the scale on the Plastigage package to determine the bearing oil clearance - be sure to measure the widest part of the Plastigage and use the correct scale; it comes with both standard and metric scales

ENGINE BEARING ANALYSIS

Debris

Babbitt bearing embedded with debris from machinings

Microscopic detail of debris

Microscopic detail of gouges

Overplated copper alloy bearing gouged by cast iron debris

Aluminum bearing embedded with glass beads

Microscopic detail of glass beads

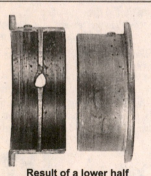

Damaged lining caused by dirt left on the bearing back

Misassembly

Result of a lower half assembled as an upper - blocking the oil flow

Excessive oil clearance is indicated by a short contact arc

Polished and oil-stained backs are a result of a poor fit in the housing bore

Result of a wrong, reversed, or shifted cap

Overloading

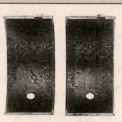

Damage from excessive idling which resulted in an oil film unable to support the load imposed

Damaged upper connecting rod bearings caused by engine lugging; the lower main bearings (not shown) were similarly affected

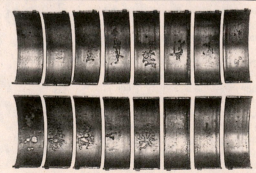

The damage shown in these upper and lower connecting rod bearings was caused by engine operation at a higher-than-rated speed under load

Misalignment

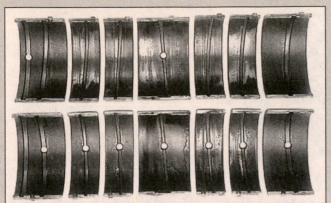

A warped crankshaft caused this pattern of severe wear in the center, diminishing toward the ends

A poorly finished crankshaft caused the equally spaced scoring shown

A tapered housing bore caused the damage along one edge of this pair

A bent connecting rod led to the damage in the "V" pattern

Lubrication

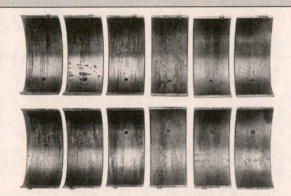

Result of dry start: The bearings on the left, farthest from the oil pump, show more damage

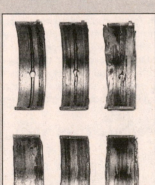

Result of a low oil supply or oil starvation

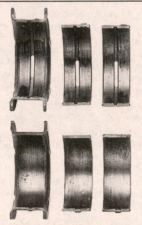

Severe wear as a result of inadequate oil clearance

Corrosion

Microscopic detail of corrosion

Corrosion is an acid attack on the bearing lining generally caused by inadequate maintenance, extremely hot or cold operation, or inferior oils or fuels

Microscopic detail of cavitation

Example of cavitation - a surface erosion caused by pressure changes in the oil film

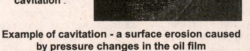

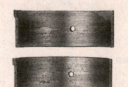

Damage from excessive thrust or insufficient axial clearance

Bearing affected by oil dilution caused by excessive blow-by or a rich mixture

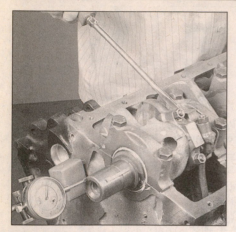

10.1 Checking crankshaft endplay with a dial indicator

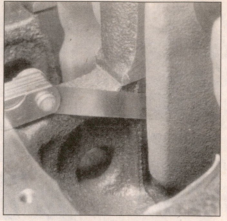

10.3 Checking the crankshaft endplay with feeler gauges at the thrust bearing journal

is usually about 0.001 to 0.002 inch. Consult an automotive machine shop for the clearance specified for the rod bearings on your engine.
42   If the clearance is not as specified, the bearing inserts may be the wrong size (which means different ones will be required). Before deciding that different inserts are needed, make sure that no dirt or oil was between the bearing inserts and the connecting rod or cap when the clearance was measured. Also, recheck the journal diameter. If the Plastigage was wider at one end than the other, the journal may be tapered. If the clearance still exceeds the limit specified, the bearing will have to be replaced with an undersize bearing. **Caution:** *When installing a new crankshaft, always use a standard size bearing.*

Final installation

43   Carefully scrape all traces of the Plastigage material off the rod journal and/or bearing face. Be very careful not to scratch the bearing - use your fingernail or the edge of a plastic card.
44   Make sure the bearing faces are perfectly clean, then apply a uniform layer of clean moly-base grease or engine assembly lube to both of them. You'll have to push the piston into the cylinder to expose the face of the bearing insert in the connecting rod.
45   Slide the connecting rod back into place on the journal, install the rod cap, install the **new** bolts and tighten them to the torque listed in this Chapter's Specifications.
46   Repeat the entire procedure for the remaining pistons/connecting rods.
47   The important points to remember are:

a) *Keep the back sides of the bearing inserts and the insides of the connecting rods and caps perfectly clean when assembling them.*
b) *Make sure you have the correct piston/ rod assembly for each cylinder.*
c) *The arrow or mark on the piston must face the front (timing chain on four-cylinder engines or timing belt on V6 engines) of the engine.*
d) *Lubricate the cylinder walls liberally with clean oil.*

e) *Lubricate the bearing faces when installing the rod caps after the oil clearance has been checked.*

48   After all the piston/connecting rod assemblies have been correctly installed, rotate the crankshaft a number of times by hand to check for any obvious binding.
49   As a final step, check the connecting rod endplay, as described in Step 3. If it was correct before disassembly and the original crankshaft and rods were reinstalled, it should still be correct. If new rods or a new crankshaft were installed, the endplay may be inadequate. If so, the rods will have to be removed and taken to an automotive machine shop for resizing.

10   Crankshaft - removal and installation

Removal

Refer to illustrations 10.1 and 10.3

Note: *The crankshaft can be removed only after the engine has been removed from the vehicle. It's assumed that the flywheel or driveplate, crankshaft pulley, timing belt or timing chain, oil pan, baffle plate, oil screen, oil pump body, crankshaft position sensor (on 1.8L engines), oil filter and piston/connecting rod assemblies have already been removed. On 2005 and earlier Civics and 2006 and earlier CR-V models, the rear main oil seal retainer must be unbolted and separated from the block before proceeding with crankshaft removal.*
1   Before the crankshaft is removed, measure the endplay. Mount a dial indicator with the indicator in line with the crankshaft and just touching the end of the crankshaft as shown **(see illustration)**.
2   Pry the crankshaft all the way to the rear and zero the dial indicator. Next, pry the crankshaft to the front as far as possible and check the reading on the dial indicator. The distance traveled is the endplay. A typical crankshaft

endplay will fall between 0.004 to 0.014 inch (0.10 to 0.35 mm). If it is greater than that, check the crankshaft thrust surfaces for wear after it's removed. If no wear is evident, new main bearings should correct the endplay.
3   If a dial indicator isn't available, feeler gauges can be used. Gently pry the crankshaft all the way to the front of the engine. Slip feeler gauges between the crankshaft and the front face of the thrust bearing or washer to determine the clearance **(see illustration)**.
4   On 1.8L, 2.0L and 2.4L engines, loosen the main bearing bridge perimeter bolts and the main bearing inner bolts or the main bearing bridge bolts on 1.7L engines, 1/4-turn at a time each, until they can be removed by hand. Follow the reverse of the tightening sequence **(see illustrations 10.19a, 10.19b, 10.19c and 10.19d)**.
5   Remove the main bearing bridge. Try not to drop the bearing inserts if they come out with the main bearing bridge assembly.
6   Carefully lift the crankshaft out of the engine. It may be a good idea to have an assistant available, since the crankshaft is quite heavy and awkward to handle. **Note:** *On 1.8L engines, remove the crankshaft position sensor (CKP) pulse plate mounting bolts and remove the plate from the rear of the crankshaft before servicing.* With the bearing inserts in place inside the engine block and main bearing bridge, reinstall the bridge or lower crankcase onto the engine block and tighten the bolts finger tight.

Installation

7   Crankshaft installation is the first step in engine reassembly. It's assumed at this point that the engine block and crankshaft have been cleaned, inspected and repaired or reconditioned.
8   Position the engine block with the bottom facing up.
9   Remove the mounting bolts and lift off the lower crankcase or bearing bridge assembly.
10   If they're still in place, remove the original bearing inserts from the block and from the main bearing bridge. Wipe the bearing surfaces of the block and main bearing bridge saddle with a clean, lint-free cloth. They must be kept spotlessly clean. This is critical for determining the correct bearing oil clearance.

Main bearing oil clearance check

Refer to illustrations 10.17, 10.19a, 10.19b, 10.19c, 10.19d and 10.21

11   Without mixing them up, clean the back sides of the new upper main bearing inserts (with grooves and oil holes) and lay one in each main bearing saddle in the engine block. Each upper bearing (engine block) has an oil groove and oil hole in it. **Caution:** *The oil holes in the block must line up with the oil holes in the engine block inserts.* The thrust washer or thrust bearing insert must be installed in the correct location. **Note:** *On 1.7L engines, the*

thrust bearing is located on the engine block number 5 journal. On 1.8L engines and all DOHC engines, the thrust bearing is located on the 4th journal in the engine block (upper). Clean the back sides of the lower main bearing inserts and lay them in the corresponding location in the main bearing bridge. Make sure the tab on the bearing insert fits into the recess in the block or main bearing caps. **Caution:** *Do not hammer the bearing insert into place and don't nick or gouge the bearing faces. DO NOT apply any lubrication at this time.*

12   Clean the faces of the bearing inserts in the block and the crankshaft main bearing journals with a clean, lint-free cloth.

13   Check or clean the oil holes in the crankshaft, as any dirt here can go only one way - straight through the new bearings.

14   Once you're certain the crankshaft is clean, carefully lay it in position in the cylinder block.

15   Before the crankshaft can be permanently installed, the main bearing oil clearance must be checked.

16   Cut several strips of the appropriate size of Plastigage. They must be slightly shorter than the width of the main bearing journal.

17   Place one piece on each crankshaft main bearing journal, parallel with the journal axis as shown **(see illustration)**.

18   Clean the faces of the bearing inserts in the lower crankcase or main bearing caps. Hold the bearing inserts in place and install the lower crankcase or caps onto the crankshaft and cylinder block. DO NOT disturb the Plastigage.

19   Apply clean engine oil to all bolt threads prior to installation, then install all bolts finger-tight. Tighten the main bearing bridge bolts in the sequence shown **(see illustrations)** progressing in steps, to the torque listed in this Chapter's Specifications. DO NOT rotate the crankshaft at any time during this operation.

10.17 Place the Plastigage onto the crankshaft bearing journal as shown

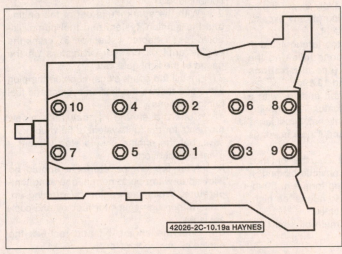

10.19a Main bearing cap bolt tightening sequence on 1.7L SOHC engines

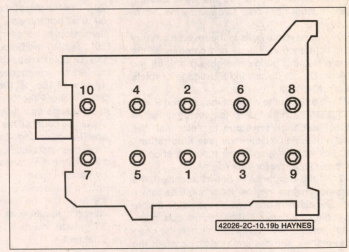

10.19b Main bearing bridge bolt tightening sequence on 1.8L SOHC and all DOHC engines - inner bolts

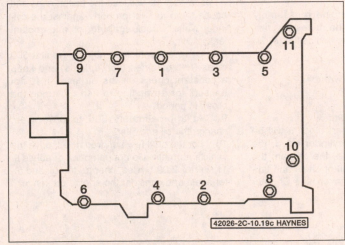

10.19c Main bearing bridge bolt tightening sequence on 1.8L SOHC engines - outer bolts

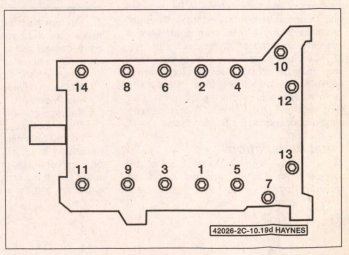

10.19d Main bearing bridge bolt tightening sequence on DOHC engines - outer bolts

10.21 Use the scale on the Plastigage package to determine the bearing oil clearance - be sure to measure the widest part of the Plastigage and use the correct scale; it comes with both standard and metric scales

Note: *Be sure to torque the main bearing bridge inner bolts first, followed by the perimeter bolts.*

20   Remove the bolts in the *reverse* order of the tightening sequence and carefully lift the main bearing bridge straight up and off the block. Do not disturb the Plastigage or rotate the crankshaft.

21   Compare the width of the crushed Plastigage on each journal to the scale printed on the Plastigage envelope to determine the main bearing oil clearance **(see illustration)**. Check with an automotive machine shop for the oil clearance for your engine.

22   If the clearance is not as specified, the bearing inserts may be the wrong size (which means different ones will be required). Before deciding if different inserts are needed, make sure that no dirt or oil was between the bearing inserts and the caps or block when the clearance was measured. If the Plastigage was wider at one end than the other, the crankshaft journal may be tapered. If the clearance still exceeds the limit specified, the bearing insert(s) will have to be replaced with an undersize bearing insert(s). **Caution:** *When installing a new crankshaft always install a standard bearing insert set.*

23   Carefully scrape all traces of the Plastigage material off the main bearing journals and/or the bearing insert faces. Be sure to remove all residue from the oil holes. Use your fingernail or the edge of a plastic card - don't nick or scratch the bearing faces.

Final installation

24   Carefully lift the crankshaft out of the cylinder block. On 1.8L engines, install the crankshaft position sensor (CKP) pulse plate

mounting bolts and tighten the bolts to the torque listed in this Chapter's Specifications.

25   Clean the bearing insert faces in the cylinder block, then apply a thin, uniform layer of moly-base grease or engine assembly lube to each of the bearing surfaces. Be sure to coat the thrust faces as well as the journal face of the thrust bearing.

26   Make sure the crankshaft journals are clean, then lay the crankshaft back in place in the cylinder block.

27   Clean the bearing insert faces and apply the same lubricant to them. Clean the engine block and the mating surface of the lower crankcase or the bearing caps thoroughly. The surfaces must be free of oil residue.

28   Apply liquid gasket or equivalent to the lower main bearing bridge and inside edge of the threaded bolt holes. Install the lower main bearing bridge. **Note:** *Once the liquid gasket has been applied, the bearing bridge must be installed within a few minuets or the gasket must be removed, parts cleaned and applied again.*

29   Prior to installation, apply clean engine oil to all bolt threads, wiping off any excess, then install all bolts finger-tight.

30   Tighten the bolts to the torque listed in this Chapter's Specifications following the correct torque sequence **(see illustrations 10.19a, 10.19b, 10.19c and 10.19d)**.

31   Recheck the crankshaft endplay with a feeler gauge or a dial indicator. The endplay should be correct if the crankshaft thrust faces aren't worn or damaged and if new bearings have been installed.

32   Rotate the crankshaft a number of times by hand to check for any obvious binding. It should rotate with a running torque of 50 in-lbs or less. If the running torque is too high, correct the problem at this time.

33   Install the new rear main oil seal (see Chapter 2A).

11   Engine overhaul - reassembly sequence

1   Before beginning engine reassembly, make sure you have all the necessary new parts, gaskets and seals as well as the following items on hand:

Common hand tools
A 1/2-inch drive torque wrench
New engine oil
Gasket sealant
Thread locking compound

2   If you obtained a short block it will be necessary to install the cylinder head, the oil pump and pick-up tube, the oil pan, the water pump, the timing belt or chain and timing cover, and the valve cover (see Chapter

2A or 2B). In order to save time and avoid problems, the external components must be installed in the following general order:

Thermostat and housing cover
Water pump
Intake and exhaust manifolds
Fuel injection components
Emission control components
Spark plug wires and spark plugs
Ignition coils or coil packs
Oil filter
Engine mounts and mount brackets
Clutch and flywheel (manual transaxle)
Driveplate (automatic transaxle)

12   Initial start-up and break-in after overhaul

Warning: *Have a fire extinguisher handy when starting the engine for the first time.*

1   Once the engine has been installed in the vehicle, double-check the engine oil and coolant levels.

2   With the spark plugs out of the engine and the ignition system and fuel pump disabled (see Chapter 4, Section 3), crank the engine until oil pressure registers on the gauge or the light goes out.

3   Install the spark plugs, hook up the plug wires and restore the ignition system and fuel pump functions.

4   Start the engine. It may take a few moments for the fuel system to build up pressure, but the engine should start without a great deal of effort.

5   After the engine starts, it should be allowed to warm up to normal operating temperature. While the engine is warming up, make a thorough check for fuel, oil and coolant leaks.

6   Shut the engine off and recheck the engine oil and coolant levels.

7   Drive the vehicle to an area with minimum traffic, accelerate from 30 to 50 mph, then allow the vehicle to slow to 30 mph with the throttle closed. Repeat the procedure 10 or 12 times. This will load the piston rings and cause them to seat properly against the cylinder walls. Check again for oil and coolant leaks.

8   Drive the vehicle gently for the first 500 miles (no sustained high speeds) and keep a constant check on the oil level. It is not unusual for an engine to use oil during the break-in period.

9   At approximately 500 to 600 miles, change the oil and filter.

10   For the next few hundred miles, drive the vehicle normally. Do not pamper it or abuse it.

11   After 2,000 miles, change the oil and filter again and consider the engine broken in.

COMMON ENGINE OVERHAUL TERMS

B

Backlash - The amount of play between two parts. Usually refers to how much one gear can be moved back and forth without moving the gear with which it's meshed.

Bearing Caps - The caps held in place by nuts or bolts which, in turn, hold the bearing surface. This space is for lubricating oil to enter.

Bearing clearance - The amount of space left between shaft and bearing surface. This space is for lubricating oil to enter.

Bearing crush - The additional height which is purposely manufactured into each bearing half to ensure complete contact of the bearing back with the housing bore when the engine is assembled.

Bearing knock - The noise created by movement of a part in a loose or worn bearing.

Blueprinting - Dismantling an engine and reassembling it to EXACT specifications.

Bore - An engine cylinder, or any cylindrical hole; also used to describe the process of enlarging or accurately refinishing a hole with a cutting tool, as to bore an engine cylinder. The bore size is the diameter of the hole.

Boring - Renewing the cylinders by cutting them out to a specified size. A boring bar is used to make the cut.

Bottom end - A term which refers collectively to the engine block, crankshaft, main bearings and the big ends of the connecting rods.

Break-in - The period of operation between installation of new or rebuilt parts and time in which parts are worn to the correct fit. Driving at reduced and varying speed for a specified mileage to permit parts to wear to the correct fit.

Bushing - A one-piece sleeve placed in a bore to serve as a bearing surface for shaft, piston pin, etc. Usually replaceable.

C

Camshaft - The shaft in the engine, on which a series of lobes are located for operating the valve mechanisms. The camshaft is driven by gears or sprockets and a timing chain. Usually referred to simply as the cam.

Carbon - Hard, or soft, black deposits found in combustion chamber, on plugs, under rings, on and under valve heads.

Cast iron - An alloy of iron and more than two percent carbon, used for engine blocks and heads because it's relatively inexpensive and easy to mold into complex shapes.

Chamfer - To bevel across (or a bevel on) the sharp edge of an object.

Chase - To repair damaged threads with a tap or die.

Combustion chamber - The space between the piston and the cylinder head, with the piston at top dead center, in which air-fuel mixture is burned.

Compression ratio - The relationship between cylinder volume (clearance volume) when the piston is at top dead center and cylinder volume when the piston is at bottom dead center.

Connecting rod - The rod that connects the crank on the crankshaft with the piston. Sometimes called a con rod.

Connecting rod cap - The part of the connecting rod assembly that attaches the rod to the crankpin.

Core plug - Soft metal plug used to plug the casting holes for the coolant passages in the block.

Crankcase - The lower part of the engine in which the crankshaft rotates; includes the lower section of the cylinder block and the oil pan.

Crank kit - A reground or reconditioned crankshaft and new main and connecting rod bearings.

Crankpin - The part of a crankshaft to which a connecting rod is attached.

Crankshaft - The main rotating member, or shaft, running the length of the crankcase, with offset throws to which the connecting rods are attached; changes the reciprocating motion of the pistons into rotating motion.

Cylinder sleeve - A replaceable sleeve, or liner, pressed into the cylinder block to form the cylinder bore.

D

Deburring - Removing the burrs (rough edges or areas) from a bearing.

Deglazer - A tool, rotated by an electric motor, used to remove glaze from cylinder walls so a new set of rings will seat.

E

Endplay - The amount of lengthwise movement between two parts. As applied to a crankshaft, the distance that the crankshaft can move forward and back in the cylinder block.

F

Face - A machinist's term that refers to removing metal from the end of a shaft or the face of a larger part, such as a flywheel.

Fatigue - A breakdown of material through a large number of loading and unloading cycles. The first signs are cracks followed shortly by breaks.

Feeler gauge - A thin strip of hardened steel, ground to an exact thickness, used to check clearances between parts.

Free height - The unloaded length or height of a spring.

Freeplay - The looseness in a linkage, or an assembly of parts, between the initial application of force and actual movement. Usually perceived as slop or slight delay.

Freeze plug - See Core plug.

G

Gallery - A large passage in the block that forms a reservoir for engine oil pressure.

Glaze - The very smooth, glassy finish that develops on cylinder walls while an engine is in service.

H

Heli-Coil - A rethreading device used when threads are worn or damaged. The device is installed in a retapped hole to reduce the thread size to the original size.

I

Installed height - The spring's measured length or height, as installed on the cylinder head. Installed height is measured from the spring seat to the underside of the spring retainer.

J

Journal - The surface of a rotating shaft which turns in a bearing.

K

Keeper - The split lock that holds the valve spring retainer in position on the valve stem.

Key - A small piece of metal inserted into matching grooves machined into two parts fitted together - such as a gear pressed onto a shaft - which prevents slippage between the two parts.

Knock - The heavy metallic engine sound, produced in the combustion chamber as a result of abnormal combustion - usually detonation. Knock is usually caused by a loose or worn bearing. Also referred to as detonation, pinging and spark knock. Connecting rod or main bearing knocks are created by too much oil clearance or insufficient lubrication.

L

Lands - The portions of metal between the piston ring grooves.

Lapping the valves - Grinding a valve face and its seat together with lapping compound.

Lash - The amount of free motion in a gear train, between gears, or in a mechanical assembly, that occurs before movement can begin. Usually refers to the lash in a valve train.

Lifter - The part that rides against the cam to transfer motion to the rest of the valve train.

M

Machining - The process of using a machine to remove metal from a metal part.

Main bearings - The plain, or babbit, bearings that support the crankshaft.

Main bearing caps - The cast iron caps, bolted to the bottom of the block, that support the main bearings.

O

O.D. - Outside diameter.

Oil gallery - A pipe or drilled passageway in the engine used to carry engine oil from one area to another.

Oil ring - The lower ring, or rings, of a piston; designed to prevent excessive amounts of oil from working up the cylinder walls and into the combustion chamber. Also called an oil-control ring.

Oil seal - A seal which keeps oil from leaking out of a compartment. Usually refers to a dynamic seal around a rotating shaft or other moving part.

O-ring - A type of sealing ring made of a special rubberlike material; in use, the O-ring is compressed into a groove to provide the sealing action.

Overhaul - To completely disassemble a unit, clean and inspect all parts, reassemble it with the original or new parts and make all adjustments necessary for proper operation.

P

Pilot bearing - A small bearing installed in the center of the flywheel (or the rear end of the crankshaft) to support the front end of the input shaft of the transmission.

Pip mark - A little dot or indentation which indicates the top side of a compression ring.

Piston - The cylindrical part, attached to the connecting rod, that moves up and down in the cylinder as the crankshaft rotates. When the fuel charge is fired, the piston transfers the force of the explosion to the connecting rod, then to the crankshaft.

Piston pin (or wrist pin) - The cylindrical and usually hollow steel pin that passes through the piston. The piston pin fastens the piston to the upper end of the connecting rod.

Piston ring - The split ring fitted to the groove in a piston. The ring contacts the sides of the ring groove and also rubs against the cylinder wall, thus sealing space between piston and wall. There are two types of rings: Compression rings seal the compression pressure in the combustion chamber; oil rings scrape excessive oil off the cylinder wall.

Piston ring groove - The slots or grooves cut in piston heads to hold piston rings in position.

Piston skirt - The portion of the piston below the rings and the piston pin hole.

Plastigage - A thin strip of plastic thread, available in different sizes, used for measuring clearances. For example, a strip of plastigage is laid across a bearing journal and mashed as parts are assembled. Then parts are disassembled and the width of the strip is measured to determine clearance between journal and bearing. Commonly used to measure crankshaft main-bearing and connecting rod bearing clearances.

Press-fit - A tight fit between two parts that requires pressure to force the parts together. Also referred to as drive, or force, fit.

Prussian blue - A blue pigment; in solution, useful in determining the area of contact between two surfaces. Prussian blue is commonly used to determine the width and location of the contact area between the valve face and the valve seat.

R

Race (bearing) - The inner or outer ring that provides a contact surface for balls or rollers in bearing.

Ream - To size, enlarge or smooth a hole by using a round cutting tool with fluted edges.

Ring job - The process of reconditioning the cylinders and installing new rings.

Runout - Wobble. The amount a shaft rotates out-of-true.

S

Saddle - The upper main bearing seat.

Scored - Scratched or grooved, as a cylinder wall may be scored by abrasive particles moved up and down by the piston rings.

Scuffing - A type of wear in which there's a transfer of material between parts moving against each other; shows up as pits or grooves in the mating surfaces.

Seat - The surface upon which another part rests or seats. For example, the valve seat is the matched surface upon which the valve face rests. Also used to refer to wearing into a good fit; for example, piston rings seat after a few miles of driving.

Short block - An engine block complete with crankshaft and piston and, usually, camshaft assemblies.

Static balance - The balance of an object while it's stationary.

Step - The wear on the lower portion of a ring land caused by excessive side and back-clearance. The height of the step indicates the ring's extra side clearance and the length of the step projecting from the back wall of the groove represents the ring's back clearance.

Stroke - The distance the piston moves when traveling from top dead center to bottom dead center, or from bottom dead center to top dead center.

Stud - A metal rod with threads on both ends.

T

Tang - A lip on the end of a plain bearing used to align the bearing during assembly.

Tap - To cut threads in a hole. Also refers to the fluted tool used to cut threads.

Taper - A gradual reduction in the width of a shaft or hole; in an engine cylinder, taper usually takes the form of uneven wear, more pronounced at the top than at the bottom.

Throws - The offset portions of the crankshaft to which the connecting rods are affixed.

Thrust bearing - The main bearing that has thrust faces to prevent excessive endplay, or forward and backward movement of the crankshaft.

Thrust washer - A bronze or hardened steel washer placed between two moving parts. The washer prevents longitudinal movement and provides a bearing surface for thrust surfaces of parts.

Tolerance - The amount of variation permitted from an exact size of measurement. Actual amount from smallest acceptable dimension to largest acceptable dimension.

U

Umbrella - An oil deflector placed near the valve tip to throw oil from the valve stem area.

Undercut - A machined groove below the normal surface.

Undersize bearings - Smaller diameter bearings used with re-ground crankshaft journals.

V

Valve grinding - Refacing a valve in a valve-refacing machine.

Valve train - The valve-operating mechanism of an engine; includes all components from the camshaft to the valve.

Vibration damper - A cylindrical weight attached to the front of the crankshaft to minimize torsional vibration (the twist-untwist actions of the crankshaft caused by the cylinder firing impulses). Also called a harmonic balancer.

W

Water jacket - The spaces around the cylinders, between the inner and outer shells of the cylinder block or head, through which coolant circulates.

Web - A supporting structure across a cavity.

Woodruff key - A key with a radiused backside (viewed from the side).

Chapter 3
Cooling, heating and air conditioning systems

Contents

	Section
Air conditioning and heating system - check and maintenance.....	3
Air conditioning compressor - removal and installation	13
Air conditioning condenser - removal and installation	15
Air conditioning pressure switch - replacement	16
Air conditioning receiver-drier - removal and installation	14
Blower motor power transistor and blower motor - replacement ...	10
Coolant reservoir - removal and installation	6
Coolant temperature sending unit - check and replacement	9
Engine cooling fans and switch - replacement	5

	Section
General information	1
Heater core - replacement..	12
Heater/air conditioning control assembly - removal and installation	11
Radiator - removal and installation......................................	7
Thermostat - check and replacement..................................	4
Troubleshooting...	2
Water pump - replacement..	8

Specifications

General

Radiator cap pressure rating	14 to 18 psi (93 to 123 kPa)
Thermostat rating (opening to fully open temperature range)	
2005 and earlier Civic and all CR-V models	169 to 194 degrees F (76 to 90 degrees C)
2006 and later Civic models...	176 to 203 degrees F (80 to 95 degrees C)
Cooling system capacity...	See Chapter 1
Refrigerant type...	R-134a
Refrigerant capacity...	Refer to HVAC specification tag

Torque specifications

Note: *One foot-pound (ft-lb) of torque is equivalent to 12 inch-pounds (in-lbs) of torque. Torque values below approximately 15 ft-lbs are expressed in inch-pounds, since most foot-pound torque wrenches are not accurate at these smaller values.*

Condenser inlet and outlet nuts..	86 in-lbs	9.5 Nm
Thermostat housing cover bolts		
Coupe and sedan models	104 in-lbs	11.5 Nm
CR-V and hatchback models	86 in-lbs	9.5 Nm
Water pump bolts	104 in-lbs	11.5 Nm
Water pump pulley bolts (1.8L engines)	120 in-lbs	13.5 Nm

Cooling, heating and air conditioning components - 2003 Civic sedan

1	Air conditioning line service port (high side)	4	Radiator cap
2	Air conditioning line service port (low side)	5	Coolant reservoir
3	Radiator (below radiator support cover)	6	Thermostat housing
		7	Fuse and relay box

Cooling, heating and air conditioning components - 2006 Civic with a 1.8L engine

1 Fuse and relay box
2 Coolant reservoir
3 Radiator cap
4 Radiator (below radiator support cover)

5 Thermostat housing
6 Water pump (right end of engine)
7 Air conditioning line service port (high side)
8 Air conditioning line service port (low side)

Cooling, heating and air conditioning components - early CR-V

1	Fuse and relay box	4	Coolant reservoir
2	Radiator cap	5	Air conditioning line service port (high side)
3	Thermostat (in housing below intake manifold)	6	Air conditioning line service port (low side)

1   General information

Warning: *Do not allow antifreeze to come in contact with your skin or painted surfaces of the vehicle. Rinse off spills immediately with plenty of water. Antifreeze is highly toxic if ingested. Never leave antifreeze lying around in an open container or in puddles on the floor; children and pets are attracted by it's sweet smell and may drink it. Check with local authorities about disposing of used antifreeze. Many communities have collection centers which will see that antifreeze is disposed of safely. Never dump used antifreeze on the ground or pour it into drains.*

Engine cooling system

All modern vehicles employ a pressurized engine cooling system with thermostatically controlled coolant circulation. The cooling system consists of a radiator, an expansion tank or coolant reservoir, a pressure cap (located on the expansion tank or radiator), a thermostat, a cooling fan, and a water pump.

The water pump circulates coolant through the engine. The coolant flows around each cylinder and around the intake and exhaust ports, near the spark plug areas and in close proximity to the exhaust valve guides.

A thermostat controls engine coolant temperature. During warm up, the closed thermostat prevents coolant from circulating through the radiator. As the engine nears normal operating temperature, the thermostat opens and allows hot coolant to travel through the radiator, where it's cooled before returning to the engine.

Heating system

The heating system consists of a blower fan and heater core located in a housing under the dash, the hoses connecting the heater core to the engine cooling system and the heater/air conditioning control head on the dashboard. Hot engine coolant is circulated through the heater core. When the heater mode is activated, a flap door in the housing opens to expose the heater core to the passenger compartment through air ducts. A fan switch on the control head activates the blower motor, which forces air through the core, heating the air.

Air conditioning system

The air conditioning system consists of a condenser mounted in front of the radiator, an evaporator mounted adjacent to the heater core, a compressor mounted on the engine, a receiver-drier or accumulator and the plumbing connecting all of the above components.

A blower fan forces the warmer air of the passenger compartment through the evaporator core (sort of a radiator-in-reverse), transferring the heat from the air to the refrigerant.

The liquid refrigerant boils off into low pressure vapor, taking the heat with it when it leaves the evaporator.

2   Troubleshooting

Coolant leaks

Refer to illustration 2.2

1   A coolant leak can develop anywhere in the cooling system, but the most common causes are:

a) *A loose or weak hose clamp*
b) *A defective hose*
c) *A faulty pressure cap*
d) *A damaged radiator*
e) *A bad heater core*
f) *A faulty water pump*
g) *A leaking gasket at any joint that carries coolant*

2   Coolant leaks aren't always easy to find. Sometimes they can only be detected when the cooling system is under pressure. Here's where a cooling system pressure tester comes in handy. After the engine has cooled completely, the tester is attached in place of the pressure cap, then pumped up to the pressure value equal to that of the pressure cap rating **(see illustration)**. Now, leaks that only exist when the engine is fully warmed up will become apparent. The tester can be left connected to locate a nagging slow leak.

Coolant level drops, but no external leaks

Refer to illustrations 2.5a and 2.5b

3   If you find it necessary to keep adding coolant, but there are no external leaks, the probable causes include:

a) *A blown head gasket*
b) *A leaking intake manifold gasket (only on engines that have coolant passages in the manifold)*
c) *A cracked cylinder head or cylinder block*

4   Any of the above problems will also usually result in contamination of the engine oil, which will cause it to take on a milk-shake-like appearance. A bad head gasket or cracked head or block can also result in engine oil contaminating the cooling system.

5   Combustion leak detectors (also known as block testers) are available at most auto parts stores. These work by detecting exhaust gases in the cooling system, which indicates a compression leak from a cylinder into the coolant. The tester consists of a large bulb-type syringe and bottle of test fluid **(see illustration)**. A measured amount of the fluid is added to the syringe. The syringe is placed over the cooling system filler neck and, with the engine running, the bulb is squeezed and a sample of the gases present in the cooling system are drawn up through the test fluid **(see illustration)**. If any combustion gases are present in the sample taken, the test fluid will change color.

6   If the test indicates combustion gas is present in the cooling system, you can be sure that the engine has a blown head gasket or a crack in the cylinder head or block, and will require disassembly to repair.

Pressure cap

Refer to illustration 2.8

Warning: *Wait until the engine is completely cool before beginning this check.*

7   The cooling system is sealed by a spring-loaded cap, which raises the boiling point of the coolant. If the cap's seal or spring are worn out, the coolant can boil and escape past the cap. With the engine completely cool, remove the cap and check the seal; if it's cracked, hardened or deteriorated in any way, replace it with a new one.

8   Even if the seal is good, the spring might not be; this can be checked with a cooling

2.2 The cooling system pressure tester is connected in place of the pressure cap, then pumped up to pressurize the system

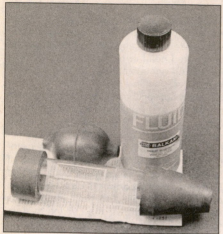

2.5a The combustion leak detector consists of a bulb, syringe and test fluid

2.5b Place the tester over the cooling system filler neck and use the bulb to draw a sample into the tester

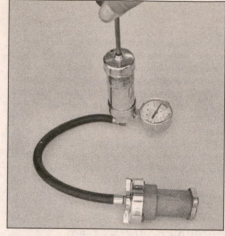

2.8 Checking the cooling system pressure cap with a cooling system pressure tester

system pressure tester **(see illustration)**. If the cap can't hold a pressure within approximately 1-1/2 lbs of its rated pressure (which is marked on the cap), replace it with a new one.

9   The cap is also equipped with a vacuum relief spring. When the engine cools off, a vacuum is created in the cooling system. The vacuum relief spring allows air back into the system, which will equalize the pressure and prevent damage to the radiator (the radiator tanks could collapse if the vacuum is great enough). If, after turning the engine off and allowing it to cool down you notice any of the cooling system hoses collapsing, replace the pressure cap with a new one.

Thermostat

Refer to illustration 2.10

10   Before assuming the thermostat **(see illustration)** is responsible for a cooling system problem, check the coolant level (see Chapter 1), drivebelt tension (see Chapter 1) and temperature gauge (or light) operation.
11   If the engine takes a long time to warm up (as indicated by the temperature gauge or heater operation), the thermostat is probably

stuck open. Replace the thermostat with a new one.
12   If the engine runs hot or overheats, a thorough test of the thermostat should be performed.
13   Definitive testing of the thermostat can only be made when it is removed from the vehicle. If the thermostat is stuck in the open position at room temperature, it is faulty and must be replaced. **Caution:** *Do not drive the vehicle without a thermostat. The computer may stay in open loop and emissions and fuel economy will suffer.*
14   To test a thermostat, suspend the (closed) thermostat on a length of string or wire in a pot of cold water.
15   Heat the water on a stove while observing thermostat. The thermostat should fully open before the water boils.
16   If the thermostat doesn't open and close as specified, or sticks in any position, replace it.

Cooling fan

Electric cooling fan

17   If the engine is overheating and the cooling fan is not coming on when the engine temperature rises to an excessive level, unplug

the fan motor electrical connector(s) and connect the motor directly to the battery with fused jumper wires. If the fan motor doesn't come on, replace the motor.
18   If the radiator fan motor is okay, but it isn't coming on when the engine gets hot, the fan relay might be defective. A relay is used to control a circuit by turning it on and off in response to a control decision by the Powertrain Control Module (PCM). These control circuits are fairly complex, and checking them should be left to a qualified automotive technician. Sometimes, the control system can be fixed by simply identifying and replacing a bad relay.
19   Locate the fan relays in the engine compartment fuse/relay box.
20   Test the relay (see Chapter 12).
21   If the relay is okay, check all wiring and connections to the fan motor. Refer to the wiring diagrams at the end of Chapter 12. If no obvious problems are found, the problem could be the Engine Coolant Temperature (ECT) sensor or the Powertrain Control Module (PCM). Have the cooling fan system and circuit diagnosed by a dealer service department or repair shop with the proper diagnostic equipment. **Note:** *These models are equipped with a cooling fan motor resistor. Have the resistor checked if the fan motor does not respond to the speed variations signaled by the PCM.*

Belt-driven cooling fan

22   Disconnect the cable from the negative terminal of the battery and rock the fan back and forth by hand to check for excessive bearing play.
23   With the engine cold (and not running), turn the fan blades by hand. The fan should turn freely.
24   Visually inspect for substantial fluid leakage from the clutch assembly. If problems are noted, replace the clutch assembly.
25   With the engine completely warmed up, turn off the ignition switch and disconnect the negative battery cable from the battery. Turn the fan by hand. Some drag should be evident. If the fan turns easily, replace the fan clutch.

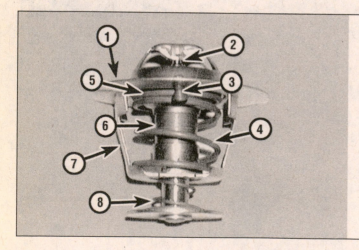

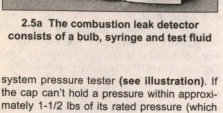

2.10 Typical thermostat:

1 Flange
2 Piston
3 Jiggle valve
4 Main coil spring
5 Valve seat
6 Valve
7 Frame
8 Secondary coil spring

2.28 The water pump weep hole is generally located on the underside of the pump

Water pump

26   A failure in the water pump can cause serious engine damage due to overheating.

Drivebelt-driven water pump

Refer to illustration 2.28

27   There are two ways to check the operation of the water pump while it's installed on the engine. If the pump is found to be defective, it should be replaced with a new or rebuilt unit.

28   Water pumps are equipped with weep (or vent) holes **(see illustration)**. If a failure occurs in the pump seal, coolant will leak from the hole.

29   If the water pump shaft bearings fail, there may be a howling sound at the pump while it's running. Shaft wear can be felt with the drivebelt removed if the water pump pulley is rocked up and down (with the engine off). Don't mistake drivebelt slippage, which causes a squealing sound, for water pump bearing failure.

Timing chain or timing belt-driven water pump

30   Water pumps driven by the timing chain or timing belt are located underneath the timing chain or timing belt cover.

31   Checking the water pump is limited because of where it is located. However, some basic checks can be made before deciding to remove the water pump. If the pump is found to be defective, it should be replaced with a new or rebuilt unit.

32   One sign that the water pump may be failing is that the heater (climate control) may not work well. Warm the engine to normal operating temperature, confirm that the coolant level is correct, then run the heater and check for hot air coming from the ducts.

33   Check for noises coming from the water pump area. If the water pump impeller shaft or bearings are failing, there may be a howling sound at the pump while the engine is running. **Note:** *Be careful not to mistake drivebelt noise (squealing) for water pump bearing or shaft failure.*

34   It you suspect water pump failure due to noise, wear can be confirmed by feeling

for play at the pump shaft. This can be done by rocking the drive sprocket on the pump shaft up and down. To do this you will need to remove the tension on the timing chain or belt as well as access the water pump.

All water pumps

35   In rare cases or on high-mileage vehicles, another sign of water pump failure may be the presence of coolant in the engine oil. This condition will adversely affect the engine in varying degrees. **Note:** *Finding coolant in the engine oil could indicate other serious issues besides a failed water pump, such as a blown head gasket or a cracked cylinder head or block.*

36   Even a pump that exhibits no outward signs of a problem, such as noise or leakage, can still be due for replacement. Removal for close examination is the only sure way to tell. Sometimes the fins on the back of the impeller can corrode to the point that cooling efficiency is diminished significantly.

Heater system

37   Little can go wrong with a heater. If the fan motor will run at all speeds, the electrical part of the system is okay. The three basic heater problems fall into the following general categories:

   a) *Not enough heat*
   b) *Heat all the time*
   c) *No heat*

38   If there's not enough heat, the control valve or door is stuck in a partially open position, the coolant coming from the engine isn't hot enough, or the heater core is restricted. If the coolant isn't hot enough, the thermostat in the engine cooling system is stuck open, allowing coolant to pass through the engine so rapidly that it doesn't heat up quickly enough. If the vehicle is equipped with a temperature gauge instead of a warning light, watch to see if the engine temperature rises to the normal operating range after driving for a reasonable distance.

39   If there's heat all the time, the control valve or the door is stuck wide open.

40   If there's no heat, coolant is probably not reaching the heater core, or the heater core is plugged. The likely cause is a collapsed or plugged hose, core, or a frozen heater control valve. If the heater is the type that flows coolant all the time, the cause is a stuck door or a broken or kinked control cable.

Air conditioning system

41   If the cool air output is inadequate:

   a) *Inspect the condenser coils and fins to make sure they're clear*
   b) *Check the compressor clutch for slippage.*
   c) *Check the blower motor for proper operation.*
   d) *Inspect the blower discharge passage for obstructions.*
   e) *Check the system air intake filter for clogging.*

42   If the system provides intermittent cooling air:

   a) *Check the circuit breaker, blower switch and blower motor for a malfunction.*

   b) *Make sure the compressor clutch isn't slipping.*
   c) *Inspect the plenum door to make sure it's operating properly.*
   d) *Inspect the evaporator to make sure it isn't clogged.*
   e) *If the unit is icing up, it may be caused by excessive moisture in the system, incorrect super heat switch adjustment or low thermostat adjustment.*

43   If the system provides no cooling air:

   a) *Inspect the compressor drivebelt. Make sure it's not loose or broken.*
   b) *Make sure the compressor clutch engages. If it doesn't, check for a blown fuse.*
   c) *Inspect the wire harness for broken or disconnected wires.*
   d) *If the compressor clutch doesn't engage, bridge the terminals of the A/C pressure switch(es) with a jumper wire; if the clutch now engages, and the system is properly charged, the pressure switch is bad.*
   e) *Make sure the blower motor is not disconnected or burned out.*
   f) *Make sure the compressor isn't partially or completely seized.*
   g) *Inspect the refrigerant lines for leaks.*
   h) *Check the components for leaks.*
   i) *Inspect the receiver-drier/accumulator or expansion valve/tube for clogged screens.*

44   If the system is noisy:

   a) *Look for loose panels in the passenger compartment.*
   b) *Inspect the compressor drivebelt. It may be loose or worn.*
   c) *Check the compressor mounting bolts. They should be tight.*
   d) *Listen carefully to the compressor. It may be worn out.*
   e) *Listen to the idler pulley and bearing and the clutch. Either may be defective.*
   f) *The winding in the compressor clutch coil or solenoid may be defective.*
   g) *The compressor oil level may be low.*
   h) *The blower motor fan bushing or the motor itself may be worn out.*
   i) *If there is an excessive charge in the system, you'll hear a rumbling noise in the high pressure line, a thumping noise in the compressor, or see bubbles or cloudiness in the sight glass.*
   j) *If there's a low charge in the system, you might hear hissing in the evaporator case at the expansion valve, or see bubbles or cloudiness in the sight glass.*

---

3   Air conditioning and heating system - check and maintenance

---

Air conditioning system

Refer to illustration 3.1

Warning: *The air conditioning system is under high pressure. Do not loosen any hose fittings or remove any components until after the system has been discharged. Air conditioning*

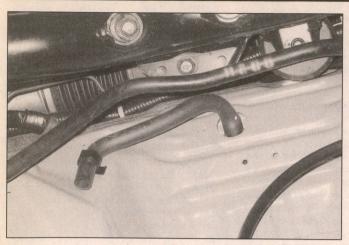

3.1 Evaporator drain hose

3.9 Insert a thermometer in the center vent, turn on the air conditioning system and wait for it to cool down; depending on the humidity, the output air should be 30 to 40 degrees cooler than the ambient air temperature

refrigerant should be properly discharged into an EPA-approved recovery/recycling unit at a dealer service department or an automotive air conditioning repair facility. Always wear eye protection when disconnecting air conditioning system fittings.
Caution 1: *All models covered by this manual use environmentally friendly R-134a. This refrigerant (and its appropriate refrigerant oils) are not compatible with R-12 refrigerant system components and must never be mixed or the components will be damaged.*
Caution 2: *When replacing entire components, additional refrigerant oil should be added equal to the amount that is removed with the component being replaced. Be sure to read the can before adding any oil to the system, to make sure it is compatible with the R-134a system.*

1   The following maintenance checks should be performed on a regular basis to ensure that the air conditioning continues to operate at peak efficiency.

 a) *Inspect the condition of the compressor drivebelt. If it is worn or deteriorated, replace it (see Chapter 1).*
 b) *Check the drivebelt tension (see Chapter 1).*
 c) *Inspect the system hoses. Look for cracks, bubbles, hardening and deterioration. Inspect the hoses and all fittings for oil bubbles or seepage. If there is any evidence of wear, damage or leakage, replace the hose(s).*
 d) *Inspect the condenser fins for leaves, bugs and any other foreign material that may have embedded itself in the fins. Use a fin comb or compressed air to remove debris from the condenser.*
 e) *Make sure the system has the correct refrigerant charge.*
 f) *If you hear water sloshing around in the dash area or have water dripping on the carpet, check the evaporator housing drain tube* **(see illustration)** *and insert a piece of wire into the opening to check for blockage.*

2   It's a good idea to operate the system for about ten minutes at least once a month. This is particularly important during the winter months because long term non-use can cause hardening, and subsequent failure, of the seals. Note that using the Defrost function operates the compressor.
3   If the air conditioning system is not working properly, proceed to Step 6 and perform the general checks outlined below.
4   Because of the complexity of the air conditioning system and the special equipment necessary to service it, in-depth troubleshooting and repairs beyond checking the refrigerant charge and the compressor clutch operation are not included in this manual. However, simple checks and component replacement procedures are provided in this Chapter. For more complete information on the air conditioning system, refer to the *Haynes Automotive Heating and Air Conditioning Manual.*
5   The most common cause of poor cooling is simply a low system refrigerant charge. If a noticeable drop in system cooling ability occurs, one of the following quick checks will help you determine if the refrigerant level is low.

Checking the refrigerant charge

Refer to illustration 3.9
6   Warm the engine up to normal operating temperature.
7   Place the air conditioning temperature selector at the coldest setting and put the blower at the highest setting.
8   After the system reaches operating temperature, feel the larger pipe exiting the evaporator at the firewall. The outlet pipe should be cold (the tubing that leads back to the compressor). If the evaporator outlet pipe is warm, the system probably needs a charge.
9   Insert a thermometer in the center air distribution duct **(see illustration)** while operating the air conditioning system at its maximum setting - the temperature of the output air should be 35 to 40 degrees F below the ambient air temperature (down to approximately 40 degrees F). If the ambient (outside)

air temperature is very high, say 110 degrees F, the duct air temperature may be as high as 60 degrees F, but generally the air conditioning is 35 to 40 degrees F cooler than the ambient air.
10   Further inspection or testing of the system requires special tools and techniques and is beyond the scope of the home mechanic.

Adding refrigerant

Refer to illustrations 3.11 and 3.13
Caution: *Make sure any refrigerant, refrigerant oil or replacement component you purchase is designated as compatible with R-134a systems.*
11   Purchase an R-134a automotive charging kit at an auto parts store **(see illustration)**. A charging kit includes a can of refrigerant, a tap valve and a short section of hose that can be attached between the tap valve and the system low side service valve. **Caution:** *Never add more than one can of refrigerant to the system. If more refrigerant than that is required, the system should be evacuated and leak tested.*
12   Back off the valve handle on the charging kit and screw the kit onto the refrigerant can,

3.11 R-134a automotive air conditioning charging kit

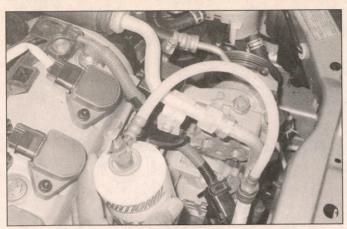

3.13 When adding refrigerant, connect the charging kit hose to the low-side port only. The location of the port varies by model and year

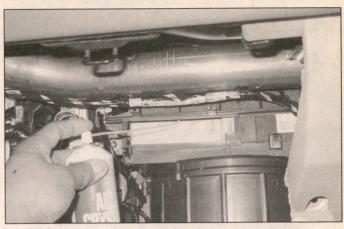

3.24 Insert the nozzle of the disinfectant can into the evaporator housing

making sure first that the O-ring or rubber seal inside the threaded portion of the kit is in place. **Warning:** *Wear protective eyewear when dealing with pressurized refrigerant cans.*

13   Remove the dust cap from the low-side charging port and attach the hose's quick-connect fitting to the port **(see illustration)**. **Warning:** *DO NOT hook the charging kit hose to the system high side! The fittings on the charging kit are designed to fit **only** on the low side of the system.*

14   Warm up the engine and turn On the air conditioning. Keep the charging kit hose away from the fan and other moving parts. **Note:** *The charging process requires the compressor to be running. If the clutch cycles off, you can put the air conditioning switch on High and leave the car doors open to keep the clutch on and compressor working. The compressor can be kept on during the charging by removing the connector from the pressure switch and bridging it with a paper clip or jumper wire during the procedure.*

15   Turn the valve handle on the kit until the stem pierces the can, then back the handle out to release the refrigerant. You should be able to hear the rush of gas. Keep the can upright at all times, but shake it occasionally. Allow stabilization time between each addition. **Note:** *The charging process will go faster if you wrap the can with a hot-water-soaked rag to keep the can from freezing up.*

16   If you have an accurate thermometer, you can place it in the center air conditioning duct inside the vehicle and keep track of the output air temperature. A charged system that is working properly should cool down to approximately 40 degrees F. If the ambient (outside) air temperature is very high, say 110 degrees F, the duct air temperature may be as high as 60 degrees F, but generally the air conditioning is 35 to 40 degrees F cooler than the ambient air.

17   When the can is empty, turn the valve handle to the closed position and release the connection from the low-side port. Reinstall the dust cap.

18   Remove the charging kit from the can

and store the kit for future use with the piercing valve in the UP position, to prevent inadvertently piercing the can on the next use.

Heating systems

19   If the carpet under the heater core is damp, or if antifreeze vapor or steam is coming through the vents, the heater core is leaking. Remove it (see Section 12) and install a new unit (most radiator shops will not repair a leaking heater core).

20   If the air coming out of the heater vents isn't hot, the problem could stem from any of the following causes:

a) *The thermostat is stuck open, preventing the engine coolant from warming up enough to carry heat to the heater core. Replace the thermostat (see Section 4).*

b) *There is a blockage in the system, preventing the flow of coolant through the heater core. Feel both heater hoses at the firewall. They should be hot. If one of them is cold, there is an obstruction in one of the hoses or in the heater core, or the heater control valve is shut. Detach the hoses and back flush the heater core with a water hose. If the heater core is clear but circulation is impeded, remove the two hoses and flush them out with a water hose.*

c) *If flushing fails to remove the blockage from the heater core, the core must be replaced (see Section 12).*

Eliminating air conditioning odors

Refer to illustration 3.24

21   Unpleasant odors that often develop in air conditioning systems are caused by the growth of a fungus, usually on the surface of the evaporator core. The warm, humid environment there is a perfect breeding ground for mildew to develop.

22   The evaporator core on most vehicles is difficult to access, and factory dealerships have a lengthy, expensive process for eliminating the fungus by opening up the evapora-

tor case and using a powerful disinfectant and rinse on the core until the fungus is gone. You can service your own system at home, but it takes something much stronger than basic household germ-killers or deodorizers.

23   Aerosol disinfectants for automotive air conditioning systems are available in most auto parts stores, but remember when shopping for them that the most effective treatments are also the most expensive. The basic procedure for using these sprays is to start by running the system in the RECIRC mode for ten minutes with the blower on its highest speed. Use the highest heat mode to dry out the system and keep the compressor from engaging by disconnecting the wiring connector at the compressor.

24   The disinfectant can usually comes with a long spray hose. Insert the nozzle into an intake port inside the cabin, and spray according to the manufacturer's recommendations **(see illustration)**. Follow the manufacturer's recommendations for the length of spray and waiting time between applications.

25   Once the evaporator has been cleaned, the best way to prevent the mildew from coming back again is to make sure your evaporator housing drain tube is clear **(see illustration 3.1)**.

Automatic heating and air conditioning systems

26   Some vehicles are equipped with an optional automatic climate control system. This system has its own computer that receives inputs from various sensors in the heating and air conditioning system. This computer, like the PCM, has self-diagnostic capabilities to help pinpoint problems or faults within the system. Vehicles equipped with automatic heating and air conditioning systems are very complex and considered beyond the scope of the home mechanic. Vehicles equipped with automatic heating and air conditioning systems should be taken to dealer service department or other qualified facility for repair.

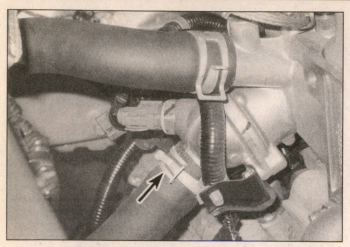

4.9 Use pliers to squeeze the coolant hose clamp and slide the clamp away from the thermostat housing

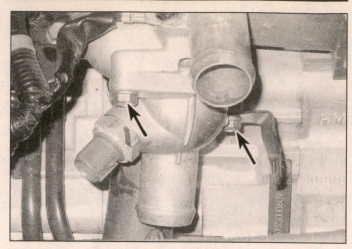

4.11 Location of the thermostat housing cover bolts - 1.7L engine shown, others similar

4   Thermostat - check and replacement

Warning: *Do not remove the radiator cap, drain the coolant or replace the thermostat until the engine has cooled completely.*

Check

1   Before assuming the thermostat is to blame for a cooling system problem, check the coolant level, drivebelt tension (DOHC engines only, see Chapter 1) and temperature gauge operation.

2   If the engine seems to be taking a long time to warm up, based on heater output or temperature gauge operation, the thermostat is probably stuck open. Replace the thermostat with a new one.

3   If the engine runs hot, use your hand to check the temperature of the lower radiator hose. If the hose isn't hot, but the engine is, the thermostat is probably stuck closed, preventing the coolant inside the engine from escaping to the radiator. Replace the thermostat. **Caution:** *Don't drive the vehicle without a thermostat. The computer may stay in open loop and emissions and fuel economy will suffer.*

4   If the lower radiator hose is hot, it means that the coolant is flowing and the thermostat is open. Consult the *Troubleshooting* Section at the front of this manual for cooling system diagnosis.

Replacement

Refer to illustrations 4.9, 4.11, 4.12 and 4.14

5   Disconnect the cable from the negative battery terminal (see Chapter 5).

6   Drain the cooling system (see Chapter 1). If the coolant is relatively new or in good condition, save it and reuse it. Read the **Warning** in Section 1.

7   If you're working on a CR-V or Hatchback, access to the thermostat is from the underside of the engine compartment. Raise the front of the vehicle and support it securely on jackstands, then remove the under-vehicle splash shield.

8   Follow the lower radiator hose to the engine to locate the thermostat housing cover.

9   Loosen the hose clamp, then detach the hose from the fitting **(see illustration)**. If it's stuck, grasp it near the end with a pair of adjustable pliers and twist it to break the seal, then pull it off. If the hose is old or deteriorated, cut it off and install a new one.

10   If the outer surface of the large fitting that mates with the hose is deteriorated (corroded, pitted, etc.), it may be damaged further by hose removal. If it is, the thermostat housing cover will have to be replaced.

11   Remove the thermostat cover bolts **(see illustration)** and detach the housing cover. If the cover is stuck, tap it with a soft-face hammer to jar it loose. Be prepared for some coolant to spill as the gasket seal is broken.

12   On coupe and sedan models, note how it's installed - with the jiggle pin up - then remove the thermostat **(see illustration)**.

Note: *The thermostat on CR-V and hatchback models is an integral component of the thermostat cover. Replace the cover and thermostat as one complete assembly.*

13   Remove all traces of old gasket material and/or sealant from the housing and cover.

14   On coupe and sedan models, install a new rubber seal over the thermostat **(see illustration)**. Make sure the cutout is aligned correctly with the jiggle valve. **Note:** *On CR-V and hatchback models, install a new O-ring into the housing before installation.*

15   On coupe and sedan models, install the new thermostat in the housing without using sealant. Make sure the jiggle pin is at the top and the spring end is directed into the engine **(see illustration 3.12)**. **Note:** *On CR-V and hatchback models, the thermostat is positioned correctly by the manufacturer. Make sure the mating surfaces on the thermostat housing are perfectly clean to insure a tight seal before installing the thermostat assembly.*

16   Install the thermostat housing (coupes and sedans) or the thermostat assembly

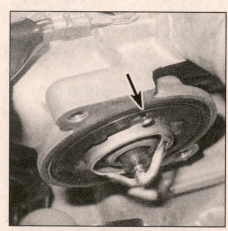

4.12 Note the location of the jiggle valve (it should be at the top) - 1.7L engine shown, others similar

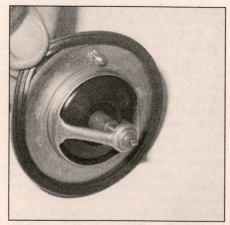

4.14 Install a new rubber seal over the thermostat

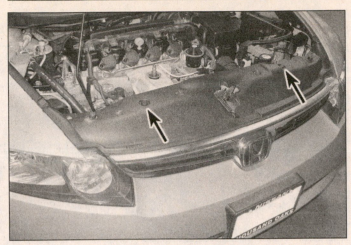

5.3 Radiator cover mounting fasteners

5.5 Disconnect the radiator fan electrical connector and remove the harness from the fan shroud bracket

(CR-V and hatchbacks) and bolts. Tighten the bolts to the torque listed in this Chapter's Specifications.

17   Reattach the hose and tighten the hose clamp securely. Install all components that were removed for access.

18   Refill the cooling system (see Chapter 1).

19   Reconnect the battery (see Chapter 5).

20   Start the engine and allow it to reach normal operating temperature, then check for leaks and proper thermostat operation (as described in Steps 2 through 4).

---

5   Engine cooling fans and switch - replacement

Warning: *To avoid possible injury or damage, DO NOT operate the engine with a damaged fan. Do not attempt to repair fan blades - replace a damaged fan with a new one.*
Note: *All air-conditioned models have two complete fan circuits - one for the condenser*

fan and one for the radiator fan. The following procedures apply to both.

Cooling fans

Refer to illustrations 5.3, 5.5, 5.8a, 5.8b, 5.9, 5.10a, 5.10b, 5.11 and 5.12

Warning: *Wait until the engine is completely cool before beginning this procedure.*

1   Disconnect the cable from the negative battery terminal (see Chapter 5).

2   Set the parking brake and block the rear wheels to prevent the vehicle from rolling. Raise the front of the vehicle and support it securely with jackstands. Remove the lower splash pan, if equipped, from under the radiator (see Chapter 2A).

3   Remove the radiator support cover push pins and remove the cover **(see illustration)**. **Note:** *On 2005 and earlier coupes and sedans, the radiator support cover is an integral component of the front bumper cover (see Chapter 11). If you're just removing the radiator fan (not the condenser fan) from a sedan or coupe model, the bumper cover does not*

have to be removed. The radiator support cover on other models can be removed separately by removing the pushpins.

4   Drain the cooling system (see Chapter 1). If the coolant is relatively new or in good condition, save it and reuse it. Read the **Warning** in Section 1.

5   Remove the wiring harness clamp and position the harness off to the side **(see illustration)**.

6   On 2006 and later Civic models, remove the battery and the battery tray, and position the wiring harness off to the side (see Chapter 5).

7   Disconnect the fan wiring connectors located near the top of the cooling fan shroud. On 2006 and later Civics and 2007 and later CR-Vs, remove the radiator crossmember.

8   Remove the upper and lower radiator hoses. Loosen the hose clamps, then detach the radiator hoses from the fittings **(see illustrations)**. If they're stuck, grasp each hose near the end with a pair of slip-joint pliers and twist it to break the seal, then pull it off - be

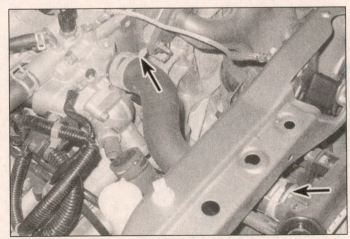

5.8a Use pliers to squeeze the hose clamps and slide the clamps off the inlet housing (neck) of the radiator and the coolant housing on the engine block

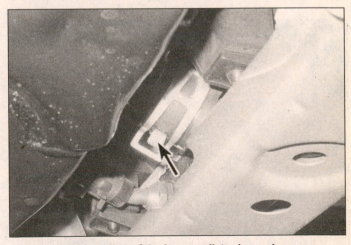

5.8b Location of the lower radiator hose clamp

5.9 Location of the radiator fan mounting bolts (condenser fan similar)

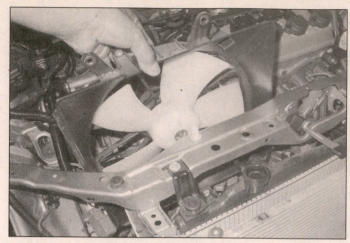

5.10a Lift the radiator fan from the engine compartment - sedan model shown

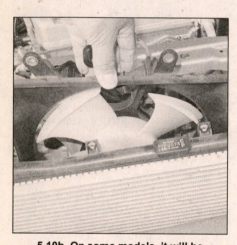

5.10b On some models, it will be necessary to remove the radiator and condenser brackets and angle the radiator and condenser toward the front of the vehicle to lift the condenser fan out of the engine compartment

careful not to damage the radiator fittings! If the hoses are old or deteriorated, cut them off and install new ones. Also disconnect the small hose to the coolant reservoir. **Note:** *If you're just removing the radiator fan (not the condenser fan) from a sedan or coupe model, the lower radiator hose does not have to be removed.*

9   Unbolt the engine cooling fan(s) from the radiator at the top **(see illustration)**.

10   Carefully lift the fan out of the engine compartment **(see illustration)**. **Note:** *On some models, it will be necessary to remove the radiator and condenser brackets (see Section 7) and tilt the radiator slightly to remove one of the cooling fans* **(see illustration)**.

11   To detach the fan from the motor, remove the motor shaft nut **(see illustration)**. **Note:** *On 2006 and later Civic models, the condenser fan does not have a replaceable fan blade or motor and must be replaced as an assembly.*

12   To detach the fan motor from the shroud, remove the mounting screws **(see illustration)**.

13   Installation is the reverse of removal.

14   Refill the cooling system (see Chapter 1).

15   Reconnect the battery (see Chapter 5).

Cooling fan switch

Warning: *Wait until the engine is completely cool before beginning this procedure.*

16   Drain the cooling system (see Chapter 1).

17   If you're working on a 1.8L, 2.0L or 2.4L engine, raise the front of the vehicle and support it securely on jackstands. Remove the splash shield from under the engine compartment.

18   Disconnect the electrical connector, then unscrew the switch from the thermostat housing cover (1.7L engine) or from the radiator (1.8L, 2.0L and 2.4L engines).

19   Installation is the reverse of removal, noting the following points:

a) *Use a new sealing ring when installing the switch.*

b) *Refill the cooling system (see Chapter 1).*

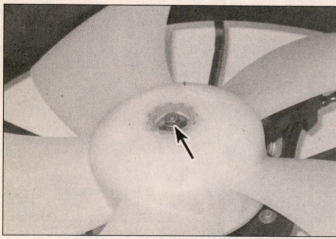

5.11 To remove the fan, unscrew the nut in the center, then pull the fan blade from the motor shaft

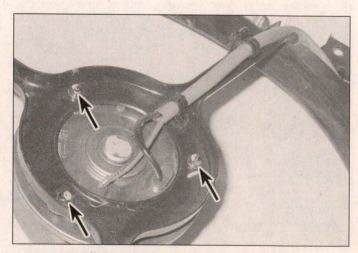

5.12 Engine cooling fan motor mounting screws

6.3 Coolant reservoir mounting fasteners

7.5a Location of the transaxle cooling hose on the right side of the radiator . . .

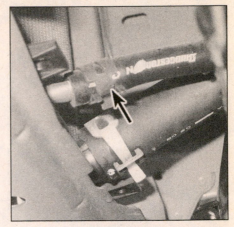

7.5b . . . and the left side of the radiator

c) *Start the engine and allow it to reach normal operating temperature, then verify proper operation of the fans.*

6 Coolant reservoir - removal and installation

Refer to illustration 6.3

Warning: *Wait until the engine is completely cool before beginning this procedure.*

1   Disconnect the reservoir hose from the radiator filler neck. Plug the hose to prevent leakage.

2   On 2006 and later models, remove the radiator support cover push pins and remove the cover **(see illustration 5.3)**. **Note:** *On some models it is necessary to remove the battery for access to the reservoir (see Chapter 5).*

3   Remove the mounting fasteners **(see illustration)**.

4   Lift the reservoir out of the engine compartment.

5   Clean out the tank with soapy water and a brush to remove any deposits inside. Inspect the reservoir carefully for cracks. If you find a crack, replace the reservoir.

6   Installation is the reverse of removal.

7 Radiator - removal and installation

Warning: *Wait until the engine is completely cool before beginning this procedure.*

Removal

Refer to illustrations 7.5a, 7.5b, 7.6, 7.7 and 7.11

1   Disconnect the cable from the negative

battery terminal (see Chapter 5).

2   Set the parking brake and block the rear wheels. Raise the front of the vehicle and support it securely on jackstands. Remove the splash shield beneath the radiator.

3   Drain the cooling system (see Chapter 1). If the coolant is relatively new or in good condition, save it and reuse it. Read the **Warning** in Section 1.

4   Remove the engine cooling fans (see Section 5).

5   On automatic transaxle models, disconnect the transaxle fluid cooling lines from the bottom of the radiator **(see illustrations)**.

6   On 2006 and later Civic models and 2007 CR-V models, remove the front grille plastic pushpins, radiator brackets, hood latch (see Chapter 11), radiator cap and the radiator support **(see illustration)**.

7   Remove the radiator brackets **(see illustration)**.

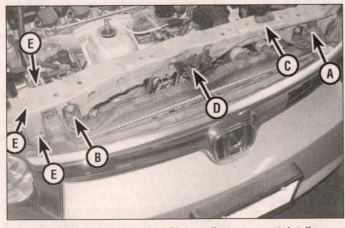

7.6 Typical 2006 and later Civic radiator support details

A   *Front grille plastic pushpins (left side shown right side the same)*
B   *Radiator mounting bracket (right side shown left side the same)*
C   *Radiator filler neck mounting fasteners*
D   *Hood latch assembly*
E   *Radiator support mounting bolts (right side shown left side the same)*

7.7 Radiator mounting bracket bolts (early model shown)

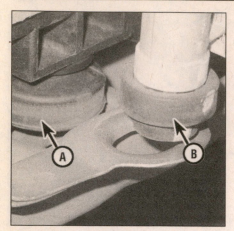

7.11 Location of the radiator (A) and the condenser (B) rubber mounts

8.7 Hold the water pump pulley and remove the mounting bolts

9.1 The Engine Coolant Temperature (ECT) sensor is mounted on the coolant passage housing on coupes and sedans

8   Carefully lift out the radiator. Don't spill coolant on the vehicle or scratch the paint.

9   Inspect the radiator for leaks and damage. If it needs repair, have a radiator shop or dealer service department perform the work as special techniques are required.

10   Bugs and dirt can be removed from the radiator by spraying with a garden hose nozzle from the back side. The radiator should be flushed out with a garden hose before reinstallation.

11   Check the radiator mounts **(see illustration)** for deterioration and replace if necessary.

Installation

12   Installation is the reverse of the removal procedure. Guide the radiator into the mounts until they seat properly.

13   After installation, fill the cooling system with the proper mixture of antifreeze and water (see Chapter 1).

14   Reconnect the battery (see Chapter 5).

15   Start the engine and check for leaks. Allow the engine to reach normal operating temperature, indicated by the upper radiator hose becoming hot. Recheck the coolant level and add more if required.

16   Check and add transaxle fluid as needed.

8   Water pump - replacement

Warning: *Wait until the engine is completely cool before beginning this procedure.*

1   Disconnect the cable from the negative battery terminal (see Chapter 5).

2   Drain the cooling system (see Chapter 1). If the coolant is relatively new or in good condition, save it and reuse it. Read the **Warning** in Section 1.

3   Remove the drivebelts (see Chapter 1).

1.7L engines

4   Remove the timing belt and the timing belt tensioner (see Chapter 2A).

5   Remove the bolts and detach the water pump from the engine. Check the impeller on the backside for evidence of corrosion or missing fins.

1.8L, 2.0L and 2.4L engines

Refer to illustration 8.7

6   Remove the drivebelt tensioner (see Chapter 1).

7   On 1.8L engines, remove the water pump pulley bolts and pulley **(see Illustration)**.

8   Remove the crankshaft pulley (see Chapter 2B).

9   Remove the bolts and detach the water pump from the engine. Check the impeller on the backside for evidence of corrosion or missing fins.

All models

10   Clean the bolt threads and the threaded holes in the engine to remove corrosion and sealant.

11   Compare the new pump to the old one to make sure they're identical.

12   Remove all traces of old gasket sealant and O-ring from the engine.

13   Clean the engine and new water pump mating surfaces with brake system cleaner.

14   Apply a thin layer of RTV sealant to the O-ring groove of the new pump, then carefully set a new O-ring in the groove.

15   Carefully attach the pump to the engine and thread the bolts into the holes finger tight. Use a small amount of RTV sealant on the bolt threads, and make sure that the dowel pins are in their original locations.

16   Tighten the bolts, a little at a time, to the torque listed in this Chapter's Specifications. Don't overtighten the bolts or the pump may be distorted.

17   Reinstall all parts removed for access to the pump.

18   Refill the cooling system and check the drivebelt tension (see Chapter 1).

19   Reconnect the battery (see Chapter 5). Run the engine and check for leaks.

9   Coolant temperature sending unit - check and replacement

Refer to illustration 9.1

Warning: *Wait until the engine is completely cool before beginning this procedure.*

1   The coolant temperature indicator system consists of a warning light or a temperature gauge on the dash and a coolant temperature sending unit mounted on the engine **(see illustration)**. On the models covered by this manual, the Engine Coolant Temperature (ECT) sensor, which is an information sensor for the Powertrain Control Module (PCM), also functions as the coolant temperature sending unit.

2   If an overheating indication occurs, check the coolant level in the system and then make sure all connectors in the wiring harness between the sending unit and the indicator light or gauge are tight.

3   When the ignition switch is turned to START and the starter motor is turning, the indicator light (if equipped) should come on. This doesn't mean the engine is overheated; it just means that the bulb is good.

4   If the light doesn't come on when the ignition key is turned to START, the bulb might be burned out, the ignition switch might be faulty or the circuit might be open.

5   As soon as the engine starts, the indicator light should go out and remain off, unless the engine overheats. If the light doesn't go out, the wire between the sending unit and the light could be grounded; the sending unit might be defective (in which case a trouble code will most likely have been set, illuminating the CHECK ENGINE light on the instrument panel - see Chapter 6); or the ignition switch might be faulty (see Chapter 12). Check the coolant to make sure it's correctly mixed; plain water, with no antifreeze, or coolant that's mainly water, might have too low a boiling point to activate the sending unit (see Chapter 1).

6   See Chapter 6 for the replacement procedure.

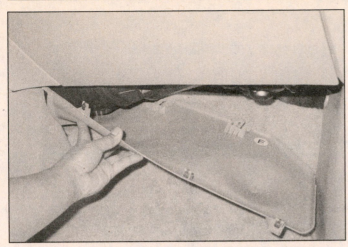

10.2 To remove the lower dash panel, pull it straight down to disengage the retaining clips

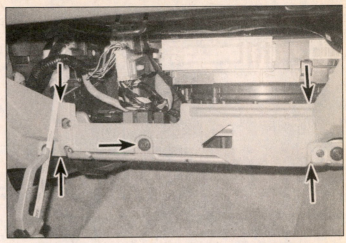

10.4 Cut off the piece of plastic where indicated using a hacksaw or panel cutters, remove the single retaining bolt and discard the plastic (the absence of this plastic cross brace will not weaken the structure)

---

10   Blower motor power transistor and blower motor - replacement

Warning: *The models covered by this manual are equipped with Supplemental Restraint Systems (SRS), more commonly known as airbags. Always disable the airbag system before working in the vicinity of any airbag system component to avoid the possibility of accidental deployment of the airbag, which could cause personal injury (see Chapter 12).*

Blower motor power transistor

Refer to illustrations 10.2, 10.4, 10.5 and 10.7

1   Disconnect the cable from the negative battery terminal (see Chapter 5).
2   Working in the passenger compartment under the glove box, remove the lower dash panel **(see illustration)**.
3   Remove the right side kick panel and the glove box (see Chapter 11).

4   Remove the plastic cross brace from the dash frame structure **(see illustration)**.
5   Detach the relay bracket from the metal cross brace, then remove the cross brace from the dash frame structure **(see illustration)**.
6   Remove the PCM (see Chapter 6).
7   Disconnect the electrical connector from the blower motor power transistor **(see illustration)**.
8   Remove the blower motor power transistor mounting screws and remove it from the blower housing.
9   Installation is the reverse of removal.
10   Reconnect the battery (see Chapter 5).

Blower motor

11   Perform Steps 1 through 6 of this Section.
12   Disconnect the electrical connector from the blower motor **(see illustration 10.7)**.
13   Remove the blower motor mounting

screws and then remove the blower motor assembly.
14   Remove the blower motor circlip and remove the blower fan from the motor.
15   Installation is the reverse of removal.
16   Reconnect the battery (see Chapter 5).

---

11   Heater/air conditioning control assembly - removal and installation

Refer to illustrations 11.3a, 11.3b, 11.5a, 11.5b and 11.5c

Warning: *The models covered by this manual are equipped with Supplemental Restraint Systems (SRS), more commonly known as airbags. Always disable the airbag system before working in the vicinity of any airbag system component to avoid the possibility of accidental deployment of the airbag, which*

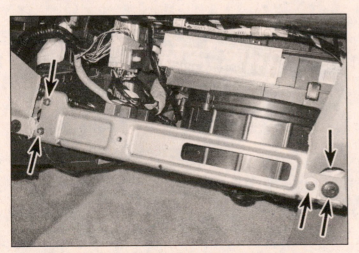

10.5 Remove the metal cross brace mounting screws

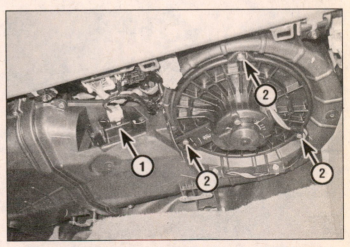

10.7 Location of the power transistor (1) and the blower fan mounting screws (2) - sedan model shown

11.3a Disconnect the electrical connectors from the blower motor and mode control switches . . .

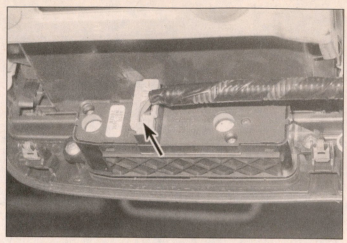

11.3b . . . and the air conditioning selection switch

could cause personal injury (see Chapter 12).

1   Disconnect the cable from the negative battery terminal (see Chapter 5).

Civic models

2   Remove the dashboard center trim panel far enough to access the electrical connectors (see Chapter 11).

3   Disconnect the electrical connectors from the blower motor switch, mode control switch and the temperature control module **(see illustrations)**.

4   Pull the knobs off of the front of the unit.

5   Remove the heater/air conditioner control assembly retaining screws **(see illustrations)**.

6   Installation is the reverse of removal.

7   Reconnect the battery (see Chapter 5).

CR-V models

2006 and earlier models

8   Remove the dashboard center trim panel (see Chapter 11).

9   Remove the screws and detach the control unit from the instrument panel, then disconnect the electrical connector.

10   Installation is the reverse of removal.

11   Reconnect the battery (see Chapter 5).

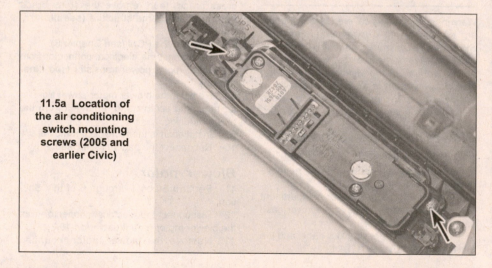

11.5a Location of the air conditioning switch mounting screws (2005 and earlier Civic)

2007 and later models

12   Apply a piece of tape to the trim panel on each side of the control unit to protect it from scratches.

13   Insert a flat-blade screwdriver into the

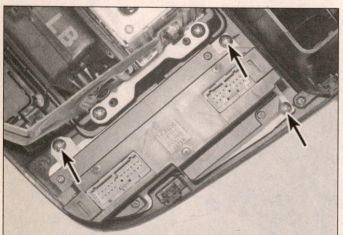

11.5b Location of the blower selection switch mounting screws (2005 and earlier Civic)

11.5c Location of the 2006 and later model HVAC control unit mounting screws (2006 and later Civic)

12.5 Disconnect the heater control valve and rotate the valve to fully OPEN

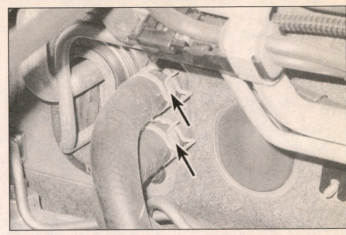

12.6 Disconnect the heater hoses from the heater core inside the engine compartment

notch in each side of the control unit (near the knobs) and carefully pull the unit out of the instrument panel. **Caution:** *Don't use the screwdrivers as prybars, as you could mar the trim panel.*

14   Disconnect the electrical connector.
15   Installation is the reverse of removal.
16   Reconnect the battery (see Chapter 5).

---

12 Heater core - replacement

Refer to illustrations 12.5, 12.6, 12.8, 12.11, 12.13a, 12.13b, 12.14, 12.15, 12.16a and 12.16b

Warning: *The models covered by this manual are equipped with Supplemental Restraint Systems (SRS), more commonly known as airbags. Always disable the airbag system before working in the vicinity of any airbag system component to avoid the possibility of accidental deployment of the airbag, which could cause personal injury (see Chapter 12).*

Warning: *The air conditioning system is under high pressure. DO NOT loosen any fittings or remove any components until after the system has been discharged. Air conditioning refrigerant must be properly discharged into an EPA-approved container at a dealer service department or an automotive air conditioning repair facility. Always wear eye protection when disconnecting air conditioning system fittings.*

Warning: *Wait until the engine is completely cool before beginning this procedure.*

Note: *The following procedure covers the typical heater core removal for Civics. However, the heater core removal on CR-Vs is similar.*

1   If so equipped, have the air conditioning system discharged by a dealer service department or an automotive air conditioning shop before proceeding (see **Warning** above).
2   Disconnect the cable from the negative battery terminal (see Chapter 5).
3   Drain the cooling system (see Chapter 1).
4   Disconnect the air conditioning evaporator lines at the dash inside the engine compartment.

5   Disconnect the heater control valve cable, if equipped (**see illustration**). **Note:** *Turn the heater valve to the fully open position after the cable has been disconnected.*
6   Disconnect the heater hoses from the heater core inside the engine compartment (**see illustration**).
7   Remove the mounting nut from the heater control valve bracket and position the assembly off to the side.
8   Remove the heater control unit mounting nut on the inside of the engine compartment (**see illustration**), taking care not to damage the fuel or brake lines.
9   On 2005 and earlier models, remove the PCM (see Chapter 6).
10   Remove the instrument panel (see Chapter 11).
11   Disconnect the blower motor and power transistor electrical connectors. Remove the blower assembly mounting bolts (**see illustration**) and remove the assembly from the vehicle.
12   Remove the evaporator drain.

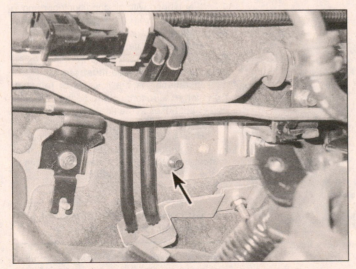

12.8 Working on the inside of the engine compartment, remove the heater control unit mounting nut

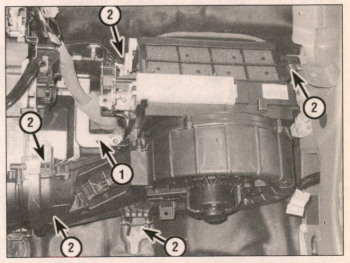

12.11 First remove the bolts from the brace (1) and next, remove the blower unit mounting bolts (2)

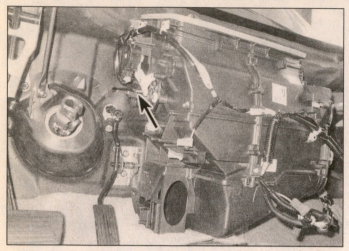

12.13a Disconnect the heater control cable from the heater/air conditioning unit . . .

12.13b . . . then remove the mounting bolts

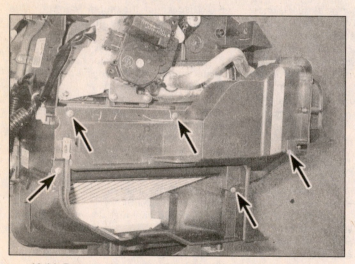

12.14 Remove the screws from the expansion valve cover

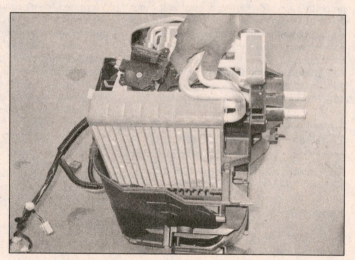

12.15 Lift the evaporator from the heater/air conditioning unit

13   Disconnect the electrical connectors or heater control cable from the heater/air conditioning unit, if equipped **(see illustration)**, remove the mounting bolts **(see illustration)** and lift the heater/air conditioning unit from the vehicle.

14   Remove the heater core cover **(see illustration)**.

15   If equipped with air conditioning, remove the evaporator from the heater/air conditioning unit **(see illustration)**.

16   Remove the flange cover **(see illustration)** and lift the heater cover from the heater/air conditioning unit **(see illustration)**.

17   Installation is the reverse of removal. Don't forget to reconnect the heater core inlet and outlet hoses at the firewall.

18   Reconnect the battery (see Chapter 5).

19   Refill the cooling system (see Chapter 1).

20   If equipped, have the air conditioning system evacuated, leak tested and recharged by the shop that discharged it.

13   Air conditioning compressor - removal and installation

Warning: *The air conditioning system is under high pressure. Do not loosen any hose fittings or remove any components until after the sys-*

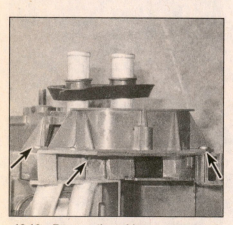

12.16a Remove the rubber grommet and the flange cover mounting screws and separate the flange cover from the heater/AC unit

12.16b Lift the heater core from the heater/AC unit

13.9 Location of the compressor clutch electrical connector

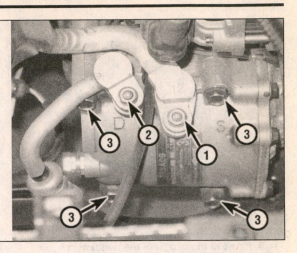

13.10 Air conditioning compressor mounting details

1   Suction line (Low side)
2   Discharge line
    (High side)
3   Compressor mounting bolts

tem has been discharged. Air conditioning refrigerant must be properly discharged into an EPA-approved recovery/recycling unit at a dealer service department or an automotive air conditioning repair facility. Always wear eye protection when disconnecting air conditioning system fittings.

Caution: *When replacing entire components, additional refrigerant oil should be added equal to the amount that is removed with the component being replaced. Be sure to read the can before adding any oil to the system, to make sure it is compatible with the R-134a system.*

Note: *The receiver-drier should be replaced whenever the compressor is replaced.*

Removal

Refer to illustrations 13.9 and 13.10

1   Have the air conditioning system refrigerant discharged and recovered by an air conditioning technician.
2   Disconnect the cable from the negative battery terminal (see Chapter 5).
3   Set the parking brake, block the rear wheels and raise the front of the vehicle, supporting it securely on jackstands.
4   Remove the radiator cover **(see illustration 5.3)** and drivebelt (see Chapter 1).
5   On coupe, sedan and hatchback models, remove the condenser fan (see Section 5).
6   On all except 2007 and later CR-V models, remove the alternator (see Chapter 5).
7   Remove the splash shield from under the engine compartment (see Chapter 2A).
8   On 2006 and earlier CR-V models, remove the coolant reservoir (see Section 5).
9   Disconnect the compressor clutch wiring harness **(see illustration)**.
10 Disconnect the refrigerant lines from the compressor. Plug the open fittings to prevent entry of dirt and moisture **(see illustration)**.
11 Remove the compressor mounting bolts.
12 Carefully guide the compressor through the opening below the engine compartment.

Installation

13 The clutch may have to be transferred from the old compressor to the new unit.

2005 and earlier Civics and 2006 and earlier CR-Vs

Note: *2006 and later Civics and 2007 and later CR-Vs do not require oil volume adjustment when installing a new compressor. This applies to compressors supplied by Honda. Be sure to follow any specific instructions that come with a replacement compressor.*

14 Adjust the amount of refrigerant oil in the new compressor using the following calculations:
a) Drain the refrigerant oil from the old compressor through the suction fitting and measure it in ounces.
b) Subtract this number from 4-1/3 ounces.
c) The difference between these two figures is equal to the amount you should drain from the new compressor. **Caution:** *Even if no oil came out of the old compressor, don't drain more than 1-2/3 ounces from the new one.*

All models

15 Installation is the reverse of removal, using new O-rings where the line fittings attach to the compressor.
16 Have the system evacuated, recharged and leak tested by an air conditioning technician.
17 Reconnect the battery (see Chapter 5).

14 Air conditioning receiver-drier - removal and installation

Warning: *The air conditioning system is under high pressure. Do not loosen any hose fittings or remove any components until after the system has been discharged. Air conditioning refrigerant must be properly discharged into an EPA-approved recovery/recycling unit at a dealer service department or an automotive air conditioning repair facility. Always wear eye protection when disconnecting air conditioning system fittings.*

Caution: *When replacing entire components, additional refrigerant oil should be added equal to the amount that is removed with the component being replaced. Be sure to read the can before adding any oil to the system,*

to make sure it is compatible with the R-134a system.

1   Have the refrigerant discharged and recovered by an air conditioning technician.
2   Disconnect the cable from the negative battery terminal (see Chapter 5).

2005 and earlier Civic models

Refer to illustration 14.3

3   Remove the air conditioning lines from the receiver-drier **(see illustration)**.
4   Disconnect the electrical connector.
5   Remove the bracket bolts from the receiver-drier.
6   Remove the receiver-drier from the engine compartment.
7   Installation is the reverse of removal. Be sure to install new O-rings onto the air conditioning lines.

2006 and later Civic and all CR-V models

Refer to illustrations 14.9, 14.10 and 14.11

8   Remove the condenser (see Section 15).

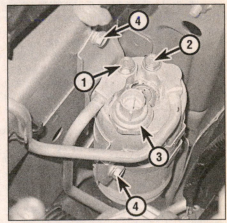

14.3 Receiver-drier mounting details (2005 and earlier Civic models)

1   Air conditioning line to condenser
2   Air conditioning line from compressor
3   Air conditioning pressure switch
4   Mounting bracket and bolts

14.9 Remove the cap from the condenser

14.10 Remove the filter from the condenser

14.11 Use pliers to remove the desiccant from the condenser

9 Remove the cap from the condenser **(see illustration)**.
10 Remove the filter from the condenser **(see illustration)**.
11 Remove the receiver-drier desiccant **(see illustration)**.
12 Installation is the reverse of removal. Be sure to install new O-rings onto the receiver-drier cap. Apply a thin film of refrigerant oil to the desiccant before installing it. Also lubricate the O-rings with refrigerant oil. If refrigerant oil must be replaced, add it to the condenser (see Section 15).

All models

13 Reconnect the battery (see Chapter 5).
14 Have the system evacuated, charged and leak tested by an air conditioning technician.

15 Air conditioning condenser - removal and installation

Warning: *The air conditioning system is under high pressure. Do not loosen any hose fittings or remove any components until after the system has been discharged. Air conditioning refrigerant must be properly discharged into an EPA-approved recovery/recycling unit at a dealer service department or an automotive air conditioning repair facility. Always wear eye protection when disconnecting air conditioning system fittings.*
Caution: *When replacing entire components, additional refrigerant oil should be added equal to the amount that is removed with the component being replaced. Be sure to read the can before adding any oil to the system, to make sure it is compatible with the R-134a system.*

Removal

Refer to illustration 15.4

1 Have the refrigerant discharged and recovered by an air conditioning technician.
2 Disconnect the cable from the negative

battery terminal (see Chapter 5).
3 Remove the front bumper (see Chapter 11).
4 Remove the condenser brackets **(see illustration)** and on CR-V models, remove the upper radiator mount brackets.
5 Disconnect the condenser line and discharge line from the condenser. Cap the fittings on the condenser and lines to prevent entry of dirt or moisture.
6 Remove the condenser by lifting it from its lower mounts.

Installation

7 Installation is the reverse of removal. Assemble all connections with new O-rings, lightly lubricated with R-134a refrigerant oil. If a new condenser was installed, add the proper amount of fresh refrigerant oil to it.
2005 and earlier Civic/2006 and earlier CR-V: 5/6-ounce
2006 and later Civic/2007 and later CR-V: 1-2/3 ounce
8 Reconnect the battery (see Chapter 5).
9 Have the system evacuated, charged and leak tested by an air conditioning technician.

16 Air conditioning pressure switch - replacement

Warning: *The air conditioning system is under high pressure. Do not loosen any hose fittings or remove any components until after the system has been discharged. Air conditioning refrigerant must be properly discharged into an EPA-approved recovery/recycling unit at a dealer service department or an automotive air conditioning repair facility. Always wear eye protection when disconnecting air conditioning system fittings.*
Note: *2006 and earlier sedans, coupes and hatchbacks are equipped with an A/C pressure switch mounted on the receiver-drier. All CR-V models and 2006 and later Civics are equipped with a receiver-drier mounted integrally with the condenser; the A/C pressure*

switch is mounted in the A/C line going from the condenser to the evaporator.
Note: *The air conditioning pressure switch detects low (28 psi) and high (455 psi) refrigerant line pressure and shuts the system off if the pressure drops below or exceeds these values.*
1 Have the refrigerant discharged and recovered by an air conditioning technician.
2 Unplug the electrical connector from the air conditioning pressure switch **(see illustration 14.3)**.
3 Unscrew the pressure switch from the receiver-drier (2005 and earlier Civic models) or the refrigerant line (CR-V and 2006 and later Civic models). On CR-V and 2006 and later Civic models, be sure to hold the stationary fitting on the line with an open-end wrench to prevent damaging the line.
4 Lubricate the sensor O-ring with clean refrigerant oil of the correct type.
5 Screw the new sensor onto the refrigerant line or receiver-drier until hand tight, then tighten it securely.
6 Reconnect the electrical connector.
7 Have the system evacuated, charged and leak tested by an air conditioning technician.

15.4 Condenser bracket and mounting bolt (left side shown)

Chapter 4
Fuel and exhaust systems

Contents

	Section		Section
Accelerator cable - removal, installation and adjustment	12	Fuel pulsation damper - removal and installation	14
Air filter housing - removal and installation	11	Fuel pump/fuel filter/fuel gauge sending unit module -	
CHECK ENGINE light on	See Chapter 6	replacement	9
Electronic throttle components (2005 and 2006 CR-V) -		Fuel pump/fuel gauge sending unit module - removal	
replacement	16	and installation	7
Exhaust system servicing - general information	6	Fuel rail and injectors - removal and installation	15
Fuel lines and fitttings - general information and disconnection	5	Fuel tank - removal and installation	10
Fuel pressure - check	4	General information	1
Fuel pressure regulator - replacement	8	Throttle body - removal and installation	13
Fuel pressure relief procedure	3	Troubleshooting	2

Specifications

Accelerator cable deflection	3/8 to 1/2 inch (10 to 12 mm)
Fuel system pressure	
1.7L engine	40 to 47 psi
1.8L engine :	55 to 63 psi
2.0L engine	
2002 to 2005 models	47 to 52 psi
2006 and later models	48 to 55 psi
2.4L engine	47 to 54 psi

Torque specifications

	Ft-lbs (unless otherwise indicated)	Nm

Note: *One foot-pound (ft-lb) of torque is equivalent to 12 inch-pounds (in-lbs) of torque. Torque values below approximately 15 ft-lbs are expressed in inch-pounds, since most foot-pound torque wrenches are not accurate at these smaller values.*

	Ft-lbs	Nm
Throttle body mounting bolts/nuts (all models)	192 in-lbs	21.5
Fuel rail mounting nuts		
1.7L engine	105 in-lbs	12
1.8L engine	84 in-lbs	9.5
2.0L and 2.4L engines	192 in-lbs	21.5

2.2a On 2005 and earlier Civic/2006 and earlier CR-V models, the PGM-FI no. 2 relay is located on a bracket behind the glove box (either above or below the PCM, depending on model)

A   PGM-FI relay no. 2
B   PGM-FI relay no. 1
C   Automatic transaxle reverse relay

2.2b On 2006 and later Civic/2007 and later CR-V, the PGM-FI no. 2 relay is located at the top of the interior fuse/relay box. Remove the driver's knee bolster for access (on some models it might be necessary to unbolt the fuse/relay box and lower it)

1   General information

Fuel system warnings

Gasoline is extremely flammable and repairing fuel system components can be dangerous. Consider your automotive repair knowledge and experience before attempting repairs which may be better suited for a professional mechanic.

- *Don't smoke or allow open flames or bare light bulbs near the work area*
- *Don't work in a garage with a gas-type appliance (water heater, clothes dryer)*
- *Use fuel-resistant gloves. If any fuel spills on your skin, wash it off immediately with soap and water*
- *Clean up spills immediately*
- *Do not store fuel-soaked rags where they could ignite*
- *Prior to disconnecting any fuel line, you must relieve the fuel pressure (see Section 3)*
- *Wear safety glasses*
- *Have a proper fire extinguisher on hand*

Fuel system

The fuel system consists of the fuel tank, electric fuel pump/fuel level sending unit (located in the fuel tank), fuel rail and fuel injectors. The fuel injection system is a multi-port system; multi-port fuel injection uses timed impulses to inject the fuel directly into the intake port of each cylinder. The Powertrain Control Module (PCM) controls the injectors. The PCM monitors various engine parameters and delivers the exact amount of fuel required into the intake ports.

Fuel is circulated from the fuel pump to the fuel rail through fuel lines running along the underside of the vehicle. Various sections of the fuel line are either rigid metal or nylon, or flexible fuel hose. The various sections of the fuel hose are connected either by quick-connect fittings or threaded metal fittings.

Exhaust system

The exhaust system consists of the exhaust manifold(s), catalytic converter(s), muffler(s), tailpipe and all connecting pipes, flanges and clamps. The catalytic converters are an emission control device added to the exhaust system to reduce pollutants.

2   Troubleshooting

Fuel pump

Refer to illustrations 2.2a and 2.2b

1   The fuel pump is located inside the fuel tank. Sit inside the vehicle with the windows closed, turn the ignition key to ON (not START) and listen for the sound of the fuel pump as it's briefly activated. You will only hear the sound for a second or two, but that sound tells you that the pump is working. Alternatively, have an assistant listen at the fuel filler cap.

2   If the pump does not come on, check the fuel pump fuse (fuse no. 17 in the interior fuse box on 2005 and earlier Civic models and 2006 and earlier CR-V models, and fuse no. 2 in the interior fuse box on 2006 and later Civic models and 2007 and later CR-V models) and the PGM-FI relay no. 2. On 2005 and earlier Civic models and 2006 and earlier CR-V models, the relay is located behind the glove box, near the PCM, attached to a bracket **(see illustration)**. On 2006 and

later Civic models and 2007 and later CR-V models, the relay is located at the top of the interior fuse/relay box **(see illustration)**. If the fuse and relay are okay, check the wiring back to the fuel pump. If the fuse, relay and wiring are okay, the fuel pump is probably defective. If the pump runs continuously with the ignition key in the ON position, the Powertrain Control Module (PCM) is probably defective. Have the PCM checked by a professional mechanic.

Fuel injection system

Refer to illustration 2.9

Note: *The following procedure is based on the assumption that the fuel pump is working and the fuel pressure is adequate (see Section 4).*

3   Check all electrical connectors that are related to the system. Check the ground wire connections for tightness.

4   Verify that the battery is fully charged (see Chapter 5).

5   Inspect the air filter element (see Chapter 1).

6   Check all fuses related to the fuel system (see Chapter 12).

7   Check the air induction system between the throttle body and the intake manifold for air leaks. Also inspect the condition of all vacuum hoses connected to the intake manifold and to the throttle body.

8   Remove the air intake duct from the throttle body and look for dirt, carbon, varnish, or other residue in the throttle body, particularly around the throttle plate. If it's dirty, clean it with carb cleaner, a toothbrush and a clean shop towel.

9   With the engine running, place an automotive stethoscope against each injector, one at a time, and listen for a clicking sound that indicates operation **(see illustration)**. **Warning:** *Stay clear of the drivebelt and any rotat-*

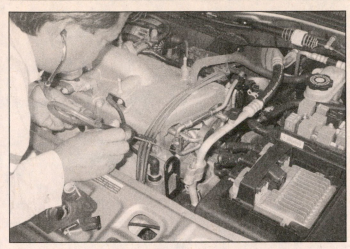

2.9 An automotive stethoscope is used to listen to the fuel injectors in operation

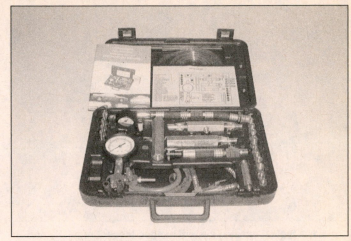

4.1a This fuel pressure testing kit contains all the necessary fittings and adapters, along with the fuel pressure gauge, to test most automotive systems

4.1b Disconnect the fuel supply hose quick-connect fitting (arrow) from the fuel rail pipe, then attach the fuel pressure gauge setup to the fuel line and fuel rail fitting (2007 Civic shown)

ing or hot components.

10   If you can hear the injectors operating, but the engine is misfiring, the electrical circuits are functioning correctly, but the injectors might be dirty or clogged. Try a commercial injector cleaning product (available at auto parts stores). If cleaning the injectors doesn't help, replace the injectors.

11   If an injector is not operating (it makes no sound), disconnect the injector electrical connector and measure the resistance across the injector terminals with an ohmmeter. Compare this measurement to the other injectors. If the resistance of the non-operational injector is quite different from the other injectors, replace it.

12   If the injector is not operating, but the resistance reading is within the range of resistance of the other injectors, the PCM or the circuit between the PCM and the injector might be faulty.

3   Fuel pressure relief procedure

1   Locate the PGM-FI main relay No. 2 **(see illustrations 2.2a and 2.2b)**, then remove/unplug it.

2   Start the engine and allow it to die. The fuel pressure is now relieved, but there is still fuel in the lines, so be sure to have shop rags handy to mop up any spilled fuel when disconnecting fuel lines. **Note:** *If the Malfunction Indicator Light (Check Engine light) on the instrument cluster comes on while you're cranking the engine, ignore it. If the light remains on after reconnecting the battery, erase the code as described in Chapter 6, Section 3.*

3   Remove the fuel filler neck cap to relieve the pressure inside the fuel tank.

4   Disconnect the cable from the negative terminal of the battery (see Chapter 5). It's now safe to work on the fuel system.

4   Fuel pressure - check

Refer to illustrations 4.1a and 4.1b

Warning: *Gasoline is extremely flammable. See* **Fuel system warnings** *in Section 1.*

Note: *The following procedure assumes that the fuel pump is receiving voltage and runs.*

1   Relieve the fuel system pressure (see Section 3), then disconnect the fuel line quick-connect fitting at the fuel rail. Using the proper adapters, tee-in a fuel pressure gauge between the fuel line and the fuel rail **(see illustrations)**.

2   Start the engine and allow it to idle. Note the gauge reading as soon as the pressure stabilizes, and compare it with the pressure listed in this Chapter's Specifications.

3   If the fuel pressure is not within specifications, check the following:

a)   *If the pressure is lower than specified, check for a restriction in the fuel sys-*

tem (kinked fuel line, plugged fuel pump inlet strainer or clogged fuel filter). If no restrictions are found, replace the fuel pressure regulator and fuel filter (see Sections 8 and 9).

b)   *Recheck the fuel pressure. If it is still lower than specified, replace the fuel pump (see Section 9).*

c)   *If the fuel pressure is higher than specified, replace the fuel pressure regulator (see Section 8).*

4   Turn off the engine. Fuel pressure should not fall more than 8 psi over five minutes. If it does, the problem could be a leaky fuel injector, fuel line leak, or faulty fuel pump module.

5   Relieve the fuel pressure (see Section 3), then disconnect the fuel pressure gauge. Wipe up any spilled gasoline.

5   Fuel lines and fittings - general information and disconnection

Warning: *Gasoline is extremely flammable. See* **Fuel system warnings** *in Section 1.*

1   Relieve the fuel pressure before servicing fuel lines or fittings (see Section 3), then disconnect the cable from the negative battery terminal (see Chapter 5) before proceeding.

2   The fuel supply line connects the fuel pump in the fuel tank to the fuel rail on the engine. The Evaporative Emission (EVAP) system lines connect the fuel tank to the EVAP canister and connect the canister to the intake manifold.

3   Whenever you're working under the vehicle, be sure to inspect all fuel and evaporative emission lines for leaks, kinks, dents and other damage. Always replace a damaged fuel or EVAP line immediately.

4   If you find signs of dirt in the lines during disassembly, disconnect all lines and blow them out with compressed air. Inspect the fuel strainer on the fuel pump pick-up unit for damage and deterioration.

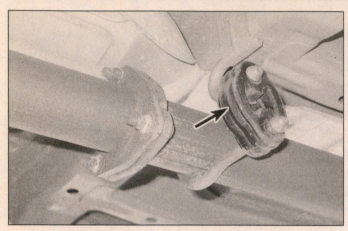

6.1 A typical exhaust system hanger. Inspect regularly and replace at the first sign of damage or deterioration

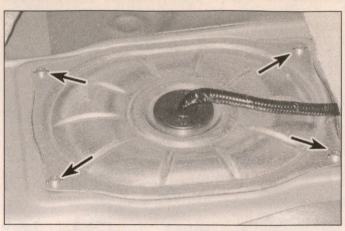

7.4 To detach the fuel pump access cover, remove these screws

Steel tubing

5   It is critical that the fuel lines be replaced with lines of equivalent type and specification.
6   Some steel fuel lines have threaded fittings. When loosening these fittings, hold the stationary fitting with a wrench while turning the tube nut.

Plastic tubing

7   When replacing fuel system plastic tubing, use only original equipment replacement plastic tubing. **Caution:** *When removing or installing plastic fuel line tubing, be careful not to bend or twist it too much, which can damage it. Also, plastic fuel tubing is NOT heat resistant, so keep it away from excessive heat.*

Flexible hoses

8   When replacing fuel system flexible hoses, use only original equipment replacements.
9   Don't route fuel hoses (or metal lines) within four inches of the exhaust system or

7.5 To disconnect the electrical connector from the fuel pump/fuel gauge sending unit, depress this release tab and pull the connector straight up

within ten inches of the catalytic converter. Make sure that no rubber hoses are installed directly against the vehicle, particularly in places where there is any vibration. If allowed to touch some vibrating part of the vehicle, a hose can easily become chafed and it might start leaking. A good rule of thumb is to maintain a minimum of 1/4-inch clearance around a hose (or metal line) to prevent contact with the vehicle underbody.

6   Exhaust system servicing - general information

Refer to illustration 6.1
Warning: *Allow exhaust system components to cool before inspection or repair. Also, when working under the vehicle, make sure it is securely supported on jackstands.*
1   The exhaust system consists of the exhaust manifolds, catalytic converter, muffler, tailpipe and all connecting pipes, flanges and clamps. The exhaust system is isolated from the vehicle body and from chassis components by a series of rubber hangers (**see illustration**). Periodically inspect these hangers for cracks or other signs of deterioration, replacing them as necessary.
2   Conduct regular inspections of the exhaust system to keep it safe and quiet. Look for any damaged or bent parts, open seams, holes, loose connections, excessive corrosion or other defects which could allow exhaust fumes to enter the vehicle. Do not repair deteriorated exhaust system components; replace them with new parts.
3   If the exhaust system components are extremely corroded, or rusted together, a cutting torch is the most convenient tool for removal. Consult a properly-equipped repair shop. If a cutting torch is not available, you can use a hacksaw, or if you have compressed air, there are special pneumatic cutting chisels that can also be used. Wear safety goggles to protect your eyes from metal chips and wear work gloves to protect your hands.

4   Here are some simple guidelines to follow when repairing the exhaust system:
a) *Work from the back to the front when removing exhaust system components.*
b) *Apply penetrating oil to the exhaust system component fasteners to make them easier to remove.*
c) *Use new gaskets, hangers and clamps.*
d) *Apply anti-seize compound to the threads of all exhaust system fasteners during reassembly.*
e) *Be sure to allow sufficient clearance between newly installed parts and all points on the underbody to avoid overheating the floor pan and possibly damaging the interior carpet and insulation. Pay particularly close attention to the catalytic converter and heat shield.*

7   Fuel pump/fuel gauge sending unit module - removal and installation

Refer to illustrations 7.4, 7.5, 7.7, 7.8 and 7.10
Warning: *Gasoline is extremely flammable, so take extra precautions when you work on any part of the fuel system. See the **Fuel system warnings** in Section 1.*
1   Relieve the fuel system pressure (see Section 3), then remove the fuel filler cap to relieve any pressure inside the fuel tank.
2   Disconnect the cable from the negative battery terminal (see Chapter 5).
3   On Civic models, remove the rear seat cushion (see Chapter 11). On CR-Vs, fold the rear seats forward and pull back the carpet to expose the fuel pump access cover.
4   Remove the fuel pump access cover screws (**see illustration**) and remove the fuel pump access cover. **Note:** *On 2006 and later Civics, remove the floor upper crossmember mounting fasteners and crossmember.*
5   Disconnect the fuel pump/fuel gauge sending unit electrical connector (**see illustration**).

Disconnecting Fuel Line Fittings

Two-tab type fitting; depress both tabs with your fingers, then pull the fuel line and the fitting apart

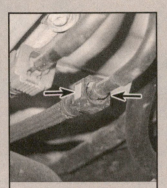

On this type of fitting, depress the two buttons on opposite sides of the fitting, then pull it off the fuel line

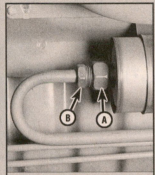

Threaded fuel line fitting; hold the stationary portion of the line or component (A) while loosening the tube nut (B) with a flare-nut wrench

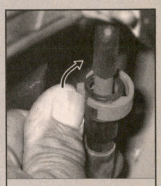

Plastic collar-type fitting; rotate the outer part of the fitting

Metal collar quick-connect fitting; pull the end of the retainer off the fuel line and disengage the other end from the female side of the fitting . . .

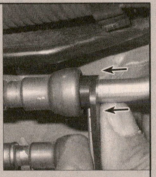

. . . insert a fuel line separator tool into the female side of the fitting, push it into the fitting and pull the fuel line off the pipe

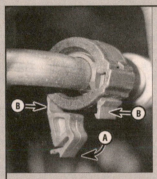

Some fittings are secured by lock tabs. Release the lock tab (A) and rotate it to the fully-opened position, squeeze the two smaller lock tabs (B) . . .

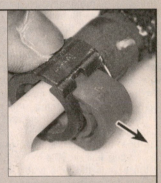

. . . then push the retainer out and pull the fuel line off the pipe

Spring-lock coupling; remove the safety cover, install a coupling release tool and close the tool around the coupling . . .

. . . push the tool into the fitting, then pull the two lines apart

Hairpin clip type fitting: push the legs of the retainer clip together, then push the clip down all the way until it stops and pull the fuel line off the pipe

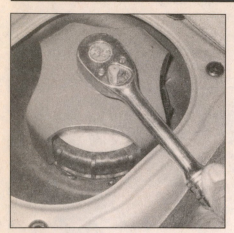

7.7 This special tool for loosening and tightening the fuel pump/fuel gauge sending unit locknut is available at most auto parts stores

7.8 Being careful not to damage the fuel gauge sending unit float arm and float, remove the fuel pump/fuel gauge sending unit module from the tank. After removing the pump/sending unit, inspect the condition of the seal around the top of the module; if the seal is cracked, torn or deteriorated, replace it

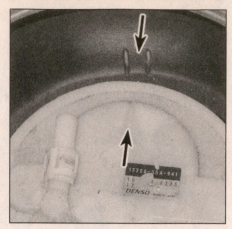

7.10 When installing the fuel pump/fuel gauge sending unit module, be sure to align the index mark on top of the module between the two marks on the edge of the hole

6   Disconnect the quick-connect fitting for the fuel supply line and set the supply line aside (see *Disconnecting Fuel Line Fittings*).

7   Remove the fuel pump/fuel gauge sending unit locknut **(see illustration)**.

8   Remove the fuel pump/fuel gauge sending unit module from the tank **(see illustration)**. When removing the pump/sending unit from the tank, carefully angle the module as shown in the accompanying illustration to protect the float arm and float from damage. After removing the pump/sending unit module, inspect the seal for cracks, tears and deterioration. If it's damaged, replace it.

9   Before installing the fuel pump/fuel gauge sending unit module in the fuel tank, install the seal in the hole first. Don't try to install it with the module, which might cause it to become pinched or distorted.

10   When installing the fuel pump/fuel gauge sending unit module, be sure to align the index mark on top of the module between the two marks on the edge of the hole **(see illustration)**.

11   Installation is otherwise the reverse of removal. Be sure to tighten the module locknut securely.

12   Installation is otherwise the reverse of removal, but before installing the fuel pump access cover, be sure to connect the cable to the negative battery terminal (see Chapter 5), start the engine and check for fuel leaks at the pump fuel line connection. If there are no leaks, install the access cover, the carpet and the rear seat (CR-V) or the seat cushion (coupe, sedan and hatchback).

---

8   Fuel pressure regulator - replacement

Warning: *Gasoline is extremely flammable, so take extra precautions when you work on*

any part of the fuel system. See the **Fuel system warnings** *in Section 1.*

1   Relieve the system fuel pressure (see Section 3), then remove the fuel filler neck cap to relieve any pressure inside the fuel tank.

2   Disconnect the cable from the negative battery terminal (see Chapter 5).

3   Remove the fuel pump/fuel gauge sending unit module from the fuel tank (see Section 7) and place it on a clean workbench.

2005 and earlier Civic models

Refer to illustrations 8.4, 8.5, 8.6, 8.7 and 8.8

4   Disconnect the pressure regulator's return hose fitting from the fuel pump housing **(see illustration)**.

5   Detach the fuel pressure regulator's inlet hose fitting from the fuel pump housing **(see illustration)**.

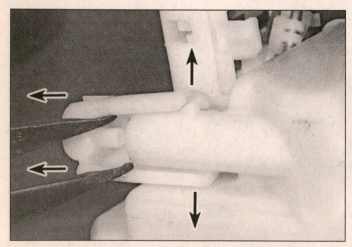

8.4 To disconnect the fuel pressure regulator's return hose fitting from the fuel pump case, spread the locking tabs apart, then pull off the fitting

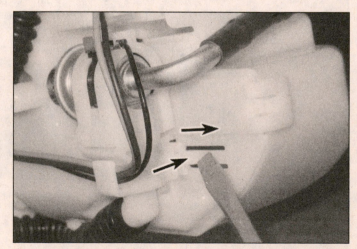

8.5 To detach the fuel pressure regulator's inlet fitting from the fuel pump housing, depress this locking tab with a small screwdriver and slide the fitting to the right

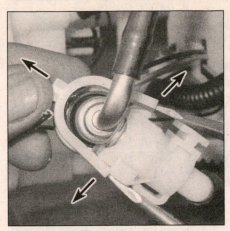

8.6 To detach this clip from the fuel pressure regulator, spread the sides apart with a small screwdriver, then pull the clip straight up and pull the pressure regulator out of the inlet hose fitting

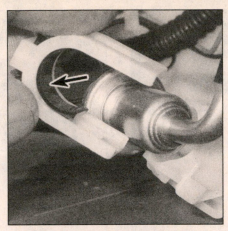

8.7 Remove the smaller clip from the larger clip and store both of them in a plastic bag for reassembly

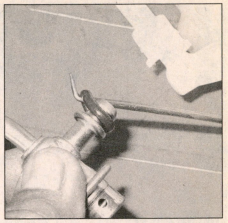

8.8 Remove and discard the old fuel pressure regulator O-ring; be sure to use a new O-ring when installing the regulator (whether you're installing the old regulator or a new unit)

6   Remove the clip from the fuel pressure regulator (see illustration) and pull the regulator out of the inlet hose fitting.
7   Note the smaller clip (see illustration) that fits inside the larger clip that you just removed. You need *both* clips to reconnect the fuel pressure regulator to its inlet hose fitting, so it's a good idea to store both of them in a plastic bag.
8   Remove the old pressure regulator O-ring (see illustration) and discard it. Be sure to use a new O-ring when you install the pressure regulator (regardless of whether you're installing the old regulator or a new unit).
9   Installation is the reverse of removal.
10   Reconnect the cable to the negative battery terminal, then perform the idle learn procedure (see Chapter 5).

2006 and later Civic models

11   From the bottom of the fuel pump housing remove the pressure regulator mounting clip.
12   Slide the ground ring off of the pressure regulator.
13   Pull the regulator out of the fuel tank unit.
14   Remove the old pressure regulator O-rings and discard them. Be sure to use new O-rings and a new mounting clip when you install the pressure regulator (regardless of whether you're installing the old regulator or a new unit).
15   Installation is the reverse of removal.
16   Reconnect the cable to the negative battery terminal, then perform the idle learn procedure (see Chapter 5).

CR-V models

Refer to illustrations 8.18, 8.19a and 8.19b

17   On 2007 and later CR-V models, depress the locking tabs and remove the reservoir/fuel gauge sending unit.
18   On 2007 and later CR-V models, remove the fuel pressure regulator housing, then disconnect the ground wire from the regulator (see illustration).
19   Remove the regulator mounting clip (see illustration) and pull the regulator out of the housing (see illustration).
20   Remove the old pressure regulator O-rings and discard them. Be sure to use new O-rings when you install the pressure regulator (regardless of whether you're installing the old regulator or a new unit). Inspect the condition

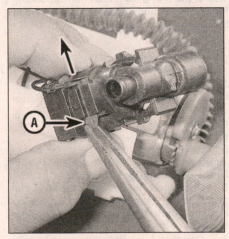

8.18 Squeeze the locking tab (A) flat and push the ground wire up and out of the regulator housing

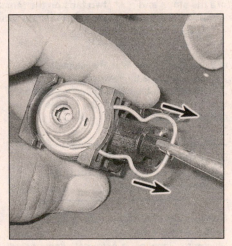

8.19a Remove the fuel pressure regulator retaining clip . . .

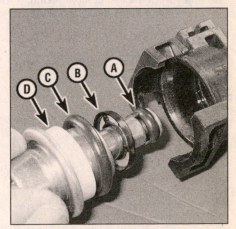

8.19b . . . and remove the fuel pressure regulator

A   O-ring
B   Mesh screen filter (if equipped)
C   O-ring
D   Spacer

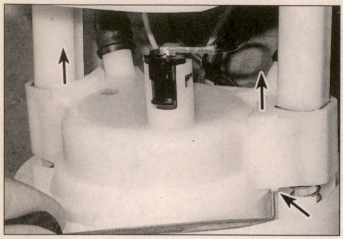

9.5a To remove the fuel filter assembly, turn the filter upside down, disengage the locking tabs for the two stops with a small screwdriver or an awl (left stop has already been released and pushed up) . . .

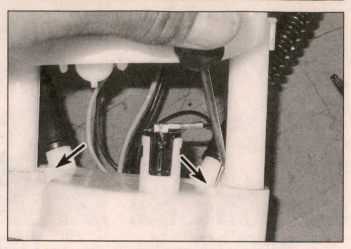

9.5b . . . release these two hooks . . .

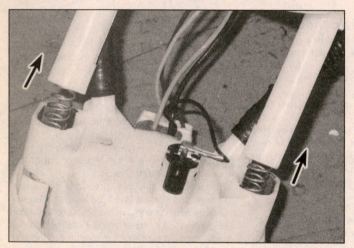

9.5c . . . and separate the spring-loaded legs of the filter assembly from the fuel pump housing, then store the stops and the springs in a plastic bag for reassembly

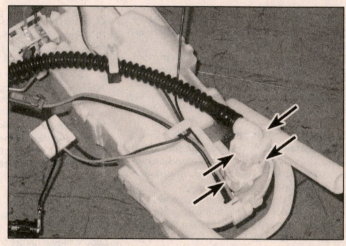

9.6 To disconnect the fuel pump outlet hose fitting, disengage the two tabs on the female side of the fitting from their corresponding slots in the male side of the fitting (fitting already disconnected in this photo for clarity)

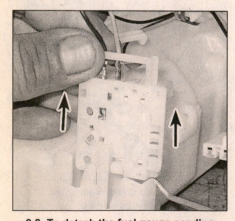

9.8 To detach the fuel gauge sending unit from its mounting bracket on the fuel pump housing, release the locking tab with a small screwdriver, then carefully lift up and remove the sending unit assembly

of the spacer screen filter (if equipped).

21   Installation is the reverse of removal.

22   Reconnect the cable to the negative battery terminal, then perform the idle learn procedure (see Chapter 5).

9   Fuel pump/fuel filter/fuel gauge sending unit module - replacement

Refer to illustrations 9.5a, 9.5b, 9.5c, 9.6, 9.8, 9.9a, 9.9b and 9.11

Warning: *Gasoline is extremely flammable, so take extra precautions when you work on any part of the fuel system. See the* **Fuel system warnings** *in Section 1.*

1   Relieve the system fuel pressure (see Section 3), then remove the fuel filler neck cap to relieve any pressure inside the fuel tank.

2   Disconnect the cable from the negative battery terminal (see Chapter 5).

3   Remove the fuel pump/fuel gauge sending unit module from the fuel tank (see Section 7) and place it on a clean workbench.

4   Disconnect and remove the fuel pressure regulator (see Section 8).

5   Remove the stops, release the hooks and separate the fuel filter assembly from the fuel pump housing **(see illustrations)**.

6   Disconnect the fitting for the hose that connects the fuel pump outlet to the fuel filter **(see illustration)** and set the fuel filter assembly aside.

7   Disconnect the electrical connectors for the fuel pump and for the fuel gauge sending unit from the fuel filter assembly.

8   Remove the fuel gauge sending unit from the fuel pump housing **(see illustration)**.

Note: *On 2006 and later models, the filter housing and fuel pump can't be serviced sep-*

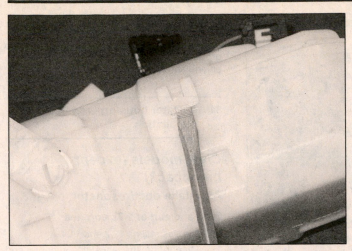

9.9a Release the four locking clips (one on each side of the housing) with a small screwdriver . . .

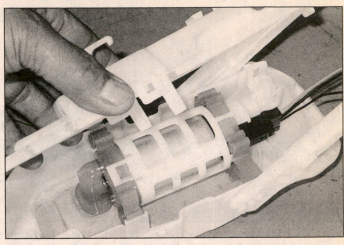

9.9b . . . and separate the housing halves

arately from the module and must be replaced as a unit.

9   Disassemble the fuel pump housing **(see illustrations)**.

10   Remove the fuel pump from the lower half of the housing.

11   Remove the fuel inlet sock (strainer) from the fuel pump **(see illustration)**.

12   Wash the fuel inlet strainer thoroughly in clean solvent, dry it off and inspect it for tears, cracks, clogging and any other damage. If the strainer is damaged or worn, replace it.

13   When installing the fuel pump strainer, be sure to use a new retainer clip.

14   When installing the fuel pump in the housing, make sure that the four tabs on the pump insulators are inserted into their respective slots in the lower half of the housing.

15   Installation is otherwise the reverse of removal. Before installing the fuel pump access cover, be sure to connect the cable to the negative battery terminal (see Chapter 5), start the engine and check for fuel leaks at the pump fuel line connection. If there are

no leaks, install the access cover, the carpet and the rear seat (CR-V) or the seat cushion (coupe, sedan and hatchback).

10 Fuel tank - removal and installation

Warning: *Gasoline is extremely flammable, so take extra precautions when you work on any part of the fuel system. See the **Fuel system warnings** in Section 1.*

Note: *The following procedure is much easier to perform if the fuel tank is empty. The tank has no drain plug, so the fuel must be siphoned from the tank with a siphoning kit, which is available at most auto parts stores. NEVER try to start the siphoning action with your mouth!*

1   Relieve the fuel system pressure (see Section 3).

2   Disconnect the cable from the negative battery terminal (see Chapter 5).

3   Raise the vehicle and place it securely on jackstands.

4   If the fuel tank is empty or nearly empty, it's not necessary to siphon the remaining fuel from the tank. But if there *is* a lot of fuel in the tank, drain the fuel by removing the fuel pump/fuel gauge sending unit (see Section 7) and siphoning it out through the hole for the pump/sending unit. **Warning:** *Always siphon fuel into an approved gasoline container. Also, never start the siphoning action by mouth - use a siphoning pump (available at most auto parts stores).*

Civic models

Refer to illustrations 10.5a, 10.5b, 10.6 and 10.9

5   Remove the fuel filler neck cover **(see illustration)**, then disconnect and remove the fuel filler neck hose and the fuel tank vapor hose **(see illustration)**. Inspect these two hoses for cracks, tears and other deterioration. If either hose is damaged or worn, replace it.

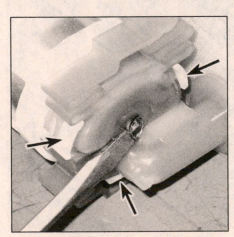

9.11 Carefully pry off and discard this retainer (always use a new retainer when installing the strainer), then disengage the three tabs on the strainer

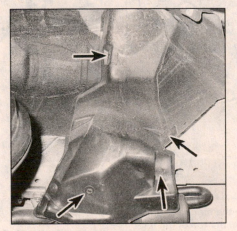

10.5a To detach the fuel filler neck cover, remove these four fasteners

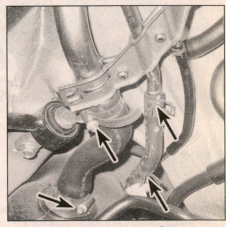

10.5b To disconnect the fuel filler neck hose and the fuel tank vapor hose, loosen these hose clamps and pull off both hoses

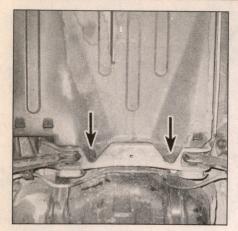

10.6 Remove the lower cover rear fasteners

10.9 To detach the fuel tank from the underside of the vehicle, remove the fuel tank strap bolts (rear shown, front similar)

6   Remove the lower rear cover mounting fasteners and pull the back of the cover down, if equipped **(see illustration)**.

7   On 2006 and later models, remove the EVAP canister guard.

8   Support the fuel tank with a transmission jack. If you don't have a transmission jack, use a floor jack. If you're going to use a floor jack, put a piece of plywood between the jack head and the fuel tank to protect the tank.

9   Unbolt the fuel tank retaining straps **(see illustration)** and remove them.

10   Carefully lower the fuel tank.

11   If you need to remove the fuel pump/fuel gauge sending unit module, but haven't yet done so, refer to Sections 7 and 9.

12   Installation is the reverse of removal.

13   Reconnect the cable to the negative battery terminal and perform the PCM idle learn procedure (see Chapter 5), then start the engine and check for fuel leaks.

CR-V models

14   Remove the fuel tank guard fasteners and guard at the front of the tank.

15   Remove the exhaust pipe mounting bolts and pipe.

16   On 4WD models remove the driveshaft (see Chapter 8).

17   If you're working on a 2007 or later model, remove the exhaust pipe.

18   Support the fuel tank with a transmission jack. If you don't have a transmission jack, use a floor jack. If you're going to use a floor jack, put a piece of plywood between the jack head and the fuel tank to protect the tank.

19   Unbolt the fuel tank retaining straps and remove them.

20   Carefully lower the fuel tank.

21   If you need to remove the fuel pump/fuel gauge sending unit module, but haven't yet done so, refer to Sections 7 and 9.

22   Installation is the reverse of removal.

23   Reconnect the cable to the negative battery terminal and perform the PCM idle learn procedure (see Chapter 5), then start the engine and check for fuel leaks.

---

11   Air filter housing - removal and installation

Civic models (except hatchback)

Air intake duct/resonator

2005 and earlier 1.7L engines

Refer to illustrations 11.2 and 11.4

1   Disengage the accelerator cable and cruise control cable from the cable guide at the right rear corner of the valve cover, disengage the accelerator cable from the guide at the right rear corner of the engine compartment (next to the cruise control actuator), then set both cables aside.

2   Detach the fresh air inlet duct from the air intake/resonator. You don't *have* to detach the fresh air inlet duct from the air intake duct/resonator in order to remove the intake duct/resonator, but you do have detach the harness from the inlet duct; the intake duct/resonator is easier to remove if the fresh air inlet duct is out of the way. Clearly label all cables and hoses **(see illustration)** that are attached or connected to the air intake duct, then detach or disconnect them and set them aside.

3   Detach the harness from the bracket at the lower left rear corner of the air intake duct/resonator.

4   Remove the air intake duct/resonator mounting bolts **(see illustration)** and remove the intake duct/resonator.

5   Installation is the reverse of removal.

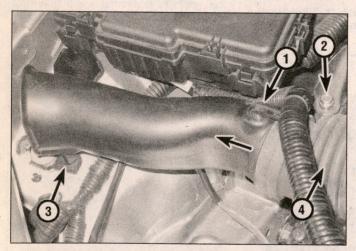

11.2 To detach the fresh air inlet duct from the air intake duct/resonator, detach the harness guide (1) from the top of the inlet duct by pulling it straight up, remove the duct mounting bolt (2), pull the locator pin (3) out of its grommet in the right fender, then pull off the duct to the right (toward the fender); if the pleated rubber boot (4) doesn't come off with the duct, remove it now also

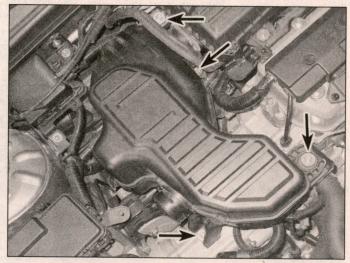

11.4 To detach the air intake duct/resonator from a coupe or sedan, remove these bolts

2006 and later 1.8L and 2.0L engines

6   Remove the front bumper (see Chapter 11).

7   Remove the upper intake air duct-to-resonator fasteners and air duct.

8   Remove the intake air resonator fasteners and withdraw the resonator from the vehicle.

9   Installation is the reverse of removal.

Air filter housing

Warning: *Wait until the engine is completely cool before beginning this procedure.*

2005 and earlier 1.7L engines

Refer to illustrations 11.11, 11.12, 11.13a and 11.13b

10   Remove the fresh air inlet duct and the air intake duct/resonator assembly (see Steps 1 through 4).

11   Disconnect the electrical connector for the Intake Air Temperature (IAT) sensor **(see illustration)**.

12   Disconnect the Positive Crankcase Ventilation (PCV) fresh air inlet hose from the valve cover **(see illustration)**.

13   Remove the air filter housing mounting bolts, loosen the screw on the hose clamp that secures the filter housing to the throttle body and remove the air filter housing **(see illustrations)**.

14   Installation is the reverse of removal.

2006 and later 1.8L and 2.0L engines

Refer to illustrations 11.16 and 11.19

15   Disconnect the MAF/IAT sensor electrical connector.

16   Disconnect the upper air intake duct clamp and separate the lower inlet hose **(see illustration)**.

17   Disconnect the air cleaner housing cover clamps, then remove the cover and filter.

18   Remove the air inlet pipe mounting fas-

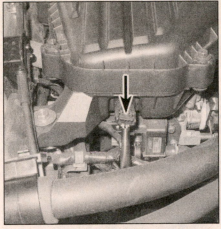

11.11 To disconnect the electrical connector from the Intake Air Temperature (IAT) sensor, depress this release tab and pull off the connector

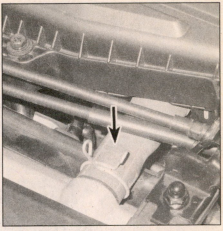

11.12 To disconnect the PCV system fresh air inlet hose from the valve cover of a coupe or sedan, loosen this hose clamp and pull off the hose

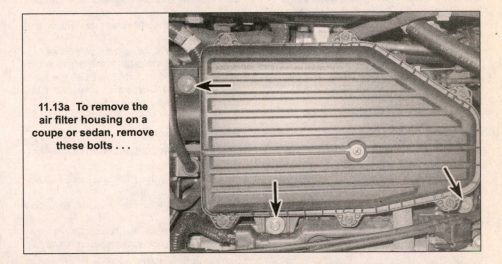

11.13a To remove the air filter housing on a coupe or sedan, remove these bolts . . .

11.13b . . . loosen this hose clamp screw and lift the air filter housing up and off the throttle body

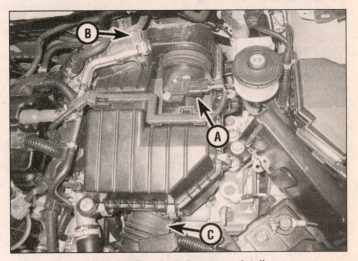

11.16 Air filter housing cover details

A   MAF/IAT sensor electrical connector
B   Upper air intake duct clamp
C   Lower inlet hose

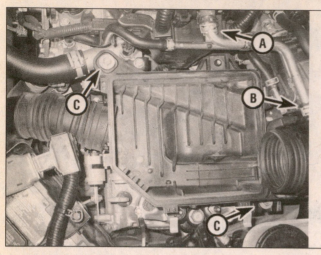

11.19 Air filter housing details

A *Pipe mounting bracket*
B *Pipe-to-housing cover clamp*
C *Air cleaner housing fasteners*

41 Remove the battery and battery tray (see Chapter 5).
42 Disconnect the MAF/IAT sensor electrical connector.
43 Disconnect the upper air intake duct clamp and separate the lower inlet hose.
44 Remove the air filter housing fasteners and lift the housing out.
45 Installation is the reverse of removal.
46 Reconnect the cable to the negative battery terminal and perform the PCM idle learn procedure (see Chapter 5), then start the engine and check for fuel leaks.

tener and disconnect the pipe-to housing clamp.
19 Remove the air filter housing fasteners and lift the housing out **(see illustration)**.
20 Installation is the reverse of removal.

Hatchback and CR-V models

Air intake duct/resonator

Hatchback models

21 Loosen the hose clamp at the air filter housing-end of the duct.
22 Loosen the hose clamp at the throttle body-end of the duct.
23 Remove the air intake duct.
24 Installation is the reverse of removal.

2006 and earlier CR-V models

25 Loosen the hose clamp at the air filter housing-end of the duct.
26 Loosen the hose clamp at the throttle body-end of the duct.
27 Remove the air intake duct.
28 Installation is the reverse of removal.

2007 and later CR-V models

29 Disconnect the cable from the negative battery terminal (see Chapter 5).

30 Remove the battery and battery tray (see Chapter 5).
31 Remove the lower air intake duct.
32 Remove the front bumper (see Chapter 11).
33 Remove the resonator fasteners and resonator.
34 Installation is the reverse of removal.
35 Reconnect the cable to the negative battery terminal and perform the PCM idle learn procedure (see Chapter 5), then start the engine and check for fuel leaks.

Air filter housing

Hatchback and 2006 and earlier CR-V models

36 Disconnect the PCV hose (see Chapter 6).
37 Remove the air filter housing mounting nut and bolts.
38 Remove the air filter housing.
39 Installation is the reverse of removal.

2007 and later CR-V models

40 Disconnect the cable from the negative battery terminal (see Chapter 5).

12 Accelerator cable - removal, installation and adjustment

Removal and installation

2005 and earlier Civic and 2004 and earlier CR-V models

Refer to illustrations 12.2, 12.3, 12.4, 12.5, 12.6a and 12.6b

1 Remove the air intake duct and the air filter housing (see Section 11). On CR-Vs, also remove the two throttle lever cover bolts and remove the cover.
2 Rotate the throttle lever cam until the cable is lined up with the slot in the cam, then disengage the cable from the cam **(see illustration)**.
3 Loosen the accelerator cable locknut at the cable bracket **(see illustration)** and disengage the accelerator cable from its bracket. **Note:** *If the cable bracket has an "L" shape to it, like the bracket in the accompanying illustration, there is no need to use a back-up wrench to hold the other nut (the adjustment nut) because the kink in the bracket prevents the adjustment nut from turning. If, however, the cable bracket does NOT have an L shape, you will need to use a back-up wrench to prevent the adjustment nut from turning when you loosen the locknut.*

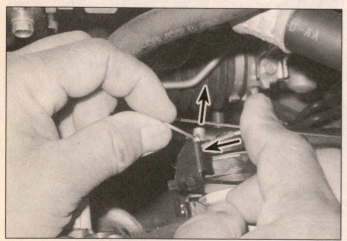

12.2 Rotate the throttle lever cam to put some slack into the accelerator cable, then slide the cable end plug out of its slot in the throttle lever cam

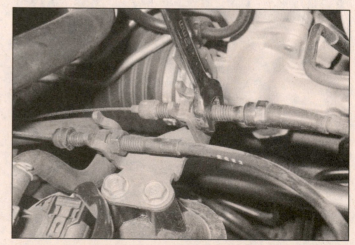

12.3 To disengage the accelerator cable from the cable bracket, loosen the locknut and pull out the cable

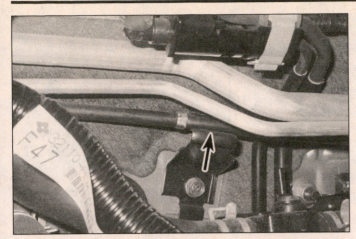

12.4 After noting the routing of the accelerator cable, trace the cable from the cable bracket all the way to the point at which the cable goes through the firewall and disengage the cable from any clips, clamps or cable guides, such as this one on the firewall of a sedan

12.5 Disengage the plastic retainer from the accelerator pedal arm by squeezing these two locking tabs together and pulling the cable to the rear, then separate the cable from the pedal arm

4   Note the routing of the accelerator cable, then trace the cable from the cable bracket back to the firewall, detaching or disengaging it from any clamps, clips or cable guides (see illustration).

5   Using a flashlight so that you can see underneath the dash, locate the cable connection at the top of the accelerator pedal, push the upper end of the pedal forward and disengage the cable from the pedal arm (see illustration).

6   Unlock the accelerator cable ferrule by turning it counterclockwise until the tabs on the ferrule are aligned with the slots in the firewall (see illustration), then pull cable out from the engine compartment side (see illustration).

7   Installation is the reverse of removal. After installing the cable, be sure to adjust it.

2005 and 2006 CR-V models

8   Remove the two throttle cable cover bolts and remove the cover from the Accelerator Pedal Position (APP) sensor on the firewall.

9   Loosen the accelerator cable locknut at the cable bracket.

10   Fully open the throttle valve and disengage the throttle cable from the throttle link.

11   Remove the cable housing from the cable bracket.

12   Note the routing of the accelerator cable, then trace the cable from the APP sensor and disengage it from the clamp on the firewall.

13   Using a flashlight so that you can see under the dash, locate the cable connection at the top of the accelerator pedal, push the upper end of the pedal forward and disengage the cable from the pedal arm.

14   Unlock the accelerator cable ferrule by

turning it counterclockwise until the tabs on the ferrule align with the slots in the firewall (see illustration 12.6a), then pull the cable out from the engine compartment side (see illustration 12.6b).

15   Installation is the reverse of removal. After installing the cable, be sure to adjust it.

Adjustment (all models)

Refer to illustrations 12.17a and 12.17b

16   Put the shift lever in Park or Neutral, start the engine, hold it at 3000 rpm until the radiator fan comes on, then allow it to idle.

17   Back off the locknut, then place the accelerator cable in the cable bracket with both the adjusting nut and the locknut on the side of the cable bracket facing away from the throttle body. Turn the adjusting nut until there is no freeplay between the adjusting nut and

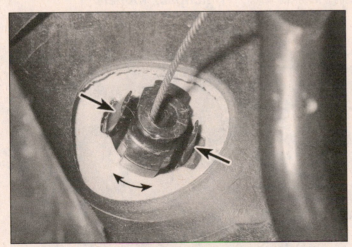

12.6a To unlock the cable ferrule from the firewall, squeeze the two locking tabs and rotate it until the bosses on the ferrule are aligned with their corresponding slots in the firewall . . .

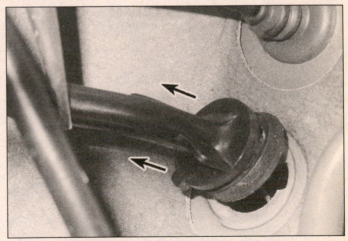

12.6b . . . then pull out the accelerator cable from the engine compartment side (coupe/sedan shown, CR-V and hatchback similar)

the cable bracket **(see illustration)**. When the freeplay is zero, lift up the adjusting nut, place it on the other side of the cable bracket, then tighten the locknut **(see illustration)**.

18   Once the accelerator cable has been installed and adjusted, verify that the throttle valve opens fully when the accelerator pedal is depressed and that it returns to its idle position when the pedal is released.

13   Throttle body - removal and installation

Warning: *Wait until the engine is completely cool before beginning this procedure.*

2005 and earlier Civic models

Refer to illustrations 13.2, 13.6, 13.7 and 13.9

1   Remove the air intake duct/resonator and the filter housing (see Section 11).
2   Disconnect the electrical connectors from the Idle Air Control (IAC) valve, the Evaporative Emissions (EVAP) canister purge valve and the Throttle Position (TP) sensor **(see illustration)**.
3   Clamp off the two coolant bypass hoses to the throttle body **(see illustration 13.2)**, then disconnect them. Be prepared for a little coolant spillage.
4   Disconnect the vacuum hoses from the EVAP canister purge valve **(see illustration 13.2)**.
5   Disconnect the accelerator and cruise control cables from the throttle lever cam. Disconnecting the cruise control cable from the throttle lever cam is the same procedure as disconnecting the accelerator cable **(see illustrations 12.2 and 12.3)**.
6   Remove the three throttle body mounting fasteners **(see illustration)** and remove the throttle body.
7   Remove the old throttle body gasket **(see illustration)** and discard it.
8   Remove all traces of old gasket material from the throttle body and the intake manifold.
9   Before installing the old throttle body (if you're installing the old unit), spray the bore

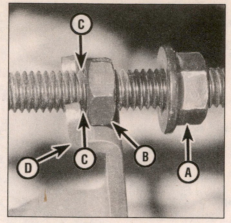

12.17a   To adjust the accelerator cable on a coupe or sedan, place the accelerator cable in the cable bracket with the adjusting nut and the locknut on the same side of the bracket (the side facing away from the throttle body), then tighten the adjusting nut until there is zero freeplay between the adjusting nut and the cable bracket (coupe/sedan shown, CR-V and hatchback similar)

A   *Locknut*
B   *Adjusting nut*
C   *Zero clearance between adjusting nut and cable bracket*
D   *Accelerator cable bracket*

with carburetor cleaner or some other suitable solvent and thoroughly clean the bore, particularly the area below the throttle valve, by wiping off the oily residue, varnish and/or carbon deposits with a clean shop rag **(see illustration)**. **Caution:** *Unless the throttle body that you're cleaning is stripped of all external components such as the Throttle Position (TP) sensor, EVAP canister purge valve and MAP sensor, make sure that you don't spray any of these devices with carb cleaner. Solvent will damage the plastic housings for these units and might even damage the delicate electronics inside them.*

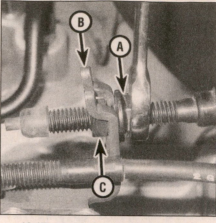

12.17b   Once the accelerator cable freeplay is correctly adjusted, lift the cable out of the cable bracket and put the adjusting nut on the other side of the cable bracket (the side facing toward the throttle body), then tighten the locknut securely (coupe/sedan shown, CR-V and hatchback similar)

A   *Locknut*
B   *Accelerator cable bracket*
C   *Adjusting nut*

10   Installation is the reverse of removal. Be sure to use new gaskets and tighten the throttle body mounting fasteners to the torque listed in this Chapter's Specifications.
11   Check the coolant level and top it up if necessary (see Chapter 1).
12   Check the accelerator cable adjustment and adjust it if necessary (see Section 12).
13   Perform the PCM idle learn procedure (see Chapter 5).
14   Start the engine and check for air and coolant leaks.

2002 through 2005 CR-V and Hatchback models

15   On CR-Vs, remove the throttle linkage cover.

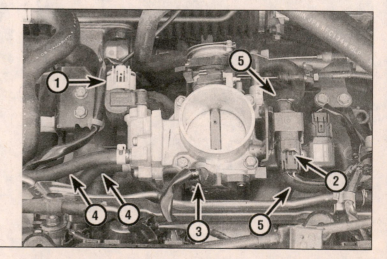

13.2 Throttle body removal (coupe and sedan):

1   *Disconnect the electrical connector from the Idle Air Control (IAC) valve*
2   *Disconnect the electrical connector from the Evaporative Emissions (EVAP) canister purge valve*
3   *Disconnect the electrical connector from the Throttle Position (TP) sensor*
4   *Disconnect the coolant bypass hoses from the throttle body*
5   *Disconnect the vacuum hoses from the EVAP canister purge valve*

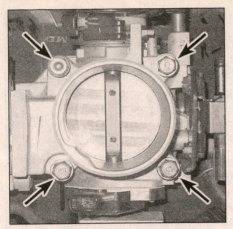

13.6 To detach the throttle body from the intake manifold on a coupe or sedan, remove these fasteners

13.7 After removing the throttle body from the intake manifold, remove and discard the old gasket; always use a new gasket when installing the throttle body to prevent air leaks

16   Loosen the hose clamp and disconnect the air intake duct from the throttle body.
17   Disconnect the electrical connectors from the Evaporative Emission (EVAP) canister purge valve, the Manifold Absolute Pressure (MAP) sensor, the Throttle Position (TP) sensor and the Idle Air Control (IAC) valve.
18   Disconnect the vacuum hoses from the EVAP canister purge valve and from the throttle body.
19   Clamp off the two coolant bypass hoses to the throttle body, then disconnect them. Be prepared for a little coolant spillage.
20   Disconnect the accelerator cable and, if equipped, the cruise control cable from the throttle lever cam (see Section 12).
21   Remove the four throttle body mounting bolts (CR-V) or two mounting bolts and two mounting nuts (hatchback) and remove the throttle body.

22   Remove the old throttle body gasket and discard it.
23   Remove all traces of old gasket material from the throttle body and the intake manifold.
24   Installation is the reverse of removal. Be sure to use new gaskets and tighten the throttle body mounting bolts and nut to the torque listed in this Chapter's Specifications.
25   Check the coolant level and top it up if necessary (see Chapter 1).
26   Check the accelerator cable adjustment and adjust it if necessary (see Section 12).
27   Perform the PCM idle learn procedure (see Chapter 5).
28   Start the engine and check for air and coolant leaks.

All 2006 and later models

Refer to illustration 13.30

29   Loosen the hose clamp and disconnect the air intake duct from the throttle body.
Note: *On Civic models, remove the air cleaner housing (see Section 11).*
30   Disconnect all electrical connectors from the throttle body **(see illustration)**.
31   Clamp off the two coolant bypass hoses to the throttle body, then disconnect them. Be prepared for a little coolant spillage. Plug the ends of the hoses.
32   Disconnect the vacuum hose and remove the harness clip from the throttle body.
33   Remove the throttle body mounting bolts and nuts and remove the throttle body.
34   Remove the old throttle body gasket and discard it.
35   Remove all traces of old gasket material from the throttle body and intake manifold.
36   Installation is the reverse of removal. Be sure to use a new gasket and tighten the throttle body mounting bolts and nuts to the torque listed in this Chapter's Specifications.
37   Check the coolant level and top it up if necessary (see Chapter 1).
38   Perform the PCM idle learn procedure (see Chapter 5).
39   Start the engine and check for vacuum and coolant leaks.

14 Fuel pulsation damper - removal and installation

1.7L and 1.8L engines

1   The fuel pulsation damper is an integral part of the fuel rail; it is not available separately. To replace the fuel pulsation damper, you must replace the fuel rail (see Section 15).

13.9 To clean the bore of the throttle body, spray it with carburetor cleaner or some other suitable solvent and wipe out the bore, particularly the area below the throttle valve (shown) with a clean shop rag. Make sure that you remove any oily residue, varnish and/or carbon deposits

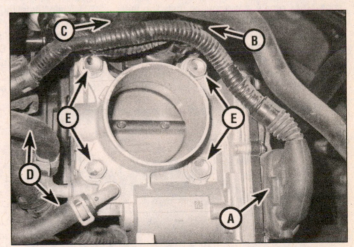

13.30 Typical throttle body mounting details - 1.8L shown, others similar

A   Throttle body actuator connector
B   EVAP purge control valve connector
C   Vacuum hose
D   Water bypass hoses
E   Throttle body mounting bolts

15.6 Ignition coil cover harness cover screws (2006 and later 1.8L engines)

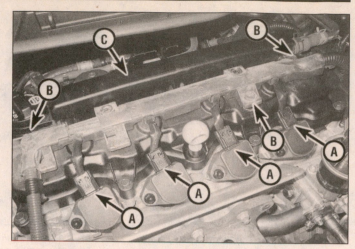

15.7 Ignition coil harness details (2006 and later 1.8L engines)

A   *Ignition coil electrical connectors*
B   *Ignition coil harness mounting details*
C   *Fuel rail cover*

2004 and earlier 2.4L engines

2   Relieve the system fuel pressure (see Section 3), then disconnect the cable from the negative battery terminal (see Chapter 5).

3   Locate the fuel pulsation damper at the left end of the fuel rail.

4   Disconnect the quick-connect fitting (see Section 5) that connects the fuel supply line to the fuel pulsation damper.

5   Using a back-up wrench on the big hex at the end of the fuel rail to protect the fuel rail from damage, loosen the pulsation damper with another wrench, then unscrew and remove the damper.

6   Remove and discard the old pulsation damper sealing washer.

7   Installation is the reverse of removal. Be sure to use a new washer when installing the pulsation damper, and tighten it securely.

8   Reconnect the cable to the negative battery terminal, then perform the PCM idle learn procedure (see Chapter 5).

9   Check for leaks around the pulsation damper.

All other models

10   Relieve the system fuel pressure (see Section 3), then disconnect the cable from the negative battery terminal (see Chapter 5).

11   Remove the engine cover (see Chapter 2B).

12   Remove the fuel rail mounting nuts (see Section 15).

13   Disconnect the ground cable.

14   Raise the fuel rail assembly slightly.

15   Using a back-up wrench on the pulsation damper junction block to protect the fuel rail, loosen the fuel pulsation damper with another wrench. Then unscrew and remove the pulsation damper from the junction block.

16   Remove and discard the old pulsation damper sealing washers.

17   When installing the pulsation damper, make sure that the drain hole on the damper faces down. Installation is otherwise the reverse of removal. Be sure to use new sealing washers and tighten the fuel pulsation damper securely.

18   Reconnect the cable to the negative bat-

tery cable, then perform the PCM idle learn procedure (see Chapter 5).

19   Check the area around the fuel pulsation damper for leaks.

---

15   Fuel rail and injectors - removal and installation

Warning: *Gasoline is extremely flammable, so take extra precautions when you work on any part of the fuel system. See the Fuel system warnings in Section 1.*

1   Relieve the system fuel pressure (see Section 3), then disconnect the cable from the negative battery terminal (see Chapter 5).

2005 and earlier 1.7L engines

2   Remove the air intake duct/resonator and filter housing (see Section 11).

3   Disconnect the electrical connectors from the Evaporative Emissions (EVAP) canister purge valve and the Throttle Position (TP) sensor and disconnect the electrical connector from the Manifold Absolute Pressure (MAP) sensor (see Chapter 6).

4   Disconnect the vacuum hoses from both ends of the pipe that's welded to the fuel rail.

2006 and later 1.8L engines

Refer to illustrations 15.6, 15.7 and 15.8

5   Remove the engine cowl panel (see Chapter 11).

6   Remove the ignition coil harness cover fasteners and cover **(see illustration)**.

7   Disconnect the ignition coil connectors at each coil (see Chapter 5), remove the coil harness fasteners **(see illustration)** and place the harness out of the way.

8   Remove the injector harness fasteners and remove the fuel rail/line cover **(see illustration)**.

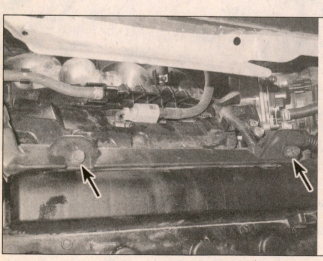

15.8 Injector harness mounting fastener location (2006 and later 1.8L engines)

15.9a Fuel injector electrical connectors - 2005 and earlier 1.7L engines

15.9b Fuel injector electrical connectors - 2006 and later 1.8L engines

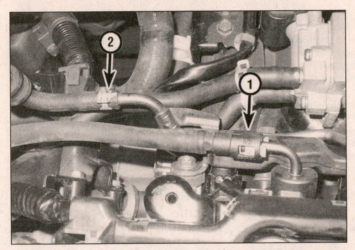

15.10a Disconnect the quick-connect fitting (1) from the fuel pulsation damper, then disconnect the vacuum hoses (2) from both ends of the vacuum pipe that's welded to the fuel rail

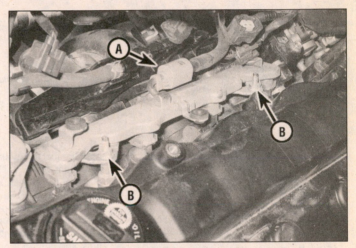

15.10b Fuel rail details (2006 and later 1.8L engines)

A   Fuel rail quick-connect fitting (under cover)
B   Fuel rail mounting nuts

All models

Refer to illustrations 15.9a, 15.9b, 15.10a, 15.10b, 15.11, 15.12, 15.13a, 15.13b and 15.14

9   Disconnect the electrical connectors from the fuel injectors **(see illustrations)** and, on models so equipped, remove the harness fasteners.

10   Disconnect the quick-connect fitting that connects the fuel supply line to the fuel rail **(see illustrations)**. See *Disconnecting Fuel Line Fittings* earlier in this Chapter.

11   Remove the fuel rail mounting fasteners **(see accompanying illustration and illustration 15.10b)**.

12   Remove the fuel rail and the fuel injectors as a single assembly **(see illustration)**. If any of the injectors are difficult to extract from their bores, carefully pry them loose by wiggling them from side to side and pulling

15.11 Fuel rail mounting fasteners (2005 and earlier 1.7L engines)

15.12 Remove the fuel rail and injectors as a single assembly

15.13a To detach an injector from the fuel rail, pull off the retainer clip with a pair of pliers . . .

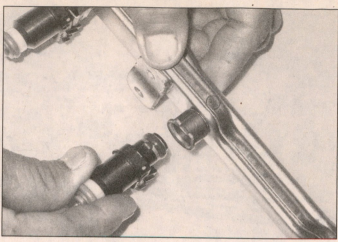

15.13b . . . then carefully work the injector out of its bore in the fuel rail

15.14 Be sure to remove the old O-rings and discard them. Always use new O-rings when installing an injector (1.7L and 1.8L engines use two O-rings per injector; 2.0L and 2.4L engines use three O-rings per injector)

up at the same time. After removing the fuel rail/injector assembly, remove the two spacers (on models so equipped) and store them in a plastic bag until you need them again for reassembly.

13 To remove each injector from the fuel rail, remove the retainer clip, then pull the injector out of its bore in the fuel rail **(see illustrations)**.

14 Remove and discard the upper and lower O-rings from each injector **(see illustration)**, discard them and install new O-rings. Coat each new O-ring with clean engine oil to make it easier to slide the O-ring into place on the injector. Repeat this procedure for each injec-

tor. **Note:** *Even if you only removed the fuel rail assembly to replace a single injector or a leaking O-ring, it's a good idea to remove all of the injectors from the fuel rail and replace all the O-rings, cushion rings and seal rings at the same time.*

15 Coat the upper O-rings with clean engine oil, then insert each injector into its corresponding bore in the fuel rail.

16 If equipped, install the plastic spacers onto the fuel rail mounting studs.

17 Coat the lower O-rings with clean engine oil, then guide the fuel rail and injectors into place.

18 Once the fuel rail assembly is in place, with all four injectors fully seated in their respective bores, install the fuel rail mounting nuts and tighten them to the torque listed in this Chapter's Specifications.

19 The remainder of installation is the reverse of removal.

20 Reconnect the cable to the negative battery terminal (see Chapter 5).

21 Turn the ignition switch to ON to activate the fuel pump and build up fuel pressure in the fuel lines and the fuel rail, but DON'T operate the starter yet. Repeat this step two or three times, then check the fuel lines, fuel rails and injectors for fuel leaks.

22 Start the engine and perform the PCM idle learn procedure (see Chapter 5).

---

16 Electronic throttle components (2005 and 2006 CR-V) - replacement

---

Note: *2005 and 2006 CR-V models use an electronically actuated throttle body. On these models, there is no direct cable link between*

the accelerator pedal and the throttle body. Instead, an electric actuator within the throttle body operates the throttle based on a signal it receives from the Throttle Actuator Control Module (TACM). The Accelerator Pedal Position (APP) sensor provides input to the TACM of the actual position of the accelerator pedal. **Note:** *On 2006 and later Civic and 2007 and later CR-V models, the electronic throttle body components are not serviceable separately, and the throttle body must be replaced as a unit.*

Throttle Actuator Control Module

1 Open the glove box door.

2 On the right side, push on the tab and disconnect the electrical connector from the throttle actuator control module.

3 Remove the throttle actuator control module mounting bolts and remove the throttle actuator control module.

4 Installation is the reverse of removal. Tighten the bolts securely.

Accelerator Pedal Position (APP) sensor

5 The Accelerator Pedal Position (APP) sensor is located in the engine compartment, on the passenger's side of the firewall.

6 Disconnect the accelerator cable from the APP sensor (see Section 12).

7 Disconnect the electrical connector from the APP sensor.

8 Remove the bolts and remove the APP sensor.

9 Installation is the reverse of removal.

Chapter 5
Engine electrical systems

Contents

	Section		Section
Alternator - removal and installation	7	General information	1
Battery - disconnection and reconnection	3	Ignition coils - replacement	6
Battery - removal and installation	4	Starter motor - removal and installation	8
Battery cables - replacement	5	Troubleshooting	2

1 General information and precautions

General information

Ignition system

The electronic ignition system consists of the Crankshaft Position (CKP) sensor, the Camshaft Position (CMP) sensor, the Knock Sensor (KS), the Powertrain Control Module (PCM), the ignition switch, the battery, the individual ignition coils or a coil pack, and the spark plugs. For more information on the CKP, CMP and KS sensors, as well as the PCM, refer to Chapter 6.

Charging system

The charging system includes the alternator (with an integral voltage regulator), the Powertrain Control Module (PCM), the Body Control Module (BCM), a charge indicator light on the dash, the battery, a fuse or fusible link and the wiring connecting all of these components. The charging system supplies electrical power for the ignition system, the lights, the radio, etc. The alternator is driven by a drivebelt.

Starting system

The starting system consists of the battery, the ignition switch, the starter relay, the Powertrain Control Module (PCM), the Transmission Range (TR) switch, the starter motor and solenoid assembly, and the wiring connecting all of the components.

Precautions

Always observe the following precautions when working on the electrical system:

a) *Be extremely careful when servicing engine electrical components. They are easily damaged if checked, connected or handled improperly.*

b) *Never leave the ignition switched on for long periods of time when the engine is not running.*

c) *Never disconnect the battery cables while the engine is running.*

d) *Maintain correct polarity when connecting battery cables from another vehicle during jump starting - see the "Booster battery (jump) starting" Section at the front of this manual.*

e) *Always disconnect the cable from the negative battery terminal before working on the electrical system, but read the battery disconnection procedure first (see Section 3).*

It's also a good idea to review the safety-related information regarding the engine electrical systems located in the *Safety first!* Section at the front of this manual before beginning any operation included in this Chapter.

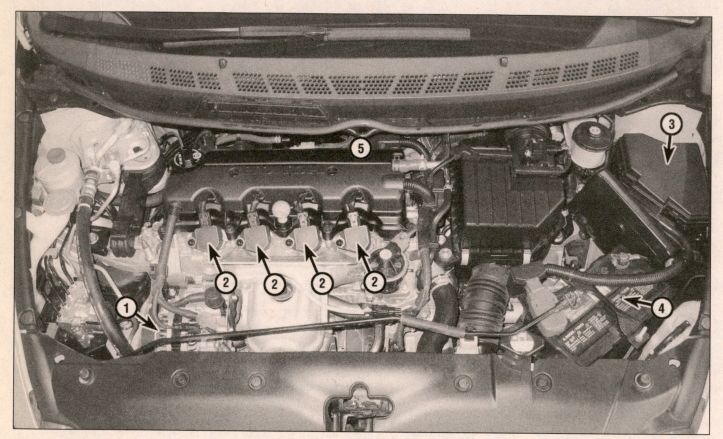

Electrical system components - 1.8L engine

1	Alternator	4	Battery
2	Ignition coil	5	Starter motor (side of engine
3	Fuse/relay block		block)

2 Troubleshooting

Ignition system

1   If a malfunction occurs in the ignition system, do not immediately assume that any particular part is causing the problem. First, check the following items:

a) *Make sure that the cable clamps at the battery terminals are clean and tight.*

b) *Test the condition of the battery (see Steps 21 through 24). If it doesn't pass all the tests, replace it.*

c) *Check the ignition coil or coil pack connections.*

d) *Check any relevant fuses in the engine compartment fuse and relay box (see Chapter 12). If they're burned, determine the cause and repair the circuit.*

Check

Refer to illustration 2.3

Warning: *Because of the high voltage generated by the ignition system, use extreme care when performing a procedure involving ignition components.*

Note 1: *The ignition system components on these vehicles are difficult to diagnose. In the event of ignition system failure that you can't diagnose, have the vehicle tested at a dealer service department or other qualified auto repair facility.*

Note 2: *You'll need a spark tester for the following test. Spark testers are available at most auto supply stores.*

2   If the engine turns over but won't start, verify that there is sufficient ignition voltage to fire the spark plugs as follows.

3   On models with a coil-over-plug type ignition system, remove a coil and install the tester between the boot at the lower end of the coil and the spark plug **(see illustration)**. On models with spark plug wires, disconnect a spark plug wire from a spark plug and install the tester between the spark plug wire boot and the spark plug.

4   Crank the engine and note whether or not the tester flashes. **Caution:** *Do NOT crank the engine or allow it to run for more than five seconds; running the engine for more than five seconds may set a Diagnostic Trouble Code (DTC) for a cylinder misfire.*

Models with a coil-over-plug type ignition system

5   If the tester flashes during cranking, the coil is delivering sufficient voltage to the spark plug to fire it. Repeat this test for each cylinder to verify that the other coils are OK.

6   If the tester doesn't flash, remove a coil from another cylinder and swap it for the one being tested. If the tester now flashes, you know that the original coil is bad. If the tester still doesn't flash, the PCM or wiring harness is probably defective. Have the PCM checked out by a dealer service department or other qualified repair shop (testing the PCM is beyond the scope of the do-it-yourselfer because it requires expensive special tools).

7   If the tester flashes during cranking but a misfire code (related to the cylinder being tested) has been stored, the spark plug could be fouled or defective.

Models with spark plug wires

8   If the tester flashes during cranking, sufficient voltage is reaching the spark plug to fire it.

9   Repeat this test on the remaining cylinders.

10   Proceed on this basis until you have verified that there's a good spark from each spark plug wire. If there is, then you have verified that the coils in the coil pack are functioning correctly and that the spark plug wires are OK.

11   If there is no spark from a spark plug wire, then either the coil is bad, the plug wire is bad or a connection at one end of the plug wire is loose. Assuming that you're using new plug wires or known good wires, then the coil is probably defective. Also inspect the coil pack electrical connector. Make sure that it's clean, tight and in good condition.

12   If all the coils are firing correctly, but the engine misfires, then one or more of the plugs might be fouled. Remove and check the spark plugs or install new ones (see Chapter 1).

13   No further testing of the ignition system is possible without special tools. If the problem persists, have the ignition system tested by a dealer service department or other qualified repair shop.

Charging system

14   If a malfunction occurs in the charging system, do not automatically assume the alternator is causing the problem. First check the following items:

a) *Check the drivebelt tension and condition, as described in Chapter 1. Replace it if it's worn or deteriorated.*

b) *Make sure the alternator mounting bolts are tight.*

c) *Inspect the alternator wiring harness and the connectors at the alternator and voltage regulator. They must be in good condition, tight and have no corrosion.*

d) *Check the fusible link (if equipped) or main fuse in the underhood fuse/relay box. If it is burned, determine the cause, repair the circuit and replace the link or fuse (the vehicle will not start and/or the accessories will not work if the fusible link or main fuse is blown).*

e) *Start the engine and check the alternator for abnormal noises (a shrieking or squealing sound indicates a bad bearing).*

f) *Check the battery. Make sure it's fully charged and in good condition (one bad cell in a battery can cause overcharging by the alternator).*

g) *Disconnect the battery cables (negative first, then positive). Inspect the battery posts and the cable clamps for corrosion. Clean them thoroughly if necessary (see Chapter 1). Reconnect the cables (positive first, negative last).*

Alternator - check

15   Use a voltmeter to check the battery voltage with the engine off. It should be at least 12.6 volts **(see illustration 2.21)**.

16   Start the engine and check the battery voltage again. It should now be approximately 13.5 to 15 volts.

17   If the voltage reading is more or less than the specified charging voltage, the voltage regulator is probably defective, which will require replacement of the alternator (the voltage regulator is not replaceable separately). Remove the alternator and have it bench tested (most auto parts stores will do this for you).

18   The charging system (battery) light on the instrument cluster lights up when the ignition key is turned to ON, but it should go out when the engine starts.

19   If the charging system light stays on after the engine has been started, there is a problem with the charging system. Before replacing the alternator, check the battery condition, alternator belt tension and electrical cable connections.

20   If replacing the alternator doesn't restore voltage to the specified range, have the charging system tested by a dealer service department or other qualified repair shop.

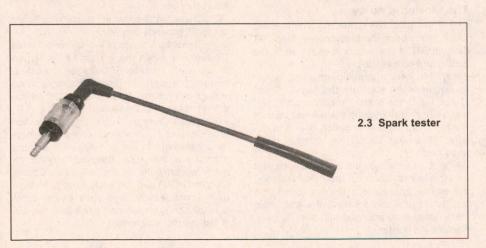

2.3 Spark tester

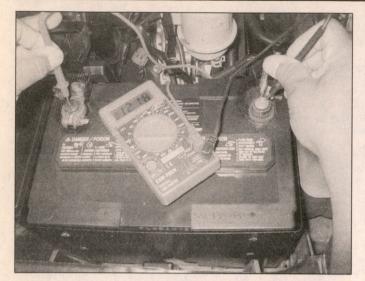

2.21 To test the open circuit voltage of the battery, touch the black probe of the voltmeter to the negative terminal and the red probe to the positive terminal of the battery; a fully charged battery should be at least 12.6 volts

2.23 Connect a battery load tester to the battery and check the battery condition under load following the tool manufacturer's instructions

Battery - check

Refer to illustrations 2.21 and 2.23

21   Check the battery state of charge. Visually inspect the indicator eye on the top of the battery (if equipped with one); if the indicator eye is black in color, charge the battery as described in Chapter 1. Next perform an open circuit voltage test using a digital voltmeter. **Note:** *The battery's surface charge must be removed before accurate voltage measurements can be made. Turn on the high beams for ten seconds, then turn them off and let the vehicle stand for two minutes.* With the engine and all accessories Off, touch the negative probe of the voltmeter to the negative terminal of the battery and the positive probe to the positive terminal of the battery **(see illustration)**. The battery voltage should be 12.6 volts or slightly above. If the battery is less than the specified voltage, charge the battery before proceeding to the next test. Do not proceed with the battery load test unless the battery charge is correct.

22   Disconnect the negative battery cable, then the positive cable from the battery.

23   Perform a battery load test. An accurate check of the battery condition can only be performed with a load tester **(see illustration)**. This test evaluates the ability of the battery to operate the starter and other accessories during periods of high current draw. Connect the load tester to the battery terminals. Load test the battery according to the tool manufacturer's instructions. This tool increases the load demand (current draw) on the battery.

24   Maintain the load on the battery for 15 seconds and observe that the battery voltage does not drop below 9.6 volts. If the battery condition is weak or defective, the

tool will indicate this condition immediately. **Note:** *Cold temperatures will cause the minimum voltage reading to drop slightly. Follow the chart given in the manufacturer's instructions to compensate for cold climates. Minimum load voltage for freezing temperatures (32 degrees F) should be approximately 9.1 volts.*

Starting system

The starter rotates, but the engine doesn't

25   Remove the starter (see Section 8). Check the overrunning clutch and bench test the starter to make sure the drive mechanism extends fully for proper engagement with the flywheel ring gear. If it doesn't, replace the starter.

26   Check the flywheel ring gear for missing teeth and other damage. With the ignition turned off, rotate the flywheel so you can check the entire ring gear.

The starter is noisy

27   If the solenoid is making a chattering noise, first check the battery (see Steps 21 through 24). If the battery is okay, check the cables and connections.

28   If you hear a grinding, crashing metallic sound when you turn the key to Start, check for loose starter mounting bolts. If they're tight, remove the starter and inspect the teeth on the starter pinion gear and flywheel ring gear. Look for missing or damaged teeth.

29   If the starter sounds fine when you first turn the key to Start, but then stops rotating the engine and emits a zinging sound, the problem is probably a defective starter drive that's not staying engaged with the ring gear. Replace the starter.

The starter rotates slowly

30   Check the battery (see Steps 21 through 24).

31   If the battery is okay, verify all connections (at the battery, the starter solenoid and motor) are clean, corrosion-free and tight. Make sure the cables aren't frayed or damaged.

32   Check that the starter mounting bolts are tight so it grounds properly. Also check the pinion gear and flywheel ring gear for evidence of a mechanical bind (galling, deformed gear teeth or other damage).

The starter does not rotate at all

33   Check the battery (see Steps 21 through 24).

34   If the battery is okay, verify all connections (at the battery, the starter solenoid and motor) are clean, corrosion-free and tight. Make sure the cables aren't frayed or damaged.

35   Check all of the fuses in the underhood fuse/relay box.

36   Check that the starter mounting bolts are tight so it grounds properly.

37   Check for voltage at the starter solenoid "S" terminal when the ignition key is turned to the start position. If voltage is present, replace the starter/solenoid assembly. If no voltage is present, the problem could be the starter relay, the Transmission Range (TR) switch (see Chapter 6) or clutch start switch (see Chapter 8), or with an electrical connector somewhere in the circuit (see the wiring diagrams at the end of Chapter 12). Also, on many modern vehicles, the Powertrain Control Module (PCM) and the Body Control Module (BCM) control the voltage signal to the starter solenoid; on such vehicles a special scan tool is required for diagnosis.

3   Battery - disconnection and reconnection

Warning: *Always disconnect the cable from the negative battery terminal FIRST and hook it up LAST or the battery may be shorted by the tool being used to loosen the cable clamps.*

Some systems on the vehicle require battery power to be available at all times, either to maintain continuous operation (alarm system, power door locks, etc.), or to maintain control unit memory (radio station presets, Powertrain Control Module and other control units). When the battery is disconnected, the power that maintains these systems is cut. So, before you disconnect the battery, please note that on a vehicle with power door locks, it's a wise precaution to remove the key from the ignition and to keep it with you, so that it does not get locked inside if the power door locks should engage accidentally when the battery is reconnected!

Devices known as "memory-savers" can be used to avoid some of these problems. Precise details vary according to the device used. The typical memory saver is plugged into the cigarette lighter and is connected to a spare battery. Then the vehicle battery can be disconnected from the electrical system. The memory saver will provide sufficient current to maintain audio unit security codes, PCM memory, etc. and will provide power to always hot circuits such as the clock and radio memory circuits. **Warning 1:** *Some memory savers deliver a considerable amount of current in order to keep vehicle systems operational after the main battery is disconnected. If you're using a memory saver, make sure that the circuit concerned is actually open before servicing it.* **Warning 2:** *If you're going to work near any of the airbag system components, the battery MUST be disconnected and a memory saver must NOT be used. If a memory saver is used, power will be supplied to the airbag, which means that it could accidentally deploy and cause serious personal injury.*

Disconnection

To disconnect the battery for service procedures requiring power to be cut from the vehicle, loosen the cable end bolt and disconnect the cable from the negative battery terminal. Isolate the cable end to prevent it from coming into accidental contact with the battery terminal.

Reconnection

After reconnecting the battery, perform the following relearning procedures:

Powertrain Control Module (PCM) idle learn procedure

1   Make sure that the PCM learns the engine idle characteristics after you perform

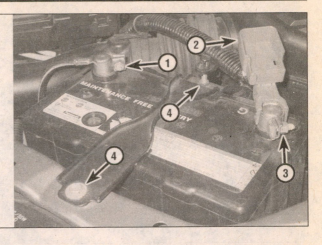

4.1 Battery details:

1   *Negative battery cable*
2   *Positive terminal cover*
3   *Positive battery cable*
4   *Battery hold-down clamp fasteners*

any of the following procedures:

> *Disconnect the battery*
> *Replace (or reset) the PCM*
> *Replace the throttle body*
> *Replace the Idle Air Control (IAC) valve*
> *Remove the No. 6 (15 amp) PCM fuse (in the engine compartment fuse and relay box)*
> *Remove the No. 19 (120-amp) BATTERY fuse (in the engine compartment fuse and relay box)*
> *Remove the PGM-FI main relay No. 1*
> *Remove any of the wires from the engine compartment fuse and relay box*
> *Disconnect any of the connectors from the engine compartment fuse and relay box*
> *Disconnect the electrical connector between the engine compartment wire harness and the PCM wire harness*
> *Disconnect the battery ground wire from the transmission housing*
> *Disconnect the ground wire from the body*
> *Disconnect the ground wire from the cylinder head*

2   Make sure that all electrical components (air conditioning system, lights, rear window defogger, sound system, etc.) are turned OFF.

3   Start the engine, bring it up to 3000 rpm and hold it there, with no load (in PARK or NEUTRAL), until the radiator fan comes on or until the engine coolant temperature reaches 194-degrees F.

4   Allow the engine to idle for at least five minutes with no load on it and with the throttle fully closed. **Note:** *If the radiator fan comes on during this five-minute period, don't include the time during which the fan runs as part of the five minutes.*

Resetting the power window control unit

5   On CR-V models through 2006 and on 2004 hatchbacks, you must reset the power window control unit after you perform any of the following procedures:

> *Disconnect the battery*
> *Remove the No. 6 (7.5 amp) and/or the*

> *No. 23 (20 amp) fuse from the under-dash fuse and relay box*
> *Disconnect the driver's door wiring harness*

6   Turn the ignition switch to OFF, then turn it to ON.

7   Fully open the driver's window by holding the driver's switch in the AUTO DOWN position. After the window reaches its fully open position, hold the driver's switch in the AUTO DOWN position for two seconds.

8   Fully close the driver's window by holding the driver's switch in the AUTO UP position. After the window reaches its fully closed position, hold the driver's switch in the AUTO UP position for two seconds.

9   If the window doesn't operate in AUTO, reset the power window control unit by repeating this entire procedure.

4   Battery - removal and installation

Refer to illustration 4.1

1   Disconnect the cable from the negative battery terminal first, then disconnect the cable from the positive battery terminal **(see illustration)**.

2   Remove the battery hold-down clamp.

3   Lift out the battery. Be careful - it's heavy. **Note:** *Battery straps and handlers are available at most auto parts stores for reasonable prices. They make it easier to remove and carry the battery.*

4   If you are replacing the battery, make sure you get one that's identical, with the same dimensions, amperage rating, cold cranking rating, etc.

5   Installation is the reverse of removal. Be sure to connect the positive cable first and the negative cable last.

5   Battery cables - replacement

1   When removing the cables, always disconnect the cable from the negative battery terminal first and hook it up last, or you might accidentally short out the battery with the tool you're using to loosen the cable

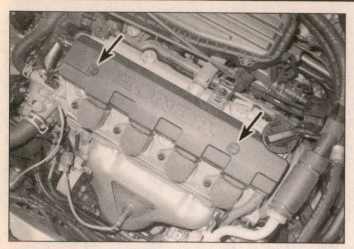

6.1a Ignition coil cover fasteners (2005 and earlier models shown)

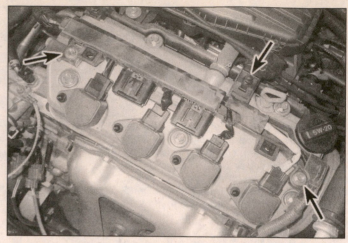

6.1b Ignition coil harness fasteners (2005 and earlier models shown)

clamps. Even if you're only replacing the cable for the positive terminal, be sure to disconnect the negative cable from the battery first.

2   Disconnect the old cables from the battery, then trace each of them to their opposite ends and disconnect them. Be sure to note the routing of each cable before disconnecting it to ensure correct installation.

3   If you are replacing any of the old cables, take them with you when buying new cables. It is vitally important that you replace the cables with identical parts.

4   Clean the threads of the solenoid or ground connection with a wire brush to remove rust and corrosion. Apply a light coat of battery terminal corrosion inhibitor or petroleum jelly to the threads to prevent future corrosion.

5   Attach the cable to the solenoid or ground connection and tighten the mounting nut/bolt securely.

6   Before connecting a new cable to the battery, make sure that it reaches the battery post without having to be stretched.

7   Connect the cable to the positive battery terminal first, *then* connect the ground cable to the negative battery terminal.

6   Ignition coils - replacement

Refer to illustrations 6.1a, 6.1b and 6.2

1   Remove the ignition coil cover **(see illustrations)**. **Note:** *On 2006 and later Civics with 1.8L engines, there is no ignition coil cover.*

2   Disconnect the electrical connector from the ignition coil **(see illustration)**.

3   Remove the ignition coil mounting fasteners.

4   Remove the ignition coil from the spark plug.

5   Installation is the reverse of removal. Be sure to tighten the ignition coil mounting nut securely.

7   Alternator - removal and installation

All models

1   Disconnect the cable from the negative terminal of the battery (see Section 3).

Coupe and sedan models
2005 and earlier models

Refer to illustrations 7.3, 7.6a and 7.6b

2   Remove the power steering pump belt (see Chapter 1), then remove the power steering pump (see Chapter 10) and set the pump aside. **Note:** *Do NOT disconnect any of the power steering hoses.*

3   Disconnect the harness clip that secures the harness to the alternator, remove the nut that attaches the alternator output cable to the stud on the backside of the alternator and disconnect the electrical connector from the alternator **(see illustration)**. Set the alternator output cable aside.

4   Remove the alternator/air conditioning compressor drivebelt (see Chapter 1).

5   Loosen the lug nuts on the left front wheel, raise the front of the vehicle, place it securely on jackstands and remove the left front wheel.

6   Remove the lock bolt and adjusting bolt **(see illustration)** from the bracket between the alternator and the air conditioning compressor. Remove the alternator upper mounting bolt **(see illustration)** and remove the alternator.

7   If you're replacing the alternator, take the old one with you when purchasing the replacement unit. Make sure that the new/rebuilt unit looks identical to the old alternator. Look at the terminals - they should be the same in number, size and location as the terminals on the old alternator.

8   Many new/rebuilt alternators DO NOT have a pulley installed, so you might have to swap the pulley from the old unit to the new/rebuilt one. When buying an alternator, find out the store's policy regarding pulley swaps. Some stores perform this service free of charge. If your local auto parts store doesn't offer this service, you'll have to purchase a puller for removing the pulley and do it yourself.

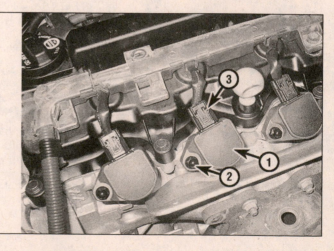

6.2 Ignition coil details

1   *Ignition coil*
2   *Ignition coil mounting bolt*
3   *Connector*

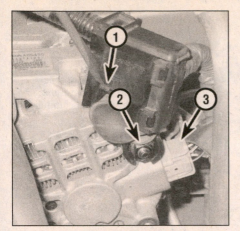

7.3 Alternator electrical connection details

1   Output cable clip mounting nut
2   Alternator output cable to the stud terminal (on the backside of the alternator)
3   Alternator electrical connector

7.6a Alternator lower mounting bracket details

1   Lock bolt
2   Adjusting bolt

7.6b Alternator upper mounting bolt

9   Installation is the reverse of removal. Be sure to tighten the alternator adjusting and mounting bolts securely. Tighten the wheel lug nuts to the torque listed in the Chapter 1 Specifications.
10   Reconnect the cable to the negative terminal of the battery (see Section 3). Check the charging voltage (see Section 2) to verify that the alternator is operating correctly.

2006 and later models

1.8L engines

Refer to illustration 7.12

11   Remove the drivebelt (see Chapter 1).
12   Disconnect the electrical connectors and the positive alternator cable **(see illustration)**. Detach the harness clip from the alternator and set the electrical harness aside.
13   Remove the alternator mounting bolts and the alternator from the vehicle.
14   Installation is the reverse of removal. Tighten the alternator mounting bolts securely.
15   Reconnect the cable to the negative terminal of the battery (see Section 3). Check the charging voltage (see Section 2) to verify that the alternator is operating correctly.

2.0L engines

16   Remove the drivebelt (see Chapter 1).
17   Remove the front grille (see Chapter 11).
18   Disconnect the cooling fan motor harness from the radiator support. Remove the radiator cap base bolts and the radiator upper brackets from the support.
19   Remove the radiator crossmember (or bulkhead) mounting bolts and remove the support.
20   Remove the alternator mounting bolts.
21   Disconnect the electrical connector and the positive alternator cable. Detach the har-

ness clip from the alternator and set the electrical harness aside. Remove the alternator.
22   Installation is the reverse of removal. Tighten the alternator mounting bolts securely.
23   Reconnect the cable to the negative terminal of the battery (see Section 3). Check the charging voltage (see Section 2) to verify that the alternator is operating correctly.

Hatchback models

24   Remove the front bumper cover (see Chapter 11).
25   Remove the right headlight housing (see Chapter 12).
26   Remove the coolant reservoir (see Chapter 3).
27   Remove the accessory drivebelt (see Chapter 1).
28   Remove the three alternator mounting bolts.
29   Disconnect the electrical connector and the black wire from the alternator (the black wire goes to the ELD unit in the engine compartment fuse and relay box). Detach the har-

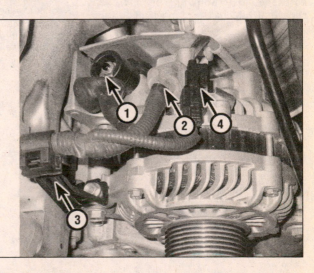

7.12 Alternator details - 1.8L engines

1   Positive alternator cable
2   Alternator electrical connector
3   Harness clamp
4   Harness connector

ness clip from the alternator and set the electrical harness aside. Remove the alternator.
30   Refer to Steps 7 and 8.
31   Installation is the reverse of removal. Tighten the alternator mounting bolts to the torque listed in this Chapter's Specifications.
32   Reconnect the cable to the negative terminal of the battery (see Section 3). Check the charging voltage (see Section 2) to verify that the alternator is operating correctly.

CR-V models

2006 and earlier models

33   Unscrew the battery ground strap bolt from the radiator crossmember, remove the cover from the radiator crossmember and remove the upper radiator mounting brackets and rubber insulators (see "Radiator - removal and installation" in Chapter 3).
34   Remove the alternator mounting bolts (removing the mounting bolts first will give you a little wiggle room for disconnecting the electrical connections).
35   Disconnect the electrical connector and

the black wire from the alternator (the black wire goes to the ELD unit in the engine compartment fuse and relay box). Detach the harness clip from the alternator and set the electrical harness aside. Remove the alternator.

36   Installation is the reverse of removal. Tighten the alternator mounting bolts securely.

37   Reconnect the cable to the negative terminal of the battery (see Section 3). Check the charging voltage (see Section 2) to verify that the alternator is operating correctly.

2007 and later models

38   Remove the drivebelt and tensioner (see Chapter 1).

39   Remove the alternator mounting bolts.

40   Disconnect the electrical connector and the black wire from the alternator (the black wire goes to the ELD unit in the engine compartment fuse and relay box). Detach the harness clip from the alternator and set the electrical harness aside. Remove the alternator.

41   Installation is the reverse of removal. Tighten the alternator mounting bolts securely.

42   Reconnect the cable to the negative terminal of the battery (see Section 3). Check the charging voltage (see Section 2) to verify that the alternator is operating correctly.

---

8   Starter motor - removal and installation

All models

1   Disconnect the cable from the negative terminal of the battery (see Section 3).

Coupe and sedan models

2005 and earlier models

Refer to illustration 8.3

2   Remove the air intake resonator (see "Air filter housing - removal and installation" in Chapter 4).

3   Clearly label, then disconnect the wires from the terminals on the starter motor solenoid **(see illustration)**. Also disconnect any clips that attach the wiring to the starter assembly.

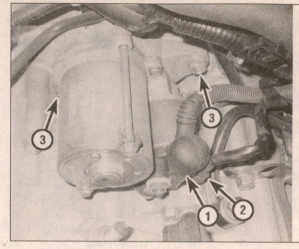

8.3 Starter motor details - 2006 and earlier models shown, other models similar

1   Positive battery cable
2   Solenoid wires
3   Starter motor mounting bolts

4   Remove the starter mounting bolts and detach the starter.

5   Installation is the reverse of removal. Be sure to tighten the starter mounting bolts securely, then reconnect the cable to the negative terminal of the battery (see Section 3).

2006 and later models

6   Raise the vehicle and support it securely on jackstands and remove the splash shield.

7   On 1.8L engines, remove the exhaust pipe (see Chapter 4).

8   On all engines, remove the intake manifold support bracket bolts and bracket.

9   Clearly label, then disconnect the wires from the terminals on the starter motor solenoid. Also disconnect any clips that attach the wiring to the starter assembly.

10   Remove the starter mounting bolts and remove the starter motor.

11   Installation is the reverse of removal. Be sure to tighten the starter mounting bolts securely, then reconnect the cable to the negative terminal of the battery (see Section 3).

CR-V and hatchback models

2006 and earlier model CR-V and hatchback

12   Disconnect the knock sensor electrical connector (see Chapter 6).

13   On hatchbacks, remove the bolt that attaches the harness bracket and the intake manifold bracket, then remove the intake manifold bracket.

14   Clearly label, then disconnect the wires from the terminals on the starter motor solenoid. Also disconnect any clips that attach the wiring to the starter assembly.

15   Remove the starter mounting bolts and remove the starter motor.

16   Installation is the reverse of removal. Be sure to tighten the starter mounting bolts securely, then reconnect the cable to the negative terminal of the battery (see Section 3).

2007 and later CR-V

17   Raise the vehicle and support it securely on jackstands and remove the splash shield.

18   Remove the exhaust pipe (see Chapter 4) and remove the intake manifold support bracket bolts and bracket.

19   The starter is located on the side of the engine near the radiator.

20   Clearly label, then disconnect the wires from the terminals on the starter motor solenoid. Also disconnect any clips that attach the wiring to the starter assembly.

21   Remove the starter mounting bolts and remove the starter motor from under the vehicle.

22   Installation is the reverse of removal. Be sure to tighten the starter mounting bolts securely, then reconnect the cable to the negative terminal of the battery (see Section 3).

Chapter 6
Emissions and engine control systems

Contents

	Section
Accelerator Pedal Position (APP) sensor - replacement	4
Camshaft Position (CMP) sensor - replacement	5
Catalytic converter - replacement	20
Crankshaft Position (CKP) sensor - replacement	6
Engine Coolant Temperature (ECT) sensor(s) - replacement	7
Evaporative Emissions Control (EVAP) system - component replacement	21
Exhaust Gas Recirculation (EGR) valve - replacement	22
General information	1
Idle Air Control (IAC) valve (2005 and earlier Civics, 2004 and earlier CR-V models) - replacement	18
Input shaft (mainshaft) speed sensor - replacement	9
Intake Manifold Runner Control (IMRC) or Intake Manifold Tuning (IMT) system - component replacement	19
Knock sensor - replacement	10

	Section
Manifold Absolute Pressure (MAP) sensor - replacement	11
Mass Air Flow (MAF) sensor/Intake Air Temperature (IAT) sensor - replacement	8
Obtaining and clearing Diagnostic Trouble Codes (DTCs)	3
On Board Diagnosis (OBD) system	2
Output shaft (countershaft) speed sensor - replacement	12
Oxygen sensors - replacement	13
Positive Crankcase Ventilation (PCV) valve - replacement	23
Power Steering Pressure (PSP) switch - replacement	14
Powertrain Control Module (PCM) - removal and installation	17
Throttle Position (TP) sensor - replacement	15
Transmission range switch - replacement and adjustment	16
Variable Valve Timing and Lift Electronic Control (VTEC) system - description and component replacement	24

Specifications

Torque specifications

Note: *One foot-pound (ft-lb) of torque is equivalent to 12 inch-pounds (in-lbs) of torque. Torque values below approximately 15 ft-lbs are expressed in inch-pounds, since most foot-pound torque wrenches are not accurate at these smaller values.*

	Ft-lbs (unless otherwise indicated)	Nm
Coolant outlet bolts	105 in-lbs	12
Knock sensor		
Coupe and sedan	16	22
CR-V and hatchback	23	31

1   General information

To prevent pollution of the atmosphere from incompletely burned and evaporating gases, and to maintain good driveability and fuel economy, a number of emission control systems are incorporated. They include the:

Catalytic converter

A catalytic converter is an emission control device in the exhaust system that reduces certain pollutants in the exhaust gas stream. There are two types of converters: oxidation converters and reduction converters.

Oxidation converters contain a monolithic substrate (a ceramic honeycomb) coated with the semi-precious metals platinum and palladium. An oxidation catalyst reduces unburned hydrocarbons (HC) and carbon monoxide (CO) by adding oxygen to the exhaust stream as it passes through the substrate, which, in the presence of high temperature and the catalyst materials, converts the HC and CO to water vapor (H_2O) and carbon dioxide (CO_2).

Reduction converters contain a monolithic substrate coated with platinum and rhodium. A reduction catalyst reduces oxides of nitrogen (NOx) by removing oxygen, which in the presence of high temperature and the catalyst material produces nitrogen (N) and carbon dioxide (CO_2).

Catalytic converters that combine both types of catalysts in one assembly are known as "three-way catalysts" or TWCs. A TWC can reduce all three pollutants.

Evaporative Emissions Control (EVAP) system

The Evaporative Emissions Control (EVAP) system prevents fuel system vapors (which contain unburned hydrocarbons) from escaping into the atmosphere. On warm days, vapors trapped inside the fuel tank expand until the pressure reaches a certain threshold. Then the fuel vapors are routed from the fuel tank through the fuel vapor vent valve and the fuel vapor control valve to the EVAP canister, where they're stored temporarily until the next time the vehicle is operated. When the conditions are right (engine warmed up, vehicle up to speed, moderate or heavy load on the engine, etc.) the PCM opens the canister purge valve, which allows fuel vapors to be drawn from the canister into the intake manifold. Once in the intake manifold, the fuel vapors mix with incoming air before being drawn through the intake ports into the combustion chambers where they're burned up with the rest of the air/fuel mixture. The EVAP system is complex and virtually impossible to troubleshoot without the right tools and training.

Exhaust Gas Recirculation (EGR) system

The EGR system reduces oxides of nitrogen by recirculating exhaust gases from the exhaust manifold, through the EGR valve and intake manifold, then back to the combustion chambers, where it mixes with the incoming air/fuel mixture before being consumed. These recirculated exhaust gases dilute the incoming air/fuel mixture, which cools the combustion chambers, thereby reducing NOx emissions.

The EGR system consists of the Powertrain Control Module (PCM), the EGR valve, the EGR valve position sensor and various other information sensors that the PCM uses to determine when to open the EGR valve. The degree to which the EGR valve is opened is referred to as "EGR valve lift." The PCM is programmed to produce the ideal EGR valve lift for varying operating conditions. The EGR valve position sensor, which is an integral part of the EGR valve, detects the amount of EGR valve lift and sends this information to the PCM. The PCM then compares it with the appropriate EGR valve lift for the operating conditions. The PCM increases current flow to the EGR valve to increase valve lift and reduces the current to reduce the amount of lift. If EGR flow is inappropriate to the operating conditions (idle, cold engine, etc.) the PCM simply cuts the current to the EGR valve and the valve closes.

Powertrain Control Module (PCM)

The Powertrain Control Module (PCM) is the brain of the engine management system. It also controls a wide variety of other vehicle systems. In order to program the new PCM, the dealer needs the vehicle as well as the new PCM. If you're planning to replace the PCM with a new one, there is no point in trying to do so at home because you won't be able to program it yourself.

Positive Crankcase Ventilation (PCV) system

The Positive Crankcase Ventilation (PCV) system reduces hydrocarbon emissions by scavenging crankcase vapors, which are rich in unburned hydrocarbons. A PCV valve or orifice regulates the flow of gases into the intake manifold in proportion to the amount of intake vacuum available.

The PCV system generally consists of the fresh air inlet hose, the PCV valve or orifice and the crankcase ventilation hose (or PCV hose). The fresh air inlet hose connects the air intake duct to a pipe on the valve cover. The crankcase ventilation hose (or PCV hose) connects the PCV valve or orifice in the valve cover to the intake manifold.

Emissions and engine control system components

1	Integral exhaust manifold/catalytic converter assembly	5	Exhaust Gas Recirculation (EGR) valve
2	Upstream oxygen sensor	6	Engine Coolant Temperature (ECT) sensor 1
3	EVAP canister purge valve	7	Powertrain Control Module (PCM)
4	VTEC solenoid valve	8	Mass Air Flow (MAF) sensor/Intake Air Temperature (IAT) sensor

Information Sensors

Accelerator Pedal Position (APP) sensor - as you press the accelerator pedal, the APP sensor alters its voltage signal to the PCM in proportion to the angle of the pedal, and the PCM commands a motor inside the throttle body to open or close the throttle plate accordingly

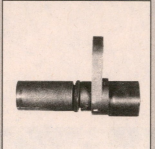

Camshaft Position (CMP) sensor - produces a signal that the PCM uses to identify the number 1 cylinder and to time the firing sequence of the fuel injectors

Crankshaft Position (CKP) sensor - produces a signal that the PCM uses to calculate engine speed and crankshaft position, which enables it to synchronize ignition timing with fuel injector timing, and to detect misfires

Engine Coolant Temperature (ECT) sensor - a thermistor (temperature-sensitive variable resistor) that sends a voltage signal to the PCM, which uses this data to determine the temperature of the engine coolant

Fuel tank pressure sensor - measures the fuel tank pressure and controls fuel tank pressure by signaling the EVAP system to purge the fuel tank vapors when the pressure becomes excessive

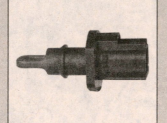

Intake Air Temperature (IAT) sensor - monitors the temperature of the air entering the engine and sends a signal to the PCM to determine injector pulse-width (the duration of each injector's on-time) and to adjust spark timing (to prevent spark knock)

Knock sensor - a piezoelectric crystal that oscillates in proportion to engine vibration which produces a voltage output that is monitored by the PCM. This retards the ignition timing when the oscillation exceeds a certain threshold

Manifold Absolute Pressure (MAP) sensor - monitors the pressure or vacuum inside the intake manifold. The PCM uses this data to determine engine load so that it can alter the ignition advance and fuel enrichment

Mass Air Flow (MAF) sensor - measures the amount of intake air drawn into the engine. It uses a hot-wire sensing element to measure the amount of air entering the engine

Oxygen sensors - generates a small variable voltage signal in proportion to the difference between the oxygen content in the exhaust stream and the oxygen content in the ambient air. The PCM uses this information to maintain the proper air/fuel ratio. A second oxygen sensor monitors the efficiency of the catalytic converter

Throttle Position (TP) sensor - a potentiometer that generates a voltage signal that varies in relation to the opening angle of the throttle plate inside the throttle body. Works with the PCM and other sensors to calculate injector pulse width (the duration of each injector's on-time)

Photos courtesy of Wells Manufacturing, except APP and MAF sensors.

2.4a Simple code readers are an economical way to extract trouble codes when the CHECK ENGINE light comes on

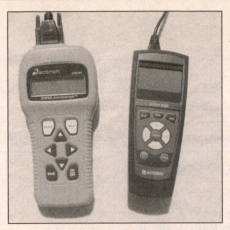

2.4b Hand-held scan tools like these can extract computer codes and also perform diagnostics

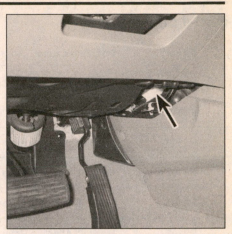

3.1 The Data Link Connector (DLC) is located under the lower edge of the dash, to the right of the steering column

2 On Board Diagnosis (OBD) system

General description

1   All models are equipped with the second generation OBD-II system. This system consists of an on-board computer known as the Powertrain Control Module (PCM), and information sensors, which monitor various functions of the engine and send data to the PCM. This system incorporates a series of diagnostic monitors that detect and identify fuel injection and emissions control system faults and store the information in the computer memory. This system also tests sensors and output actuators, diagnoses drive cycles, freezes data and clears codes.

2   The PCM is the brain of the electronically controlled fuel and emissions system. It receives data from a number of sensors and other electronic components (switches, relays, etc.). Based on the information it receives, the PCM generates output signals to control various relays, solenoids (fuel injectors) and other actuators. The PCM is specifically calibrated to optimize the emissions, fuel economy and driveability of the vehicle.

3   It isn't a good idea to attempt diagnosis or replacement of the PCM or emission control components at home while the vehicle is under warranty. Because of a federally-mandated warranty which covers the emissions system components and because any owner-induced damage to the PCM, the sensors and/or the control devices may void this warranty, take the vehicle to a dealer service department if the PCM or a system component malfunctions.

Scan tool information

Refer to illustrations 2.4a and 2.4b

4   Because extracting the Diagnostic Trouble Codes (DTCs) from an engine management system is now the first step in troubleshooting many computer-controlled systems and components, a code reader, at the very least, will be required **(see illustration)**. More powerful scan tools can also perform many of the diagnostics once associated with expensive factory scan tools **(see illustration)**. If you're planning to obtain a generic scan tool for your vehicle, make sure that it's compatible with OBD-II systems. If you don't plan to purchase a code reader or scan tool and don't have access to one, you can have the codes extracted by a dealer service department or an independent repair shop. **Note:** *Some auto parts stores even provide this service.*

3 Obtaining and clearing Diagnostic Trouble Codes (DTCs)

All models covered by this manual are equipped with on-board diagnostics. When the PCM recognizes a malfunction in a monitored emission or engine control system, component or circuit, it turns on the Malfunction Indicator Light (MIL) on the dash. The PCM will continue to display the MIL until the problem is fixed and the Diagnostic Trouble Code (DTC) is cleared from the PCM's memory. You'll need a scan tool to access any DTCs stored in the PCM.

Before outputting any DTCs stored in the PCM, thoroughly inspect ALL electrical connectors and hoses. Make sure that all electrical connections are tight, clean and free of corrosion. And make sure that all hoses are correctly connected, fit tightly and are in good condition (no cracks or tears).

Accessing the DTCs

Refer to illustration 3.1

1   The Diagnostic Trouble Codes (DTCs) can only be accessed with a code reader or scan tool. Professional scan tools are expensive, but relatively inexpensive generic code readers or scan tools **(see illustrations 2.4a and 2.4b)** are available at most auto parts stores. Simply plug the connector of the scan tool into the diagnostic connector **(see illustration)**. Then follow the instructions included with the scan tool to extract the DTCs.

2   Once you have outputted all of the stored DTCs, look them up on the accompanying DTC chart.

3   After troubleshooting the source of each DTC, make any necessary repairs or replace the defective component(s).

Clearing the DTCs

4   Clear the DTCs with the code reader or scan tool in accordance with the instructions provided by the tool's manufacturer.

Diagnostic Trouble Codes

5   The accompanying tables are a list of the Diagnostic Trouble Codes (DTCs) that can be accessed by a do-it-yourselfer working at home (there are many, many more DTCs available to professional mechanics with proprietary scan tools and software, but those codes cannot be accessed by a generic scan tool). If, after you have checked and repaired the connectors, wire harness and vacuum hoses (if applicable) for an emission-related system, component or circuit, the problem persists, have the vehicle checked by a dealer service department or other qualified repair shop.

OBD-II trouble codes

Code	Possible cause
P0010	Variable Valve Timing Control (VTC) oil control solenoid valve malfunction
P0011	Variable Valve Timing Control (VTC) system malfunction
P0101	Mass air flow or volume air flow circuit, range or performance problem
P0102	Mass air flow or volume air flow circuit, low input
P0103	Mass air flow or volume air flow circuit, high input
P0107	Manifold Absolute Pressure (MAP) sensor circuit, low voltage
P0108	Manifold Absolute Pressure (MAP) sensor circuit, high voltage
P0111	Intake Air Temperature (IAT) sensor circuit, range performance problem
P0112	Intake Air Temperature (IAT) sensor circuit, low voltage
P0113	Intake Air Temperature (IAT) sensor circuit, high voltage
P0116	Engine Coolant Temperature (ECT) sensor range/performance problem
P0117	Engine Coolant Temperature (ECT) sensor circuit, low voltage
P0118	Engine Coolant Temperature (ECT) sensor circuit, high voltage
P0122	Throttle Position (TP) sensor circuit, low voltage
P0123	Throttle Position (TP) sensor circuit, high voltage
P0125	Engine Coolant Temperature (ECT) sensor, slow response
P0128	Cooling system malfunction
P0131	Upstream oxygen sensor circuit, low voltage
P0132	Upstream oxygen sensor circuit, high voltage
P0133	Upstream oxygen sensor circuit, slow response
P0133	Air/Fuel (A/F) ratio sensor circuit, slow response
P0134	Air/Fuel (A/F) ratio sensor circuit, no activity detected
P0135	Upstream oxygen sensor, heater circuit malfunction
P0135	Air/Fuel (A/F) ratio sensor, heater circuit malfunction
P0137	Downstream oxygen sensor circuit, low voltage
P0138	Downstream oxygen sensor circuit, high voltage
P0139	Downstream oxygen sensor circuit, slow response
P0141	Downstream oxygen sensor, heater circuit malfunction

Code	Possible cause
P0143	Third oxygen sensor circuit, low voltage
P0144	Third oxygen sensor circuit, high voltage
P0145	Third oxygen sensor circuit, slow response
P0147	Third oxygen sensor, heater circuit malfunction
P0171	Fuel system too lean
P0172	Fuel system too rich
P0222	Throttle Position Sensor (TP) sensor circuit, low voltage
P0223	Throttle Position Sensor (TP) sensor circuit, high voltage
P0300	Random misfire detected
P0301	Cylinder no. 1 misfire detected
P0302	Cylinder no. 2 misfire detected
P0303	Cylinder no. 3 misfire detected
P0304	Cylinder no. 4 misfire detected
P0325	Knock sensor circuit malfunction
P0335	Crankshaft Position (CKP) sensor circuit, no signal
P0336	Crankshaft Position (CKP) sensor circuit, intermittent interruption
P0339	Crankshaft Position (CKP) sensor circuit, intermittent interruption
P0340	Camshaft Position (CMP) sensor, no signal
P0340	Camshaft Position (CMP) sensor A, no signal
P0341	Variable Valve Timing Control (VTC) phase gap
P0344	Camshaft Position (CMP) sensor, intermittent interruption
P0344	Camshaft Position (CMP) sensor A, intermittent interruption
P0365	Camshaft Position (CMP) sensor B, no signal
P0369	Camshaft Position (CMP) sensor B, intermittent interruption
P0401	Exhaust Gas Recirculation (EGR) system, insufficient flow
P0404	Exhaust Gas Recirculation (EGR) valve, insufficient lift
P0406	Exhaust Gas Recirculation (EGR) valve position sensor circuit, high voltage
P0420	Catalyst system efficiency below threshold
P0443	Evaporative emission control system, purge control valve circuit malfunction

OBD-II trouble codes (continued)

Code	Possible cause
P0451	Fuel tank pressure sensor, range or performance problem
P0452	Fuel tank pressure sensor circuit, low voltage
P0453	Fuel tank pressure sensor circuit, high voltage
P0455	Evaporative emission (EVAP) control system leak detected (no purge flow or large leak)
P0456	Evaporative emission (EVAP) control system leak detected (very small leak)
P0457	Evaporative emission control system leak detected (fuel cap loose/off)
P0461	Fuel level sensor circuit, range or performance problem
P0462	Fuel level sensor circuit, low input
P0463	Fuel level sensor circuit, high input
P0496	Evaporative emission system - high purge flow
P0497	Evaporative Emission (EVAP) system, low purge flow
P0498	Evaporative emission system, vent control - circuit low
P0499	Evaporative emission system, vent control - circuit high
P0500	Vehicle Speed Sensor (VSS), circuit malfunction
P0501	Vehicle Speed Sensor (VSS), range or performance problem
P0502	Vehicle Speed Sensor (VSS), no signal
P0505	Idle control system malfunction
P0506	Idle control system, rpm lower than expected
P0507	Idle control system, rpm higher than expected
P0511	Idle Air Control (IAC) valve, circuit malfunction
P0532	A/C refrigerant pressure sensor, low input
P0533	A/C refrigerant pressure sensor, high input
P0562	System voltage low
P0563	System voltage high
P0600	Serial communication link malfunction
P0602	Engine Control Module (ECM), programming error
P0603	Engine Control Module (ECM), internal circuit malfunction
P0606	Engine Control Module (ECM), processor malfunction

Code	Possible cause
P0607	Powertrain Control Module (PCM) internal circuit malfunction
P0630	VIN not programmed, or mismatched
P0661	Intake Manifold Runner Control (IMRC) valve position sensor circuit, low voltage
P0662	Intake Manifold Runner Control (IMRC) valve position sensor circuit, high voltage
P0685	PCM power control circuit - internal circuit malfunction

Automatic transmission diagnostic trouble codes

Code	Possible cause
P0705	Transmission Range (TR) switch, multiple shift position input
P0706	Transmission Range (TR) switch, open circuit
P0710	Automatic Transmission Fluid (ATF) temperature sensor
P0711	Transmission fluid temperature sensor circuit, range or performance problem
P0713	Transmission fluid temperature sensor circuit, high input
P0715	Input shaft (mainshaft) speed sensor
P0716	Input shaft (mainshaft) speed sensor, range or performance problem
P0717	Input shaft (mainshaft) speed sensor, no signal input
P0718	Input/turbine speed sensor circuit, intermittent signal
P0720	Output shaft (countershaft) speed sensor
P0721	Output shaft (countershaft) speed sensor, range or performance problem
P0722	Output shaft (countershaft) speed sensor, no signal input
P0723	Output speed sensor circuit, intermittent signal
P0730	Shift control system
P0731	Incorrect gear ratio, first gear
P0732	Incorrect gear ratio, second gear
P0733	Incorrect gear ratio, third gear
P0734	Incorrect gear ratio, fourth gear
P0735	Incorrect gear ratio, fifth gear
P0740	Lock-up control system
P0741	Lock-up control system

Automatic transmission diagnostic trouble codes (continued)

Code	Possible cause
P0745	Mechanical problem in hydraulic system
P0747	Pressure control solenoid, stuck in On position
P0748	Automatic transmission clutch pressure control solenoid valve A
P0750	Mechanical problem in hydraulic system
P0752	Shift solenoid A, stuck in On position
P0753	Shift control solenoid valve A
P0756	Shift solenoid B, performance problem or stuck in Off position
P0757	Shift solenoid B, stuck in On position
P0758	Shift control solenoid valve B
P0761	Shift solenoid C, performance problem or stuck in Off position
P0771	Shift solenoid E, performance problem or stuck in Off position
P0776	Pressure control solenoid "B" performance or stuck in Off position
P0777	Pressure control solenoid "B" stuck On
P0778	Automatic transmission clutch pressure control solenoid valve B
P0780	Mechanical problem in hydraulic system
P0795	Mechanical problem in hydraulic system
P0796	Transmission fluid pressure (TFP) solenoid "C" - performance or stuck Off
P0797	Transmission fluid pressure (TFP) solenoid "C" - stuck On
P0798	Automatic transmission clutch pressure control solenoid valve C
P0840	2nd clutch transmission fluid pressure switch
P0842	Transmission fluid pressure sensor/switch "A" circuit low
P0843	Transmission fluid pressure sensor/switch "A" circuit high
P0845	3rd clutch transmission fluid pressure switch
P0847	Transmission fluid pressure sensor/switch "B" circuit low
P0848	Transmission fluid pressure sensor/switch "B" circuit high
P0962	Clutch pressure control solenoid valve A, short or open circuit
P0963	Clutch pressure control solenoid valve A
P0966	Clutch pressure control solenoid valve B

Code	Possible cause
P0967	Clutch pressure control solenoid valve C
P0970	Pressure control (PC) solenoid C - control circuit low
P0971	Pressure control (PC) solenoid C - control circuit high
P0973	Shift solenoid valve A, short circuit
P0974	Shift solenoid valve A, open circuit
P0976	Shift solenoid valve B, short circuit
P0977	Shift solenoid valve B, open circuit
P0979	Shift solenoid (SS) C - control circuit low
P0982	Shift solenoid (SS) D - control circuit low
P0983	Shift solenoid (SS) D - control circuit high
P0985	Shift solenoid (SS) E - control circuit low
P0986	Shift solenoid (SS) E - control circuit high

4 Accelerator Pedal Position (APP) sensor - replacement

Note: *The APP sensor is located at the top of the accelerator pedal module. The module and sensor are not available separately and must be replaced as a unit.*

2008 and earlier Civic models

Refer to illustrations 4.2 and 4.3

1   Disconnect the electrical connector from the APP sensor.
2   Remove the APP sensor module mounting nuts **(see illustration)** and remove the sensor module.
3   Push the pedal locking clip back **(see illustration)** and lift the pedal module out from the floor.
4   Installation is the reverse of removal.

2009 Civic models

5   Disconnect the electrical connector from the APP sensor.
6   Remove the APP sensor module mounting nuts.
7   Remove the pedal cover clip from the front of the pedal.

4.2 Accelerator pedal module details

A   Accelerator pedal position (APP) sensor
B   Accelerator pedal module mounting nuts

8   Press down on the holding tab and lift the pedal assembly from the pedal stop. **Note:** *Do not reuse the pedal cover clip.*
9   Remove the APP sensor module.
10   Installation is the reverse of removal.

4.3 Push the retaining clip back and remove the pedal module assembly from the floor

2007 and later CR-V models

11   Disconnect the electrical connector from the APP sensor.
12   Remove the APP sensor module mounting nuts and remove the sensor module.
13   Installation is the reverse of removal.

5.3 To detach the Camshaft Position (CMP) sensor from the cylinder head, remove the mounting bolt

6.4 To detach the Crankshaft Position (CKP) sensor from the engine, remove this mounting bolt. When installing the CKP sensor, make sure that the rubber weather seal is correctly seated to prevent moisture from entering the timing belt area

5   Camshaft Position (CMP) sensor - replacement

1.7L engines

Refer to illustration 5.3

1   Remove the rubber grommet from the timing belt cover and disconnect the Camshaft Position (CMP) sensor electrical connector.
2   Remove the upper timing belt cover (see Chapter 2A).
3   Remove the CMP sensor mounting bolt **(see illustration)** and remove the CMP sensor.
4   Installation is the reverse of removal. Be sure to tighten the CMP sensor mounting bolts securely.
5   Perform the PCM idle learn procedure (see Chapter 5).

1.8L engines

6   Remove the cowl cover (see Chapter 11).
7   Disconnect the Camshaft Position (CMP) sensor electrical connector located on the back side of the cylinder head.
8   Remove the CMP sensor mounting bolt and remove the CMP sensor.
9   Installation is the reverse of removal. Be sure to use a new O-ring on the sensor and tighten the CMP sensor mounting bolt securely.

2.0L engines

Note: *On 2006 and later models, there are two Camshaft Position (CMP) sensors; sensor "A" used for the intake camshaft and sensor "B" used for the exhaust camshaft.*

10   Remove the air cleaner (see Chapter 4).
11   Disconnect the Camshaft Position (CMP) sensor electrical connector.
12   Remove the CMP sensor mounting bolt and remove the CMP sensor.

13   Installation is the reverse of removal. Be sure to use a new O-ring on the sensor and tighten the CMP sensor mounting bolt securely.

CR-V models

Note: *There are two Camshaft Position (CMP) sensors; sensor "A" used for the intake camshaft and sensor "B" used for the exhaust camshaft.*

14   Remove the EGR valve (see Section 22).
15   Disconnect the Camshaft Position (CMP) sensor electrical connector from the back of the cylinder head.
16   Remove the CMP sensor mounting bolt and remove the CMP sensor from the cylinder head.
17   Installation is the reverse of removal. Be sure to use a new O-ring on the sensor and tighten the CMP sensor mounting bolt securely.

6   Crankshaft Position (CKP) sensor - replacement

Replacement

2005 and earlier models

Refer to illustration 6.4

1   Raise the front of the vehicle and place it securely on jackstands.
2   The Crankshaft Position (CKP) sensor electrical connector is located at the left end of the engine, behind the lower timing belt cover, near the crankshaft. To release the connector, depress this tab and pull off the connector.
3   Remove the timing belt cover and the timing belt (see Chapter 2A or 2B).
4   Remove the CKP sensor mounting bolt **(see illustration)** and remove the CKP sensor.

5   Installation is the reverse of removal. Be sure to tighten the CKP sensor mounting bolt securely.

2006 and later models

Note: *After the Crankshaft Position (CKP) sensor is replaced, perform the CKP learn procedure (see Steps 14 through 19).*

1.8L engines

6   Raise the front of the vehicle and place it securely on jackstands. Remove the splash shield.
7   Disconnect the Crankshaft Position (CKP) sensor electrical connector at the lower rear of the engine block.
8   Remove the CKP sensor mounting bolt and remove the CKP sensor.
9   Installation is the reverse of removal. Be sure to use a new O-ring on the sensor, tighten the CMP sensor mounting bolt securely and perform the CKP learn procedure.

2.0L and 2.4L engines

10   Raise the front of the vehicle and place it securely on jackstands.
11   Disconnect the Crankshaft Position (CKP) sensor electrical connector, located at the bottom side of the crankshaft pulley.
12   Remove the CKP sensor mounting bolt and remove the CKP sensor.
13   Installation is the reverse of removal. Be sure to use a new O-ring on the sensor, tighten the CMP sensor mounting bolt securely and perform the CKP learn procedure.

Crankshaft Position (CKP) sensor learn procedure (without Honda Diagnostic System equipment)

14   Start the engine. Wait for the engine to fully warm up or the cooling fan to come on (air conditioning off).
15   Drive on a level road.

16   Place the transmission in 2 (automatic transmission) or 1 (manual transmission), accelerate until 2,500 rpm is reached, then allow the vehicle to decelerate back down to 1,000 rpm.

17   Place the transmission in 2 (automatic transmission) or 1 (manual transmission), accelerate until 5,000 rpm is reached, then allow the vehicle to decelerate back down to 3,000 rpm.

18   Repeat Steps 16 and 17 several more times.

19   Stop the vehicle and turn the ignition to the OFF position, then turn the ignition to ON position (without starting the engine) and wait 30 seconds. Learn procedure should be established.

7   Engine Coolant Temperature (ECT) sensor(s) - replacement

Warning: *Wait until the engine has cooled completely before beginning this procedure.*

Engine Coolant Temperature (ECT) sensor 1

Refer to illustration 7.1

1   The Engine Coolant Temperature (ECT) sensor 1 is located at the right end of the cylinder head on 1.7L and 1.8L engines and at the left end of the cylinder head on 2.0L and 2.4L engines **(see illustration)**.

2   Drain the engine coolant (see Chapter 1). **Note:** *If you don't drain the coolant, some coolant will run out when you remove the ECT sensor, so install the new sensor as quickly as possible.*

3   Disconnect the electrical connector from the ECT sensor.

4   Unscrew the ECT sensor. **Caution:** *If you're planning to reuse the old ECT sensor, handle it with care. Damage to the ECT sensor will adversely affect the operation of the PGM-FI system.*

5   Remove and discard the old ECT sensor O-ring. Whether you're planning to reuse the old ECT sensor or install a new unit, be sure to use a new O-ring.

7.1 The Engine Coolant Temperature (ECT) sensor is located at the right end of the cylinder head on 1.7L and 1.8L engines (shown) and on the left end of the cylinder head on 2.0L and 2.4L engines

6   Installation is the reverse of removal. Be sure to tighten the ECT sensor securely.

7   Refill the cooling system (see Chapter 1).

Engine Coolant Temperature (ECT) sensor 2

All 2006 and later models

8   The Engine Coolant Temperature (ECT) sensor 2, is located in the lower radiator tank next to the radiator hose.

9   Drain the engine coolant (see Chapter 1). **Note:** *If you don't drain the coolant, some coolant will run out when you remove the ECT sensor, so install the new sensor as quickly as possible.*

10   Disconnect the electrical connector from the ECT sensor.

11   Unscrew the ECT sensor. **Caution:** *If you're planning to reuse the old ECT sensor, handle it with care. Damage to the ECT sensor will adversely affect the operation of the PGM-FI system.*

12   Remove and discard the old ECT sensor O-ring. Whether you're planning to reuse the

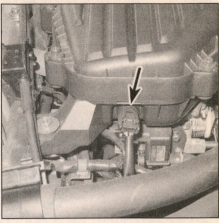

8.1 On 2005 and earlier 1.7L and 1.8L engines, the IAT sensor is located on the left end of the air filter housing

old ECT sensor or install a new unit, be sure to use a new O-ring.

13   Installation is the reverse of removal. Be sure to tighten the ECT sensor securely.

14   Refill the cooling system (see Chapter 1).

8   Mass Air Flow (MAF) sensor/ Intake Air Temperature (IAT) sensor - replacement

2005 and earlier models

Refer to illustration 8.1

1   Locate the IAT sensor **(see illustration)**, which is on the left end of the air filter housing on 1.7L and 1.8L engines and on the air intake duct on 2.0L and 2.4L engines.

2   Disconnect the electrical connector from the IAT sensor.

3   Pull the IAT sensor out of its mounting grommet.

4   Remove the IAT sensor mounting grommet and inspect it for cracks, tears and other deterioration. If the grommet is damaged or worn, replace it.

5   Installation is the reverse of removal.

2006 and later models

Refer to illustration 8.6

6   Locate the MAF sensor/IAT sensor **(see illustration)** on the air filter inlet housing.

7   Disconnect the electrical connector from the MAF sensor/IAT sensor.

8   Remove the fasteners and pull the MAF sensor/IAT sensor out of the housing.

9   Remove and discard the old MAF sensor/IAT sensor O-ring. Whether you're planning to reuse the old MAF sensor/IAT sensor or install a new unit, be sure to use a new O-ring.

10   Installation is the reverse of removal. Be sure to tighten the MAF sensor/IAT sensor fasteners securely.

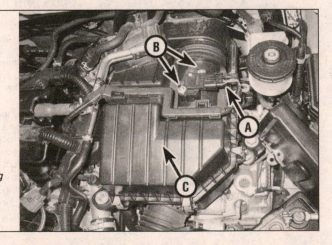

8.6 MAF sensor/IAT sensor details

A   MAF sensor/IAT sensor electrical connector

B   MAF sensor/IAT sensor fasteners

C   Air filter inlet housing

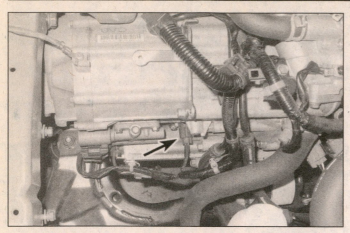

9.1 On 2005 and earlier models, the input shaft (mainshaft) speed sensor is located on the front of the transaxle on coupes and sedans (shown) or on the backside of the transaxle on CR-Vs and hatchbacks

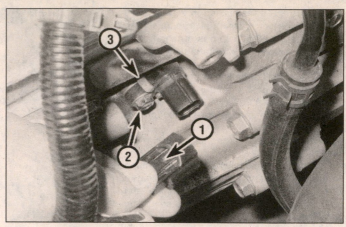

9.4 To remove the input shaft (mainshaft) speed sensor, depress the tab and disconnect the electrical connector (1), remove the mounting bolt (2), remove the sensor and, on SLXA transaxles, remove and bag the special spacer washer (3)

9 Input shaft (mainshaft) speed sensor - replacement

2005 and earlier models

Refer to illustrations 9.1, 9.4 and 9.6

1 Locate the input shaft (mainshaft) speed sensor **(see illustration)** on the front side of the transaxle on coupes and sedans, or on the backside of the transaxle on hatchback and CR-V models.

2 On coupes and sedans, remove the air intake resonator (see "Air filter housing - removal and installation" in Chapter 4) and remove the battery (see Chapter 5). For even more working room, you might want to remove the battery tray as well, but it's not absolutely necessary to do so.

3 On CR-Vs and hatchbacks, raise the vehicle and place it securely on jackstands, then remove the splash shield, if equipped, from underneath the engine/transaxle assembly.

4 Disconnect the electrical connector from the input shaft speed sensor **(see illustration)**.

5 Remove the input shaft speed sensor mounting bolt and remove the sensor.

6 On models with an SLXA (not a BMXA) transaxle, remove the special spacer washer from the input shaft sensor **(see illustration)** and save it for reassembly. To determine whether your vehicle has an SLXA or a BMXA transaxle, look at the tag on top of the transaxle.

7 Remove and discard the sensor O-ring.

8 Installation is the reverse of removal. Be sure to use a new O-ring and, if you're installing the sensor on an SLXA transaxle, make sure you install the special spacer washer, then tighten the sensor mounting bolt securely.

9 If you're servicing a coupe or sedan, install the battery tray (if removed), the battery (see Chapter 5) and the air intake resonator (see "Air filter housing - removal and installation" in Chapter 4).

10 If you're servicing a CR-V or a hatchback, lower the vehicle.

2006 and later models

11 Locate the input shaft (mainshaft) speed sensor on the back side of the transaxle (towards the engine).

12 Remove the air filter housing (see Chapter 4).

13 Disconnect the electrical connector from the input shaft speed sensor.

14 Remove the input shaft speed sensor mounting bolt and remove the sensor.

15 Remove and discard the sensor O-ring.

16 Installation is the reverse of removal. Be sure to use a new O-ring and tighten the sensor mounting bolt securely

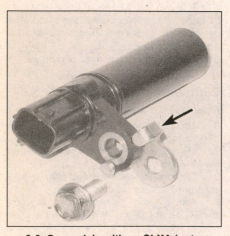

9.6 On models with an SLXA (not a BMXA) automatic transaxle, the input shaft (mainshaft) speed sensor uses a special spacer washer that you'll need when installing the sensor again

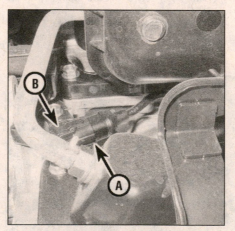

10.4 To disconnect the knock sensor electrical connector (A), depress this release button (B) with your finger or with a flat-blade screwdriver

10 Knock sensor - replacement

2005 and earlier models

Refer to illustrations 10.4 and 10.5

1 Locate the knock sensor, which is located on the backside of the engine block on 1.7L engines, and on the front side of the block on 2.0L and 2.4L engines.

2 Raise the vehicle and place it securely on jackstands.

3 Remove the under-engine splash shield, if equipped (see Chapter 2).

4 Disconnect the knock sensor electrical connector **(see illustration)**.

5 On 1.7L SOHC engines, remove the knock sensor retaining bolt and detach the sensor **(see illustration)**. On DOHC engines, unscrew the sensor.

6 Installation is the reverse of removal. Be sure to tighten the knock sensor retaining bolt

10.5 Knock sensor retaining bolt (oil filter removed for clarity) (1.7L engine shown)

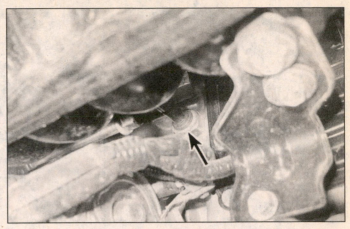

10.7 The knock sensor is located on the backside of the engine block behind the intake manifold

or sensor to the torque listed in this Chapter's Specifications

2006 and later models

1.8L engines

Refer to illustration 10.7

7   Locate the knock sensor on the backside of the engine block under the intake manifold **(see illustration)**.
8   Remove the intake manifold (see Chapter 4).
9   Disconnect the knock sensor electrical connector.
10   Unscrew the sensor. Installation is the reverse of removal. Be sure to tighten the knock sensor to the torque listed in this Chapter's Specifications

2.0L and 2.4L engines

11   Raise the vehicle and place it securely on jackstands.
12   Remove the under-engine splash shield,

if equipped (see Chapter 2).
13   Locate the knock sensor on the front side of the block.
14   Disconnect the knock sensor electrical connector.
15   Unscrew the sensor. Installation is the reverse of removal. Be sure to tighten the knock sensor to the torque listed in this Chapter's Specifications

11   Manifold Absolute Pressure (MAP) sensor - replacement

2005 and earlier models

Refer to illustration 11.2

1   Remove the air filter housing (see Chapter 4).
2   Disconnect the electrical connector from the MAP sensor **(see illustration)**.

3   Remove the MAP sensor retaining screw and remove the MAP sensor.
4   Remove the old MAP sensor O-ring and discard it.
5   Installation is the reverse of removal. Be sure to use a new O-ring and tighten the MAP sensor mounting screw securely.

2006 and later models

Refer to illustration 11.7

6   On 1.8L engines, remove the cowl cover (see Chapter 11).
7   Disconnect the electrical connector from the Manifold Absolute Pressure (MAP) sensor **(see illustration)**.
8   Remove the MAP sensor retaining screw and remove the MAP sensor.
9   Remove the old MAP sensor O-ring and discard it.
10   Installation is the reverse of removal. Be sure to use a new O-ring and tighten the MAP sensor mounting screw securely.

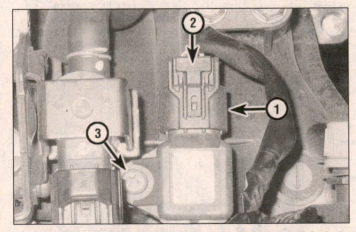

11.2 To remove the MAP sensor, disconnect the electrical connector (1) by depressing the release tab (2), then remove the sensor mounting screw (3). After removing the MAP sensor, be sure to remove and discard the old O-ring; always use a new O-ring when installing the MAP sensor

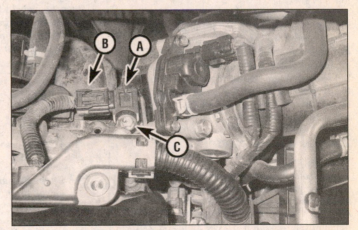

11.7 Manifold Absolute Pressure (MAP) sensor details - 1.8L engine shown, others similar

A   *Manifold Absolute Pressure (MAP) sensor*
B   *Sensor electrical connector*
C   *Sensor mounting bolt*

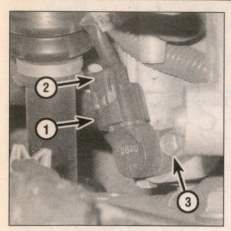

12.3 Output shaft (countershaft) speed sensor mounting details (coupe/sedan shown, CR-V similar)

1   *Electrical connector*
2   *Tab (depress to release connector)*
3   *Mounting bolt*

12   Output shaft (countershaft) speed sensor - replacement

2005 and earlier models

Refer to illustration 12.3

1   Locate the output shaft (countershaft) speed sensor on top of the transaxle, near the transaxle fluid level dipstick (on coupes and sedans) or on the backside of the transaxle (on CR-Vs).
2   If you're replacing the output shaft sensor on a coupe or sedan, remove the air intake resonator (see "Air filter housing - removal and installation" in Chapter 4). If you're replacing the output shaft sensor on a CR-V, raise the vehicle and place it securely on jackstands, then remove any splash shield, if equipped, that's in the way.
3   Disconnect the electrical connector from the output shaft (countershaft) speed sensor **(see illustration)**.
4   Remove the output shaft sensor mounting bolt and remove the sensor.
5   Remove and discard the sensor O-ring.
6   Installation is the reverse of removal. Be sure to use a new O-ring and tighten the sensor mounting bolt securely.

2006 and later models

Refer to illustration 12.7

7   Locate the output shaft (countershaft) speed sensor **(see illustration)** on the back side of the transaxle (towards the fender).
8   On 1.8L engines, remove the air filter housing (see Chapter 4). On 2.0L and 2.4L engines, raise the vehicle and place it securely on jackstands, then remove the splash shield.
9   Disconnect the electrical connector from the input shaft speed sensor.
10   Remove the output shaft speed sensor mounting bolt and remove the sensor.

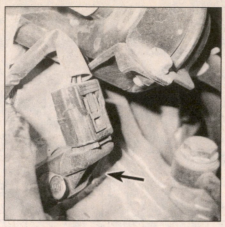

12.7 On 2006 and later models, the output shaft (mainshaft) speed sensor is located under the air filter housing and on the back side of the transaxle

11   Remove and discard the sensor O-ring.
12   Installation is the reverse of removal. Be sure to use a new O-ring and tighten the sensor mounting bolt securely

13   Oxygen sensors - replacement

Note: *Because it is installed in the exhaust manifold or pipe, both of which contract when cool, an oxygen sensor might be very difficult to loosen when the engine is cold. Rather than risk damage to the sensor or its mounting threads, start and run the engine for a minute or two, then shut it off. Be careful not to burn yourself during the following procedure.*

1   Remove the key from the ignition key lock cylinder. Raise the vehicle and place it securely on jackstands.
2   Special care must be taken whenever a sensor is serviced.

a)   *Oxygen sensors have a permanently attached pigtail and an electrical connector that cannot be removed. Damaging or removing the pigtail or electrical connector will render the sensor useless.*

b)   *Keep grease, dirt and other contaminants away from the electrical connector and the louvered end of the sensor.*
c)   *Do not use cleaning solvents of any kind on an oxygen sensor.*
d)   *Oxygen sensors are extremely delicate. Do not drop a sensor, throw it around or handle it roughly.*
e)   *Make sure the silicone boot on the sensor is installed in the correct position. Otherwise, the boot might melt and prevent the sensor from operating correctly.*

2005 and earlier Civic models

3   On coupes and sedans with non-VTEC (D17A1) engines, there are two oxygen sensors. The upstream oxygen sensor - also referred to by Honda as the "Air/Fuel (A/F) ratio sensor" - is located above the catalytic converter (which is an integral part of the exhaust manifold), and the downstream sensor is located below the catalyst. On coupes and sedans with VTEC engines, there are either two oxygen sensors (D17A2 engines) or three oxygen sensors (D17A6 engines). On VTEC models with two oxygen sensors, the sensors are located ahead of and on the catalyst, which is located underneath the vehicle (these models do not use the integral exhaust manifold/catalyst assembly). VTEC models with three oxygen sensors use the same integral exhaust manifold/catalyst as non-VTEC models, and their upstream and downstream oxygen sensors are installed at the same locations as the upstream and downstream sensors on non-VTEC models. But these models have a *third* oxygen sensor, which is located at the second catalyst (in the same location [underneath the vehicle] as the catalyst on VTEC models with only two sensors).

Upstream oxygen sensor

Refer to illustration 13.4

4   Disconnect the upstream oxygen sensor electrical connector **(see illustration)**.
5   Remove the upstream oxygen sensor.
6   If you're going to install the old sensor, apply anti-seize compound to the threads of

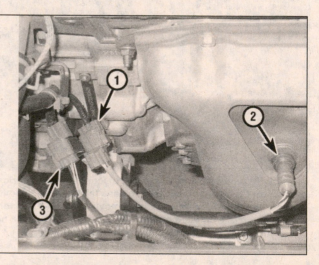

13.4 Oxygen sensor details

1   *Electrical connector (upstream)*
2   *Oxygen sensor (upstream)*
3   *Electrical connector (downstream)*

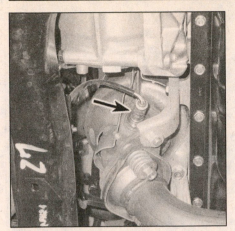

13.10 If you're removing the downstream oxygen sensor on a coupe or sedan with a D17A1 (non-VTEC) or a D17A6 (VTEC) engine, you'll find the sensor directly above the exhaust manifold-to-exhaust pipe flange. The downstream oxygen sensor of a D17A2 VTEC engine is at the rear end of the catalytic converter

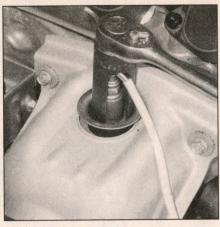

13.19 Use an oxygen sensor socket to remove the oxygen sensor - 1.8L shown, others similar

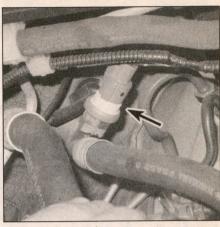

14.3 The Power Steering Pressure (PSP) switch is located on the pressure line for the power steering system, right above the steering rack (coupe/sedan shown, CR-V similar)

the sensor to facilitate future removal. If you're going to install a new oxygen sensor, it's not necessary to apply anti-seize compound to the threads. The threads on new sensors already have anti-seize compound on them.

7   Installation is the reverse of removal. Be sure to tighten the upstream oxygen sensor securely.

Downstream oxygen sensor

Refer to illustration 13.10

8   Disconnect the electrical connector **(see illustration 13.4).**
9   Raise the front of the vehicle and place it securely on jackstands.
10   Locate the downstream oxygen sensor at the lower end of the exhaust manifold **(see illustration).**
11   Remove the downstream oxygen sensor from the exhaust manifold.
12   If you're going to install the old sensor, apply anti-seize compound to the threads of the sensor to facilitate future removal. If you're going to install a new oxygen sensor, it's not necessary to apply anti-seize compound to the threads. The threads on new sensors already have anti-seize compound on them.
13   Installation is the reverse of removal. Be sure to tighten the oxygen sensor securely

Third oxygen sensor (D17A6 engine only)

14   Raise the vehicle and place it securely on jackstands.
15   Disconnect the oxygen sensor electrical connector.
16   Unscrew the oxygen sensor from the catalytic converter.
17   If you're going to install the old sensor, apply anti-seize compound to the threads of the sensor to facilitate future removal. If you're going to install a new oxygen sensor, it's not

necessary to apply anti-seize compound to the threads. The threads on new sensors already have anti-seize compound on them.
18   Installation is the reverse of removal. Be sure to tighten the oxygen sensor securely.

CR-V, hatchback and all 2006 and later Civics

Refer to illustration 13.19

19   The upstream oxygen sensor - also referred to by Honda as the "Air/Fuel (A/F) ratio sensor" - is located at the upstream end of the catalytic converter. The downstream oxygen sensor is located at the middle of the catalyst. On 1.8L engines, the catalyst is an integral part of the exhaust manifold and the sensor is located on the top of the engine **(see illustration).** On all 2.0L and 2.4L engines, the catalyst is located underneath the vehicle.
20   Raise the vehicle and place it securely on jackstands.
21   Disconnect the electrical connector for the upstream or downstream oxygen sensor.
22   Unscrew and remove the upstream or downstream oxygen sensor.
23   If you're going to install the old sensor, apply anti-seize compound to the threads of the sensor to facilitate future removal. If you're going to install a new oxygen sensor, it's not necessary to apply anti-seize compound to the threads. The threads on new sensors already have anti-seize compound on them.
24   Installation is the reverse of removal. Be sure to tighten the oxygen sensor securely.

14 Power Steering Pressure (PSP) switch - replacement

Refer to illustrations 14.3 and 14.5
Note: *This procedure does not apply to hatchbacks, which are equipped with Electri-*

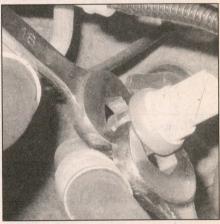

14.5 To remove the PSP switch from the power steering pressure line, put a back-up wrench on the junction block to prevent kinking the pressure line when you loosen the switch (use the back-up wrench when you install the switch, too)

cal Power Steering.

1   On coupes and sedans, remove the air filter housing (see Chapter 4).
2   On CR-Vs, raise the front end of the vehicle and place it securely on jackstands.
3   Find the power steering pressure switch **(see illustration)**, which is located in the pressure line for the power steering system, just above the steering rack.
4   Disconnect the electrical connector from the PSP switch.
5   Using a back-up wrench, unscrew the PSP switch **(see illustration).**
6   Installation is the reverse of removal. Be sure to tighten the PSP switch securely.
7   Lower the vehicle and check the power steering fluid level, adding fluid of the proper type if necessary (see Chapter 1).

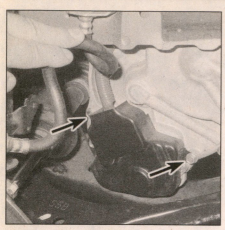

16.4 To detach the transmission range switch cover, remove these two bolts (2005 and earlier Civic shown, other models similar)

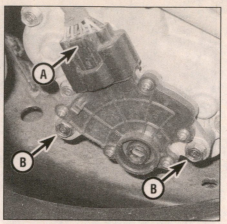

16.5 To disconnect the electrical connector from the transmission range switch, depress the locking tab (A) and pull off the connector; to detach the transmission range switch from the transaxle, remove the two bolts (B) (2005 and earlier Civic shown, other models similar)

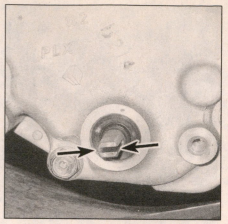

16.6 Once you have removed the transmission range switch from the transaxle, do NOT move the control shaft from the Neutral position (shown)

15   Throttle Position (TP) sensor - replacement

The TP sensor is not removable. If it's defective, replace the throttle body (see Chapter 4).

16   Transmission range switch - replacement and adjustment

Refer to illustrations 16.4, 16.5, 16.6 and 16.8

1   On 2005 and earlier Civic models, loosen the lug nuts for the right front wheel. On all 2006 and later Civic and CR-V models, loosen the lug nuts for the left front wheel. Raise the vehicle and place it securely on jackstands, then remove the appropriate front wheel.

16.8 When installing the transmission range switch, align the slot in the control shaft with the cutouts in the rotary frame and the switch housing

2   Remove the inner fender splash shield (see Chapter 11).
3   Put the shift lever inside the vehicle in the Neutral position.
4   Remove the cover from the transmission range switch **(see illustration)**.
5   Disconnect the electrical connector from the transmission range switch **(see illustration)**.
6   Remove the transmission range switch mounting bolts and remove the switch. **Caution:** *While the transmission range switch is removed, do NOT rotate the control shaft* **(see illustration)** *on the transaxle.*
7   Before installing the transmission range switch, make sure that the switch is in the Neutral position. You'll hear/feel a click when you put the switch into Neutral. Also make sure that the control shaft is in the Neutral position before installing the transmission range switch. To do so, rotate the control shaft in a clockwise direction until it stops. As you rotate the shaft, it clicks into each gear position. Rotate it counterclockwise to the third position (third click), which is Neutral.
8   Install the transmission range switch and loosely install the switch mounting bolts. Then use a long, thin drill bit or a metal rod to align the control shaft with the rotary frame **(see illustration)** and to lock them together while you tighten the switch mounting bolts securely. **Note:** *Be careful not to move the transmission range switch while tightening the switch mounting bolts.*
9   The remainder of installation is the reverse of removal.
10   Turn the ignition switch to ON, move the shift lever through all the gears and verify that the transmission range switch is correctly synchronized with the gear position indicator on the instrument cluster. Then verify that the engine will NOT start in any gear position other than Park or

Neutral, and that the back-up lights come on when the shift lever is in the Reverse position. If the vehicle fails to meet any of these criteria, readjust the transmission range switch.

17   Powertrain Control Module (PCM) - removal and installation

Warning: *All models covered by this manual are equipped with a Supplemental Restraint System (SRS), more commonly known as airbags. Always disarm the airbag system before working in the vicinity of any airbag system component to avoid the possibility of accidental deployment of the airbag, which could cause personal injury (see Chapter 12).*
Caution: *To avoid electrostatic discharge damage to the PCM, handle the PCM only by its case. Do not touch the electrical terminals during removal and installation. If available, ground yourself to the vehicle with an anti-static ground strap, available at computer supply stores.*
Note: *The PCM is a component of the immobilizer (vehicle security) system. If a new PCM is installed in the vehicle, the immobilizer code must be programmed into the new PCM by a dealership service department or other qualified repair facility before the engine will start. The technician will need the vehicle, the new PCM unit and all of the vehicle keys to program the new PCM unit.*
1   Disconnect the cable from the negative battery terminal (see Chapter 5).
2   Disable the airbag system (see Chapter 12).
3   On coupes, sedans and hatchbacks, remove the passenger's dashboard lower cover (see "Dashboard trim panels - removal and installation" in Chapter 11). On all models, remove the glove box (see same Section in Chapter 11).

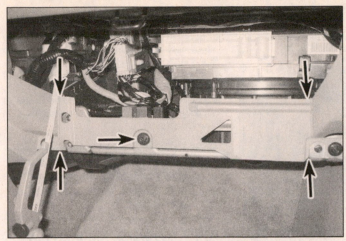

17.4 On coupes and sedans, cut off this piece of plastic where indicated, remove the single retaining bolt and discard the plastic

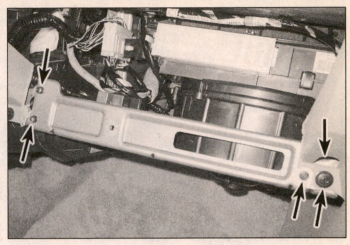

17.5a On coupes and sedans, unbolt and remove the glove box frame . . .

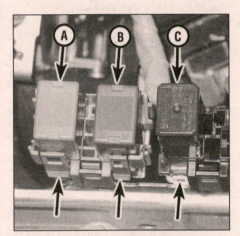

17.5b . . . depress the relay release tabs, detach the relays from the frame and set it aside (unlike the plastic that was covering it, the frame is structural, so you will need to install it after you have replaced the PCM)

A PGM-FI main relay No. 2
B PGM-FI main relay No. 1
C Automatic transmission reverse relay

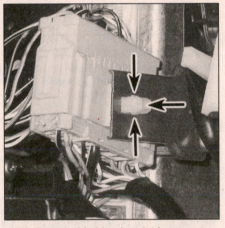

17.6 Detach this big electrical connector from the PCM mounting bracket by squeezing the two release tabs together (into the locator pin) and pushing the locator pin from the bracket

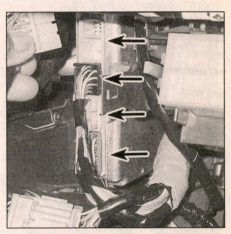

17.7 Disconnect the four electrical connectors from the PCM (coupe/sedan shown; CR-V similar)

2005 and earlier models
Coupe, sedan and CR-V

Refer to illustrations 17.4, 17.5a, 17.5b, 17.6, 17.7 and 17.8

4   On coupes and sedans, cut off and unbolt the section of plastic that covers up the glove box frame **(see illustration)**. The manufacturer leaves this piece of plastic intact when the dash is assembled, but it's not structural, so you're not weakening the dash when you remove it.

5   On coupes and sedans, unbolt the glove box frame **(see illustration)**, detach the relays from it **(see illustration)** and remove the frame. Unlike the plastic piece that was covering it, this frame *is* structural, so you

will have to install it again after replacing the PCM.

6   Detach the big electrical connector from the PCM mounting bracket **(see illustration)**.

7   Disconnect the electrical connectors from the PCM **(see illustration)**.

8   Remove the PCM mounting bolt and the two mounting nuts **(see illustration)** and remove the PCM. **Caution:** *Avoid any static electricity damage to the computer by grounding yourself to the body before touching the PCM and using a special anti-static pad to store the PCM on once it is removed.*

9   Installation is the reverse of removal.

10 Reconnect the cable to the negative battery terminal and perform the PCM idle learn procedure (see Chapter 5).

17.8 PCM mounting fasteners (2005 and earlier models)

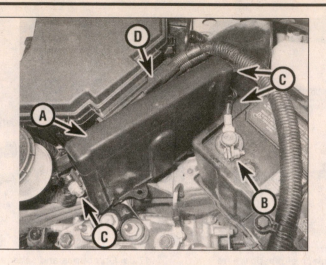

17.16 To detach the PCM from a coupe, sedan or CR-V, remove these fasteners

A   *PCM cover*
B   *Negative battery cable*
C   *PCM mounting fasteners*
D   *Electrical connectors*

Hatchback

11   Disconnect the electrical connectors from the underside of the PCM.
12   Remove the three PCM mounting bolts and remove the PCM.
13   Installation is the reverse of removal.

2006 and later models

Refer to illustration 17.16

14   Remove the battery (see Chapter 5). On CR-V models, remove the fuse/relay box from the engine compartment.
15   Slide the cover off the PCM.
16   Remove the PCM mounting bolts **(see illustration)**. **Caution:** *Avoid any static electricity damage to the computer by grounding yourself to the body before touching the PCM and using a special anti-static pad to store the PCM on once it is removed.*
17   On CR-V models, detach the harness mounting bracket.
18   Disconnect the electrical connectors from the PCM and remove the PCM.
19   Installation is the reverse of removal.
20   Reconnect the cable to the negative battery terminal and perform the PCM idle learn procedure (see Chapter 5).

18 Idle Air Control (IAC) valve (2005 and earlier Civics, 2004 and earlier CR-V models) - replacement

Refer to illustrations 18.4 and 18.5
Warning: *Wait until the engine is completely cool before beginning this procedure.*

1   Remove the air filter housing (see Chapter 4).
2   Clamp off the coolant hoses to the IAC valve, then detach the hoses from the valve. Be prepared for a little coolant spillage.
3   On CR-Vs and hatchbacks, remove the throttle body from the intake manifold (see Chapter 4). On coupes and sedans, the IAC valve is on the front side of the throttle body, so it's not necessary to remove the throttle body in order to remove the IAC valve. On CR-Vs and hatchbacks, the IAC valve is mounted on the underside of the throttle body, so you must first remove the throttle body before you can remove the IAC valve from it.
4   Remove the IAC valve mounting screws **(see illustration)** and remove the IAC valve.

5   Remove the old IAC valve gasket **(see illustration)** and discard it.
6   When installing the IAC valve, be sure to use a new gasket and tighten the IAC valve mounting screws securely.
7   Installation is otherwise the reverse of removal.
8   Check the coolant level and add some, if necessary, to bring it to the appropriate level (see Chapter 1).

19 Intake Manifold Runner Control (IMRC) or Intake Manifold Tuning (IMT) system - component replacement

IMRC/IMT valve position sensor

1   Disconnect the electrical connector from the IMRC/IMT valve position sensor.
2   Remove the two valve position sensor mounting screws and remove the sensor.
3   Remove and discard the old sensor O-ring.
4   Install a new O-ring.
5   When installing the valve position sensor, make sure that the projection inside the IMRC/IMT valve is aligned with the groove in the sensor.
6   Installation is otherwise the reverse of removal. Be sure to tighten the IMRC/IMT valve position sensor mounting screws securely.

IMRC/IMT actuator/valve assembly

7   Remove the intake manifold (see Chapter 2A or 2B).
8   Remove the three IMRC/IMT actuator/valve assembly mounting bolts.
9   Remove the actuator/valve assembly.
10   Remove and discard the old O-rings and install new O-rings.
11   When installing the actuator/valve assembly, make sure that the pilot bearing is in place.

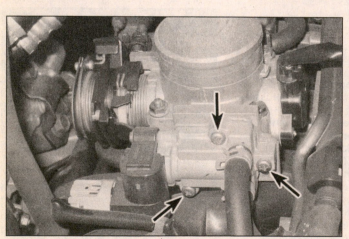

18.4 IAC valve mounting screws (coupe/sedan shown, CR-V and hatchback IAC valve similar, except that it's on the underside of the throttle body and has two screws instead of three)

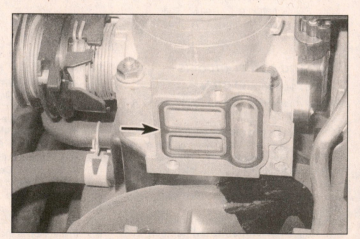

18.5 After removing the IAC valve from the throttle body, remove this gasket and replace it

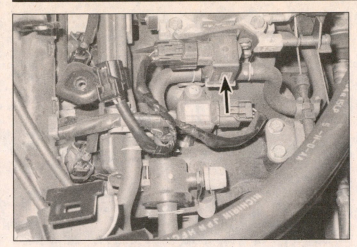

21.2a The EVAP canister purge valve is located on the side of the throttle body (1.7L engines)

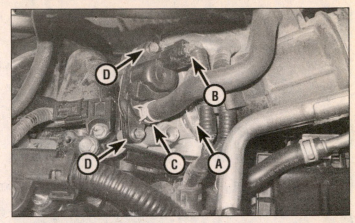

21.2b The EVAP canister purge valve details (1.8L engines)

A   Throttle body
B   Canister purge valve electrical connector
C   Vacuum hose
D   Canister purge valve fasteners

12   Also, when installing the actuator/valve assembly, make sure that the hole is visible.
13   Installation is otherwise the reverse of removal. Be sure to tighten the actuator/valve assembly mounting bolts securely.

20 Catalytic converter - replacement

Note: *Because of a Federally mandated extended warranty which covers emissions-related components like the catalytic converter, check with a dealer service department before replacing the converter at your own expense.*

Integral exhaust manifold/ catalytic converter assembly (1.7L D17A1, D17A6 and 1.8L R18A1 engines only)

1   Remove the upstream and downstream oxygen sensors (see Section 13).
2   Remove the exhaust manifold (see Chapter 2A). The catalyst is an integral part of the exhaust manifold.
3   Installation is the reverse of removal.

Under-vehicle catalytic converter (all except models with 1.7L D17A1, D17A6 and 1.8L R18A1 engines)

4   Raise the vehicle and place it securely on jackstands.
5   Remove the upstream and downstream oxygen sensors (see Section 13). On models with a D17A6 engine, remove the third oxygen sensor (see Section 13).
6   Remove the spring-loaded bolts from the front mounting flange and the nuts from the rear flange and remove the catalytic converter.
7   If you're planning to *replace* (rather than

just remove) the catalytic converter, remove the heat shield bolts and remove the heat shield, then install the heat shield on the new unit.
8   Installation is the reverse of removal. Be sure to replace any rusted or damaged fasteners and to tighten all fasteners securely.

21 Evaporative Emissions Control (EVAP) system - component replacement

EVAP canister purge valve
1.7L and 1.8L engines
Refer to illustrations 21.2a and 21.2b
1   Remove the air filter housing (see Chapter 4). On 2006 and later models, remove the cowl cover (see Chapter 11).
2   Locate the EVAP purge control valve on the side of the throttle body **(see illustrations)**.
3   Disconnect the electrical connector from the purge control valve.
4   Disconnect the vacuum hose(s) from the purge control valve.
5   Remove the purge control valve fasteners and remove the purge control valve.
6   Installation is the reverse of removal.

2.0L and 2.4L engines
7   Remove the engine cover and air filter housing (see Chapter 4).
8   On 2006 and later models, relieve the fuel pressure and disconnect the fuel line (see Chapter 4).
9   Disconnect the electrical connector from the EVAP canister purge valve.
10   Disconnect the vacuum hoses from the EVAP canister purge valve.
11   Remove the EVAP canister purge valve mounting screws.
12   Remove the EVAP canister purge valve.
13   On 2005 and earlier models, remove

and discard the EVAP canister purge valve O-ring.
14   Using a new O-ring (if equipped), install the EVAP canister purge valve and tighten the mounting screws securely.
15   Installation is otherwise the reverse of removal.

EVAP canister air filter (2005 and earlier models)
Refer to illustration 21.17
16   Raise the vehicle and place it securely on jackstands.
17   Clearly label the two hoses connected to the EVAP canister air filter **(see illustration)**, then disconnect them.
18   Remove the canister air filter mounting bolt and remove the air filter from its mounting bracket.
19   Installation is the reverse of removal.

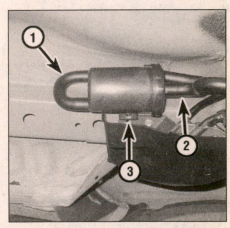

21.17 EVAP canister air filter details:
1   Fresh air inlet hose
2   Outlet hose (goes to the vent shut valve on the EVAP canister)
3   Air filter mounting bolt

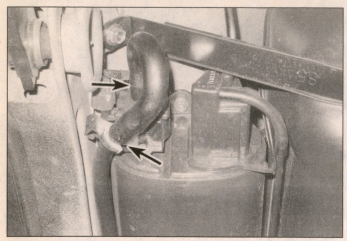

21.21 Disconnect the vapor hose from the EVAP canister vent shut valve and disengage it from this hose clip

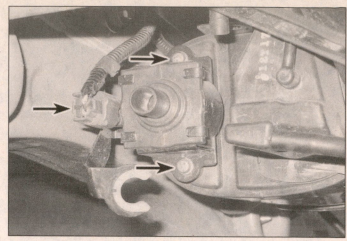

21.22 Disconnect the electrical connector from the EVAP canister vent shut valve, then remove the vent shut valve mounting screws and remove the valve from the EVAP canister

EVAP canister vent shut valve
2005 and earlier models
Refer to illustrations 21.21 and 21.22

20   Raise the vehicle and place it securely on jackstands.

21   Disconnect the vapor hose from the EVAP canister vent shut valve **(see illustration)**.

22   Disconnect the electrical connector from the EVAP canister vent shut valve **(see illustration)**.

23   Remove the EVAP canister vent shut valve mounting screws and remove the shut valve from the EVAP canister.

24   Replace the O-ring on the vent shut valve.

25   Installation is the reverse of removal.

2006 and later models

26   Remove the EVAP canister.

27   Use a small screwdriver and release the vent shut valve cap locking tabs and remove the cap.

28   Rotate the vent shut valve clockwise and pull the valve from the EVAP canister.

29   Replace the O-ring on the vent shut valve.
Caution: *Do not coat the O-rings with oil.*

30   Installation is the reverse of removal.

EVAP two-way valve/bypass solenoid valve (2005 and earlier models)
Refer to illustrations 21.32 and 21.33

31   Raise the vehicle and place it securely on jackstands.

32   Disconnect the vapor hoses from the two-way valve **(see illustration)**.

33   Disconnect the electrical connector from the bypass solenoid valve **(see illustration)**.

34   Disconnect the vapor hose that connects the fuel tank pressure sensor to the two-way valve.

35   Remove the two-way valve mounting screws and remove the two-way valve/bypass solenoid valve assembly.

36   Installation is the reverse of removal.

EVAP fuel tank pressure (FTP) sensor
2005 and earlier models
Refer to illustration 21.38

37   Remove the EVAP two-way valve/bypass solenoid valve assembly (see Steps 31

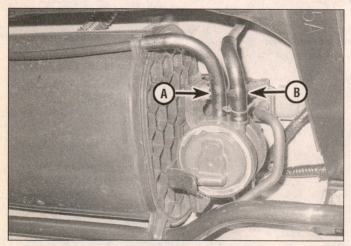

21.32 Clearly label and then disconnect the two vapor hoses from the two-way valve

A   *To EVAP canister*
B   *To EVAP valve on top of fuel tank*

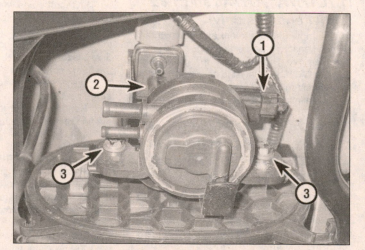

21.33 EVAP two-way/bypass solenoid valve installation details

1   *Bypass solenoid electrical connector*
2   *Vapor hose from the fuel tank pressure sensor to the two-way valve*
3   *Two-way valve mounting screws*

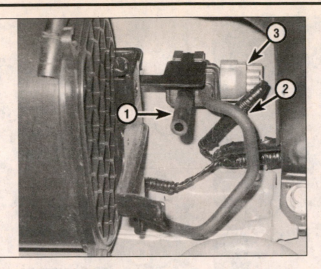

21.38 EVAP fuel tank pressure sensor installation details

1 *Hose from the fuel tank pressure sensor to the two-way valve*
2 *Vent hose*
3 *Electrical connector*

through 35).

38 Disconnect the vapor hoses from the fuel tank pressure sensor (**see illustration**).
39 Disconnect the electrical connector from the fuel tank pressure sensor.
40 Remove the fuel tank pressure sensor from its mounting bracket by pushing it straight up.
41 Installation is the reverse of removal.

2006 and later models

42 Raise the vehicle and remove the cover.
43 Locate the FTP sensor at the side of the

EVAP canister and disconnect the electrical connector.
44 Remove the FTP sensor retaining clip and remove the sensor.
45 Replace the O-ring on the sensor. **Caution:** *Do not coat the O-rings with oil.*
46 Installation is the reverse of removal.

EVAP canister

Refer to illustrations 21.49a and 21.49b

47 Raise the vehicle and place it securely on jackstands.
48 On 2006 and later models, remove the

lower cover and canister bracket.
49 Disconnect the vapor hose and the electrical connector from the vent shut valve and disconnect the two vapor hoses from the right end of the EVAP canister (**see illustrations**).
50 On 2005 and earlier models, detach the two-way valve/bypass solenoid valve assembly from the left end of the EVAP canister. It's not necessary to actually remove the two-way valve/bypass solenoid assembly - just remove the two bracket mounting screws and pull the bracket away from the canister.
51 Disengage any vapor hoses that are attached to the sides of the canister.
52 Remove the EVAP canister mounting bolt, then remove the canister.
53 If you're planning to replace the EVAP canister, be sure to remove the vent shut valve, and any other EVAP system components attached to the canister, and install them on the new canister.
54 Installation is the reverse of removal.

22 Exhaust Gas Recirculation (EGR) valve - replacement

Refer to illustration 22.3

1 Locate the EGR valve on the coolant housing at the right end of the engine.
2 Disconnect the electrical connector from the EGR valve.
3 Remove the EGR valve mounting nuts

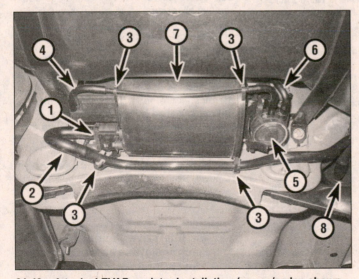

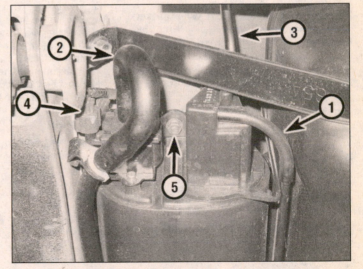

21.49a A typical EVAP canister installation (coupe/sedan shown, other models similar)

1 Vent shut valve
2 Vent shut valve-to-air filter hose
3 Hose guides
4 EVAP canister-to-two-way valve hose
5 Two-way valve/bypass solenoid valve assembly (bypass solenoid, on top of two-way valve, not visible in this photo)
6 Two-way valve-to-EVAP valve (EVAP valve, on top of fuel tank, not visible in this photo)
7 EVAP canister
8 Air filter

21.49b EVAP canister installation details (right end)

1 Hose from the EVAP canister to the two-way valve
2 Hose from the vent shut valve to the air filter
3 Hose from the EVAP canister to the canister purge valve in the engine compartment
4 Vent shut valve electrical connector
5 EVAP canister mounting bolt

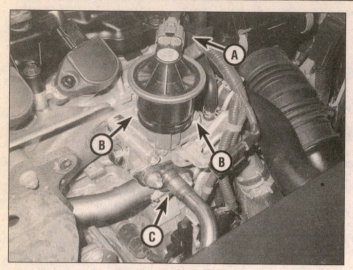

22.3 Typical EGR mounting details

A   *EGR electrical connector*
B   *EGR mounting bolts*
C   *EGR tube and mounting bolts*

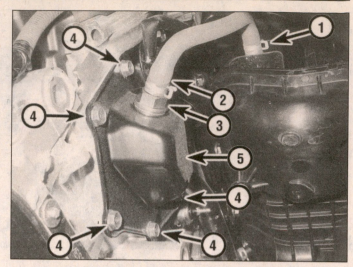

23.5 Typical PCV system crankcase ventilation hose, PCV valve and air/oil separator installation details

1   *Hose clamp at air filter housing*
2   *Hose clamp at PCV valve*
3   *PCV valve*
4   *Air/oil separator mounting bolts (upper bolt is not visible in this photo)*
5   *Air/oil separator*

and remove the EGR valve from the coolant housing **(see illustration)**.
4   Remove and discard the old EGR valve gasket.
5   Installation is the reverse of removal. Be sure to use a new EGR valve gasket, and tighten the EGR valve mounting nuts securely.

23 Positive Crankcase Ventilation (PCV) valve - replacement

Fresh air inlet hose

1   On coupes and sedans, remove the air filter housing (see Chapter 4).
2   Loosen the hose clamps at both ends of the hose, slide them back and disconnect the hose from the valve cover and from the air filter housing.
3   Installation is the reverse of removal. Make sure that both hose clamps are in good condition. If either one is loose, replace it.

Crankcase ventilation hose

Coupe and sedan

Refer to illustration 23.5

4   Raise the front of the vehicle and place it securely on jackstands.
5   Loosen the hose clamps at both ends of the crankcase ventilation hose **(see illustration)**, then disconnect the hose from the PCV valve and from the intake manifold.
6   Installation is the reverse of removal. Make sure that both hose clamps are in good condition. If either one is loose, replace it.

CR-V and hatchback

7   On CR-Vs, remove the intake manifold cover (see Chapter 2B). On these models, the crankcase ventilation hose is routed across the top of the intake manifold.
8   Loosen the hose clamps at both ends of the crankcase ventilation hose, then disconnect the hose from the PCV valve and from the intake manifold.
9   Installation is the reverse of removal. Make sure that both hose clamps are in good condition. If either one is loose, replace it.

PCV valve

Coupe and sedan

10   Raise the front of the vehicle and place it securely on jackstands.
11   Disconnect the crankcase ventilation hose from the PCV valve **(see illustration 23.5)**.
12   Unscrew the PCV valve from the air/oil separator.
13   Installation is the reverse of removal. Be sure to tighten the PCV valve securely.

CR-V and hatchback

14   Disconnect the crankcase ventilation hose from the PCV valve.
15   Unscrew and remove the PCV valve.
16   Installation is the reverse of removal. Be sure to tighten the PCV valve securely.

Air/oil separator (coupe and sedan only)

17   Raise the front of the vehicle and place it securely on jackstands.
18   Remove the crankcase ventilation hose

and the PCV valve **(see illustration 23.5)**.
19   Unbolt the air/oil separator and remove it.
20   Using solvent and a gasket scraper, remove all residual liquid gasket material from the gasket mating surfaces of the separator and the block, then blow dry with compressed air.
21   Apply a fresh coat of liquid gasket to the mating surface of the separator and to the inner threads of the bolt holes in the block, then install the separator within the interval of time specified by the manufacturer of the liquid gasket. If you wait too long - more than four minutes, for example - some liquid gaskets will not seal correctly.
22   Installation is otherwise the reverse of removal. Be sure to tighten the air/oil separator mounting bolts securely.

24 Variable Valve Timing and Lift Electronic Control (VTEC) system - description and component replacement

Description

1   A low-lift, short-duration camshaft intake lobe produces good torque, quick response, good fuel economy and low emissions at lower engine speeds, but can't deliver sufficient air/fuel mixture to the combustion chamber at higher engine speeds. A high-lift, long-duration intake cam lobe produces good power at high engine speeds, but produces a lumpy idle and poor driveability, wastes fuel

and produces unacceptable emissions at lower engine speeds. That's why camshaft intake lobe profiles are always a compromise between economy and performance. But Honda's **V**ariable Valve **T**iming and Lift **E**lectronic **C**ontrol (VTEC) system allows an engine to operate economically *and* make good power at the same time.

2   The VTEC system is used on some coupe and sedan engines (D17A2 and D17A6) and on all 1.8L engines, CR-V and hatchback engines. The principal differences between VTEC and non-VTEC engines are in the cylinder head, the camshaft(s) and the rocker arms. The block, the lubrication and cooling systems and most other components are identical on VTEC and non-VTEC engines. For more information about the cylinder head, the camshaft(s) and the rocker arms, refer to Chapter 2. This Section is intended to familiarize you with how VTEC works and to show you how to replace the PCM-controlled components (the VTEC solenoid valve and the VTC oil control solenoid valve) in the VTEC system. If you don't know whether your vehicle is equipped with VTEC, look for the letters "VTEC" on top of the valve cover.

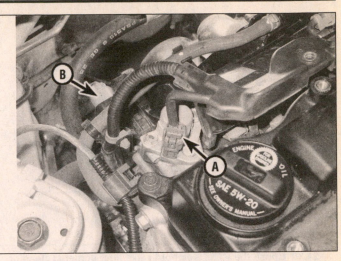

24.22 Typical 1.8L rocker arm oil control valve details

A   Rocker arm oil control valve electrical connector
B   Rocker arm oil pressure sensor

VTEC system on SOHC models (coupes and sedans)

3   On D17A2 and D17A6 SOHC engines (D17A1 SOHC engines do not use VTEC), there are two cam lobes for each pair of intake valves. On R18A1 SOHC engines, there are five camshaft lobes, three for the intake rocker arm and two for the exhaust rocker arms. These "primary" and "secondary" lobe profiles differ in lift and duration: the secondary lobe has lower lift and less duration (it opens later and closes sooner), while the primary lobe has higher lift and more duration (opens sooner and closes later). Each lobe operates its own rocker arm, which in turn pushes on its own valve. At low speeds, the secondary camshaft lobe operates one intake valve and the primary cam lobe operates the other valve. The low-lift, short-duration lobe produces good low-end torque and responsiveness.

4   When more power is needed at higher engine speeds, the PCM activates the VTEC solenoid valve, which allows higher oil pressure to a hydraulically-operated, spring-loaded pin inside the primary rocker arm. **Note:** *On 2006 and later models, the VTEC solenoid is called the rocker arm oil control valve.* When hydraulic pressure overcomes spring pressure, the pin slides sideways and locks the secondary rocker arm to the primary rocker arm. The two rocker arms are both activated by the primary cam lobe; the secondary rocker arm no longer contacts its own camshaft lobe again until the system is disengaged. So both valves are now opened by the primary camshaft lobe with its higher lift and longer duration, increasing performance.

5   The PCM turns the VTEC solenoid on and off in accordance with engine rpm, vehicle speed, throttle opening angle, engine load

and coolant temperature. Although diagnosis of the VTEC system is beyond the scope of the home mechanic, it's not difficult to replace the VTEC solenoid valve or to clean the filter for the system, both of which are outlined below.

Intelligent Variable Valve Timing and Lift Electronic Control (i-VTEC) system on DOHC models (CR-Vs and hatchbacks)

6   The "intelligent" VTEC (i-VTEC) system used on the DOHC engines in these two models is similar in operation to the SOHC VTEC system used on coupes and sedans, except that they also employ Variable Valve Timing Control (VTC).

Variable Valve Timing Control (VTC)

7   The VTEC system changes the *valve lift and duration* of the intake camshaft by using two different cam profiles. The VTC system, which is employed only on i-VTEC systems, changes the *phase* of the intake camshaft, which is another way of saying that it changes the cam timing, except that it does so *continuously*, not just when engine speed exceeds a certain threshold, as with the VTEC system. The VTC system, which is also operated by hydraulic (oil) pressure, improves fuel efficiency even more than VTEC alone, and it reduces exhaust emissions at all combinations of engine speed, vehicle speed and engine load.

8   When the engine is under a light load, the VTC control actuator (located inside the intake cam timing chain sprocket) is at its base position. The angle of the intake cam lobes is retarded to reduce the entry of exhaust gases into the intake ports and to achieve stable fuel consumption during lean burn.

9   When the engine is under a medium-to-high load, the VTC control actuator is at its advance control position. Cam angle is advanced slightly to reduce the effect of a diluted charge when the EGR system is operating by reducing the accompanying pumping loss. The intake valve is closed quickly to help reduce the entry of air/fuel mixture into

the intake port and to improve the charging effect.

10   When the engine is operating at higher speeds, the VTC control actuator is at its advance-base position. The cam phase angle is controlled for maximum valve timing and maximum engine power.

Component replacement

1.7L engines

VTEC solenoid valve

11   Remove the air intake resonator (see "Air filter housing - removal and installation" in Chapter 4).

12   The VTEC solenoid valve is located at the right rear corner of the cylinder head.

13   Disconnect the electrical connector from the VTEC solenoid valve.

14   Remove the VTEC solenoid valve mounting bolts and remove the VTEC solenoid valve from the cylinder head.

15   Remove the VTEC solenoid valve filter.

16   Inspect the filter for clogging and, if necessary, clean it with fresh solvent. If the filter is too dirty to be cleaned, replace it, and replace the engine oil and the engine oil filter (see Chapter 1).

17   Remove the three solenoid mounting bolts and separate the solenoid from the valve.

18   Remove the old O-ring between the solenoid and the valve and discard it. Always install a new O-ring when you disassemble the solenoid and the valve.

19   Using a new O-ring and, if necessary, a new filter, install the VTEC solenoid valve.

20   Installation is otherwise the reverse of removal. Be sure to tighten the solenoid-to-valve bolts and the VTEC solenoid valve mounting bolts securely.

1.8L engines

Rocker arm oil control valve

Refer to illustration 24.22

21   Remove the cowl cover.

22   Disconnect the electrical connector from the rocker arm oil control valve **(see illustration)**.

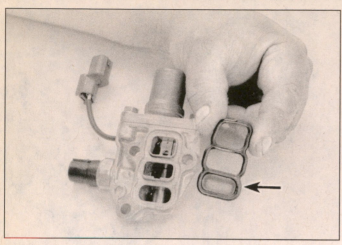

24.30 Check the VTEC solenoid valve filter screens; clean or replace the screens as necessary

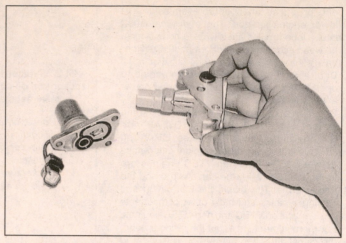

24.31 The plunger in the solenoid should move freely

23   Remove the rocker arm oil control valve mounting bolts and remove the valve from the cylinder head.

24   Remove the two control valve mounting bolts and separate the control valve from the housing.

25   Remove the old O-ring between the solenoid and the valve and discard it. Always install a new O-ring when you disassemble the solenoid and the valve.

26   Using a new O-ring, install the valve.

27   Installation is otherwise the reverse of removal. Be sure to tighten the solenoid-to-valve bolts and the rocker arm oil control valve mounting bolts securely.

2.0L and 2.4L engines

VTEC solenoid valve

Refer to illustrations 24.30 and 24.31

28   Locate the VTEC solenoid valve at the right rear corner of the cylinder head and disconnect the electrical connector.

29   Remove the VTEC solenoid valve mounting bolts, remove the solenoid valve heat shield and remove the VTEC solenoid from the cylinder head.

30   Remove the VTEC solenoid valve filter **(see illustration)**. Inspect the filter for clogging and, if necessary, clean it with fresh solvent. If the filter is too dirty to be cleaned, replace it, and replace the engine oil and the engine oil filter (see Chapter 1).

31   Remove the solenoid-to-valve mounting bolts and separate the solenoid from the valve. Depress the plunger into the valve with your finger **(see illustration)**. It should move freely in its bore in the valve. If it doesn't, replace the VTEC solenoid valve.

32   Installation is the reverse of removal. Be sure to tighten the VTEC solenoid valve mounting bolts securely.

VTC oil control solenoid valve

33   Locate the VTC oil control solenoid valve on the right end of the cylinder head.

34   Disconnect the electrical connector from the VTC oil control solenoid valve.

35   Remove the VTC oil control solenoid mounting bolt and remove the solenoid valve.

36   Remove and discard the old VTC oil control solenoid valve O-ring.

37   Inspect the VTC oil control solenoid valve for clogging. If the oil control solenoid valve is clogged, replace it and inspect the VTC oil strainer.

38   Using a new O-ring, install the VTC oil control solenoid valve, tighten the mounting bolt securely and plug in the electrical connector.

VTC oil strainer

39   Locate the VTC oil control solenoid oil strainer on the right front corner of the cylinder head.

40   Remove the VTC oil strainer cover bolts and remove the cover.

41   Remove the VTC oil strainer and inspect it for clogging. If the strainer is clogged, clean it in fresh solvent. If the strainer is too dirty to clean, replace it, then replace the engine oil and the oil filter (see Chapter 1).

42   Installation is the reverse of removal. Be sure to tighten the VTC oil strainer cover bolts securely.

Chapter 7 Part A
Manual transaxle

Contents

	Section			Section
Back-up light switch - replacement	5	Manual transaxle overhaul - general information		7
Driveaxle oil seals - replacement	2	Manual transaxle - removal and installation		6
General information	1	Shift cables - removal and installation		4
Lubricant change	See Chapter 1	Transaxle mount - check and replacement		3
Lubricant level check	See Chapter 1			

Specifications

Torque specifications

	Ft-lbs (unless otherwise indicated)	Nm
Starter bolts	See Chapter 5	
Subframe mounting bolts	See Chapter 10	
Transaxle-to-engine mounting bolts	47	64

1 General information

Vehicles covered by this manual are equipped with either a five- or six-speed manual transaxle, a four- or five-speed automatic transaxle, or a Continuously Variable Transaxle (CVT).

All information on the manual transaxle is included in this Part of Chapter 7. Service procedures for the four- and five-speed automatic transaxle, and Continuously Variable Transaxle (CVT) can be found in Chapter 7, Part B. You'll also find certain procedures common to both transaxles - such as oil seal replacement - in this Chapter.

Depending on the expense involved in having a transaxle overhauled, it might be a better idea to consider replacing it with either a new or rebuilt unit. Your local dealer or transaxle shop should be able to supply information concerning cost, availability and exchange policy. Regardless of how you decide to remedy a transaxle problem, you can still save a lot of money by removing and installing the unit yourself.

2 Driveaxle oil seals - replacement

Refer to illustrations 2.4 and 2.6

1 Oil leaks frequently occur due to wear of the driveaxle oil seals. Replacement of these seals is relatively easy, since the repair can usually be performed without removing the transaxle from the vehicle.

2 Driveaxle oil seals are located at the sides of the transaxle, where the driveaxles are attached. If leakage at the seal is suspected, raise the vehicle and support it

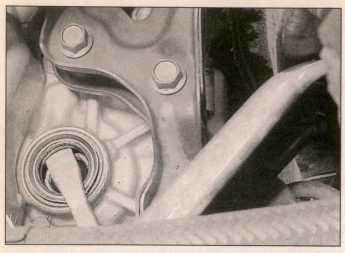

2.4 Insert the tip of a large screwdriver or prybar behind the oil seal and very carefully pry it out

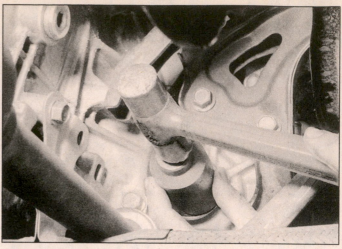

2.6 Using a large socket or a section of pipe, drive the new seal squarely into the bore

securely on jackstands. If the seal is leaking, lubricant will be found on the sides of the transaxle, below the seals.

3   Refer to Chapter 8 and remove the driveaxles.

4   Use a screwdriver or prybar to carefully pry the oil seal out of the transaxle bore **(see illustration)**.

5   If the oil seal cannot be removed with a screwdriver or prybar, a special oil seal removal tool (available at auto parts stores) will be required.

6   Using a large section of pipe or a large deep socket (slightly smaller than the outside diameter of the seal) as a drift, install the new oil seal **(see illustration)**. Drive it into the bore squarely and make sure it's completely seated. Coat the seal lip with transaxle lubricant.

7   Install the driveaxle(s). Be careful not to damage the lip of the new seal.

---

3   Transaxle mount - check and replacement

1   Raise the front of the vehicle and place it securely on jackstands.

2   Insert a large screwdriver or prybar between the mount support arm and the frame and try to lever the support arm.

3   The transaxle support arm should not move up more than about 1/2 to 3/4-inch within the mount. If it does, replace the mount.

4   To replace the mount, support the transaxle with a jack, remove the nuts and bolts and remove the mount. **Warning:** *Do not place any part of your body under the transaxle when it's supported only by a jack.*

5   Installation is the reverse of removal.

4   Shift cables - removal and installation

1   Remove the center console (see Chapter 11).

2   Remove the cotter pins and detach the cable ends from the lock pins on the shift lever. **Note:** *Hatchback models are equipped with clamps that snap fit over the cable ends while coupes and sedans are equipped with cotter pins.*

3   Pry off the spring clips and detach the cables from the shift lever housing. Rotate the cables until the squared edge aligns with the slot in the shift lever housing cutout.

4   On 2005 and earlier models, pull back the carpet and dislodge the grommet from the floorpan.

5   Raise the front of the vehicle and support it securely on jackstands.

6   Working under the vehicle, unscrew the nut and detach the cable bracket from the floorpan. On 2006 and later models, remove the fasteners securing the grommet to the floorpan.

7   Remove the clip(s) and washer(s) and detach the cable(s) from the shift lever(s) on the transaxle.

8   Pry off the spring clip(s) and detach the cable(s) from the bracket on the transaxle.

9   Guide the cable(s) through the floorpan.

10 Installation is the reverse of removal

5   Back-up light switch - replacement

1   Unplug the back-up light switch electrical connector, located just below the shift levers on the transaxle.

2   Unscrew the back-up light switch.

3   If equipped, discard the old washer. Using a new washer, install the new switch. On models without a washer, apply RTV sealant or Teflon tape to the threads of the new switch to prevent leakage.

4   Plug in the connector.

---

6   Manual transaxle - removal and installation

Removal

1   Remove the air intake duct and the air filter housing (see Chapter 4).

2   Remove the battery and the battery tray (see Chapter 5).

3   Remove the clutch release cylinder and hydraulic line, without disconnecting any fittings. Support the cylinder out of the way with a length of wire or rope. **Caution:** *Don't depress the clutch pedal while the release cylinder is removed.*

4   Remove the starter (see Chapter 5).

5   Clearly label and disconnect all vacuum lines, emissions hoses, electrical connectors and wiring harness clamps/brackets that may interfere with transaxle removal. Masking tape and/or a touch up paint applicator work well for marking items. Take instant photos or sketch the locations of components and brackets.

6   Support the engine with an engine support fixture or an engine hoist (an engine support fixture is recommended, as it doesn't have legs that extend under the vehicle that would get in the way). Connect the sling or chain to the lifting hook at the end of the engine near the transaxle, not to the lifting eye on the transaxle. If no lifting hook is provided, use the threaded hole(s) in the cylinder head to attach the sling or chain.

7   Loosen the front wheel lug nuts, then

raise the vehicle and support it securely on jackstands. Remove the wheels.

8   Remove the engine splash shield (see Chapter 2A, Section 5) and the inner fender splash shields (see Chapter 11). Cover the fenders and cowl using special pads. An old bedspread or blanket will also work.

9   Drain the transaxle fluid (see Chapter 1).

10   Remove the front section of the exhaust pipe, between the exhaust manifold(s) and the downstream catalytic converter.

11   Remove the driveaxles and, on 4WD CR-V models, the driveshaft (see Chapter 8).

12   Disconnect the shift cables from the transaxle (see Section 4).

13   Remove all of the powertrain mounts except the mount at the timing belt (or chain) end of the engine (see Chapter 2A).

14   Remove the subframe (see Chapter 10).

15   Support the transaxle with a jack, preferably one made for this purpose. Secure the transaxle to the jack with straps or chains.

16   Remove the transaxle-to-engine bolts.

17   Move the transaxle away from the engine to disengage the transaxle input shaft from the clutch disc, and far enough to clear the pressure plate. Lower the transaxle from the vehicle. **Note:** *It may be necessary to slowly lower the engine a slight amount while the jack supporting the transaxle is being lowered. This will provide more clearance between the transaxle and the body.*

Installation

18   If removed, install the clutch components (see Chapter 8).

19   Make sure the dowel pins are installed in the engine block. With the transaxle secured to the jack with a chain, raise it into position behind the engine, then carefully slide it forward, engaging the two dowel pins on the transaxle with the corresponding holes in the block and the input shaft with the clutch plate hub splines. Do not use excessive force to install the transaxle - if the input shaft does not slide into place, readjust the angle of the transaxle so it is level and/or turn the input shaft so the splines engage properly with the clutch plate hub.

20   Install the transaxle-to-engine bolts and tighten them to the torque listed in this Chapter's Specifications.

21   The remainder of installation is the reverse of removal, noting the following points:

a) *Refill the transaxle with the specified type of lubricant (see Chapter 1).*

b) *Tighten the driveaxle/hub nuts to the torque listed in the Chapter 8 Specifications.*

c) *Tighten the wheel lug nuts to the torque listed in the Chapter 1 Specifications.*

d) *Road test the vehicle for proper operation and check for leaks.*

7   Manual transaxle overhaul - general information

1   Overhauling a manual transaxle is a difficult job for the do-it-yourselfer. It involves the disassembly and reassembly of many small parts. Numerous clearances must be precisely measured and, if necessary, changed with select fit spacers and snap-rings. As a result, if transaxle problems arise, it can be removed and installed by a competent do-it-yourselfer, but overhaul should be left to a transaxle repair shop. Rebuilt transaxles may be available - check with your dealer parts department and auto parts stores. At any rate, the time and money involved in an overhaul is almost sure to exceed the cost of a rebuilt unit.

2   Nevertheless, it's not impossible for an inexperienced mechanic to rebuild a transaxle if the special tools are available and the job is done in a deliberate step-by-step manner so nothing is overlooked.

3   The tools necessary for an overhaul include internal and external snap-ring pliers, a bearing puller, a slide hammer, a set of pin punches, a dial indicator and possibly a hydraulic press. In addition, a large, sturdy workbench and a vise or transaxle stand will be required.

4   During disassembly of the transaxle, make careful notes of how each piece comes off, where it fits in relation to other pieces and what holds it in place. Noting how the parts are installed when you remove them will make it much easier to get the transaxle back together.

5   Before taking the transaxle apart for repair, it will help if you have some idea what area of the transaxle is malfunctioning. Certain problems can be closely tied to specific areas in the transaxle, which can make component examination and replacement easier. Refer to the *Troubleshooting* Section at the front of this manual for information regarding possible sources of trouble.

Notes

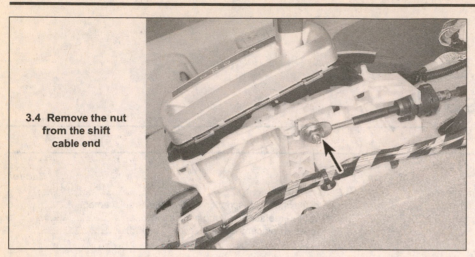

Chapter 7 Part B
Automatic transaxle

Contents

	Section
Automatic transaxle and Continuously Variable Transaxle (CVT) - removal and installation	6
Automatic transaxle overhaul - general information	7
Diagnosis - general	2
General information	1
Interlock system - description and solenoid replacement	5
Shift cable - replacement and adjustment	3
Shift lever - replacement	4

Specifications

General

Fluid type and capacity	See Chapter 1

Torque specifications

	Ft-lbs (unless otherwise indicated)	Nm

Note: *One foot-pound (ft-lb) of torque is equivalent to 12 inch-pounds (in-lbs) of torque. Torque values below approximately 15 ft-lbs are expressed in inch-pounds, since most foot-pound torque wrenches are not accurate at these smaller values.*

	Ft-lbs (unless otherwise indicated)	Nm
Driveplate-to-torque converter bolts	108 in-lbs	12
Flywheel-to-driveplate bolts (Continuously Variable Transaxle)	108 in-lbs	12
Subframe mounting bolts	See Chapter 10	
Transaxle mounting bolts	47	64

1 General information

The vehicles covered by this manual are equipped with either a five- or six-speed manual transaxle, a four- or five-speed automatic transaxle, or a Continuously Variable Transaxle (CVT). All information on automatic transaxles and the Continuously Variable Transaxle is included in this Part of Chapter 7. Information for the manual transaxle can be found in Part A of this Chapter. Information related to the transfer case on 4WD CR-V models can be found in Chapter 8.

Due to the complexity of the automatic transaxles and Continuously Variable Transaxles covered in this manual and the specialized equipment necessary to perform most service operations, this Chapter contains only those procedures related to general diagnosis, routine maintenance, adjustment and removal and installation.

If the transaxle requires major repair work, this should be left to a dealer service department or an automotive or transmission repair shop. You can, however, remove and install the transaxle yourself and save the expense, even if a transmission shop does the repair work (but be sure a proper diagnosis has been made before removing the transaxle).

2 Diagnosis - general

1 Automatic transaxle malfunctions may be caused by five general conditions:

a) *Poor engine performance*
b) *Improper adjustments*
c) *Hydraulic malfunctions*
d) *Mechanical malfunctions*
e) *Malfunctions in the computer or its signal network*

2 Diagnosis of these problems should always begin with a check of the easily repaired items: fluid level and condition (see Chapter 1), shift cable adjustment and shift lever installation. Next, perform a road test to determine if the problem has been corrected or if more diagnosis is necessary. If the problem persists after the preliminary tests and corrections are completed, additional diagnosis should be performed by a dealer service department or other qualified transmission repair shop. Refer to the *Troubleshooting* Section at the front of this manual for information on symptoms of transaxle problems.

Preliminary checks

3 Drive the vehicle to warm the transaxle to normal operating temperature.

4 Check the fluid level as described in Chapter 1:

a) *If the fluid level is unusually low, add enough fluid to bring the level within the designated area of the dipstick, then check for external leaks (see "Fluid leak diagnosis" below).*
b) *If the fluid level is abnormally high, drain off the excess, then check the drained fluid for contamination by coolant. The presence of engine coolant in the automatic transmission fluid indicates that a failure has occurred in the internal radiator walls that separate the coolant from the transmission fluid (see Chapter 3).*
c) *If the fluid is foaming, drain it and refill the transaxle, then check for coolant in the fluid, or a high fluid level.*

5 Make sure the engine idle speed is correct. If the idle speed is incorrect, have it adjusted by a dealer service department or other qualified repair shop before proceeding.

6 Inspect the shift cable. Make sure that it's properly adjusted and operates smoothly (see Section 3).

Fluid leak diagnosis

7 Most fluid leaks are easy to locate visually. Repair usually consists of replacing a seal or gasket. If a leak is difficult to find, the following procedure may help.

8 Identify the fluid. Make sure it's transmission fluid and not engine oil or brake fluid (auto-

3.4 Remove the nut from the shift cable end

matic transmission fluid is a deep red color).

9   Try to pinpoint the source of the leak. Drive the vehicle several miles, then park it over a large sheet of cardboard. After a minute or two, you should be able to locate the leak by determining the source of the fluid dripping onto the cardboard.

10   Make a careful visual inspection of the suspected component and the area immediately around it. Pay particular attention to gasket mating surfaces. A mirror is often helpful for finding leaks in areas that are hard to see.

11   If the leak still cannot be found, clean the suspected area thoroughly with a degreaser or solvent, then dry it.

12   Drive the vehicle for several miles at normal operating temperature and varying speeds. After driving the vehicle, visually inspect the suspected component again.

13   Once the leak has been located, the cause must be determined before it can be properly repaired. If a gasket is replaced but the sealing flange is bent, the new gasket will not stop the leak. The bent flange must be straightened.

14   Before attempting to repair a leak, check to make sure that the following conditions are corrected or they may cause another leak. **Note:** *Some of the following conditions cannot be fixed without highly specialized tools and expertise. Such problems must be referred to a transmission shop or a dealer service department.*

Seal leaks

15   If a transaxle seal is leaking, the fluid level or pressure may be too high, the vent may be plugged, the seal bore may be damaged, the seal itself may be damaged or improperly installed, the surface of the shaft protruding through the seal may be damaged or a loose bearing may be causing excessive shaft movement.

16   Make sure the dipstick tube seal is in good condition and the tube is properly seated. Periodically check the area around the speedometer gear or sensor for leakage. If transmission fluid is evident, check the O-ring for damage.

Case leaks

17   If the case itself appears to be leaking, the casting is porous and will have to be repaired or replaced.

18   Make sure the oil cooler hose fittings are tight and in good condition.

Fluid comes out vent pipe or fill tube

19   If this condition occurs, the transaxle is overfilled, there is coolant in the fluid, the case is porous, the dipstick is incorrect, the vent is plugged or the drain-back holes are plugged.

---

3   Shift cable - replacement and adjustment

Warning: *These models are equipped with a Supplemental Restraint System (SRS), more commonly known as airbags. Always disable the airbag system before working in the vicinity of any airbag system component to avoid the possibility of accidental deployment of the airbag(s), which could cause personal injury (see Chapter 12).*
Warning: *Do not use a memory saving device to preserve the PCM or radio memory when working on or near airbag system components*

1   Raise the vehicle and support it securely on jackstands.

Sedan and coupe models
Replacement

Refer to illustrations 3.4, 3.5a, 3.5b, 3.6, 3.7a, 3.7b, 3.8a and 3.8b

2   Set the parking brake, then place the shift lever in the Neutral position.

3   Remove the center console panels. Remove the center console (see Chapter 11).

4   Remove the nut that secures the shift cable end **(see illustration)**.

5   On 2005 and earlier models, rotate the socket holder 1/4 turn until the flattened edge of the cable grommet guide aligns with the base and slide the assembly out of the slotted recess **(see illustration)**. On 2006 and later

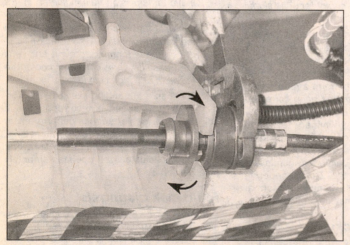

3.5a Rotate the socket holder 1/4 turn until the flattened edge of the cable grommet guide aligns with the base

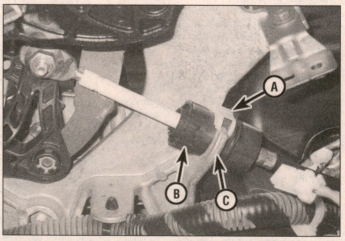

3.5b Pry the cable lock (A) up, then rotate the socket holder (B) counterclockwise and push the socket against the mounting bracket (C)

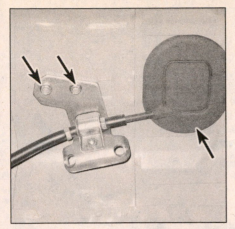

3.6 Remove the shift cable guide bracket bolts and the rubber grommet

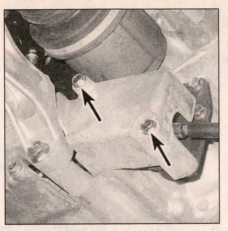

3.7a Remove the shift cable holder cover bolts . . .

3.7b . . . then remove the holder bolts and separate the assembly from the transaxle

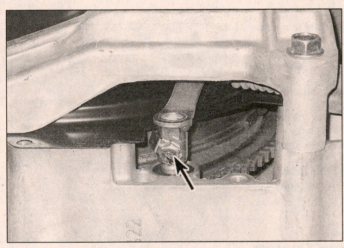

3.8a Bend back the metal tab and remove the lock bolt from the control shaft

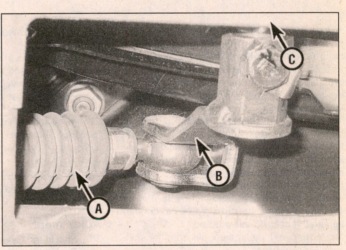

3.8b After the lock bolt is removed from the control shaft (C), the shift cable (A) and the control lever (B) will be removed as one unit

models, pry the lock up and rotate the socket holder counterclockwise, then push the socket in and slide the assembly out of the slotted recess **(see illustration)**.

6   Remove the shift cable guide bracket mounting bolts **(see illustration)**.
7   Remove the shift cable holder **(see illustrations)**.

8   Remove the lock washer and lock bolt and the control lever from the transaxle control shaft and remove the shift cable together with the control lever **(see illustrations)**.
9   Pull the rubber grommet and shift cable out of the vehicle.
10   Installation is the reverse of the removal procedure, noting the following points:
   a)   *Install a new lock washer, then bend the locking tang against the bolt head.*
   b)   *Be sure to adjust the cable before reattaching it to the shift lever (see Steps 11 through 17).*

Adjustment

Refer to illustrations 3.12, 3.13 and 3.14

11   Shift to the Neutral position, then remove the lock nut from the cable and disconnect it from the mounting bracket (see Step 4).
12   Push the shift cable until it stops and release your hand. Pull back two clicks until the cable stops (locks-in) in position **(see illustration)**. This is the NEUTRAL position.

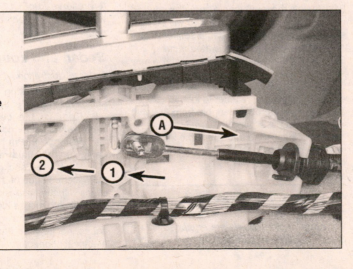

3.12 First, push the shift cable until it stops (A), pull back two clicks until the cable locks-in the Neutral position

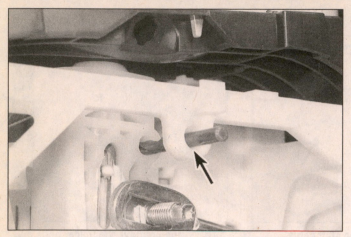

3.13 Insert a 0.24 inch (6.0 mm) pin into the positioning hole on the shift lever bracket base

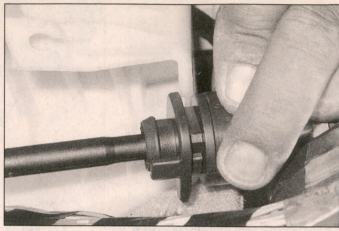

3.14 Rotate the shift cable socket holder 1/4 turn to align it with the slotted recess

13　Insert a 0.24 inch (6.0 mm) pin into the positioning hole on the shift lever bracket base **(see illustration)**. Once the pin is slid through the positioning hole on the shift lever bracket base, align the shift lever and slide the pin into the shift lever positioning hole to lock the assembly into place.

14　Install the shift cable into the mounting bracket, then install the cable end to the shift lever mounting bolt and align the square surface with the alignment casting on the mounting bolt. **Note:** *It will be necessary to rotate the shift cable socket holder 1/4 turn to align it with the slotted recess* **(see illustration)**.

15　Install the lock nut on the cable and tighten the cable in this position.

16　Remove the alignment pin from the shift lever bracket base.

17　Start the engine and check the shift lever in all gears. If any gear doesn't work properly, refer to Section 2.

CR-V models

Replacement

18　Set the parking brake, then place the shift lever in the Reverse position.

19　Remove the dashboard lower cover on the driver's side and the instrument panel (see Chapter 11).

20　Slide the lock tab down over the shift cable end holder.

21　On 2006 and earlier models, use needle-nose pliers to grasp the middle of the lock tab and lift the lock tab off the shift cable end holder. Be sure to replace the lock tab with a new part on reassembly. On 2007 and later models, pry the lock retainer up and rotate the socket holder counterclockwise, then push the socket in and slide the assembly out of the slotted recess **(see illustration 3.5b)**.

22　Remove the shift cable end from the cable holder.

23　Rotate the socket holder 1/4 turn until the flattened edge of the cable grommet guide aligns with the base and slide the assembly out of the slotted recess.

24　Remove the shift cable guide bracket and mounting bolts and separate it from the vehicle body.

25　Remove the shift cable cover, remove the spring clip and separate the shift cable from the control lever.

26　Pull the rubber grommet and shift cable out of the vehicle.

27　Installation is the reverse of the removal procedure, noting the following points:

a)　*Install a new lock tab on the shift cable end holder.*

b)　*Be sure to adjust the cable before reattaching it to the shift lever (see Steps 28 through 34).*

Adjustment

28　Shift to the Reverse position.

29　Push the shift cable until it stops and release your hand. Pull back one click until the cable stops (locks-in) in position. This is the REVERSE position.

30　Insert a 0.24 inch (6.0 mm) pin into the positioning hole on the shift lever bracket base. Once the pin is slid through the positioning hole on the shift lever bracket base, align the shift lever and slide the pin into the shift lever positioning hole to lock the assembly into place.

31　Install the shift cable into the slotted recess of the cable base. **Note:** *It will be necessary to rotate the shift cable socket holder 1/4 turn to align it with the slotted recess.*

32　On 2006 and earlier models, install a new shift cable lock to secure the shift cable end in the shift cable holder. On 2007 and later models, push in the lock retainer to lock it.

33　Remove the alignment pin from the shift lever bracket base.

34　Start the engine and check the shift lever in all gears. If any gear doesn't work properly, refer to Section 2.

4　Shift lever - replacement

Warning: *These models are equipped with a Supplemental Restraint System (SRS), more*

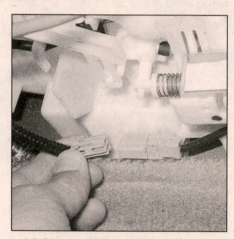

4.5 Disconnect the shift lock solenoid electrical connector

commonly known as airbags. Always disable the airbag system before working in the vicinity of any airbag system component to avoid the possibility of accidental deployment of the airbag(s), which could cause personal injury (see Chapter 12).

Warning: *Do not use a memory saving device to preserve the PCM or radio memory when working on or near airbag system components*

Sedan and coupe models

Refer to illustrations 4.5, 4.6a and 4.6b

1　Set the parking brake, then place the shift lever in the Neutral position.

2　Remove the center console panels. Remove the center console (see Chapter 11).

3　Remove the nut that secures the shift cable end **(see illustration 3.4)**.

4　Rotate the socket holder 1/4 turn until the flattened edge of the cable grommet guide aligns with the base and slide the assembly out of the slotted recess **(see illustration 3.5)**.

5　Disconnect the shift lock solenoid electrical connector **(see illustration)** and park pin electrical connector.

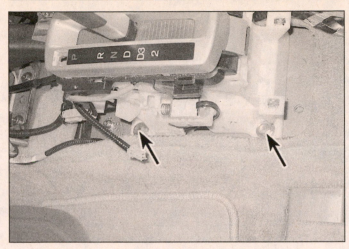

4.6a Remove the shift lever assembly mounting bolts from the left side . . .

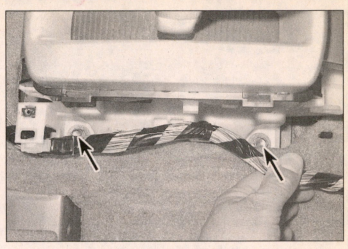

4.6b . . . and the right side

6   Remove the four bolts and remove the shift lever assembly from the floor (see illustrations).
7   Installation is the reverse of the removal procedure, but note the following points:
 a) Verify the indicator for the neutral position lights with the ignition switch on.
 b) Adjust the shift cable, if necessary (see Section 3).

CR-V models

8   Set the parking brake, then place the shift lever in the Reverse position.
9   Remove the dashboard lower cover on the driver's side and the instrument panel (see Chapter 11).
10   Disconnect the O/D switch electrical connector.
11   On 2006 and earlier models, use needle-nose pliers to grasp the middle of the lock tab and lift the lock tab off the shift cable end holder. Be sure to replace the lock tab with a new part on reassembly. On 2007 and later models, pry the lock retainer up and rotate the socket holder counterclockwise, then push the socket in and slide the assembly out of the slotted recess (see illustration 3.5b).
12   Remove the shift cable end from the cable holder.
13   Rotate the socket holder 1/4 turn until the flattened edge of the cable grommet guide aligns with the base and slide the assembly out of the slotted recess.
14   Remove the bolts and remove the shift lever assembly.
15   Installation is the reverse of the removal procedure, but note the following points:
 a) Verify the indicator for the neutral position lights with the ignition switch on.
 b) Adjust the shift cable, if necessary (see Section 3).

5   Interlock system - description and solenoid replacement

Warning: These models are equipped with a Supplemental Restraint System (SRS), more commonly known as airbags. Always disable the airbag system before working in the vicinity of any airbag system component to avoid the possibility of accidental deployment of the airbag(s), which could cause personal injury (see Chapter 12).
Warning: Do not use a memory saving device to preserve the PCM or radio memory when working on or near airbag system components

Description

1   Vehicles equipped with an automatic transaxle have an interlock system to prevent unintentional shifting. The interlock system consists of two subsystems: a shift lock system and a key interlock system.

Key interlock system

2   The key interlock system prevents the ignition key from being removed from the ignition switch unless the shift lever is in the Park position.

Shift lock system

3   The shift lock system prevents the shift lever from moving from the Park position unless the brake pedal is depressed. Nor can the shift lever be shifted when the brake pedal and the accelerator pedal are depressed at the same time. In the event of a system malfunction, you can release the shift lever by inserting a screwdriver into the release slot near the shift lever (sedans/coupes) or into the slot in the upper steering column cover (CR-V).

Solenoid replacement

Note: The following procedure pertains only to the shift lock solenoid. For information on how to replace the key interlock solenoid, refer to the "Ignition switch/key lock cylinder replacement" Section in Chapter 12. The key interlock solenoid isn't available separately.

Coupe and sedan models

4   Remove the center console panels. Remove the center console (see Chapter 11).
5   Disconnect the shift lock solenoid electrical connector.
6   Pry the plastic lock tabs and slide the shift lock solenoid, clear the tabs and remove the solenoid.
7   Installation is the reverse of removal. Install the plunger and plunger spring into the new shift lock solenoid.
8   Align the shift lock solenoid plunger with the tip of the shift lock stop.
9   Connect the shift lock solenoid electrical connector.

CR-V models

10   Remove the lower instrument panel, knee bolster and the steering column covers (see Chapter 11).
11   Remove the shift lever assembly (see Section 4).
12   Remove the harness band clamp from the shift lever bracket base.
13   Disconnect the O/D switch/shift lock solenoid/park pin switch connector.
14   Using two small screwdrivers, release the locking tabs retaining the shift lock solenoid and remove the solenoid.
15   Installation is the reverse of removal. Install the plunger and plunger spring into the new shift lock solenoid.
16   Align the shift lock solenoid plunger with the tip of the shift lock stop.
17   Install the lock connector.
18   Installation is the reverse of removal.

6.6 Install an engine support fixture to support the engine while the transaxle is removed

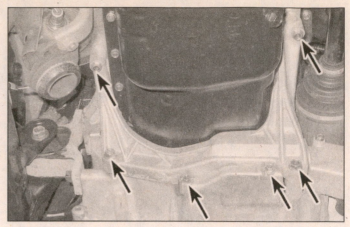

6.13a Remove the transaxle brace mounting bolts . . .

6 Automatic transaxle and Continuously Variable Transaxle (CVT) - removal and installation

Warning: *These models are equipped with a Supplemental Restraint System (SRS), more commonly known as airbags. Always disable the airbag system before working in the vicinity of any airbag system component to avoid the possibility of accidental deployment of the airbag(s), which could cause personal injury (see Chapter 12).*

Warning: *Do not use a memory saving device to preserve the PCM or radio memory when working on or near airbag system components*

Note: *Read through the entire Section before beginning this procedure. The engine and transaxle are removed as a unit from below, then separated outside the vehicle.*

Removal

Refer to illustrations 6.6, 6.13a, 6.13b, 6.14 and 6.15

1   Open the hood and cover the fenders and cowl using special pads. An old bed-spread or blanket will also work. Remove the air intake duct and the air filter housing (see Chapter 4).

2   Remove the battery and the battery tray (see Chapter 5).

3   Remove the starter (see Chapter 5).

4   Clearly label and disconnect all vacuum lines, emissions hoses, electrical connectors and wiring harness clamps/brackets that may interfere with transaxle removal. Masking tape and/or a touch up paint applicator work well for marking items. Take instant photos or sketch the locations of components and brackets.

5   Disconnect the automatic transaxle fluid cooler lines from the transaxle. Be sure to position a pan to catch excess fluid. Plug the lines to prevent leakage.

6   Support the engine with an engine support fixture or an engine hoist (an engine support fixture is recommended, as it doesn't have legs that extend under the vehicle that would get in the way) **(see illustration)**. Connect the sling or chain to the lifting hook at the end of the engine near the transaxle, not to the lifting eye on the transaxle. If no lifting hook is provided, use the threaded hole(s) in the cylinder head to attach the sling or chain.

7   Loosen the front wheel lug nuts, then raise the vehicle and support it securely on jackstands. Remove the wheels.

8   Remove the engine splash shield (see Chapter 2A, Section 5) and the inner fender splash shields (see Chapter 11, Section 12).

9   Disconnect the shift cable from the transaxle (see Section 3).

10   Drain the transaxle fluid (see Chapter 1). Be sure to use a new sealing washer when you reinstall the drain plug.

11   Remove the front section of the exhaust pipe, between the exhaust manifold and the downstream catalytic converter.

12   Remove the driveaxles and, on 4WD CR-V models, the driveshaft (see Chapter 8).

13   Remove the transaxle brace and the torque converter cover **(see illustrations)**.

14   Mark the relationship of the torque converter (conventional transaxle) or the flywheel (CVT) to the driveplate so that they can be reinstalled in the same relationship to one another **(see illustration)**.

15   Remove the torque converter-to-drive-

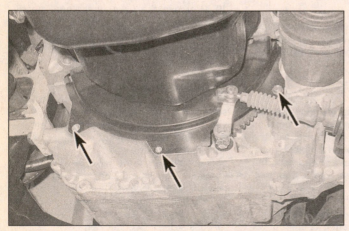

6.13b . . . and the torque converter driveplate cover - note several bolts have been removed along with the transaxle brace

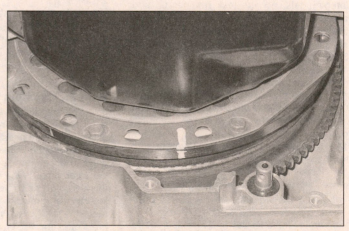

6.14 Mark the relationship of the torque converter to the driveplate - sedan model shown

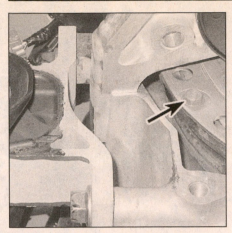

6.15 Location of one of the torque converter bolts

plate bolts **(see illustration)** one at a time by rotating the crankshaft pulley for access to each bolt.

16 Remove all of the powertrain mounts except the mount at the timing belt (or chain) end of the engine (see Chapter 2A).

17 Remove the subframe (see Chapter 10).

18 Support the transaxle with a jack, preferably one made for this purpose. Secure the transaxle to the jack with straps or chains.

19 Remove the transaxle-to-engine bolts.

20 Move the transaxle back to disengage it from the engine block dowel pins and make sure the torque converter is detached from the driveplate. Secure the torque converter to the transaxle so it will not fall out during removal. Lower the transaxle from the vehicle. **Note:** *It may be necessary to slowly lower the engine a slight amount while the jack supporting the transaxle is being lowered. This will provide more clearance between the transaxle and the body.*

Installation

21 Honda recommends flushing the transaxle cooler and the cooler hoses and lines with solvent whenever the transaxle is removed from the vehicle. Flush the lines and fluid cooler thoroughly and make sure no solvent remains in the lines or cooler after flushing. It's a good idea to repeat the flushing procedure with clean automatic transaxle fluid to ensure that no solvent remains in the lines or cooler.

22 Prior to installation, make sure that the torque converter hub is securely engaged in the transaxle pump. With the transaxle secured to the jack, raise it into position. Be sure to keep it level so the torque converter does not slide out.

23 Line-up the marks you made on the torque converter and driveplate.

24 Make sure the dowel pins are still installed, then move the transaxle forward carefully until the dowel pins are engaged with the holes in the engine block.

25 Install the transaxle-to-engine bolts and tighten them to the torque listed in this Chapter's Specifications. **Caution:** *Don't use the bolts to force the transaxle and engine together. If the transaxle doesn't slide easily up against the engine, find out why before you tighten the bolts*

26 The remainder of installation is the reverse of the removal procedure, noting the following points:

a) *Tighten subframe mounting bolts to the torque listed in this Chapter 10 Specifications.*

b) *Install all of the driveplate bolts before tightening any of them. Tighten the driveplate bolts to the torque listed in this Chapter's Specifications.*

c) *Tighten the driveaxle/hub nuts to the torque listed in the Chapter 8 Specifications.*

d) *Tighten the wheel lug nuts to the torque listed in the Chapter 1 Specifications.*

e) *Refill the transaxle with the specified type and amount of lubricant (see Chapter 1). Note that the transaxle may require more fluid than in a normal fluid and filter change, since the torque converter may be empty (the converter is not drained during a fluid change).*

f) *Start the engine, set the parking brake and shift the transaxle through all gears three times. Make sure the shift cable is adjusted properly (see Section 3).*

g) *Allow the engine to reach its proper operating temperature with the transaxle in Park or Neutral, then turn it off and check the fluid level again.*

h) *Road test the vehicle and check for fluid leaks.*

7 Automatic transaxle overhaul - general information

In the event of a problem occurring, it will be necessary to establish whether the fault is electrical, mechanical or hydraulic in nature, before repair work can be contemplated. Diagnosis requires detailed knowledge of the transmission's operation and construction, as well as access to specialized test equipment, and so is deemed to be beyond the scope of this manual. It is therefore essential that problems with the automatic transmission are referred to a dealer service department or other qualified repair facility for assessment.

Note that a faulty transmission should not be removed before the vehicle has been diagnosed by a knowledgeable technician equipped with the proper tools, as troubleshooting must be performed with the transmission installed in the vehicle.

Notes

Chapter 8
Clutch and driveline

Contents

	Section		Section
Clutch - description and check	2	Clutch start switch - replacement	9
Clutch components - removal, inspection and installation	6	Differential (4WD CR-V models) - removal and installation	14
Clutch hydraulic system - bleeding	5	Differential oil seals (4WD CR-V models) - replacement	13
Clutch master cylinder - removal and installation	3	Driveaxle boot - replacement	11
Clutch pedal adjustment	8	Driveaxles - removal and installation	10
Clutch release bearing and lever - removal, inspection and installation	7	Driveshaft (4WD CR-V models) - removal and installation	12
Clutch release cylinder - removal and installation	4	General information	1
		Transfer case (4WD CR-V models) - removal and installation	15

Specifications

Clutch fluid type	See Chapter 1
Driveshaft runout limit (4WD CR-V models)	0.06 inch (1.5 mm)
Clutch pedal	
Pedal height	
2001 to 2005 all except Hatchback models	7.8 inches (198 mm)
2002 to 2005 Hatchback models	7.6 inches (193 mm)
2002 to 2006 CR-V models	7.87 inches (200 mm)
2006 and later models (except Si models)	6.27 inches (159 mm)
2006 and later Si models	6.35 inches (161 mm)
Pedal freeplay	
2001 to 2005 (all except Hatchback models)	0.59 to 0.79 inch (15 to 20 mm)
2002 to 2005 Hatchback models	0.39 to 0.63 inch (10 to 16 mm)
2006 and later models (except CR-V models)	0.35 to 0.47 inch (9 to 12 mm)
2002 to 2006 CR-V models	0.24 to 0.67 inch (6 to 17 mm)

Torque specifications

Note: *One foot-pound (ft-lb) of torque is equivalent to 12 inch-pounds (in-lbs) of torque. Torque values below approximately 15 ft-lbs are expressed in inch-pounds, since most foot-pound torque wrenches are not accurate at these smaller values.*

	Ft-lbs (unless otherwise indicated)	Nm
Clutch master cylinder mounting nuts	108 in-lbs	13
Clutch pressure plate-to-flywheel bolts	19	25
Clutch release cylinder mounting fasteners	16	22
Differential mounting bracket-to-floorpan mounting bolts (4WD CR-V models)	36	49
Differential pinion flange nut (4WD CR-V models)		
2006 and earlier models	87	118
2007 and later models	108	147
Driveshaft center support bearing mounting bolts (4WD CR-V models)	29	39
Driveshaft-to-differential pinion flange mounting bolts (4WD CR-V models)	24	32
Driveshaft-to-transfer case pinion flange mounting bolts (4WD CR-V models)	24	24
Driveaxle hub/nut		
All models except CR-V and 2006 and later Si models	134	181
2006 and later Si models	181	245
CR-V models		
Front		
2006 and earlier models	181	245
2007 and later models	242	328
Rear (4WD CR-V models)		
2006 and earlier models	134	181
2007 and later models	181	245

Torque specifications (continued)

Ft-lbs (unless otherwise indicated)   **Nm**

Note: *One foot-pound (ft-lb) of torque is equivalent to 12 inch-pounds (in-lbs) of torque. Torque values below approximately 15 ft-lbs are expressed in inch-pounds, since most foot-pound torque wrenches are not accurate at these smaller values.*

Intermediate shaft bearing support mounting bolts	29	39
Transfer case mounting bolts	33	44
Wheel lug nuts	See Chapter 1	

---

1 General information

The information in this Chapter deals with the components from the rear of the engine to the front wheels, except for the transaxle, which is dealt with in the previous Chapter. For the purposes of this Chapter, these components are grouped into two categories - clutch and driveaxles. Separate Sections within this Chapter offer general descriptions and checking procedures for components in each of the two groups.

Since nearly all the procedures covered in this Chapter involve working under the vehicle, make sure it's securely supported on sturdy jackstands or on a hoist where the vehicle can be easily raised and lowered.

2 Clutch - description and check

1   All vehicles with a manual transaxle use a single dry-plate, diaphragm-spring type clutch. The clutch disc has a splined hub which allows it to slide along the splines of the transaxle input shaft. The clutch and pressure plate are held in contact by spring pressure exerted by the diaphragm in the pressure plate.

2   The clutch release system is operated by hydraulic pressure. The hydraulic release system consists of the clutch pedal, a master cylinder and fluid reservoir, the hydraulic line, a release (or slave) cylinder which actuates the clutch release lever and the clutch release (or throwout) bearing.

3   When pressure is applied to the clutch pedal to release the clutch, hydraulic pressure is exerted against the outer end of the clutch release lever. As the lever pivots the shaft fingers push against the release bearing. The bearing pushes against the fingers of the diaphragm spring of the pressure plate assembly, which in turn releases the clutch plate.

4   Terminology can be a problem when discussing the clutch components because common names are in some cases different from those used by the manufacturer. For example, the driven plate is also called the clutch plate or disc, the clutch release bearing is sometimes called a throwout bearing, the release cylinder is sometimes called the operating or slave cylinder.

5   Other than to replace components with obvious damage, some preliminary checks should be performed to diagnose clutch problems. These checks assume that the transaxle is in good working condition.

a) *The first check should be of the fluid level in the clutch master cylinder (see Chapter 1). If the fluid level is low, add fluid as necessary and inspect the hydraulic system for leaks. If the master cylinder reservoir has run dry, bleed the system as described in Section 5 and retest the clutch operation.*

b) *To check clutch spin-down time, run the engine at normal idle speed with the transaxle in Neutral (clutch pedal up - engaged). Disengage the clutch (pedal down), wait several seconds and shift the transaxle into Reverse. No grinding noise should be heard. A grinding noise would most likely indicate a problem in the pressure plate or the clutch disc.*

c) *To check for complete clutch release, run the engine (with the parking brake applied to prevent movement) and hold the clutch pedal approximately 1/2-inch from the floor. Shift the transaxle between 1st gear and Reverse several times. If the shift is rough, component failure is indicated. Check the release cylinder pushrod travel. With the clutch pedal depressed completely, the release cylinder pushrod should extend substantially. If it doesn't, check the fluid level in the clutch master cylinder.*

d) *Visually inspect the pivot bushing at the top of the clutch pedal to make sure there is no binding or excessive play.*

e) *Crawl under the vehicle and make sure the clutch release lever is solidly mounted on the ball stud.*

3 Clutch master cylinder - removal and installation

Removal

1   Working inside the engine compartment, clamp a pair of locking pliers onto the clutch fluid feed hose, a couple of inches downstream of the reservoir. The pliers should be just tight enough to prevent fluid flow when the hose is disconnected.

2   On 2006 and later Civic models, remove the battery and battery tray (see Chapter 5).

3   On models with the air filter housing mounted in the left side of the engine compartment, remove the air filter housing (see Chapter 4).

4   Remove the hydraulic line retaining clip holder and retaining clip, then disconnect the hydraulic line at the cylinder. Loosen the fluid feed hose clamp and detach the hose from the cylinder. Have rags handy as some fluid will be lost as the line is removed. Cap or plug the ends of the lines (and/or hose) to prevent fluid leakage and the entry of contaminants. **Caution:** *Don't allow brake fluid to come into contact with the paint as it will damage the finish.*

5   Working under the dashboard, remove the cotter pin or spring clip from the master cylinder pushrod clevis. Pull out the clevis pin to disconnect the pushrod from the pedal. Unscrew the two clutch master cylinder retaining nuts and remove the cylinder.

Installation

6   Installation is the reverse of removal, noting the following points:

a) *Use new gasket between the master cylinder and the firewall. Tighten the master cylinder mounting nuts to the torque listed in this Chapter's Specifications.*

b) *Install a new O-ring seal on the hydraulic line fitting at the master cylinder.*

c) *Fill the clutch master cylinder reservoir with brake fluid conforming to DOT 3 specifications and bleed the clutch system as outlined in Section 5.*

---

4 Clutch release cylinder - removal and installation

Removal

1   If you're working on a 2005 and earlier CR-V or hatchback model, remove the battery and battery tray (see Chapter 5), then remove the air filter housing and intake duct (see Chapter 4). Disconnect the hydraulic line mounting bracket.

2   Remove the release cylinder line bracket mounting bolt and bracket.

3   Remove the roll pins securing the hydraulic line to the release cylinder, then disconnect the line. Have a small can and rags handy - some fluid will be spilled as the line is

removed. Plug the line to prevent excessive fluid loss.

4   Remove the two release cylinder mounting bolts and remove the release cylinder.

Installation

5   Lightly lubricate the release cylinder pushrod and the release fork pocket with high temperature grease. Install the release cylinder on the clutch housing. Make sure the pushrod is seated in the release fork pocket, then tighten the mounting bolts to the torque listed in this Chapter's Specifications.

6   Install a new O-ring on the hydraulic line, then connect the hydraulic line to the release cylinder and install the roll pins.

7   Install the hydraulic line bracket and tighten the bolt securely.

8   The remainder of installation is the reverse of removal, noting the following points:

   a) *Fill the clutch master cylinder with brake fluid conforming to DOT 3 specifications.*
   b) *Bleed the system as described in Section 5.*
   c) *If you're working on a CR-V or hatchback model, before reconnecting the battery, refer to Chapter 5.*

---

5   Clutch hydraulic system - bleeding

1   Bleed the hydraulic system whenever any part of the system has been removed or the fluid level has fallen so low that air has been drawn into the master cylinder. The bleeding procedure is very similar to bleeding a brake system.

2   Fill the master cylinder with new brake fluid conforming to DOT 3 specifications. **Caution:** *Do not re-use any of the fluid coming from the system during the bleeding operation or use fluid which has been inside an open container for an extended period of time.*

3   If you're working on a CR-V or hatchback model, remove the battery and battery tray (see Chapter 5), then remove the air filter housing and intake duct (see Chapter 4).

4   Remove the dust cap from the bleeder valve and push a length of plastic hose over the valve. Place the other end of the hose into a clear container with about two inches of brake fluid. The hose end must be in the fluid at the bottom of the container.

5   Have an assistant depress the clutch pedal and hold it. Open the bleeder valve on the release cylinder, allowing fluid to flow through the hose. Close the bleeder valve when the flow of fluid (and bubbles) ceases. Once closed, have your assistant release the pedal.

6   Continue this process until all air is evacuated from the system, indicated by a solid stream of fluid being ejected from the bleeder valve each time with no air bubbles in the hose or container. Keep a close watch on the fluid level inside the clutch master cylinder reservoir - if the level drops too far, air will

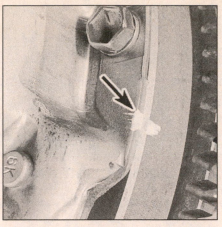

6.5 Mark the relationship of the pressure plate to the flywheel (if you're planning to re-use the old pressure plate)

get into the system and you'll have to start all over again.

7   Check carefully for proper operation before placing the vehicle into normal service.

8   If you're working on a CR-V or hatchback model, before reconnecting the battery, refer to Chapter 5.

---

6   Clutch components - removal, inspection and installation

Warning: *Dust produced by clutch wear is hazardous to your health. DO NOT blow it out with compressed air and DO NOT inhale it. DO NOT use gasoline or petroleum-based solvents to remove the dust. Brake system cleaner should be used to flush the dust into a drain pan. After the clutch components are wiped clean with a rag, dispose of the contaminated rags and cleaner in a covered, marked container.*

Removal

Refer to illustration 6.5

1   Access to the clutch components is normally accomplished by removing the transaxle, leaving the engine in the vehicle. If the engine is being removed for major overhaul, check the clutch for wear and replace worn components as necessary. However, the relatively low cost of the clutch components compared to the time and trouble spent gaining access to them warrants their replacement anytime the engine or transaxle is removed, unless they are new or in near-perfect condition. The following procedures are based on the assumption the engine will stay in place.

2   Remove the transaxle from the vehicle (see Chapter 7, Part A). Support the engine while the transaxle is out. Preferably, an engine support fixture or a hoist should be used to support it from above.

3   The clutch fork and release bearing can remain attached to the transaxle housing for the time being.

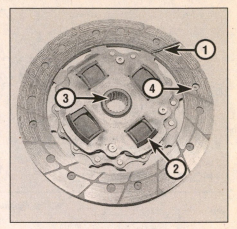

6.9 The clutch disc

1   **Lining** - *this will wear down in use*
2   **Springs or dampers** - *check for cracking and deformation*
3   **Splined hub** - *the splines must not be worn and should slide smoothly on the transaxle input shaft splines*
4   **Rivets** - *these secure the lining and will damage the flywheel or pressure plate if allowed to contact the surfaces*

4   To support the clutch disc during removal, install a clutch alignment tool through the clutch disc hub.

5   Carefully inspect the flywheel and pressure plate for indexing marks. The marks are usually an X, an O or a white letter. If they cannot be found, scribe or paint marks yourself so the pressure plate and the flywheel will be in the same alignment during installation **(see illustration)**.

6   Turning each bolt a little at a time, loosen the pressure plate-to-flywheel bolts. Work in a criss-cross pattern until all spring pressure is relieved. Then hold the pressure plate securely and completely remove the bolts, followed by the pressure plate and clutch disc.

Inspection

Refer to illustrations 6.9, 6.11a and 6.11b

7   Ordinarily, when a problem occurs in the clutch, it can be attributed to wear of the clutch driven plate assembly (clutch disc). However, all components should be inspected at this time.

8   Inspect the flywheel for cracks, heat checking, grooves and other obvious defects. If the imperfections are slight, a machine shop can machine the surface flat and smooth, which is highly recommended regardless of the surface appearance. Refer to Chapter 2 for the flywheel removal and installation procedure.

9   Inspect the lining on the clutch disc. There should be at least 1/16-inch of lining above the rivet heads. Check for loose rivets, distortion, cracks, broken springs and other obvious damage **(see illustration)**. As mentioned earlier in this Section, ordinarily the clutch disc is routinely replaced, so if in doubt about the condition, replace it with a new one.

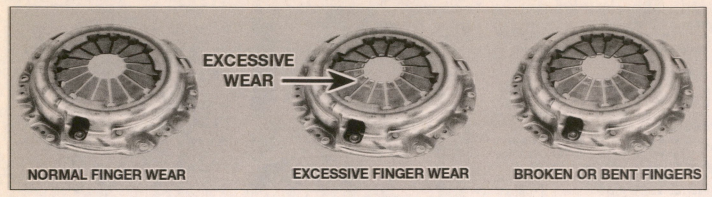

EXCESSIVE
WEAR

NORMAL FINGER WEAR   EXCESSIVE FINGER WEAR   BROKEN OR BENT FINGERS

6.11a Replace the pressure plate if excessive wear or damage is noted

6.11b Inspect the pressure plate surface for excessive score marks, cracks and signs of overheating

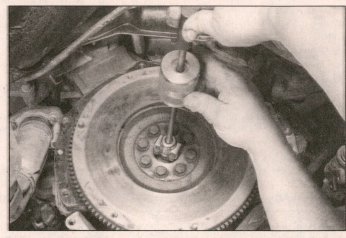

6.16 A small slide hammer is handy for removing a pilot bearing

10   The release bearing should also be replaced along with the clutch disc (see Section 7).

11   Check the machined surfaces and the diaphragm spring fingers of the pressure plate **(see illustrations)**. If the surface is grooved or otherwise damaged, replace the pressure

6.17 Tap the bearing into place with a bearing driver or a socket that is slightly smaller than the outside diameter of the bearing

plate. Also check for obvious damage, distortion, cracking, etc. Light glazing can be removed with emery cloth or sandpaper. If a new pressure plate is required, new and remanufactured units are available.

Pilot bearing replacement
2005 and earlier models

12   Remove the flywheel (see Chapter 2A).

13   Using a hammer and drift, drive the pilot bearing out of the flywheel, from the friction surface side toward the crankshaft side).

14   Lubricate the outer surface of the new pilot bearing with clean engine oil, then drive it into the flywheel (from the crankshaft side) - using a bearing driver or a socket with a diameter slightly smaller than that of the bearing - until it seats.

15   Install the flywheel (see Chapter 2A).

2006 and later models

Refer to illustrations 6.16 and 6.17

16   Remove the pilot bearing using a slide hammer and puller attachment **(see illustration)**, which are available at most auto parts stores or tool rental yards.

17   To install a new pilot bearing, lightly lubricate the outside surface with grease, then

drive it into the recess with a bearing driver or a socket **(see illustration)**.

Installation

Refer to illustration 6.19

18   Before installation, clean the flywheel and pressure plate machined surfaces with brake cleaner. It's important that no oil or grease is on these surfaces or the lining of the clutch disc. Handle the parts only with clean hands.

19   Position the clutch disc and pressure plate against the flywheel with the clutch held in place with an alignment tool **(see illustration)**. Make sure the disc is installed properly (most replacement clutch discs will be marked "flywheel side" or something similar - if not marked, install the clutch disc with the damper springs toward the transaxle).

20   Tighten the pressure plate-to-flywheel bolts only finger tight, working around the pressure plate.

21   Center the clutch disc by ensuring the alignment tool extends through the splined hub and into the pilot bearing in the crankshaft. Wiggle the tool up, down or side-to-side as needed to center the disc. Tighten the pressure plate-to-flywheel bolts a little at a time, working in a criss-cross pattern to prevent distorting the cover. After all of the bolts

6.19 Center the clutch disc in the pressure plate with a clutch alignment tool

7.4 Hold the bearing by the outer race and rotate the inner race while applying pressure - if the bearing doesn't turn smoothly or if it's noisy, replace the bearing

are snug, tighten them to the torque listed in this Chapter's Specifications. Remove the alignment tool.

22 Using high-temperature grease, lubricate the inner groove of the release bearing (see Section 7). Also place a small amount of grease on the release lever contact areas and the transaxle input shaft bearing retainer.

23 Install the clutch release bearing (see Section 7).

24 Install the transaxle and all components removed previously.

7 Clutch release bearing and lever - removal, inspection and installation

Warning: *Dust produced by clutch wear is hazardous to your health. DO NOT blow it out with compressed air and DO NOT inhale it. DO NOT use gasoline or petroleum-based solvents to remove the dust. Brake system cleaner should be used to flush the dust into a drain pan. After the clutch components are wiped clean with a rag, dispose of the contaminated rags and cleaner in a covered, marked container.*

Removal

1 Remove the transaxle (see Chapter 7A).

2 Pull the clutch release fork off the ball-stud and slide the release bearing off the input shaft along with the release fork.

Inspection

Refer to illustration 7.4

3 Wipe off the bearing with a clean rag and inspect it for damage, wear and cracks. Don't immerse the bearing in solvent - it's sealed for life and immersion in solvent will ruin it.

4 Hold the center of the bearing and rotate the outer portion while applying pressure **(see illustration)**. If the bearing doesn't turn smoothly or if it's noisy or rough, replace it.

Note: *Considering the difficulty involved with*

replacing the release bearing, we recommend replacing the release bearing whenever the clutch components are replaced.

Installation

5 Lightly lubricate the friction surfaces of the release bearing, ballstud and the input shaft bearing retainer with high-temperature grease.

6 Install the release lever and bearing onto the input shaft.

7 The remainder of installation is the reverse of removal.

8 Clutch pedal adjustment

Pedal height

Refer to illustration 8.1

1 The height of the clutch pedal is the distance the pedal sits off the floor with the carpet pulled back **(see illustration)**. If the pedal height is not within the specified range, it must be adjusted.

2 To adjust the clutch pedal, loosen the

locknut on the clutch start switch or adjusting bolt and back the switch out until it no longer touches the pedal, then loosen the locknut on the clutch pushrod. Turn the pushrod to adjust the pedal height, then tighten the locknut.

3 Turn the switch or bolt clockwise until it just contacts the pedal arm, then turn it in an additional 3/4 to 1 turn. Tighten the locknut.

4 Adjust the clutch start switch as described in Section 9.

Pedal freeplay

Refer to illustration 8.5

5 The freeplay is the pedal slack, or the distance the pedal can be depressed before it begins to have any effect on the clutch system **(see illustration)**. If the pedal freeplay is not within the specified range, it must be adjusted.

6 To adjust the pedal freeplay, loosen the locknut on the clutch pushrod. Then back off the pushrod to adjust the pedal freeplay to the specified range and retighten the locknut.

7 Check and, if necessary, adjust the clutch start switch (see Section 9).

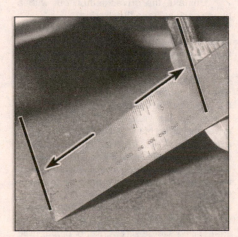

8.1 Pedal height is the distance between the pedal and the floor

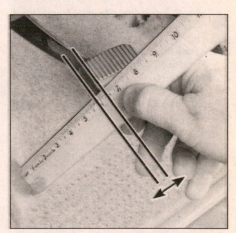

8.5 Pedal freeplay is the distance the pedal travels before resistance is felt

10.2 Use a punch or chisel and unstake the driveaxle/hub nut

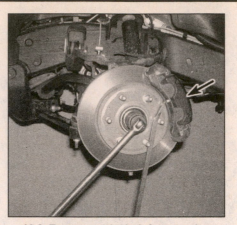

10.3 To prevent the hub from turning while you're loosening the driveaxle/hub nut, wedge a prybar between two of the wheel studs

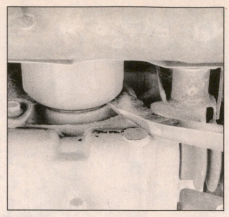

10.6a Use a large screwdriver or a prybar to pop the inner end of the driveaxle from the transaxle, or . . .

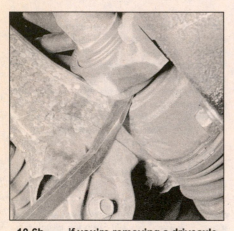

10.6b . . . if you're removing a driveaxle from a vehicle equipped with an intermediate shaft, insert the prybar between the intermediate shaft bearing and the driveaxle to pop it loose

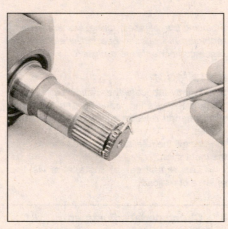

10.8a Pry the old spring clip from the inner end of the driveaxle with a small screwdriver or awl

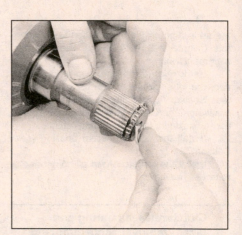

10.8b To install the new spring clip, start one end in the groove and work the clip over the shaft end, into the groove

9   Clutch start switch - replacement

1   Unplug the switch electrical connector, if you haven't already done so.
2   Loosen the locknut and unscrew the switch from the clutch pedal bracket.
3   Installation is the reverse of removal. To adjust the switch, loosen the locknut and turn the switch in or out, as necessary, to provide continuity through the switch when the clutch pedal is depressed.

10   Driveaxles - removal and installation

Front
Removal
Refer to illustrations 10.2, 10.3, 10.6a and 10.6b

1   Loosen the front wheel lug nuts, raise the

vehicle and support it securely on jackstands. Remove the wheel.
2   Unstake the driveaxle/hub nut with a punch or chisel **(see illustration)**.
3   Loosen the driveaxle/hub nut with a large socket and breaker bar **(see illustration)**, then remove the driveaxle/hub nut from the axle and discard it.
4   Separate the lower control arm from the steering knuckle (see Chapter 10).
5   Swing the knuckle/hub assembly out (away from the vehicle) until the end of the driveaxle is free of the hub. **Note:** *If the drive-axle splines stick in the hub, tap on the end of the driveaxle with a plastic hammer.* Support the outer end of the driveaxle with a piece of wire to avoid unnecessary strain on the inner CV joint.
6   Pry the inner CV joint out of the transaxle (or, on models so equipped, the intermediate shaft) using a large screwdriver or prybar **(see illustrations)**.
7   Support the CV joints and carefully remove the driveaxle from the vehicle.

Installation
Refer to illustrations 10.8a and 10.8b

8   Pry the old spring clip from the inner end of the driveaxle (or, on models so equipped, the outer end of the intermediate shaft) and install a new one **(see illustrations)**.
9   Installation is the reverse of removal, but with the following additional points:

a) *Remove the old set-ring from the drive-axle or intermediate shaft (depending on which model you're working on) and install a new one.*
b) *Apply a film of multi-purpose grease around the splines of the joints.*
c) *When installing the driveaxle, hold the driveaxle straight out, then push it in sharply to seat the driveaxle set-ring.*
d) *Clean all foreign matter from the drive-axle outer CV joint threads and coat the splines with multi-purpose grease. Guide the driveaxle into the hub splines and install the new driveaxle/hub nut. Tighten the nut securely but not to the specified torque at this time.*

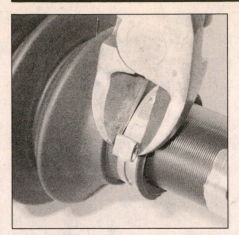

11.3a Cut off the boot clamps and discard them - don't try to re-use old clamps

11.3b Slide the boot down the driveaxle, out of the way

e) *Reconnect the control arm, then tighten the suspension fasteners to the torque listed in the Chapter 10 Specifications.*

f) *Install the wheel and lug nuts, then lower the vehicle.*

g) *Tighten the driveaxle/hub nut to the torque listed in this Chapter's Specifications.*

h) *Tighten the wheel lug nuts to the torque listed in the Chapter 1 Specifications.*

i) *Add transaxle lubricant if it was drained or if any fluid spilled out (see Chapter 1).*

Intermediate shaft

Removal

10   Loosen the right front wheel lug nuts, raise the vehicle and support it securely on jackstands. Remove the wheel.

11   Unstake the driveaxle/hub nut with a punch or chisel **(see illustration 10.2)**.

12   Loosen the driveaxle/hub nut with a large socket and breaker bar **(see illustration 10.3)**, then remove the driveaxle/hub nut from the axle and discard it.

13   Separate the lower control arm from the steering knuckle (see Chapter 10).

14   Swing the knuckle/hub assembly out (away from the vehicle) until the end of the driveaxle is free of the hub. **Note:** *If the driveaxle splines stick in the hub, tap on the end of the driveaxle with a plastic hammer. Support the outer end of the driveaxle with a piece of wire to avoid unnecessary strain on the inner CV joint.*

15   Remove the driveaxle (see Step 7).

16   Remove the intermediate shaft heat shield mounting bolts, then remove the heat shield.

17   Remove the bearing support mounting bolts and slide the intermediate shaft out of the transaxle. Be careful not to damage the transaxle seal when pulling the shaft out.

18   Check the support bearing for smooth operation by turning the shaft while holding the bearing. If you feel any roughness, take the intermediate shaft to an automotive machine shop or other qualified repair facility to have a new bearing installed.

Installation

19   Lubricate the lips of the transaxle seal with multi-purpose grease. Carefully guide the intermediate shaft into the transaxle side gear then install the mounting nuts for the bearing support. Tighten the nuts to the torque listed in this Chapter's Specifications.

20   The remainder of installation is the reverse of removal.

Rear (4WD CR-V models)

Removal

21   Remove the wheel cover or hub cap. Unstake the driveaxle/hub nut with a punch or chisel **(see illustration 10.2)**, then break the hub nut loose with a socket and large breaker bar.

22   Block the front wheels to prevent the vehicle from rolling. Loosen the wheel lug nuts, raise the rear of the vehicle and support it securely on jackstands. Remove the wheel.

23   Remove the driveaxle/hub nut from the axle and discard it.

24   Detach the trailing arm from the knuckle (see Chapter 10), then pry the knuckle outward and remove the outer end of the driveaxle from the hub. **Caution:** *Don't let the driveaxle hang by the inner CV joint.*

25   Place a drain pan under the rear differential. Pry the inner end of the driveaxle out of the differential and remove it from the vehicle.

Installation

26   Pry the old spring clip from the inner end of the driveaxle and install a new one **(see illustrations 10.8a and 10.8b)**.

27   Apply a light film of grease to the area on the inner CV joint stub shaft where the seal rides, then insert the splined end of the inner CV joint into the differential. Make sure the spring clip locks in its groove.

28   Apply a light film of grease to the outer CV joint splines, pry the trailing arm outward and insert the outer end of the driveaxle into the hub.

29   Connect the trailing arm to the knuckle and install the bolts. Using a floor jack, raise the trailing arm to simulate normal ride height, then tighten the bolt to the torque listed in the Chapter 10 Specifications.

30   Install a new driveaxle/hub nut. Tighten the hub nut securely, but don't try to tighten it to the actual torque specification until you've lowered the vehicle to the ground.

31   Install the wheel and lug nuts, then lower the vehicle. Tighten the lug nuts to the torque listed in the Chapter 1 Specifications.

32   Tighten the driveaxle/hub nut to the torque listed in this Chapter's Specifications, then, using a hammer and a punch, stake the collar of the nut into the slot in the driveaxle. Install the wheel cover or hub cap.

33   Check the differential lubricant, adding as necessary to bring it to the appropriate level (see Chapter 1).

---

11   Driveaxle boot - replacement

Note: *If the CV joints are worn, indicating the need for an overhaul (usually due to torn boots), explore all options before beginning the job. Complete rebuilt driveaxles are available on an exchange basis, which eliminates much time and work. If you decide to rebuild a CV joint, check on the cost and availability of parts before disassembling the driveaxle.*

Note: *Some auto parts stores carry split type replacement boots, which can be installed without removing the driveaxle from the vehicle. This is a convenient alternative; however, the driveaxle should be removed and the CV joint disassembled and cleaned to ensure the joint is free from contaminants such as moisture and dirt which will accelerate CV joint wear.*

1   Remove the driveaxle from the vehicle (see Section 10).

2   Mount the driveaxle in a vise. The jaws of the vise should be lined with wood or rags to prevent damage to the driveaxle.

Inner CV joint and boot (front driveaxle) or inner and outer CV joint and boot (rear driveaxle)

Disassembly

Refer to illustrations 11.3a, 11.3b and 11.6

3   If you have any doubts about the condition of the outer boot this would be a good time to replace it as well. Cut off both boot clamps and slide the boot towards the center of the driveaxle **(see illustrations)**.

4   Scribe or paint alignment marks on the outer race and the tri-pot bearing assembly so they can be returned to their original position, then slide the outer race off the tri-pot bearing assembly.

5   Remove the snap-ring from the end of the axleshaft.

11.6 Secure the bearing rollers with tape and drive the tri-pot off the shaft with a hammer and brass drift, then remove the stop-ring

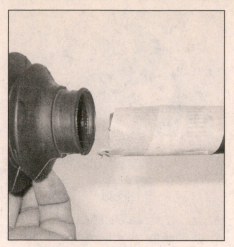

11.10a Wrap the splined area of the axleshaft with tape to prevent damage to the boot when installing it

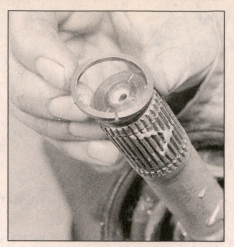

11.10b Install the stop-ring on the axleshaft, making sure it seats in its groove

11.12 Install the tri-pot assembly on the axleshaft, then install the snap-ring

11.13 Use plenty of CV joint grease to hold the needle bearings in place when you install the roller assemblies on the tri-pot, and make sure you put each roller in its original position

11.14 Pack the outer race with grease and slide it over the tri-pot assembly - make sure the match marks on the outer race and tri-pot line up

6   Secure the bearing rollers with tape, then remove the tri-pot bearing assembly from the axleshaft with a brass drift and a hammer **(see illustration)**. Remove the tape, but don't let the rollers fall off and get mixed up.

7   Remove the stop-ring (if equipped), slide the old boot off the driveaxle and discard it.

Inspection

8   Clean the old grease from the outer race and the tri-pot bearing assembly. Carefully disassemble each section of the tri-pot assembly, one at a time so as not to mix up the parts, and clean the needle bearings with solvent.

9   Inspect the rollers, tri-pot, bearings and outer race for scoring, pitting or other signs of abnormal wear, which will warrant the replacement of the inner CV joint.

Reassembly

Refer to illustrations 11.10a, 11.10b, 11.12, 11.13, 11.14, 11.16, 11.17a, 11.17b 11.17c, 11.17d and 11.17e

10   Wrap the splines of the axleshaft with tape to avoid damaging the new boot, then slide the boot onto the axleshaft **(see illustration)**. Remove the tape and slide the inner stop-ring (if equipped) into place **(see illustration)**.

11   Slide the tri-pot assembly onto the axleshaft.

12   Install the outer snap-ring **(see illustration)**.

13   Apply a coat of CV joint grease to the inner bearing surfaces to hold the needle bearings in place when reassembling the tri-pot assembly **(see illustration)**. Make sure each roller is installed on the same post as

before. **Note:** *If the rollers are equipped with a flat, rectangular shaped surface, make sure the flat sides are positioned closest to the driveaxle.*

14   Pack the outer race with half of the grease furnished with the new boot and place the remainder in the boot. Install the outer race **(see illustration)**. Make sure the marks you made on the tri-pot assembly and the outer race are aligned.

15   Seat the boot in the grooves in the outer race and the axleshaft, then position the driveaxle (front) or CV joint (rear) midway through its travel.

16   With the CV joint set mid-way through its travel, equalize the pressure in the boot by inserting a blunt screwdriver between the boot and the outer race **(see illustration)**. Don't damage the boot with the tool.

11.16 Equalize the pressure inside the boot by inserting a small, dull screwdriver between the boot and the outer race

11.17a To install fold-over type clamps, bend the tang down . . .

11.17b . . . and flatten the tabs to hold it in place

11.17c You'll need a special tightening tool to install band type boot clamps. Install the band with its end pointing in the direction of axle rotation and tighten it securely . . .

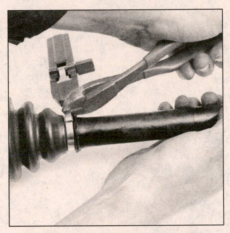

11.17d . . . bend back the end of the clamp, cut off the excess, then place a dimple in the center of the folded-over portion with a hammer and center punch

11.17e If you're installing crimp-type boot clamps, you'll need a pair of special crimping pliers (available at most auto parts stores)

17   Install and tighten the new boot clamps **(see illustrations)**.

18   Install the driveaxle assembly (see Section 10).

Outer CV joint and boot (front driveaxle)

Disassembly

19   Following Steps 3 through 7, remove the inner CV joint from the driveaxle and disassemble it.

20   If the driveaxle is equipped with a dynamic damper, scribe or paint a location mark on the axleshaft along the outer edge of the damper (the side facing the outer CV joint), cut the retaining clamp and slide the damper off. **Note:** *If you're planning to replace the axleshaft and outer CV joint assembly, measure the distance between the inner CV joint boot and the dynamic damper so the damper can be placed in the proper position on the new driveaxle.*

21   Cut the boot clamps from the outer CV joint. Slide the boot off the shaft. **Note:** *The outer CV joint can't be disassembled or removed from the shaft.*

Inspection

Refer to illustration 11.23

22   Thoroughly wash the inner and outer CV joints in clean solvent and blow them dry with compressed air, if available. **Warning:** *Wear eye protection when using compressed air.* **Note:** *Because the outer joint can't be disassembled, it is difficult to wash away all the old grease and to rid the bearing of solvent once it's clean. But it is imperative that the job be done thoroughly, so take your time and do it right.*

23   Bend the outer CV joint housing at an angle to the axleshaft to expose the bearings, inner race and cage **(see illustration)**. Inspect the bearing surfaces for signs of wear. If the bearings are damaged or worn, replace the driveaxle.

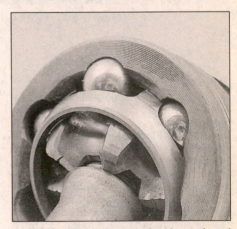

11.23 After the old grease has been rinsed away and the solvent has been blown out with compressed air, rotate the outer joint assembly through its full range of motion and inspect the bearing surfaces for wear and damage - if any of the ball bearings, the race or the cage look damaged, replace the driveaxle and outer joint assembly

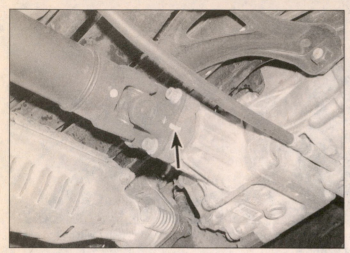

12.2 Mark the relationship of the driveshaft to the differential pinion flange and the transfer case flange

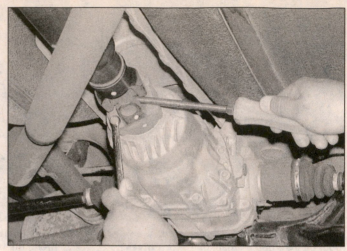

12.3 Immobilize the driveshaft by placing a screwdriver into the universal joint while loosening the bolts

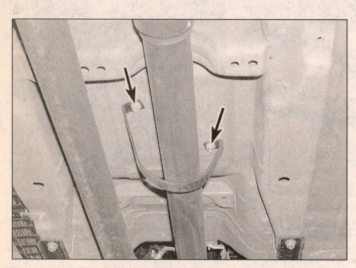

12.4 Remove the driveshaft safety loops

12.5 The driveshaft center support bearing is retained by two bolts

Reassembly

24   Slide the new outer boot onto the axle-shaft. It's a good idea to wrap tape around the splines of the shaft to prevent damage to the boot (see illustration 11.10a). When the boot is in position, add the specified amount of grease (included in the boot replacement kit) to the outer joint and the boot (pack the joint with as much grease as it will hold and put the rest into the boot). Slide the boot on the rest of the way and install the new clamps (see illustrations 11.17a through 11.17e).
25   Slide the dynamic damper, if equipped, onto the shaft. Make sure its outer edge is aligned with the previously applied mark. **Note:** *If you're using a new axleshaft and outer CV joint assembly, install the damper on the shaft to the distance from the inner CV joint boot measured in Step 20.* Install a new

retaining clamp.
26   Clean and reassemble the inner CV joint by following Steps 8 through 17, then install the driveaxle as outlined in Section 10.

12 Driveshaft (4WD CR-V models) - removal and installation

Refer to illustrations 12.2, 12.3, 12.4 and 12.5
1   Raise the rear of the vehicle and support it securely on jackstands. Place the transaxle in Neutral with the parking brake off. Block the front wheels to prevent the vehicle from rolling.
2   Make reference marks on the driveshaft flanges, the differential pinion flange and the transfer case pinion flange in line with each other (see illustration). This is to make sure

the driveshaft is reinstalled in the same position to preserve the balance.
3   Remove the rear universal joint bolts. Turn the driveshaft (or wheels) as necessary to bring the bolts into the most accessible position. Insert a screwdriver into the joint while loosening the bolts to prevent the shaft from turning (see illustration).
4   Unbolt the driveshaft safety loops from the floorpan (see illustration).
5   Unbolt the center support bearing from the floorpan (see illustration).
6   Unbolt the front of the driveshaft from the transfer case flange and remove the driveshaft assembly.
7   Installation is the reverse of the removal procedure. Be sure to align the marks on the flanges and tighten all fasteners to the torque values listed in this Chapter's Specifications.

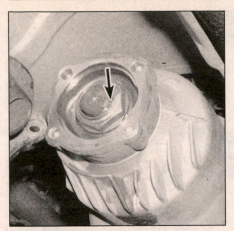

13.3 Insert a punch into the slot and unstake the pinion flange nut before unscrewing it

13.4 A chain wrench can be used to prevent the pinion flange from turning when loosening the nut

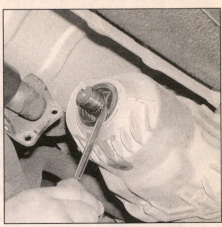

13.7 Carefully pry out the old seal . . .

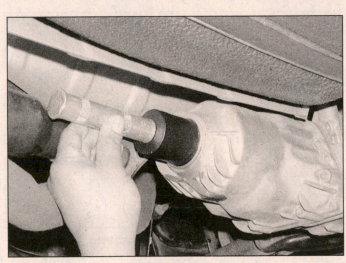

13.8 . . . and drive the new one in with a seal installation tool or a socket with an outside diameter slightly smaller than that of the seal

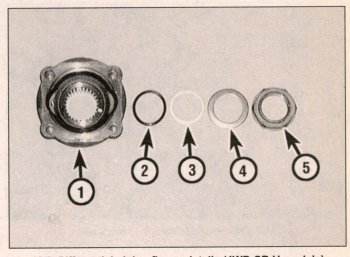

13.9 Differential pinion flange details (4WD CR-V models)

1 *Pinion flange*
2 *O-ring*
3 *Back-up ring*

4 *Spring washer*
5 *Nut*

13 Differential oil seals (4WD CR-V models) - replacement

Pinion oil seal

Refer to illustrations 13.3, 13.4, 13.7, 13.8 and 13.9

1 Raise the rear of the vehicle and support it securely on jackstands. Place the transaxle in Neutral with the parking brake off. Block the front wheels to prevent the vehicle from rolling.

2 Mark the relationship of the driveshaft to the pinion flange, then unbolt the driveshaft from the flange (see Section 12). Suspend the driveshaft with a piece of wire (don't let it hang by the center support bearing).

3 Using a hammer and a punch, unstake the pinion flange nut **(see illustration)**.

4 A flange holding tool will be required to keep the companion flange from moving while the self-locking pinion nut is loosened. A chain wrench will also work **(see illustration)**.

5 Remove the pinion nut, spring washer, back-up ring and O-ring.

6 Withdraw the flange. It may be necessary to use a two-jaw puller engaged behind the flange to draw it off. Do not attempt to pry or hammer behind the flange or hammer on the end of the pinion shaft.

7 Pry out the old seal and discard it **(see illustration)**.

8 Lubricate the lips of the new seal and fill the space between the seal lips with wheel bearing grease, then tap it evenly into position with a seal installation tool or a large socket **(see illustration)**. Make sure it enters the housing squarely and is tapped in to its full depth.

9 Install the pinion flange, a new O-ring (lubricated with clean differential lubricant),

the back-up ring, spring washer (with the concave side facing the flange), and a new nut **(see illustration)**. If necessary, tighten the pinion nut to draw the flange into place. Do not try to hammer the flange into position.

10 Tighten the nut to the torque listed in this Chapter's Specifications, then stake the collar of the nut into the slot in the pinion shaft.

11 Reconnect the driveshaft to the pinion flange (see Section 12).

12 Check the differential lubricant level and add some, if necessary, to bring it to the appropriate level (see Chapter 1).

Driveaxle oil seals

Refer to illustrations 13.15 and 13.16

13 Raise the rear of the vehicle and support it securely on jackstands. Place the transaxle in Neutral with the parking brake off. Block the front wheels to prevent the vehicle from rolling.

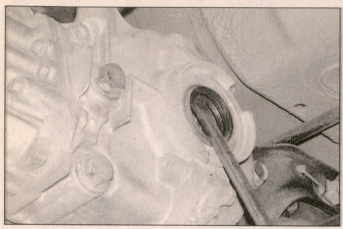

13.15 Carefully pry out the driveaxle oil seal with a seal removal tool or a large screwdriver; make sure you don't scratch the seal bore

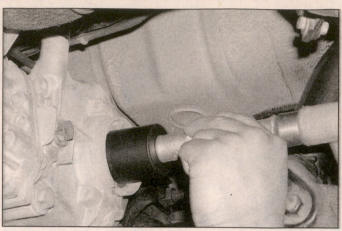

13.16 Use a seal installer or a large socket to install the new seal - whatever type of tool you use, make sure it doesn't contact the raised seal lip

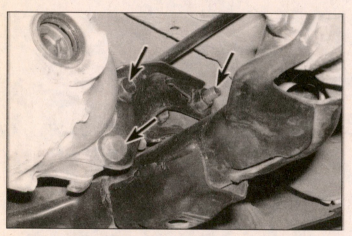

14.8 Differential mounting bracket bolts

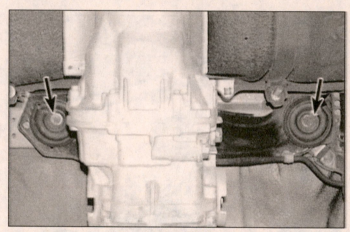

14.9 Differential-to-floorpan bolts

14   Remove the driveaxle(s) (see Section 10).

15   Pry the seal from the differential housing **(see illustration)**.

16   Using a seal installer or a large deep socket as a drift, install the new oil seal. Drive it into the bore squarely and make sure it's completely seated **(see illustration)**.

17   Lubricate the lip of the new seal with multi-purpose grease, then install the driveaxle. Be careful not to damage the lip of the new seal.

18   Check the differential lubricant level and add some, if necessary, to bring it to the appropriate level (see Chapter 1).

14   Differential (4WD CR-V models) - removal and installation

Refer to illustrations 14.8 and 14.9

1   Raise the rear of the vehicle and support it securely on jackstands. Place the transaxle in Neutral with the parking brake off. Block the front wheels to prevent the vehicle from rolling.

2   Drain the differential lubricant (see Chapter 1).

3   Remove the driveaxles (see Section 10).

4   Mark the relationship of the driveshaft to the pinion flange, then unbolt the driveshaft from the flange (see Section 12). Suspend the driveshaft with a piece of wire (don't let it hang by the center support bearing).

5   Remove the EVAP canister and mounting bracket (see Chapter 6).

6   Unbolt the damper weight from the differential.

7   Detach the breather tube from the fitting on the floorpan.

8   Support the differential with a floor jack. Remove the nuts and bolts from the mounting bracket at the rear of the differential **(see illustration)**.

9   Remove the differential-to-floorpan bolts **(see illustration)**. Slowly lower the jack and remove the differential out from under the vehicle.

10   Installation is the reverse of the removal procedure. Tighten all fasteners to the torque values listed in this Chapter's Specifications. Fill the differential with the proper lubricant (see Chapter 1).

15   Transfer case (4WD CR-V models) - removal and installation

1   Raise the front of the vehicle and support it securely on jackstands.

2   Mark the relationship of the driveshaft to the transfer case flange, then unbolt the driveshaft from the flange (see Section 12). Suspend the driveshaft with a piece of wire (don't let it hang by the center support bearing).

3   Drain the transaxle lubricant (see Chapter 1).

4   Remove the bolts securing the transfer case to the transaxle, then carefully remove the transfer case from the transaxle.

5   Installation is the reverse of removal, noting the following points:

a)   Install a new O-ring to the case.

b)   Tighten the mounting bolts to the torque listed in this Chapter's Specifications.

c)   Refill the transaxle with the proper type and amount of lubricant (see Chapter 1).

Chapter 9   Brakes

Contents

	Section
Anti-lock Brake System (ABS) and Vehicle Stability Assist (VSA) system – general information	15
Brake disc – inspection, removal and installation	5
Brake hoses and lines – inspection and replacement	9
Brake hydraulic system – bleeding	10
Brake light switch – replacement	13
Brake pedal – adjustment	14
Disc brake caliper – removal and installation	4

	Section
Disc brake pads – replacement	3
Drum brake shoes/parking brake shoes – replacement	6
General information	1
Master cylinder – removal and installation	8
Parking brake – adjustment	12
Power brake booster – removal and installation	11
Troubleshooting	2
Wheel cylinder – removal and installation	7

Specifications

General

Brake fluid type	See Chapter 1
Power brake booster pushrod-to-master cylinder piston clearance (with 20 in-Hg of vacuum applied to the booster)	0.0 to 0.020 inch (0.0 to 0.5 mm)
Brake pedal height	
Civic (2001 to 2005 models)	
Manual transaxle	7 1/4 inches (184 mm)
Automatic transaxle	7 3/8 inches (188 mm)
Civic (2006 to 2010 models)	
Manual transaxle	6 inches (153 mm)
Automatic transaxle	6 1/4 inches (158 mm)
CR-V (2002 to 2006 models)	6 13/16 inches (173 mm)
CR-V (2007 to 2009 models)	6 1/2 inches (165 mm)
Brake pedal freeplay	1/16 to 3/16 inch (1 to 5 mm)

Disc brakes

Brake pad minimum thickness	See Chapter 1
Disc lateral runout limit	0.004 inch (0.10 mm)
Disc minimum thickness	Cast into disc
Parallelism (thickness variation) limit	0.0006 inch (0.015 mm)

Drum brakes

Maximum drum diameter	Cast into drum
Shoe lining minimum thickness	See Chapter 1

Torque specifications

Note: *One foot-pound (ft-lb) of torque is equivalent to 12 inch-pounds (in-lbs) of torque. Torque values below approximately 15 ft-lbs are expressed in inch-pounds, since most foot-pound torque wrenches are not accurate at these smaller values.*

	Ft-lbs (unless otherwise indicated)	Nm
Caliper mounting bracket bolts		
Front	80	108
Rear		
2005 and earlier models	41	55
2006 and later models	54	74
Caliper mounting guide pins/bolts		
Front	25	34
Rear	17	23
Master cylinder mounting nuts	132 in-lbs	15
Power brake booster mounting bolts	108 in-lbs	13
Wheel cylinder mounting bolt		
2005 and earlier models	132 in-lbs	15
2006 and later models	84 in-lbs	9
Wheel lug nuts	See Chapter 1	

1   General information

General

The vehicles covered by this manual are equipped with hydraulically operated front and rear brake systems. Both front and rear brakes are disc-type and are self-adjusting.

Hydraulic system

The hydraulic system consists of two separate circuits. The master cylinder has separate reservoirs for the two circuits, and, in the event of a leak or failure in one hydraulic circuit, the other circuit will remain operative and a warning indicator will light up on the instrument panel when a substantial amount of brake fluid is lost, showing that a failure has occurred.

Power brake booster

The power brake booster uses engine manifold vacuum to provide assistance to the brakes. It is mounted on the firewall in the engine compartment, directly behind the master cylinder.

Parking brake

Control cables are routed to the rear axle, where they operate small drum brake shoes that apply pressure to the inner diameter of the rear brake discs.

Service

After completing any operation involving disassembly of any part of the brake system, always test drive the vehicle to check for proper braking performance before resuming normal driving. When testing the brakes, perform the tests on a clean, dry, flat surface. Conditions other than these can lead to inaccurate test results.

Test the brakes at various speeds with both light and heavy pedal pressure. The vehicle should stop evenly without pulling to one side or the other. Under hard braking, the ABS system may engage, resulting in brake pedal pulsation. This is considered normal operation.

Tires, vehicle load and wheel alignment are factors which also affect braking performance.

Precautions

There are some general cautions and warnings involving the brake system on this vehicle:

a) *Use only brake fluid conforming to DOT 3 specifications.*

b) *The brake pads and linings contain fibers which are hazardous to your health if inhaled. Whenever you work on brake system components, clean all parts with brake system cleaner. Do not allow the fine dust to become airborne. Also, wear an approved filtering mask.*

c) *Safety should be paramount whenever any servicing of the brake components is performed. Do not use parts or fasteners which are not in perfect condition, and be sure that all clearances and torque specifications are adhered to. If you are at all unsure about a certain procedure, seek professional advice. Upon completion of any brake system work, test the brakes carefully in a controlled area before putting the vehicle into normal service. If a problem is suspected in the brake system, don't drive the vehicle until it's fixed.*

d) *Used brake fluid is considered a hazardous waste and it must be disposed of in accordance with federal, state and local laws. **DO NOT pour it down the sink, into septic tanks or storm drains, or on the ground.***

e) *Clean up any spilled brake fluid immediately and then wash the area with large amounts of water. This is especially true for any finished or painted surfaces.*

2   Troubleshooting

PROBABLE CAUSE	CORRECTIVE ACTION

No brakes - pedal travels to floor

1 Low fluid level 2 Air in system	1 and 2 Low fluid level and air in the system are symptoms of another problem - a leak somewhere in the hydraulic system. Locate and repair the leak
3 Defective seals in master cylinder	3 Replace master cylinder
4 Fluid overheated and vaporized due to heavy braking	4 Bleed hydraulic system (temporary fix). Replace brake fluid (proper fix)

Brake pedal slowly travels to floor under braking or at a stop

1 Defective seals in master cylinder	1 Replace master cylinder
2 Leak in a hose, line, caliper or wheel cylinder	2 Locate and repair leak
3 Air in hydraulic system	3 Bleed the system, inspect system for a leak

Brake pedal feels spongy when depressed

1 Air in hydraulic system	1 Bleed the system, inspect system for a leak
2 Master cylinder or power booster loose	2 Tighten fasteners
3 Brake fluid overheated (beginning to boil)	3 Bleed the system (temporary fix). Replace the brake fluid (proper fix)
4 Deteriorated brake hoses (ballooning under pressure)	4 Inspect hoses, replace as necessary (it's a good idea to replace all of them if one hose shows signs of deterioration)

Brake pedal feels hard when depressed and/or excessive effort required to stop vehicle

1 Power booster faulty	1 Replace booster
2 Engine not producing sufficient vacuum, or hose to booster clogged, collapsed or cracked	2 Check vacuum to booster with a vacuum gauge. Replace hose if cracked or clogged, repair engine if vacuum is extremely low
3 Brake linings contaminated by grease or brake fluid	3 Locate and repair source of contamination, replace brake pads or shoes
4 Brake linings glazed	4 Replace brake pads or shoes, check discs and drums for glazing, service as necessary
5 Caliper piston(s) or wheel cylinder(s) binding or frozen	5 Replace calipers or wheel cylinders
6 Brakes wet	6 Apply pedal to boil-off water (this should only be a momentary problem)
7 Kinked, clogged or internally split brake hose or line	7 Inspect lines and hoses, replace as necessary

Excessive brake pedal travel (but will pump up)

1 Drum brakes out of adjustment	1 Adjust brakes
2 Air in hydraulic system	2 Bleed system, inspect system for a leak

Excessive brake pedal travel (but will not pump up)

1 Master cylinder pushrod misadjusted	1 Adjust pushrod
2 Master cylinder seals defective	2 Replace master cylinder
3 Brake linings worn out	3 Inspect brakes, replace pads and/or shoes
4 Hydraulic system leak	4 Locate and repair leak

Brake pedal doesn't return

1 Brake pedal binding	1 Inspect pivot bushing and pushrod, repair or lubricate
2 Defective master cylinder	2 Replace master cylinder

Troubleshooting (continued)

PROBABLE CAUSE	CORRECTIVE ACTION

Brake pedal pulsates during brake application

PROBABLE CAUSE	CORRECTIVE ACTION
1 Brake drums out-of-round	1 Have drums machined by an automotive machine shop
2 Excessive brake disc runout or disc surfaces out-of-parallel	2 Have discs machined by an automotive machine shop
3 Loose or worn wheel bearings	3 Adjust or replace wheel bearings
4 Loose lug nuts	4 Tighten lug nuts

Brakes slow to release

PROBABLE CAUSE	CORRECTIVE ACTION
1 Malfunctioning power booster	1 Replace booster
2 Pedal linkage binding	2 Inspect pedal pivot bushing and pushrod, repair/lubricate
3 Malfunctioning proportioning valve	3 Replace proportioning valve
4 Sticking caliper or wheel cylinder	4 Repair or replace calipers or wheel cylinders
5 Kinked or internally split brake hose	5 Locate and replace faulty brake hose

Brakes grab (one or more wheels)

PROBABLE CAUSE	CORRECTIVE ACTION
1 Grease or brake fluid on brake lining	1 Locate and repair cause of contamination, replace lining
2 Brake lining glazed	2 Replace lining, deglaze disc or drum

Vehicle pulls to one side during braking

PROBABLE CAUSE	CORRECTIVE ACTION
1 Grease or brake fluid on brake lining	1 Locate and repair cause of contamination, replace lining
2 Brake lining glazed	2 Deglaze or replace lining, deglaze disc or drum
3 Restricted brake line or hose	3 Repair line or replace hose
4 Tire pressures incorrect	4 Adjust tire pressures
5 Caliper or wheel cylinder sticking	5 Repair or replace calipers or wheel cylinders
6 Wheels out of alignment	6 Have wheels aligned
7 Weak suspension spring	7 Replace springs
8 Weak or broken shock absorber	8 Replace shock absorbers

Brakes drag (indicated by sluggish engine performance or wheels being very hot after driving)

PROBABLE CAUSE	CORRECTIVE ACTION
1 Brake pedal pushrod incorrectly adjusted	1 Adjust pushrod
2 Master cylinder pushrod (between booster and master cylinder) incorrectly adjusted	2 Adjust pushrod
3 Obstructed compensating port in master cylinder	3 Replace master cylinder
4 Master cylinder piston seized in bore	4 Replace master cylinder
5 Contaminated fluid causing swollen seals throughout system	5 Flush system, replace all hydraulic components
6 Clogged brake lines or internally split brake hose(s)	6 Flush hydraulic system, replace defective hose(s)
7 Sticking caliper(s) or wheel cylinder(s)	7 Replace calipers or wheel cylinders
8 Parking brake not releasing	8 Inspect parking brake linkage and parking brake mechanism, repair as required
9 Improper shoe-to-drum clearance	9 Adjust brake shoes
10 Faulty proportioning valve	10 Replace proportioning valve

Troubleshooting (continued)

PROBABLE CAUSE	CORRECTIVE ACTION

Brakes fade (due to excessive heat)

1 Brake linings excessively worn or glazed	1 Deglaze or replace brake pads and/or shoes
2 Excessive use of brakes	2 Downshift into a lower gear, maintain a constant slower speed (going down hills)
3 Vehicle overloaded	3 Reduce load
4 Brake drums or discs worn too thin	4 Measure drum diameter and disc thickness, replace drums or discs as required
5 Contaminated brake fluid	5 Flush system, replace fluid
6 Brakes drag	6 Repair cause of dragging brakes
7 Driver resting left foot on brake pedal	7 Don't ride the brakes

Brakes noisy (high-pitched squeal)

1 Glazed lining	1 Deglaze or replace lining
2 Contaminated lining (brake fluid, grease, etc.)	2 Repair source of contamination, replace linings
3 Weak or broken brake shoe hold-down or return spring	3 Replace springs
4 Rivets securing lining to shoe or backing plate loose	4 Replace shoes or pads
5 Excessive dust buildup on brake linings	5 Wash brakes off with brake system cleaner
6 Brake drums worn too thin	6 Measure diameter of drums, replace if necessary
7 Wear indicator on disc brake pads contacting disc	7 Replace brake pads
8 Anti-squeal shims missing or installed improperly	8 Install shims correctly

Note: *Other remedies for quieting squealing brakes include the application of an anti-squeal compound to the backing plates of the brake pads, and lightly chamfering the edges of the brake pads with a file. The latter method should only be performed with the brake pads thoroughly wetted with brake system cleaner, so as not to allow any brake dust to become airborne.*

Brakes noisy (scraping sound)

1 Brake pads or shoes worn out; rivets, backing plate or brake shoe metal contacting disc or drum	1 Replace linings, have discs and/or drums machined (or replace)

Brakes chatter

1 Worn brake lining	1 Inspect brakes, replace shoes or pads as necessary
2 Glazed or scored discs or drums	2 Deglaze discs or drums with sandpaper (if glazing is severe, machining will be required)
3 Drums or discs heat checked	3 Check discs and/or drums for hard spots, heat checking, etc. Have discs/drums machined or replace them
4 Disc runout or drum out-of-round excessive	4 Measure disc runout and/or drum out-of-round, have discs or drums machined or replace them
5 Loose or worn wheel bearings	5 Adjust or replace wheel bearings
6 Loose or bent brake backing plate (drum brakes)	6 Tighten or replace backing plate
7 Grooves worn in discs or drums	7 Have discs or drums machined, if within limits (if not, replace them)
8 Brake linings contaminated (brake fluid, grease, etc.)	8 Locate and repair source of contamination, replace pads or shoes
9 Excessive dust buildup on linings	9 Wash brakes with brake system cleaner
10 Surface finish on discs or drums too rough after machining (especially on vehicles with sliding calipers)	10 Have discs or drums properly machined
11 Brake pads or shoes glazed	11 Deglaze or replace brake pads or shoes

Troubleshooting (continued)

PROBABLE CAUSE	CORRECTIVE ACTION

Brake pads or shoes click

PROBABLE CAUSE	CORRECTIVE ACTION
1 Shoe support pads on brake backing plate grooved or excessively worn	1 Replace brake backing plate
2 Brake pads loose in caliper	2 Loose pad retainers or anti-rattle clips
3 Also see items listed under Brakes chatter	

Brakes make groaning noise at end of stop

PROBABLE CAUSE	CORRECTIVE ACTION
1 Brake pads and/or shoes worn out	1 Replace pads and/or shoes
2 Brake linings contaminated (brake fluid, grease, etc.)	2 Locate and repair cause of contamination, replace brake pads or shoes
3 Brake linings glazed	3 Deglaze or replace brake pads or shoes
4 Excessive dust buildup on linings	4 Wash brakes with brake system cleaner
5 Scored or heat-checked discs or drums	5 Inspect discs/drums, have machined if within limits (if not, replace discs or drums)
6 Broken or missing brake shoe attaching hardware	6 Inspect drum brakes, replace missing hardware

Rear brakes lock up under light brake application

PROBABLE CAUSE	CORRECTIVE ACTION
1 Tire pressures too high	1 Adjust tire pressures
2 Tires excessively worn	2 Replace tires
3 Defective proportioning valve	3 Replace proportioning valve

Brake warning light on instrument panel comes on (or stays on)

PROBABLE CAUSE	CORRECTIVE ACTION
1 Low fluid level in master cylinder reservoir (reservoirs with fluid level sensor)	1 Add fluid, inspect system for leak, check the thickness of the brake pads and shoes
2 Failure in one half of the hydraulic system	2 Inspect hydraulic system for a leak
3 Piston in pressure differential warning valve not centered	3 Center piston by bleeding one circuit or the other (close bleeder valve as soon as the light goes out)
4 Defective pressure differential valve or warning switch	4 Replace valve or switch
5 Air in the hydraulic system	5 Bleed the system, check for leaks
6 Brake pads worn out (vehicles with electric wear sensors - small probes that fit into the brake pads and ground out on the disc when the pads get thin)	6 Replace brake pads (and sensors)

Brakes do not self adjust

Disc brakes

PROBABLE CAUSE	CORRECTIVE ACTION
1 Defective caliper piston seals	1 Replace calipers. Also, possible contaminated fluid causing soft or swollen seals (flush system and fill with new fluid if in doubt)
2 Corroded caliper piston(s)	2 Same as above

Drum brakes

PROBABLE CAUSE	CORRECTIVE ACTION
1 Adjuster screw frozen	1 Remove adjuster, disassemble, clean and lubricate with high-temperature grease
2 Adjuster lever does not contact star wheel or is binding	2 Inspect drum brakes, assemble correctly or clean or replace parts as required
3 Adjusters mixed up (installed on wrong wheels after brake job)	3 Reassemble correctly
4 Adjuster cable broken or installed incorrectly (cable-type adjusters)	4 Install new cable or assemble correctly

Rapid brake lining wear

PROBABLE CAUSE	CORRECTIVE ACTION
1 Driver resting left foot on brake pedal	1 Don't ride the brakes
2 Surface finish on discs or drums too rough	2 Have discs or drums properly machined
3 Also see Brakes drag	

3.5 Using a large C-clamp, push the piston back into the caliper - note that one end of the clamp is on the back side of the caliper and the other end (screw end) is pressing on the outer brake pad (front caliper shown, rear calipers similar)

3.6a Before removing anything, spray the assembly with brake system cleaner to remove the dust produced by brake pad wear - DO NOT blow the dust off with compressed air!

3   Disc brake pads - replacement

Warning: *Disc brake pads must be replaced on both front and rear wheels at the same time - never replace the pads on only one side. Also, the dust created by the brake system is harmful to your health. Never blow it out with compressed air and don't inhale any of it. An approved filtering mask should be worn when working on the brakes. Do not, under any circumstances, use petroleum-based solvents to clean brake parts. Use brake system cleaner only!*
Note: *This procedure applies to front and rear disc brakes.*

1   Remove the cap from the brake fluid reservoir.
2   Loosen the wheel lug nuts, raise the front, or rear, of the vehicle and support it securely on jackstands.

3   Remove the front, or rear, wheels. Work on one brake assembly at a time, using the assembled brake for reference if necessary.
4   Inspect the brake disc carefully as outlined in Section 5. If machining is necessary, follow the information in that Section to remove the disc, at which time the calipers and pads can be removed as well.

Front pads

Refer to illustrations 3.5 and 3.6a through 3.6n
5   Push the piston back into the bore to provide room for the new brake pads. A C-clamp can be used to accomplish this **(see illustration)**. As the piston is depressed to the bottom of the caliper bore, the fluid in the master cylinder will rise. Make sure it doesn't overflow. If necessary, siphon off some of the fluid.
6   Follow the **accompanying illustrations**, beginning with 3.6a, for the actual pad replace-

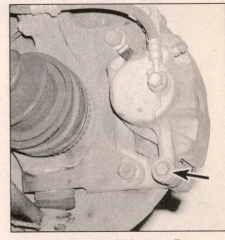

3.6b Remove the lower caliper mounting bolt . . .

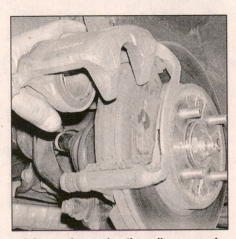

3.6c . . . then swing the caliper up and secure it to the strut with a piece of wire

3.6d Remove the outer brake pad and shim

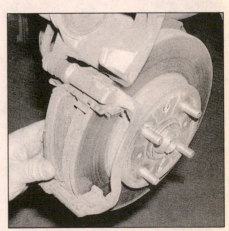

3.6e Remove the inner brake pad (some models don't have a shim on the inner pad)

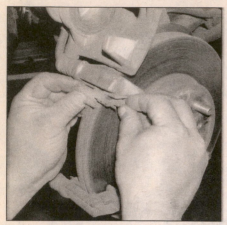

3.6f Remove and inspect the upper and lower brake pad retainer clips

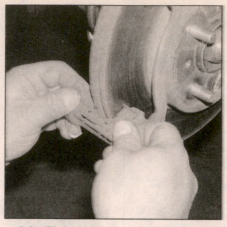

3.6g The pad retainer clips should fit snugly into their respective grooves in the caliper mounting bracket; if they don't, replace them

3.6h Inner pad (left) and outer pad and shim layout - some models have inner pad shims

3.6i Apply anti-squeal compound to the back of the pads, then install the shim(s)

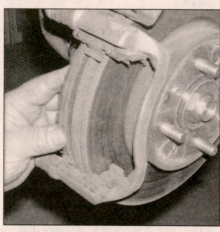

3.6j Install the new inner pad; make sure the ears on the upper and lower ends of the pad are fully engaged with their respective grooves and the pad retainer clips

3.6k Install the new outer pad and shim (if the new pad has no shim, take the shim off the old pad and install it on the new outer pad)

3.6l Before installing the caliper, remove the caliper pin dust boots and inspect them for tears and cracks; if they're damaged, replace them. If you're using the same ones, clean off the caliper sliding pins and coat them with high-temperature grease

3.6m Swing the caliper down over the disc and new pads (if the piston hits the inner pad, depress the piston further into the caliper bore with your C-clamp)

3.6n Install the lower bolt and tighten it to the torque listed in this Chapter's Specifications

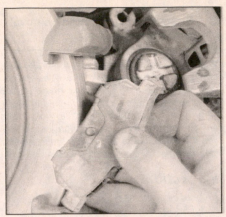

3.10 Remove the outer pad and shim

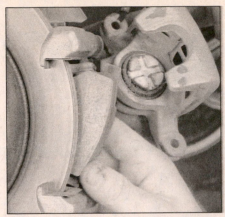

3.11 Remove the inner pad and shim

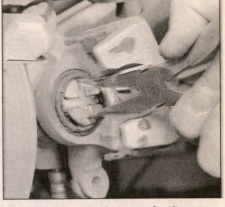

3.18 To provide clearance for the new brake pads, back the piston into the caliper bore by rotating it with a pair of needle-nose pliers

4.2a Remove the brake hose banjo bolt

4.2b Using a short piece of rubber hose of the appropriate diameter, plug the brake line banjo fitting

ment procedure. Be sure to stay in order and read the caption under each illustration. Once you have installed the new pads, proceed to Step 20.

Rear pads

Refer to illustrations 3.10, 3.11 and 3.18

7   Disconnect the brake line from its mounting bracket.

8   If you're working on a CR-V model, push the piston back into the bore to provide room for the new brake pads. A C-clamp can be used to accomplish this **(see illustration 3.5)**.

9   Remove the caliper mounting bolts while holding the caliper pins with a second wrench, then remove the caliper from its mounting bracket and hang it out of the way with a piece of wire. Don't let the caliper hang by the brake hose.

10   Remove the outer brake pad and shim **(see illustration)**.

11   Remove the inner brake pad and shim(s) **(see illustration)**.

12   Remove and inspect the upper and lower pad retainer clips. **Note:** *On 2004 CR-V models, the upper and lower pad retainers are different. Make note of the position before removing.*

13   Install the pad retainer clips. They should fit snugly in the caliper mounting bracket; if

they don't, replace them. Apply a thin film of high-temperature grease to the retainer.

14   Apply a small amount of high-temperature grease to both sides of the shims.

15   Install the new inner pad and shim(s). Make sure the ears on the upper and lower ends of the pad are fully engaged with their respective grooves and the pad retainer clips.

16   Install the new outer pad and shim.

17   Before installing the caliper, remove the caliper pin dust boots and inspect them for tears and cracks; if they're damaged, replace them.

18   If you're working on a Civic Si, hatchback, or 2006 and later Civic, retract the piston by engaging the tips of a pair of needlenose pliers with two of the grooves in the face of the piston and turning it clockwise until it bottoms in the bore **(see illustration)**. Now, rotate the piston out until one of its grooves is aligned with the tab on the inner brake pad when you install the caliper. You may have to adjust the piston position by turning it back and forth to fit the tab in the groove. If the piston dust boot becomes distorted when the piston is turned, turn the piston in the opposite direction to restore the shape of the boot, but make sure the groove is aligned properly.

19   Install the caliper mounting bolts while holding the caliper pins with a second wrench. Tighten them to the torque listed in this Chapter's Specifications. If the brake line was disconnected from its mounting bracket, reconnect the line and tighten the bolt securely.

Front or rear pads

20   Install the wheel and lug nuts, lower the vehicle and tighten the lug nuts to the torque listed in the Chapter 1 Specifications.

21   Apply and release the brake pedal several times to bring the pads into contact with the brake discs. Check the brake fluid level and add fluid, if necessary (see Chapter 1).

22   Check the operation of the brakes in an isolated area before driving the vehicle in traffic.

4   Disc brake caliper - removal and installation

Warning: *The dust created by the brake system is harmful to your health. Never blow it out with compressed air and don't inhale any of it. An approved filtering mask should be worn when working on the brakes. Do not, under any circumstances, use petroleum-based solvents to clean brake parts. Use brake system cleaner only!*

Note: *Always replace the calipers in pairs - never replace just one of them.*

Front

Removal

Refer to illustrations 4.2a and 4.2b

1   Loosen - but don't remove - the lug nuts on the front wheels. Raise the front of the vehicle and place it securely on jackstands. Remove the front wheels.

2   Disconnect the brake line from the caliper and plug it to keep contaminants out of the brake system and to prevent losing any more brake fluid than is necessary **(see illustrations)**. **Note:** *If you're simply removing the caliper for access to other components, don't disconnect the hose.*

5.2 Caliper mounting bracket-to-steering knuckle bolts

5.3 The brake pads on this vehicle were obviously neglected, as they wore down completely and cut deep grooves into the disc - wear this severe means the disc must be replaced

5   Brake disc - inspection, removal and installation

Warning: *The dust created by the brake system is harmful to your health. Never blow it out with compressed air and don't inhale any of it. An approved filtering mask should be worn when working on the brakes. Do not, under any circumstances, use petroleum-based solvents to clean brake parts. Use brake system cleaner only!*

Inspection

Refer to illustrations 5.2, 5.3, 5.4a, 5.4b and 5.5

3   Remove the caliper mounting bolts while holding the caliper pins with a second wrench.

4   Detach the caliper from its mounting bracket.

Installation

5   Install the caliper by reversing the removal procedure. Remember to replace the sealing washers on either side of the brake line fitting with new ones. Tighten the caliper mounting bolts and the banjo bolt to the torque listed in this Chapter's Specifications.

6   Bleed the brake system (see Section 10).

7   Install the wheels and lug nuts and lower the vehicle. Tighten the lug nuts to the torque listed in the Chapter 1 Specifications.

Rear

Removal

8   Loosen - but don't remove - the lug nuts on the rear wheels. Raise the rear of the vehicle and place it securely on jackstands. Remove the rear wheels.

9   Remove the clip securing the parking brake cable to the caliper parking brake lever,

then separate the cable from the caliper.

10   Unscrew the banjo bolt and detach the brake line from the caliper. Plug the fitting to prevent fluid loss and contamination **(see illustration 4.2b)**. **Note:** *If you're simply removing the caliper for access to other components, don't disconnect the hose.*

11   Remove the caliper mounting bolts while holding the caliper pins with a second wrench.

12   Detach the caliper from its mounting bracket.

Installation

13   Install the caliper by reversing the removal procedure. Remember to replace the sealing washers on either side of the brake line fitting with new ones. Tighten the caliper mounting bolts and the banjo bolt to the torque listed in this Chapter's Specifications.

14   Bleed the brake system (see Section 10).

15   Install the wheels and lug nuts. Lower the vehicle and tighten the lug nuts to the torque listed in the Chapter 1 Specifications.

1   Loosen the wheel lug nuts, raise the vehicle and support it securely on jackstands. Remove the wheel and install the lug nuts to hold the disc in place against the hub flange. **Note:** *If the lug nuts don't contact the disc when screwed on all the way, install washers under them. If you're checking the rear disc, release the parking brake.*

2   Remove the brake caliper as outlined in Section 4. It isn't necessary to disconnect the brake hose. After removing the caliper bolts, suspend the caliper out of the way with a piece of wire. Remove the two caliper mounting bracket-to-steering knuckle bolts **(see illustration)** or, on rear calipers, the bracket-to-knuckle bolts and remove the mounting bracket.

3   Visually inspect the disc surface for score marks and other damage. Light scratches and shallow grooves are normal after use and may not always be detrimental to brake operation, but deep scoring requires disc removal and refinishing by an automotive machine shop. Be sure to check both sides of the disc **(see illustration)**. If pulsating has been noticed during application of the brakes, suspect disc runout.

4   To check disc runout, place a dial indicator at a point about 1/2-inch from the outer edge of the disc **(see illustration)**. Set the indicator to zero and turn the disc. The indicator reading should not exceed the specified

5.4a To check disc runout, mount a dial indicator as shown and rotate the disc

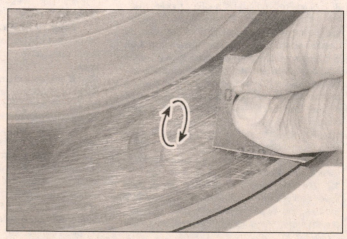

5.4b Using a swirling motion, remove the glaze from the disc surface with sandpaper or emery cloth

5.5 Use a micrometer to measure disc thickness

5.6a If the disc retaining screws are stuck, use an impact screwdriver to loosen them

allowable runout limit. If it does, the disc should be refinished by an automotive machine shop. **Note:** *The discs should be resurfaced regardless of the dial indicator reading, as this will impart a smooth finish and ensure a perfectly flat surface, eliminating any brake pedal pulsation or other undesirable symptoms related to questionable discs. At the very least, if you elect not to have the discs resurfaced, remove the glaze from the surface with emery cloth or sandpaper, using a swirling motion* **(see illustration).**

5   It's absolutely critical that the disc not be machined to a thickness under the specified minimum thickness. The minimum (or discard) thickness is cast or stamped into the disc. The disc thickness can be checked with a micrometer **(see illustration).**

Removal

Refer to illustrations 5.6a and 5.6b

6   Remove the lug nuts which were installed to hold the disc in place, or remove the two disc retaining screws **(see illustration)** and remove the disc from the hub. If the disc is stuck to the hub and won't come off, thread two bolts into the holes provided **(see illustration)** and tighten them. Alternate between the bolts, turning them a couple of turns at a time, until the disc is free. Remove the disc from the hub.

Installation

7   Place the disc in position over the threaded studs. Install the disc retaining screws and tighten them securely.

8   Install the caliper mounting bracket and caliper, tightening the bolts to the torque values listed in this Chapter's Specifications.

9   Install the wheel, then lower the vehicle to the ground. Tighten the lug nuts to the torque listed in the Chapter 1 Specifications. Depress the brake pedal a few times to bring the brake pads into contact with the disc. Bleeding won't be necessary unless the brake hose was disconnected from the caliper.

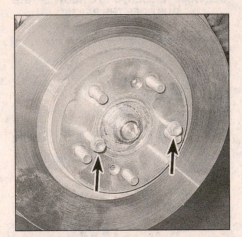

5.6b If the disc is stuck, thread two bolts into the disc and tighten them to force the disc off the hub

Check the operation of the brakes carefully before driving the vehicle.

---

6   Drum brake shoes/parking brake shoes - replacement

Refer to illustrations 6.4, 6.5, 6.6a through 6.6p and 6.7

Warning: *Drum brake shoes must be replaced on both wheels at the same time - never replace the shoes on only one wheel. Also, the dust created by the brake system is harmful to your health. Never blow it out with compressed air and don't inhale any of it. An approved filtering mask should be worn when working on the brakes. Do not, under any circumstances, use petroleum-based solvents to clean brake parts. Use brake system cleaner only!*

Caution: *Whenever the brake shoes are replaced, the return and hold-down springs should also be replaced. Due to the continuous heating/cooling cycle the springs are sub-*

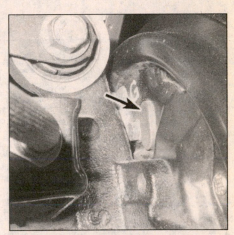

6.4 Remove this plug for access to the adjuster star wheel

jected to, they can lose tension over a period of time and may allow the shoes to drag on the drum and wear at a much faster rate than normal.

1   Loosen the wheel lug nuts, raise the rear of the vehicle and support it securely on jackstands. Block the front wheels to keep the vehicle from rolling.

2   Release the parking brake.

3   Remove the wheel. **Note:** *All four rear brake shoes must be replaced at the same time, but to avoid mixing up parts, work on only one brake assembly at a time.*

4   Remove the brake drum. **Note:** *If the brake drum cannot be easily pulled off the axle and shoe assembly, make sure the parking brake is completely released. If the drum still cannot be pulled off, the brake shoes will have to be retracted. This is done by first removing the plug from the backing plate* **(see illustration).** *With the plug removed, push the lever off the adjuster star wheel with a screwdriver while turning the adjuster wheel with another screwdriver, moving the shoes away from the drum. The drum should now come off.*

5   Clean the brake shoe assembly with brake system cleaner before beginning work **(see illustration)**.

6   Follow the accompanying illustrations for the brake shoe replacement procedure **(see illustrations 6.6a through 6.6p)**. Be sure to stay in order and read the caption under each illustration.

7   Before reinstalling the drum, it should be checked for cracks, score marks, deep scratches and hard spots, which will appear as small discolored areas. If the hard spots cannot be removed with fine emery cloth or if any of the other conditions listed above exist, the drum must be taken to an automotive machine shop to have it resurfaced. **Note:** *Professionals recommend resurfacing the drums each time a brake job is done. Resurfacing will eliminate the possibility of out-of-round drums. If the drums are worn so much that they can't be resurfaced without exceed-*

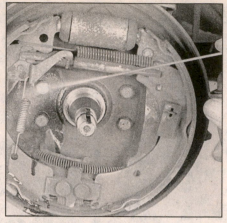

6.5 Before removing anything, clean the brake assembly with brake cleaner and allow it to dry - position a drain pan under the brake to catch the residue - DO NOT USE COMPRESSED AIR TO BLOW BRAKE DUST OFF THE PARTS!

6.6a Push down on the retainer spring with a screwdriver, then turn the hold-down pin to align its blade with the slot in the retainer spring - the spring should pop off (repeat this on the other spring)

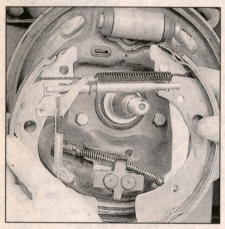

6.6b Pull the shoe assembly away from the backing plate (hub removed for clarity) . . .

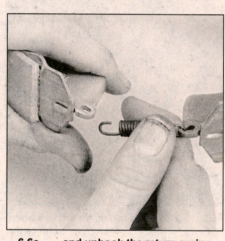

6.6c . . . and unhook the return spring

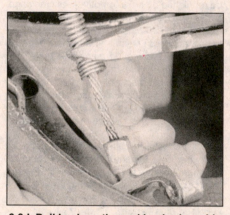

6.6d Pull back on the parking brake cable spring and squeeze the pliers just enough to grip the cable, holding the spring in the compressed position (diagonal cutting pliers are being used because they grip the cable well - be careful not to cut the cable); unhook the cable end from the parking brake lever

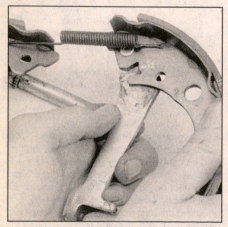

6.6e Swing the parking brake lever away from the trailing shoe, which will force the adjuster bolt clevis out of its groove in the shoe; the two shoes can now be separated

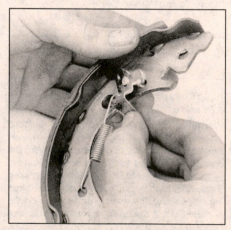

6.6f Remove the self-adjuster lever and spring from the leading shoe

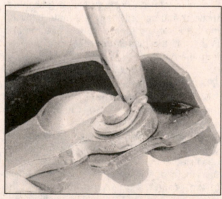

6.6g Pry open the parking brake lever retaining clip and separate the lever from the shoe; be careful not to lose the wave washer that is under the clip

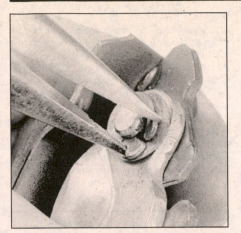

6.6h Put the new trailing shoe on the lever, place the wave washer over the pin, then install the retaining clip; crimp the ends of the clip together with a pair of needle-nose pliers

6.6i Clean the adjuster bolt and clevis, then lubricate the threads and ends with high-temperature grease

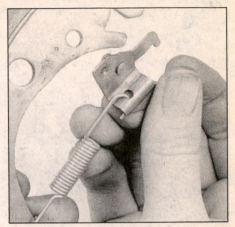

6.6j Connect the self-adjuster lever spring to the leading brake shoe, then insert the pin on the lever into its hole in the shoe

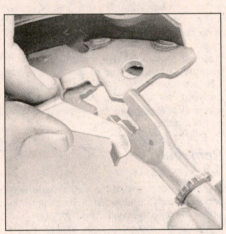

6.6k Insert the short clevis of the adjuster bolt into its slot in the leading shoe, making sure it catches the self-adjuster lever

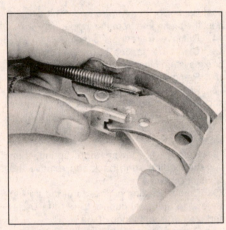

6.6l Connect the upper return spring between the two shoes, pry the lower ends of the shoes apart and insert the clevis at the other end of the adjuster bolt into the slot in the shoe; note the position of the stepped portion of the clevis opening

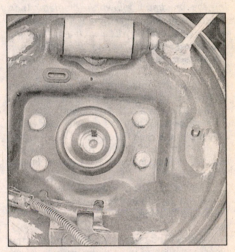

6.6m Lubricate the brake shoe contact areas on the backing plate with high-temperature grease

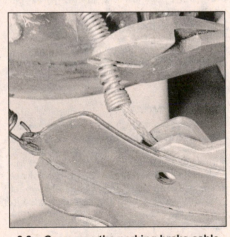

6.6n Compress the parking brake cable spring, hold it in position and connect the cable end to the parking brake lever (again, if you use diagonal cutting pliers, be careful not to cut or nick the cable)

6.6o Place the brake shoe assembly against the backing plate, engaging the upper ends of the shoes in the slots in the wheel cylinder pistons. Connect the lower return spring between the shoes

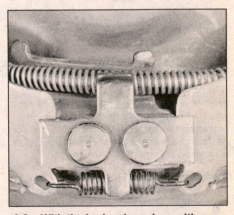

6.6p With the brake shoes in position on the backing plate, pass the hold-down pins through the holes in the backing plate and brake shoes, then install the retainer springs (see illustration 6.6a) - make sure the parking brake cable spring and the lower return spring are seated behind the anchor plate, as shown here

6.7 The maximum allowable drum diameter is cast into the drum (typical)

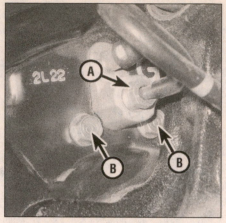

7.4 Unscrew the brake line fitting (A), then remove the wheel cylinder mounting bolts (B)

ing the maximum allowable diameter **(see illustration)**, then new ones will be required. At the very least, if you elect not to have the drums resurfaced, remove the glaze from the surface with emery cloth using a swirling motion.

8   Install the brake drum on the hub flange. Using a screwdriver inserted through the adjusting hole in the brake backing plate **(see illustration 6.4)**, turn the adjuster star wheel until the brake shoes drag on the drum as the drum is rotated, then back off the star wheel until the shoes don't drag. Reinstall the plug in the backing plate.

9   Mount the wheel and install the lug nuts. Lower the vehicle and tighten the lug nuts to the torque listed in the Chapter 1 Specifications.

10   Make a number of forward and reverse stops and operate the parking brake to adjust the brakes until satisfactory pedal action is obtained.

11   Check the operation of the brakes carefully before driving the vehicle.

Parking brake shoes (CR-V models)

Warning: *The dust created by the brake system is harmful to your health. Never blow it out with compressed air and don't inhale any of it. An approved filtering mask should be worn when working on the brakes. Do not, under any circumstances, use petroleum-based solvents to clean brake parts. Use brake system cleaner only!*

Removal

12   Loosen the rear wheel lug nuts, raise the rear of the vehicle and support it securely on jackstands. Block the front wheels and remove the rear wheels. Release the parking brake.
Note: *All four parking brake shoes must be replaced at the same time, but to avoid mixing up parts, work on only one brake assembly at a time.*

13   Remove the rear calipers (see Section 4). Support the caliper assemblies with a

coat hanger or heavy wire and don't disconnect the brake line from the caliper.

14   Remove the rear discs (see Section 5).

15   Clean the parking brake assembly with brake system cleaner.

16   Remove the two upper return springs.

17   Push the hold-down clips on the shoes and turn the pins 90-degrees, then remove the clips.

18   Remove the connecting rod and rod spring.

19   Remove the lower return spring, then pull the leading shoe back and remove the adjuster screw.

20   On the backing plate side of the trailing shoe, use diagonal cutters to pry the U-clip and washer from the top of the shoe.

21   Remove the parking brake lever from the trailing shoe and remove the shoe.

Installation

22   With the backing plate cleaned, apply light dabs of high-temperature grease to the shoe contact areas **(see illustration 6.6m)**.

23   Lubricate the parking brake lever pin, then assemble the parking brake lever to the new trailing shoe.

24   Position the trailing shoe against the stationary stop at the top of the backing plate, then insert the hold-down pin through the backing plate and install the hold-down clip.

25   Clean the adjuster bolt and clevis, then lubricate the threads and ends with high-temperature grease.

26   Install the adjuster and lower return spring on each shoe, then position the leading shoe and insert the hold-down pin through the backing plate and install the hold-down clip.

27   Place the rod spring on the connecting rod, then separate the shoes and install the connecting rod.

28   Connect the two upper return springs to the top of each shoe.

29   Install the disc and caliper. Tighten the caliper mounting bolts to the torque listed in this Chapter's Specifications.

30   Using a screwdriver inserted through the

adjusting hole in the disc, turn the adjuster star wheel until the brake shoes drag on the drum as the drum is rotated, then back off the star wheel until the shoes don't drag.

31   Mount the wheel and install the lug nuts. Lower the vehicle and tighten the lug nuts to the torque listed in the Chapter 1 Specifications.

32   Make a number of forward and reverse stops and operate the parking brake to adjust the brakes until satisfactory pedal action is obtained.

33   Check the operation of the brakes carefully before driving the vehicle.

7   Wheel cylinder - removal and installation

Warning: *The dust created by the brake system is harmful to your health. Never blow it out with compressed air and don't inhale any of it. An approved filtering mask should be worn when working on the brakes. Do not, under any circumstances, use petroleum-based solvents to clean brake parts. Use brake system cleaner only!*
Note: *If replacement is indicated (usually because of fluid leakage or sticky operation), it is recommended that the wheel cylinders be replaced, not overhauled. Always replace the wheel cylinders in pairs - never replace just one of them.*

Removal

Refer to illustration 7.4

1   Raise the rear of the vehicle and support it securely on jackstands. Block the front wheels to keep the vehicle from rolling.

2   Remove the brake shoe assembly (see Section 6).

3   Remove all dirt and foreign material from around the wheel cylinder.

4   Disconnect the brake line **(see illustration)**. Don't pull the brake line away from the wheel cylinder.

5   Remove the wheel cylinder mounting bolts.

6   Detach the wheel cylinder from the brake backing plate and immediately plug the brake line to prevent fluid loss and contamination.

Installation

7   Apply a small amount of RTV sealant between the backing plate and wheel cylinder, then place the wheel cylinder in position and install the bolts finger tight. Connect the brake line to the cylinder, being careful not to cross thread the fitting. Tighten the wheel cylinder mounting bolts to the torque listed in this Chapter's Specifications. Now tighten the brake line fitting securely.

8   Install the brake shoe assembly (see Section 6).

9   Bleed the brakes (see Section 10).

10   Check the operation of the brakes carefully before driving the vehicle.

8.2 Remove the fasteners securing the strut bar, then remove the bar

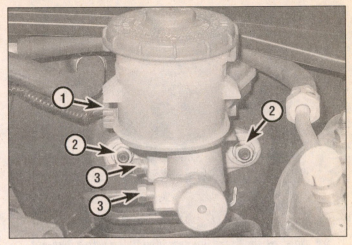

8.6 Master cylinder mounting details

1 Electrical connector   3 Brake line fittings
2 Mounting nuts

8 Master cylinder - removal and installation

Removal

Refer to illustrations 8.2 and 8.6

1 The master cylinder is located in the engine compartment, mounted to the power brake booster.

2 If you're working on a 2006 or earlier CR-V model, remove the strut bar **(see illustration)**. Some other models require removal of the air filter housing cover (or the entire housing) to gain adequate access to the master cylinder (see Chapter 4).

3 Disconnect the electrical connector from the fluid level warning switch.

4 Using a syringe or equivalent, remove the brake fluid from the master cylinder reservoir and dispose of it properly. **Caution:** *Brake fluid will damage paint. Cover all painted surfaces and avoid spilling fluid during this procedure. If you do spill fluid, wash it off with water immediately.*

5 If you're working on a hatchback model, separate the clutch master cylinder reservoir and the engine wire harness clip from the master cylinder mounting base. Remove the bolt attaching the brake reservoir to the mounting base.

6 Place rags under the fluid fittings and prepare caps or plastic bags to cover the ends of the lines once they are disconnected. Loosen the fittings at the ends of the brake lines where they enter the master cylinder **(see illustration)**. To prevent rounding off the corners on these nuts, the use of a flare-nut wrench, which wraps around the nut, is preferred. Pull the brake lines slightly away from the master cylinder and plug the ends to prevent contamination.

7 Remove the nuts attaching the master cylinder to the power booster. Pull the mas-

ter cylinder off the studs and out of the engine compartment. Again, be careful not to spill the fluid as this is done.

8 If a new master cylinder is being installed, remove the reservoir from the master cylinder and transfer it to the new master cylinder. **Note:** *On coupes, sedans and CR-V models, be sure to install new seals when transferring the reservoir.*

Installation

Refer to illustration 8.10

9 Bench bleed the new master cylinder before installing it. Mount the master cylinder in a vise, with the jaws of the vise clamping on the mounting flange.

10 Attach a pair of master cylinder bleeder tubes to the outlet ports of the master cylinder **(see illustration)**.

11 Fill the reservoir with brake fluid of the recommended type (see Chapter 1).

12 Slowly push the pistons into the master cylinder (a large Phillips screwdriver can be used for this) - air will be expelled from the pressure chambers and into the reservoir. Because the tubes are submerged in fluid, air can't be drawn back into the master cylinder when you release the pistons.

13 Repeat the procedure until no more air bubbles are present.

14 Remove the bleed tubes, one at a time, and install plugs in the open ports to prevent fluid leakage and air from entering. Install the reservoir cap.

15 Install the master cylinder over the studs on the power brake booster and tighten the attaching nuts only finger tight at this time. **Note:** *Be sure to install a new rod seal on the master cylinder.*

16 Thread the brake line fittings into the master cylinder. Since the master cylinder is still a bit loose, it can be moved slightly in order for the fittings to thread in easily. Do not strip the threads as the fittings are tightened.

17 Fully tighten the mounting nuts, then the brake line fittings. Tighten the nuts to the torque listed in this Chapter's Specifications.

18 Fill the master cylinder reservoir with fluid, then bleed the master cylinder and the brake system as described in Section 10. To bleed the cylinder on the vehicle, have an assistant depress the brake pedal and hold the pedal to the floor. Loosen the fitting to allow air and fluid to escape. Repeat this procedure on both fittings until the fluid is clear of air bubbles. **Caution:** *Have plenty of rags on hand to catch the fluid - brake fluid will ruin painted surfaces. After the bleeding procedure is completed, rinse the area under the master cylinder with clean water.*

19 The remainder of installation is the reverse of removal. Test the operation of the brake system carefully before placing the vehicle into normal service. **Warning:** *Do not operate the vehicle if you are in doubt about the effectiveness of the brake system.* On

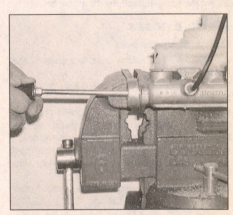

8.10 The best way to bleed air from the master cylinder before installing it on the vehicle is with a pair of bleeder tubes that direct brake fluid into the reservoir during bleeding

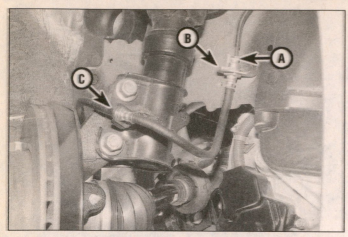

9.3 Unscrew the brake line threaded fitting with a flare-nut wrench to protect the fitting corners from being rounded off (A), then pull off the U-clip (B) with a pair of pliers and remove the brake line mounting bolt (C)

10.8 When bleeding the brakes, a hose is connected to the bleed screw at the caliper and submerged in brake fluid - air will be seen as bubbles in the tube and container (all air must be expelled before moving to the next wheel)

models equipped with ABS, it is possible for air to become trapped in the anti-lock brake system hydraulic control unit, so, if the pedal continues to feel spongy after repeated bleedings or the BRAKE or ANTI-LOCK light stays on, have the vehicle towed to a dealer service department or other qualified shop to be bled with the aid of a scan tool.

9   Brake hoses and lines - inspection and replacement

1   About every six months, with the vehicle raised and placed securely on jackstands, the flexible hoses which connect the steel brake lines with the front and rear brake assemblies should be inspected for cracks, chafing of the outer cover, leaks, blisters and other damage. These are important and vulnerable parts of the brake system and inspection should be complete. A light and mirror will be needed for a thorough check. If a hose exhibits any of the above defects, replace it with a new one.

Flexible hoses

Refer to illustration 9.3
2   Clean all dirt away from the ends of the hose.
3   To disconnect a brake hose from the brake line, unscrew the metal tube nut with a flare nut wrench, then remove the U-clip from the female fitting at the bracket and remove the hose from the bracket **(see illustration).**
4   Disconnect the hose from the caliper, discarding the sealing washers on either side of the fitting.
5   Using new sealing washers, attach the new brake hose to the caliper.
6   To reattach a brake hose to the metal line, insert the end of the hose through the frame bracket, make sure the hose isn't twisted, then attach the metal line by tightening the tube nut fitting securely. Install the U-clip at the frame bracket.

7   Carefully check to make sure the suspension or steering components don't make contact with the hose. Have an assistant push down on the vehicle and also turn the steering wheel lock-to-lock during inspection.
8   Bleed the brake system (see Section 10).

Metal brake lines

9   When replacing brake lines, be sure to use the correct parts. Don't use copper tubing for any brake system components. Purchase steel brake lines from a dealer parts department or auto parts store.
10   Prefabricated brake line, with the tube ends already flared and fittings installed, is available at auto parts stores and dealer parts departments. These lines can be bent to the proper shapes using a tubing bender.
11   When installing the new line make sure it's well supported in the brackets and has plenty of clearance between moving or hot components.
12   After installation, check the master cylinder fluid level and add fluid as necessary. Bleed the brake system as outlined in Section 10 and test the brakes carefully before placing the vehicle into normal operation.

10   Brake hydraulic system - bleeding

Refer to illustration 10.8
Warning: *If air has found its way into the hydraulic control unit on models with ABS, the system must be bled with the use of a scan tool. If the brake pedal feels spongy even after bleeding the brakes, or the ABS light on the instrument panel does not go off, or if you have any doubts whatsoever about the effectiveness of the brake system, have the vehicle towed to a dealer service department or other repair shop equipped with the necessary tools for bleeding the system.*

Warning: *Wear eye protection when bleeding the brake system. If the fluid comes in contact with your eyes, immediately rinse them with water and seek medical attention.*
Note: *Bleeding the brake system is necessary to remove any air that's trapped in the system when it's opened during removal and installation of a hose, line, caliper, wheel cylinder or master cylinder.*
1   It will probably be necessary to bleed the system at all four brakes if air has entered the system due to low fluid level, or if the brake lines have been disconnected at the master cylinder.
2   If a brake line was disconnected only at a wheel, then only that caliper or wheel cylinder must be bled.
3   If a brake line is disconnected at a fitting located between the master cylinder and any of the brakes, that part of the system served by the disconnected line must be bled.
4   Remove any residual vacuum (or hydraulic pressure) from the brake power booster by applying the brake several times with the engine off.
5   Remove the master cylinder reservoir cap and fill the reservoir with brake fluid. Reinstall the cap. **Note:** *Check the fluid level often during the bleeding operation and add fluid as necessary to prevent the fluid level from falling low enough to allow air bubbles into the master cylinder.*
6   Have an assistant on hand, as well as a supply of new brake fluid, an empty clear plastic container, a length of plastic, rubber or vinyl tubing to fit over the bleeder valve and a wrench to open and close the bleeder valve.
7   Beginning at the front left wheel, loosen the bleeder screw slightly, then tighten it to a point where it's snug but can still be loosened quickly and easily.
8   Place one end of the tubing over the bleeder screw fitting and submerge the other end in brake fluid in the container **(see illustration).**

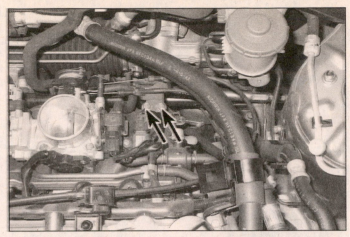

11.8 Remove the bolts securing the throttle cable bracket

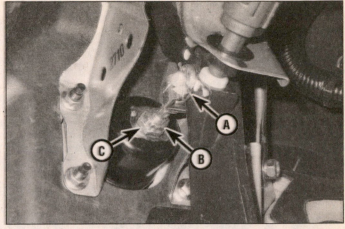

11.9 Remove the clevis pin retaining clip (A) and clevis pin, disconnect the pushrod from the pedal - (B) is the star locknut and (C) is the adjuster mentioned in Step 15

9   Have the assistant slowly depress the brake pedal and hold it in the depressed position.

10   While the pedal is held depressed, open the bleeder screw just enough to allow a flow of fluid to leave the valve. Watch for air bubbles to exit the submerged end of the tube. When the fluid flow slows after a couple of seconds, tighten the screw and have your assistant release the pedal.

11   Repeat Steps 9 and 10 until no more air is seen leaving the tube, then tighten the bleeder screw and proceed to the right front wheel, the right rear wheel and the left rear wheel, in that order, and perform the same procedure. Be sure to check the fluid in the master cylinder reservoir frequently.

12   Never use old brake fluid. It contains moisture which can boil, rendering the brake system inoperative.

13   Refill the master cylinder with fluid at the end of the operation.

14   Check the operation of the brakes. The pedal should feel solid when depressed, with no sponginess. If necessary, repeat the entire process. **Warning:** *Do not operate the vehicle if you are in doubt about the effectiveness of the brake system. On models equipped with ABS, it's possible for air to become trapped in the anti-lock brake system hydraulic control unit, so, if the pedal continues to feel spongy after repeated bleedings or the BRAKE or ANTI-LOCK light stays on, have the vehicle towed to a dealer service department or other qualified shop to be bled with the aid of a scan tool.*

11   Power brake booster - removal and installation

Operating check

1   Depress the brake pedal several times with the engine off and make sure there is no change in the pedal reserve distance.

2   Depress the pedal and start the engine. If the pedal goes down slightly, operation is normal.

Airtightness check

3   Start the engine and turn it off after one or two minutes. Depress the brake pedal several times slowly. If the pedal goes down farther the first time but gradually rises after the second or third depression, the booster is airtight.

4   Depress the brake pedal while the engine is running, then stop the engine with the pedal depressed. If there is no change in the pedal reserve travel after holding the pedal for 30 seconds, the booster is airtight.

Removal

Refer to illustrations 11.8, 11.9 and 11.10

5   Power brake booster units should not be disassembled. They require special tools not normally found in most automotive repair shops. They are fairly complex and because of their critical relationship to brake performance it is best to replace a defective booster unit with a new or rebuilt one.

6   To remove the booster, first remove the brake master cylinder as described in Section 8. On coupe or sedan models equipped with ABS, remove the master cylinder brake lines from the ABS hydraulic unit.

7   Disconnect the hose leading from the engine to the booster. Be careful not to damage the hose when removing it from the booster fitting.

8   If you're working on a coupe or sedan model, remove the bolts securing the throttle cable bracket, then remove the power steering and air conditioning lines from their holders **(see illustration)**.

9   Locate the pushrod clevis pin connecting the booster to the brake pedal **(see illustration)**. Remove the clevis pin retaining clip with pliers and pull out the pin.

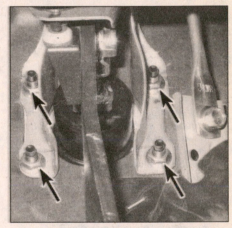

11.10 Remove the four booster mounting nuts

10   Remove the four nuts **(see illustration)** holding the brake booster to the firewall.

11   Slide the booster straight out from the firewall until the studs clear the holes and pull the booster, brackets and gaskets from the engine compartment area.

Installation

Refer to illustrations 11.14a, 11.14b and 11.14c

12   If a new booster is being installed, measure the length of the input rod, from the booster mounting surface to the hole in the clevis; it should be as listed in this Chapter's Specifications. If it isn't, loosen the locknut and turn the clevis one way or the other until the length is correct.

13   Installation procedures are the reverse of those for removal. Tighten the booster mounting nuts to the torque listed in this Chapter's Specifications. Also, be sure to use a new cotter pin on the clevis pin.

14   If a new power brake booster unit is being installed, the booster pushrod-to-master cylinder clearance must be as specified - if there is

11.14a Measure the distance that the pushrod protrudes from the brake booster at the master cylinder mounting surface (including the gasket, if equipped)

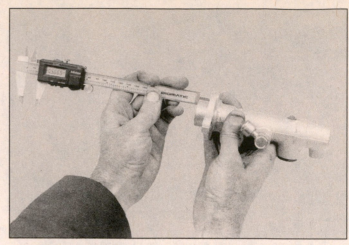

11.14b Measure the distance from the mounting flange to the end of the master cylinder

interference between the two, the brakes may drag; if there is too much clearance, there will be excessive brake pedal travel. Check the pushrod clearance as follows:

a) *Using a hand-held vacuum pump, apply a vacuum of 20 in-Hg to the booster. Measure the distance that the push-rod protrudes from the master cylinder mounting surface on the front of the power brake booster, including the gasket (if used). Write down this measurement* **(see illustration).** *This is "dimension A."*

b) *Measure the distance from the mounting flange to the end of the master cylinder* **(see illustration).** *Write down this measurement. This is "dimension B."*

c) *Measure the distance from the end of the master cylinder to the bottom of the pocket in the piston* **(see illustration).** *Write down this measurement. This is "dimension C."*

d) *Subtract measurement B from measurement C, then subtract measurement A from the difference between B and C. This is the pushrod clearance.*

e) *Compare your calculated pushrod clearance to the pushrod clearance listed in this Chapter's Specifications. If necessary, adjust the pushrod length to achieve the correct clearance (see the next Step).*

15   If the clearance is more or less than specified, loosen the star locknut **(see illustration 11.9)** and turn the adjuster on the power booster pushrod until the clearance is within the specified limit. After adjustment, tighten the locknut. Recheck the clearance. Repeat this step as often as necessary until the clearance is correct.

16   After the final installation of the master cylinder and brake hoses and lines, bleed the brakes as described in Section 10.

12   Parking brake - adjustment

2005 and earlier models (except Civic Si models)

Refer to illustrations 12.1 and 12.3

1   Remove the center console rear cover **(see illustration).**

2   Block the front wheels, raise the rear of the vehicle and support it securely on jackstands. Apply the parking brake lever until you hear one click.

3   Tighten the adjusting nut on the equalizer while rotating the rear wheels **(see illustration).** Stop turning the nut when the brakes just start to drag on the rear wheels.

4   Release the parking brake lever and check to see that the brakes don't drag when the rear wheels are turned. The travel on the parking brake lever should be as listed in

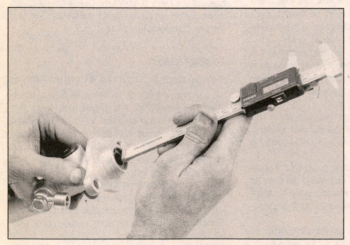

11.14c Measure the distance from the piston pocket to the end of the master cylinder

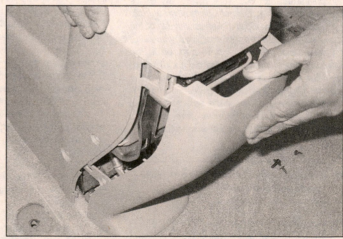

12.1 Remove the fasteners securing the center console rear cover, then detach the rear cover

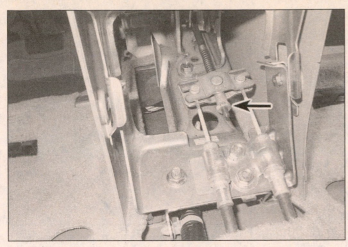

12.3 The parking brake adjusting nut is on the equalizer assembly on 2005 and earlier models

12.11 2006 and later parking brake adjusting nut location

the Chapter 1 Specifications when properly adjusted.

5   Lower the vehicle and reinstall the center console rear cover.

Civic Si models and all 2006 and later Civic models

Refer to illustration 12.11

6   Remove the center console (see Chapter 11).

7   Release the parking brake lever and loosen the parking brake lever adjusting nut.

8   Start the engine, then set the self-adjusting brake by depressing the brake several times. Turn off the engine.

9   Block the front wheels, raise the rear of the vehicle and support it securely on jackstands.

10   At the rear caliper, be sure the parking brake arm is contacting the brake caliper pin.

11   Apply the parking brake lever until you hear one click. Tighten the adjusting nut **(see illustration)** while rotating the rear wheels. Stop turning the nut when the brakes just start to drag on the rear wheels.

12   Release the parking brake lever and check to see that the brakes don't drag when the rear wheels are turned. The travel on the parking brake lever should be as listed in the Chapter 1 Specifications when properly adjusted.

13   Lower the vehicle and reinstall the center console.

CR-V models

14   Block the front wheels, raise the rear of the vehicle and support it securely on jackstands.

2005 and earlier models

15   Working inside the vehicle, pull the driver's seat all the way forward and pull back the carpet under the seat.

16   Remove the fasteners securing the parking brake equalizer cover, then remove the cover.

17   With the parking brake lever fully released, remove the return spring from the parking brake equalizer.

18   Apply the parking brake lever or pedal until you hear one click.

19   Tighten the adjusting nut on the equalizer while rotating the rear wheels. Stop turning the nut when the brakes just start to drag on the rear wheels.

20   Release the parking brake lever and check to see that the brakes don't drag when the rear wheels are turned. The travel on the parking brake lever should be as listed in the Chapter 1 Specifications when properly adjusted.

21   Lower the vehicle and reinstall the equalizer return spring and cover.

2006 and later models

22   Working inside the vehicle, under the dash, fully release the parking brake pedal.

23   Tighten the adjusting nut on the side of the parking brake pedal while rotating the rear wheels. Stop turning the nut when the brakes just start to drag on the rear wheels.

24   Release the parking brake pedal and check to see that the brakes don't drag when the rear wheels are turned. The travel on the parking brake lever should be as listed in the Chapter 1 Specifications when properly adjusted.

25   Lower the vehicle.

13   Brake light switch - replacement

Refer to illustration 13.1

1   Disconnect the electrical connector from the brake light switch **(see illustration)**.

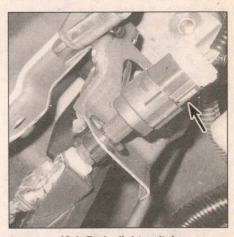

13.1 Brake light switch electrical connector

2   Rotate the switch counterclockwise slightly, so it unlocks from its holder, then pull it out of the holder.

3   To install the switch, insert it into its holder (canted slightly counterclockwise as during removal) and push it in until the switch body contacts the bracket on the brake pedal. Rotate the switch 45-degrees clockwise to lock it into place.

4   Plug the electrical connector into the switch.

14   Brake pedal - adjustment

Brake pedal height

Refer to illustrations 14.2a and 14.2b

1   Disconnect the brake light switch electrical connector, then remove the brake light switch (see Section 13).

2   Pull the carpet back and find the insulator cutout, then with the brake pedal fully

14.2a With the brake pedal fully released, measure the distance from the top of the pedal pad to the floor

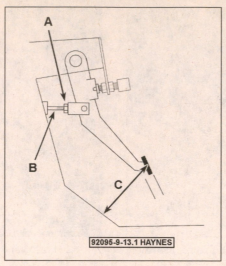

92095-9-13.1 HAYNES

14.2b Brake pedal details:

A   Pushrod/clevis locknut
B   Brake power booster push rod (turn this rod to raise or lower the pedal)
C   Pedal height measurement points

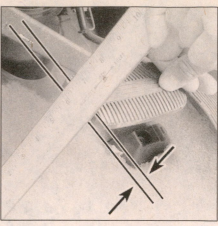

14.8 To measure brake pedal freeplay, press down lightly on the pedal and measure the distance that it moves freely before resistance is felt

released, measure the distance from the top of the pad to the floor **(see illustrations).**

3   If the height is not as listed in this Chapter's Specifications, it must be adjusted.

4   Loosen the locknut just in front of the clevis on the power brake booster pushrod.

5   Turn the booster pushrod until the pedal height is correct.

6   Tighten the locknut.

7   After adjusting the pedal height, check the freeplay, then install the brake light switch (see Section 13).

Brake pedal freeplay

Refer to illustration 14.8

8   Press down lightly on the brake pedal and measure the distance that it moves freely before resistance is felt **(see illustration).** The freeplay should be within the specified limits. If it isn't, check the clevis, clevis pin and the hole in the brake pedal arm for excessive wear.

---

15   Anti-lock Brake System (ABS) and Vehicle Stability Assist (VSA) system - general information

---

General information

1   Some models are equipped with an Anti-lock Brake System (ABS). 2005 and later CR-V models and 2006 and later Civic models are equipped with a combined ABS/VSA system. These systems are designed to maintain vehicle steerability, directional stability and optimum deceleration under severe braking and handling conditions. It does so by monitoring the rotational speed of each wheel and controlling the brake line pressure to each wheel during braking. This prevents the wheels from locking up.

2   The ABS or VSA systems have three main components - the wheel speed sensors,

the electronic control (ECU) and the hydraulic unit. Starting in 2006, the hydraulic unit is called the Modulator Control Unit (MCU). Four wheel speed sensors - one at each wheel - send a variable voltage signal to the control unit, which monitors these signals, compares them to its program and determines whether a wheel is about to lock up. When a wheel is about to lock up, the control unit signals the hydraulic unit to reduce hydraulic pressure (or not increase it further) at that wheel's brake caliper. Pressure modulation is handled by electrically-operated solenoid valves.

3   If a problem develops within the system, an "ABS" or "VSA" warning light will glow on the dashboard. Sometimes, a visual inspection of the ABS or VSA can help you locate the problem. Carefully inspect the ABS or VSA wiring harness. Pay particularly close attention to the harness and connections near each wheel. Look for signs of chafing and other damage caused by incorrectly routed wires. If a wheel sensor harness is damaged, the sensor must be replaced. **Warning:** *Do NOT try to repair an ABS/VSA wiring harness. The ABS/VSA system is sensitive to even the smallest changes in resistance. Repairing the harness could alter resistance values and cause the system to malfunction. If the ABS/VSA wiring harness is damaged in any way, it must be replaced.* **Caution:** *Make sure the ignition is turned off before unplugging or reattaching any electrical connections.*

Diagnosis and repair

4   If the dashboard warning light comes on and stays on while the vehicle is in operation, the ABS or VSA system requires attention. Although special electronic ABS or VSA diag-

nostic testing tools are necessary to properly diagnose the system, you can perform a few preliminary checks before taking the vehicle to a dealer service department.

a) Check the brake fluid level in the reservoir.
b) Verify that the computer electrical connectors are securely connected.
c) Check the electrical connectors at the hydraulic control unit.
d) Check the fuses.
e) Follow the wiring harness to each wheel and verify that all connections are secure and that the wiring is undamaged.

5   If the above preliminary checks do not rectify the problem, the vehicle should be diagnosed by a dealer service department or other qualified repair shop. Due to the complex nature of this system, all actual repair work must be done by a qualified automotive technician.

Wheel speed sensor - removal and installation

6   Loosen the wheel lug nuts, raise the vehicle and support it securely on jackstands. Remove the wheel.

7   Make sure the ignition key is turned to the Off position.

8   Trace the wiring back from the sensor, detaching all brackets and clips while noting its correct routing, then disconnect the electrical connector.

9   Remove the mounting bolt and carefully pull the sensor out from the knuckle or brake backing plate.

10   Installation is the reverse of the removal procedure. Tighten the mounting bolt securely.

11   Install the wheel and lug nuts, tightening them securely. Lower the vehicle and tighten the lug nuts to the torque listed in the Chapter 1 Specifications.

Chapter 10
Suspension and steering systems

Contents

	Section			Section
Coil spring (rear) (2006 and later Civic models) - removal and installation	10		Stabilizer bar and bushings (rear) - removal, inspection and installation	13
Control arm (front) - removal and installation	5		Steering column - removal and installation	15
General information	1		Steering gear - removal and installation	17
Hub and bearing assembly (front) - replacement	7		Steering knuckle and hub - removal and installation	6
Hub and bearing assembly (rear) - removal and installation	12		Steering wheel - removal and installation	14
Power steering pump - removal and installation	18		Strut assembly (front) - removal, inspection and installation	3
Power steering system - bleeding	19		Strut/spring assembly - replacement	4
Shock absorber (rear) (2006 and later Civic models) - removal and installation	9		Subframe - removal and installation	20
Shock absorber/coil spring assembly (rear) - removal, component replacement and installation	8		Suspension arms (rear) and rear knuckle - removal and installation	11
Stabilizer bar and bushings (front) - removal, inspection and installation	2		Tie-rod ends - removal and installation	16
			Wheel alignment - general information	22
			Wheels and tires - general information	21

Specifications

General
Power steering fluid type .... See Chapter 1

Torque specifications

Ft-lbs (unless otherwise indicated)   **Nm**

Note: *One foot-pound (ft-lb) of torque is equivalent to 12 inch-pounds (in-lbs) of torque. Torque values below approximately 15 ft-lbs are expressed in inch-pounds, since most foot-pound torque wrenches are not accurate at these smaller values.*

Front suspension

	Ft-lbs	Nm
Strut		
Damper rod nut*	33	44
Strut upper mounting nuts*	33	44
Strut-to-steering knuckle bolts/nuts		
Coupe and Sedan models		
2002 and earlier models	76	103
2003 to 2005 models	116	157
2006 and later models	67	90
Hatchback and CR-V models	116	157
Stabilizer bar		
Civic		
Stabilizer bar link nuts*		
2005 and earlier models	29	39
2006 and later models		
Upper	28	38
Lower	25	34
Stabilizer bar bracket bolts	29	39
CR-V		
Stabilizer bar link nuts*		
2006 and earlier models	29	39
2007 and later models	58	78
Stabilizer bar bracket bolts		
2006 and earlier models	29	39
2007 and later models	58	78

* The manufacturer recommends that these fasteners(s) be replaced with new ones whenever they are loosened or removed.

Torque specifications

	Ft-lbs (unless otherwise indicated)	Nm
Control arm		
Arm-to-subframe		
All models except 2007 and later CR-V models	61	83
2007 and later CR-V models		
Front arm-to-subframe bolt...	76	103
Rear arm-to-subframe bolts	43	59
Balljoint-to-control arm nut	43 to 51	59 to 69
Lower balljoint mounting nuts/bolts (2006 and later Civic/2007		
and later CR-V)*	38	53
Subframe bolts*		
Main bolts..	76	103
Mid-bracket bolts (2)	47	64
Driveaxle/hub nut..	See Chapter 8	

The manufacturer recommends that these fasteners(s) be replaced with new ones whenever they are loosened or removed.

Rear suspension

	Ft-lbs	Nm
Rear hub retaining nut*...	134	181
Rear hub mounting bolts		
2006 and later models...	47	64
Shock absorber mounting fasteners*		
Civic		
2005 and earlier models		
Upper...	43	59
Lower	45	61
2006 and later models		
Upper...	22	29
Lower		
Except Si models	43	59
Si models	51	69
CR-V		
Upper...	54	74
Lower	69	93
Damper rod nut (all models)*	22	29
Stabilizer bar		
Clamp bolts	16	22
Link-to-trailing arm nuts*	29	39
Link-to-stabilizer bar nuts*		
Coupe, Sedan and Hatchback models	28	38
CR-V models	22	29
Trailing arm-to-chassis mounting bolts*		
Coupe, Sedan and Hatchback models	80	108
CR-V models	85	115
Trailing arm-to-chassis pivot bolt*	43	59
Trailing arm-to-knuckle bolts*	43	59
Upper arm-to-knuckle pivot bolt*	43	59
Upper arm-to-chassis mounting bolts (Coupe, Sedan and		
Hatchback models)*	80	108
Upper arm-to-chassis pivot bolt (CR-V models)*................................	69	93

The manufacturer recommends that these fasteners(s) be replaced with new ones whenever they are loosened or removed.

Steering system

	Ft-lbs	Nm
Airbag module-to-steering wheel fasteners..	86 in-lbs	9.5
Electronic Power Steering (EPS) motor fasteners.................................	14	20
Power steering pump-to-engine bracket mounting fasteners.................	14	20
Coupe and Sedan models...	17	24
CR-V models	16	22
Power steering motor bolts (Hatchback models)....................................	14	20
Steering gear mounting bolts/nuts		
2005 and earlier models...	45	61
2006 and later Civic models...	40	54
2006 and later CR-V models..	52	71
Tie-rod end-to-steering knuckle nut		
2005 and earlier models...	32	43
2006 and later models...	40	54
Intermediate shaft-to-universal joint pinch-bolt	21 to 22	28 to 29
Steering gear input shaft-to-universal joint pinch-bolt	21 to 22	28 to 29
Steering column mounting fasteners...	132 in-lbs	16
Steering wheel mounting bolt/nut..	29	39

1.1 Front suspension components (Civic model shown)

1 Stabilizer bar   3 Strut/coil spring assembly   4 Control arm
2 Subframe

1 General information

Refer to illustrations 1.1, 1.2a and 1.2b

The front suspension is a MacPherson strut design. The upper end of each strut is attached to the vehicle's body strut support. The lower end of the strut is connected to the upper end of the steering knuckle. The steering knuckle is attached by a balljoint mounted to the outer end of the suspension control arm. A stabilizer bar connected to each control arm and mounted to the suspension crossmember reduces body roll during cornering **(see illustration)**.

The rear suspension employs a trailing arm, upper control arms and either shock absorber/coil spring assemblies on 2005 and earlier models **(see illustration)** or shock absorbers with independent coil springs on 2006 and later models **(see illustration)**. A stabilizer bar is clamped to a suspension support and connected to the trailing arms

by two links.

The power-assisted rack-and-pinion steering gear is attached to the front suspension subframe. There are two types of power steering, the first is hydraulic and the second is electric. On hydraulic models, the power assist comes from an engine-mounted hydraulic pump. On models with Electric Power Steering (EPS), the assist comes from an electric motor mounted to the steering gear. All models and years were available with hydraulic power steering. 2002 through 2005 Si models, and all 2006 and later models have the option of the Electric Power Steering. The steering gear actuates the tie-rods, which are attached to the steering knuckles. The steering column is designed to collapse in the event of an accident.

Frequently, when working on the suspension or steering system components, you may come across fasteners that seem impossible to loosen. These fasteners on the underside of the vehicle are continually subjected to water, road grime, mud, etc., and can become

rusted or frozen, making them extremely difficult to remove. In order to unscrew these stubborn fasteners without damaging them (or other components), be sure to use lots of penetrating oil and allow it to soak for a while. Using a wire brush to clean exposed threads will also ease removal of the nut or bolt and prevent damage to the threads. Sometimes a sharp blow with a hammer and punch will break the bond between a nut and bolt threads, but care must be taken to prevent the punch from slipping off the fastener and ruining the threads. Heating the stuck fastener and surrounding area with a torch sometimes helps too, but isn't recommended because of the obvious dangers associated with fire. Long breaker bars and extension, or cheater, pipes will increase leverage, but never use an extension pipe on a ratchet - the ratcheting mechanism could be damaged. Sometimes tightening the nut or bolt first will help to break it loose. Fasteners that require drastic measures to remove should always be replaced with new ones.

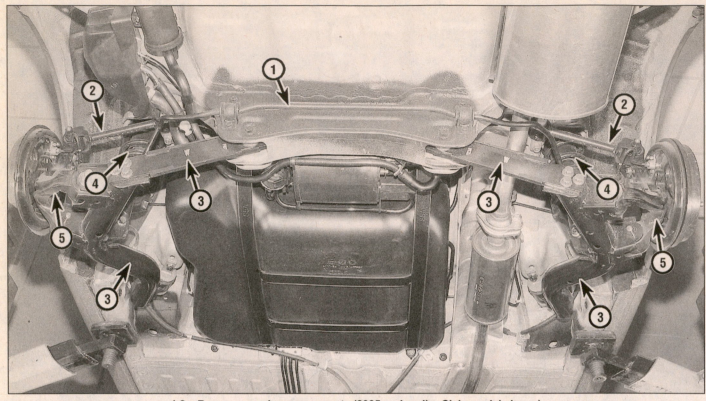

1.2a Rear suspension components (2005 and earlier Civic model shown)

1	Stabilizer bar	3	Trailing arm	5	Rear knuckle (hub and bearing)
2	Upper arm	4	Shock absorber/coil spring assembly		

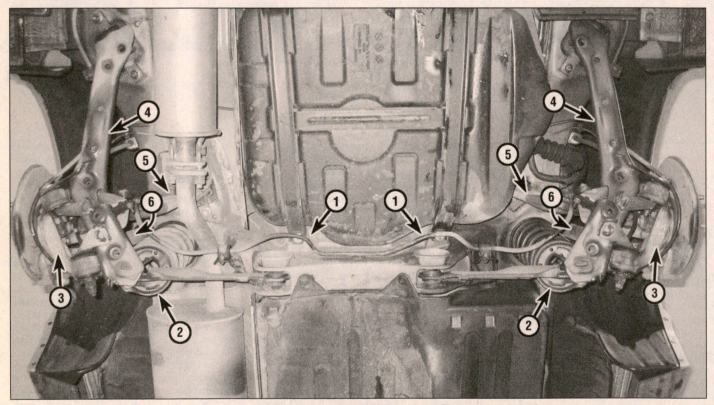

1.2b Rear suspension components (2006 and later Civic model shown)

1	Stabilizer bar	3	Rear knuckle (hub and bearing)	5	Upper arm
2	Coil spring	4	Trailing arm	6	Shock absorber

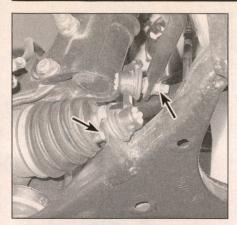

2.2 Stabilizer bar link attaching nuts

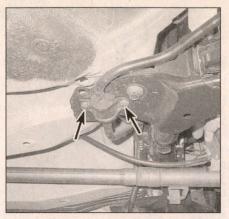

2.3 Stabilizer bar bushing clamps

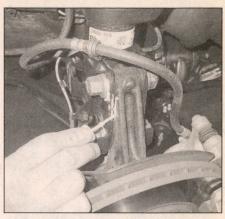

3.4 Mark the position of the strut to the steering knuckle, around the bolt heads and where the strut meets the knuckle

Since most of the procedures dealt with in this Chapter involve jacking up the vehicle and working underneath it, a good pair of jackstands will be needed. A hydraulic floor jack is the preferred type of jack to lift the vehicle, and it can also be used to support certain components during various operations. **Warning:** *Never, under any circumstances, rely on a jack to support the vehicle while working on it. Whenever any of the suspension or steering fasteners are loosened or removed they must be inspected and, if necessary, replaced with new ones of the same part number or of original equipment quality and design. Torque specifications must be followed for proper reassembly and component retention. Never attempt to heat or straighten any suspension or steering components. Instead, replace any bent or damaged part with a new one.*

2 Stabilizer bar and bushings (front) - removal, inspection and installation

All except 2007 and later CR-V models

Removal
Refer to illustrations 2.2 and 2.3
1 Loosen the front wheel lug nuts, raise the front of the vehicle and support it securely on jackstands. Apply the parking brake and block the rear wheels to keep the vehicle from rolling off the stands. Remove the front wheels.
2 Remove the nuts and the stabilizer bar links from the lower control arms **(see illustration). Note:** *Use an Allen wrench to prevent the ballstud from turning when removing the nut.*
3 Remove the stabilizer bar bushing retainer bolts **(see illustration).**
4 Remove the stabilizer bar from the vehicle.

Inspection
5 Inspect for cracked, torn, or distorted stabilizer bar bushings, bushing retainers,

and worn or damaged stabilizer bar links.
6 To replace damaged stabilizer bar bushings, remove the retainer, open the bushing slit and peel the bushing from the stabilizer bar. On some models, it will be necessary to bend back the tabs holding the retainer together. **Caution:** *Install the new bushings with the slits facing the same way that the original bushing slits faced.*

Installation
7 Guide the stabilizer bar into position. Install the retainer bolts, tightening them to the torque listed in this Chapter's Specifications.
8 Connect the stabilizer bar links to the lower control arms. Tighten the nuts to the torque listed in this Chapter's Specifications.
9 Install the wheels and lug nuts. Lower the vehicle and tighten the lug nuts to the torque listed in the Chapter 1 Specifications.

2007 and later CR-V models
10 Loosen the front wheel lug nuts. Raise the front of the vehicle and support it securely on jackstands. Remove the wheels.
11 Attach an engine support fixture or an engine hoist to the engine (see Chapter 2C, Section 7).
12 Support the front and rear of the subframe with floor jacks.
13 Make alignment marks from each corner of the subframe to the vehicle body. Remove the subframe mid-bracket bolts and loosen the subframe mounting bolts until the undersides of the bolt heads are 1-3/16 inches (30 mm) from the subframe **(see illustration 20.12)**. Slowly lower the subframe 1-3/16 inches (30 mm). **Warning:** *The jacks must remain in position, supporting the subframe. Don't allow the weight of the subframe to rest on the loosened bolts.*
14 Remove the nuts and detach the stabilizer bar links from the stabilizer bar. **Note:** *Use an Allen wrench to prevent the ballstud from turning when removing the nut.*
15 Remove the stabilizer bar bushing retainer bolts.

16 Remove the stabilizer bar from the vehicle.
17 Inspect the components as described in Steps 5 and 6.
18 Installation is the reverse of removal. Tighten the stabilizer bar fasteners and subframe mounting fasteners to the torque listed in this Chapter's Specifications. **Note:** *The manufacturer recommends replacing the subframe bolts with new ones whenever they are loosened or removed. Replace them one at a time.*
19 Install the wheels and lug nuts. Lower the vehicle and tighten the lug nuts to the torque listed in the Chapter 1 Specifications.
20 Have the front end alignment checked and, if necessary, adjusted.

3 Strut assembly (front) - removal, inspection and installation

Removal
Refer to illustrations 3.4 and 3.6
Note: *If both strut assemblies are going to be removed, mark the assemblies Right and Left so they will be reinstalled on the correct side.*
1 Loosen the wheel lug nuts, raise the vehicle and support it securely on jackstands. Remove the wheels.
2 Unbolt the brake hose bracket from the strut. If the vehicle is equipped with ABS, detach the speed sensor wiring harness from the strut by removing the clamp bracket bolt.
3 On 2005 and earlier Civic models and 2006 and earlier CR-V models, disconnect the tie-rod end from the steering arm on the strut (see Section 16). On 2007 and later CR-V models, detach the stabilizer bar link from the strut.
4 Mark the position of the strut to the steering knuckle **(see illustration). Note:** *This is only necessary if special camber adjusting bolts have been installed in place of the regular strut-to-knuckle bolts.* Remove the strut-to-knuckle nuts, then knock the bolts out with a hammer and punch.

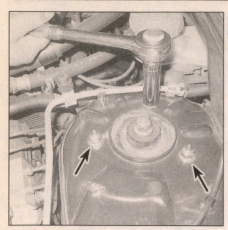

3.6 Support the strut and remove the upper mounting nuts (DON'T remove the nut in the center)

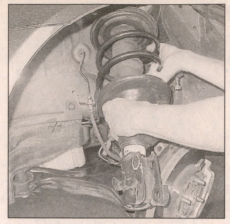

3.10 Carefully guide the strut assembly up into the fenderwell

4.3 Install the spring compressor following the tool manufacturer's instructions; compress the spring until all pressure is relieved from the upper spring seat (you can verify the spring is loose by wiggling it)

5   Separate the strut from the steering knuckle. Be careful not to overextend the inner CV joint. Also, don't let the steering knuckle fall outward and strain the brake hose.

6   Support the strut and spring assembly with one hand and remove the three strut-to-body nuts **(see illustration)**. Remove the assembly out from the fenderwell.

Inspection

7   Check the strut body for leaking fluid, dents, cracks and other obvious damage which would warrant repair or replacement.

8   Check the coil spring for chips or cracks in the spring coating (this will cause premature spring failure due to corrosion). Inspect the spring seat for cuts, hardness and general deterioration.

9   If any undesirable conditions exist, proceed to the strut disassembly procedure (see Section 4).

Installation

Refer to illustration 3.10

10   Guide the strut assembly up into the fenderwell and insert the upper mounting studs through the holes in the body **(see illustration)**. Once the studs protrude, install the nuts so the strut won't fall back through. This is most easily accomplished with the help of an assistant, as the strut is quite heavy and awkward.

11   Slide the steering knuckle into the strut flange and insert the two bolts. Install the nuts, align the previously made matchmarks and tighten them to the torque listed in this Chapter's Specifications.

12   The remainder of installation is the reverse of removal. Tighten all fasteners to the torque values listed in this Chapter's Specifications.

13   Install the wheel and lug nuts, then lower the vehicle and tighten the lug nuts to the torque listed in the Chapter 1 Specifications.

14   Tighten the upper mounting nuts to the torque listed in this Chapter's Specifications.

15   Have the front end alignment checked and, if necessary, adjusted.

---

4   Strut/spring assembly - replacement

Warning: *Struts and/or coil springs must be replaced in pairs - never replace just one of them.*

1   If the struts or coil springs exhibit the tell-tale signs of wear (leaking fluid, loss of damping capability, chipped, sagging or cracked coil springs) explore all options before beginning any work. The strut/shock absorber assemblies are not serviceable and must be replaced if a problem develops. However, strut assemblies complete with springs may be available on an exchange basis, which eliminates much time and work. Whichever route you choose to take, check on the cost and availability of parts before disassembling your vehicle. **Warning:** *Disassembling a strut is potentially dangerous and utmost attention must be directed to the job, or serious injury may result. Use only a high-quality spring compressor and carefully follow the manufacturer's instructions furnished with the tool. After removing the coil spring from the strut assembly, set it aside in a safe, isolated area.*

Disassembly

Refer to illustrations 4.3, 4.5, 4.6 and 4.7

2   Remove the strut and spring assembly (see Section 3). Mount the strut assembly in a vise. Line the vise jaws with wood or rags to prevent damage to the unit and don't tighten the vise excessively.

3   Following the tool manufacturer's instructions, install the spring compressor (which can be obtained at most auto parts stores or equipment yards on a daily rental basis) on the spring and compress it sufficiently to relieve all pressure from the upper spring seat **(see illustration)**. This can be verified by wiggling the spring.

4   Hold the damper rod with an Allen wrench, and unscrew the damper rod nut with a box-end wrench.

5   Remove the nut and upper mount **(see illustration)**. Lay the parts out in the exact order in which they are removed. Inspect the bearing in the suspension support for smooth operation. If it doesn't turn smoothly, replace the upper mount. Check the rubber portion of the upper mount for cracking and general deterioration. If there is any separation of the rubber, replace it.

6   Remove the upper spring seat from the damper rod **(see illustration)**. Check the spring seat for cracking and hardness; replace it if necessary. Remove the upper insulator from the damper shaft.

7   Carefully lift the compressed spring from the assembly **(see illustration)** and set it in a safe place. **Warning:** *When removing the compressed spring, lift it off carefully and set it in a safe place. Keep the ends of the spring away from your body.* **Note:** *If you are disas-*

4.5 Lift the upper mount off the damper rod

4.6 Remove the upper spring seat and insulator from the damper rod

4.7 Remove the compressed spring from the strut/shock absorber assembly - keep the ends of the spring pointed away from your body

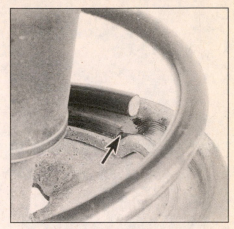

4.11 When installing the spring, make sure the end fits into the recessed portion of the lower seat

sembling both struts, mark the springs LEFT and RIGHT so you don't mix them up (they're different).

8   Remove the dust cover plate and dust cover.
9   Slide the rubber bump stop off the damper rod. Check the bump stop for cracking and general deterioration. If there is any deterioration of the rubber, replace it.

Reassembly

Refer to illustration 4.11

10   Extend the damper rod to its full length and install the rubber bump stop, dust cover and dust cover plate.
11   Carefully place the compressed coil spring onto the lower seat of the damper, with the end of the spring resting in the lowest part of the seat **(see illustration)**.
12   Install the upper insulator and spring seat.

13   Install the bearing and suspension support.
14   Install the washer and damper rod nut and tighten it to the torque listed in this Chapter's Specifications. Remove the spring compressor tool.
15   Install the strut/spring assembly (see Section 3).

5   Control arm (front) - removal and installation

Refer to illustrations 5.4, 5.5 and 5.7

1   Loosen the wheel lug nuts, raise the vehicle and support it securely on jackstands. Remove the wheel.
2   Detach the stabilizer bar link from the control arm (see Section 2).
3   On 2005 and earlier Civic/2006 and ear-

lier CR-V, remove the lock-pin from the castle nut on the balljoint stud. Loosen the nut, but don't remove it yet. Using a puller, separate the control arm from the balljoint in the steering knuckle. Remove the nut.
4   On 2006 and later Civic/2007 and later CR-V, remove the fasteners securing the balljoint to the control arm **(see illustration)**.
5   Remove the control arm-to-subframe mounting bolts **(see illustration)**.
6   Remove the control arm.
7   On 2005 and earlier Civic/2006 and earlier CR-V, installation is the reverse of removal, noting the following points:

a) *Raise the control arm with a floor jack to simulate normal ride height before tightening the fasteners to the specified torque. Do not place the jack in a position so that it interferes with the tightening of the balljoint nut.*

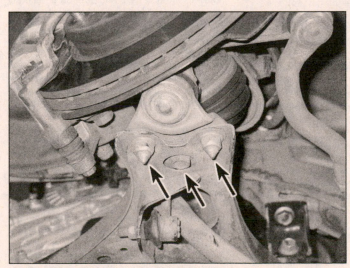

5.4 Lower balljoint mounting details (2006 and later Civic/2007 and later CR-V)

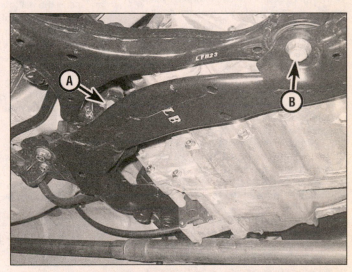

5.5 Remove the control arm rear pivot bolt (A) and the front mounting bolt (B)

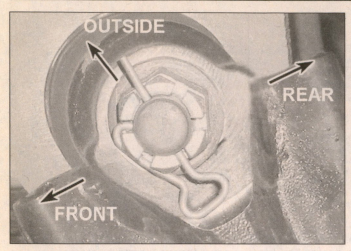

5.7 Install the lock pin from the inside of the vehicle to the outside

8.2 Remove the nuts from the shock absorber mounting studs - DON'T remove the nut in the center (2005 and earlier Civic and all CR-V models)

b) *Position the lock-pin so that it's facing the specified direction* **(see illustration)**. **Note:** *If necessary, tighten the nut a little more to allow lock pin insertion. Never loosen the nut in order to align the hole in the balljoint with the castellations in the nut.*

c) *Install the wheel and lug nuts, lower the vehicle and tighten the lug nuts to the torque listed in the Chapter 1 Specifications.*

8   On 2006 and later Civic/2007 and later CR-V, tighten the balljoint mounting fasteners to the torque listed in this Chapter's Specifications. The remainder of installation is the reverse of removal.

---

6   Steering knuckle and hub - removal and installation

Warning: *Dust created by the brake system is harmful to your health. Never blow it out with compressed air and don't inhale any of it. Do not, under any circumstances, use petroleum-based solvents to clean brake parts. Use brake system cleaner only.*

Removal

1   Loosen the wheel lug nuts, raise the vehicle and support it securely on jackstands. Remove the wheel.

2   Remove the driveaxle/hub nut (see Chapter 8). Remove the brake caliper and support it with a piece of wire as described in Chapter 9. Remove the caliper mounting bracket, then remove the brake disc from the hub.

3   Mark the strut to the steering knuckle, then loosen, but do not remove the strut-to-steering knuckle bolts **(see illustration 3.4)**.

4   If the vehicle is equipped with ABS, remove the speed sensor (see Chapter 8).

5   Separate the control arm from the balljoint (see Section 5). On 2006 and later Civics and 2007 and later CR-Vs, detach the tie-rod end from the steering knuckle (see Section 16).

6   On 2005 and earlier Civics and 2006 and earlier CR-Vs, disconnect the stabilizer bar attaching link from the lower control arm (see Section 2). The strut-to-knuckle bolts can now be removed.

7   Push the driveaxle from the hub as described in Chapter 8. Support the end of the driveaxle with a piece of wire.

8   Remove the bolts and separate the steering knuckle from the strut.

Installation

9   Guide the knuckle and hub assembly into position, inserting the driveaxle into the hub.

10   Push the knuckle into the strut flange and install the bolts and nuts, but don't tighten them yet.

11   Connect the balljoint to the control arm and install the nut (don't tighten it yet).

12   Tighten the strut bolt nuts, the balljoint-to-control arm nut and the tie-rod nut to the torque values listed in this Chapter's Specifications.

13   Place the brake disc on the hub and install the caliper mounting bracket and caliper as outlined in Chapter 9.

14   Install the driveaxle/hub nut and tighten it to the torque listed in the Chapter 8 Specifications.

15   Install the wheel and lug nuts. Lower the vehicle and tighten the lug nuts to the torque listed in the Chapter 1 Specifications.

16   Have the front wheel alignment checked and, if necessary, adjusted.

---

7   Hub and bearing assembly (front) - replacement

Due to the special tools and expertise required to press the hub and bearing from the steering knuckle, this job should be left to a professional mechanic. However, the steering knuckle and hub may be removed and the assembly taken to an automotive machine shop or other qualified repair facility equipped with the necessary tools. See Section 6 for the steering knuckle and hub removal procedure.

---

8   Shock absorber/coil spring assembly (rear) - removal, component replacement and installation

---

Note: *This procedure applies to 2005 and earlier Civic and all CR-V models.*

Removal

Refer to illustrations 8.2 and 8.3

1   Loosen the rear wheel lug nuts. Raise the rear of the vehicle and support it securely on jackstands. Block the front wheels to prevent the vehicle from rolling. Remove the wheel.

2   Remove the side trim panels from the trunk (Coupe and Sedan models) or from the cargo area (CR-V and Hatchback models). Remove the shock absorber upper mounting nuts **(see illustration)**.

3   Remove the shock absorber lower mounting bolt **(see illustration)**, then remove the shock absorber/coil spring assembly.

4   Check the shock body for leaking fluid, dents, cracks and other obvious damage which would warrant repair or replacement.

5   Check the coil spring for chips or cracks in the spring coating (this will cause premature spring failure due to corrosion). Inspect the spring seat for cuts, hardness and general deterioration.

6   If any undesirable conditions exist, proceed to the component replacement procedure.

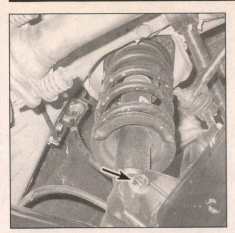

8.3 Rear shock absorber lower mounting bolt (2005 and earlier Civic and all CR-V models)

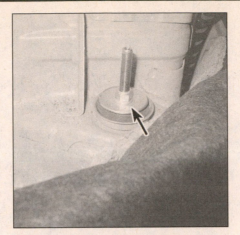

9.4 Rear shock absorber upper mounting nut (2006 and later Civic models)

9.5 Rear shock absorber lower mounting bolt (2006 and later Civic models)

Component replacement

Warning: *Disassembling a shock/coil spring is potentially dangerous and utmost attention must be directed to the job, or serious injury may result. Use only a high-quality spring compressor and carefully follow the manufacturer's instructions furnished with the tool. After removing the coil spring from the shock absorber, set it aside in a safe, isolated area.*

Note: *If the shocks or coil springs exhibit the telltale signs of wear (leaking fluid, loss of damping capability, chipped, sagging or cracked coil springs), explore all options before beginning any work. The shock absorber/coil spring assemblies are not serviceable and must be replaced if a problem develops. However, assemblies complete with springs may be available on an exchange basis, which eliminates much time and work. Whichever route you choose to take, check on the cost and availability of parts before disassembling your vehicle.*

7   Mount the shock/coil spring assembly in a vise. Line the vise jaws with wood or rags to prevent damage to the unit and don't tighten the vise excessively.

8   Following the tool manufacturer's instructions, install the spring compressor (which can be obtained at most auto parts stores or equipment yards on a daily rental basis) on the spring and compress it sufficiently to relieve all pressure from the upper spring seat. This can be verified by wiggling the spring. **Note:** *Note the orientation of the upper mount in relation to the lower mounting eye (when reassembling the unit, the mount will have to be in the same position). Make a sketch or some matchmarks to help you get the mount positioned properly when reinstalling it.*

9   Hold the shock damper rod with an Allen wrench, and unscrew the retaining nut with a box-end wrench.

10   Disassemble the parts from the damper, taking care to lay the parts out in the exact order in which they are removed. **Warning:** *When removing the compressed spring, lift it*

off carefully and set it in a safe place. Keep the ends of the spring away from your body

11   Reassembly is the reverse of removal, noting the following points:

  a) *Carefully place the spring onto the shock absorber body with the end of the spring resting in the lowest part of the seat.*

  b) *Use a new self-locking nut, then tighten the nut to the torque listed in this Chapter's Specifications.*

  c) *Before releasing the spring compressor, make sure the upper mount is oriented as it was before removal in Step 8.*

Installation

12   Guide the shock absorber/coil spring assembly up into the fenderwell and insert the upper mounting studs through the holes in the body. Once the studs protrude from the holes, install the nuts so the assembly won't fall back through, but don't tighten the nuts completely yet. The shock absorber is heavy and awkward, so get an assistant to help you, if possible.

13   Connect the shock to the trailing arm. Raise the trailing arm with the floor jack to simulate normal ride height, Tighten the shock absorber lower mounting bolt to the torque listed in this Chapter's Specifications.

14   Install the wheel and lug nuts, lower the vehicle and tighten the lug nuts to the torque listed in the Chapter 1 Specifications.

15   Tighten the upper mounting nuts to the torque listed in this Chapter's Specifications.

9   Shock absorber (rear) (2006 and later Civic models) - removal and installation

Refer to illustrations 9.4 and 9.5

1   Loosen the rear wheel lug nuts. Raise the rear of the vehicle and support it securely on jackstands. Block the front wheels to prevent the vehicle from rolling. Remove the wheel.

2   Remove the trunk side trim panel.

3   Support the lower arm with a floor jack placed under the rear knuckle. **Warning:** *Do not move the jack while it is supporting the lower arm and the coil spring tension.*

4   Remove the shock absorber damper mounting nut **(see illustration)**.

5   Remove the shock absorber lower mounting bolt **(see illustration)**, then remove the shock absorber.

6   Check the shock body for leaking fluid, dents, cracks and other obvious damage which would warrant repair or replacement.

7   Guide the shock absorber up into the fenderwell and insert the damper through the hole in the body. Once the damper protrudes from the hole, install the nut so the assembly won't fall back through.

8   Connect the shock to the trailing arm. Tighten the shock absorber lower mounting bolt and damper mounting nut to the torque listed in this Chapter's Specifications.

9   Install the wheel and lug nuts, lower the vehicle and tighten the lug nuts to the torque listed in the Chapter 1 Specifications.

10   Coil spring (rear) (2006 and later Civic models) - removal and installation

1   Loosen the rear wheel lug nuts. Raise the rear of the vehicle and support it securely on jackstands. Block the front wheels to prevent the vehicle from rolling. Remove the wheel.

2   Remove the rear wheel speed sensor and brake hose mounting bolts.

3   Place a floor jack under the rear knuckle. Slowly raise the jack until the spring begins to compress.

4   Remove the shock absorber lower mounting bolt **(see illustration 9.5)**.

5   Disconnect the rear stabilizer link (see Section 13).

6   Remove the upper arm to knuckle

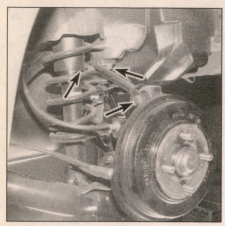

11.4 Upper arm pivot and mounting bolts

11.6 Mark the relationship of the toe adjusting cam to the trailing arm (2005 and earlier Civic and all CR-V models)

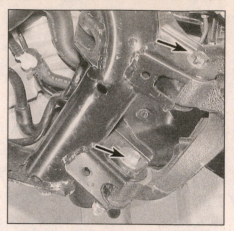

11.7 Remove the knuckle-to-trailing arm bolts (2005 and earlier Civic and all CR-V models)

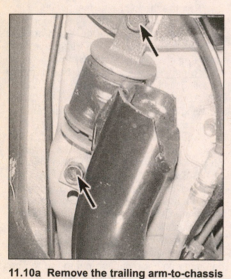

11.10a Remove the trailing arm-to-chassis front mounting bolts . . .

11.10b . . . and the trailing arm-to-chassis pivot bolt (2005 and earlier Civic and all CR-V models)

mounting bolt and trailing arm-to-chassis front mounting bolts **(see illustration 11.17)**.

7　Slowly lower the jack and remove the coil spring

8　Check the coil spring for chips or cracks in the spring coating (this will cause premature spring failure due to corrosion). Inspect the spring seat for cuts, hardness and general deterioration, replacing it if necessary.

9　Installation is the reverse of removal, noting the following points:

a) *Be sure to position the lower end of the coil spring in the depressed area of the trailing arm.*

b) *Raise the outer end of the lower arm with a floor jack to simulate normal ride height, then tighten all of the mounting bolts to the torque listed in this Chapter's Specifications.*

c) *Tighten the wheel and lug nuts to the torque listed in the Chapter 1 Specifications.*

11　Suspension arms (rear) and rear knuckle - removal and installation

1　Loosen the rear wheel lug nuts. Raise the rear of the vehicle and support it securely on jackstands. Block the front wheels to prevent the vehicle from rolling. Remove the wheel.

Upper arm

Refer to illustration 11.4

2　On models with ABS, remove the ABS wheel speed sensor and unbolt the harness bracket from the upper arm.

3　Support the trailing arm with a floor jack. **Warning:** *The jack must remain in this position until the new arm is installed.*

4　Remove the upper arm-to-knuckle bolt, then remove the mounting/pivot bolt(s) from the inner end of the arm **(see illustration)**. **Note:** *On 2006 and later Civic models, some upper arms are stamped "C" and some arms*

are not. If replacing the upper arm, make sure the new one is stamped the same as the old one.

5　Installation is the reverse of removal, noting the following points:

a) *Before fully tightening the fasteners, raise the trailing arm with the floor jack to simulate normal ride height.*

b) *Tighten all fasteners to the proper torque specifications.*

c) *Tighten the wheel lug nuts to the torque listed in the Chapter 1 Specifications.*

d) *Have the rear wheel alignment checked and, if necessary, adjusted.*

Trailing arm

2005 and earlier Civic and all CR-V models

Refer to illustrations 11.6, 11.7, 11.10a and 11.10b

6　Mark the relationship of the toe adjusting cam to the trailing arm **(see illustration)**, then support the trailing arm with a floor jack.

7　Remove the trailing arm-to-knuckle bolts, then disconnect the arm from the knuckle **(see illustration)**. **Note:** *Suspend the knuckle with a bungee cord or piece of wire.*

8　Disconnect the stabilizer bar link from the trailing arm (see Section 13).

9　Remove the shock absorber lower mounting bolt and disconnect the shock from the trailing arm **(see illustration 8.3)**.

10　Remove the trailing arm-to-chassis front mounting bolts, then remove the trailing arm-to-chassis pivot bolt **(see illustrations)**.

11　Remove the trailing arm.

12　Installation is the reverse of removal, noting the following points:

a) *Align the mark you made on the adjuster cam with the mark on the trailing arm.*

b) *Before fully tightening the fasteners, raise the trailing arm with the floor jack to simulate normal ride height.*

c) *Tighten all fasteners to the proper torque specifications.*

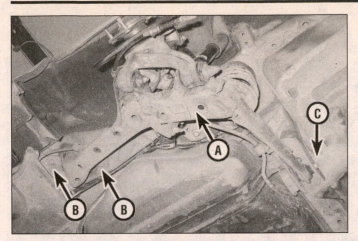

11.17 Rear trailing arm details (2006 and later Civic models)

A *Rear trailing arm*
B *Trailing arm-to-chassis front mounting bolts*
C *Trailing arm-to-chassis pivot bolt*

12.3a Using a hammer and chisel, remove the dust cover (2005 and earlier Civic models)

d) *Tighten the wheel lug nuts to the torque listed in the Chapter 1 Specifications.*
e) *Have the rear wheel alignment checked and, if necessary, adjusted.*

2006 and later Civic models

Refer to illustration 11.17

13   Support the trailing arm with a floor jack. Raise the jack just enough to begin to take some of the spring force.
14   Unbolt the rear knuckle from the trailing arm.
15   Disconnect the stabilizer bar link from the trailing arm (see Section 13).
16   Remove the shock absorber lower mounting bolt, then remove the trailing arm-to-chassis front mounting bolts. Slowly lower the floor jack and remove the coil spring.
17   Remove the trailing arm-to-chassis pivot bolt **(see illustration)**.
18   Remove the trailing arm.
19   Installation is the reverse of removal, noting the following points:
a) *Before fully tightening the fasteners, raise the trailing arm with the floor jack to simulate normal ride height.*
b) *Tighten all fasteners to the proper torque specifications.*
c) *Tighten the wheel lug nuts to the torque listed in the Chapter 1 Specifications.*
d) *Have the rear wheel alignment checked and, if necessary, adjusted.*

Rear knuckle

20   If you're working on a 4WD model, loosen the rear driveaxle/hub nut (see Chapter 8).
21   Remove the brake drum or brake caliper and disc (see Chapter 9).
22   On 2005 and earlier Civic and 2006 and earlier 2WD CR-V models, unstake and remove the hub retaining nut.
23   Remove the parking brake shoes (if equipped), wheel speed sensor and parking brake cable (see Chapter 9).

24   Support the trailing arm with a floor jack, then disconnect the suspension arms from the knuckle (see Steps 1 through 18).
25   On 4WD models, carefully separate the driveaxle from the knuckle and hub assembly as described in Chapter 8. Support the end of the driveaxle with a piece of wire.
26   Remove the knuckle along with the brake backing plate from the vehicle.
27   Installation is the reverse of removal, noting the following points:
a) *Before fully tightening the suspension arm fasteners, raise the trailing arm with a floor jack to simulate normal ride height.*
b) *Align the matchmarks on the toe adjusting cam (see Section 11).*
c) *Tighten all fasteners to the proper torque specifications.*
d) *On 2005 and earlier Civic and 2006 and earlier 2WD CR-V models, install a new hub retaining nut and tighten it to the torque listed in this Chapter's Specifications. Stake the new hub nut in place. If you're working on a 4WD CR-V model, install a new driveaxle/hub nut and tighten it to the torque listed in the Chapter 8 Specifications.* **Note:** *Apply a little clean engine oil to the seating surface of the hub retaining nut before installing it.*
e) *Tighten the caliper mounting bolts to the torque listed in the Chapter 9 Specifications.*
f) *It won't be necessary to bleed the brakes unless a hydraulic fitting was loosened.*
g) *Have the rear wheel alignment checked and, if necessary, adjusted.*

12   Hub and bearing assembly (rear) - removal and installation

Warning: *Dust created by the brake system is harmful to your health. Never blow it out with compressed air and don't inhale any of it. Do not, under any circumstances, use petroleum-*

12.3b Unstake the hub nut (2005 and earlier Civic models)

based solvents to clean brake parts. Use brake system cleaner only.
Note: *The rear hub and bearing are combined into a single assembly. The bearing is sealed for life and requires no lubrication or attention. If the bearing is worn or damaged, replace the entire hub and bearing assembly.*

1   Loosen the rear wheel lug nuts, raise the rear of the vehicle and support it securely on jackstands. Block the front wheels to prevent the vehicle from rolling. Remove the wheels.
2   Remove the brake drum or disc (see Chapter 9).

Civic models

2005 and earlier models

Refer to illustrations 12.3a, 12.3b and 12.5

3   Remove the dust cover, then unstake and remove the hub retaining nut **(see illustrations)**.
4   Remove the hub and bearing assembly from the spindle.

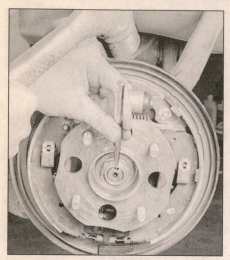

12.5 Stake the collar of the hub nut back into the groove in the spindle (2005 and earlier Civic models)

12.7 Hub and bearing mounting bolts (2006 and later Civic/2007 and later CR-V models)

13.2a Stabilizer bar link attaching nuts

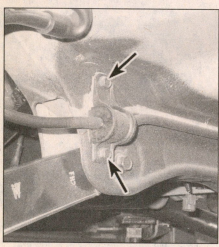

13.2b Stabilizer bar bracket bolts

5   Installation is the reverse of removal, noting the following points:

a) *Install a new hub retaining nut and tighten it to the torque listed in this Chapter's Specifications. Stake the new hub nut in place* **(see illustration). Note:** *Apply a little clean engine oil to the seating surface of the hub retaining nut before installing it.*

b) *Install the dust cover by tapping lightly around the edge until it is seated.*

c) *On models with rear disc brakes, tighten the caliper mounting bolts to the torque listed in the Chapter 9 Specifications.*

d) *Install the wheel and lug nuts. Lower the vehicle and tighten the lug nuts to the torque listed in the Chapter 1 Specifications.*

2006 and later models

Refer to illustration 12.7

6   On disc brake models, remove the rear

brake caliper, caliper mounting bracket and brake disc (see Chapter 9).

7   Remove the hub and bearing mounting bolts and remove the hub assembly from the rear knuckle **(see illustration)**.

8   Installation is the reverse of removal, noting the following points:

a) *Install a new O-ring.* **Note:** *Apply a little clean engine oil to the seating surface of the hub retaining nut before installing it.*

b) *On models with rear disc brakes, tighten the caliper mounting bolts to the torque listed in the Chapter 9 Specifications.*

c) *Install the wheel and lug nuts. Lower the vehicle and tighten the lug nuts to the torque listed in the Chapter 1 Specifications.*

CR-V models

2006 and earlier models

Note: *Due to the special tools and expertise required to press the hub and bearing from the knuckle, this job should be left to a professional mechanic. However, the knuckle and hub may be removed and the assembly taken to an automotive machine shop or other qualified repair facility equipped with the necessary tools.*

2007 and later models

9   If you're working on a 4WD model, loosen and remove the rear driveaxle/hub nut (see Chapter 8).

10   Remove the rear brake caliper, caliper mounting bracket and brake disc (see Chapter 9).

11   Remove the hub and bearing mounting bolts from the back of the knuckle and remove the hub assembly **(see illustration 12.7)**.

12   Installation is the reverse of removal, noting the following points:

a) *Install a new O-ring.* **Note:** *Apply a little clean engine oil to the seating surface of the hub retaining nut before installing it.*

b) *On models with rear disc brakes, tighten the caliper mounting bolts to the torque listed in the Chapter 9 Specifications.*

c) *Install the wheel and lug nuts. Lower the vehicle and tighten the lug nuts to the torque listed in the Chapter 1 Specifications.*

13 Stabilizer bar and bushings (rear) - removal, inspection and installation

Refer to illustrations 13.2a and 13.2b

1   Loosen the rear wheel lug nuts. Raise the rear of the vehicle and support it securely on jackstands. Block the front wheels to prevent the vehicle from rolling. Remove the rear wheels.

2   Remove the stabilizer bar-to-link nuts and the stabilizer bar-to-body clamp bolts and remove the stabilizer bar **(see illustrations)**.

3   Pull the brackets off the stabilizer bar and inspect the bushings for cracks, hardness and other signs of deterioration. If the bushings are damaged, replace them.

4   Installation is the reverse of removal.

14 Steering wheel - removal and installation

Warning: *These models are equipped with a Supplemental Restraint System (SRS), more commonly known as airbags. Always disable the airbag system before working in the vicinity of any airbag system component to avoid the possibility of accidental deployment of the airbag(s), which could cause personal injury (see Chapter 12).*

Warning: *Do not use a memory saving device to preserve the PCM or radio memory when working on or near airbag system components.*

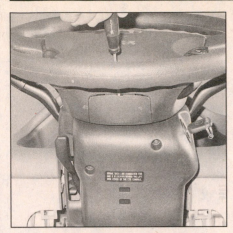

14.2 Remove the panel from the underside of the steering wheel

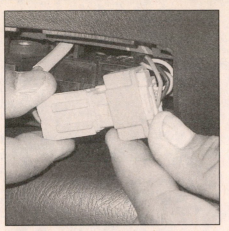

14.3 Disconnect the electrical connector for the airbag module

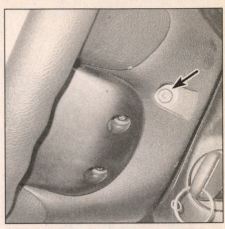

14.4 Remove the airbag fasteners on each side of the steering wheel

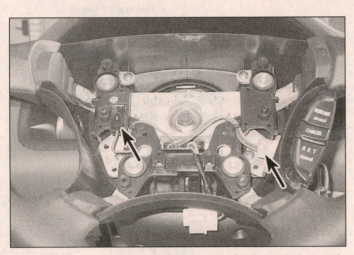

14.6 Disconnect the electrical connectors for the cruise control and horn

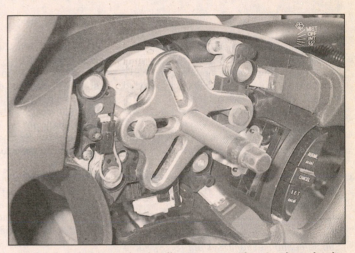

14.8 Use a steering wheel puller to remove the steering wheel

Removal

Refer to illustrations 14.2, 14.3, 14.4, 14.6 and 14.8

1   Make sure the front wheels are pointed straight ahead, then disconnect the cable from the negative terminal of the battery (see Chapter 5). Wait at least three minutes before proceeding.

2   Remove the airbag connector access panel from the bottom of the steering wheel **(see illustration)**.

3   Unplug the airbag module connector **(see illustration)**.

4   On each side of the steering wheel, remove the fasteners retaining the airbag module to the steering wheel **(see illustration)**.

5   Pull off the airbag module, then carefully set it in a safe location. **Warning:** *Carry the airbag module with the trim side facing away from you, and set the steering wheel/ airbag module down with the trim side facing up. Don't place anything on top of the airbag module.*

6   Disconnect the connectors for the horn and the cruise control switch **(see illustration)**.

7   Loosen the steering wheel retaining bolt until about 1/2-inch of threads are showing between the bolt head and the steering wheel.

8   Remove the steering wheel using a steering wheel puller **(see illustration)**. The puller screw must be contacting the steering wheel bolt or shaft. **Caution:** *Don't thread the bolts of the puller into the steering wheel more than five turns, as they could contact the airbag clockspring and damage it.* **Caution:** *While the steering wheel is removed, DO NOT turn the steering shaft. If you do so, the airbag clockspring could be damaged.* Once the steering wheel has been released from the shaft, remove the puller and retaining bolt, make a mark indicating the relationship of the steering wheel hub to the steering shaft, then pull the steering wheel off the shaft.

9   If it is necessary to remove the clockspring, remove the steering column covers (see Chapter 11).

10   Unplug the clockspring electrical connectors, then release the locking tabs and detach it from the column.

Installation

11   With the front wheels pointed straight ahead, make sure that the airbag clockspring is centered with the arrow on the clockspring pointing up. This shouldn't be a problem as long as you have not turned the steering shaft while the wheel was removed. If for some reason the shaft was turned, center the clockspring as follows:

a) *Rotate the clockspring clockwise until it stops.*

b) *Rotate the clockspring counterclockwise about 2-1/2 to 3 turns until the arrow on the clockspring points straight up.*

12   Be sure to align the index mark on the steering wheel hub with the mark on the shaft when you slip the wheel onto the shaft. Make sure the locating pins on the turn signal canceling cam engage the holes in the backside of the steering wheel, and the notches in the steering wheel hub engage the tabs on the turn signal canceling cam. Install a NEW steering wheel bolt and tighten it to the torque listed in this Chapter's Specifications.

15.7 Mark the relationship of the intermediate shaft to the steering gear U-joint (A), then remove the pinch bolt (B)

16.2 Using a back-up wrench to prevent the tie-rod end from turning, loosen the jam nut

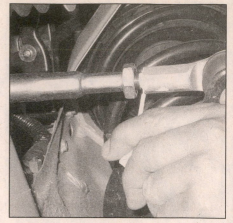

16.3 Back off the jam nut and mark the exposed threads to ensure that the new tie-rod end is threaded on the same number of turns

13   Connect the horn and the cruise control switch connectors.

14   Reattach the airbag module using NEW fasteners and tighten them to the torque listed in this Chapter's Specifications.

15   Plug in the electrical connector for the airbag module.

16   Reconnect the negative battery cable (see Chapter 5).

15   Steering column - removal and installation

Warning: *These models are equipped with a Supplemental Restraint System (SRS), more commonly known as airbags. Always disable the airbag system before working in the vicinity of any airbag system component to avoid the possibility of accidental deployment of the airbag(s), which could cause personal injury (see Chapter 12).*

Warning: *Do not use a memory saving device to preserve the PCM or radio memory when working on or near airbag system components.*

Removal

Refer to illustration 15.7

1   Park the vehicle with the wheels pointing straight ahead. Disconnect the cable from the negative terminal of the battery (see Chapter 5).

2   Adjust the steering wheel tilt to the Neutral position, approximately 8 mm down from the uppermost position.

3   Remove the steering wheel (see Section 14). Prevent the steering shaft from turning. **Caution:** *If this is not done, the airbag clockspring could be damaged.*

4   Remove the steering column covers (see Chapter 11).

5   Remove the clockspring (see Section 14).

6   Remove the steering column switches (see Chapter 12).

7   Mark the relationship of the intermediate shaft to the steering gear U-joint, then remove the pinch bolt **(see illustration).**

8   Remove the steering column mounting fasteners, lower the column and pull it to the rear, making sure nothing is still connected, then remove the column.

Installation

9   Guide the steering column into position, then install the steering column mounting fasteners and tighten them to the torque listed in this Chapter's Specifications.

10   Connect the U-joint to the intermediate shaft. Install the intermediate shaft pinch bolt and nut, tightening it to the torque listed in this Chapter's Specifications.

11   The remainder of installation is the reverse of removal. Reconnect the negative battery cable (see Chapter 5).

16   Tie-rod ends - removal and installation

Removal

Refer to illustrations 16.2, 16.3 and 16.4

1   Loosen the wheel lug nuts, raise the front of the vehicle and support it securely on jackstands. Apply the parking brake and block the rear wheels to keep the vehicle from rolling off the jackstands. Remove the wheel.

2   Loosen the tie-rod end jam nut **(see illustration).**

3   Mark the relationship of the tie-rod end to the threaded portion of the tie-rod. This will ensure the toe-in setting is restored when reassembled **(see illustration).**

4   Remove the cotter pin and loosen the nut from the tie-rod end ballstud a few turns. Disconnect the tie-rod end ballstud from the steering arm with a puller **(see illustration).**

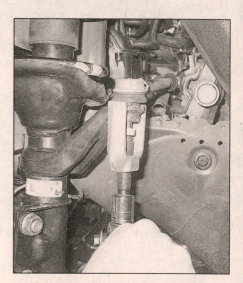

16.4 Use a two-jaw puller or balljoint separator to push the tie-rod end out of the steering arm

5   Remove the nut from the ballstud, separate the tie-rod end from the steering knuckle, then unscrew the tie-rod end from the tie-rod.

Installation

6   Thread the tie-rod end onto the tie-rod to the marked position and connect the tie-rod end to the steering arm. Install the nut on the ballstud and tighten it to the torque listed in this Chapter's Specifications. Install a new cotter pin. **Note:** *If necessary, tighten the nut a little more to allow insertion of the cotter pin. Never loosen the nut to align the cotter pin holes.*

7   Tighten the jam nut securely and install the wheel. Lower the vehicle and tighten the lug nuts to the torque listed in the Chapter 1 Specifications.

8   Have the front end alignment checked and, if necessary, adjusted.

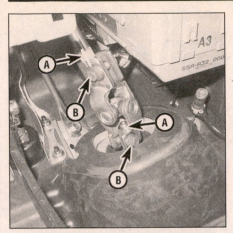

17.3 Mark the relationship of the intermediate shaft and the steering gear output shaft to the steering gear U-joint (A), then remove the pinch bolts (B)

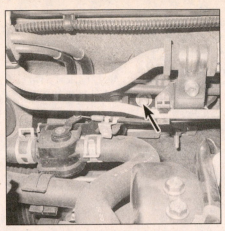

17.5 Remove the fastener securing the clamp and release the heater valve from the firewall

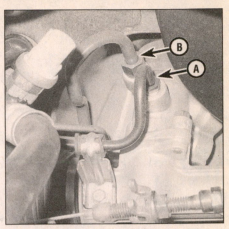

17.6 Disconnect the pressure (A) and return (B) lines from the steering gear (Sedan model shown, other models similar)

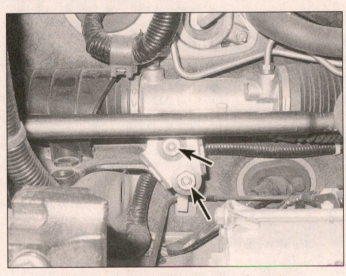

17.9a Remove the steering gear mounting nuts . . .

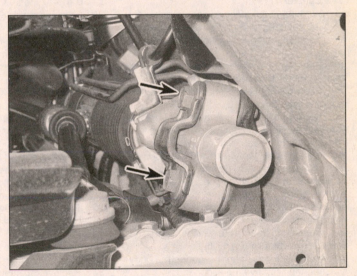

17.9b . . . and bolts

17 Steering gear - removal and installation

Warning: *Make sure the steering shaft is not turned while the steering gear is removed or you could damage the clockspring for the airbag system. To prevent the shaft from turning, place the ignition key in the lock position or thread the seat belt through the steering wheel and clip it into place.*

Removal

1 Park the vehicle with the front wheels pointing straight ahead. Loosen the front wheel lug nuts, raise the front of the vehicle and support it securely on jackstands. Apply the parking brake and remove the wheels.
2 Disconnect the cable from the negative terminal of the battery (see Chapter 5).

Hydraulic power steering

Refer to illustrations 17.3, 17.5, 17.6, 17.9a and 17.9b

3 Mark the relationship of the universal joint to the steering gear input shaft and the intermediate shaft. Remove the universal joint pinch bolts and separate the shafts from the joint **(see illustration)**.
4 Remove the air filter housing assembly (see Chapter 4).
5 Separate the heater valve from the firewall **(see illustration)**.
6 Place a drain pan under the steering gear. Detach the power steering pressure and return lines **(see illustration)** and cap the ends to prevent excessive fluid loss and contamination.
7 Separate the tie-rod ends from the steering arms (see Section 16).
8 Disconnect the pressure line clamp and

engine harness from the steering gear.
9 Remove the steering gear mounting nuts and bolts **(see illustrations)**, then pull on the steering gear to release it from the right-side mounting stud.
10 Remove the bolts securing the right-side bracket, then remove the bracket.
11 Lower the steering gearbox, then rotate the steering gear so that the input shaft is pointing upward. Carefully guide the steering gear assembly through the right wheel opening and remove it from the vehicle.

Electric Power Steering (EPS)

2005 and earlier models

12 Mark the relationship of the universal joint to the steering gear input shaft and the intermediate shaft. Remove the universal joint pinch bolts and separate the shafts from the joint **(see illustration 17.3)**.

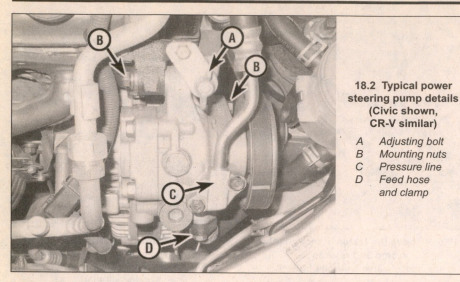

18.2 Typical power steering pump details (Civic shown, CR-V similar)

A   Adjusting bolt
B   Mounting nuts
C   Pressure line
D   Feed hose and clamp

13   Remove the air filter housing assembly (see Chapter 4).
14   Working at the steering gear, remove the bracket securing the power steering motor electrical connector, then disconnect the connector.
15   Remove the fasteners securing the power steering motor, then remove the motor.
16   Separate the tie-rod ends from the steering arms (see Section 16).
17   Remove the exhaust heat shield from the floor pan and let it rest on the exhaust pipe.
18   Disconnect the electrical connector for the steering gear, then separate the connector mounting bracket. Remove the ground connection at the steering gear.
19   Working in the engine compartment, separate the engine wire harness from the mounting brackets securing it to the firewall.
20   Separate the heater valve from the firewall **(see illustration 17.5)**.
21   Remove the fasteners securing the body stiffener, then remove the stiffener.
22   Remove the steering gear mounting nuts and bolts, then pull on the steering gear to release it from the right-side mounting stud.
23   Lower the steering gearbox, then rotate the steering gear so that the input shaft is pointing upward. Carefully guide the steering gear assembly through the right wheel opening, then raise the left side of the steering gear up through the engine compartment and remove it from the vehicle.

2006 and later models

24   Mark the relationship of the universal joint to the steering gear input shaft and the intermediate shaft. Remove the universal joint pinch bolts and separate the shafts from the joint **(see illustration 17.3)**.
25   Remove the steering wheel and driver's side airbag (see Section 14).
26   Adjust the steering column to the full tilt position (down). Insert a piece of wire from the top steering yoke to the bottom and wire the two together to prevent the slider shaft from pulling out.
27   Raise the column, lock the tilt lever and remove the lower joint bolt.

28   Separate the lower steering joint from the steering gear shaft.
29   Remove the air cleaner and mounting bracket (see Chapter 4).
30   Separate the tie-rod ends from the steering arms (see Section 16).
31   Remove the exhaust heat shield from the floor pan and let it rest on the exhaust pipe.
32   Disconnect the electrical connector for the steering gear, then separate the connector mounting bracket. Remove the ground connection at the steering gear.
33   Working in the engine compartment, separate the engine wire harness from the mounting brackets securing it to the firewall.
34   Support the engine using an engine holding fixture or equivalent (see Chapter 2C).
35   Remove the lower balljoint mounting nuts/bolts and separate the control arm (see Section 5).
36   On 2.0L engines, remove the exhaust hangers.
37   Remove the subframe (see Section 20).
38   Remove the steering gear mounting nuts and bolts, and electrical harness clips.
39   Lower the steering gearbox, then rotate the steering gear down and remove it from the vehicle.
40   Disconnect the electrical connectors to the EPS motor.
41   Remove the EPS motor mounting fasteners and remove the motor and O-ring.

Installation

42   Installation is the reverse of removal, noting the following points:

a) *Raise the steering gear into position and connect the U-joint, aligning the marks.*
b) *Install the mounting bolts and nuts and tighten them to the torque listed in this Chapter's Specifications.*
c) *Install the U-joint pinch bolts and tighten them to the torque listed in this Chapter's Specifications.*
d) *If you're working on an EPS model, be sure to use a new O-ring when installing the power steering motor.*

e) *Install the wheels and lug nuts. Lower the vehicle, then tighten the lug nuts to the torque listed in the Chapter 1 Specifications.*
f) *If you're working on a hydraulic power steering model, fill the power steering pump reservoir with the recommended fluid (see Chapter 1), then bleed the steering system (see Section 19).*
g) *Have the front wheel alignment checked and, if necessary, adjusted.*

18   Power steering pump - removal and installation

Refer to illustration 18.2

1   Disconnect the cable from the negative battery terminal (see Chapter 5).
2   Clamp the power steering feed hose shut so fluid loss will be minimized when the hose is disconnected, then disconnect the fluid hoses at the pump **(see illustration)**. Note the difference between the pressure and the return hoses; the return hose is held to the pump with a spring type clamp, and the pressure line has two bolts holding it to the pump body. Cap or plug both hoses to prevent leakage or contamination. Install a new O-ring on the end of the pressure line.
3   Remove the pump adjusting bolt.
4   Remove the pump mounting nuts/bolts and remove the pump from the engine.
5   Installation is the reverse of removal. Be sure to adjust the drivebelt tension (see Chapter 1) and bleed the power steering system (see Section 19).

19   Power steering system - bleeding

1   The power steering system must be bled whenever a line has been disconnected. Bubbles can be seen in power steering fluid that has air in it and the fluid will often have a frothy or milky appearance. Low fluid level can cause air to mix with the fluid, resulting in a noisy pump as well as foaming of the fluid.
2   Open the hood and check the fluid level in the reservoir, adding the specified fluid necessary to bring it up to the proper level (see Chapter 1).
3   Start the engine and slowly turn the steering wheel several times from left-to-right and back again. Do not turn the wheel completely from lock-to-lock. Check the fluid level, topping it up as necessary until it remains steady and no more bubbles are visible.

20   Subframe - removal and installation

Warning: *The manufacturer recommends replacing the subframe bolts with new ones whenever they are removed.*

Removal

Refer to illustration 20.12

1   Disconnect the cable from the negative battery terminal (see Chapter 5).

2   Loosen the front wheel lug nuts, raise the front of the vehicle and support it securely on jackstands. Remove both front wheels. **Note:** *The jackstands must be behind the front suspension subframe, not supporting the vehicle by the subframe.*

3   Remove the engine splash shield (see Chapter 2A).

4   Remove the exhaust pipe from the exhaust manifold to the catalytic converter (see Chapter 6).

5   Disconnect the stabilizer bar links from the control arms (see Section 2).

6   Disconnect the control arms from the steering knuckles (see Section 5).

7   On automatic transaxle models, disconnect the shift control cable from the transaxle (see Chapter 7B).

8   Carefully mark the position of the subframe in relation to the vehicle chassis.

9   Using two floor jacks, support the subframe. Position one jack on each side of the subframe, midway between the front and rear mounting points.

10   Attach an engine support fixture or a hoist to the engine with a lengths of heavy-duty chain. If the engine is equipped with lifting brackets, use them. If not, you'll have to fasten the chain to some substantial part of the engine - one that is strong enough to take the weight, but in a location that will provide good balance. If you're attaching the chain to a stud on the engine, or are using a bolt passing through the chain and into a threaded hole, place a washer between the nut or bolt head and the chain, and tighten the nut or bolt securely. Take up the slack in the chain, but don't lift the engine. **Warning:** *DO NOT place any part of your body under the engine when it's supported only by a hoist or other lifting device.*

11   Remove the engine mount and the transaxle mount (see Chapter 2A or 2B).

12   Make alignment marks from each corner of the subframe to the vehicle body. With the jacks sufficiently supporting the subframe, remove the subframe-to-chassis mounting bolts **(see illustration)**.

13   Lower the jacks until the subframe is resting on the ground.

Installation

14   Installation is the reverse of removal, noting the following points:

   a) *Replace the subframe bolts with new ones. Align the reference marks on the subframe then tighten the subframe mounting bolts to the torque listed in this Chapter's Specifications.*

   b) *Reconnect the negative battery cable (see Chapter 5).*

   c) *Have the front end alignment checked and, if necessary, adjusted.*

20.12 Subframe details (Coupe and Sedan models shown, CR-V and Hatchback similar)

A   *Subframe main bolts*

B   *Subframe mid-bracket bolts (not visible)*

C   *Alignment reference holes*

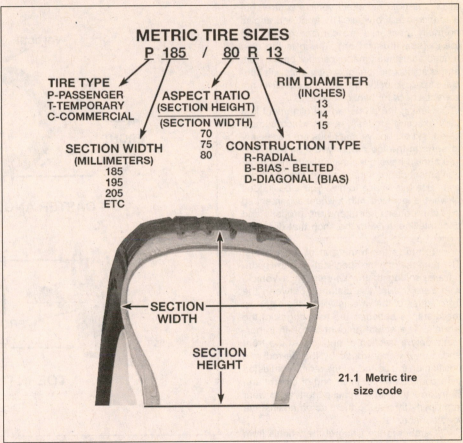

METRIC TIRE SIZES

P 185 / 80 R 13

TIRE TYPE
P-PASSENGER
T-TEMPORARY
C-COMMERCIAL

ASPECT RATIO (SECTION HEIGHT) / (SECTION WIDTH)
70
75
80

RIM DIAMETER (INCHES)
13
14
15

SECTION WIDTH (MILLIMETERS)
185
195
205
ETC

CONSTRUCTION TYPE
R-RADIAL
B-BIAS - BELTED
D-DIAGONAL (BIAS)

SECTION WIDTH

SECTION HEIGHT

21.1 Metric tire size code

21 Wheels and tires - general information

Refer to illustration 21.1

1   All vehicles covered by this manual are equipped with metric-sized fiberglass or steel belted radial tires **(see illustration)**. Use of other size or type of tires may affect the ride and handling of the vehicle. Don't mix different types of tires, such as radials and bias belted, on the same vehicle as handling may be seriously affected. It's recommended that tires be replaced in pairs on the same axle, but if only one tire is being replaced, be sure it's the same size, structure and tread design as the other.

2   Because tire pressure has a substantial effect on handling and wear, the pressure on all tires should be checked at least once a month or before any extended trips (see Chapter 1).

3   Wheels must be replaced if they are bent, dented, leak air, have elongated bolt holes, are heavily rusted, out of vertical symmetry or if the lug nuts won't stay tight. Wheel repairs that use welding or peening are not recommended.

4   Tire and wheel balance is important in the overall handling, braking and performance of the vehicle. Unbalanced wheels can adversely affect handling and ride characteristics as well as tire life. Whenever a tire is installed on a wheel, the tire and wheel should be balanced by a shop with the proper equipment.

22   Wheel alignment - general information

Refer to illustration 22.1

A wheel alignment refers to the adjustments made to the wheels so they are in proper angular relationship to the suspension and the ground. Wheels that are out of proper alignment not only affect vehicle control, but also increase tire wear. The front end angles normally measured are camber, caster and toe-in **(see illustration)**. Toe-in is the only routine adjustment made; camber on the front end is adjustable, but only after installing special strut-to-knuckle bolts. If the caster is not correct, check for bent components.

Getting the proper wheel alignment is a very exacting process, one in which complicated and expensive machines are necessary to perform the job properly. Because of this, you should have a technician with the proper equipment perform these tasks. We will, however, use this space to give you a basic idea of what is involved with a wheel alignment so you can better understand the process and deal intelligently with the shop that does the work.

Toe-in is the turning in of the wheels. The purpose of a toe specification is to ensure parallel rolling of the wheels. In a vehicle with zero toe-in, the distance between the front edges of the wheels will be the same as the distance between the rear edges of the wheels. The actual amount of toe-in is normally only a fraction of an inch. At the front end, toe-in is controlled by the tie-rod end position on the tie-rod. At the rear, it's adjusted by a cam bolt at the inner end of control arm B. Incorrect toe-in will cause the tires to wear improperly by making them scrub against the road surface.

Camber is the tilting of the wheels from vertical when viewed from one end of the vehicle. When the wheels tilt out at the top, the camber is said to be positive (+). When the wheels tilt in at the top the camber is negative (-). The amount of tilt is measured in degrees from vertical and this measurement is called the camber angle. This angle affects the amount of tire tread which contacts the road and compensates for changes in the suspension geometry when the vehicle is cornering or traveling over an undulating surface. On the front end it is adjusted using special

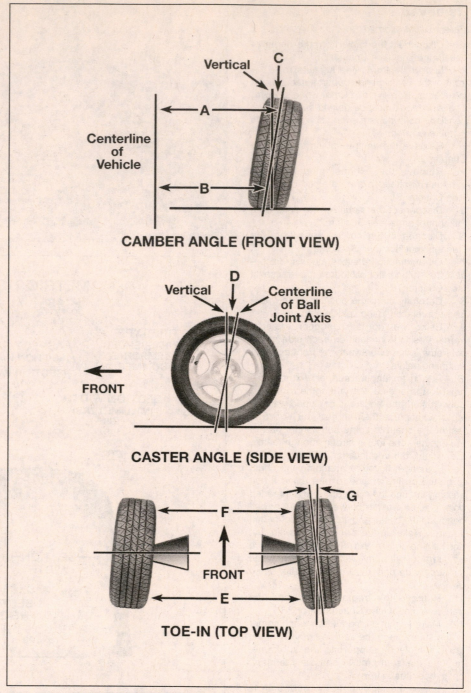

22.1 Camber, caster and toe-in angles

A minus B = C (degrees camber)
D = degrees caster

E minus F = toe-in (measured in inches)
G = toe-in (expressed in degrees)

camber adjusting bolts, which alter the relationship between the strut and the steering knuckle. At the rear end camber is not adjustable.

Caster is the tilting of the front steering axis from vertical. A tilt toward the rear is positive caster and a tilt toward the front is negative caster.

Chapter 11 Body

Contents

	Section
Body repair - major damage	4
Body repair - minor damage	3
Bumper covers - removal and installation	10
Center console - removal and installation	24
Cowl cover - removal and installation	12
Dashboard trim panels - removal and installation	25
Door - removal, installation and adjustment	19
Door latch, lock cylinder and handles - removal and installation	20
Door trim panels - removal and installation	18
Door window glass - removal and installation	21
Door window glass regulator - removal and installation	22
Fastener and trim removal	6
Front fender - removal and installation	11
General information	1
Hood - removal, installation and adjustment	7
Hood latch and cable - removal and installation	8
Instrument panel - removal and installation	27
Liftgate (hatchback models) - removal, installation and adjustment	14
Liftgate handle, latch and lock cylinder (hatchback models) - removal and installation	13
Mirrors - removal and installation	23
Radiator grille - removal and installation	9
Rear shelf trim panel - removal and installation	32
Rear tailgate glass and support struts (CR-V models) - removal, installation and adjustment	31
Repair minor paint scratches	2
Seats - removal and installation	28
Steering column covers - removal and installation	26
Tailgate/liftgate and assist strut (CR-V models) - removal, installation and adjustment	30
Tailgate latch, lock cylinder and handle (CR-V models) - removal and installation	29
Trunk lid (coupe and sedan models) - removal, installation and adjustment	16
Trunk lid latch and lock cylinder (coupe and sedan models) - removal and installation	15
Trunk release lever and fuel door cables - removal and installation	17
Upholstery, carpets and vinyl trim - maintenance	5

1   General information

Warning: *The models covered by this manual are equipped with Supplemental Restraint Systems (SRS), more commonly known as airbags. Always disable the airbag system before working in the vicinity of any airbag system components to avoid the possibility of accidental deployment of the airbags, which could cause personal injury (see Chapter 12).*

Certain body components are particularly vulnerable to accident damage and can be unbolted and repaired or replaced. Among these parts are the hood, doors, tailgate, liftgate, bumpers and front fenders.

Only general body maintenance practices and body panel repair procedures within the scope of the do-it-yourselfer are included in this Chapter.

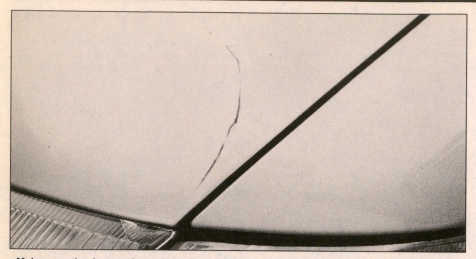

Make sure the damaged area is perfectly clean and rust free. If the touch-up kit has a wire brush, use it to clean the scratch or chip. Or use fine steel wool wrapped around the end of a pencil. Clean the scratched or chipped surface only, not the good paint surrounding it. Rinse the area with water and allow it to dry thoroughly

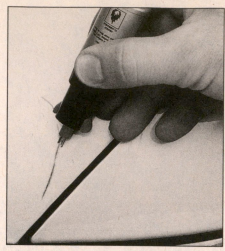

Thoroughly mix the paint, then apply a small amount with the touch-up kit brush or a very fine artist's brush. Brush in one direction as you fill the scratch area. Do not build up the paint higher than the surrounding paint

2   Repair minor paint scratches

No matter how hard you try to keep your vehicle looking like new, it will inevitably be scratched, chipped or dented at some point. If the metal is actually dented, seek the advice of a professional. But you can fix minor scratches and chips yourself. Buy a touch-up paint kit from a dealer service department or an auto parts store. To ensure that you get the right color, you'll need to have the specific make, model and year of your vehicle and, ideally, the paint code, which is located on a special metal plate under the hood or in the door jamb.

3   Body repair - minor damage

Plastic body panels

The following repair procedures are for minor scratches and gouges. Repair of more serious damage should be left to a dealer service department or qualified auto body shop. Below is a list of the equipment and materials necessary to perform the following repair procedures on plastic body panels.

Wax, grease and silicone removing solvent
Cloth-backed body tape
Sanding discs
Drill motor with three-inch disc holder
Hand sanding block
Rubber squeegees
Sandpaper
Non-porous mixing palette
Wood paddle or putty knife
Curved-tooth body file
Flexible parts repair material

Flexible panels (bumper trim)

1   Remove the damaged panel, if necessary or desirable. In most cases, repairs can be car-

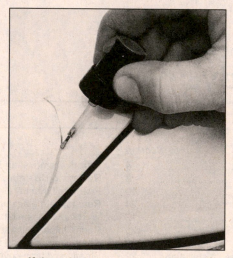

If the vehicle has a two-coat finish, apply the clear coat after the color coat has dried

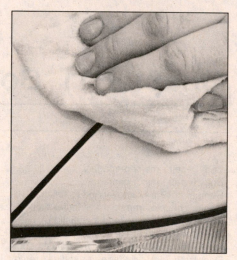

Wait a few days for the paint to dry thoroughly, then rub out the repainted area with a polishing compound to blend the new paint with the surrounding area. When you're happy with your work, wash and polish the area

ried out with the panel installed.
2   Clean the area(s) to be repaired with a wax, grease and silicone removing solvent applied with a water-dampened cloth.
3   If the damage is structural, that is, if it extends through the panel, clean the backside of the panel area to be repaired as well. Wipe dry.
4   Sand the rear surface about 1-1/2 inches beyond the break.
5   Cut two pieces of fiberglass cloth large enough to overlap the break by about 1-1/2 inches. Cut only to the required length.
6   Mix the adhesive from the repair kit according to the instructions included with the kit, and apply a layer of the mixture approximately 1/8-inch thick on the backside of the panel. Overlap the break by at least 1-1/2 inches.
7   Apply one piece of fiberglass cloth to the adhesive and cover the cloth with additional adhesive. Apply a second piece of fiberglass

cloth to the adhesive and immediately cover the cloth with additional adhesive in sufficient quantity to fill the weave.
8   Allow the repair to cure for 20 to 30 minutes at 60-degrees to 80-degrees F.
9   If necessary, trim the excess repair material at the edge.
10   Remove all of the paint film over and around the area(s) to be repaired. The repair material should not overlap the painted surface.
11   With a drill motor and a sanding disc (or a rotary file), cut a "V" along the break line approximately 1/2-inch wide. Remove all dust and loose particles from the repair area.
12   Mix and apply the repair material. Apply a light coat first over the damaged area; then continue applying material until it reaches a level

slightly higher than the surrounding finish.

13   Cure the mixture for 20 to 30 minutes at 60-degrees to 80-degrees F.

14   Roughly establish the contour of the area being repaired with a body file. If low areas or pits remain, mix and apply additional adhesive.

15   Block sand the damaged area with sandpaper to establish the actual contour of the surrounding surface.

16   If desired, the repaired area can be temporarily protected with several light coats of primer. Because of the special paints and techniques required for flexible body panels, it is recommended that the vehicle be taken to a paint shop for completion of the body repair.

Steel body panels

See photo sequence

Repair of dents

17   When repairing dents, the first job is to pull the dent out until the affected area is as close as possible to its original shape. There is no point in trying to restore the original shape completely as the metal in the damaged area will have stretched on impact and cannot be restored to its original contours. It is better to bring the level of the dent up to a point that is about 1/8-inch below the level of the surrounding metal. In cases where the dent is very shallow, it is not worth trying to pull it out at all.

18   If the backside of the dent is accessible, it can be hammered out gently from behind using a soft-face hammer. While doing this, hold a block of wood firmly against the opposite side of the metal to absorb the hammer blows and prevent the metal from being stretched.

19   If the dent is in a section of the body which has double layers, or some other factor makes it inaccessible from behind, a different technique is required. Drill several small holes through the metal inside the damaged area, particularly in the deeper sections. Screw long, self-tapping screws into the holes just enough for them to get a good grip in the metal. Now pulling on the protruding heads of the screws with locking pliers can pull out the dent.

20   The next stage of repair is the removal of paint from the damaged area and from an inch or so of the surrounding metal. This is easily done with a wire brush or sanding disk in a drill motor, although it can be done just as effectively by hand with sandpaper. To complete the preparation for filling, score the surface of the bare metal with a screwdriver or the tang of a file or drill small holes in the affected area. This will provide a good grip for the filler material. To complete the repair, see the Section on filling and painting.

Repair of rust holes or gashes

21   Remove all paint from the affected area and from an inch or so of the surrounding metal using a sanding disk or wire brush mounted in a drill motor. If these are not available, a few sheets of sandpaper will do the job just as effectively.

22   With the paint removed, you will be able to determine the severity of the corrosion and

decide whether to replace the whole panel, if possible, or repair the affected area. New body panels are not as expensive as most people think and it is often quicker to install a new panel than to repair large areas of rust.

23   Remove all trim pieces from the affected area except those which will act as a guide to the original shape of the damaged body, such as headlight shells, etc. Using metal snips or a hacksaw blade, remove all loose metal and any other metal that is badly affected by rust. Hammer the edges of the hole in to create a slight depression for the filler material.

24   Wire-brush the affected area to remove the powdery rust from the surface of the metal. If the back of the rusted area is accessible, treat it with rust inhibiting paint.

25   Before filling is done, block the hole in some way. This can be done with sheet metal riveted or screwed into place, or by stuffing the hole with wire mesh.

26   Once the hole is blocked off, the affected area can be filled and painted. See the following subsection on filling and painting.

Filling and painting

27   Many types of body fillers are available, but generally speaking, body repair kits which contain filler paste and a tube of resin hardener are best for this type of repair work. A wide, flexible plastic or nylon applicator will be necessary for imparting a smooth and contoured finish to the surface of the filler material. Mix up a small amount of filler on a clean piece of wood or cardboard (use the hardener sparingly). Follow the manufacturer's instructions on the package, otherwise the filler will set incorrectly.

28   Using the applicator, apply the filler paste to the prepared area. Draw the applicator across the surface of the filler to achieve the desired contour and to level the filler surface. As soon as a contour that approximates the original one is achieved, stop working the paste. If you continue, the paste will begin to stick to the applicator. Continue to add thin layers of paste at 20-minute intervals until the level of the filler is just above the surrounding metal.

29   Once the filler has hardened, the excess can be removed with a body file. From then on, progressively finer grades of sandpaper should be used, starting with a 180-grit paper and finishing with 600-grit wet-or-dry paper. Always wrap the sandpaper around a flat rubber or wooden block, otherwise the surface of the filler will not be completely flat. During the sanding of the filler surface, the wet-or-dry paper should be periodically rinsed in water. This will ensure that a very smooth finish is produced in the final stage.

30   At this point, the repair area should be surrounded by a ring of bare metal, which in turn should be encircled by the finely feathered edge of good paint. Rinse the repair area with clean water until all of the dust produced by the sanding operation is gone.

31   Spray the entire area with a light coat of primer. This will reveal any imperfections in the surface of the filler. Repair the imperfections with

fresh filler paste or glaze filler and once more smooth the surface with sandpaper. Repeat this spray-and-repair procedure until you are satisfied that the surface of the filler and the feathered edge of the paint are perfect. Rinse the area with clean water and allow it to dry completely.

32   The repair area is now ready for painting. Spray painting must be carried out in a warm, dry, windless and dust free atmosphere. These conditions can be created if you have access to a large indoor work area, but if you are forced to work in the open, you will have to pick the day very carefully. If you are working indoors, dousing the floor in the work area with water will help settle the dust that would otherwise be in the air. If the repair area is confined to one body panel, mask off the surrounding panels. This will help minimize the effects of a slight mismatch in paint color. Trim pieces such as chrome strips, door handles, etc., will also need to be masked off or removed. Use masking tape and several thickness of newspaper for the masking operations.

33   Before spraying, shake the paint can thoroughly, then spray a test area until the spray painting technique is mastered. Cover the repair area with a thick coat of primer. The thickness should be built up using several thin layers of primer rather than one thick one. Using 600-grit wet-or-dry sandpaper, rub down the surface of the primer until it is very smooth. While doing this, the work area should be thoroughly rinsed with water and the wet-or-dry sandpaper periodically rinsed as well. Allow the primer to dry before spraying additional coats.

34   Spray on the top coat, again building up the thickness by using several thin layers of paint. Begin spraying in the center of the repair area and then, using a circular motion, work out until the whole repair area and about two inches of the surrounding original paint is covered. Remove all masking material 10 to 15 minutes after spraying on the final coat of paint. Allow the new paint at least two weeks to harden, then use a very fine rubbing compound to blend the edges of the new paint into the existing paint. Finally, apply a coat of wax

4   Body repair - major damage

1   Major damage must be repaired by an auto body shop specifically equipped to perform body and frame repairs. These shops have the specialized equipment required to do the job properly.

2   If the damage is extensive, the frame must be checked for proper alignment or the vehicle's handling characteristics may be adversely affected and other components may wear at an accelerated rate.

3   Due to the fact that all of the major body components (hood, fenders, etc.) are separate and replaceable units, any seriously damaged components should be replaced rather than repaired. Sometimes the components can be found in a wrecking yard that specializes in used vehicle components, often at considerable savings over the cost of new parts.

These photos illustrate a method of repairing simple dents. They are intended to supplement *Body repair - minor damage* in this Chapter and should not be used as the sole instructions for body repair on these vehicles.

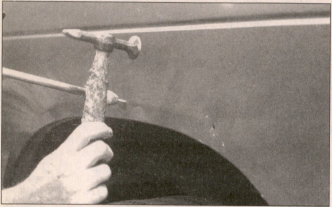

1 If you can't access the backside of the body panel to hammer out the dent, pull it out with a slide-hammer-type dent puller. Tap with a hammer near the edge of the dent to help 'pop' the metal back to its original shape, about 1/8-inch below the surface of the surrounding metal

2 Using coarse-grit sandpaper, remove the paint down to the bare metal. Clean the repair area with wax/silicone remover.

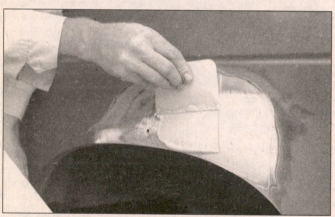

3 Following label instructions, mix up a batch of plastic filler and hardener, then quickly press it into the metal with a plastic applicator. Work the filler until it matches the original contour and is slightly above the surrounding metal

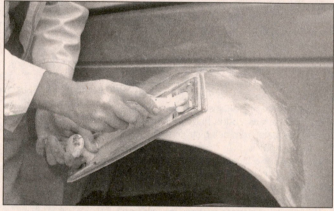

4 Let the filler harden until you can just dent it with your fingernail. File, then sand the filler down until it's smooth and even. Work down to finer grits of sandpaper - always using a board or block - ending up with 360 or 400 grit

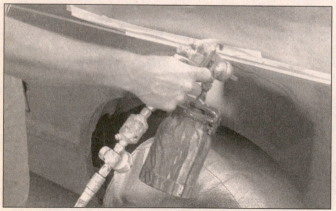

5 When the area is smooth to the touch, clean the area and mask around it. Apply several layers of primer to the area. A professional-type spray gun is being used here, but aerosol spray primer works fine

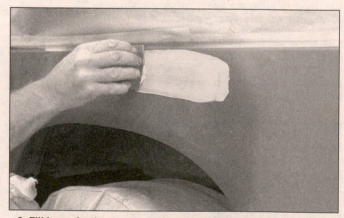

6 Fill imperfections or scratches with glazing compound. Sand with 360 or 400-grit and re-spray. Finish sand the primer with 600 grit, clean thoroughly, then apply the finish coat. Don't attempt to rub out or wax the repair area until the paint has dried completely (at least two weeks)

5 Upholstery, carpets and vinyl trim - maintenance

Upholstery and carpets

1 Every three months remove the floor-mats and clean the interior of the vehicle (more frequently if necessary). Use a stiff whiskbroom to brush the carpeting and loosen dirt and dust, then vacuum the upholstery and carpets thoroughly, especially along seams and crevices.

2 Dirt and stains can be removed from carpeting with basic household or automotive carpet shampoos available in spray cans. Follow the directions and vacuum again, then use a stiff brush to bring back the "nap" of the carpet.

3 Most interiors have cloth or vinyl upholstery, either of which can be cleaned and maintained with a number of material-specific cleaners or shampoos available in auto supply stores. Follow the directions on the product for usage, and always spot-test any upholstery cleaner on an inconspicuous area (bottom edge of a backseat cushion) to ensure that it doesn't cause a color shift in the material.

4 After cleaning, vinyl upholstery should be treated with a protectant. **Note:** *Make sure the protectant container indicates the product can be used on seats - some products may make a seat too slippery.* **Caution:** *Do not use protectant on vinyl-covered steering wheels.*

5 Leather upholstery requires special care. It should be cleaned regularly with saddle-soap or leather cleaner. Never use alcohol, gasoline, nail polish remover or thinner to clean leather upholstery.

6 After cleaning, regularly treat leather upholstery with a leather conditioner, rubbed in with a soft cotton cloth. Never use car wax on leather upholstery.

7 In areas where the interior of the vehicle is subject to bright sunlight, cover leather seating areas of the seats with a sheet if the vehicle is to be left out for any length of time.

Vinyl trim

8 Don't clean vinyl trim with detergents, caustic soap or petroleum-based cleaners. Plain soap and water works just fine, with a soft brush to clean dirt that may be ingrained. Wash the vinyl as frequently as the rest of the vehicle.

9 After cleaning, application of a high-quality rubber and vinyl protectant will help prevent oxidation and cracks. The protectant can also be applied to weather-stripping, vacuum lines and rubber hoses, which often fail as a result of chemical degradation, and to the tires.

6 Fastener and trim removal

Refer to illustration 6.4

1 There is a variety of plastic fasteners used to hold trim panels, splash shields and other parts in place in addition to typical screws, nuts and bolts. Once you are familiar with them, they can usually be removed without too much difficulty.

2 The proper tools and approach can prevent added time and expense to a project by minimizing the number of broken fasteners and/or parts.

3 The following illustration shows various types of fasteners that are typically used on most vehicles and how to remove and install them **(see illustration)**. Replacement fasteners are commonly found at most auto parts stores, if necessary.

Fasteners

This tool is designed to remove special fasteners. A small pry tool used for removing nails will also work well in place of this tool

A Phillips head screwdriver can be used to release the center portion, but light pressure must be used because the plastic is easily damaged. Once the center is up, the fastener can easily be pried from its hole

Here is a view with the center portion fully released. Install the fastener as shown, then press the center in to set it

This fastener is used for exterior panels and shields. The center portion must be pried up to release the fastener. Install the fastener with the center up, then press the center in to set it

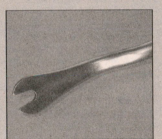

This type of fastener is used commonly for interior panels. Use a small blunt tool to press the small pin at the center in to release it . . .

. . . the pin will stay with the fastener in the released position

Reset the fastener for installation by moving the pin out. Install the fastener, then press the pin flush with the fastener to set it

This fastener is used for exterior and interior panels. It has no moving parts. Simply pry the fastener from its hole like the claw of a hammer removes a nail. Without a tool that can get under the top of the fastener, it can be very difficult to remove

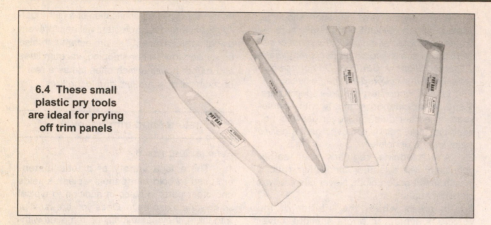

6.4 These small plastic pry tools are ideal for prying off trim panels

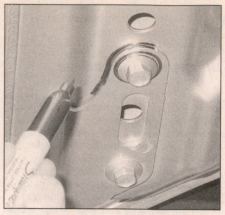

7.2 Scribe or draw alignment marks around the bolt heads and the hood hinges to ensure proper alignment of the hood when it's reinstalled

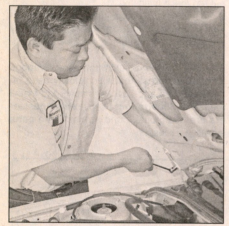

7.4 Support the hood with your shoulder while removing the hood bolts

4   Trim panels are typically made of plastic and their flexibility can help during removal. The key to their removal is to use a tool to pry the panel near its retainers to release it without damaging surrounding areas or breaking-off any retainers. The retainers will usually snap out of their designated slot or hole after force is applied to them. Stiff plastic tools designed for prying on trim panels are available at most auto parts stores **(see**

illustration). Tools that are tapered and wrapped in protective tape, such as a screwdriver or small pry tool, are also very effective when used with care.

---

7   Hood - removal, installation and adjustment

Removal and installation

Refer to illustrations 7.2 and 7.4
Note: *The hood is heavy and somewhat awkward to remove and install - at least two people should perform this procedure.*
1   Use blankets or pads to cover the fenders and cowl areas. This will protect the body and paint as the hood is lifted off.
2   Scribe or draw alignment marks around the bolt heads to ensure proper alignment during installation **(see illustration)**.
3   Disconnect any cables or wire harnesses, which will interfere with removal.
4   Have an assistant support one side of the hood. Take turns removing the hinge-to-hood bolts and lift off the hood **(see illustration)**.
5   Lift off the hood.
6   Installation is the reverse of removal. If you position the hood so that the hinges fit within the scribe marks you made before loosening the bolts, in the same location they were

in prior to removal, then the hood should still be aligned. Of course, if you're installing a new hood, or forgot to scribe the hinge positions, then you'll need to readjust the hood position.

Adjustment

Refer to illustrations 7.8, 7.10 and 7.11
7   You can adjust the hood fore-and-aft and right-and-left by means of the elongated holes in the hinges.
8   Scribe a line around the entire hinge plate so you can judge the amount of movement. On 2006 and later Civic and 2007 and later CR-V models, remove the fender trim, front grille cover (see Section 9) and cowl cover (see Section 12) **(see illustration)**.
9   Loosen the bolts and move the hood into correct alignment. Move it only a little at a time. Tighten the hinge bolts or nuts and carefully lower the hood to check the alignment.
10   If necessary after installation, the entire hood latch assembly can be adjusted up-and-down as well as from side-to-side on the upper radiator support so the hood closes securely and is flush with the fenders **(see illustration)**. To do this, scribe a line around

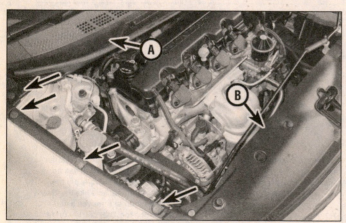

7.8 On 2006 and later Civic and 2007 and later CR-V models, remove the cowl cover (A), front grille cover (B), fender trim fasteners and both fender trim pieces

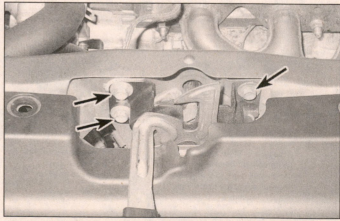

7.10 Scribe a line around the hood latch so you can judge the movement, then loosen the bolts and adjust the latch position

7.11 To adjust the vertical height of the leading edge of the hood so it's flush with the fenders, turn each edge cushion clockwise (to lower the hood) or counterclockwise (to raise the hood)

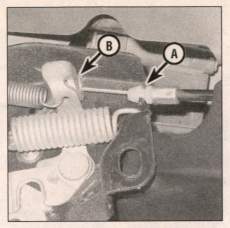

8.2 Detach the cable (A) then unhook the end from the latch (B)

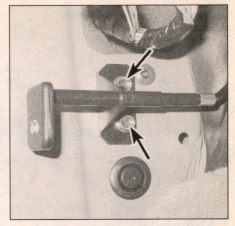

8.6 Remove the release lever bolts and detach the cable and lever

the hood latch mounting bolts to provide a reference point. Then loosen the bolts and reposition the latch assembly as necessary. Following adjustment, retighten the mounting bolts.

11   Adjust the vertical height of the leading edge of the hood by screwing the edge cushions in or out so that the hood, when closed, is flush with the fenders **(see illustration)**.

12   The hood latch assembly, as well as the hinges, should be periodically lubricated with white lithium-base grease to prevent sticking and wear.

8   Hood latch and cable - removal and installation

Latch

Refer to illustration 8.2

1   Remove the radiator grille opening cover (if equipped), then scribe a line around the latch to aid alignment when installing, detach the latch retaining bolts from the radiator support **(see illustration 7.10)** and remove the latch.

2   Disconnect the hood release cable by disengaging the cable from the latch assembly **(see illustration)**.

3   Installation is the reverse of removal. **Note:** *Adjust the latch so the hood engages securely when closed and the hood bumpers are slightly compressed.*

Cable

Refer to illustration 8.6

4   Disconnect the hood release cable from the latch assembly **(see illustration 8.2)**, then detach the cable from any retaining clips securing it to the radiator support.

5   Attach a piece of wire or string to the latch end of the cable.

6   Working in the passenger's compartment, remove the driver's side kick panel. Then remove the release lever mounting bolts and detach the hood release lever **(see illustration)**.

7   Remove the left side inner fender splash

shield (see Section 11). Detach the cable from the retaining clip.

8   Push the grommet through the body and pull the cable into the passenger compartment. Ensure that the new cable has a grommet attached, then remove the old cable from the wire and replace it with the new cable.

9   Pull the wire back through the body.

10   Installation is the reverse of removal. **Note:** *Push on the grommet to seat it in the body completely.*

9   Radiator grille - removal and installation

Refer to illustrations 9.2a and 9.2b

1   On 2005 and earlier Civic and all CR-V models, remove the front bumper cover (see Section 10).

2   On 2006 and later model Civic models, remove the front grille cover **(see illustration)** and remove the front grille-to-radiator support push-pin fasteners **(see illustration)**.

9.2a Remove the push-pin fasteners and lift the grille cover off

9.2b Remove the grille-to-radiator support push-pin fasteners

10.2 Bumper cover lower retaining fasteners

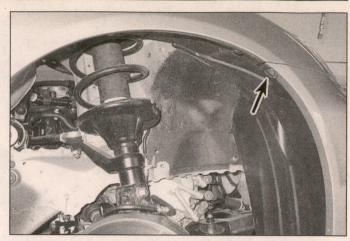

10.3 Remove the outer fastener securing the bumper cover to the inner fender (sedan model shown)

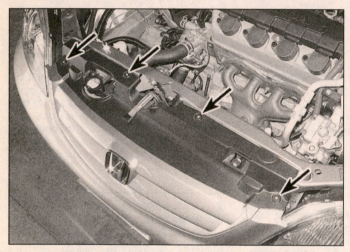

10.4a Bumper cover upper fasteners (Civic models)

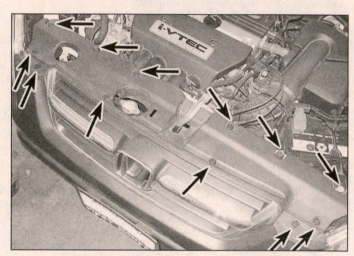

10.4b Bumper cover upper fasteners (CR-V models)

3   Remove the fasteners securing the edges of the grille to the bumper cover.
4   Pull the grille forward to disengage it from the bumper.
5   Installation is the reverse of removal.

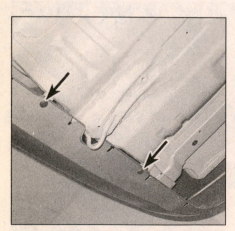

10.7 Remove the push-pins from the lower section of the bumper cover

10   Bumper covers - removal and installation

Front

Refer to illustrations 10.2, 10.3, 10.4a and 10.4b

1   Raise the vehicle and support it securely on jackstands.
2   Working under the vehicle, detach the push pins, bolts or screws securing the lower edges of the bumper cover **(see illustration)**.
3   Working in the front wheel opening, remove the retaining screw securing the bumper cover to the fenderwell **(see illustration)**.
4   Remove the front grille cover, if equipped **(see illustration 9.2a)**. Remove the fasteners securing the upper portion of the bumper cover **(see illustrations)**. Pull the bumper cover corners out and away, then remove it from the vehicle.
5   Installation is the reverse of removal.

Rear

Refer to illustrations 10.7, 10.8 and 10.9

6   Raise the vehicle and support it securely on jackstands.
7   Working under the vehicle, detach the plastic clips and screws securing the lower edge of the bumper cover **(see illustration)**.
8   Remove the screws securing the bumper cover in the rear wheel openings **(see illustration)**.
9   Open the trunk or rear liftgate and remove the screws and clips securing the upper edge of the bumper cover **(see illustration)**. Pull the bumper cover out and away from the vehicle.
10   Installation is the reverse of removal.

11   Front fender - removal and installation

Refer to illustrations 11.3, 11.4a, 11.4b, 11.4c and 11.4d

1   Loosen the wheel lug nuts, raise the

10.8 The ends of the bumper cover are retained by screws

10.9 Remove the screws along the upper edge of the bumper cover

11.3 Remove the fasteners retaining the inner fender splash shield

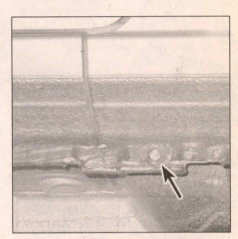

11.4a The lower rear corner of the fender is retained by a bolt

front of the vehicle and support it securely on jackstands. Remove the wheel.

2   Remove the front bumper cover (see Section 10).

3   Remove the fasteners securing the inner fender splash shield and detach the shield **(see illustration).**

4   Remove the fender mounting bolts **(see illustrations).**

5   Detach the fender. It's a good idea to have an assistant support the fender while it's being moved away from the vehicle to prevent damage to the surrounding body panels.

6   Installation is the reverse of removal.

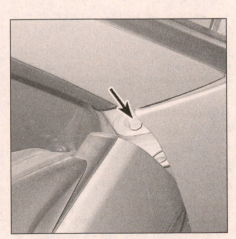

11.4b The upper rear corner of the fender is retained to the A-pillar with a bolt

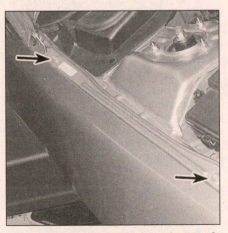

11.4c Remove the bolts along the top of the fender

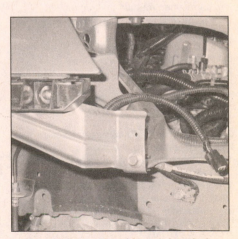

11.4d Remove the bolt and detach the bracket behind the headlight

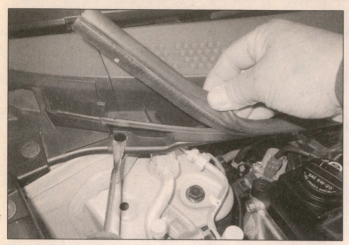

12.2a Pry out the push-pin fasteners and remove the hood seal . . .

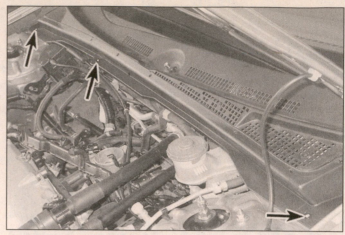

12.2b . . . then detach the plastic fasteners and remove the cowl (sedan model shown, other models similar)

12 Cowl cover - removal and installation

Refer to illustrations 12.2a and 12.2b

1   Remove the windshield wiper arms (see Chapter 12, Section 19).
2   Remove the hood seal and the push-pin fasteners securing the cowl cover **(see illustrations).**
3   Installation is the reverse of removal.

13 Liftgate handle, latch and lock cylinder (hatchback models) - removal and installation

1   Open the liftgate.
2   On the inside of the liftgate, remove the liftgate lower trim cover.

Handle

3   Remove the fasteners securing the hatch lock cylinder and rear license trim panel.
4   Remove the clips securing the license trim panel, then remove the trim panel.
5   Remove the rear window wiper motor (see Chapter 12).
6   Detach the liftgate release cable from the liftgate handle.
7   Remove the liftgate handle retaining nuts and remove the handle.
8   Installation is the reverse of removal.

Latch

9   Disconnect the liftgate release cable and lock cylinder rod from the latch.
10   Disconnect the liftgate latch electrical connectors.
11   Remove the bolts securing the liftgate latch and remove the latch.
12   Installation is the reverse of removal.

Lock cylinder

13   Remove the rear license trim panel (see Step 3).

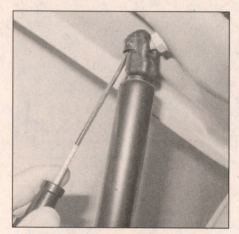

14.3 Release the strut support clip and detach it from the ballstud

14   Disconnect the lock cylinder rod from the cylinder.
15   Working outside of the liftgate, remove the bolt securing the lock cylinder.
16   Working inside the liftgate, remove the lock cylinder from inside of the liftgate.
17   Installation is the reverse of removal.

14 Liftgate (hatchback models) - removal, installation and adjustment

Note: *The liftgate is heavy and somewhat awkward to hold - at least two people should perform this procedure.*

Removal and installation

Refer to illustration 14.3

1   Open the liftgate and support it securely.
2   Remove the upper trim molding from the liftgate opening and disconnect all wiring har-

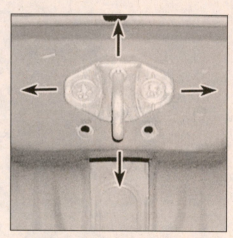

14.8 To adjust the liftgate striker, loosen the screws and move the striker as necessary

ness connectors leading to the liftgate.
3   While an assistant supports the liftgate, detach both ends of the support struts **(see illustration).**
4   Remove the C-pillar trim panels, then carefully pull down the rear portion of the headliner.
5   Detach the liftgate hinge-to-body bolts and remove the liftgate from the vehicle.
6   Installation is the reverse of removal.

Adjustment

Refer to illustrations 14.8 and 14.9

7   Adjustments are made by loosening the liftgate hinge-to-body bolts and moving the liftgate. Proper alignment is achieved when the edges of the liftgate are parallel with the rear quarter panels and the roof panel.
8   Remove the rear trim panel and adjust the latch striker assembly as necessary to provide positive engagement with the latch mechanism **(see illustration).**

14.9 Screw the bumpers in-or-out to make final adjustments to the liftgate

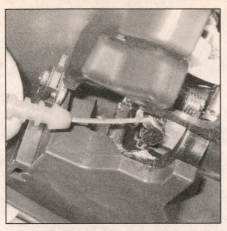

15.2 Detach the cable and unhook the end from the latch

15.3 Trunk lid latch retaining bolts

9   Finally, adjust the height of the liftgate in relation to the body by screwing the rubber bumpers in-or-out **(see illustration)**.

15 Trunk lid latch and lock cylinder (coupe and sedan models) - removal and installation

Trunk lid latch

Refer to illustrations 15.2 and 15.3

1   Open the trunk and scribe a line around the trunk lid latch assembly for a reference point to aid the installation procedure.
2   Disconnect the latch cable from the latch **(see illustration)**.
3   Disconnect the electrical connector, then remove the bolts retaining the trunk lid latch **(see illustration)**.
4   Installation is the reverse of removal.

Trunk lock cylinder

Refer to illustration 15.5

5   Open the trunk. Look upward through the trunk lid access hole and detach the rod from the lock cylinder **(see illustration)**.
6   Remove the mounting bolts and remove it from the trunk lid.
7   Installation is the reverse of removal.

16 Trunk lid (coupe and sedan models) - removal, installation and adjustment

Note: *The trunk lid is heavy and somewhat awkward to remove and install - at least two people should perform this procedure.*

Removal and installation

Refer to illustrations 16.3 and 16.4

1   Open the trunk lid and cover the edges of the trunk compartment with pads or cloths

to protect the painted surfaces when the lid is removed.
2   Disconnect any cables or wire harness connectors attached to the trunk lid that would interfere with removal.
3   Remove the hinge trim cover (if equipped) and make alignment marks around the hinge **(see illustration)**.
4   While an assistant supports the trunk lid, remove the lid-to-hinge bolts on both sides and lift it off **(see illustration)**.
5   Installation is the reverse of removal.
Note: *When reinstalling the trunk lid, align the lid-to-hinge bolts with the marks made during removal.*

Adjustment

6   Fore-and-aft and side-to-side adjustment of the trunk lid is accomplished by moving the lid in relation to the hinge after loosening the bolts or nuts.
7   Scribe a line around the hinge plate as described earlier in this Section so you can determine the amount of movement.

15.5 Pry the rod from its clip

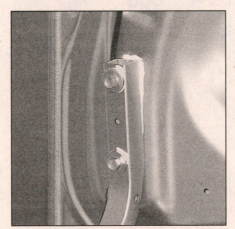

16.3 Draw around the hinge with a marking pen before loosening the bolts to ensure proper alignment of the trunk lid when it's reinstalled

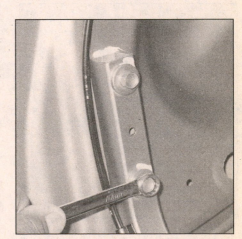

16.4 With an assistant holding the trunk lid, remove the four trunk lid retaining bolts

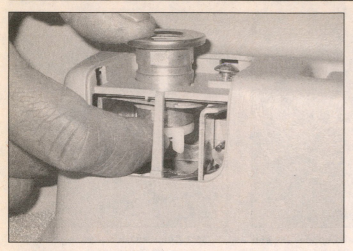

17.1a Remove the lock cylinder, then remove the trim panel

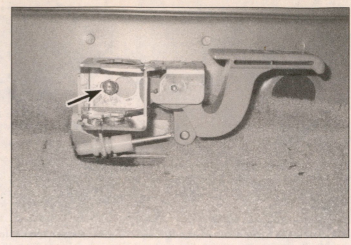

17.1b Remove the fastener and detach the release lever assembly

8   Loosen the bolts and move the trunk lid into correct alignment. Move it only a little at a time. Tighten the hinge bolts or nuts and carefully lower the trunk lid to check the alignment.

9   If necessary after installation, the entire trunk lid striker assembly can be adjusted up and down as well as from side to side on the trunk lid so the lid closes securely and is flush with the rear quarter panels. To do this, scribe a line around the trunk lid striker assembly to provide a reference point, then loosen the bolts and reposition the striker as necessary. Following adjustment, retighten the mounting bolts.

10   The trunk lid latch assembly, as well as the hinges, should be periodically lubricated with white lithium-base grease to prevent sticking and wear.

11   Finally, adjust the height of the trunk lid in relation to the body by screwing the rubber bumpers in-or-out.

---

17 Trunk release lever and fuel door cables - removal and installation

---

Release lever (coupe, sedan and hatchback models)

Refer to illustrations 17.1a and 17.1b

1   Detach the lower trim panel for access to the release cable and lever, then remove the lever retaining bolt **(see illustrations)**. Detach the cable from the release assembly.

2   Installation is the reverse of removal.

Cables

Refer to illustration 17.5

3   If you're working on a CR-V model, remove the driver's side kick panel, then remove the fasteners securing the release handle.

4   Working in the trunk or rear compartment, remove the plastic clips securing the driver's side and rear inside finishing panels

to allow access to the fuel door assembly.

5   Twist the cable 90-degrees to align the tabs on the striker assembly with the slots in the body and withdraw it into the rear compartment **(see illustration)**. Detach the trunk release cable from the trunk lid latch (see Section 15).

6   Remove the left door sill plate, the rear seat and the left rear quarter trim panel. Pull the carpet back and detach all the cable retaining clips.

7   Working in the trunk or rear compartment, pull the cable assembly towards the rear of the vehicle.

8   Installation is the reverse of removal.

---

18 Door trim panels - removal and installation

Removal

Front doors

Coupe, Sedan and Hatchback models

Refer to illustrations 18.1, 18.2a, 18.2b, 18.2c, 18.3a, 18.3b and 18.5

1   On manual window regulator equipped models, remove the window crank **(see illustration)**.

2   On Coupe and Sedan models, remove the inside door handle trim cover. Remove the mounting screws, then detach the handle rod and electrical connector **(see illustrations)**.

3   Remove the pull handle trim cover, then remove the pull handle retaining screws **(see illustrations)**. If equipped with power windows, disconnect the electrical connector from the window switch.

4   Remove the mirror trim cover (see Section 23).

5   Remove the door trim panel using a door panel removal tool **(see illustration)**. Start from the bottom of the trim panel and work around the perimeter until all the fasteners have been released from the door.

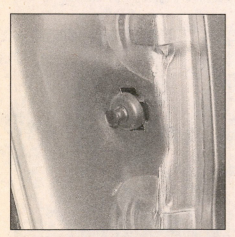

17.5 From inside the trunk or hatch area, rotate the fuel door release cable 90-degrees so the tabs line up with the slots in the body, then withdraw it

18.1 Remove the window crank by pulling this clip off with a wire hook or a special tool made for this purpose (handle removed for clarity)

18.2a Remove the door handle
trim cover . . .

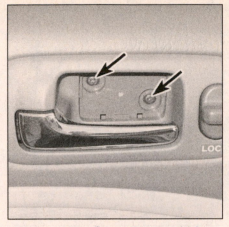

18.2b . . . then remove the screw(s) from
the inside pull handle area - 2006 and
earlier models shown, 2007 and later
models similar

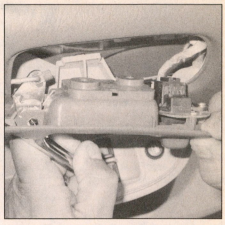

18.2c Pull the handle outward to access
the door lock switch electrical connector
and the door handle actuating rod

6   Lift the trim panel up to disengage the
panel from the upper door ridge, unplug any
electrical connectors, and remove the panel.
7   For access to the door outside handle
or the door window regulator inside the door,
raise the window fully, then carefully peel back
the plastic watershield.

CR-V models

Refer to illustration 18.9

8   Remove the window crank (if equipped)
and inside door handle trim cover. Remove
the mounting screws, then detach the handle
rod and electrical connector (**see illustrations
18.2a, 18.2b and 18.2c**). Note: *On 2007 and
later models equipped with a window crank,
use a small screwdriver pry open the cap at
the bottom of the crank handle to release the
retaining clip.*
9   Remove the armrest mounting screws
(**see illustration**).

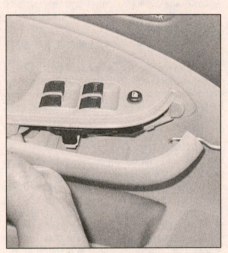

18.3a Carefully remove the pull handle
trim cover . . .

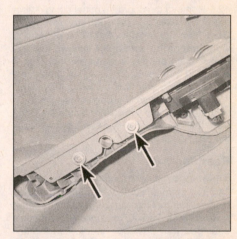

18.3b . . . to gain access to the pull handle
retaining screws - 2005 and earlier models
shown, 2006 and later models similar

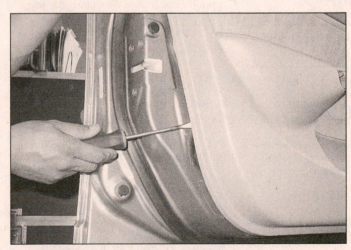

18.5 Carefully pry the clips free so the door trim panel can be
removed - 2005 and earlier models shown, 2006 and later
models similar

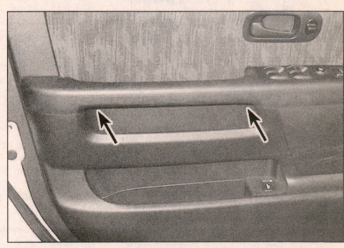

18.9 Remove the two fasteners securing the armrest - 2005 and
earlier models shown, 2006 and later models similar

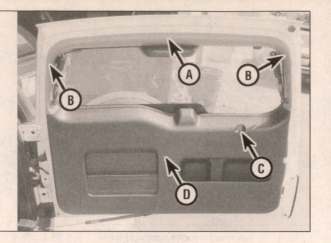

18.21 Tailgate trim panel details - 2005 and earlier model shown, later models similar

A   Upper trim panel
B   Left and right trim panels
C   Cargo hook
D   Tailgate trim panel

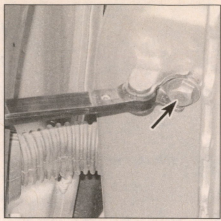

19.6 Remove the door strut retaining bolt

10   If you're working on a passenger door panel, remove the window switch.

11   Remove the mirror trim cover (see Section 23).

12   Remove the door trim panel using a door panel removal tool **(see illustration 18.5)**. Start from the bottom of the trim panel and work around the perimeter until all the fasteners have been released from the door. If equipped with power windows, disconnect the electrical connector from the window switch.

13   For access to the door outside handle or the door window regulator inside the door, raise the window fully, then carefully peel back the plastic watershield.

Rear doors

Sedan and CR-V models

14   On manual window regulator equipped models, remove the window crank **(see illustration 18.1)**. On 2007 and later CR-V models equipped with a window crank, use a small screwdriver to pry open the cap at the bottom of the crank handle to release the retaining clip.

15   Remove the inside door handle trim cover. Remove the mounting screws, then detach the handle rod and electrical connector **(see illustrations 18.2a, 18.2b and 18.2c)**.

16   On Sedan models, remove the pull handle trim cover, then remove the pull handle retaining screws. If equipped with power windows, disconnect the electrical connector from the window switch.

17   If you're working on a CR-V model, remove the armrest mounting screws, then remove the window switch and disconnect the electrical connector.

18   On CR-V models, remove the door quarter trim panel, then remove the door trim panel upper push-pin.

19   Remove the door trim panel using a door panel removal tool **(see illustration 18.5)**. Start from the bottom of the trim panel and work around the perimeter until all the fasteners have been released from the door.

20   For access to the door outside handle or the door window regulator inside the door, raise the window fully, then carefully peel back the plastic watershield.

Tailgate

Refer to illustration 18.21

21   Remove the tailgate upper trim panel, lower brake light trim panel and the left and right trim panels by carefully releasing the clips **(see illustration)**.

22   Remove the screw securing the cargo hook and remove the hook (if equipped).

23   Remove the door trim panel using a door panel removal tool. Start from the bottom of the trim panel and work around the perimeter until all the fasteners have been released from the door.

Installation

24   Prior to installation of the door trim panels and/or the tailgate trim panel, be sure to reinstall any clips in the panel which may have come out when you removed the panel.

25   Position the wire harness connectors for the power door lock switch and the power window switch (if equipped) on the back of the panel, then place the panel in position in the door. Press the door panel into place until the clips are seated.

26   The remainder of the installation is the reverse of removal.

---

19   Door - removal, installation and adjustment

Note: *On 2006 and later Civic models, 2004 hatchback models and CR-V models, you must reset the power window control unit after disconnecting the driver's door wiring harness (see Chapter 5).*

Note: *The door is heavy and somewhat awkward to remove and install - at least two people should perform this procedure.*

Removal and installation

Refer to illustrations 19.6 and 19.8

1   Lower the window completely in the door, then disconnect the cable from the negative battery terminal (see Chapter 5).

2   Open the door all the way and support it on jacks or blocks covered with rags to prevent damaging the paint.

3   Remove the door trim panel and watershield as described in Section 18.

4   Disconnect all electrical connections, ground wires and harness retaining clips from the door. **Note:** *It is a good idea to label all connections to aid the reassembly process.*

5   From the door side, detach the rubber conduit between the body and the door. Then pull the wiring harness through the conduit hole and remove it from the door.

6   Remove the door stop strut **(see illustration)**.

7   Mark around the door hinges with a pen or a scribe to facilitate realignment during reassembly.

8   With an assistant holding the door, remove the hinge-to-door bolts **(see illustration)** and lift the door off.

9   Installation is the reverse of removal.

Adjustment

Refer to illustrations 19.11 and 19.13

10   Having proper door-to-body alignment is a critical part of a well functioning door assembly. First check the door hinge pins for excessive play. Fully open the door and lift up and down on the door without lifting the body. If a door has 1/16-inch or more excessive play, the hinges should be replaced.

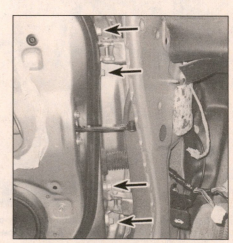

19.8 Remove the door hinge bolts

11   Door-to-body alignment adjustments are made by loosening the hinge-to-body bolts (**see illustration**) or hinge-to-door bolts and moving the door. Proper body alignment is achieved when the top of the doors are parallel with the roof section, the front door is flush with the fender, the rear door is flush with the rear quarter panel and the bottom of the doors are aligned with the lower rocker panel. If these goals can't be reached by adjusting the hinge-to-body or hinge-to-door bolts, body alignment shims may have to be purchased and inserted behind the hinges to achieve correct alignment.

12   To adjust the door closed position, scribe a line or mark around the striker plate to provide a reference point, then check that the door latch is contacting the center of the latch striker. If not, adjust the up and down position first.

13   Finally adjust the latch striker sideways position, so that the door panel is flush with the center pillar or rear quarter panel and provides positive engagement with the latch mechanism (**see illustration**).

20   Door latch, lock cylinder and handles - removal and installation

Caution: *Wear gloves when working inside the door openings to protect against cuts from sharp metal edges.*

Door latch

Refer to illustrations 20.2 and 20.4

1   Raise the window, then remove the door trim panel and watershield (see Section 18).
2   Working through the large access hole, remove the lock rod protector and glass run channel (**see illustration**).
3   On 2006 and later models, remove the small access hole tape (coupes) or plastic plug (sedans and CR-V) and use a small screwdriver to disconnect the outer handle rod.
4   Remove the screws securing the latch to

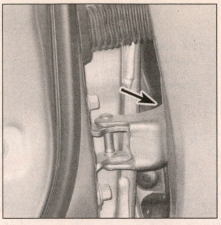

19.11 Loosen the hinge-to-body bolts to adjust the doors

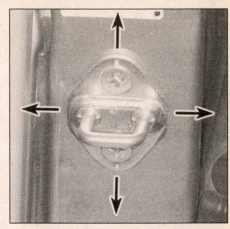

19.13 Adjust the door lock striker by loosening the mounting screws and gently tapping the striker in the desired direction

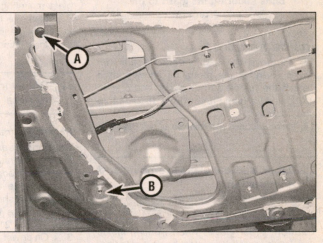

20.2 Remove the plastic pin to release the lock rod protector (A) then remove the fastener securing the glass run channel (B)

the door (**see illustration**).
5   Disengage the outside door handle-to-latch rod, outside door lock-to-latch rod, the inside handle-to-latch rod, and the lock solenoid-to-latch rod. On 2006 and later models, a cable is used for the door lock-to-latch, instead of a rod. To disconnect the cable, pull the outer tabs out while holding the center tab, then pull the cable end off.

6   All door lock rods are attached by plastic clips. The plastic clips can be removed by unsnapping the portion engaging the connecting rod, then pulling the rod out of its locating hole. On models with power door locks, disconnect the electrical connectors at the latch. Remove the latch assembly from the door.
7   Installation is the reverse of removal.

Outside handle and door lock cylinder

Refer to illustration 20.9

8   To remove the outside handle and lock cylinder assembly, raise the window and remove the door trim panel and watershield (see Section 18).
9   Working through the access hole, disengage the plastic clips that secure the outside handle-to-latch rod and the outside door lock-to-latch rod (**see illustration**).
10   The lock cylinder can be removed from the handle assembly by removing a clip on 2005 and earlier models and special security screws on 2006 and later models.
11   Remove the outside handle retaining fastener, then remove the handle from the vehicle.
12   Installation is the reverse of removal.

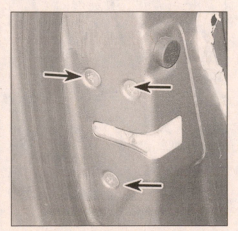

20.4 Remove the latch screws from the end of the door

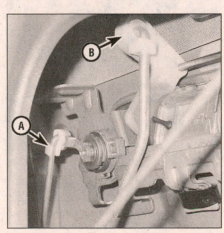

20.9 Detach the lock actuating rod (A) and handle-to-latch rod (B)

21.2 Raise the window just enough to access the glass retaining bolts through the holes in the door frame - remove the bolts securing the glass to the equalizer arm

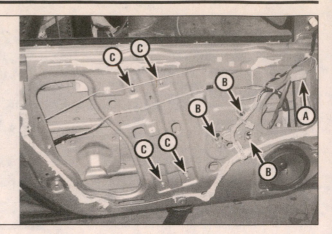

22.4 Door window glass regulator details - 2005 and earlier models shown, 2006 and later models similar

A   Regulator motor electrical connector
B   Regulator motor mounting bolts
C   Window regulator mounting bolts

Inside handle

13   Remove the inside door handle trim cover. Remove the mounting screws, then detach the handle rod or cable, and electrical connector **(see illustrations 18.2a, 18.2b and 18.2c)**.
14   Installation is the reverse of removal.

---

21   Door window glass - removal and installation

Refer to illustration 21.2
Caution: *Wear gloves when working inside the door openings to protect against cuts from sharp metal edges.*
1   Remove the door trim panel and the plastic watershield (see Section 18).
2   Raise the window glass just enough to access the window retaining bolts through the holes in the door frame **(see illustration)**.

3   Place a rag over the glass to help prevent scratching the glass and remove the two glass mounting bolts.
4   Remove the glass by tilting it slightly, pulling it up and out.
5   Installation is the reverse of removal.

---

22   Door window glass regulator - removal and installation

Refer to illustration 22.4
Caution: *Wear gloves when working inside the door openings to protect against cuts from sharp metal edges.*
1   Remove the door trim panel and the plastic watershield (see Section 18).
2   Remove the window glass assembly (see Section 21).
3   On power operated windows, disconnect the electrical connector from the window regulator motor.
4   Remove the regulator mounting bolts **(see illustration),** then slide the regulator assembly out of the service hole in the door frame to remove it.
5   Installation is the reverse of removal.

---

23   Mirrors - removal and installation

Outside door mirrors
Refer to illustrations 23.1 and 23.3
1   Pry off the mirror trim cover **(see illustration)**.
2   Disconnect the electrical connector from the mirror (if equipped). **Note:** *On some models, the electrical connector plugs directly into the mirror and can be unplugged without removing the door panel. On other models, the electrical connector is located in the wiring harness, behind the door panel. See Section 18 for door panel removal, if necessary.*
3   Remove the three mirror retaining nuts and detach the mirror from the vehicle **(see illustration)**.
4   Installation is the reverse of removal.

Inside mirror
2005 and earlier models
Refer to illustrations 23.5 and 23.6
5   Detach the cover from the retaining bracket **(see illustration)**.

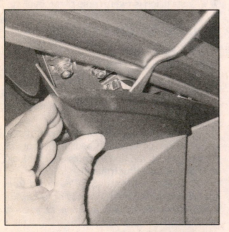

23.1 Use a small screwdriver or trim removal tool to pry off the mirror cover

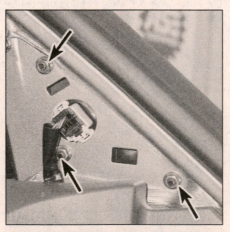

23.3 To remove the mirror, remove these three nuts - if the vehicle has power mirrors, also unplug the electrical connector

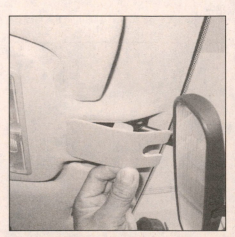

23.5 Remove the mirror cover

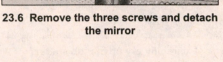

23.6 Remove the three screws and detach the mirror

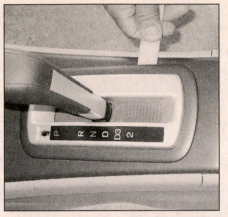

24.10 Carefully detach the clips and remove the trim ring from around the shifter (automatic transaxle)

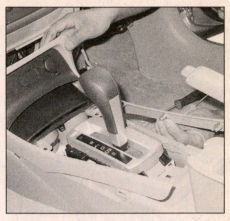

24.11a Pry off the dashboard center lower cover

6 Remove the screws and lower the mirror **(see illustration)**.

7 Installation is the reverse of removal.

2006 and later models

8 Remove the trim cover from the mirror base.

9 Loosen the set screw and slide the mirror up and off of the base mount.

10 Disconnect the electrical connector (if equipped) and remove the mirror.

11 Installation is the reverse of removal.

12 If the mounting bracket for the mirror has come off the windshield, it can be reattached with a special mirror adhesive kit available at auto parts stores. Clean the glass and support base thoroughly and follow the directions on the adhesive package, allowing the base to bond overnight before attaching the mirror.

24 Center console - removal and installation

Warning: *Models covered by this manual are equipped with a Supplemental Restraint System (SRS), more commonly known as airbags. Always disable the airbag system before working in the vicinity of any airbag system component to avoid the possibility of accidental deployment of the airbag, which could cause personal injury (see Chapter 12).*

1 Disconnect the cable from the negative terminal of the battery (see Chapter 5).

Hatchback models

Rear console

2 Slide the front seats all the way to the forward position.

3 At the rear of the console, remove the fasteners from each side.

4 Slide the front seats all the way to the rear, then carefully pull up on the front of the rear console to release the clips.

5 Remove the rear half of the console by lifting it up and toward the rear.

Front console

6 Pry out the dashboard center lower cover, remove the two console fasteners and disconnect the electrical connector.

7 Remove the mat from the console box, then remove the two fasteners from the bottom of the box.

8 At the front of the console, remove the fasteners along both sides of the console, then gently lift the console up and toward the rear to remove it from the vehicle.

9 Installation is the reverse of removal.

Coupe and sedan models

2005 and earlier models

Refer to illustrations 24.10, 24.11a, 24.11b, 24.12a, 24.12b and 24.13

10 If you're working on an automatic transaxle model, pry off the gear selector trim bezel and center console trim **(see illustration)**. On manual transaxle models, unscrew the shift lever knob.

11 Remove the dashboard center lower cover and disconnect any electrical connectors, then detach the parking brake lever trim panel **(see illustrations)**.

12 Remove the console retaining screws and surrounding fasteners **(see illustrations)**.

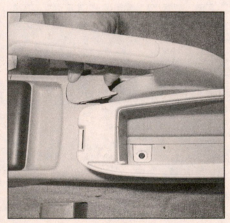

24.11b Pull up and remove the brake lever trim panel

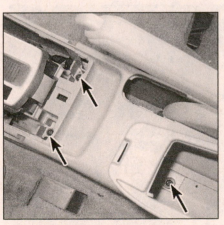

24.12a Remove the console mounting fasteners . . .

24.12b . . . from the top of the center console. Don't forget the fasteners securing the sides of the console

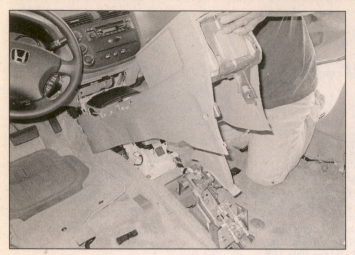

24.13 Lift the rear of the console up, then pull it out

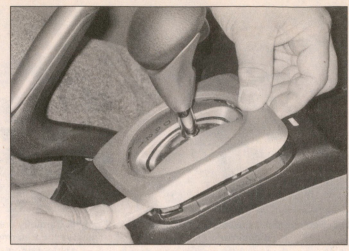

24.16a Using a trim tool, carefully pry up the top shifter trim cover . . .

13   Disconnect any electrical connections and remove the console from the vehicle **(see illustration).**
14   Installation is the reverse of removal.

24.16b . . . and lower shift cover

2006 and later models

Refer to illustrations 24.16a, 24.16b, 24.17, 24.18a and 24.18b

15   Carefully pull the passengers side lower trim panel out to disengage the retaining clips and remove the trim panel.
16   If you're working on an automatic trans-axle model, pry off the gear selector trim bezel and center console trim **(see illustrations).** On manual transaxle models, unscrew the shift lever knob. **Note:** *On Si models, loosen the jam nut, then unscrew the shift knob.*
17   Open the center console arm rest, remove the mat and retaining screws **(see illustration).**
18   Remove the upper and lower console fasteners **(see illustrations).**
19   Disconnect any electrical connections and remove the console from the vehicle.
20   Installation is the reverse of removal.

CR-V models
2007 and later models

21   Slide the front seats all the way to the rear. Using a trim tool, pry the lower front trim panels out from the console and disconnect any electrical connectors.
22   Open the center console shutter, remove the mat and rear retaining screws.
23   Slide the front seats all the way to the front and remove the console from the vehicle.
24   Installation is the reverse of removal.

25   Dashboard trim panels - removal and installation

Warning: *Models covered by this manual are equipped with a Supplemental Restraint System (SRS), more commonly known as airbags. Always disable the airbag system before working in the vicinity of any airbag system component to avoid the possibility of accidental deployment of the airbag, which*

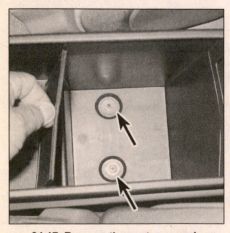

24.17 Remove the center console fasteners under the arm rest

24.18a Remove the upper console fasteners . . .

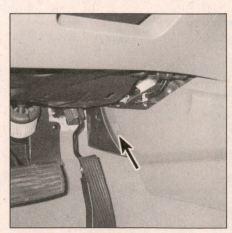

24.18b . . . and lower fasteners (driver's side lower fastener shown, passenger's side is similar)

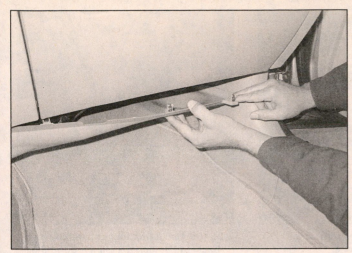

25.2 Carefully pull the panel down to release the clips (2005 and earlier sedan model shown, other models similar)

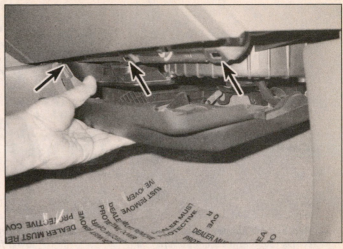

25.4 Carefully pull the passenger side lower trim panel forward to release the retaining clips (2006 and later models)

could cause personal injury (see Chapter 12).

1   Disconnect the cable from the negative battery terminal (see Chapter 5).

Passenger's lower dashboard cover

2005 and earlier models

Refer to illustration 25.2

2   Pull the edge of the panel down until the clips are disengaged and remove the panel **(see illustration).**

3   Installation is the reverse of removal.

2006 and later models

Refer to illustration 25.4

4   Pull the edge of the panel out until the clips are disengaged and remove the panel **(see illustration).**

5   Installation is the reverse of removal.

Driver's instrument panel under cover

Refer to illustration 25.6

6   Turn the locking knob and remove the panel **(see illustration).**

7   Installation is the reverse of removal.

Glovebox

Refer to illustrations 25.9a and 25.9b

8   At the bottom of the glovebox, remove the screws from the hinges.

9   Open the glovebox door and remove the glovebox stops, then lower the glovebox from the instrument panel **(see illustrations).** **Note:** *On 2005 and later CR-V models, disconnect the glovebox damper hooks from the top corners of the glovebox.*

10   Installation is the reverse of removal.

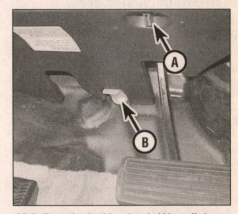

25.6 Turn the locking knob (A), pull down the front of the panel and release the rear part from the clip (B) (2005 and earlier sedan model shown, other models similar)

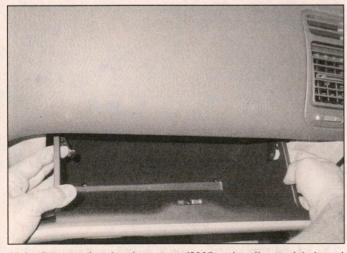

25.9a Remove the glovebox stops (2005 and earlier model shown)

25.9b Push the glovebox stops in and lower the glovebox (2006 and later models)

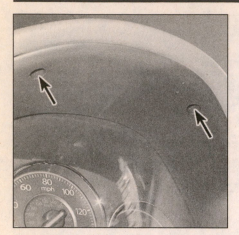

25.12 Remove the cluster bezel retaining screws (2005 and earlier sedan model shown)

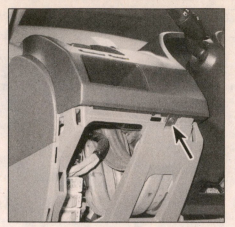

25.16a Remove the trim panel lower fastener

25.16b Use a trim tool to carefully pull back and detach the clips around the panel, then release the retaining pin (arrow) and remove the panel (2006 and later Civic)

Instrument cluster bezel

2005 and earlier Coupe and sedan models

Refer to illustration 25.12

11   Remove the steering column upper cover (see Section 26).

12   Remove the screws (see illustration), then grasp the bezel securely and pull back to detach the clips from the instrument panel.

13   Installation is the reverse of removal.

2006 and later Civic models

Refer to illustrations 25.16a and 25.16b

14   Lower the steering column using the tilt steering release.

15   Remove the driver's instrument panel lower cover (see Steps 26 and 27).

16   Remove the lower fastener (see illustration). Using a trim tool, carefully pull back and detach the clips, working your way around the panel (see illustration).

17   Unplug any electrical connectors, then remove the panel.

18   Installation is the reverse of removal.

CR-V models

19   Remove the driver's instrument panel lower cover (see Steps 29 through 31).

20   Remove the steering column upper cover (see Section 26).

21   Grasp the bezel securely and gently pull back to detach the clips from the instrument panel.

22   Installation is the reverse of removal.

Hatchback models

23   Tilt the steering wheel down to the lowest position, then remove the steering column upper cover (see Section 26).

24   Grasp the bezel securely and gently pull back to detach the clips from the instrument panel.

25   Installation is the reverse of removal.

Driver's instrument panel lower cover

Coupe and sedan models

Refer to illustrations 25.27a and 25.27b

26   Tilt the steering wheel up to the highest position.

27   On 2005 and earlier models, turn the locking knobs and remove the panel (see illustration). On 2006 and later models, carefully pull out from the bottom up to release the retaining clips (see illustration) and remove the panel.

28   Installation is the reverse of removal.

CR-V models

29   Open the access door for the under-dash fuse/relay box and remove the fastener located in the opening.

30   Open the driver's side pocket and remove the fastener located in the opening.

31   Grasp the bottom of the instrument panel

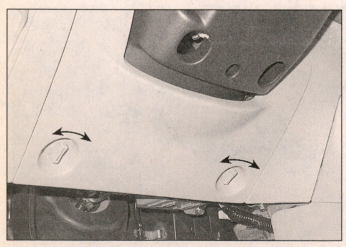

25.27a On 2005 and earlier models, give these two knobs a 1/2-turn either way, then remove the driver's dashboard lower cover and carefully pull down to release the clips

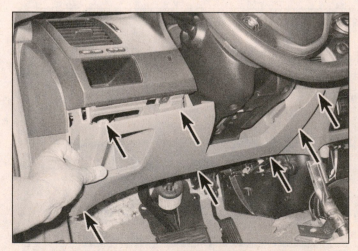

25.27b On 2006 and later models, carefully pull the panel outwards releasing the clips (arrows) on the back side of the panel

lower cover securely and gently pull back to detach the bottom clips from the instrument panel. Repeat the same for the upper clips. Unplug any electrical connectors, then remove the panel.

32   Installation is the reverse of removal.

Hatchback models

33   Tilt the steering wheel up to the highest position.

34   Turn the locking knob a 1/2-turn either way, then grasp the side of the panel and gently pull back to remove the panel.

35   Installation is the reverse of removal.

Center trim panel

2005 and earlier Coupe and sedan models

Refer to illustration 25.37

Note: *On 2006 and later model Civics, the center trim panel is one unit with the audio and heater control unit; see Chapter 12, Section 11 for removal.*

36   Remove the center console (see Section 24).

37   Remove the center trim panel mounting bolts, then release the trim panel clips **(see illustration).**

38   Carefully slide the trim panel out far enough to unplug any electrical connectors that interfere with removal, then remove the trim panel from the dashboard.

39   Installation is the reverse of removal.

CR-V models

2006 and earlier models

40   Remove the screws securing the lower edge of the center trim panel.

41   Lift the lower edge of the panel and work your way upward along the edges to detach the clips. Unplug any electrical connectors, then remove the panel.

42   Installation is the reverse of removal.

2007 and later models

43   Remove the console cover trim panel from each side (see Section 24).

25.37 Remove the center trim panel mounting bolts (arrows), then carefully pry the panel using a trim stick

44   Remove the screw securing the center trim panel.

45   Lift the lower edge of the panel and work your way upward along the edges to detach the clips. Unplug any electrical connectors, then remove the lower panel from the center panel.

46   Remove the center trim panel screws and carefully pull the trim panel out from the dash.

47   Installation is the reverse of removal.

Hatchback models

48   Remove the driver's instrument panel lower cover (see Steps 33 and 34).

49   Remove the passenger's lower dashboard cover **(see illustration 25.2).**

50   Remove the glovebox (see Steps 8 and 9).

51   Using a ratchet with an 11-inch extension or a long screwdriver, wrap the end with a towel, then carefully insert the end through the glovebox opening and gently release the clips by pushing from under the shift lever trim.

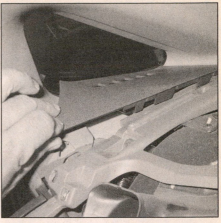

25.54 Carefully pry up and remove the instrument panel side trim

52   Remove the center panel fasteners from the driver's lower cover and glovebox openings.

53   Carefully slide the trim panel out far enough to unplug any electrical connectors that interfere with removal, then remove the trim panel from the dashboard. Installation is the reverse off removal.

Driver's instrument panel upper cover

2006 and later Civic models

Refer to illustrations 25.54, 25.56 and 25.57

54   Using a trim tool, carefully pry up and remove the instrument panel side trim **(see illustration).**

55   Remove the instrument panel lower cover (see Steps 26 and 27) and instrument cluster bezel (see Steps 14 through 17).

56   Remove the instrument panel upper fasteners **(see illustration).**

57   Detach the mounting clips by carefully pulling the panel outwards, working your way around the panel **(see illustration).**

58   Installation is the reverse of removal.

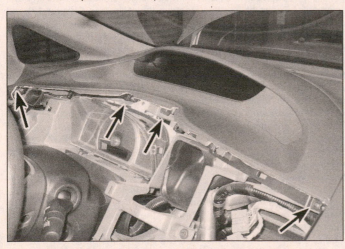

25.56 Remove the upper instrument panel fasteners

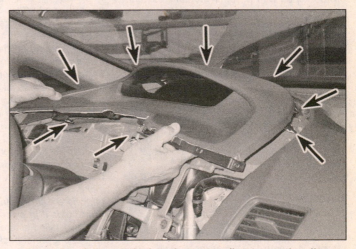

25.57 Carefully pull the housing out to disconnect the clips (arrows) and remove the panel

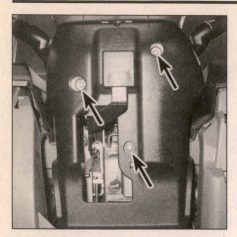

26.4 Steering column cover retaining screws (Sedan model shown, other models similar)

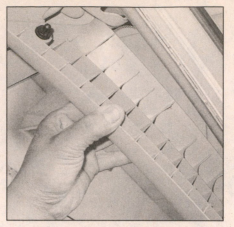

27.7 Remove the front pillar trim by carefully releasing the clips

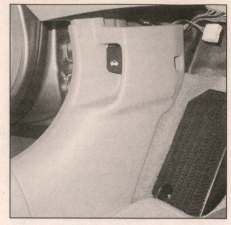

27.9 Carefully detach both side kick panels

2007 and later CR-V models

59   Using a trim tool, carefully pry the driver's vent out from the bottom.

60   Remove the instrument panel lower cover (see Steps 29 through 31) and instrument cluster bezel (see Steps 19 through 21).

61   Pull the center vent forward to release the rear clips, then lift the vent back to release the front clips and remove the center vent. **Caution:** *If the vent is pried up before releasing the rear clips, damage to the vent can occur.*

62   Grasp the bottom of the instrument panel cover securely and gently pull back to detach the bottom clips from the instrument panel. Repeat the same for the upper clips.

63   Installation is the reverse of removal.

26   Steering column covers - removal and installation

Refer to illustration 26.4

Warning: *Models covered by this manual are equipped with a Supplemental Restraint*

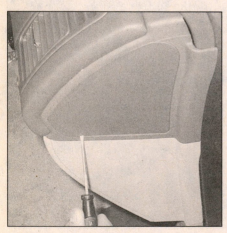

27.11 Carefully pry off both dashboard side covers

System (SRS), more commonly known as airbags. Always disable the airbag system before working in the vicinity of any airbag system component to avoid the possibility of accidental deployment of the airbag, which could cause personal injury (see Chapter 12).

1   Disconnect the cable from the negative battery terminal (see Chapter 5).

2   Remove the driver's instrument panel lower cover (see Section 25).

3   On tilt steering columns, move the column to the lowest position.

4   Remove the retaining screws, then separate the halves and remove the covers **(see illustration)**.

5   Installation is the reverse of the removal procedure.

27   Instrument panel - removal and installation

Refer to illustrations 27.7, 27.9, 27.11, 27.16, 27.17a and 27.17b

Warning: *Models covered by this manual are equipped with a Supplemental Restraint System (SRS), more commonly known as airbags. Always disable the airbag system before working in the vicinity of any airbag system component to avoid the possibility of accidental deployment of the airbag, which could cause personal injury (see Chapter 12).* **Note:** *This is a difficult procedure for the home mechanic. There are many hidden fasteners, difficult angles to work in and many electrical connectors to tag and disconnect/connect. We recommend that this procedure be done only by an experienced do-it-yourselfer.* **Note:** *During removal of the instrument panel, make careful notes of how each piece comes off, where it fits in relation to other pieces and what holds it in place. If you note how each part is installed before removing it, getting the instrument panel back together again will be much easier.* **Note:** *It is not necessary, but it is suggested*

to remove both front seats to allow additional working space and lessen the chance of damage to the seats during this procedure.

1   Disconnect the cable from the negative battery terminal (see Chapter 5).

2   Remove the steering wheel (see Chapter 10).

3   If equipped, remove the center floor console (see Section 24).

4   Remove the instrument cluster bezel (see Section 25).

5   Remove the instrument cluster (see Chapter 12).

6   Remove all of the dashboard trim panels described in Section 25.

7   Remove the front pillar trim **(see illustration)**.

8   Remove the nuts and lower the steering column (see Chapter 10).

9   Remove the side kick panels **(see illustration)**.

10   Remove the center, driver and passenger vents.

11   Remove the dashboard side covers **(see illustration)**.

12   Remove the glovebox (see Section 25).

13   Remove the radio (see Chapter 12) and the heater control assembly (see Chapter 3).

14   Remove the rear vent duct.

15   Disconnect the instrument panel electrical connectors including the passenger's side airbag (see Chapter 12). **Note:** *A number of electrical connectors must be disconnected in order to remove the instrument panel. Most are designed so that they will only fit on the matching connector (male or female), but if there is any doubt, mark the connectors with masking tape and a marking pen before disconnecting them.*

16   Remove the fasteners securing the lower center part of the instrument panel **(see illustration)**.

17   Remove the fasteners from each end of the instrument panel **(see illustrations)**.

18   Pull the instrument panel towards the rear of the vehicle and detach any electrical connectors interfering with removal.

27.16 Remove the instrument panel center brace mounting bolts (sedan model shown, other models similar)

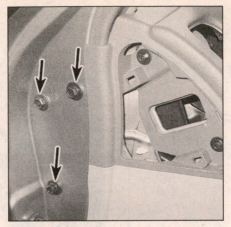

27.17a Remove the bolts from the support structure on the left . . .

27.17b . . . and the right side of the instrument panel (sedan model shown, other models similar)

19   Once all the electrical connectors are detached, lift the instrument panel, then pull it away from the windshield and take it out through the driver's door opening. **Note:** *This is a two-person job.*
20   Installation is the reverse of removal.
21   Reconnect the battery. Refer to Chapter 5.

28 Seats - removal and installation

Warning: *The front seat belts on some models are equipped with pre-tensioners, which are pyrotechnic (explosive) devices designed to retract the seat belts in the event of a collision. On models equipped with pre-tensioners, do not remove the front seat belt retractor assemblies, and do not disconnect the electrical connectors leading to the assemblies. Problems with the pre-tensioners will turn on the SRS (airbag) warning light on the dash. If any pre-tensioner problems are suspected, take the vehicle to a dealer service department.*

Warning: *On models with side-impact airbags, be sure to disarm the airbag system before beginning this procedure (see Chapter 12).*

Front seat
Refer to illustrations 28.2a and 28.2b
1   Disconnect the cable from the negative battery terminal (see Chapter 5).
2   Position the seat all the way forward, then all the way to the rear to access the seat retaining bolts **(see illustrations).**
3   Detach any bolt trim covers and remove the retaining bolts.
4   Tilt the seat upward to access the underneath, then disconnect any electrical connectors and lift the seat from the vehicle.
5   Installation is the reverse of removal.

Rear seat
Refer to illustrations 28.6a and 28.6b
6   On Coupe, Sedan and Hatchback models, remove the seat cushion bolt and remove the cushion **(see illustration).** Pull back the seat back trim cover, then remove the fasteners securing the seat hinge and remove the seat backs **(see illustration).**

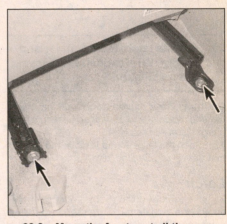

28.2a Move the front seat all the way forward to access the rear retaining bolts . . .

7   On CR-V models, tilt the seat forward and remove the retaining bolts at the front of the seat. Remove the seat from the vehicle.
8   Installation is the reverse of removal.

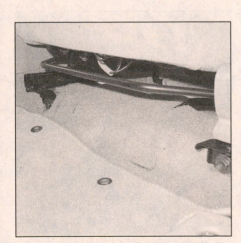

28.2b . . . then move the seat all the way to the rear to access the front retaining bolts

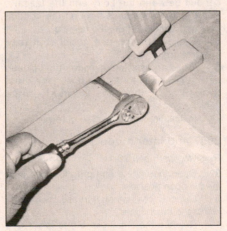

28.6a Remove the rear seat cushion retaining bolt

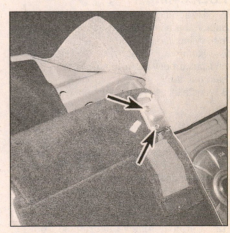

28.6b Remove the fasteners securing the seat hinge

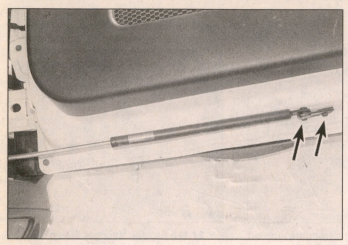

30.5 Remove the bolts securing the assist strut to the tailgate

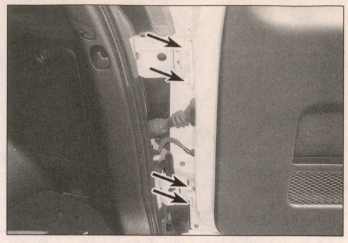

30.6 Tailgate hinge-to-tailgate bolts

29 Tailgate latch, lock cylinder and handle (CR-V models) - removal and installation

Caution: *Wear gloves when working inside the door openings to protect against cuts from sharp metal edges.*

1   Open the tailgate and remove the tailgate trim panel (see Section 18).

Latch

2   Reaching through the access hole, detach the tailgate rod and cylinder rod, then disconnect the actuator connector from the latch.

3   On 2006 and later models, remove the actuator connector and latch switch connector.

4   Remove the latch mounting screws and remove the latch from the tailgate.

5   Installation is the reverse of removal.

Lock cylinder

6   Reaching through the access hole, detach the actuating rod from the rear of the lock cylinder.

7   Remove the lock cylinder retaining clip and pull it outward to remove it from the tailgate handle.

8   Installation is the reverse of removal.

Handle

9   Reaching through the access hole, remove the lock cylinder (see Steps 6 and 7).

10   Remove the bolt securing the lock cylinder protector and handle to the tailgate. Release the clip and remove the protector.

11   Remove the bolt securing the handle and spacer handle to the tailgate.

12   Carefully remove the handle from the tailgate.

13   Installation is the reverse of removal.

30 Tailgate/liftgate and assist strut (CR-V models) - removal, installation and adjustment

Note: *The tailgate is heavy and somewhat awkward to hold - at least two people should perform this procedure.*

Removal and installation

2006 and earlier models

Refer to illustrations 30.5 and 30.6

1   Remove the spare tire from the tailgate if equipped. Open the tailgate and support it securely with several jackstands. Place pads or cloths between the jackstands and the tailgate to protect the paint.

2   Remove the tailgate trim panel (see Section 18).

3   Working through the openings in the tailgate frame, disconnect all wiring harness connectors leading to the tailgate.

4   From the tailgate side, detach the rubber conduit between the body and the tailgate. Pull the wiring harness through the conduit hole and remove it from the tailgate.

5   Remove the tailgate assist strut **(see illustration)**.

6   While an assistant supports the tailgate, detach the hinge-to-tailgate bolts **(see illustration)** and remove the tailgate from the vehicle.

7   Installation is the reverse of removal.

2007 and later models

Refer to illustration 30.11

8   Open the liftgate and prop it securely in the full open position.

9   Disconnect all wiring harness connectors leading to the tailgate.

10   Release the small clip at the lower end of the strut, then pull the strut from the mounting ball.

11   Remove the clip securing the upper half

of the support strut **(see illustration)** to the liftgate and detach the strut from the vehicle. Make sure the liftgate is supported properly before removing the struts or injury may occur.

12   While an assistant helps support the tailgate, detach the hinge-to-tailgate bolts and remove the tailgate from the vehicle.

13   Installation is the reverse of the removal procedure.

Adjustment

14   Adjustments are made by loosening the hinge-to-body bolts or the hinge-to-tailgate bolts and moving the tailgate **(see illustration 30.6)**. Proper alignment is achieved when the edges of the tailgate are parallel with the rear quarter panels and the lower door sill.

15   Adjust the latch striker assembly as necessary (up and down) to provide positive engagement with the latch mechanism.

16   Finally, adjust the tailgate wedge by slightly loosening the bolts and centering the

30.11 Use a small screwdriver to pry up the clip at each strut end, just enough to remove the strut from the ballstud

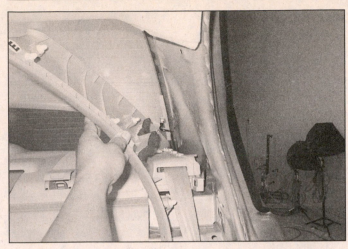

32.3a Carefully pull on the roof pillar trim pieces to detach the clips

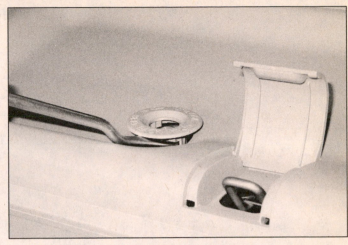

32.3b Pry or pull the plastic trim ring from around the lock cylinder

wedge between the holes in the adjustment slots. While holding the tailgate handle open, close the tailgate until it is flush with the body and the latch mechanism engages. Tighten the wedge bolts and recheck the adjustment, making sure the tailgate is flush with the body when closed.

31 Rear tailgate glass and support struts (CR-V models) - removal, installation and adjustment

Warning: *The rear tailgate glass is heavy and awkward to hold. At least two people should perform this procedure.*
Note: *On 2007 and later models, the rear tailgate glass is fixed to the tailgate. Replacement of the fixed glass requires the use of special fast-setting adhesive/caulk materials and some specialized tools and techniques. These operations should be left to a dealer service department or a shop specializing in glass work.*

Removal and installation

1   Open the rear hatch glass and support it fully in this position. If you're just replacing the glass support struts, proceed to Step 4.
2   Remove the tailgate upper trim panel and the left and right trim panels by carefully releasing the clips.
3   Remove the screws and detach the rear windshield wiper motor cover. Also remove the high mount brake light cover by pushing inward on the tabs at the side. Disconnect the electrical connector and remove the mounting nuts, then remove the high mount brake light.

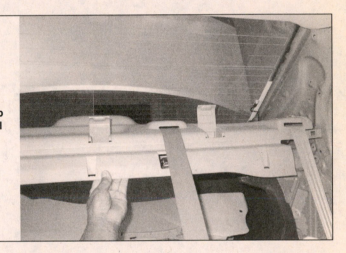

32.3c Carefully pull up on the shelf trim panel to release the clips

4   Detach the support struts at the rear hatch glass. If you're replacing the glass support struts, detach the strut from the body in the same manner as you detached the strut from the glass.
5   Remove the rear hatch glass mounting nuts, while at least one assistant, preferably two, helps you hold the rear hatch glass.
6   Installation is the reverse of the removal procedure. Be extremely careful not to overtighten the fasteners.

Adjustment

7   Adjustments are made by loosening the hinge-to-body bolts or the hinge-to-glass bolts and moving the glass. Proper alignment is achieved when the edges of the glass are parallel with the rear quarter panel pillars and the top of the tailgate.

8   Adjust the latch striker assembly as necessary (up and down) to provide positive engagement with the latch mechanism.

32 Rear shelf trim panel - removal and installation

Refer to illustrations 32.3a, 32.3b and 32.3c

1   Remove the rear seat cushion and seat back (see Section 28).
2   Open the trunk and disconnect the high mounted brake light.
3   Detach the roof pillar trim pieces on both sides, then remove the lock cylinder trim ring (if equipped) and detach the shelf trim panel **(see illustrations)**.
4   Installation is the reverse of the removal procedure.

Notes

Chapter 12
Chassis electrical system

Contents

	Section		Section
Airbag system - general information	23	Ignition switch and key lock cylinder - replacement	7
Antenna - removal and installation	12	Instrument cluster - removal and installation	10
Bulb replacement	17	Instrument panel switches - replacement	9
Circuit breakers, fuses and fusible links - general information	3	Key fob - battery replacement	6
Cruise control system - general information	20	Power door lock system - general information	22
Electrical connectors - general information	5	Power window system - general information	21
Electrical troubleshooting - general information	2	Radio and speakers - removal and installation	11
General information	1	Rear window defogger - check and repair	13
Headlight bulb - replacement	15	Relays - general information	4
Headlight housing - replacement	14	Steering column switches - replacement	8
Headlights - adjustment	16	Wiper motor - check and replacement	19
Horn - replacement	18	Wiring diagrams - general information	24

1 General information

The electrical system is a 12-volt, negative ground type. Power for the lights and all electrical accessories is supplied by a lead/acid-type battery that is charged by the alternator.

This Chapter covers repair and service procedures for the various electrical components not associated with the engine. Information on the battery, alternator, ignition system and starter motor can be found in Chapter 5.

It should be noted that when portions of the electrical system are serviced, the negative cable should be disconnected from the battery to prevent electrical shorts and/or fires.

2 Electrical troubleshooting - general information

Refer to illustrations 2.5a, 2.5b, 2.6 and 2.9

A typical electrical circuit consists of an electrical component, any switches, relays, motors, fuses, fusible links or circuit breakers related to that component and the wiring and connectors that link the component to both the battery and the chassis. To help you pinpoint an electrical circuit problem, wiring diagrams are included at the end of this Chapter.

Before tackling any troublesome electrical circuit, first study the appropriate wiring diagrams to get a complete understanding of what makes up that individual circuit. Trouble spots, for instance, can often be narrowed down by noting if other components related to the circuit

are operating properly. If several components or circuits fail at one time, chances are the problem is in a fuse or ground connection, because several circuits are often routed through the same fuse and ground connections.

Electrical problems usually stem from simple causes, such as loose or corroded connections, a blown fuse, a melted fusible link or a failed relay. Visually inspect the condition of all fuses, wires and connections in a problem circuit before troubleshooting the circuit.

If test equipment and instruments are going to be utilized, use the diagrams to plan ahead of time where you will make the necessary connections in order to accurately pinpoint the trouble spot.

The basic tools needed for electrical troubleshooting include a circuit tester or voltmeter (a 12-volt bulb with a set of test leads can also be used), a continuity tester, which includes a bulb, battery and set of test leads, and a jumper wire, preferably with a circuit breaker incorporated, which can be used to bypass electrical components **(see illustrations)**. Before attempting to locate a problem with test instruments, use the wiring diagram(s) to decide where to make the connections.

Voltage checks

Voltage checks should be performed if a circuit is not functioning properly. Connect one lead of a circuit tester to either the negative battery terminal or a known good ground. Connect the other lead to a connector in the circuit being tested, preferably nearest to the battery or fuse **(see illustration)**. If the bulb of the tester lights, voltage is present, which means that the part of the circuit between the connector and the battery is problem free. Continue checking the rest of the circuit in the same fashion. When you reach a point at which no voltage is present, the problem lies between that point and the last test point with voltage. Most of the time the problem can be traced to a loose connection. **Note:** *Keep in mind that some circuits receive voltage only when the ignition key is in the Accessory or Run position.*

Finding a short

One method of finding shorts in a circuit is to remove the fuse and connect a test light or voltmeter in place of the fuse terminals. There should be no voltage present in the circuit. Move the wiring harness from side-to-side while watching the test light. If the bulb goes on, there is a short to ground somewhere in that area, probably where the insulation has rubbed through. The same test can be performed on each component in the circuit, even a switch.

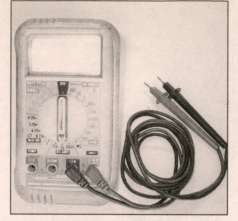

2.5a The most useful tool for electrical troubleshooting is a digital multimeter that can check volts, amps, and test continuity

Ground check

Perform a ground test to check whether a component is properly grounded. Disconnect the battery and connect one lead of a continuity tester or multimeter (set to the ohms scale), to a known good ground. Connect the other lead to the wire or ground connection being tested. If the resistance is low (less than 5 ohms), the ground is good. If the bulb on a self-powered test light does not go on, the ground is not good.

Continuity check

A continuity check is done to determine if there are any breaks in a circuit - if it is passing electricity properly. With the circuit off (no power in the circuit), a self-powered continuity tester or multimeter can be used to check the circuit. Connect the test leads to both ends of the circuit (or to the power end and a good ground), and if the test light comes on the

2.5b A test light is a very handy tool for checking voltage

circuit is passing current properly **(see illustration)**. If the resistance is low (less than 5 ohms), there is continuity; if the reading is 10,000 ohms or higher, there is a break somewhere in the circuit. The same procedure can be used to test a switch, by connecting the continuity tester to the switch terminals. With the switch turned On, the test light should come on (or low resistance should be indicated on a meter).

Finding an open circuit

When diagnosing for possible open circuits, it is often difficult to locate them by sight because the connectors hide oxidation or terminal misalignment. Merely wiggling a connector on a sensor or in the wiring harness may correct the open circuit condition. Remember this when an open circuit is indicated when troubleshooting a circuit. Intermittent problems may also be caused by oxidized or loose connections.

2.6 In use, a basic test light's lead is clipped to a known good ground, then the pointed probe can test connectors, wires or electrical sockets - if the bulb lights, the part being tested has battery voltage

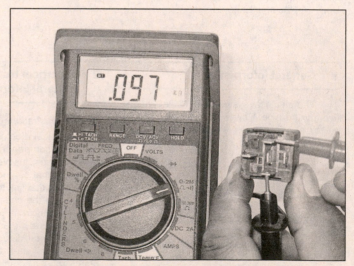

2.9 With a multimeter set to the ohms scale, resistance can be checked across two terminals - when checking for continuity, a low reading indicates continuity, a high reading indicates lack of continuity

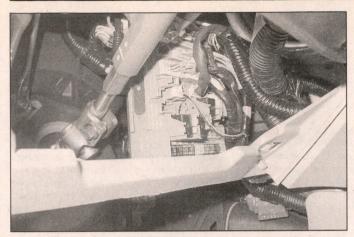

3.1a Remove the driver's dashboard lower cover to expose the under-dash fuse and relay box (on CR-Vs, the under-dash fuse/relay box is located in the same spot but has an access door in the driver's dashboard lower cover, so you don't have to remove the cover)

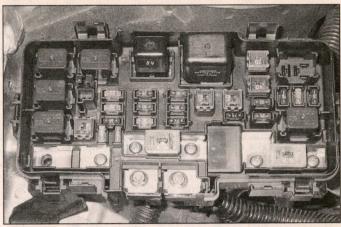

3.1b On coupes and sedans, the engine compartment fuse/relay box is located on the right side of the engine compartment. The functions and locations of the various fuses and relays are listed on the fuse/relay box cover (on CR-Vs and hatchbacks, this fuse/relay box is located on the *left* side of the engine compartment)

Electrical troubleshooting is simple if you keep in mind that all electrical circuits are basically electricity running from the battery, through the wires, switches, relays, fuses and fusible links to each electrical component (light bulb, motor, etc.) and to ground, from which it is passed back to the battery. Any electrical problem is an interruption in the flow of electricity to and from the battery.

3   Circuit breakers, fuses and fusible links - general information

Fuses

Refer to illustrations 3.1a, 3.1b and 3.3

The electrical circuits of the vehicle are protected by a combination of fuses, circuit breakers and fusible links. The main fuse/relay panel is in the engine compartment **(see illustration)**, while the interior fuse/relay panel is located inside the passenger compartment **(see illustration)**. Each of the fuses is designed to protect a specific circuit, and the various circuits are identified on the fuse panel itself.

Several sizes of fuses are employed in the fuse blocks. There are small, medium and large sizes of the same design, all with the same blade terminal design. The medium and large fuses can be removed with your fingers, but the small fuses require the use of pliers or the small plastic fuse-puller tool found in most fuse boxes.

If an electrical component fails, always check the fuse first. The best way to check the fuses is with a test light. Check for power at the exposed terminal tips of each fuse. If power is present at one side of the fuse but not the other, the fuse is blown. A blown fuse can also be identified by visually inspecting it **(see illustration)**.

Be sure to replace blown fuses with the correct type. Fuses (of the same physical size) of different ratings may be physically interchangeable, but only fuses of the proper rating should be used. Replacing a fuse with one of a higher or lower value than specified is not recommended. Each electrical circuit needs a specific amount of protection. The amperage value of each fuse is molded into the top of the fuse body.

If the replacement fuse immediately fails, don't replace it again until the cause of the problem is isolated and corrected. In most cases, this will be a short circuit in the wiring caused by a broken or deteriorated wire.

Fusible links

Some circuits are protected by fusible links. The links are used in circuits which carry high current.

Cartridge-type fusible links are located in the engine compartment fuse/relay box and are similar to a large fuse. After disconnecting the negative battery cable, simply unplug the fusible link and replace it with a fusible link of the same amperage.

Circuit breakers - general information

Circuit breakers protect certain circuits, such as the power windows or heated seats. Depending on the vehicle's accessories, there may be one or two circuit breakers, located in the fuse/relay box in the engine compartment.

Because the circuit breakers reset automatically, an electrical overload in a circuit breaker-protected system will cause the circuit to fail momentarily, then come back on. If the circuit does not come back on, check it immediately.

For a basic check, pull the circuit breaker up out of its socket on the fuse panel, but

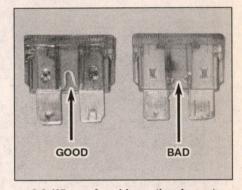

3.3 When a fuse blows, the element between the terminals melts

just far enough to probe with a voltmeter. The breaker should still contact the sockets. With the voltmeter negative lead on a good chassis ground, touch each end prong of the circuit breaker with the positive meter probe. There should be battery voltage at each end. If there is battery voltage only at one end, the circuit breaker must be replaced.

Some circuit breakers must be reset manually.

4   Relays - general information

Several electrical accessories in the vehicle, such as the fuel injection system, horns, starter, and fog lamps use relays to transmit the electrical signal to the component. Relays use a low-current circuit (the control circuit) to open and close a high-current circuit (the power circuit). If the relay is defective, that component will not operate properly. Most relays are mounted in the engine compartment and interior fuse/relay boxes **(see illustrations 3.1a and 3.1b)**.

5 Electrical connectors - general information

Most electrical connections on these vehicles are made with multiwire plastic connectors. The mating halves of many connectors are secured with locking clips molded into the plastic connector shells. The mating halves of some large connectors, such as some of those under the instrument panel, are held together by a bolt through the center of the connector.

To separate a connector with locking clips, use a small screwdriver to pry the clips apart carefully, then separate the connector halves. Pull only on the shell, never pull on the wiring harness as you may damage the individual wires and terminals inside the connectors. Look at the connector closely before trying to separate the halves. Often the locking clips are engaged in a way that is not immediately clear. Additionally, many connectors have more than one set of clips.

Each pair of connector terminals has a male half and a female half. When you look at the end view of a connector in a diagram, be sure to understand whether the view shows the harness side or the component side of the connector. Connector halves are mirror images of each other, and a terminal shown on the right side end-view of one half will be on the left side end-view of the other half.

It is often necessary to take circuit voltage measurements with a connector connected. Whenever possible, carefully insert a small straight pin (not your meter probe) into the rear of the connector shell to contact the terminal inside, then clip your meter lead to the pin. This kind of connection is called "back-probing." When inserting a test probe into a terminal, be careful not to distort the terminal opening. Doing so can lead to a poor connection and corrosion at that terminal later. Using the small straight pin instead of a meter probe results in less chance of deforming the terminal connector.

Electrical connectors

Most electrical connectors have a single release tab that you depress to release the connector

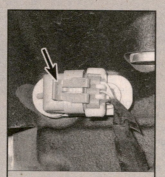

Some electrical connectors have a retaining tab which must be pried up to free the connector

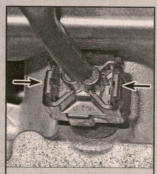

Some connectors have two release tabs that you must squeeze to release the connector

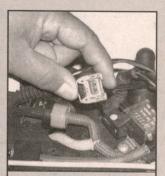

Some connectors use wire retainers that you squeeze to release the connector

Critical connectors often employ a sliding lock (1) that you must pull out before you can depress the release tab (2)

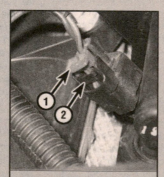

Here's another sliding-lock style connector, with the lock (1) and the release tab (2) on the side of the connector

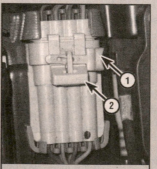

On some connectors the lock (1) must be pulled out to the side and removed before you can lift the release tab (2)

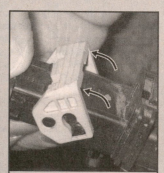

Some critical connectors, like the multi-pin connectors at the Powertrain Control Module employ pivoting locks that must be flipped open

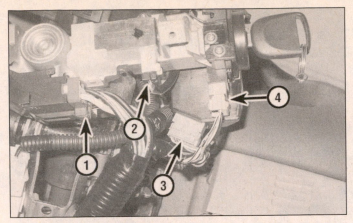

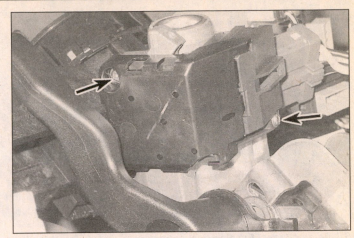

7.3 Ignition switch and key lock cylinder electrical connectors

1   *Ignition switch electrical connector*
2   *Ignition key lock cylinder electrical connector*
3   *Immobilizer control unit/receiver electrical connector*
4   *Ignition key lock cylinder/key light electrical connector*

7.4 To detach the ignition switch, remove these two screws

6   Key fob - battery replacement

1   Replace the battery when the key fob transmitter doesn't operate the locks at a distance of 10 feet. Normal range should be about 30 feet.

2   Before replacing the key fob battery, insert the key into the ignition and start the vehicle. If the vehicle starts with the key, continue to Step 3. **Note:** *If the vehicle will not start, the immobilizer and transmitter must be reprogrammed using the factory scan tool. Take the vehicle to a dealer service department or other qualified repair facility and have it reprogrammed.*

3   Using a small screwdriver, remove the screw on the key fob and carefully separate the case halves.

4   Remove the battery, noting which way it is facing before you remove it, then install the new one.

5   Snap the case halves together and install the screw.

6   Press the lock or unlock button five to six times, if the doors lock or unlock the transmitter is programmed and set. If the doors do not lock or unlock perform, the immobilizer and transmitter must be reprogrammed using a factory scan tool. Take the vehicle to a dealer service department or other qualified repair facility and have it reprogrammed.

7   Ignition switch and key lock cylinder - replacement

Warning: *All models covered by this manual are equipped with a Supplemental Restraint System (SRS), more commonly known as airbags. Always disable the airbag system before working in the vicinity of any airbag system component to avoid the possibility of accidental deployment of the airbag, which*

could cause personal injury (see Section 23).

1   Disconnect the cable from the negative battery terminal (see Chapter 5), then wait at least three minutes before proceeding.

2   Remove the driver's dashboard lower cover and the steering column covers (see Chapter 11).

Ignition switch

Refer to illustrations 7.3 and 7.4

3   Disconnect the electrical connector from the ignition switch **(see illustration)**.

4   Remove the ignition switch mounting screws **(see illustration)** and remove the switch.

5   Installation is the reverse of removal. Reconnect the cable to the negative battery terminal and perform the PCM idle learn procedure (see Chapter 5), then verify that the ignition switch operates correctly in the LOCK, ACC, ON and START positions.

Key lock cylinder

Refer to illustration 7.7

Note: *If the key lock cylinder is being replaced, the immobilizer and transmitter must be reprogrammed using the factory scan tool. Take the vehicle to a dealer service department or other qualified repair facility and have it reprogrammed.*

6   Disconnect the ignition switch electrical connector and the connectors for the ignition key lock cylinder, the immobilizer control unit/receiver and the ignition key lock cylinder/key light **(see illustration 7.3)**.

7   Center-punch the shear-head bolts that secure the key lock cylinder housing to the steering column, then drill a hole in the center of each bolt with a 3/16-inch (5 mm) drill bit **(see illustration)** and unscrew them with a screw extractor.

8   Remove the key lock cylinder assembly from the steering column.

9   Before tightening the new shear-head

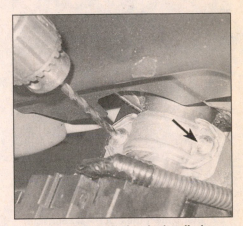

7.7 To detach the key lock cylinder housing from the steering column, drill out the bolts with a 3/16-inch (5 mm) drill bit and remove the bolts with a screw extractor

bolts, insert the ignition key and verify that the steering wheel lock mechanism functions correctly and that the ignition key turns freely in the key lock cylinder. Then tighten the shear-head bolts until the heads break off.

10   Installation is otherwise the reverse of removal. Reconnect the cable to the negative battery terminal (see Chapter 5).

8   Steering column switches - replacement

Warning: *All models covered by this manual are equipped with a Supplemental Restraint System (SRS), more commonly known as airbags. Always disable the airbag system before working in the vicinity of any airbag system component to avoid the possibility of accidental deployment of the airbag, which could cause personal injury (see Section 23).*

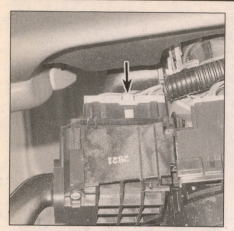

8.3 To disconnect the electrical connector from the multi-function switch, depress this release tab

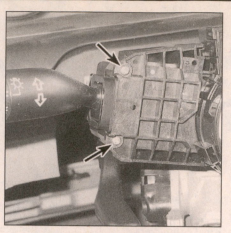

8.4 To detach the multi-function switch, remove these two screws

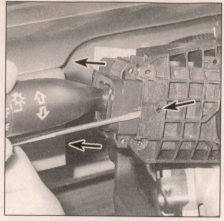

8.5 To remove the multi-function switch, carefully pry the combination switch housing off the small lug on the multi-function switch housing with a small screwdriver, then pull the multi-function switch straight out to the side

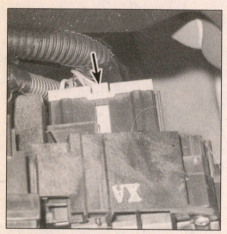

8.8 Disconnect the electrical connector from the windshield wiper/washer switch

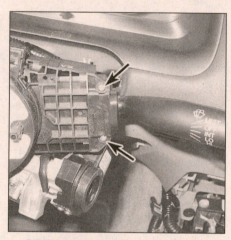

8.9 To detach the windshield wiper/ washer switch, remove these two screws

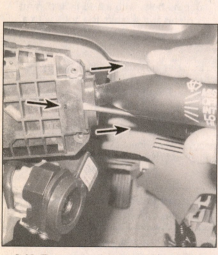

8.10 To remove the windshield wiper/ washer switch, carefully pry the combination switch housing off the small lug on the wiper switch housing with a small screwdriver, then pull the switch straight out to the right

1   Disconnect the cable from the negative battery terminal (see Chapter 5), then wait at least three minutes before proceeding.
2   Remove the driver's dashboard lower cover and the steering column covers (see Chapter 11).

Multi-function switch

Refer to illustrations 8.3, 8.4 and 8.5

3   Disconnect the electrical connector from the multi-function switch **(see illustration)**.
4   Remove the multi-function switch retaining screws **(see illustration)**.
5   Remove the multi-function switch **(see illustration)**.
6   Installation is the reverse of removal.
7   Reconnect the cable to the negative battery terminal (see Chapter 5).

Windshield wiper/washer switch

Refer to illustrations 8.8, 8.9 and 8.10

8   Disconnect the electrical connector from

the windshield wiper/washer switch **(see illustration)**.
9   Remove the windshield wiper/washer switch retaining screws **(see illustration)**.
10   Remove the windshield wiper/washer switch **(see illustration)**.
11   Installation is the reverse of removal.
12   Reconnect the cable to the negative battery terminal (see Chapter 5).

9   Instrument panel switches - replacement

Warning: *All models covered by this manual are equipped with a Supplemental Restraint System (SRS), more commonly known as airbags. Always disable the airbag system before working in the vicinity of any airbag system component to avoid the possibility of accidental deployment of the airbag, which could cause personal injury (see Section 23).*

2005 and earlier Coupe and Sedan models

Switches in driver's pocket (cruise control, moonroof and power mirrors)

Refer to illustrations 9.3a, 9.3b and 9.4

1   Disconnect the cable from the negative battery terminal (see Chapter 5), then wait at least three minutes before proceeding.
2   Remove the driver's dashboard under cover (see Chapter 11).
3   Open the driver's pocket, remove the retaining screw and remove the driver's pocket assembly **(see illustrations)**.
4   To remove the cruise control, moonroof or power mirror switch, depress the release tab on top and push the switch out from the backside of the trim piece **(see illustration)**.

9.3a Remove this retaining screw, pull out the driver's pocket assembly . . .

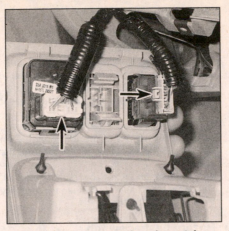

9.3b . . . then depress the release tab on each electrical connector and pull out the connectors

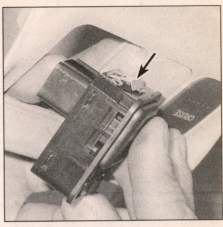

9.4 Depress the locking spring or tab with a small screwdriver from the backside of the trim panel, then push out the switch through the front side of the panel

9.8 To disconnect the electrical connector from the hazard flasher switch, depress this release tab and pull off the connector

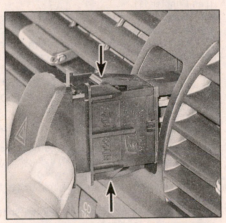

9.9 Depress these two locking tabs with a small screwdriver from the backside of the trim panel and push out the switch through the front of the trim panel

9.20 Typical 2006 and later Civic hazard flasher details

A *Hazard flasher electrical connector*
B *Hazard flasher mounting screws*

5   Installation is the reverse of removal. Reconnect the cable to the negative battery terminal (see Chapter 5).

Hazard flasher switch

Refer to illustrations 9.8 and 9.9

6   Disconnect the cable from the negative battery terminal (see Chapter 5), then wait at least three minutes before proceeding.
7   Remove the center trim panel from the dashboard (see Chapter 11).
8   Disconnect the electrical connector from the hazard flasher switch **(see illustration)**.
9   Remove the hazard flasher switch **(see illustration)**.
10   Installation is the reverse of removal. Reconnect the cable to the negative battery terminal (see Chapter 5).

Rear window defogger switch

11   The rear window defogger switch is an integral part of the heater and air conditioning control assembly. To replace the rear window defogger switch, you must replace the heater and air conditioning control assembly (see Chapter 3).

2006 and later Civic models

Driver's side switches (dash lights dimmer switch and odometer select/reset switch)

12   Disconnect the cable from the negative battery terminal (see Chapter 5), then wait at least three minutes before proceeding.
13   Remove the driver's instrument panel lower cover (see Chapter 11).
14   The switch assembly is mounted to the back of the lower cover. Remove the retaining screws and the switch assembly.
15   Installation is the reverse of removal. Reconnect the cable to the negative battery terminal (see Chapter 5).

Hazard flasher switch

Refer to illustration 9.20

16   Disconnect the cable from the negative battery terminal (see Chapter 5), then wait at least three minutes before proceeding.
17   Remove the driver's instrument panel instrument cluster bezel (see Chapter 11).
18   Remove the radio unit (see Section 11).
19   Disconnect the electrical connector from the hazard flasher switch.
20   Remove the retaining screws and the hazard flasher switch **(see illustration)**.
21   Installation is the reverse of removal. Reconnect the cable to the negative battery terminal (see Chapter 5).

Rear window defogger switch

22   The rear window defogger switch is an integral part of the heater and air conditioning control assembly. To replace the rear window defogger switch, you must replace the heater

and air conditioning control assembly (see Chapter 3).

Accessory power sockets

23 Disconnect the cable from the negative battery terminal (see Chapter 5), then wait at least three minutes before proceeding.
24 Remove the radio unit (see Section 11).
25 Disconnect the electrical connector from the power socket.
26 Pull the inner socket out from the outer collar.
27 Carefully pull the outer collar and cover from the instrument panel.
28 Installation is the reverse of removal. Reconnect the cable to the negative battery terminal (see Chapter 5).

2006 and earlier CR-V
Cruise control switch or moonroof switch

29 Disconnect the cable from the negative battery terminal (see Chapter 5), then wait at least three minutes before proceeding.
30 Remove the driver's dashboard lower cover (see Chapter 11).
31 Depress the release tabs on the cruise control switch or moonroof switch and push the switch out of the trim panel **(see illustration 9.4)**, then disconnect the electrical connector from the switch.
32 Installation is the reverse of removal. Reconnect the cable to the negative battery terminal (see Chapter 5).

Hazard flasher switch

33 Disconnect the cable from the negative battery terminal (see Chapter 5), then wait at least three minutes before proceeding.
34 Remove the center trim panel (see Chapter 11).
35 Disconnect the electrical connector from the hazard flasher switch **(see illustration 9.8)**.
36 Depress the release tabs, then push out the hazard flasher switch from behind the center trim panel **(see illustration 9.9)**.
37 Installation is the reverse of removal. Reconnect the cable to the negative battery terminal (see Chapter 5).

Seat heater switches

38 Disconnect the cable from the negative battery terminal (see Chapter 5), then wait at least three minutes before proceeding.
39 Remove the driver's dashboard lower cover (see Chapter 11).
40 Reach underneath the dash and disconnect the electrical connector from the seat heater switch.
41 Depress the seat heater switch release tabs with a small screwdriver and push the switch out of the dashboard from the backside of the dash.
42 Installation is the reverse of removal. Reconnect the cable to the negative battery terminal (see Chapter 5).

2007 and later CR-V
Power mirror switch and VSA OFF switch

43 Disconnect the cable from the negative battery terminal (see Chapter 5), then wait at least three minutes before proceeding.
44 Remove the driver's dashboard lower cover (see Chapter 11).
45 Reach behind the switch assembly and push the switch out of the trim panel, then disconnect the electrical connector from the switch.
46 Installation is the reverse of removal. Reconnect the cable to the negative battery terminal (see Chapter 5).

Hazard flasher switch

47 Disconnect the cable from the negative battery terminal (see Chapter 5), then wait at least three minutes before proceeding.
48 Remove the center vent and trim panel (see Chapter 11).
49 Disconnect the electrical connector from the hazard flasher switch.
50 Depress the release tabs, then push out the hazard flasher switch from behind center vent panel.
51 Installation is the reverse of removal. Reconnect the cable to the negative battery terminal (see Chapter 5).

Seat heater switches

52 Disconnect the cable from the negative battery terminal (see Chapter 5), then wait at least three minutes before proceeding.
53 Remove the heater A/C control unit (see Chapter 3).
54 Using a trim tool, carefully pry the shift lever panel up to release the clips and outer hooks. Disconnect the electrical connector from the seat heater switches and remove the panel.
55 Remove the retaining screws and the seat heater switch(s).
56 Installation is the reverse of removal. Reconnect the cable to the negative battery terminal (see Chapter 5).

Rear window defogger switch

57 The rear window defogger switch is an integral part of the heater and air conditioning control assembly. To replace the rear window defogger switch, you must replace the heater and air conditioning control assembly (see Chapter 3).

Accessory power sockets

58 Disconnect the cable from the negative battery terminal (see Chapter 5), then wait at least three minutes before proceeding.
59 Remove the lower center instrument panel (see Chapter 11).
60 Disconnect the electrical connector from the power socket.
61 Pull the inner socket out from the outer collar.
62 Carefully pull the outer collar and cover from the instrument panel.
63 Installation is the reverse of removal. Reconnect the cable to the negative battery terminal (see Chapter 5).

Hatchback
Hazard flasher switch

64 Disconnect the cable from the negative battery terminal (see Chapter 5), then wait at least three minutes before proceeding.
65 Remove the center trim panel (see Chapter 11).
66 Disconnect the electrical connector from the hazard warning switch **(see illustration 9.8)**.
67 Remove the two hazard warning switch mounting screws, then push out the hazard warning switch from behind the center trim panel **(see illustration 9.9)**.
68 Installation is the reverse of removal. Reconnect the cable to the negative battery terminal (see Chapter 5).

Rear window defogger switch

69 The rear window defogger switch is an integral part of the heater and air conditioning control assembly. To replace the defogger switch, you must replace the heater and air conditioning control assembly (see Chapter 3).

Cruise control main switch

70 Disconnect the cable from the negative battery terminal (see Chapter 5), then wait at least three minutes before proceeding.
71 Remove the driver's dashboard lower cover (see Chapter 11).
72 Reach underneath the dash and disconnect the electrical connector from the cruise control main switch.
73 Depress the cruise control main switch release tabs with a small screwdriver and push the switch out of the dashboard from the backside of the dash.
74 Installation is the reverse of removal. Reconnect the cable to the negative battery terminal (see Chapter 5).

Power mirror switch

75 Disconnect the cable from the negative battery terminal (see Chapter 5), then wait at least three minutes before proceeding.
76 Remove the driver's pocket.
77 Reach through the opening for the driver's pocket, depress the release tabs on the power mirror switch and push the switch out of the dash from the backside.
78 Disconnect the electrical connector from the power mirror switch.
79 Installation is the reverse of removal. Reconnect the cable to the negative battery terminal (see Chapter 5).

Moonroof switch

80 Disconnect the cable from the negative battery terminal (see Chapter 5), then wait at least three minutes before proceeding.
81 Pry the moonroof switch out of the headliner.
82 Disconnect the electrical connector from

10.3a Remove the screws and detach the instrument cluster from the dashboard (2005 and earlier Civics shown, CR-V models similar)

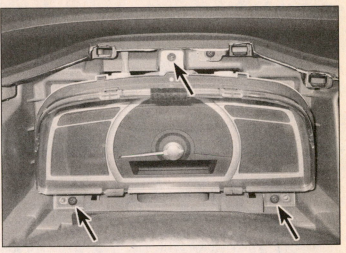

10.3b On 2006 and later Civics, remove the lower cluster fasteners . . .

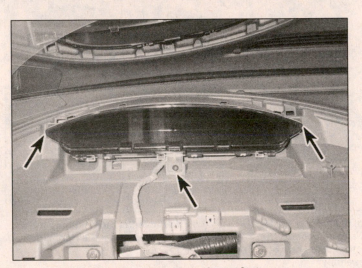

10.3c . . . and the upper cluster fasteners

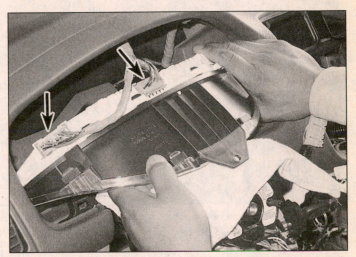

10.3d Pull out the cluster and disconnect the electrical connectors

the moonroof switch and remove the switch.
83 Installation is the reverse of removal. Reconnect the cable to the negative battery terminal (see Chapter 5).

---

10 Instrument cluster - removal and installation

Refer to illustrations 10.3a, 10.3b, 10.3c and 10.3d

Warning: *All models covered by this manual are equipped with a Supplemental Restraint System (SRS), more commonly known as airbags. Always disable the airbag system before working in the vicinity of any airbag system component to avoid the possibility of accidental deployment of the airbag, which could cause personal injury (see Section 23).*

1 Disconnect the cable from the negative battery terminal and wait at least three minutes before proceeding (see Chapter 5).
2 Remove the instrument cluster bezel (see Chapter 11).
3 Remove the instrument cluster retaining screws **(see illustrations)**, then pull out the cluster and disconnect the electrical connectors from the backside **(see illustration)**.
4 Installation is the reverse of removal.
5 Reconnect the cable to the negative battery terminal (see Chapter 5).

---

11 Radio and speakers - removal and installation

Warning: *All models covered by this manual are equipped with a Supplemental Restraint*

System (SRS), more commonly known as airbags. Always disable the airbag system before working in the vicinity of any airbag system component to avoid the possibility of accidental deployment of the airbag, which could cause personal injury (see Section 23).
Note: *Before beginning these procedures, make sure that you have the anti-theft code for the radio.*

Coupe and sedan models
Radio

1 Disconnect the cable from the negative battery terminal and wait at least three minutes before proceeding (see Chapter 5).

2005 and earlier models

Refer to illustrations 11.2 and 11.3

2 Remove the center trim panel from the dashboard (see Chapter 11), then disconnect

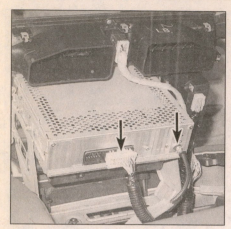

11.2 Pull out the center trim panel and disconnect the electrical connector and antenna cable from the backside of the radio

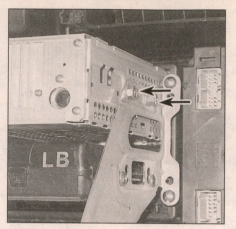

11.3 To detach the radio unit from its mounting bracket, remove the two bolts from each side

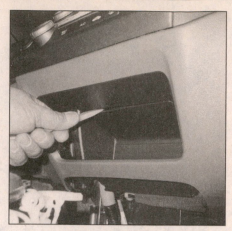

11.7a Carefully pry the pocket trim out . .

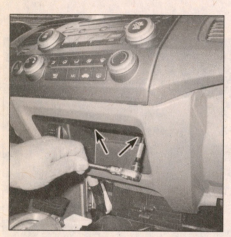

11.7b . . . and remove the mounting fasteners

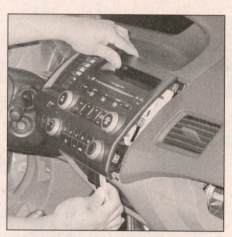

11.8 Use a trim tool to carefully pry the radio unit forward and disconnect the electrical connectors at the rear of the assembly

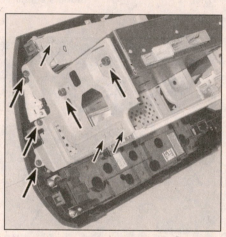

11.9a Remove the radio and mounting bracket fasteners from the right side . . .

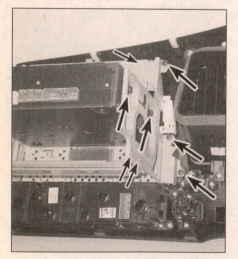

11.9b . . . and left side, then separate the radio unit from the center trim panel

the antenna and the electrical connector from the back of the radio **(see illustration)**.

3   Remove the radio mounting bolts **(see illustration)** and remove the radio from its mounting bracket.

4   Installation is the reverse of removal.

5   Reconnect the cable to the negative battery terminal and perform the PCM idle learn procedure (see Chapter 5).

2006 and later models

Refer to illustrations 11.7a, 11.7b, 11.8, 11.9a and 11.9b

6   Remove the driver's instrument panel lower cover (see Chapter 11).

7   Using a trim tool, remove the center pocket and remove the radio/navigation unit mounting screws **(see illustrations)**. **Note:** *If equipped with a navigation system, the navigation is incorporated into the radio unit; follow the radio removal and installation procedures to service the system.*

8   Carefully pry the radio unit forward **(see illustration)** enough to disconnect the electri-

cal connectors and remove the radio assembly from dash.

9   Remove the radio bracket mounting bolts **(see illustrations)** and separate the radio from the center panel.

10   Installation is the reverse of removal.

11   Reconnect the cable to the negative battery terminal (see Chapter 5).

Speakers

Tweeters (2005 and earlier models)

12   Remove the front door trim panel (see Chapter 11).

13   Disconnect the electrical connector from the tweeter.

14   Remove the mirror mount cover (see Chapter 11).

15   Remove the tweeter retaining screw and remove the tweeter.

16   Installation is the reverse of removal.

Tweeters (2006 and later models)

17   Pry the tweeter grille up and out from the corner(s) of the dashboard.

11.22 Remove the upper mounting screw (if equipped) and carefully pry the front door speaker out of the door with a panel removal tool (shown) or a large screwdriver (pry only at the top) . . .

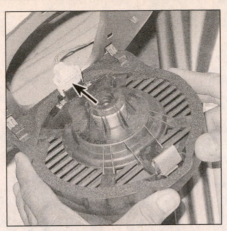

11.23 . . . then disconnect the electrical connector

11.26 To disconnect the electrical connector from a rear speaker, depress the release tabs and pull off the connector

18 Disconnect the electrical connector from the tweeter.
19 Remove the tweeter from the tweeter grille.
20 Installation is the reverse of removal.

Front door speakers

Refer to illustrations 11.22 and 11.23

21 Remove the front door trim panel (see Chapter 11).
22 Remove the mounting screw (if equipped) and working from the top, carefully pry the speaker out of the door **(see illustration)**.
23 Disconnect the electrical connector **(see illustration)** and remove the speaker from the vehicle.
24 Installation is the reverse of removal.

Rear speakers

Refer to illustrations 11.26 and 11.27

25 Remove the rear shelf trim panel (see Chapter 11).
26 Open the trunk and disconnect the electrical connector from the speaker **(see illustration)**.
27 Remove the speaker mounting screws **(see illustration)** and pull the speaker out of its receptacle.
28 Installation is the reverse of removal.

CR-V models

Radio

29 Remove the dashboard center panel (see Chapter 11).
30 Remove the four radio mounting bolts and pull out the radio.
31 Disconnect the electrical connector and the antenna lead from the radio.
32 If you're planning to replace the radio with a new unit, remove all four mounting bracket bolts from the left and right radio mounting brackets and remove the mounting brackets from both sides of the radio. Install

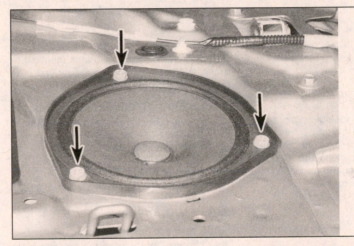

11.27 To detach a rear speaker from the rear shelf area, remove these three screws

these brackets on the new unit.
33 Installation is the reverse of removal.

Speakers

Door speakers

34 Remove the door trim panel (see Chapter 11).
35 Push down on the upper release tab and pull out the top of the speaker just enough to release the upper tab (if you pull out the speaker too far, you will damage the two lower mounting tabs). Pull the speaker straight up to disengage its two lower mounting tabs.
36 Disconnect the electrical connector from the speaker and remove the speaker.
37 Installation is the reverse of removal.

Tweeters

38 Carefully pry the tweeter speaker grille loose from the dashboard, then remove the tweeter speaker grille and the tweeter as a single assembly.
39 Disconnect the electrical connector from the tweeter and remove the tweeter.
40 Installation is the reverse of removal.

Hatchback models

Radio

Note: *Before beginning this procedure, make sure that you have the anti-theft code for the radio and that you have written down the frequencies for the radio station preset buttons.*

41 Remove the driver's dashboard lower cover (see Chapter 11).
42 Open the glovebox, remove the glovebox stops (see Chapter 11, Section 25) and let the glovebox hang down.
43 Remove the two center panel mounting bolts, then pull out the center panel.
44 Disconnect the electrical connector and the antenna lead from the radio. Disconnect the electrical connectors from the heater/air conditioner control assembly and remove the center panel, the radio and the heater/air conditioner control panel as a single assembly.
45 Remove the heater/air conditioner control panel from the center panel (see Chapter 3).
46 Remove the four radio mounting bolts and detach the radio from its mounting brackets.
47 Installation is the reverse of removal.

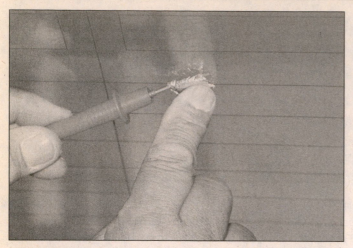

13.4 When measuring the voltage at the rear window defogger grid, wrap a piece of aluminum foil around the positive probe of the voltmeter and press the foil against the wire with your finger

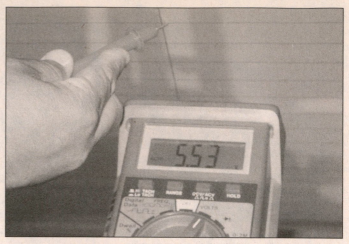

13.5 To determine if a heating element has broken, check the voltage at the center of each element; if the voltage is 5 or 6-volts, the element is unbroken, but if the voltage is 10 or 12-volts, the element is broken between the center and the ground side. If there is no voltage, the element is broken between the center and the positive side

Speakers

Door speakers

48   Remove the door trim panel (see Chapter 11).
49   Pull the top of the speaker straight out, just enough to release the upper retaining tab, then pull the speaker straight up to disengage the two lower mounting tabs. Remove the speaker from the door and disconnect the speaker electrical connector.
50   Installation is the reverse of removal.

Tweeters

51   Carefully pry the tweeter out of the mirror mounting trim cover.
52   Disconnect the electrical connector from the tweeter.
53   Installation is the reverse of removal.

Rear speakers

54   Carefully pry off the speaker cover.
55   Remove the three speaker mounting screws.
56   Pull out the speaker and disconnect the electrical connector.
57   Installation is the reverse of removal.

---

12   Antenna - removal and installation

Coupe and sedan models

Standard antenna

1   Coupes and sedans use a rear window-mounted antenna grid, which is similar to the defogger grid on the rear window. To replace the antenna, you have to replace the rear window. However, you can easily repair the antenna grid as long as the broken part is no more than one inch long. The procedure for repairing the antenna grid is identical to repairing the rear window defogger grid (see Section 13).

XM antenna (2006 and later models)

2   Carefully pry the rear window trim out.
3   Carefully pull the rear headliner down and remove the antenna mounting nut.
4   Disconnect the electrical connector and pull the XM antenna off the roof.
5   Installation is the reverse of removal.

CR-V models

2006 and earlier models

6   Unscrew and remove the antenna mast from its mounting base. If you're replacing the antenna mast, stop here. If you're replacing the entire antenna assembly, continue to Step 7.
7   Unscrew the antenna nut, the mounting base and the rubber bushing.
8   Disconnect the antenna lead electrical connector.
9   Remove the right inner fender housing panel (see Chapter 11).
10   Pull the antenna lead and weather seal grommet out of the A-pillar.
11   Remove the antenna housing bracket mounting nut and remove the antenna mounting bracket assembly.
12   Installation is the reverse of removal.

2007 and later models

13   Remove the rear, A, and B pillar trim panels (see Chapter 11).
14   Carefully pull the rear headliner down and remove the antenna mounting nut.
15   Disconnect the electrical connector and pull the antenna off the roof.
16   Installation is the reverse of removal.

Hatchback models

17   Carefully remove the rear part of the headliner.
18   Disconnect the electrical connector from the antenna.
19   Remove the antenna mounting nut.
20   Remove the antenna.
21   Installation is the reverse of removal.

---

13   Rear window defogger - check and repair

1   The rear window defogger consists of a number of horizontal elements baked onto the glass surface.
2   Small breaks in the element can be repaired without removing the rear window.

Check

Refer to illustrations 13.4, 13.5 and 13.7

3   Turn the ignition switch and defogger system switches to the ON position. Using a voltmeter, place the positive probe against the defogger grid positive terminal and the negative probe against the ground terminal. If battery voltage is not indicated, check the fuse, defogger switch and related wiring. If voltage is indicated, but all or part of the defogger doesn't heat, proceed with the following tests.
4   When measuring voltage during the next two tests, wrap a piece of aluminum foil around the tip of the voltmeter positive probe and press the foil against the heating element with your finger **(see illustration)**. Place the negative probe on the defogger grid ground terminal.
5   Check the voltage at the center of each heating element **(see illustration)**. If the voltage is 5 or 6-volts, the element is okay

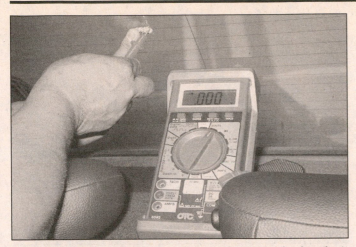

13.7 To find the break, place the voltmeter negative lead against the defogger ground terminal, place the voltmeter positive lead with the foil strip against the heating element at the positive terminal end and slide it toward the negative terminal end. The point at which the voltmeter reading changes abruptly is the point at which the element is broken

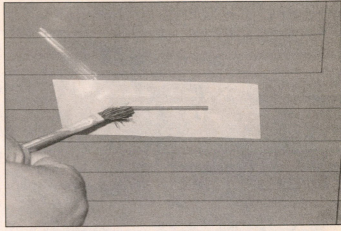

13.13 To use a defogger repair kit, apply masking tape to the inside of the window at the damaged area, then brush on the special conductive coating

(there is no break). If the voltage is zero, the element is broken between the center of the element and the positive end. If the voltage is 10 to 12-volts the element is broken between the center of the element and ground. Check each heating element.

6   Connect the negative lead to a good body ground. The reading should stay the same. If it doesn't, the ground connection is bad.

7   To find the break, place the voltmeter negative probe against the defogger ground terminal. Place the voltmeter positive probe with the foil strip against the heating element at the positive terminal end and slide it toward the negative terminal end. The point at which the voltmeter deflects from several volts to zero is the point at which the heating element is broken **(see illustration)**.

Repair

Refer to illustration 13.13

8   Repair the break in the element using a repair kit for this purpose (available at most auto parts stores). Make sure that the repair kit includes plastic conductive epoxy.

9   Prior to repairing a break, turn off the system and allow it to cool off for a few minutes.

10   Lightly buff the element area with fine steel wool, then clean it thoroughly with rubbing alcohol.

11   Use masking tape to mask off the area being repaired.

12   Thoroughly mix the epoxy, following the instructions provided with the repair kit.

13   Apply the epoxy material to the slit in the masking tape, overlapping the undamaged area about 3/4-inch on either end **(see illustration)**.

14   Allow the repair to cure for 24 hours before removing the tape and using the system.

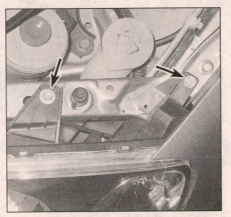

14.3a To detach the headlight housing assembly, remove the two upper mounting bolts . . .

14 Headlight housing - replacement

Refer to illustrations 14.3a, 14.3b and 14.5

1   Make sure that the headlight switch and the ignition switch are turned off.

2   Remove the front bumper cover (see Chapter 11).

3   Remove the headlight housing mounting bolts **(see illustrations)**.

4   Disconnect the electrical connectors from the headlight, turn signal and parking light bulbs.

5   If you're replacing the headlight housing, detach the corner bumper beam (the small black metal piece that's attached to the underside of the headlight housing) **(see illustration)** and install it on the new headlight housing unit.

6   Installation is the reverse of removal.

14.3b . . . and the two lower mounting bolts (2005 and earlier coupe/sedan shown, later Civics, CR-V and hatchback similar; CR-V models have *two* mounting bolts at the outer end of the corner upper beam instead of one bolt as shown here)

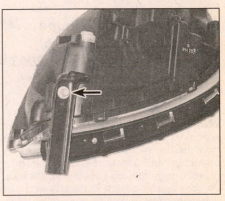

14.5 To detach the corner bumper beam from the underside of the headlight housing, remove this bolt (2005 and earlier coupe/sedan shown, later Civics, CR-V and hatchback similar)

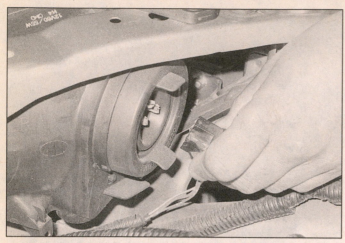

15.3 Disconnect the electrical connector from the headlight . . .

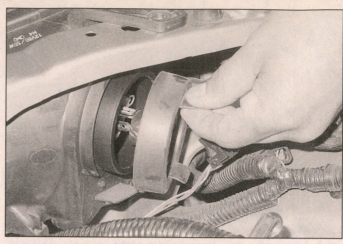

15.4 . . . then remove the rubber weather seal from the headlight assembly

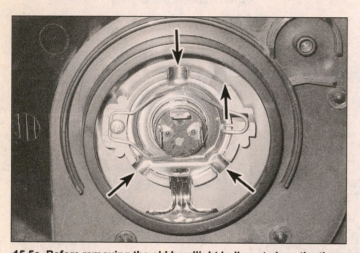

15.5a Before removing the old headlight bulb, note how the three metal tabs on the bulb mounting flange are aligned with their respective slots in the headlight mounting base. To disengage the headlight bulb retainer wire from the headlight assembly, lift the end of the wire up and out of its slot . . .

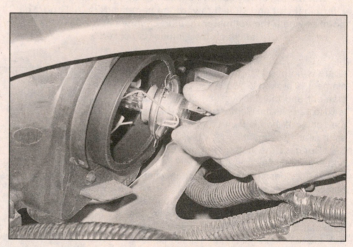

15.5b . . . then swing it open. Pull the headlight bulb out of the headlight assembly

15   Headlight bulb - replacement

2001 through 2003 Coupe and Sedan, 2002 through 2004 CR-V and 2002 and 2003 Hatchback

Refer to illustrations 15.3, 15.4, 15.5a and 15.5b

Warning: *Halogen gas filled bulbs are under pressure and can shatter if the surface is scratched or the bulb is dropped. Wear eye protection and handle the bulbs carefully, grasping only the base whenever possible. Do not touch the surface of the bulb with your fingers because the oil from your skin could cause it to overheat and fail prematurely. If you do touch the bulb surface, clean it with rubbing alcohol.*

1   Make sure that the headlight switch and the ignition switch are both turned off, then open the hood.

2   If you're going to replace the left headlight bulb, remove the power steering reservoir from its mounting bracket by pulling it straight up, then set it aside (do NOT disconnect any power steering hoses!).

3   Disconnect the electrical connector from the headlight **(see illustration)**.

4   Remove the rubber weather seal from the headlight housing **(see illustration)**.

5   Disengage the headlight bulb retainer wire, then remove the bulb from the headlight housing **(see illustrations)**.

6   Without touching the glass part of the new bulb with your bare fingers, insert the bulb into the headlight assembly. Make sure that the three metal tabs on the bulb **(see illustration 15.5a)** are aligned with the three slots in the plastic mounting base and that the bulb mounting flange is fully seated against the base.

7   Swing the bulb retainer wire back into place and engage the end with its slot.

8   Install the rubber weather seal on the back of the headlight assembly.

9   Plug in the electrical connector.

10   Verify that the new headlight bulb operates correctly.

2004 and later Civic and Hatchback, and 2005 and later CR-V models

11   Make sure that the headlight switch and the ignition switch are both turned off, then open the hood.

12   Disconnect the electrical connector from the headlight bulb socket. **Note:** *On 2006 and later Civics, the inner fender liner must be removed to replace the low beam bulb (see Chapter 11).*

13   Rotate the bulb socket counterclockwise 45-degrees and pull it out.

14   Installation is the reverse of removal.

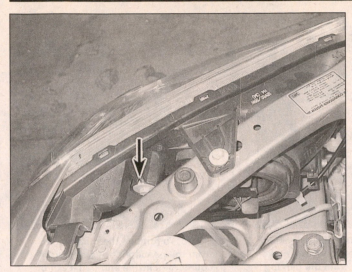

16.1a The vertical adjuster is located on the upper backside of each headlight housing

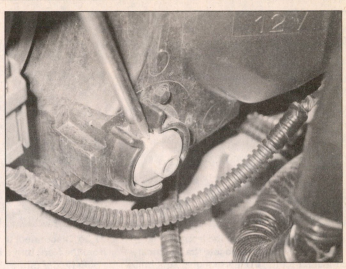

16.1b Using a Phillips screwdriver, adjust the headlight by turning the adjuster clockwise for UP and counterclockwise for DOWN

16 Headlights - adjustment

Refer to illustrations 16.1a, 16.1b and 16.3

Caution: *The headlights must be aimed correctly. If adjusted incorrectly they could blind the driver of an oncoming vehicle and cause a serious accident or seriously reduce your ability to see the road. The headlights should be checked for correct aim every 12 months and any time a new headlight is installed or front end body work is performed. It should be emphasized that the following procedure is only an interim step that will provide temporary adjustment until a properly equipped shop can adjust the headlights.*

1   The vertical adjuster **(see illustration)** is located on the upper backside of each headlight housing. Use a Phillips screwdriver to turn the adjusters **(see illustration)**. There are no horizontal adjustment screws.

2   There are several methods for adjusting the headlights. The simplest method requires masking tape, a blank wall and a level floor.

3   Position masking tape vertically on the wall in relation to the vehicle centerline and in relation to the centerlines of both headlights **(see illustration)**.

4   Position a horizontal tape line in reference to the centerline of all the headlights.

Note: *It might be easier to position the tape on the wall with the vehicle parked only a few inches away.*

5   Adjustment should be made with the vehicle parked 25 feet from the wall, sitting level, the gas tank half-full and no heavy load in the vehicle.

6   With the low beams turned on, position the high intensity zone so it is two inches below the horizontal line.

7   With the high beams on, the high intensity zone should be vertically centered with the exact center just below the horizontal line.

Note: *It might not be possible to position the headlight aim exactly for both high and low beams. If a compromise must be made, keep in mind that the low beams are the most used*

and have the greatest effect on safety.

8   If you have any difficulty adjusting the headlights, have them adjusted by a dealer service department as soon as possible.

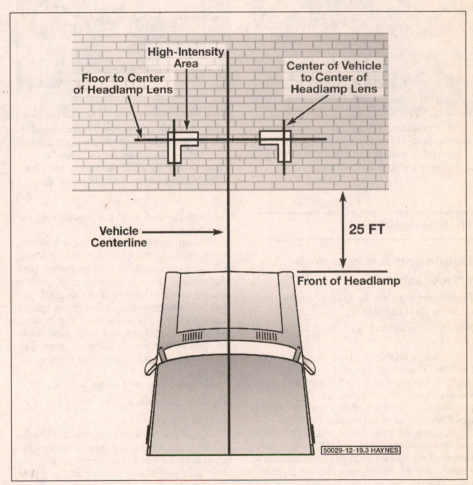

16.3 Headlight adjustment details

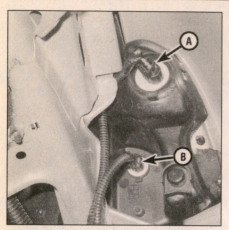

17.3a After removing the front part of the inner fender liner, locate the electrical connector for the front turn signal light bulb (A) or for the front parking light bulb (B)

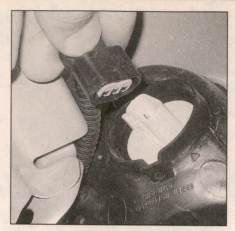

17.3b Disconnect the electrical connector from the front turn signal light/side marker bulb holder (shown) or from the parking light bulb holder

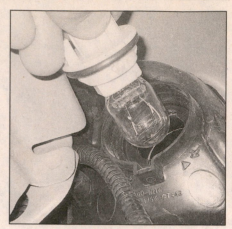

17.3c To remove the bulb holder from the headlight housing, turn it counterclockwise and pull it out of the housing

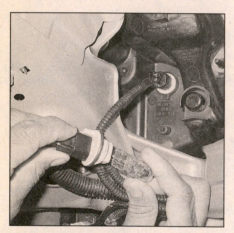

17.4 To remove the front turn signal/side marker bulb or the front parking light bulb from its holder, grasp the holder firmly and pull the bulb straight out

17.6 Disconnect the electrical connector from the high-mount brake light bulb holder, then turn the bulb holder counterclockwise to remove it from the high-mount brake light housing

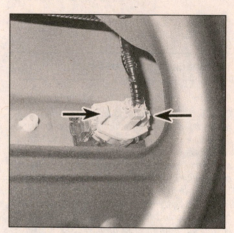

17.11 To remove the bulb holder for either license plate light, depress these two release tabs and pull the holder out of the license plate light lens (it's not necessary to disconnect the electrical connector)

17 Bulb replacement

Coupe and sedan models

Exterior light bulbs

Front turn signal/side marker and parking light bulb(s)

Refer to illustrations 17.3a, 17.3b, 17.3c and 17.4

1   If you're changing a bulb on the left side, turn the wheels all the way to the right. If you're replacing a bulb on the right side, turn the wheels all the way to the left.

2   Remove the front part of the left or right inner fender liner (see Chapter 11).

3   Locate the front turn signal bulb holder and the front parking light bulb holder **(see illustration)**. Disconnect the electrical connector from the front turn signal bulb holder **(see illustration)** or from the front parking light bulb holder. To remove the bulb holder, turn it counterclockwise **(see illustration)** and pull it out of the housing.

4   Remove the turn signal bulb from the bulb holder. On 2001 through 2003 models, pull the bulb straight out of its holder **(see illustration)**. To install a new bulb, push it straight into the bulb holder. On 2004 and later models, push the bulb into the holder, rotate it counterclockwise, then pull it out of the holder. To install a new bulb, push it into the bulb holder until it's seated, then give it a clockwise turn to lock it into place in the holder.

5   Installation is the reverse of removal.

High-mount brake light

Refer to illustration 17.6

6   Open the trunk and look for the electrical connector for the high-mount brake light, which is located in the underside of the rear shelf area, just ahead of the trunk light **(see illustration)**.

7   Disconnect the electrical connector from

the bulb holder.

8   To remove the bulb holder from the high-mount brake light assembly, rotate the bulb holder counterclockwise and pull it out.

9   To remove the old bulb from the bulb holder, pull it straight out of the holder. To install a new bulb, push it straight into the bulb holder.

10   Installation is the reverse of removal.

License plate light

Refer to illustration 17.11

11   Open the trunk and locate the electrical connector for the license plate bulb you wish to replace **(see illustration)**.

12   To remove the bulb holder, depress the release tabs on the sides of the holder **(see illustration 17.11)** and pull it out. It's not necessary to disconnect the electrical connector from the bulb holder in order to remove the holder.

13   To remove the bulb from the socket, pull it straight out.

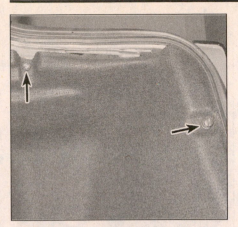

17.16 To gain access to the outer taillight bulbs, remove these two screws and carefully peel back the molded carpeting (if you have difficulty pulling back the carpeting, remove the third screw, which is located down near the floor of the trunk)

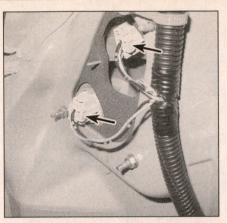

17.17a On 2005 and earlier models, when you peel back the carpeting in the trunk, you'll see two bulb holders: the upper bulb holder is for the brake/tail/rear side marker light bulb and the lower holder is for the turn signal light bulb

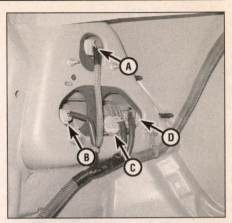

17.17b On 2006 and later models, there are four bulbs: taillight/brake light (A), backup light (B), rear turn signal light (C) and rear side marker light (D). To remove any bulb holder, turn it counterclockwise and pull it out

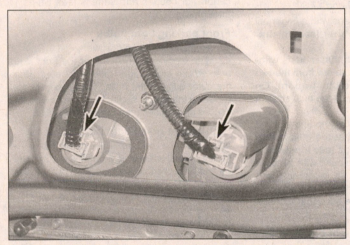

17.21 The bulb holders for the taillight and back-up light bulbs are in the trunk lid

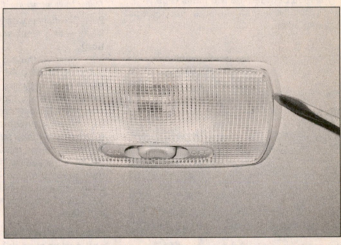

17.25 To remove the lens from the ceiling light, pry it off with a small screwdriver. Be careful not to damage the plastic trim around the edge of the lens

14   To install a new bulb in the holder, push it straight into the holder.

15   Installation is the reverse of removal.

Taillight bulbs (in rear fender)

Refer to illustrations 17.16, 17.17a and 17.17b

16   To access the outer taillight bulbs (in the vehicle's rear fender), detach and peel back the trunk carpeting **(see illustration)**.

17   After peeling back the carpeting, you'll see the bulb holders **(see illustrations)**. The upper bulb holder is for the brake/tail/rear side marker light bulb; the lower bulb holder is for the turn signal light bulb. To remove a bulb holder from an inner taillight, rotate the holder counterclockwise and pull it out.

18   To remove an inner taillight bulb from its holder, pull it straight out.

19   To install a bulb in its socket, push it straight into the socket.

20   Installation is the reverse of removal.

Taillight bulbs (in trunk lid)

Refer to illustration 17.21

21   Open the trunk lid and locate the bulb holders for the taillight and back-up light bulbs **(see illustration)**.

22   To remove either bulb holder, turn it counterclockwise and pull it out.

23   To remove either bulb from its bulb holder, pull it straight out of the holder.

24   To install either bulb in its bulb holder, push it straight into the holder.

Interior lights

Ceiling light (dome light)

Refer to illustrations 17.25 and 17.26

25   Using a fingernail file or a small screwdriver, pry off the lens **(see illustration)**. Be careful not to damage the plastic trim around the edge of the lens.

26   Remove the old bulb from the two metal clips **(see illustration)**.

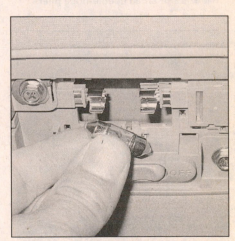

17.26 To remove the old bulb from the ceiling light, pull it straight out of the two metal clips

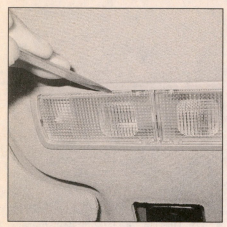

17.29 To remove the lens for the spotlight or the lens for the ceiling light/spotlight, carefully pry it loose with a small screwdriver

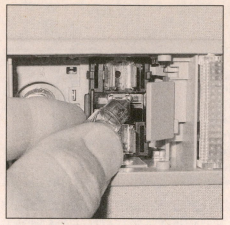

17.30 To remove a bulb from a spotlight assembly, pull it out of the two metal clips

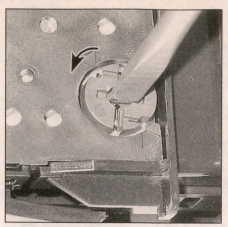

17.34a To remove the illumination bulb from the hazard flasher switch, unscrew it . . .

27   Install the new bulb. Make sure that it's fully seated between the two metal clips.
28   Install the lens. Make sure that it snaps back into place.

17.34b . . . and pull it out with a pair of tweezers or small needle-nose pliers

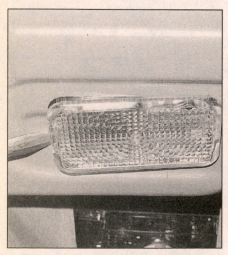

17.36 To remove the trunk light lens, carefully pry it loose from the trunk

Spotlight or ceiling light/spotlight

Refer to illustrations 17.29 and 17.30

29   Carefully pry off the lens with a fingernail file or with a small screwdriver **(see illustration)**.
30   Remove the old bulb. On models without a moonroof, pull the bulb out from the two metal retaining clips **(see illustration)**. On models with a moonroof, pull the bulb straight down from its receptacle.
31   Install a new bulb. On models without a moonroof, make sure that the bulb is fully seated in the two metal clips **(see illustration 17.26)**. If the vehicle is equipped with a moonroof, insert the bulb into its receptacle and push it straight up until it stops.
32   Install the lens. Make sure that it snaps into place.

Hazard flasher switch light bulb (2005 and earlier models)

Refer to illustrations 17.34a and 17.34b

33   Remove the hazard flasher switch (see Section 9).
34   Unscrew and remove the light bulb from the left side of the hazard flasher switch **(see illustrations)**.
35   Installation is the reverse of removal.

Trunk light bulb

Refer to illustrations 17.36 and 17.37

36   Open the trunk. Remove the trunk light lens **(see illustration)**.
37   To remove the old bulb, pull it straight out **(see illustration)**.
38   To install a new bulb, push it straight in until it stops.
39   Install the trunk light lens. Make sure that it snaps into place.

CR-V models

Exterior lights

Front side marker/turn signal light bulb

40   The electrical connector for the front side marker/turn signal light bulb is located near the headlight bulb connector. The procedure

for replacing the bulb is similar to the procedure for coupes and sedans (see Steps 1 through 4).

Front parking light bulbs

41   Remove the radiator cover.
42   The electrical connector for the front side marker/turn signal light bulb is located near the outer edge of the grille. The procedure for replacing the bulb is similar to the procedure for coupes and sedans (see Steps 1 through 4).

High-mount brake light bulb

43   Open the tailgate. To remove the high-mount brake light housing, push in on the tabs on the ends of the housing and pull off the housing. On 2007 and later models, remove the tailgate upper trim panel (see Chapter 11).
44   To remove the bulb holder, turn it counterclockwise and pull it out.
45   To remove the bulb from the holder, pull it straight out.
46   To install the new bulb in the holder, push it straight in.
47   To install the housing, place it in position and push on it until it snaps into place.

17.37 To remove the old bulb from the trunk light lens assembly, pull it straight out

License plate light bulb

48   On 2006 and earlier models, pry off the lens by inserting a small flat-tipped screwdriver between the right edge of the lens and the housing. On 2007 and later models, slide the lens from the left to the right and lift the lens off. To protect the lens from scratches, put a clean shop rag over the tip of the screwdriver or put a piece of duct tape on the tip.

49   Pull the license plate light bulb straight out of its socket.

50   Push the new bulb into the socket until it's fully seated.

51   Place the lens in position, left end first, then push on the right end until it snaps into place.

Taillight bulbs

52   Open the tailgate. Each of the two mounting screws for each taillight assembly is hidden by a trim cover. To remove the two trim covers, carefully pry off each of them with a small flat-tipped screwdriver. Put a piece of tape or a clean shop rag over the tip to protect the finish on the trim covers, then use the slot provided in each cover to pry it off.

53   Remove the two taillight assembly mounting screws and remove the taillight assembly.

54   There are four bulbs in the taillight assembly. They are, from top to bottom, the turn signal light bulb, the brake light bulb, the side marker/running light bulb and the back-up light bulb. To remove any of the bulb sockets, turn it counterclockwise and pull it out.

55   To remove a bulb from its socket, pull it straight out of the socket.

56   To install a new bulb in its socket, push it straight into the socket.

57   To install a bulb socket into the taillight assembly, insert the socket into its receptacle and give it a quarter-turn clockwise.

58   When installing the taillight assembly, make sure the locator pins on the taillight assembly are aligned with their respective holes in the pillar.

59   Installation is otherwise the reverse of removal.

Interior lights

Ceiling light and cargo area light bulbs

60   If you're replacing a ceiling light (dome light) bulb, carefully pry on the rear edge of the lens with a small flat-tipped screwdriver and remove the lens. Don't pry on the housing around the lens. If you're replacing a cargo area light bulb, pry on the front edge of the lens.

61   The ceiling light and cargo area light bulbs are identical. To remove an old bulb, pull it straight down.

62   To install a new bulb, push it straight up until it's fully seated in the two metal tabs.

63   Install the lens. Make sure that it snaps into place.

Spotlight bulbs

64   Pry on the front edge of the lens with a small flat-tipped screwdriver (just in front of the two spotlight bulbs).

65   Pull the spotlight bulb straight down to remove it.

66   Push the new spotlight bulb straight up until it's fully seated.

67   Install the lens. Make sure that it snaps into place.

Hazard switch light bulb (2006 and earlier models)

68   Remove the center panel and pull out the hazard flasher switch (see Section 9).

69   Remove the illumination bulb from the side of the hazard flasher switch.

70   Install a new illumination bulb in the switch.

71   Install the hazard flasher switch (see Section 9).

Glovebox light bulb (2006 and earlier models)

72   Open the glovebox and locate the glovebox light in the upper front part of the glovebox ceiling.

73   Remove the bulb by pulling it straight out of the two metal mounting tabs.

74   To install the new bulb, push it into the two metal tabs until it's fully seated.

Hatchback models

Exterior lights

Front turn signal bulbs

75   Using a flat-tipped screwdriver, remove the holding clip from the inner fender cover (see Chapter 11 if necessary).

76   Pull back the inner fender cover.

77   To remove the bulb socket from the headlight housing, turn it counterclockwise and pull it out.

78   To remove the old bulb from the socket, push it in and turn it counterclockwise until it unlocks, then pull it out.

79   To install the new bulb in the socket, push it in and turn it clockwise until it stops.

Front parking light bulbs

80   Open the hood and locate the electrical connector for the front parking light bulb, which is next to the headlight bulb connector.

81   To remove the bulb socket from the housing, turn it counterclockwise and pull it out of the housing.

82   To remove the old bulb from the socket, pull it straight out of the socket.

83   To install a new bulb in the socket, push it straight into the socket until it stops.

84   Insert the bulb socket into the parking light housing and turn it clockwise to lock it into place.

Front side marker bulbs

85   Push the front edge of the side marker lens toward the rear of the vehicle until the front edge of the lens pops out of the bumper cover.

86   To remove the bulb socket from the lens, turn the bulb socket counterclockwise and pull it out.

87   To remove the old bulb from the socket, pull it straight out of the socket.

88   To install a new bulb in the socket, push it straight into the socket until it stops.

89   Insert the bulb socket into the lens assembly and turn it clockwise until it stops.

90   Insert the tabbed end of the side marker assembly into the hole first, then the looped end, then press on the looped end until the assembly snaps into place.

High-mount brake light bulbs

91   Open the hatch. To remove the trim covering the high-mount brake light assembly, put your fingers between the trim and the hatch glass, then carefully pull down on the trim to unsnap the trim retaining clips from the hatch.

92   To remove the bulb holder from the high-mount brake light assembly, push the tabs on both sides and pull down the bulb holder.

93   To remove an old bulb from the holder, pull it straight out of the holder.

94   To install a new bulb in the holder, push it straight into the holder until it stops.

95   Push the bulb holder into the high-mount brake light assembly until it locks into place.

96   Align the clips on the trim with their corresponding holes in the hatch, then push the trim until the clips snap into place.

License plate light bulbs

97   To remove the license plate light assembly, slide the lens to the right until the left end pops out of the body, then pull out the license plate light assembly.

98   To remove the lens from the bulb socket, pull on the lens and squeeze the tabs on both sides of the socket at the same time.

99   To remove the old bulb from the bulb socket, pull the bulb straight out of the socket.

100 To install a new bulb in the socket, push it straight into the socket until it stops.

101 To install the lens on the bulb socket, push it into place until it latches.

102 To install the license plate light assembly, slide the right end of the assembly into the hole and push on the left end until the assembly snaps into place.

Side turn signal bulbs

103 Push the front of the side turn signal assembly toward the rear of the vehicle until it pops out of the body.

104 To remove the bulb socket from the lens, turn the socket counterclockwise.

105 To remove the old bulb from the bulb socket, pull it straight out.

106 To install a new bulb in the socket, push it straight into the socket until it stops.

107 To install the bulb socket into the lens, insert it into the hole in the lens and turn it clockwise until it stops.

108 To install the side turn signal assembly in the body, insert it into the hole rear end first, then push on the front end until it snaps into place.

Taillight bulbs

109 Open the hatch. Locate the trim cover in the corner of the cargo area. To remove the trim cover, carefully pry on the upper front edge with a small flat-tipped screwdriver.

110 You'll see three bulb sockets. The upper socket is for the turn signal light bulb, the mid-

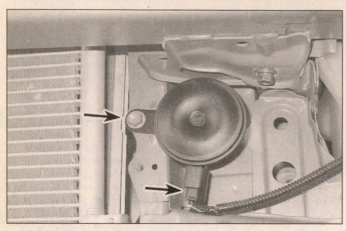

18.3 On 2005 and earlier coupes and sedans (shown), the horn is located below the left headlight. To remove the horn, disconnect the electrical connector and remove the mounting bracket bolt

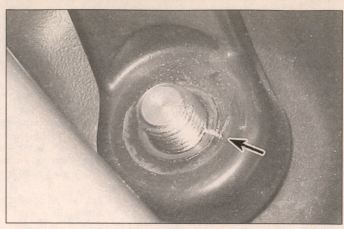

19.6 Pry off the trim caps and remove the windshield wiper arm retaining nuts, then mark the relationship of each wiper arm to its splined shaft before removing the arm

dle socket is for the back-up light bulb and the lower one is for the brake light/taillight bulb. All three sockets are removed the same way.

111 To remove a bulb socket, turn it counterclockwise and pull it out.

112 To remove an old bulb from its socket, push it in and turn it counterclockwise until it unlocks.

113 To install a new bulb into a socket, push it in and turn it clockwise until it stops.

114 Insert the bulb socket into the taillight assembly and turn it clockwise until it locks into place.

115 Install the trim cover.

Interior lights

Front ceiling light/spotlight bulbs

116 To remove the lens for the front ceiling light/spotlight, pry on the middle of the front edge of the lens.

117 To remove one of the old bulbs, pull it straight down.

118 To install a new bulb, push it straight up until it stops.

119 To install the lens, place the side with the tabs in position, then push the other side into place until it snaps into position.

Center ceiling light bulb

120 To remove the lens for the center ceiling light, pry on the middle of the side edge of the lens.

121 To remove the old bulb, pull it straight down from the two metal tabs.

122 To install a new bulb, insert it into the metal tabs until it snaps into place.

123 To install the lens, place the edge with the tabs in position, then push the other edge into place until it snaps into position.

Cargo area light bulb

124 Open the hatch. To remove the lens for the cargo area light, carefully pry on the front edge of the lens with a small screwdriver. Put a shop towel or a piece of tape on the tip of the screwdriver to protect the trim.

125 To remove the old bulb pull it straight out of the bulb holder.

126 To install a new bulb, push it straight into the holder until it's fully seated.

127 To install the lens, insert it into the mounting hole rear side first, then push on the front side until it snaps into place.

18 Horn - replacement

Refer to illustration 18.3

1   Raise the front of the vehicle and place it securely on jackstands.

2   Remove the front bumper cover (see Chapter 11).

3   There is one horn **(see illustration)** on 2005 and earlier coupes and sedans. There are two horns on 2006 and later Civics, all CR-Vs and hatchbacks, one below each headlight, and the replacement procedure is the same.

4   Disconnect the electrical connector from the horn.

5   Remove the horn mounting bracket bolt and remove the horn.

6   Installation is the reverse of removal.

19 Wiper motor - check and replacement

Wiper motor circuit check

Note: *Refer to the wiring diagrams for wire colors in the following checks. When checking for voltage, probe a grounded 12-volt test light to each terminal at a connector until it lights; this verifies voltage (power) at the terminal. If the following checks fail to locate the problem, have the system diagnosed by a dealer service department or other properly equipped repair facility.*

1   If the wipers work slowly, make sure the battery is fully charged and in good condition (see Chapter 5). If the battery is in good shape, remove the wiper motor (see below) and operate the wiper arms by hand. Check for binding linkage and pivots. Lubricate or repair the linkage or pivots as necessary. Reinstall the wiper

motor. If the wipers still operate slowly, check for loose or corroded connections, especially the ground connection. If all connections look OK, replace the motor.

2   If the wipers fail to operate when activated, check the fuse (see Section 3). If the fuse is OK, connect a jumper wire between the wiper motor's ground terminal and ground, then retest. If the motor works now, repair the ground connection. If the motor still doesn't work, turn the wiper switch to the HI position and check for voltage at the motor. **Note:** *Remove the hood seal and cowl covers (see Chapter 11) and disconnect the electrical connector (see Step 8).*

3   If there's voltage at the connector, remove the motor and check it off the vehicle with fused jumper wires from the battery. If the motor now works, check for binding linkage (see Step 1). If the motor still doesn't work, replace it. If there's no voltage to the motor, check for voltage at the wiper control relays. If there's voltage at the wiper control relays and no voltage at the wiper motor, have the switch tested. If the switch is OK, the wiper control relay is probably bad. See Section 5 for relay testing.

4   If the interval (delay) function is inoperative, check the continuity of all the wiring between the switch and the wiper control module.

5   If the wipers fail to park (if they stop at the position that they're in when the switch is turned off instead of returning to their normal off position), turn the wiper switch to OFF and the ignition switch to ON, then check for voltage at the park feed wire of the wiper motor connector. If no voltage is present, check for an open circuit between the wiper motor and the fuse panel.

Wiper motor replacement

Windshield wiper motor

Refer to illustrations 19.6, 19.8, 19.9a, 19.9b, 19.9c, 19.9d and 19.10

6   Remove the windshield wiper arm retaining nut covers, then remove the nuts. Be sure

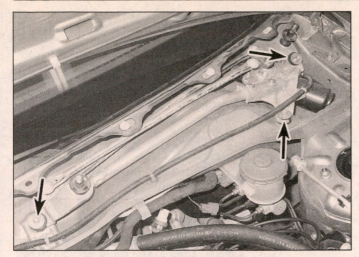

19.8 To detach the windshield wiper linkage/motor assembly from the cowl area, remove these three bolts

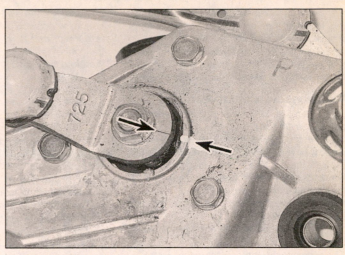

19.9a Mark the relationship of the linkage arm and the motor mounting bracket to ensure that the arm is correctly realigned during reassembly

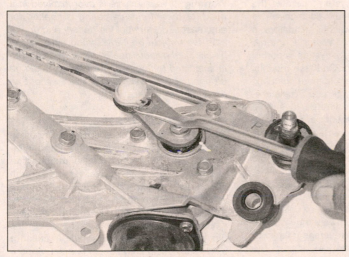

19.9b To separate the windshield wiper linkage from the linkage arm, pry the two halves of the spherical bearing apart

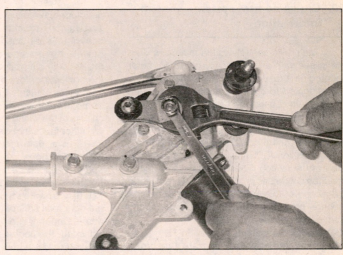

19.9c Using an adjustable wrench (shown) or a pair of large adjustable pliers to immobilize the linkage arm, loosen the arm retaining nut and remove the arm from the motor shaft

to mark the position of each wiper arm in relation to its splined shaft (see illustration), then remove the wiper arms.

7   Remove the hood seal and cowl covers (see Chapter 11).

8   Remove the windshield wiper linkage/motor assembly mounting bolts (see illustration), then disconnect the electrical connector from the windshield wiper motor.

9   Separate the windshield wiper linkage from the wiper motor (see illustrations).

10   Remove the windshield wiper motor mounting bolts (see illustration) and separate the motor from its mounting bracket.

11   Before installing the windshield wiper linkage (especially if you're installing the old linkage), be sure to grease the moving parts.

12   Installation is otherwise the reverse of removal. Be sure to align the marks you made between the linkage arm and the motor mounting bracket and between the windshield wiper arm and the motor shaft.

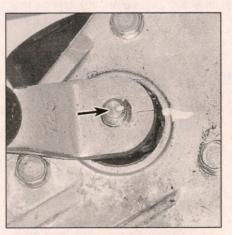

19.9d Mark the relationship of the linkage arm to the motor shaft, then remove the arm from the shaft

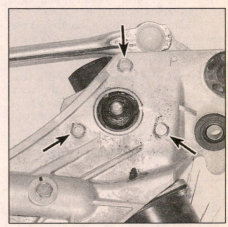

19.10 To detach the windshield wiper motor from its mounting bracket, remove these three bolts

13   Reconnect the cable to the negative battery terminal, then perform the PCM idle learn procedure (see Chapter 5).

14   Turn on the windshield wipers and verify that the wiper motor operates correctly in all modes (see your owner's manual if necessary).

Rear window wiper motor

15   Open the hatch. Remove the hatch trim panel (see Chapter 11).

16   Remove the windshield wiper arm retaining nut cover, then remove the nut. Be sure to mark the position of the wiper arm in relation to its splined shaft **(see illustration 19.6)**, then remove the wiper arm.

17   Disconnect the electrical connector from the rear window wiper motor.

18   Remove the three wiper motor mounting bolts.

19   Remove the rear window wiper motor.

20   Installation is the reverse of removal.

20 Cruise control system - general information

1   The cruise control system maintains vehicle speed with an electrically operated motor located in the engine compartment, which is connected to the throttle body by a cable. The system consists of the Powertrain Control Module, the speed control actuator, the speed control cable, the speed control indicator light, the speed control actuator switches, the Brake Pedal Position (BPP) switch and the transmission range switch. The cruise control system requires diagnostic procedures that are beyond the scope of this manual, but there are some general procedures that will help you identify common problems.

2   Check the fuses (see Section 3).

3   Have an assistant operate the brake lights while you check their operation (voltage from the brake light switch deactivates the cruise control).

4   If the brake lights don't come on or stay on all the time, correct the problem and retest the cruise control system.

5   Visually inspect the control cable between the cruise control motor and the throttle linkage for free movement. Replace it if necessary.

6   Test drive the vehicle to determine if the cruise control is now working. If it isn't, take it to a dealer service department or an automotive electrical specialist for further diagnosis.

21 Power window system - general information

The power window system operates electric motors, mounted on the doors, which lower and raise the windows. The system consists of the control switches, the motors, regulators, glass mechanisms and associated wiring.

The power windows can be lowered and raised from the master control switch by the driver or by the switch located at the passenger window. Each window has a separate motor that is reversible. The position of the control switch determines the polarity and therefore the direction of operation.

The circuit is protected by fuses and a circuit breaker. Check the fuses in the fuse panel at the left end of the instrument panel. Each motor is equipped with an internal circuit breaker; this prevents one stuck window from disabling the whole system. Refer to the wiring diagrams at the end of this Chapter. Problems within this system can only be diagnosed with a factory scan tool. If you have eliminated the obvious causes of a problem, have the vehicle checked at a dealership service department or other properly equipped repair shop.

22 Power door lock system - general information

1   A power door lock system operates the door lock actuators mounted in each door. The system consists of the switches, actuators, a control unit and associated wiring. On some models, the power door lock system is part of the security alarm system. On these models, the power door lock system is more complex, and more difficult to diagnose. Therefore, home troubleshooting is limited to simple checks of the wiring connections and actuators for minor faults that can be easily repaired.

2   Power door lock systems are operated by bi-directional solenoids located in the doors. The lock switches have two operating positions: LOCK and UNLOCK. When activated, the switch sends a ground signal to the door lock control unit to lock or unlock the doors. Depending on which way the switch is activated, the control unit reverses polarity to the solenoids, allowing the two sides of the circuit to be used alternately as the feed (positive) and ground side.

3   The following general guidelines should help you quickly identify and repair typical problems. If you're unable to locate the trouble using these guidelines, consult a dealer service department.

4   Always check the fuses first (see Section 3 and your owner's manual).

5   Operate the door lock switches in both directions (LOCK and UNLOCK) with the engine off. Listen for the click of the solenoids operating.

6   Test the switches for continuity. Remove the switches and have them checked by a dealer service department.

7   Check the wiring between the switches, control unit and solenoids for continuity. Repair the wiring if there's no continuity.

8   Check for a bad ground at the switches and at the control unit.

9   If only one lock solenoid doesn't operate, remove the trim panel from the door with the bad solenoid (see Chapter 11) and check for voltage at the solenoid while the lock switch is operated. One of the wires should have voltage in the Lock position; the other should have voltage in the Unlock position.

10   If the inoperative solenoid is receiving voltage, replace the solenoid.

11   If the inoperative solenoid isn't receiving voltage, check for an open or short in the wire between the lock solenoid and the control unit. **Note:** *Wire harnesses typically break between the body and door, because repeatedly opening and closing the door fatigues and eventually breaks the wires.*

23 Airbag system - general information

1   These models are equipped with a Supplemental Restraint System (SRS), more commonly known as airbags, designed to protect the driver and the passenger from serious injury in the event of a head-on or side collision. All models have a diagnostic control unit, located on the floor under the center console. **Warning:** *If your vehicle is ever involved in a flood, or the interior carpeting is soaked for any reason, disconnect the battery and do not start the vehicle until the airbag system can be checked by your dealer. If the SRS system is subjected to flooding, the airbags could go off upon starting the vehicle, even without an accident taking place.*

Airbag modules

2   The airbag modules consist of a housing incorporating the cushion (airbag) and inflator unit. The inflator assembly is mounted on the back of the housing over a hole through which gas is expelled, inflating the bag almost instantaneously when an electrical signal is sent from the system. The specially-wound wire on the driver's side that carries this signal to the driver's module is called a spiral cable. The spiral cable is a flat, ribbon-like electrically conductive tape that is wound many times so that it can transmit an electrical signal regardless of steering wheel position. Airbag modules are located in the steering wheel, on the passenger side above the glovebox, on 2006 and later models at the upper side of each front seat (side-impact airbags) and head-level airbags located along the roof rails (side curtain airbags). The side-impact airbag modules are mounted inside of the seats and the seat must be disassembled to gain access to the modules.

Control unit and sensors

3   The sensing/diagnostic control unit contains an on-board microprocessor which monitors the operation of the system, and the crash sensors. The crash sensors are located in the front and sides of the vehicle. It checks this system every time the vehicle is started, causing the "AIRBAG" light to illuminate for five seconds, then go off, if the system is operating properly. If there is a fault in the system, the light may not come on at all, the light will go on and continue, either illuminated steadily or blinking, and the unit will store fault codes indicating the nature of the fault.

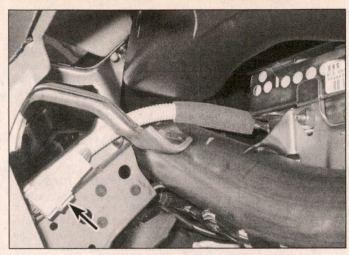

23.12 Before removing the passenger's side airbag module, be sure to disconnect the electrical connector

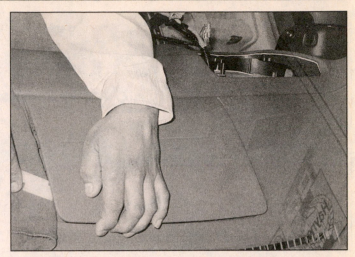

23.14 Using a shop towel to protect the dashboard, carefully pry loose the trim cover in the top of the dash, then lift out the cover and airbag module as a single assembly

Operation

4   For the airbag(s) to deploy, the impact sensor(s) must be activated. When this condition occurs, the circuit to the airbag inflator is closed and the airbag inflates.

Self-diagnosis system

5   A self-diagnosis circuit in the SRS unit displays a light on the instrument panel when the ignition switch is turned to the On position. If the system is operating normally, the light should go out after about five seconds. If the light doesn't come on, or doesn't go out after a short time, or if it comes on while you're driving the vehicle, or if it blinks at any time, there's a malfunction in the SRS system. Have it inspected and repaired as soon as possible. Do not attempt to troubleshoot or service the SRS system yourself. Even a small mistake could cause the SRS system to malfunction when you need it.

Servicing components near the SRS system

6   There are times when you need to remove the steering wheel, radio or service other components on or near the dashboard. At these times, you'll be working around components and wire harnesses for the SRS system. **Warning:** *Do not use electrical test equipment on airbag system wires; it could cause the airbag(s) to deploy.* ***ALWAYS DISABLE THE SRS SYSTEM BEFORE WORKING NEAR THE SRS SYSTEM COMPONENTS OR RELATED WIRING***.

Disabling the SRS system

Warning: *Any time you are working in the vicinity of airbag wiring or components, DISABLE THE SRS SYSTEM.*
Warning: *An auxiliary voltage input device (memory saver) must not be used when working near airbag system components.*

Caution: *Disconnecting the battery can cause driveability problems that require a scan tool to rectify. Additionally, disconnecting the battery may cause one or more warning lights on the instrument panel to illuminate, which will also require the use of a scan tool to turn off. Most scan tools available to the public do not have the capability to perform either of these tasks, which will necessitate taking the vehicle to a dealer service department or other properly equipped repair facility after service work has been performed. See Chapter 5 for other precautions related to battery disconnection.*
Caution: *These models are equipped with an anti-theft radio. Before performing a procedure that requires disconnecting the battery, make sure you have the proper activation code.*

7   To disable the airbag system, perform the following steps:

a) *Turn the steering wheel to the straight-ahead position and turn the ignition switch to the Lock position, then remove the key.*
b) *Disconnect the negative battery cable. Refer to the* **Cautions** *in Chapter 5.*
c) *Before touching any airbag system component, ground yourself to a metal part of the vehicle to discharge any static electricity built up in your body.*

Enabling the system

8   To enable the airbag system, perform the following steps:

a) *Turn the ignition switch to the On position.*
b) *Make sure nobody is inside the vehicle.*
c) *Connect the battery cable.*
d) *Turn the ignition to the Off position, then with your body out of the path of the airbag, turn the ignition switch to the On position. Confirm that the airbag warning light is functioning properly.*

e) *Take the vehicle to a dealer service department or other qualified repair facility and have the airbag system checked and the diagnostic light canceled, if it remains lit.*

Airbag module removal and installation

Driver's side airbag module and clockspring

9   Refer to Chapter 10, *Steering wheel - removal and installation*, for the driver's side airbag module and clockspring removal and installation procedures.

Passenger's side airbag module (Civic and Hatchback models)

Refer to illustration 23.12

10   Disarm the airbag system as described previously in this Section.
11   Remove the glovebox (see Chapter 11).
12   Disconnect the passenger side airbag module electrical connector **(see illustration)**.

2005 and earlier models

Refer to illustration 23.14

13   Remove the airbag module mounting nuts **(see illustration 23.18)**.
14   Working from above, carefully pry loose the trim cover in the dash **(see illustration)**, then lift the airbag trim cover and airbag module out of the dash as a single assembly. If necessary (and only if necessary), carefully separate the airbag module from the trim cover. Be sure to heed the precautions outlined previously in this Section.
15   Installation is the reverse of removal. Tighten the airbag module mounting nuts securely.
16   Reconnect the cable to the negative battery terminal (see Chapter 5).

23.18 To detach the passenger's side airbag module, remove the mounting nuts

2006 and later models

Refer to illustration 23.18

17   Remove the radio unit (see Section 11).

18   Remove the airbag module mounting nuts **(see illustration)**.

19   Carefully pry loose the trim cover in the dash, then lift the airbag trim cover and airbag module out of the dash as a single assembly.

20   Installation is the reverse of removal. Tighten the airbag module mounting nuts securely.

21   Reconnect the cable to the negative battery terminal (see Chapter 5).

Passenger's side airbag module (CR-V models)

2006 and earlier models

22   Disarm the airbag system as described previously in this Section.

23   Directly above the glovebox, you'll find a small access panel. Removing this panel provides access to the airbag module electrical connector. Carefully pry the access panel from the dashboard with a small screwdriver. Tape the end of the screwdriver to protect the dash trim.

24   Disconnect the airbag module electrical connector.

25   Remove the three airbag module mounting bracket nuts.

26   Working from above, carefully pry loose the trim cover in the dash **(see illustration 23.14)**, then lift the airbag trim cover and airbag module out of the dash as a single assembly. If necessary (and only if necessary), carefully separate the airbag module from the trim cover. Be sure to heed the precautions outlined previously in this Section.

27   Installation is the reverse of removal. Tighten the airbag module mounting nuts securely.

28   Reconnect the cable to the negative battery terminal (see Chapter 5).

2007 and later models

29   Disarm the airbag system as described previously in this Section.

30   Remove the passenger's side vent (see Chapter 11).

31   Remove the upper instrument panel center panel (see Chapter 11).

32   Disconnect the glovebox dampers and lower the glovebox (see Chapter 11).

33   Disconnect the airbag module electrical connector.

34   Remove the airbag module mounting nuts **(see illustration 23.18)**.

35   Remove the upper two module side screws.

36   Lift the front of the airbag module up, then lift the left side and right side to release the clips along the outer edge of the panel. Remove the airbag trim cover and airbag module out of the dash as a single assembly.

37   Installation is the reverse of removal. Tighten the airbag module mounting nuts securely.

38   Reconnect the cable to the negative battery terminal (see Chapter 5).

Impact seat belt retractors

39   All models are equipped with pyrotechnic (explosive) units in the front seat belt retracting mechanisms for both the lap and shoulder belts. During an impact that would trigger the airbag system, the airbag control unit also triggers the seat belt retractors. When the pyrotechnic charges go off, they accelerate the retractors to instantly take up any slack in the seat belt system to more fully prepare the driver and front seat passenger for impact.

40   The airbag system should be disabled any time work is done to or around the seats. **Caution:** *Never strike the pillars or floorpan with a hammer or use an impact-driver tool in these areas unless the system is disabled.*

---

24   Wiring diagrams - general information

Since it isn't possible to include all wiring diagrams for every year and model covered by this manual, the following diagrams are those that are typical and most commonly needed.

Prior to troubleshooting any circuits, check the fuses and circuit breakers (if equipped) to make sure they're in good condition. Make sure the battery is properly charged and check the cable connections (see Chapter 1).

When checking a circuit, make sure that all connectors are clean, with no broken or loose terminals. When disconnecting a connector, do not pull on the wires. Pull only on the connector housings themselves.

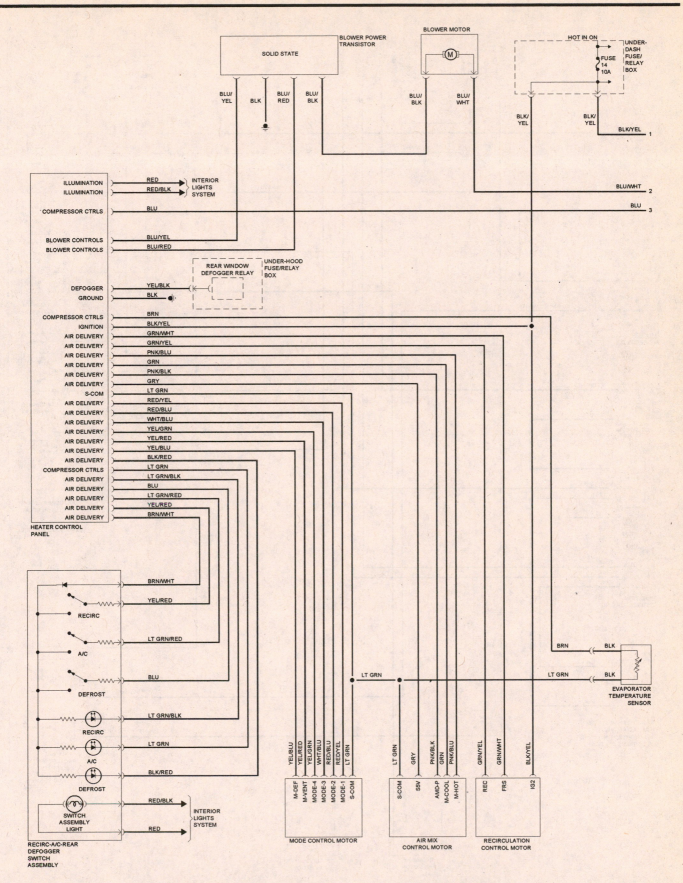

Air conditioning and engine cooling systems - 2005 and earlier coupe/sedan (1 of 2)

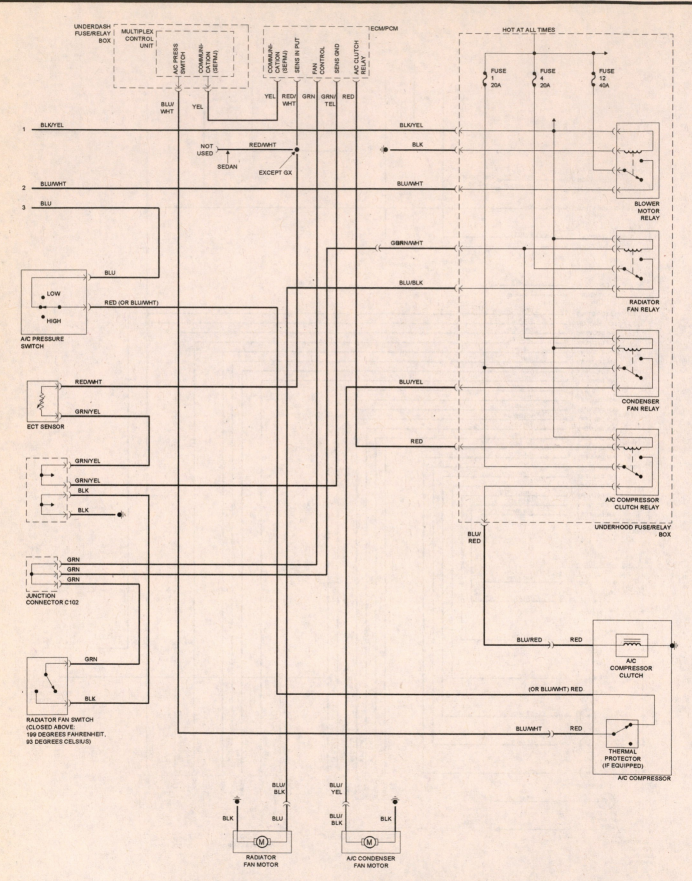

Air conditioning and engine cooling systems - 2005 and earlier coupe/sedan (2 of 2)

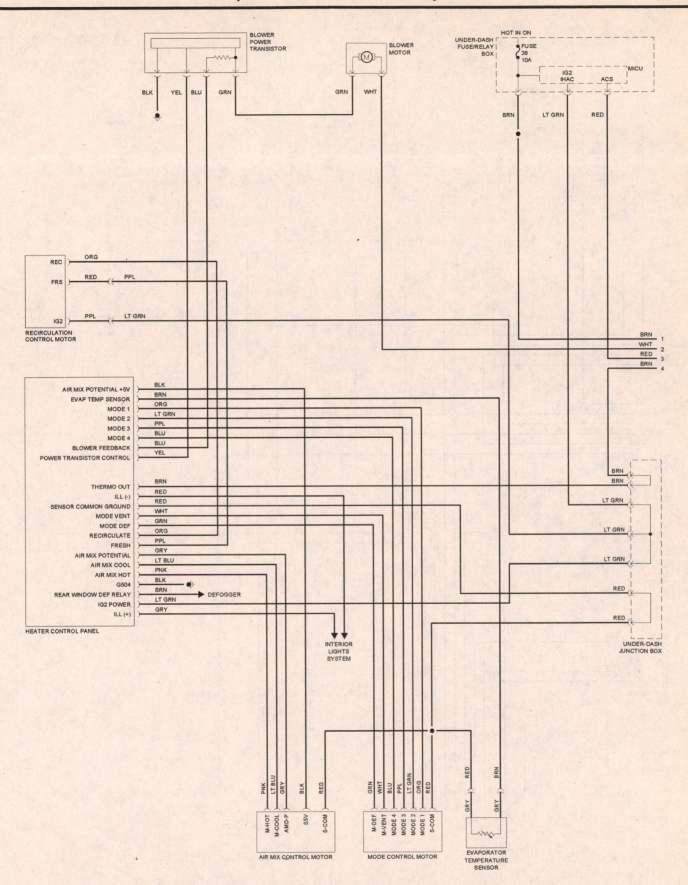

Air conditioning and engine cooling systems - 2006 and later coupe/sedan (1 of 2)

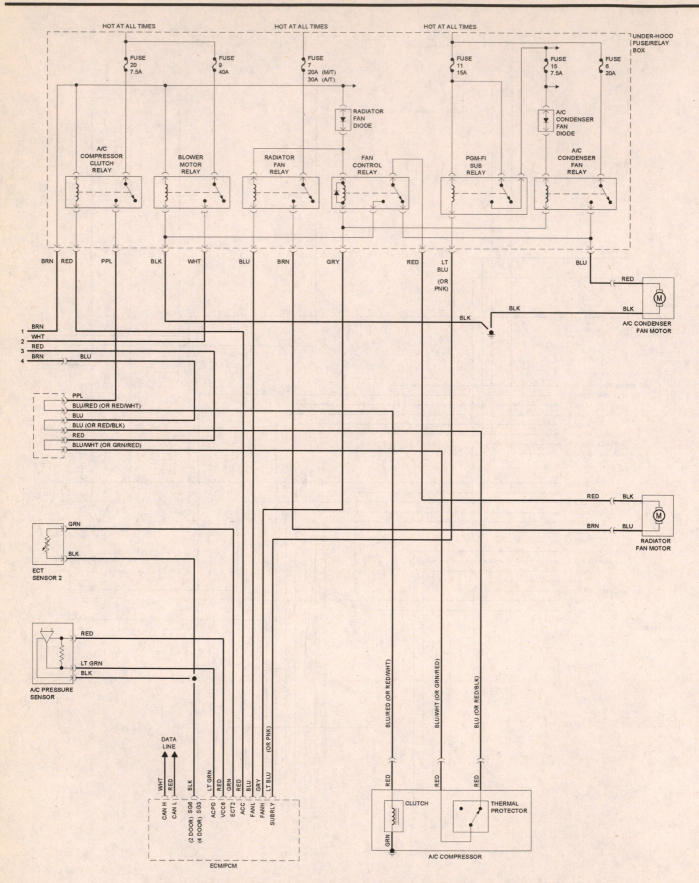

Air conditioning and engine cooling systems - 2006 and later coupe/sedan (2 of 2)

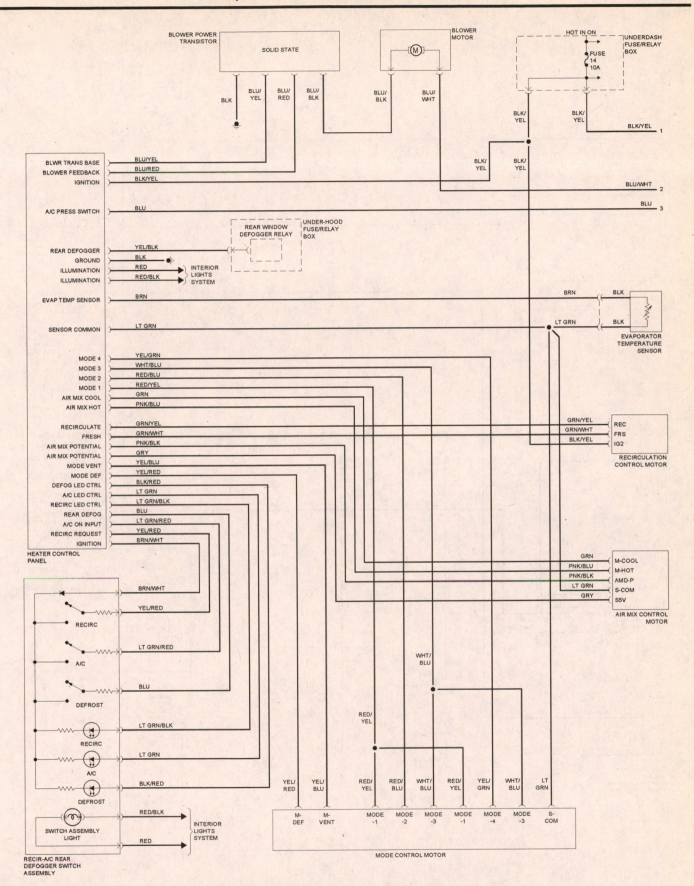

Air conditioning and engine cooling systems - hatchback (1 of 2)

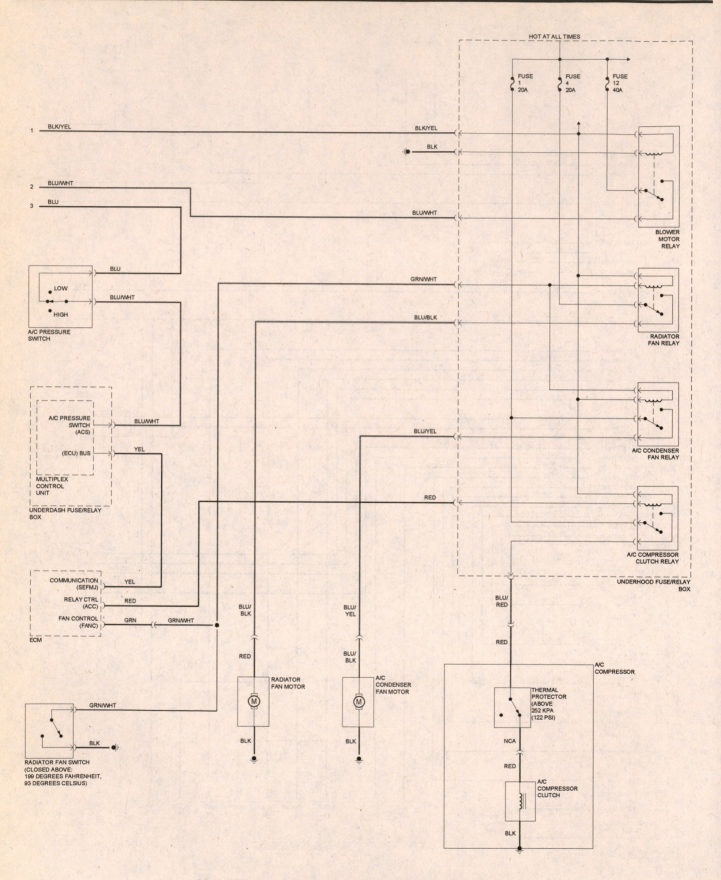

Air conditioning and engine cooling systems - hatchback (2 of 2)

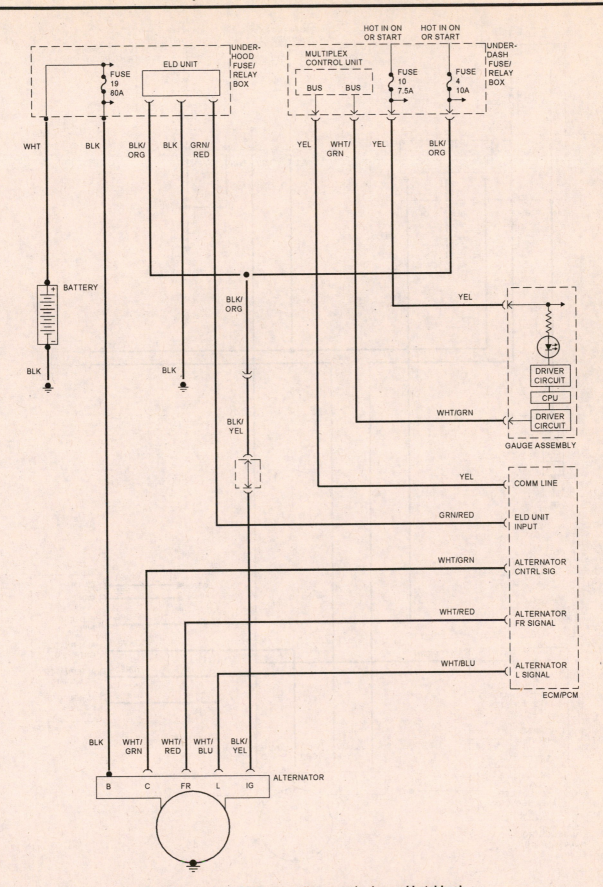

Charging system - 2005 and earlier coupe/sedan and hatchback

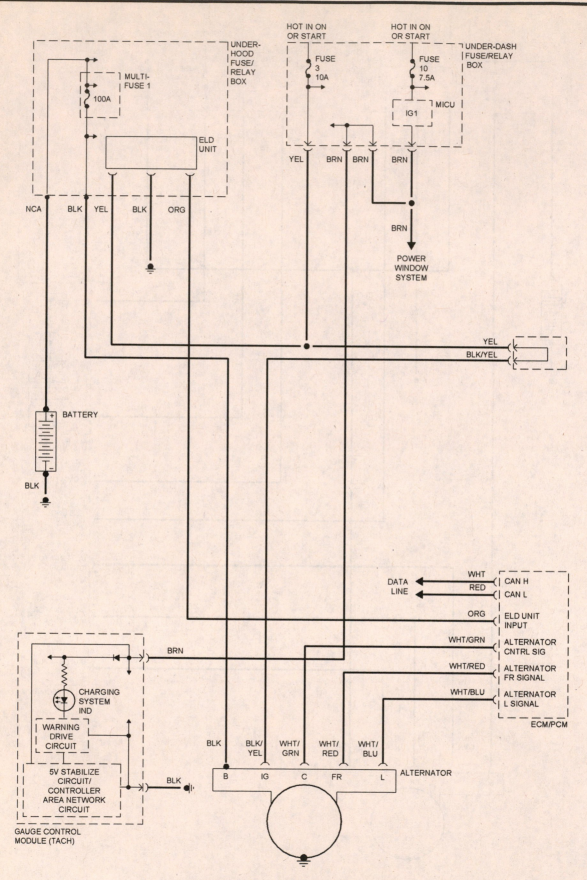

Charging system - 2006 and later coupe/sedan

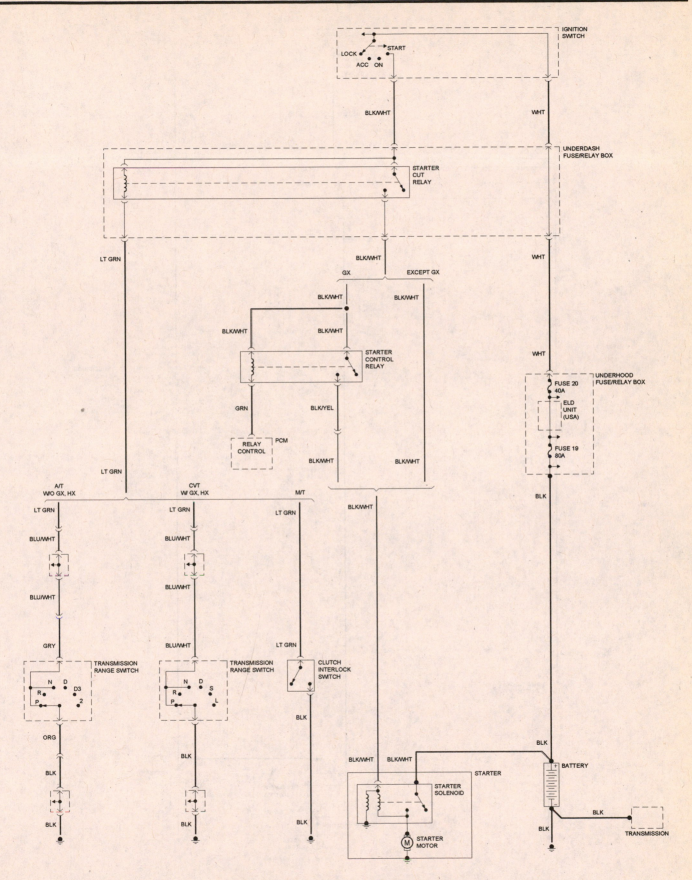

Starting system - 2005 and earlier coupe/sedan

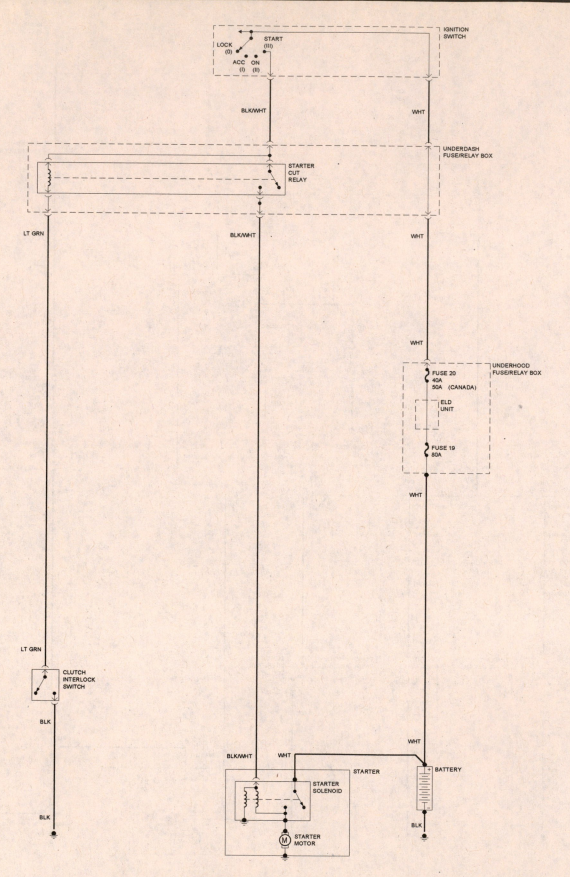

Starting system - hatchback

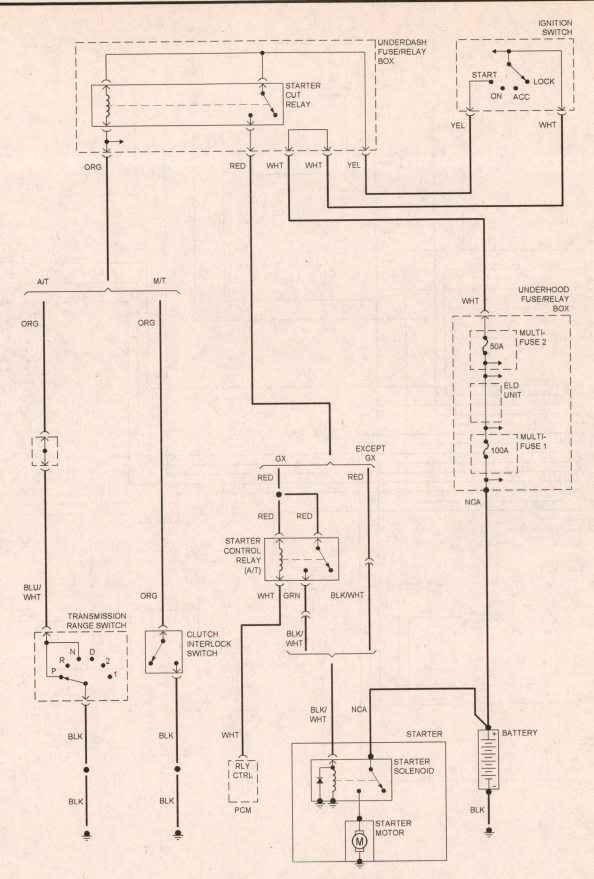

Starting system - 2006 and later coupe/sedan

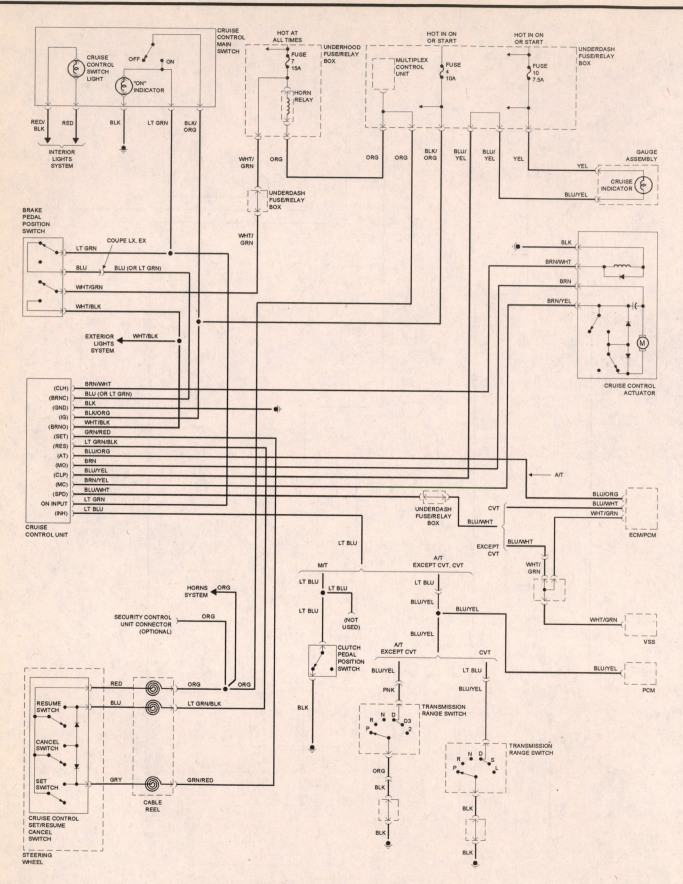

Cruise control system - 2005 and earlier coupe/sedan

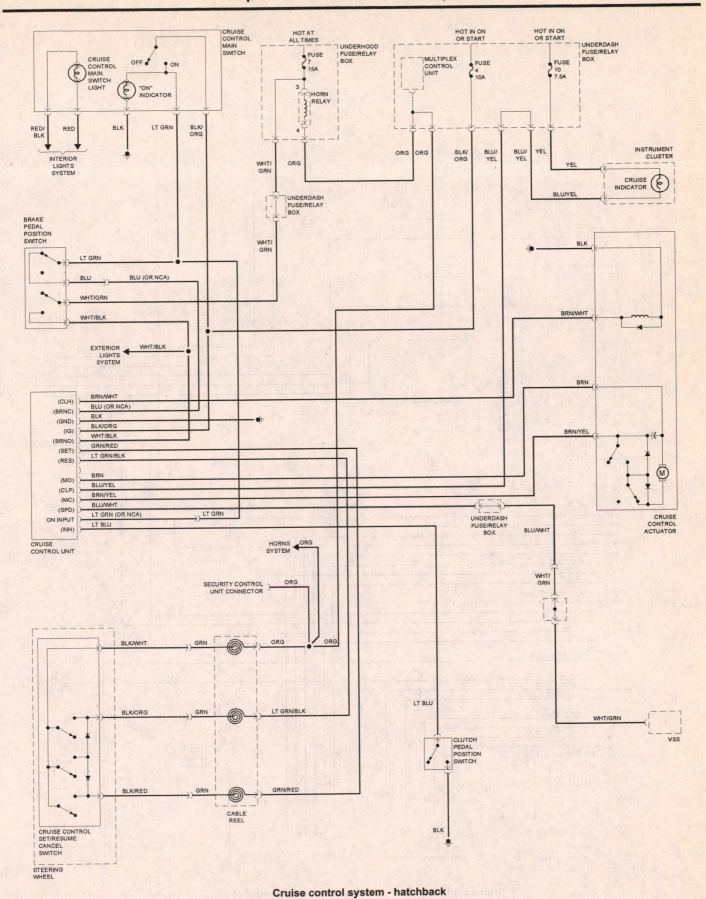

Cruise control system - hatchback

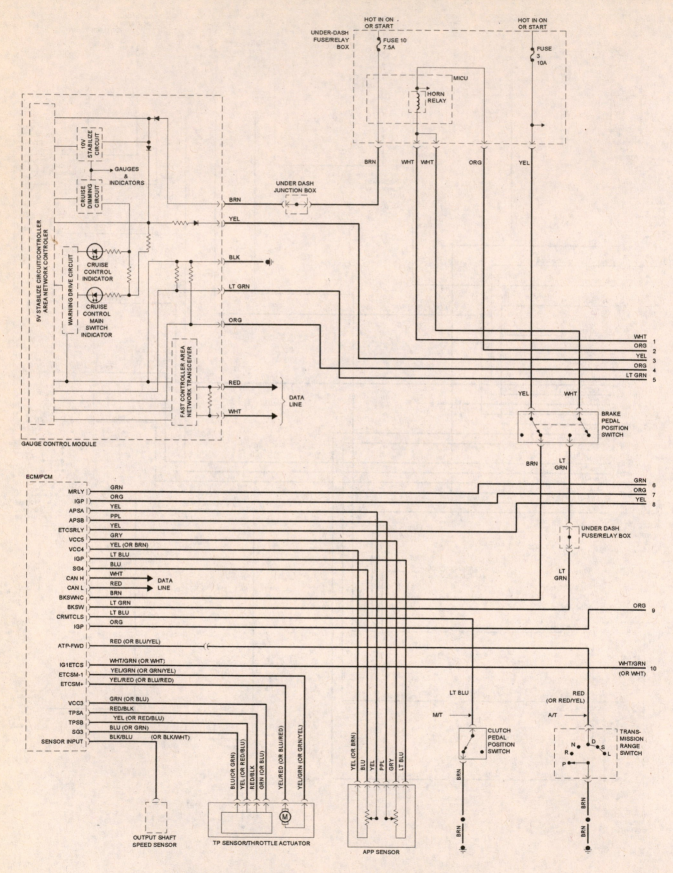

Cruise control system - 2006 and later coupe/sedan (1 of 2)

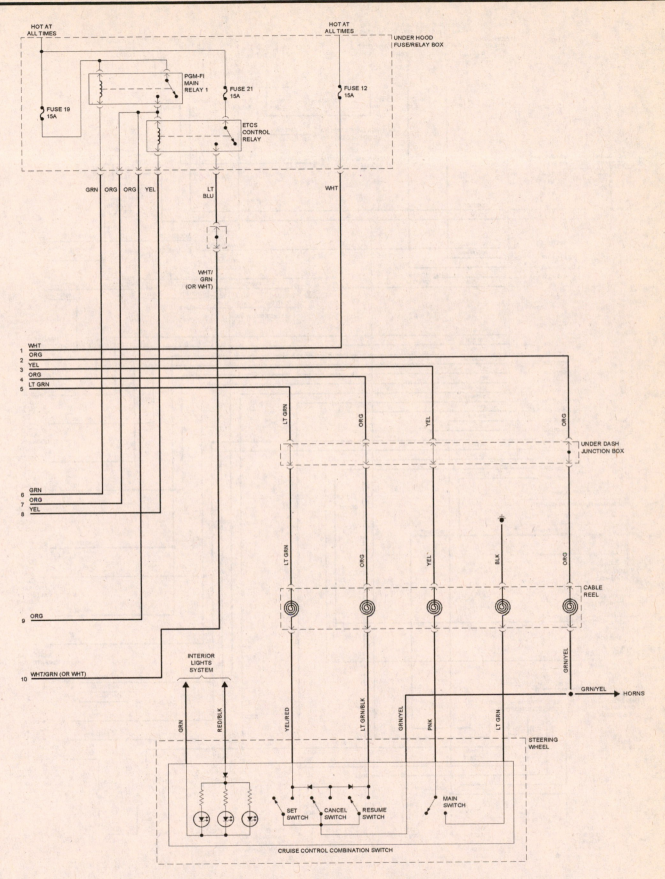

Cruise control system - 2006 and later coupe/sedan (2 of 2)

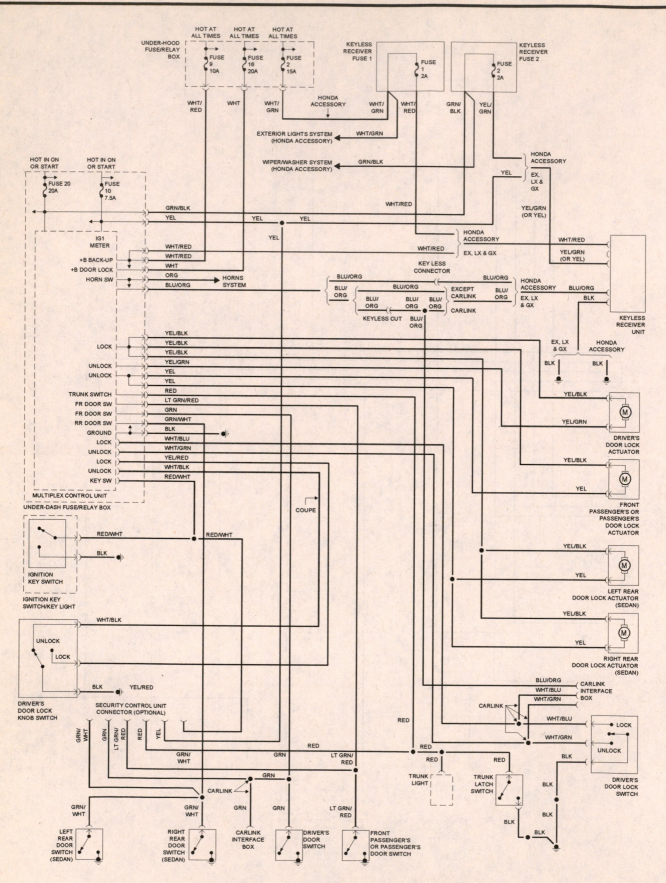

Power door lock system - 2005 and earlier coupe/sedan

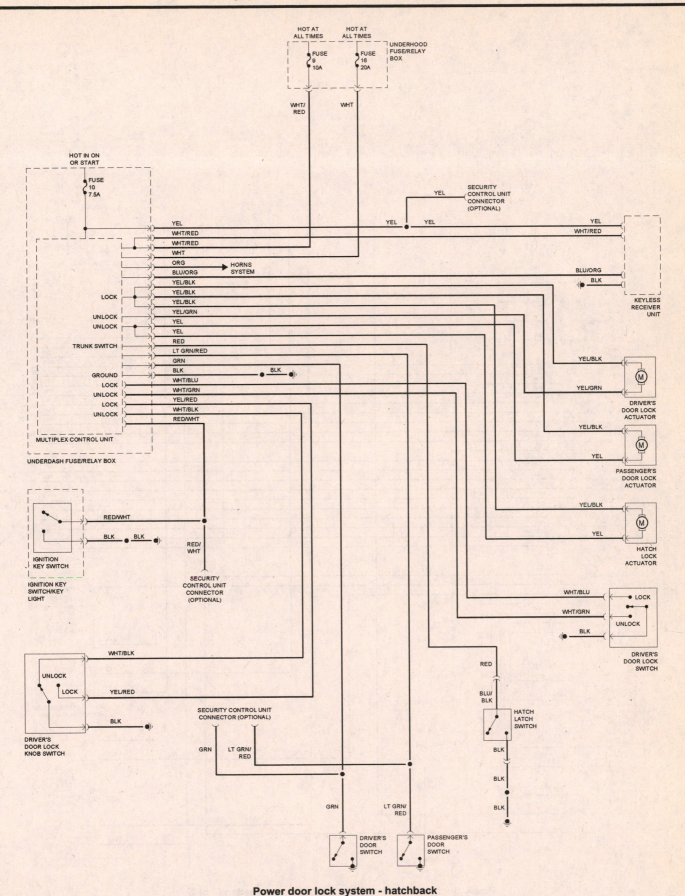

Power door lock system - hatchback

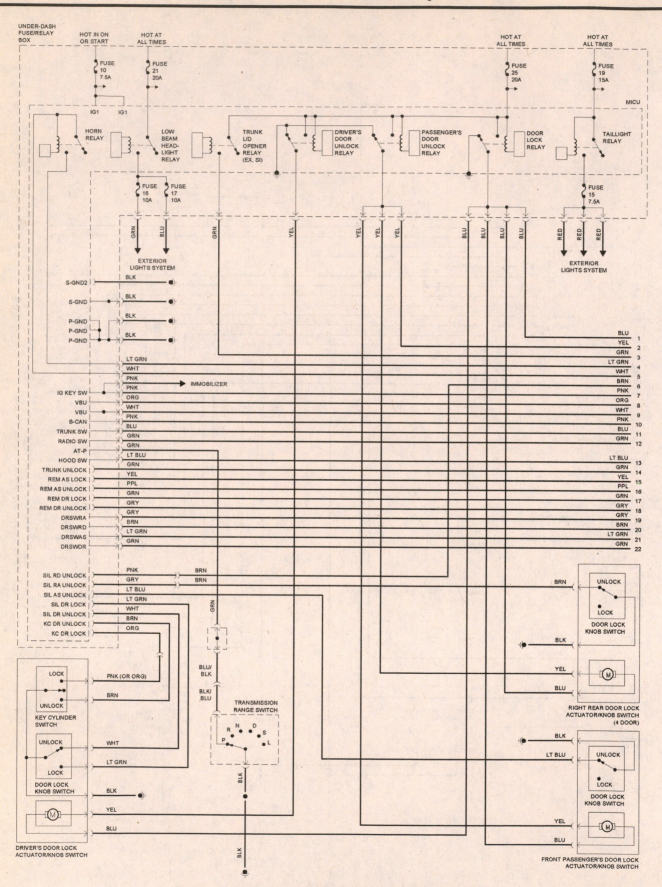

Power door lock system - 2006 and later coupe/sedan (1 of 2)

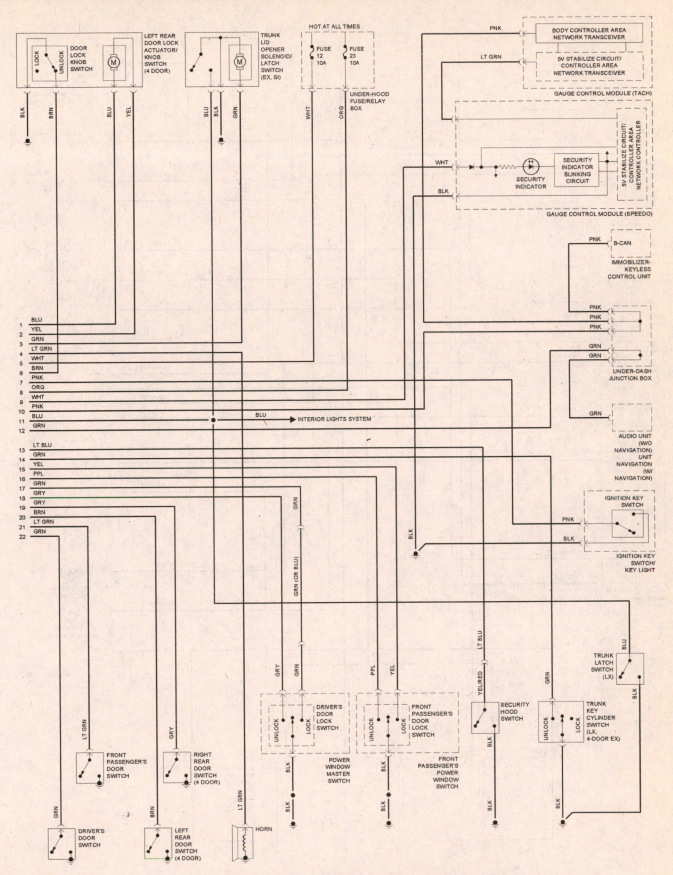

Power door lock system - 2006 and later coupe/sedan (2 of 2)

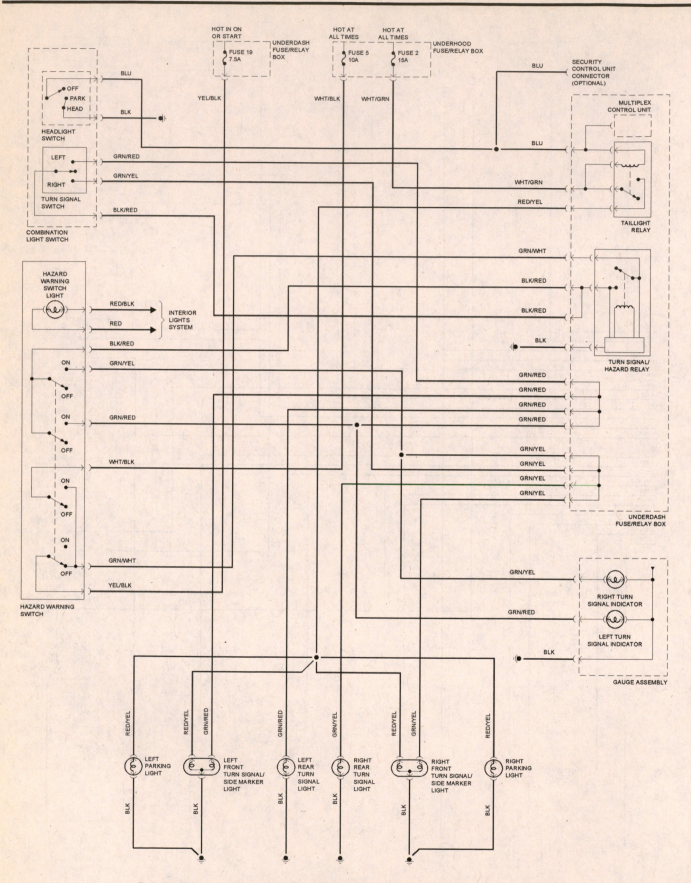

Exterior lighting system (except headlights) - 2005 and earlier coupe/sedan (1 of 2)

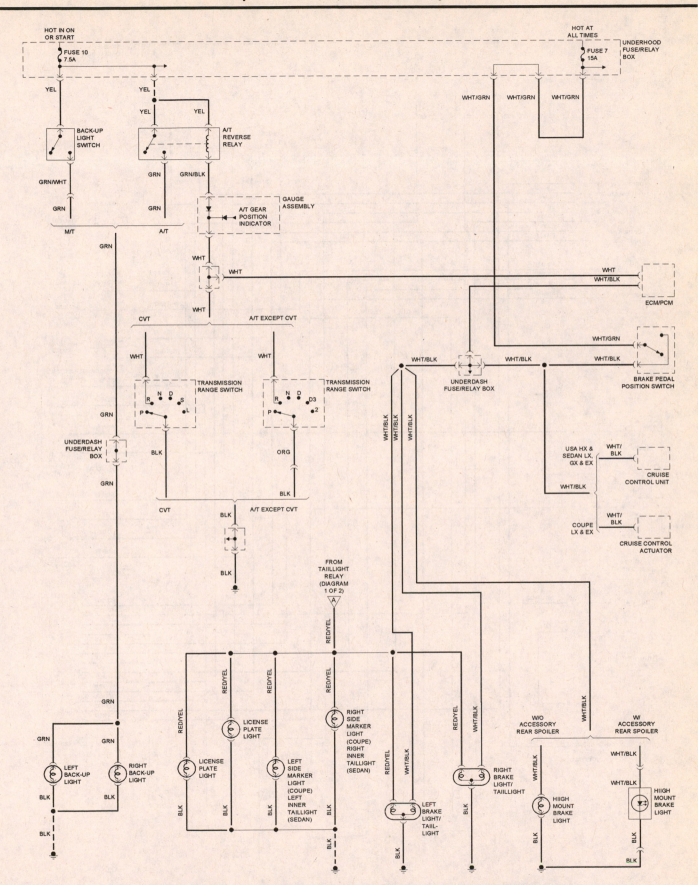

Exterior lighting system (except headlights) - 2005 and earlier coupe/sedan (2 of 2)

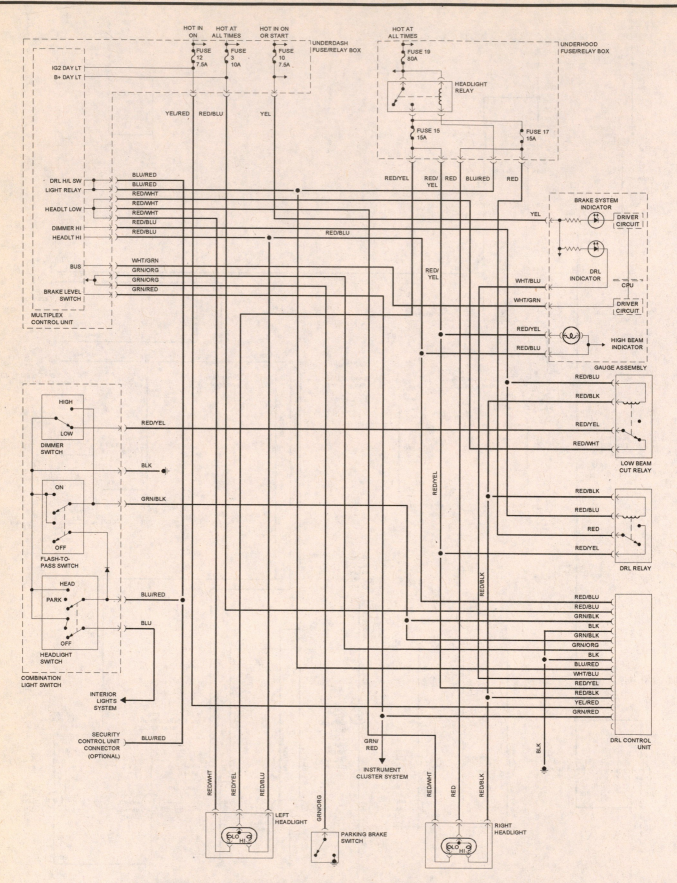

Headlight system (with Daytime Running Lights) - 2001 through 2003 coupe/sedan

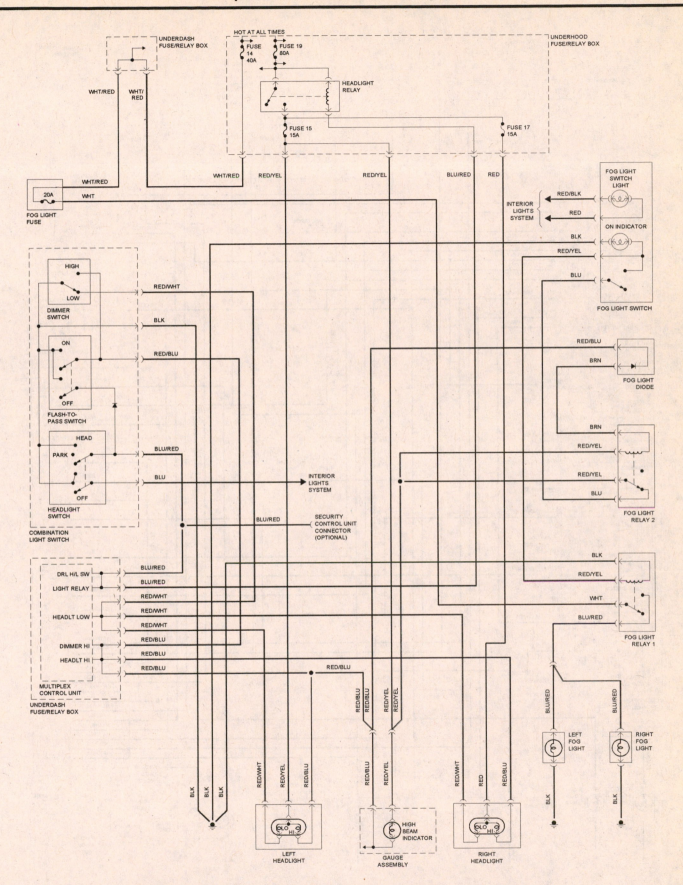

Headlight system (without Daytime Running Lights) - 2001 through 2003 coupe/sedan

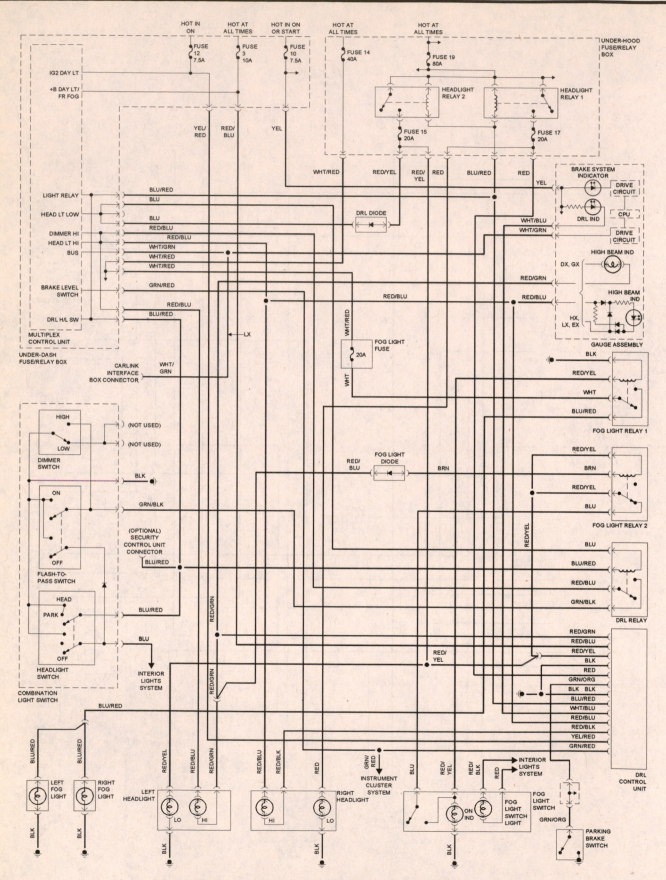

Headlight system (with Daytime Running Lights) - 2004 and 2005 coupe/sedan

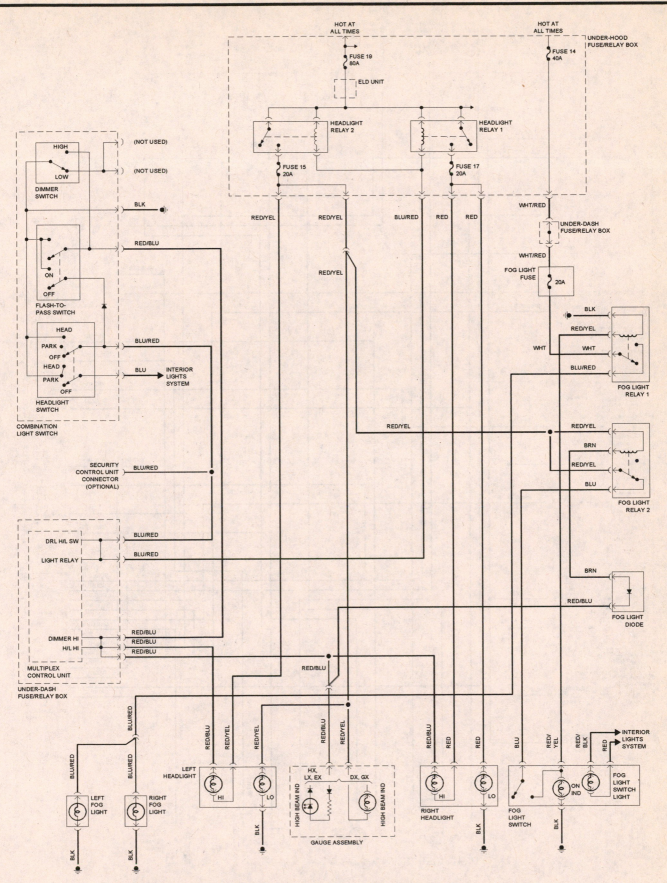

Headlight system (without Daytime Running Lights) - 2004 and 2005 coupe/sedan

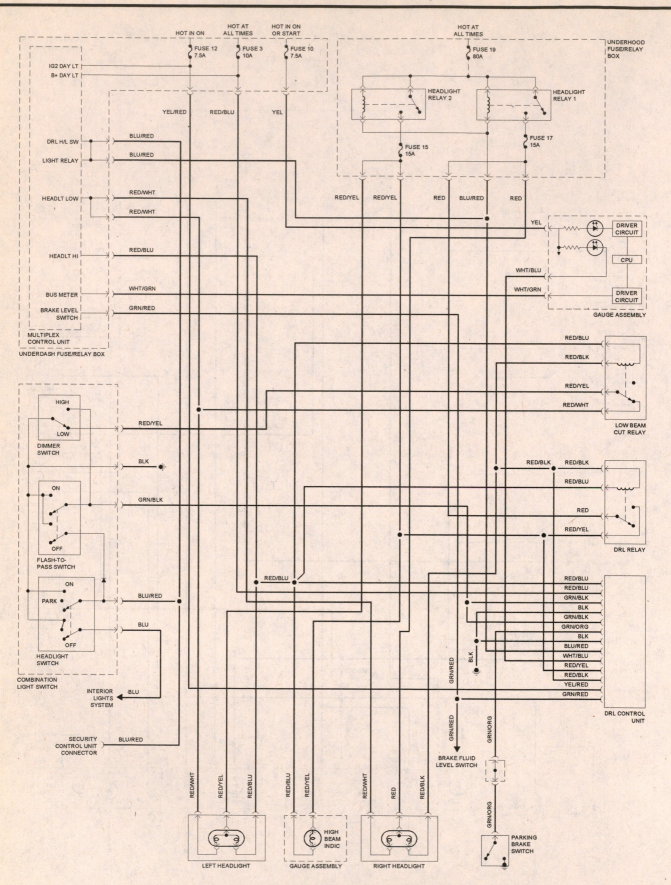

Headlight system (with Daytime Running Lights) - 2002 through 2003 hatchback

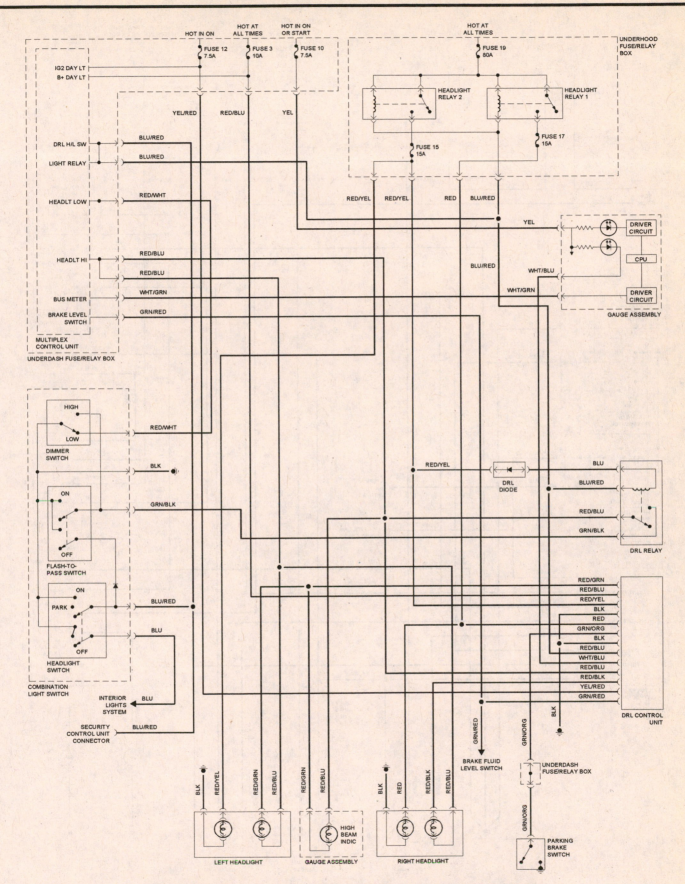

Headlight system (with Daytime Running Lights) - 2004 and 2005 hatchback

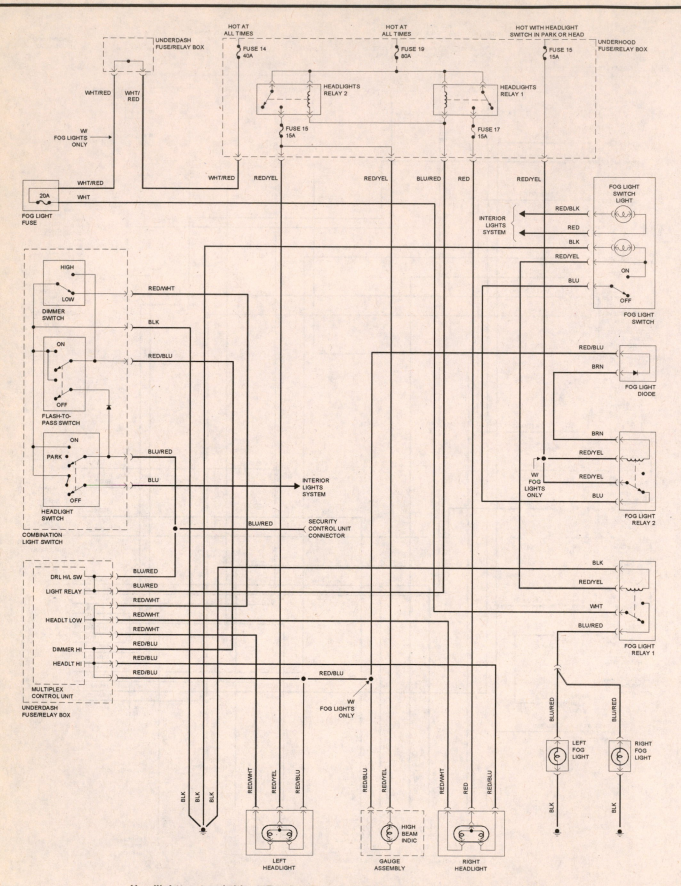

Headlight system (without Daytime Running Lights) - 2002 through 2003 hatchback

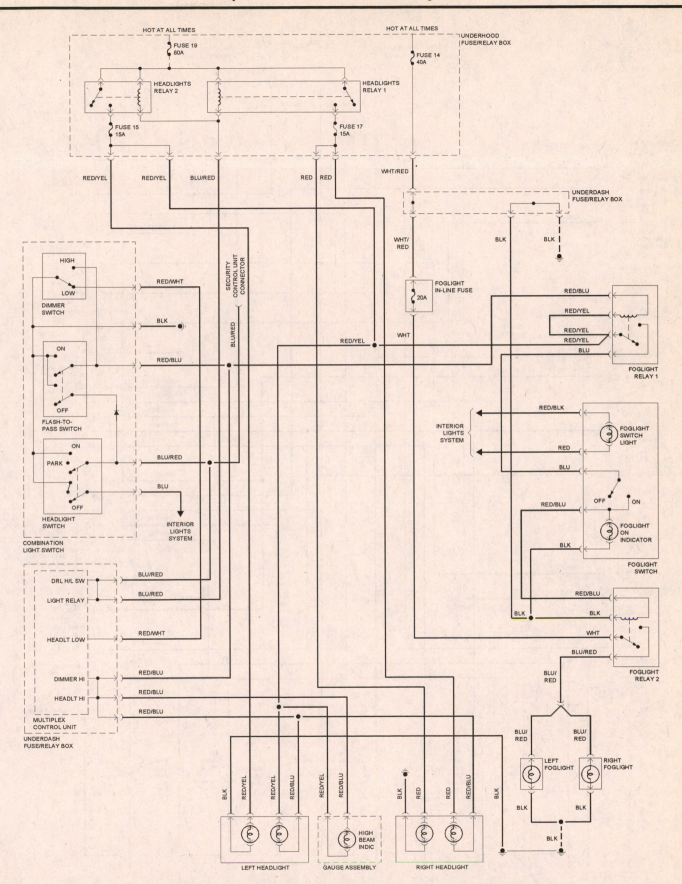

Headlight system (without Daytime Running Lights) - 2004 and 2005 hatchback

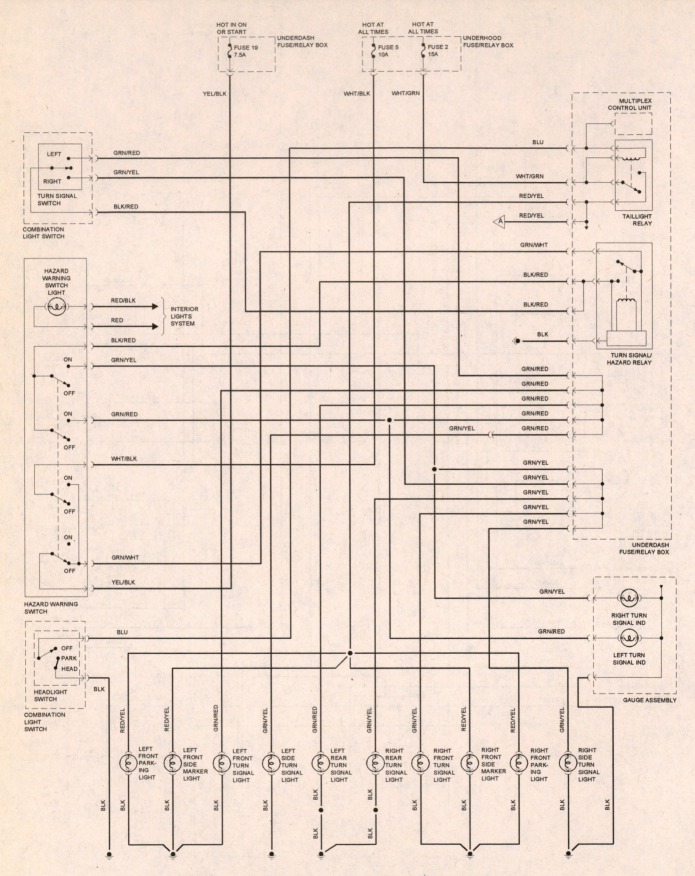

Exterior lighting systems (except headlights) - hatchback (1 of 2)

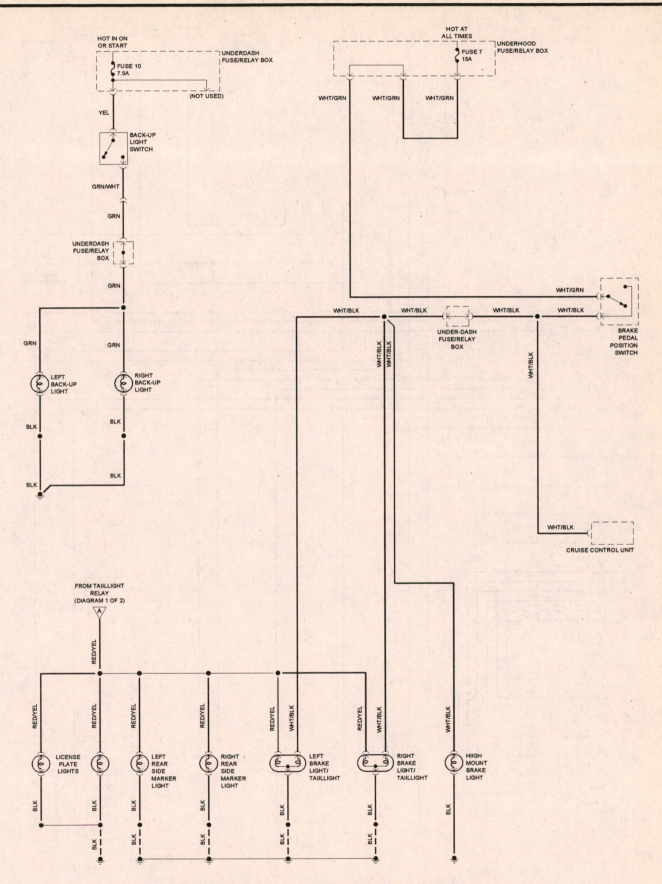

Exterior lighting systems (except headlights) - hatchback (2 of 2)

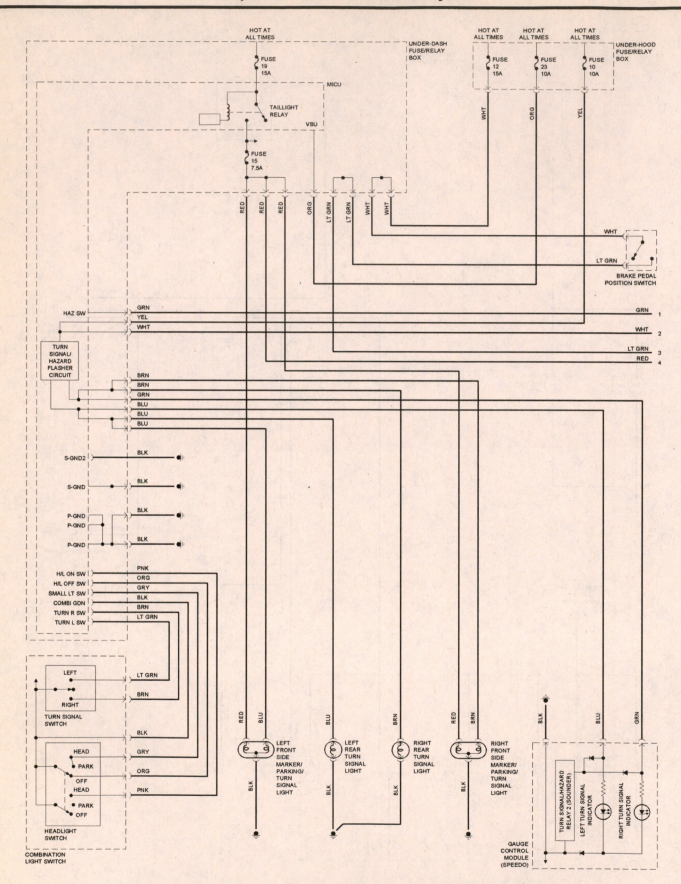

Exterior lighting system (except headlights) - 2006 and later coupe/sedan (1 of 2)

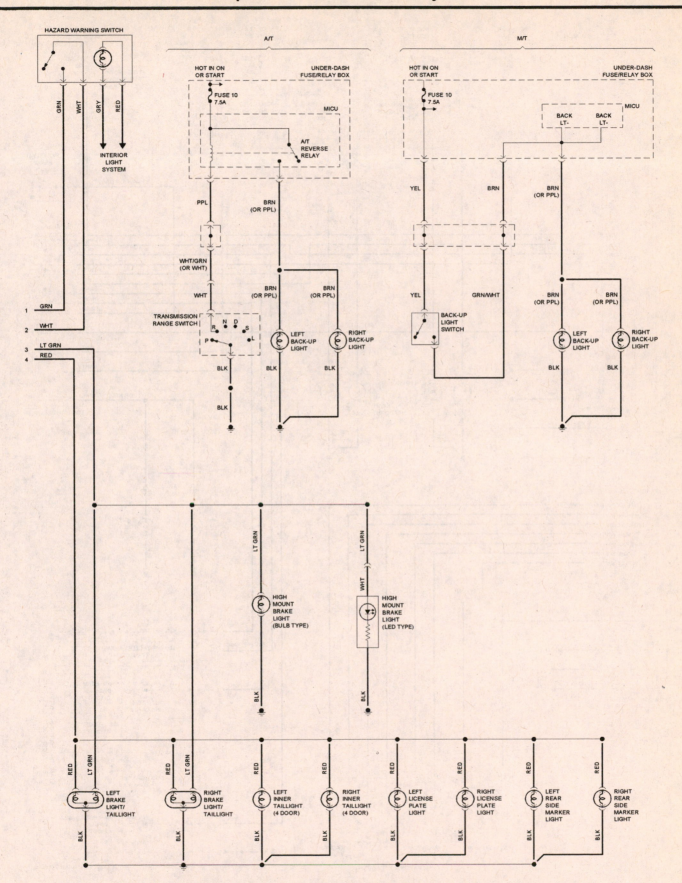

Exterior lighting system (except headlights) - 2006 and later coupe/sedan (2 of 2)

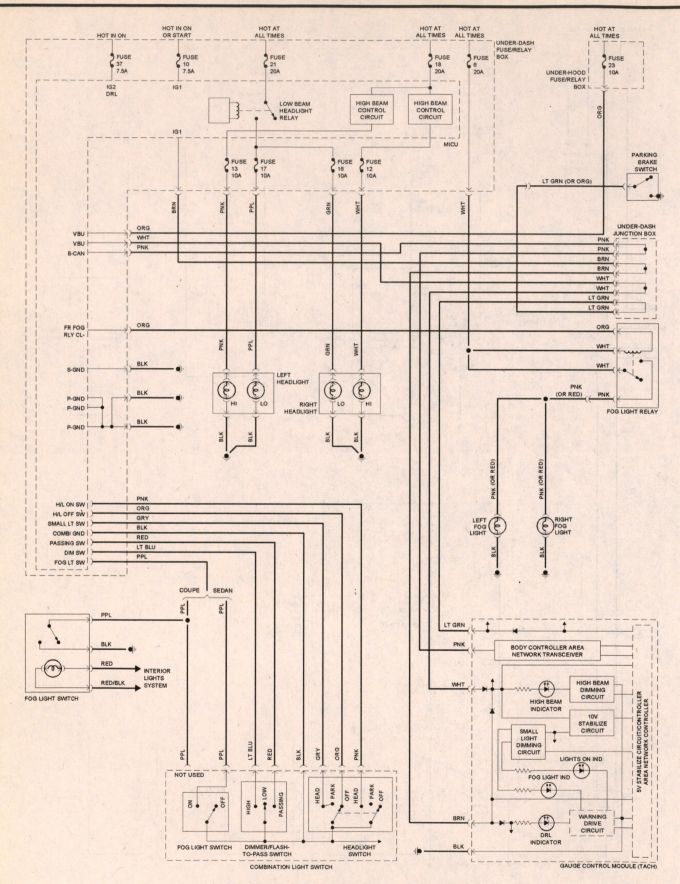

Headlight system - 2006 and later coupe/sedan

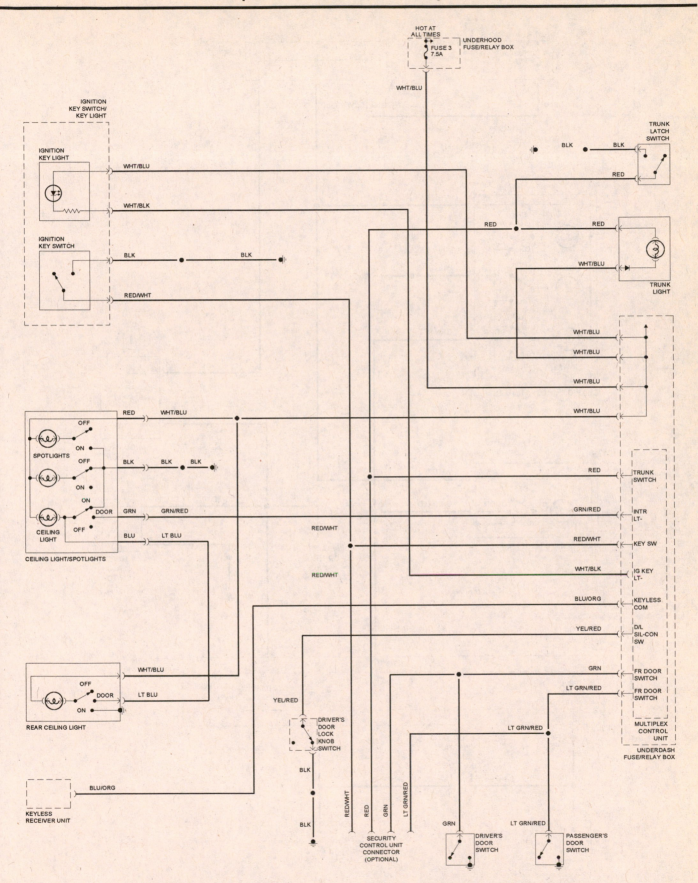

Interior lighting systems, including courtesy lights - 2005 and earlier coupe with sunroof

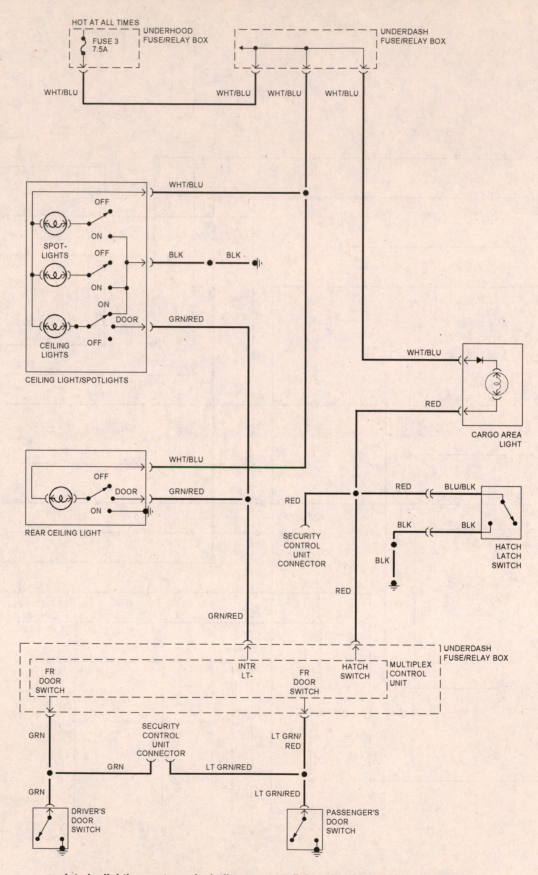

Interior lighting systems, including courtesy lights - hatchback without sunroof

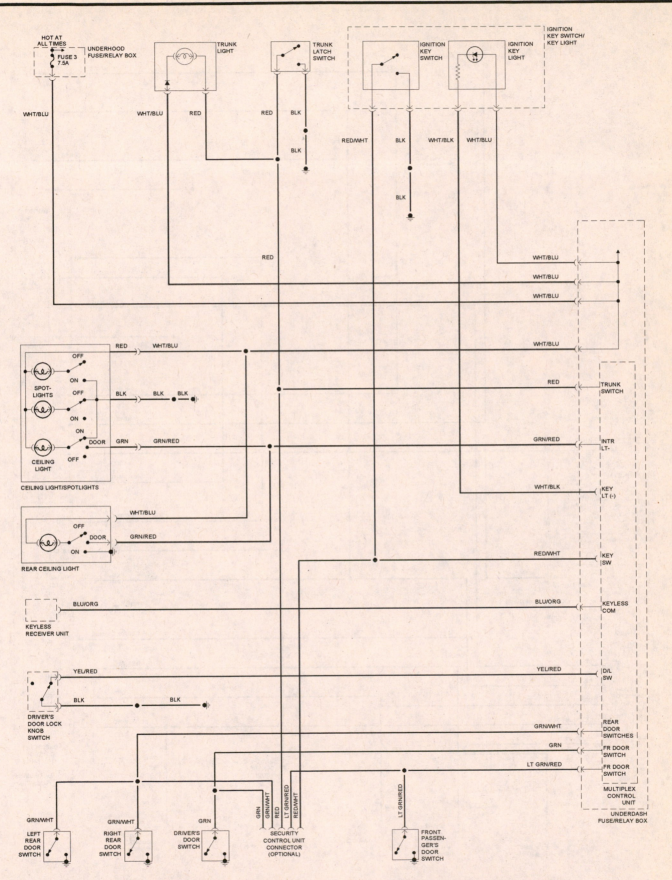

Interior lighting systems, including courtesy lights - 2005 and earlier sedan with sunroof

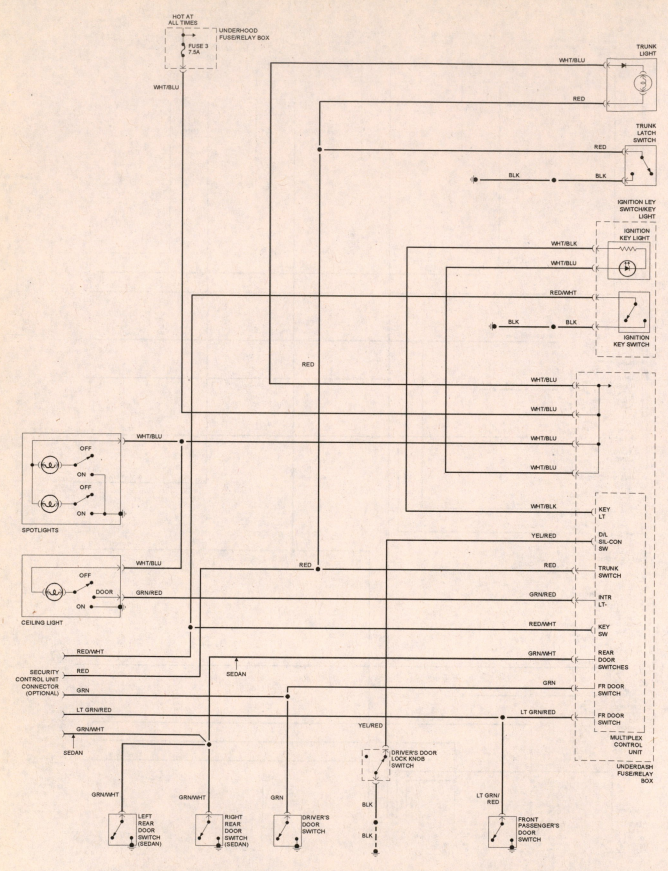

Interior lighting systems, including courtesy lights - 2005 and earlier coupe/sedan without sunroof

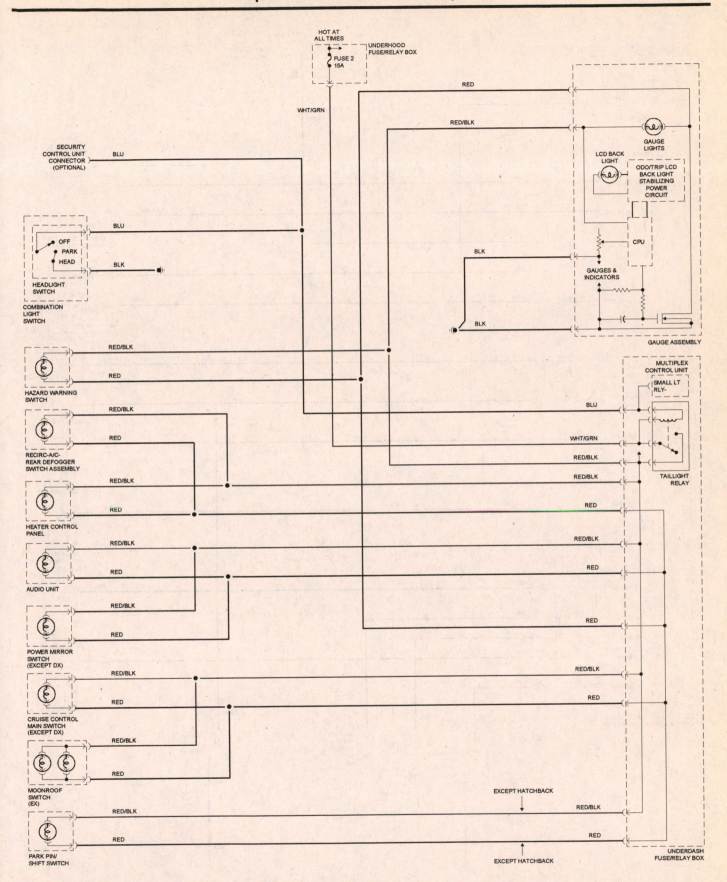

Interior lighting systems, including switch and instrument illumination lights - 2005 and earlier coupe, sedan and hatchback

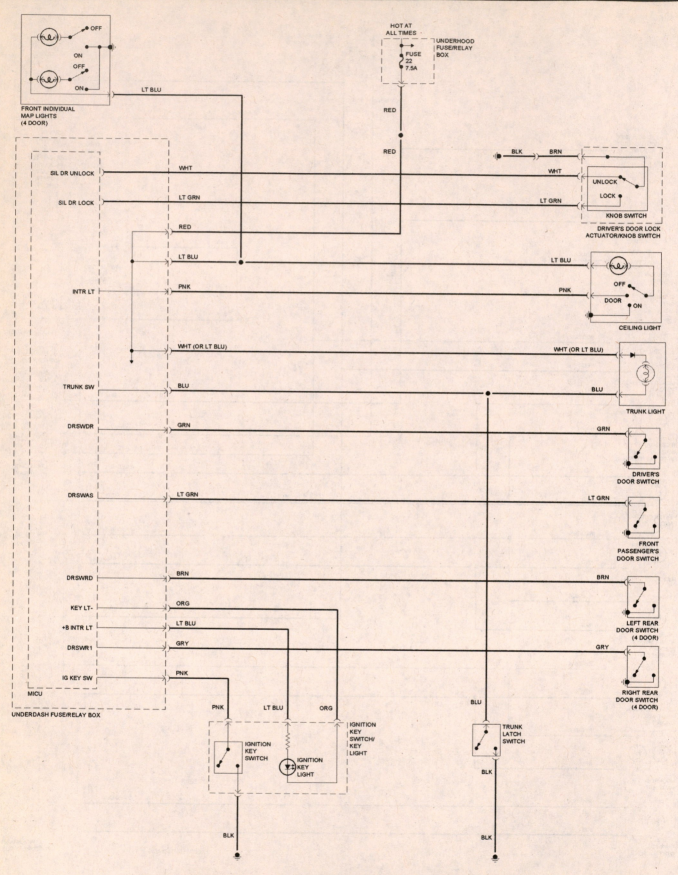

Interior lighting systems, including courtesy lights - 2006 and later coupe/sedan

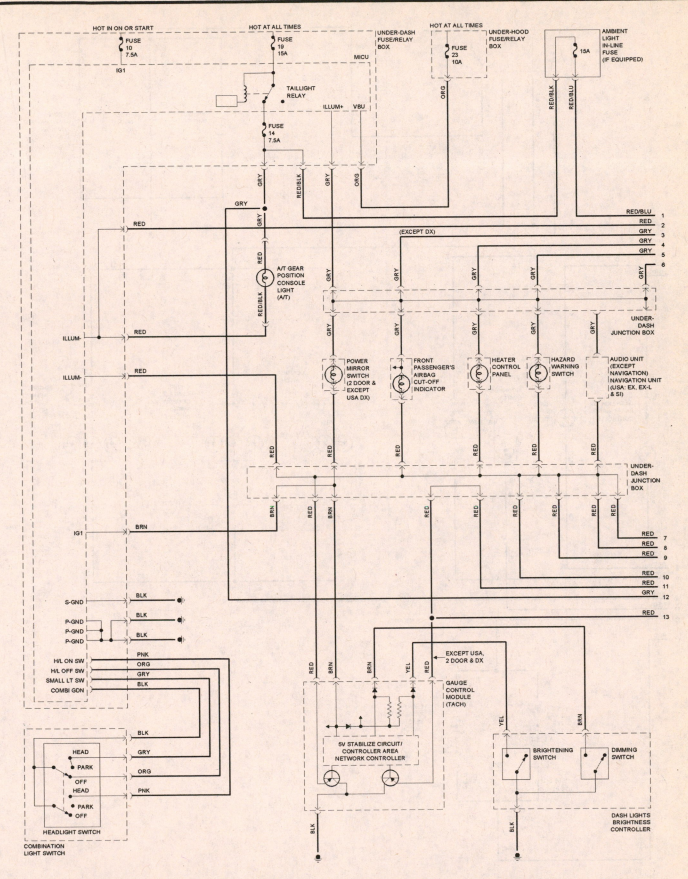

Interior lighting systems, including switch and instrument illumination lights - 2006 and later coupe/sedan (1 of 2)

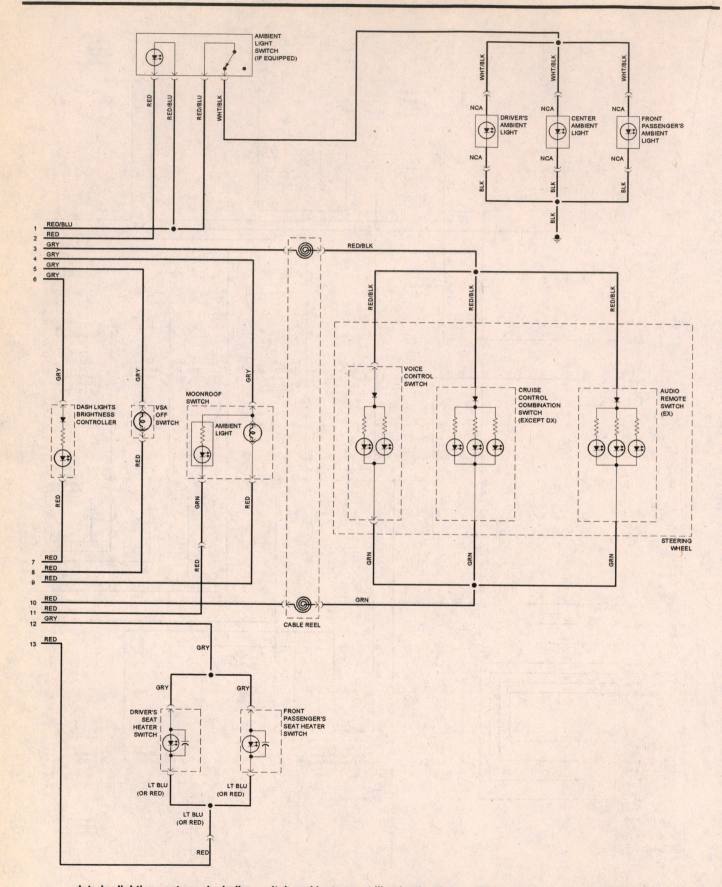

Interior lighting systems, including switch and instrument illumination lights - 2006 and later coupe/sedan (2 of 2)

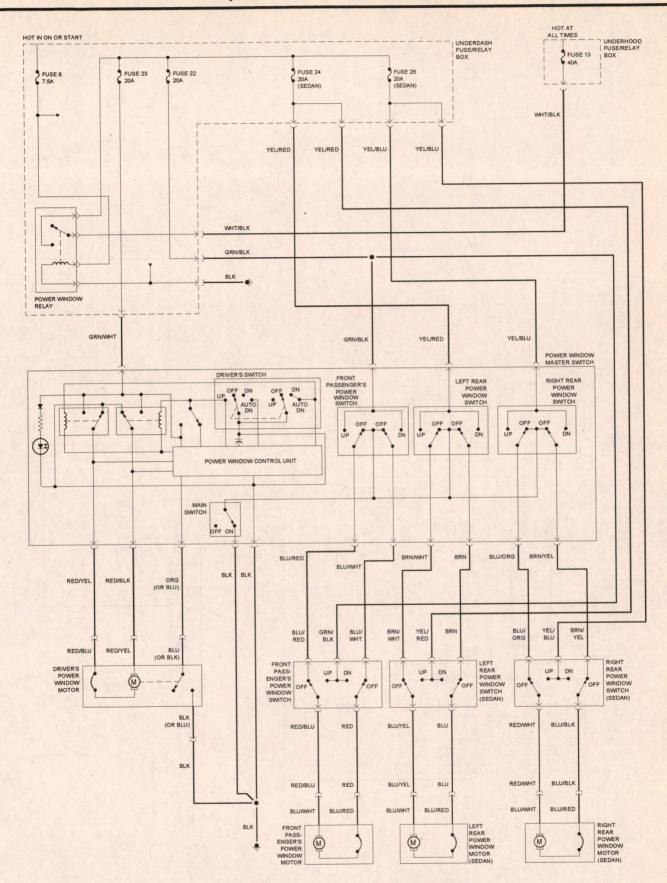

Power window systems - 2005 and earlier coupe/sedan

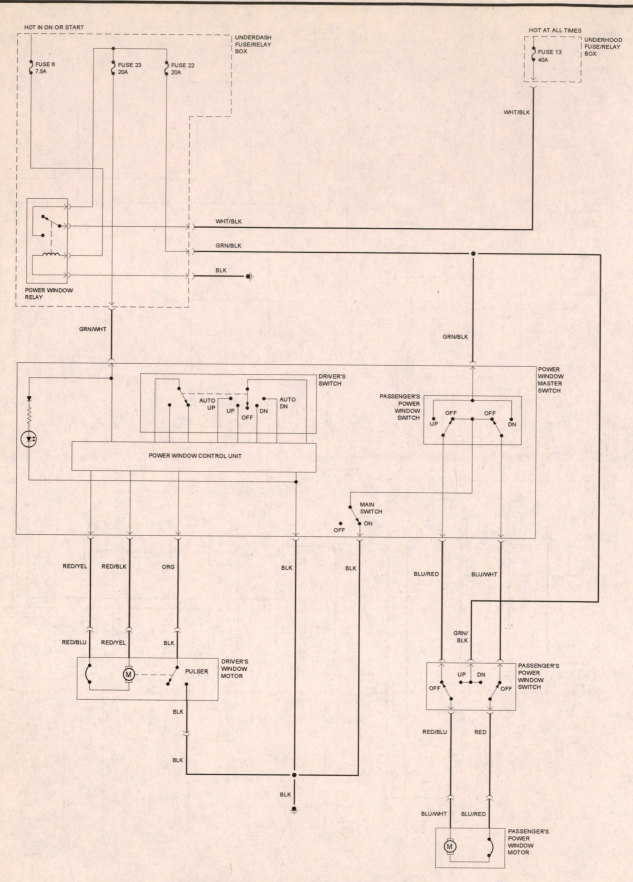

Power window systems - 2002 and 2003 hatchback

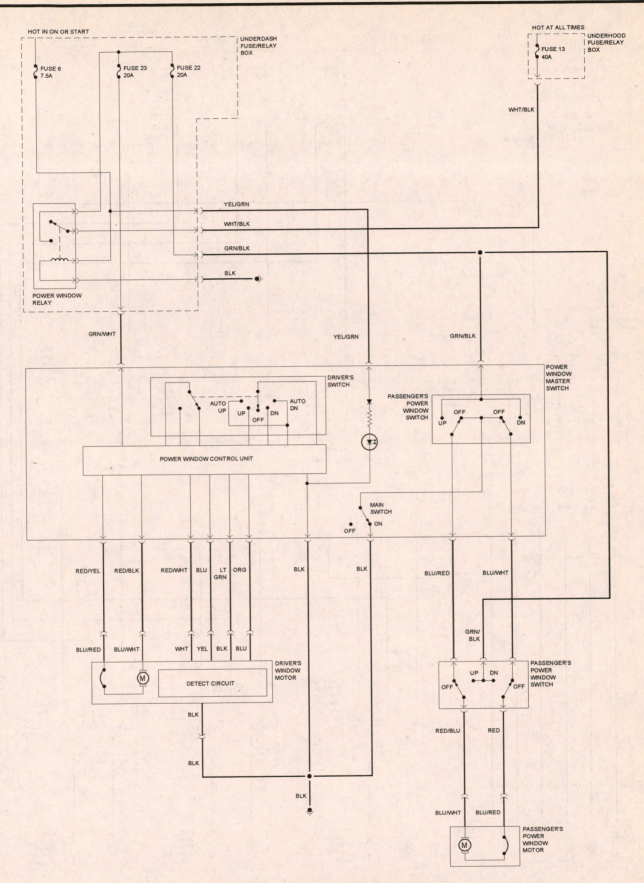

Power window systems - 2004 and 2005 hatchback

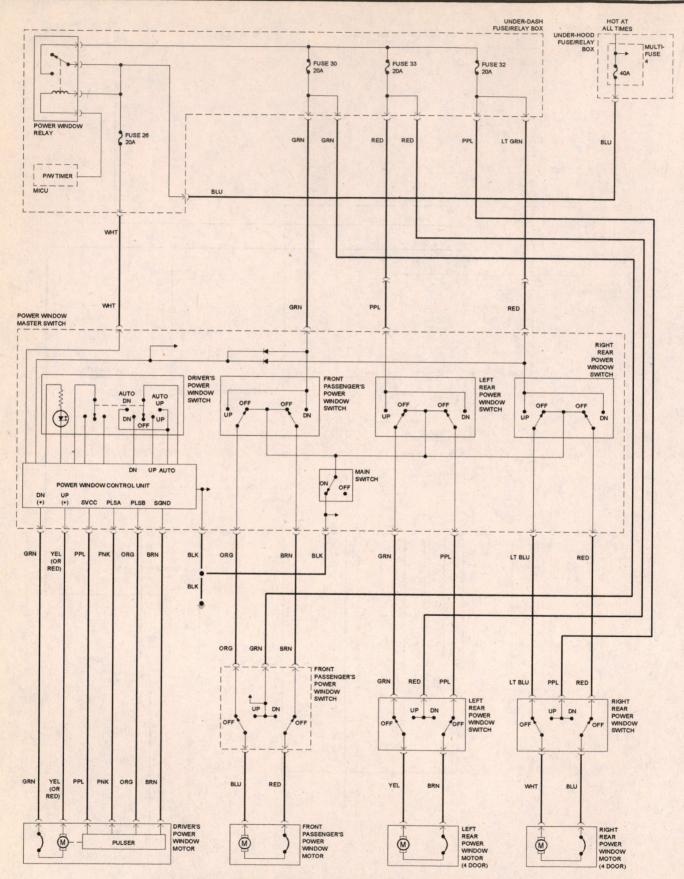

Power window systems - 2006 and later coupe/sedan (except DX models)

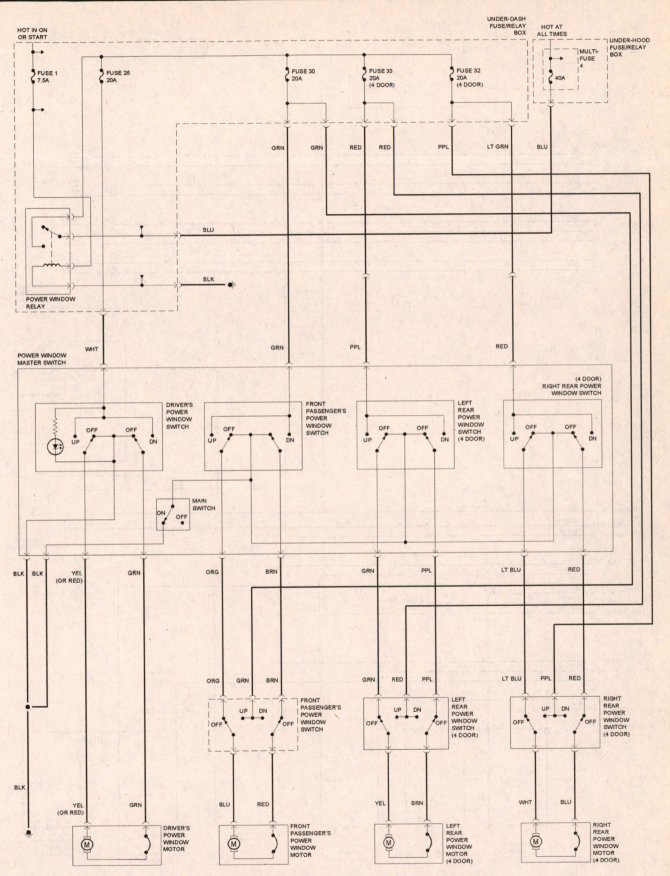

Power window systems - 2006 and later coupe/sedan (DX models)

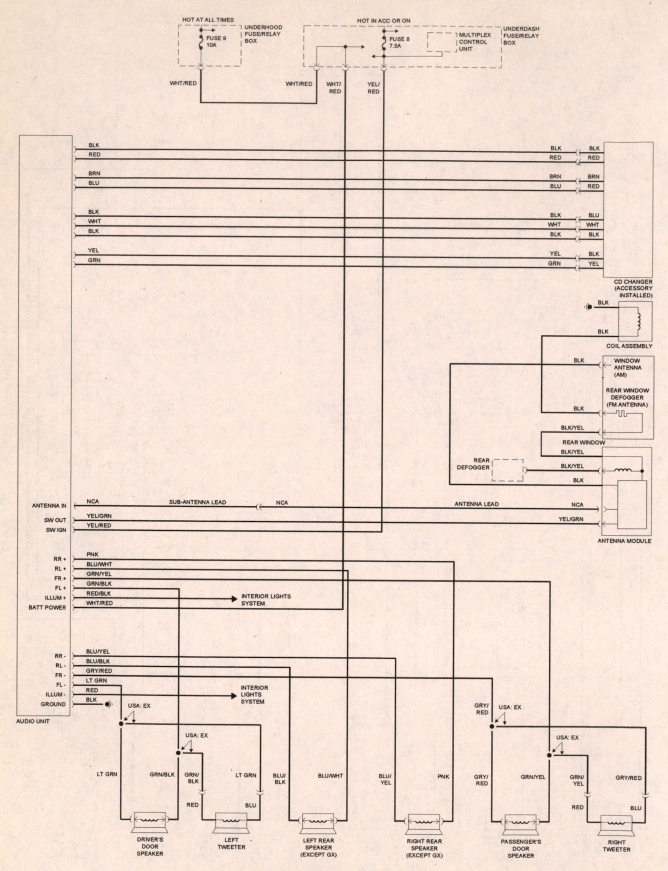

Sound system - 2005 and earlier coupe

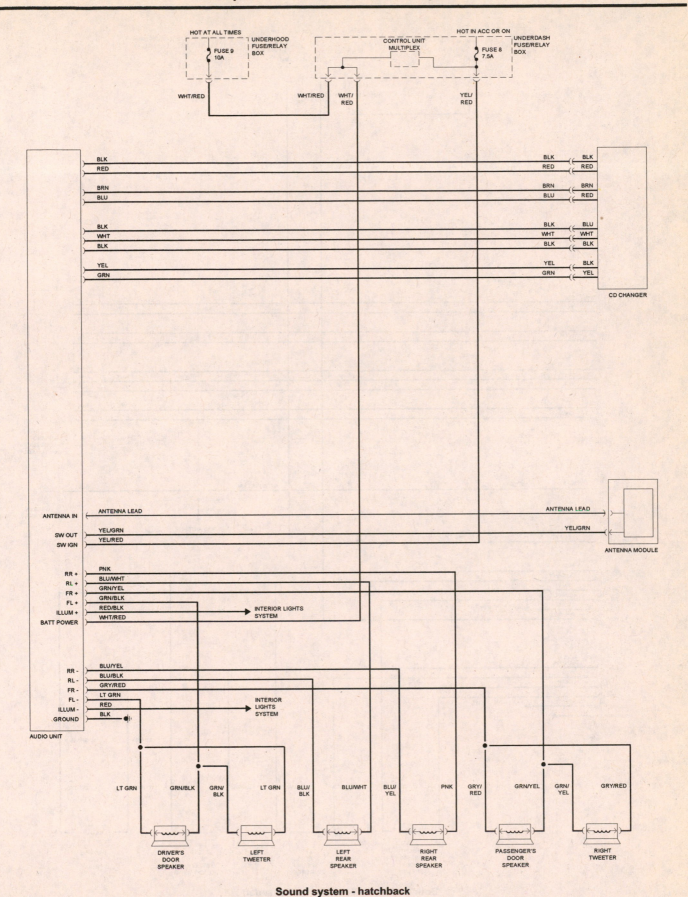

Sound system - hatchback

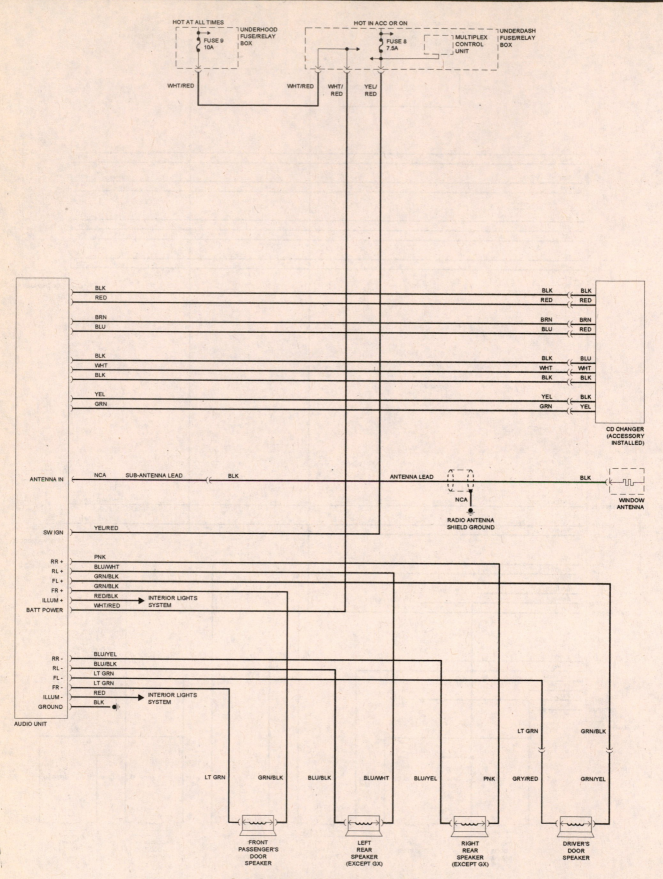

Sound system - 2005 and earlier sedan

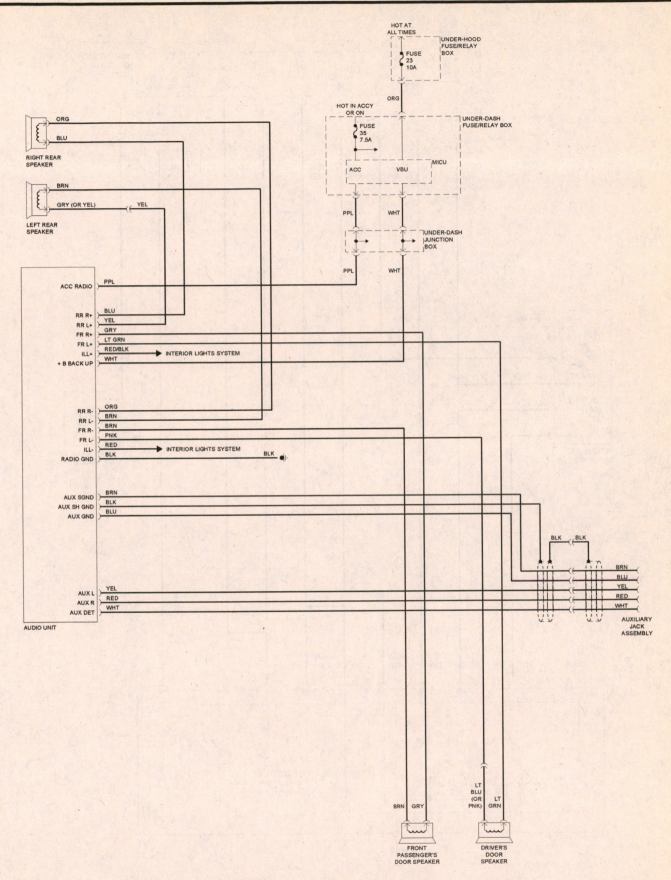

Sound system - 2006 and later coupe/sedan

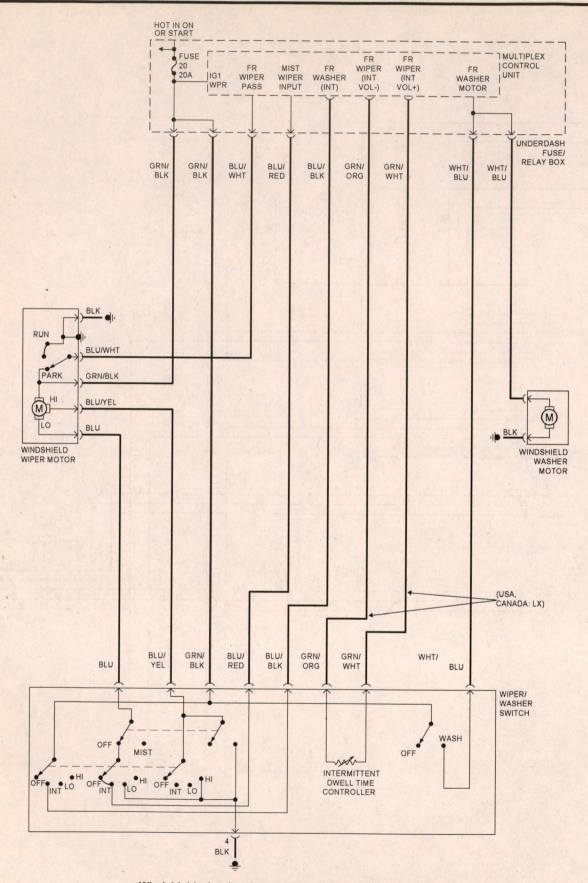

Windshield wiper/washer system - 2005 and earlier coupe/sedan

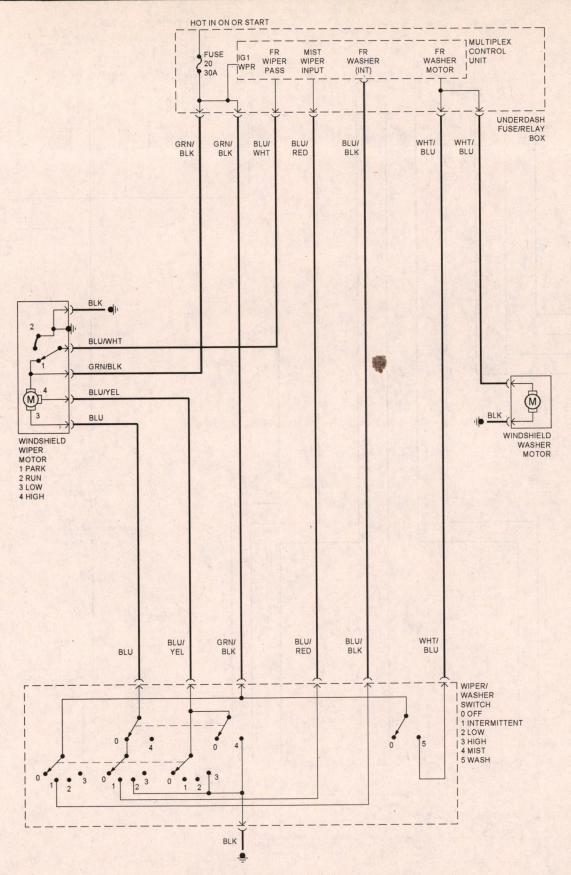

Windshield wiper/washer system - hatchback

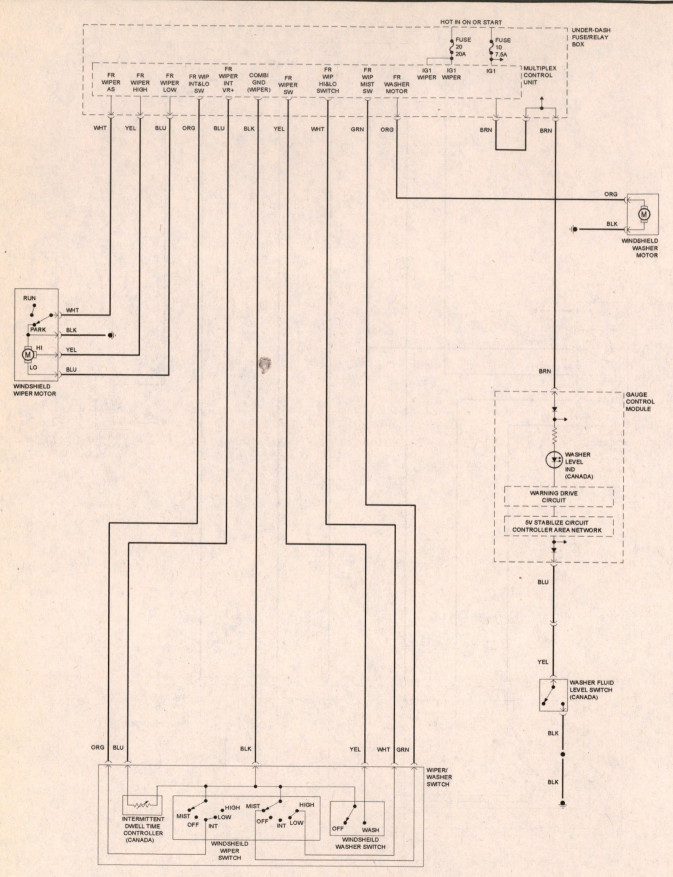

Windshield wiper/washer system - 2006 and later coupe/sedan

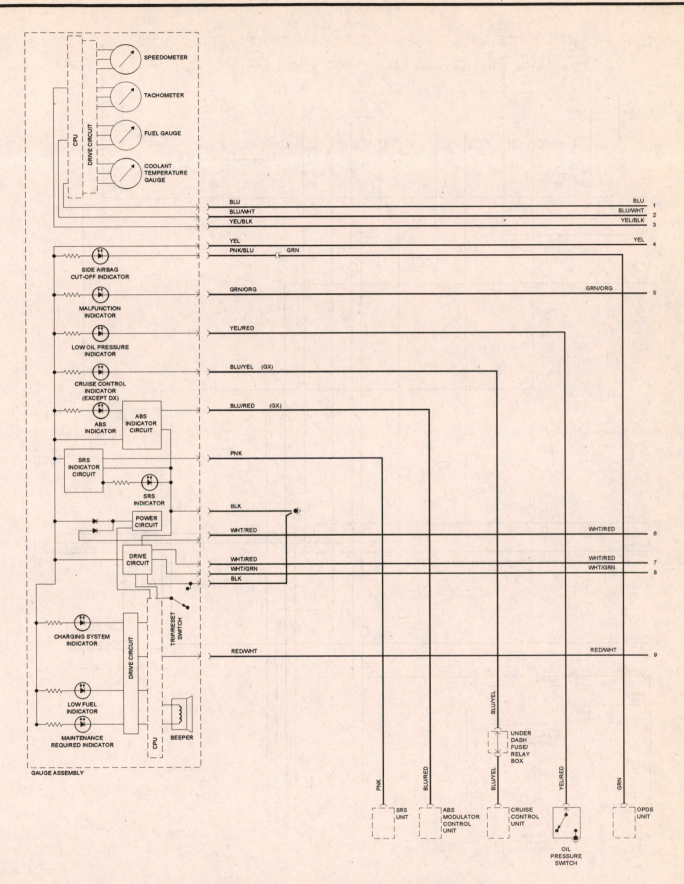

Warning systems - 2005 and earlier coupe/sedan (1 of 2)

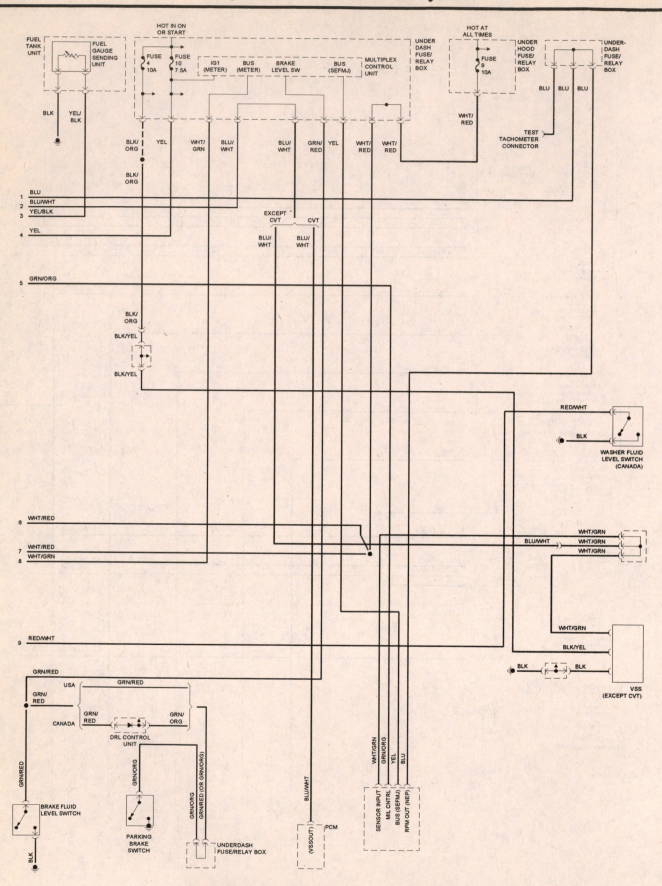

Warning systems - 2005 and earlier coupe/sedan (2 of 2)

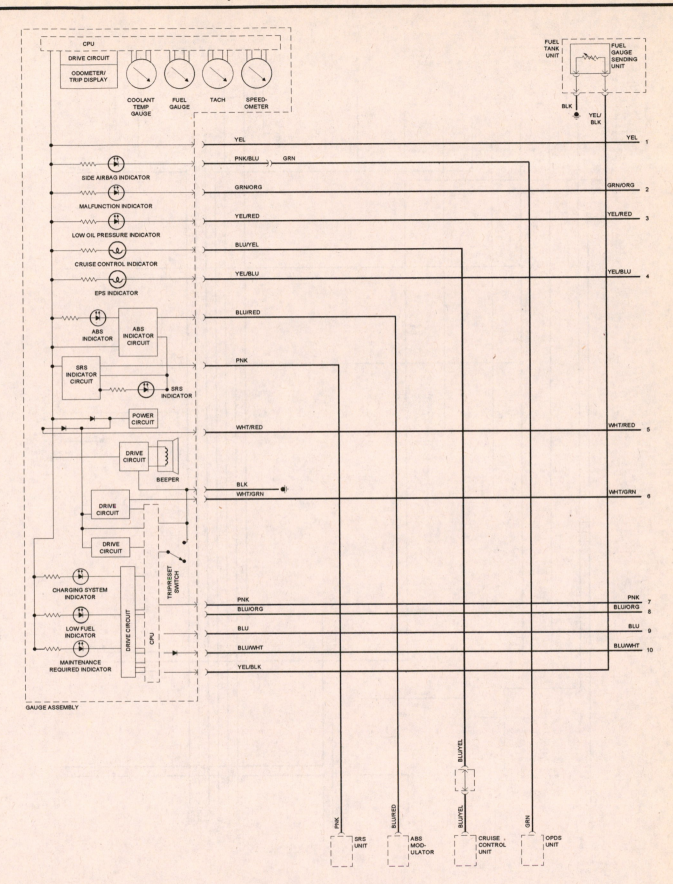

Warning systems - hatchback (1 of 2)

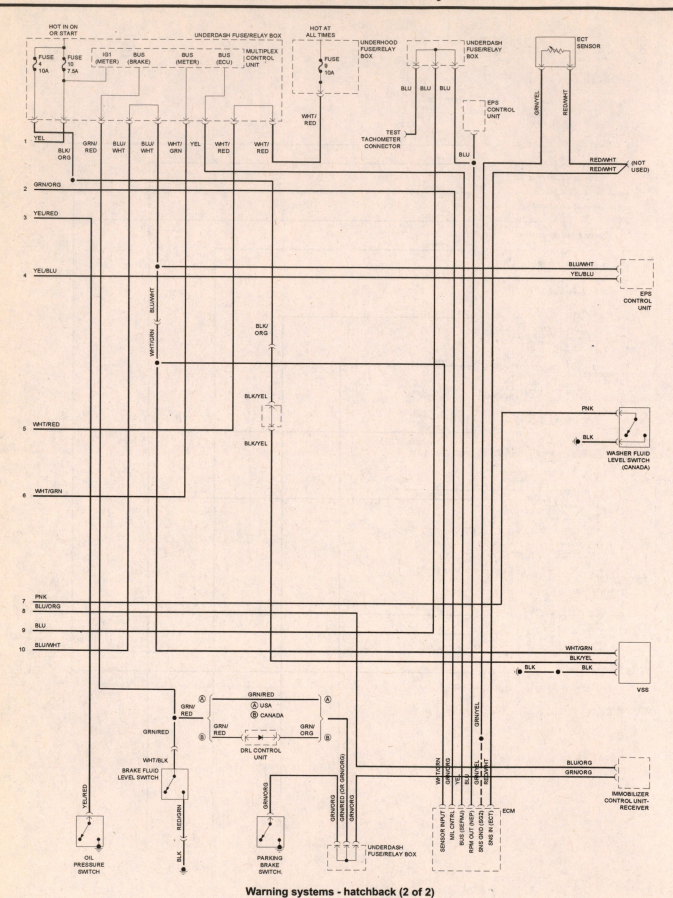

Warning systems - hatchback (2 of 2)

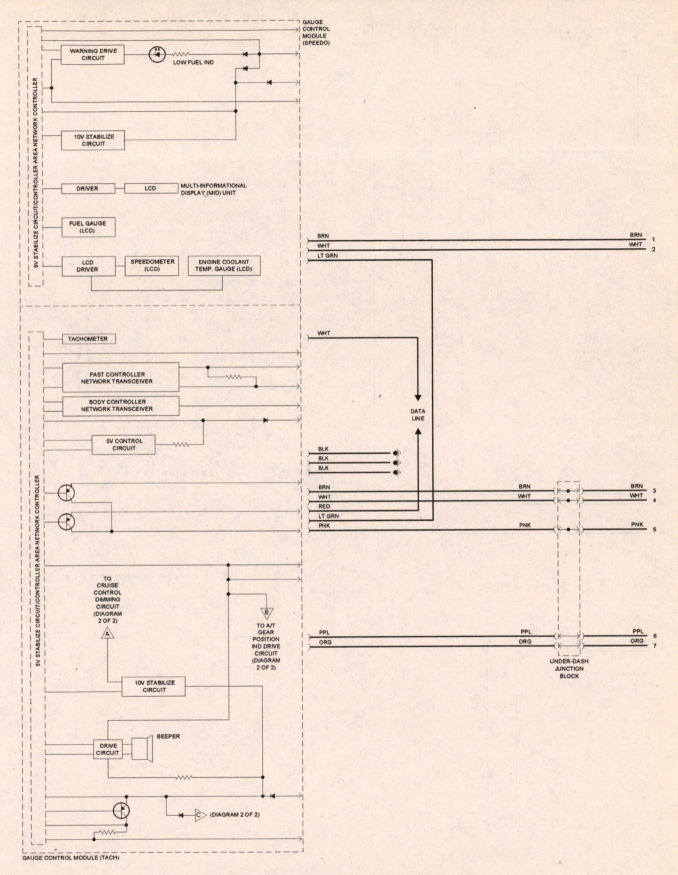

Warning systems - 2006 and later coupe/sedan (1 of 2)

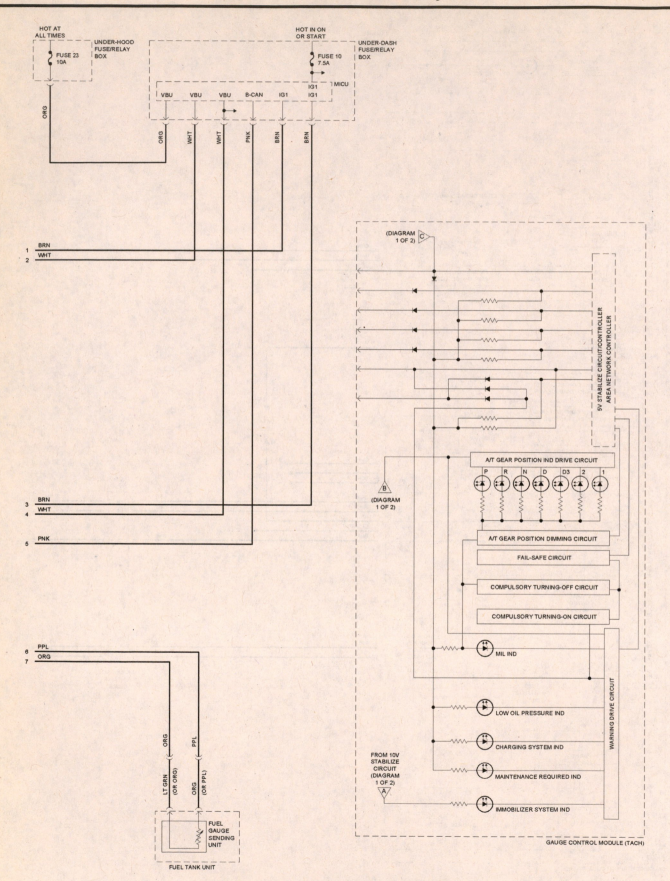

Warning systems - 1006 and later coupe/sedan (2 of 2)

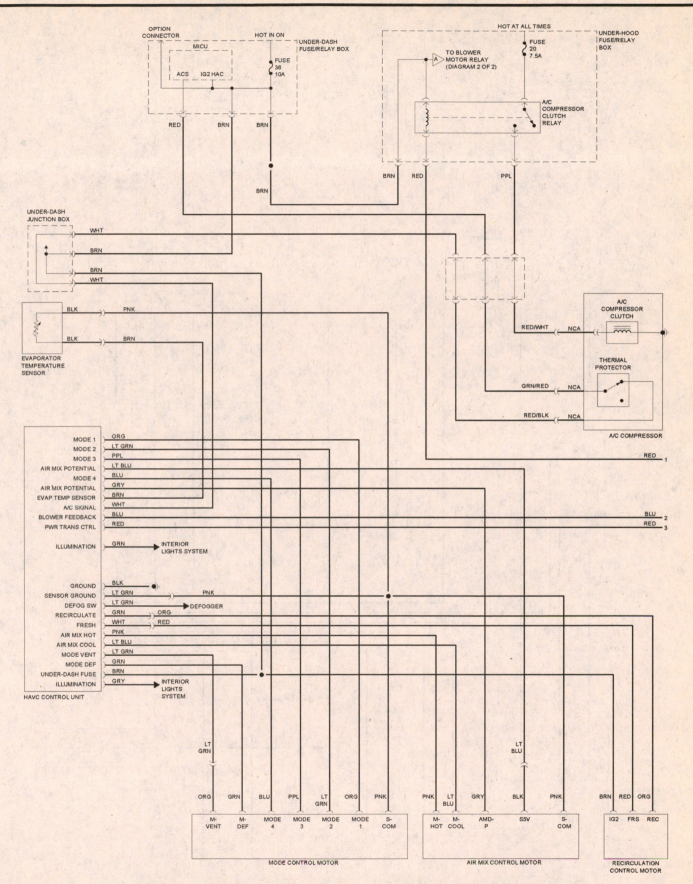

Air conditioning (manual) and engine cooling systems - 2007 and later CR-V (1 of 2)

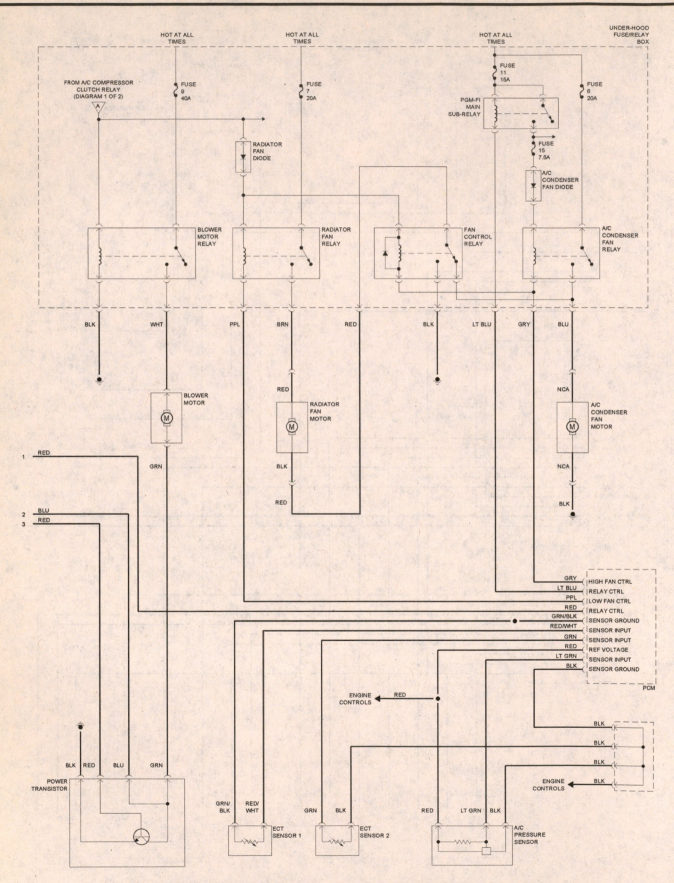

Air conditioning (manual) and engine cooling systems - 2007 and later CR-V (2 of 2)

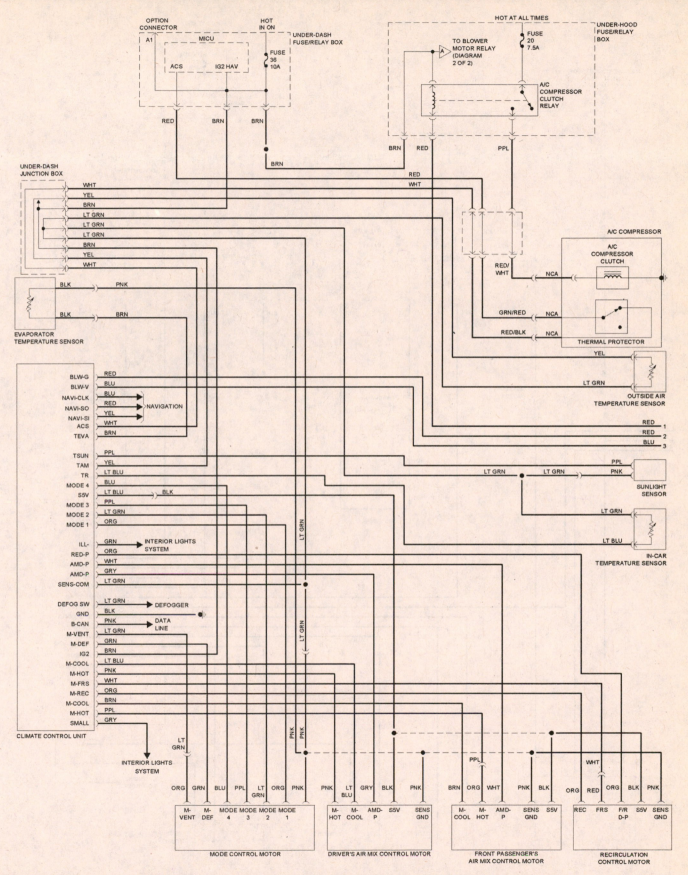

Air conditioning (automatic) and engine cooling systems - 2007 and later CR-V (1 of 2)

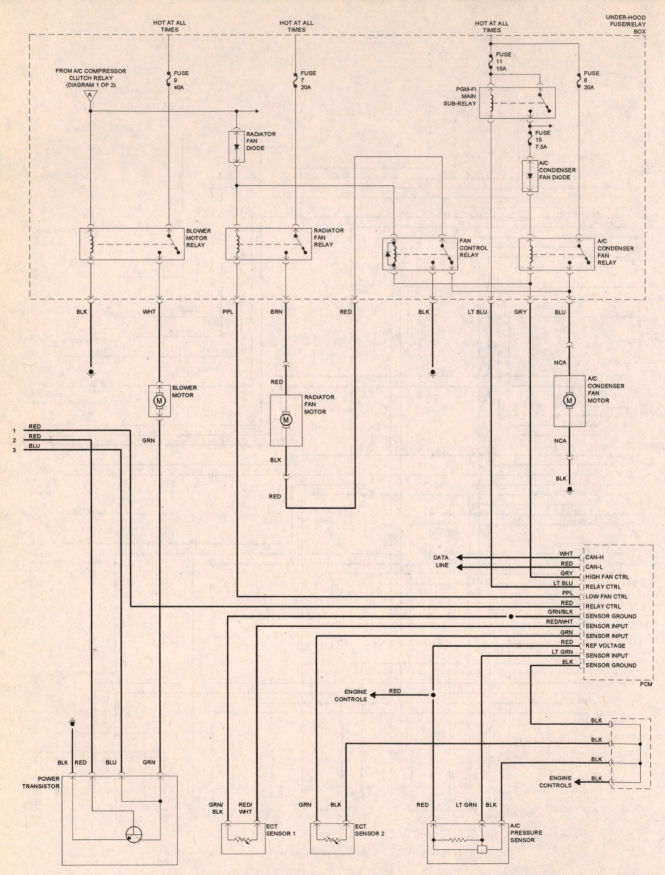

Air conditioning (automatic) and engine cooling systems - 2007 and later CR-V (2 of 2)

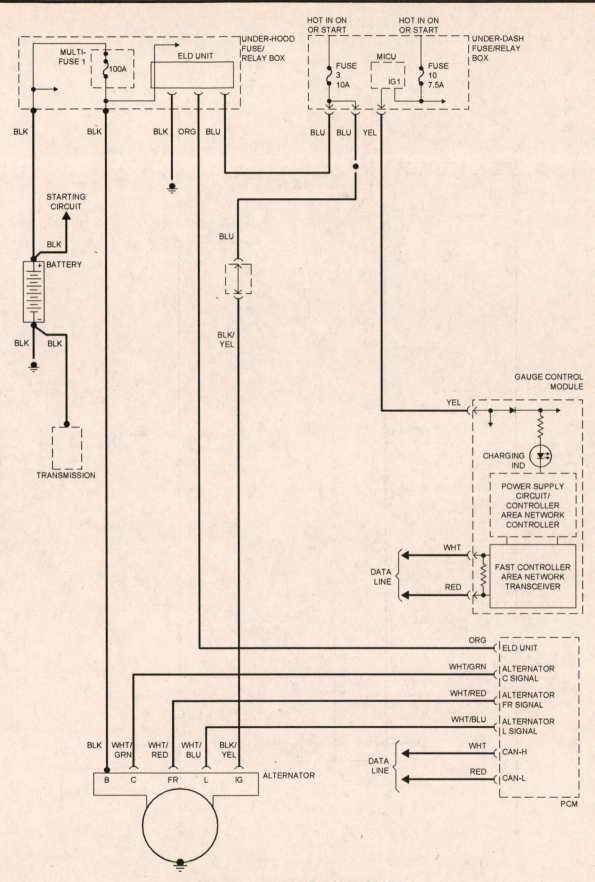

Charging system - 2007 and later CR-V

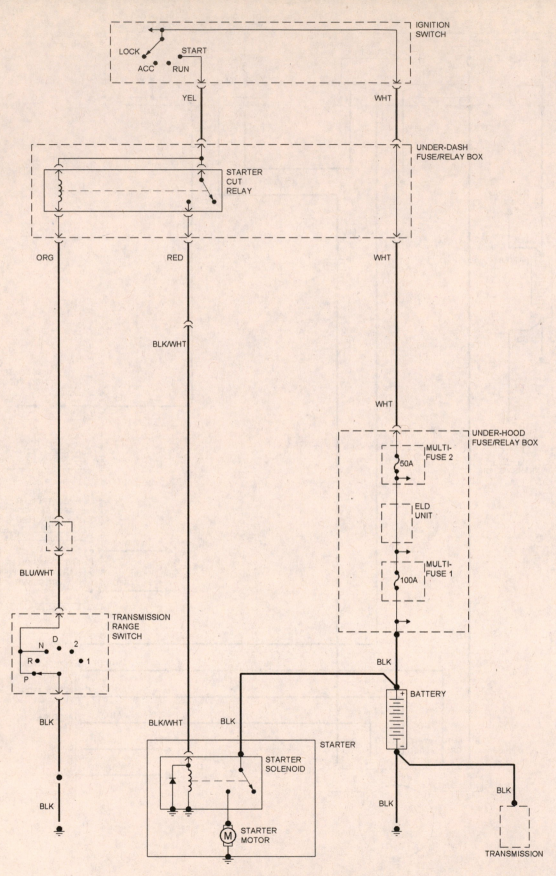

Starting system - 2007 and later CR-V

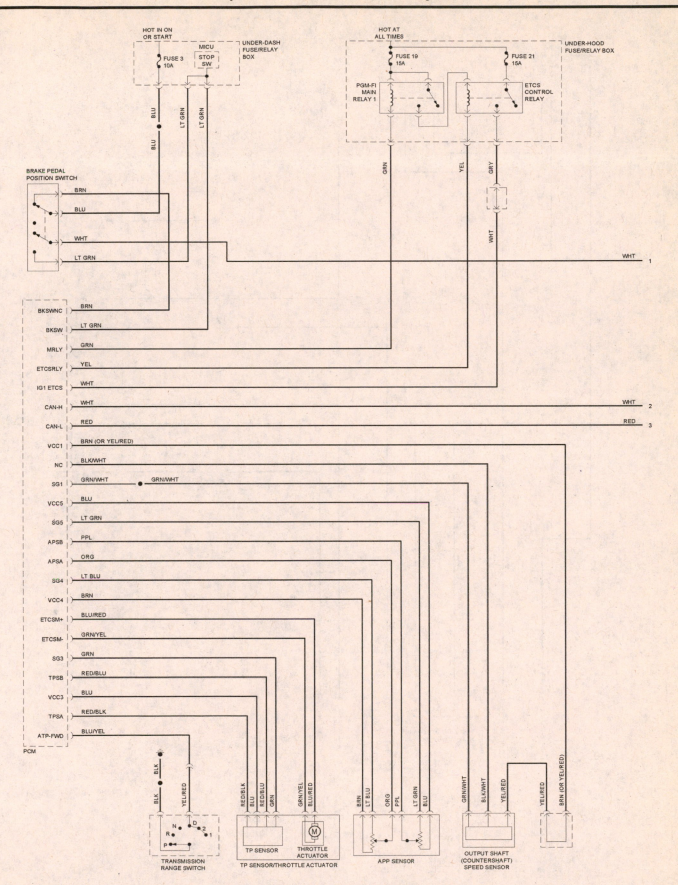

Cruise control system - 2007 and later CR-V (1 of 2)

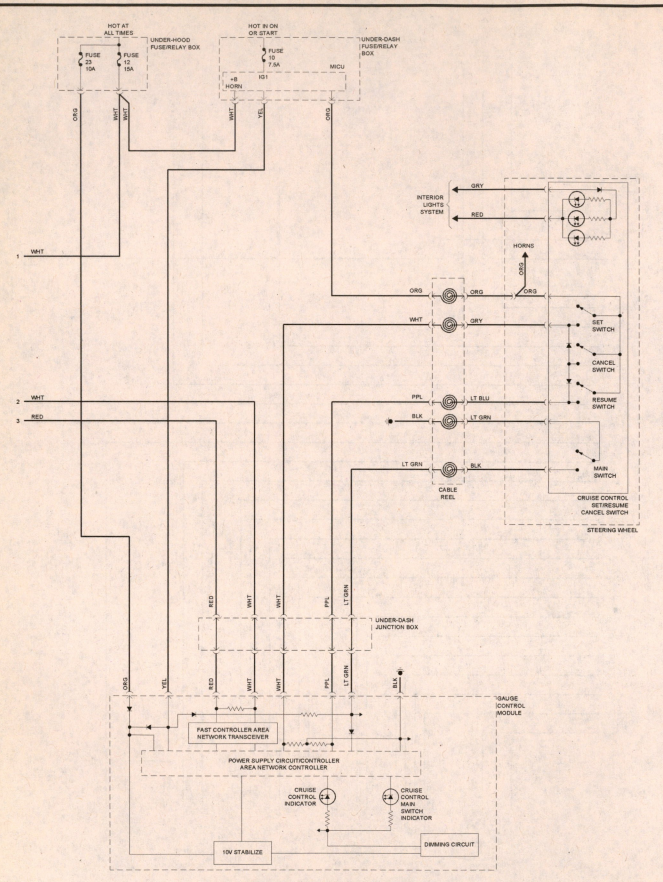

Cruise control system - 2007 and later CR-V (2 of 2)

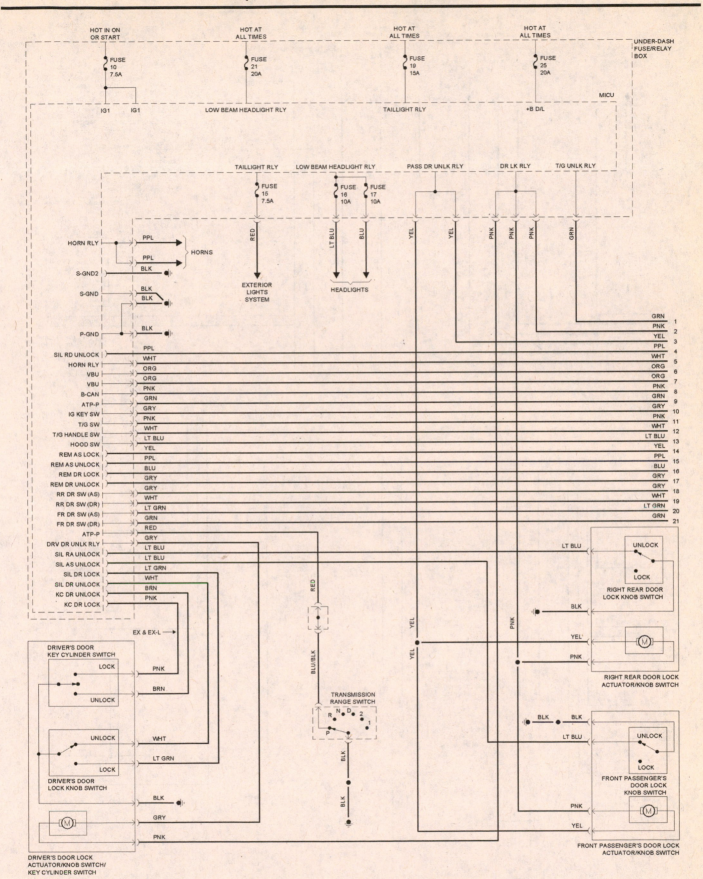

Power door lock system - 2007 and later CR-V (1 of 2)

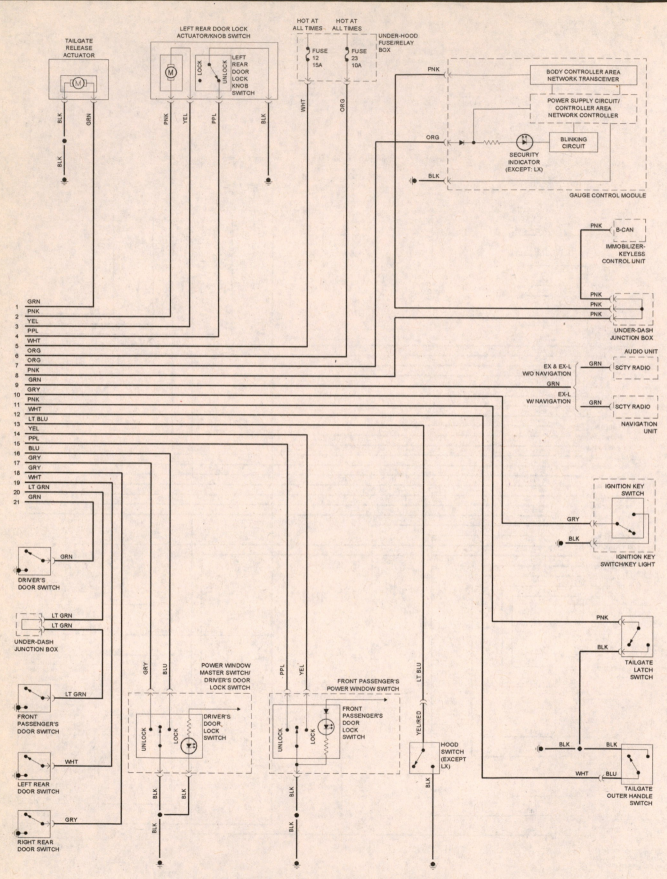

Power door lock system - 2007 and later CR-V (2 of 2)

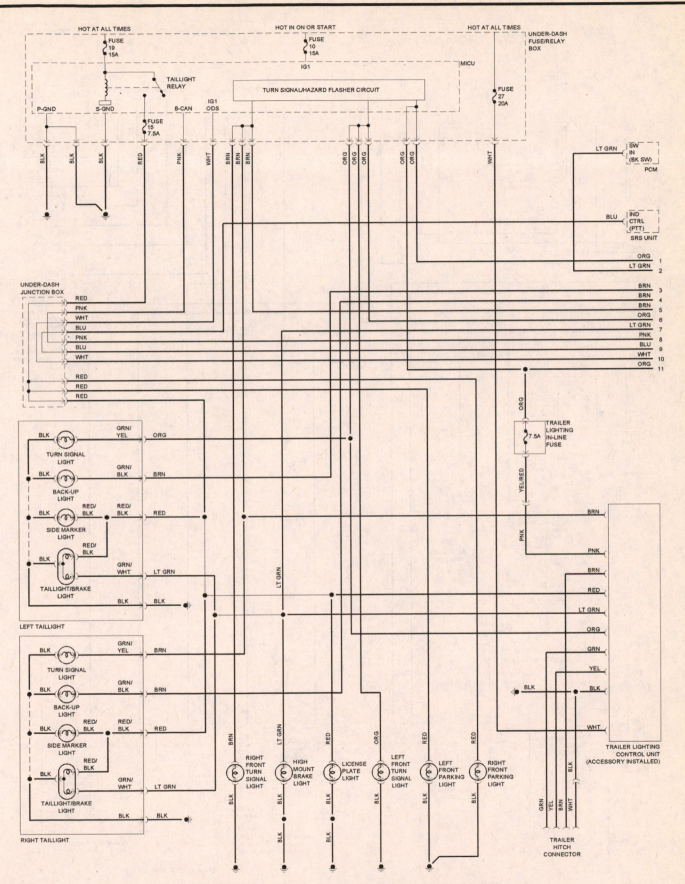

Exterior lighting system (except headlights) - 2007 and later CR-V (1 of 2)

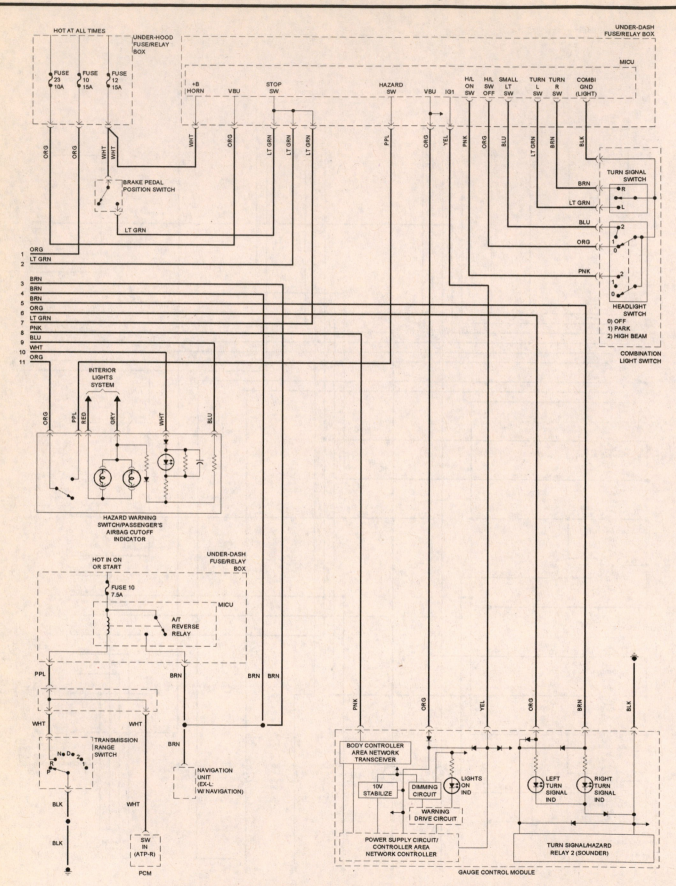

Exterior lighting system (except headlights) - 2007 and later CR-V (2 of 2)

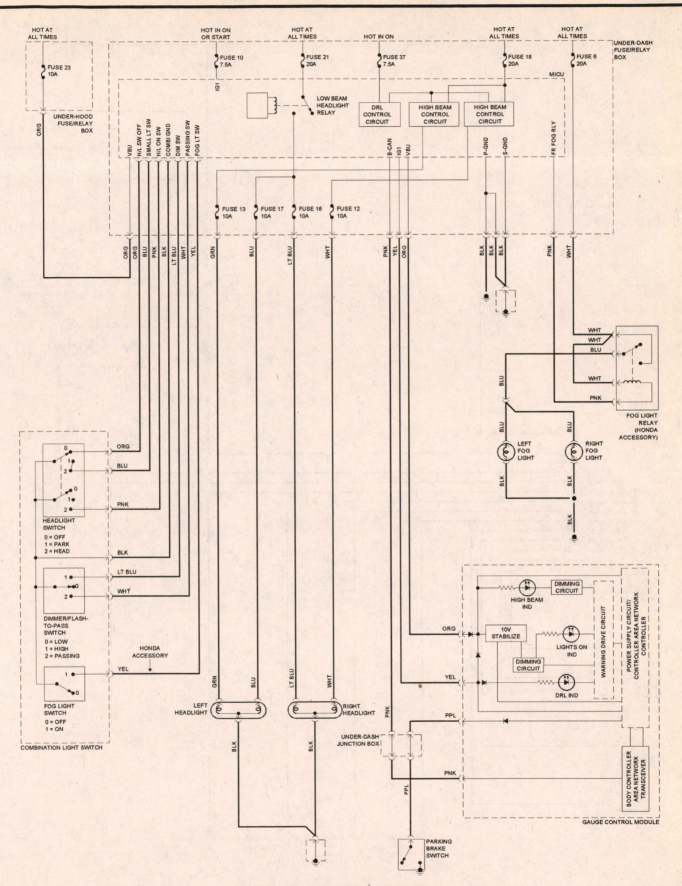

Headlight system - 2007 and later CR-V

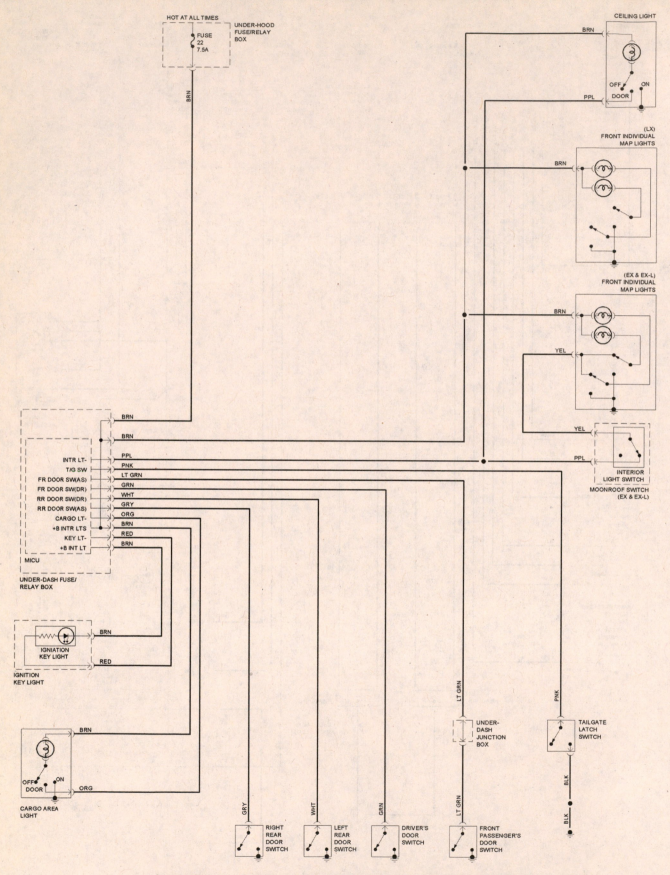

Interior lighting systems, including courtesy lights - 2007 and later CR-V

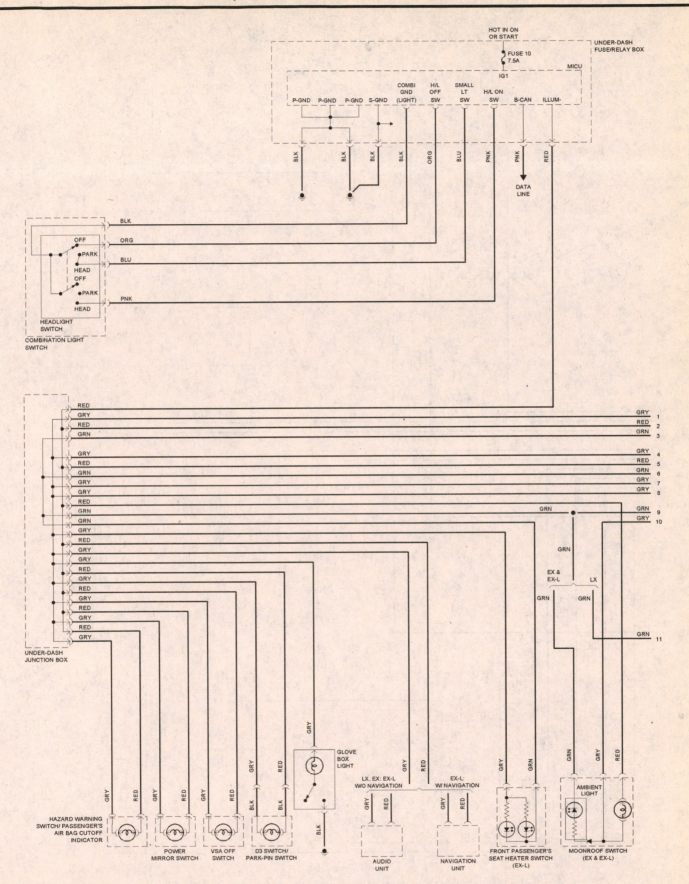

Interior lighting systems, including switch and instrument illumination lights - 2007 and later CR-V (1 of 2)

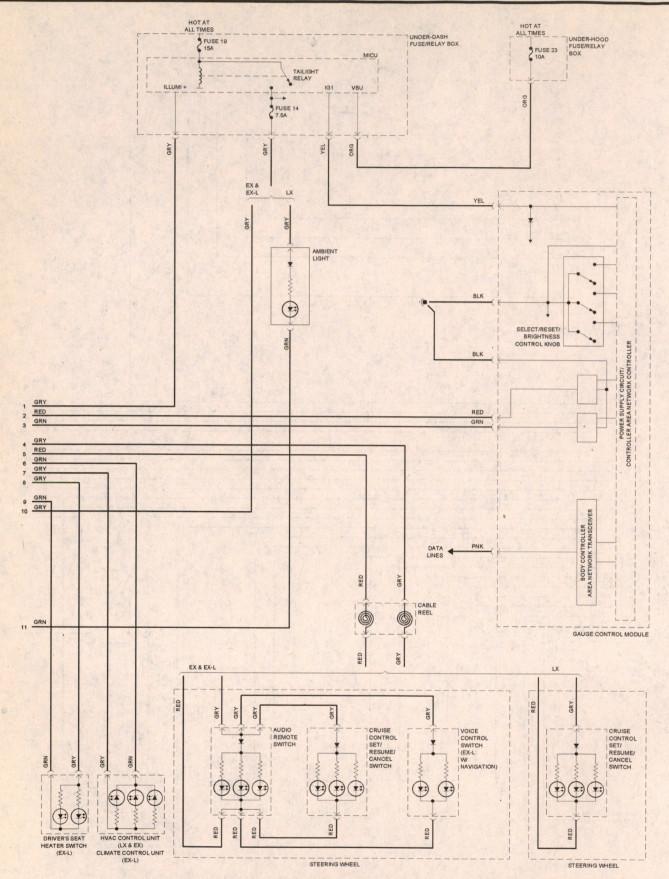

Interior lighting systems, including switch and instrument illumination lights - 2007 and later CR-V (2 of 2)

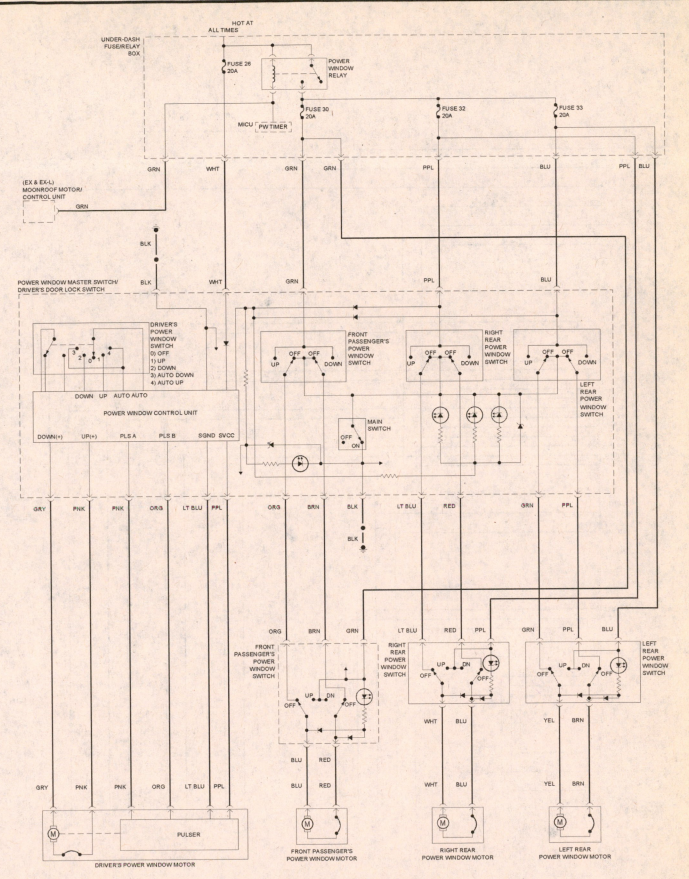

Power window system - 2007 and later CR-V

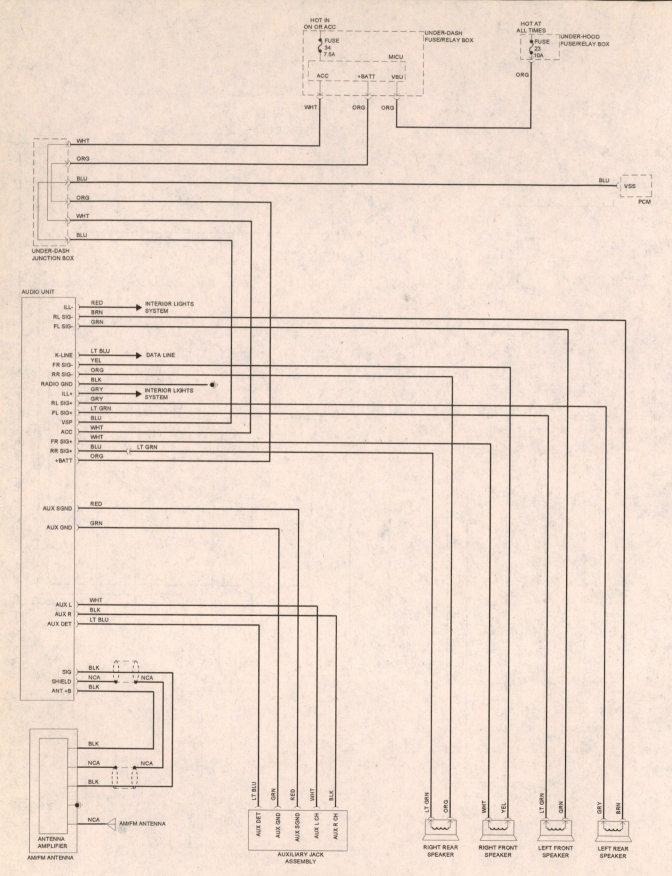

Sound system - 2007 and later CR-V

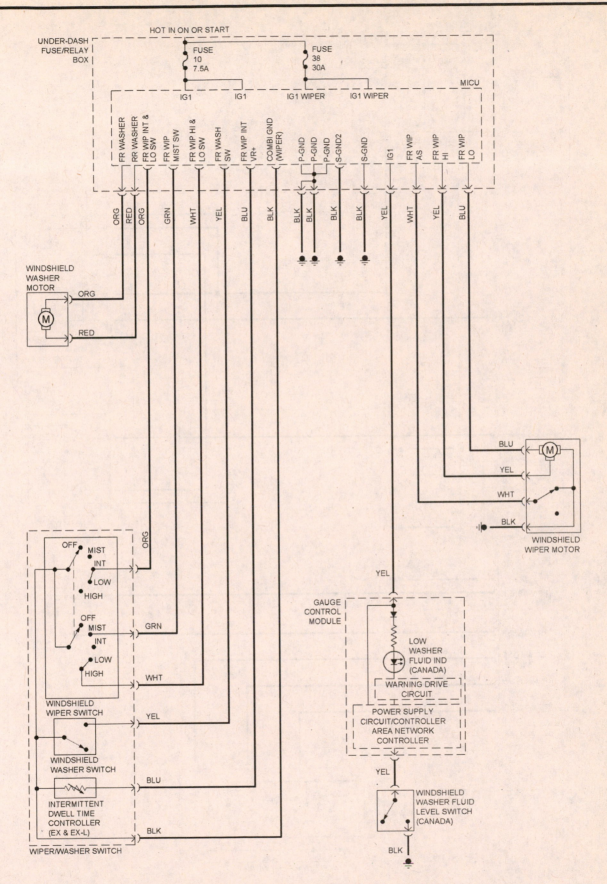

Windshield wiper/washer system - 2007 and later CR-V

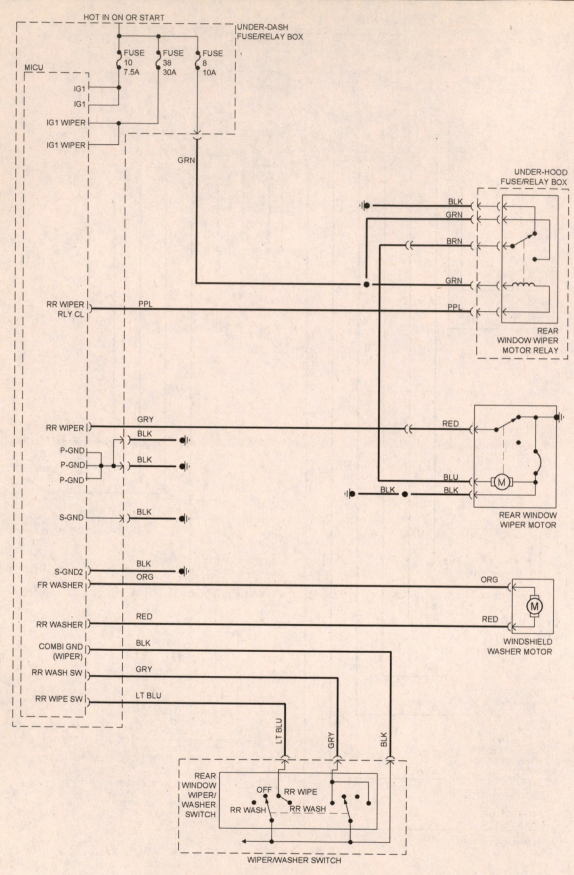

Rear window wiper/washer system - 2007 and later CR-V

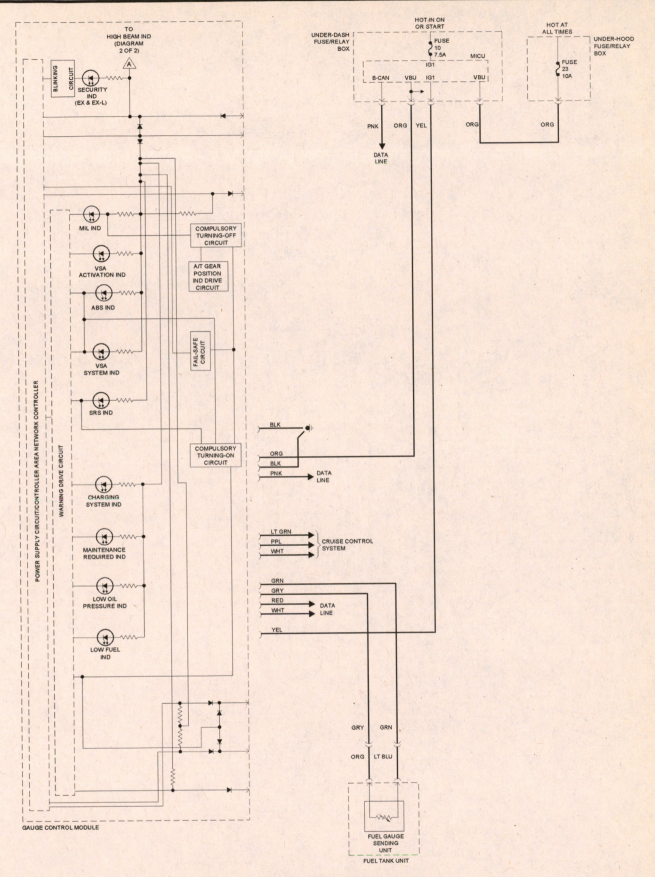

Warning systems - 2007 and later CR-V (1 of 2)

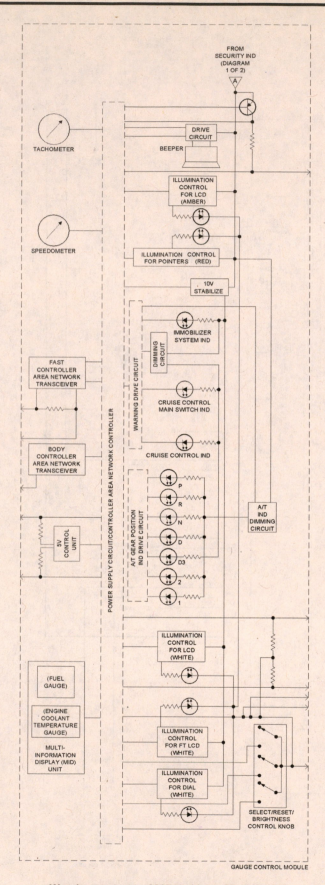

Warning systems - 2007 and later CR-V (2 of 2)

Index

A

About this manual, 0-5
Accelerator cable, removal, installation and adjustment, 4-12
Accelerator Pedal Position (APP) sensor, replacement, 6-11
Acknowledgements, 0-2
Air conditioning
    and heating system, check and maintenance, 3-7
    compressor, removal and installation, 3-18
    condenser, removal and installation, 3-20
    pressure switch, replacement, 3-20
    receiver-drier, removal and installation, 3-19
Air filter
    element, replacement, 1-20
    housing, removal and installation, 4-10
Airbag system, general information, 12-22
Alternator, removal and installation, 5-6
Antenna, removal and installation, 12-12
Anti-lock Brake System (ABS), general information, 9-20
Automatic transaxle
    diagnosis, general, 7B-1
    fluid
        change, 1-28
        level check, 1-11
        type, 1-1

    interlock system, description and solenoid replacment, 7B-5
    overhaul, general information, 7B-7
    removal and installation, 7B-6
    shift
        cable, check, replacement and adjustment, 7B-2
        lever, removal and installation, 7B-4
Automotive chemicals and lubricants, 0-22

B

Back-up light switch, replacement, 7A-2
Balance shaft assembly and balance shafts (DOHC engines), removal, inspection and installation, 2B-10
Battery
    cables, check and replacement, 5-5
    check, maintenance and charging, 1-15
    disconnection and reconnection, 5-5
    removal and installation, 5-5
Blower motor power transistor and blower motor, replacement, 3-15
Body repair
    major damage, 11-3
    minor damage, 11-2
    minor paint scratches, repairing, 11-2
Booster battery (jump) starting, 0-17

Brakes

Anti-lock Brake System (ABS) and Vehicle Stability
Assist (VSA) system, general information, 9-20

caliper, removal and installation, 9-9

disc, inspection, removal and installation, 9-10

drum/parking brake shoes, replacement, 9-11

fluid

change, 1-24

level check, 1-10

type, 1-1

general information, 9-2

hoses and lines, inspection and replacement, 9-16

hydraulic system, bleeding, 9-16

light switch, replacement, 9-19

master cylinder, removal and installation, 9-15

pads, replacement, 9-7

parking brake, adjustment, 9-18

pedal, adjustment, 9-19

power brake booster, removal and installation, 9-17

system check, 1-18

troubleshooting, 9-3

wheel cylinder, removal and installation, 9-14

Bulb replacement, 12-16

Bumper covers, removal and installation, 11-8

Buying parts, 0-11

C

Cabin air filter replacement, 1-21

Cable replacement

accelerator, 4-12

battery, 5-5

fuel door, 11-12

hood release, 11-7

shift cable

automatic transaxle, 7B-2

manual transaxle, 7A-2

trunk release, 11-12

Caliper, disc brake, removal and installation, 9-9

Camshaft Position (CMP) sensor, replacement, 6-12

Camshafts, removal, inspection and installation

DOHC engines, 2B-7

SOHC engines, 2A-16

Capacities, fluids and lubricants, 1-2

Carpets, maintenance, 11-5

Catalytic converter, replacement, 6-21

Center console, removal and installation, 11-17

Chassis electrical system, 12-1

Chemicals and lubricants, 0-22

Circuit breakers, general information, 12-3

Clutch

components, removal, inspection and installation, 8-3

description and check, 8-2

fluid

level check, 1-10

type, 1-1

hydraulic system, bleeding, 8-3

master cylinder, removal and installation, 8-2

pedal adjustment, 8-5

release bearing and lever, removal, inspection and
installation, 8-5

release cylinder, removal and installation, 8-2

start switch, check and replacement, 8-6

**Coil spring (rear, 2006 and later Civics), removal
and installation, 10-9**

Coils, ignition, replacement, 5-6

**Compressor, air conditioning, removal and
installation, 3-18**

**Condenser, air conditioning, removal and
installation, 3-20**

**Continuously Variable Transaxle (CVT), removal
and installation, 7B-6**

Control arm (front), removal and installation, 10-7

Conversion factors, 0-20

Coolant

level check, 1-10

reservoir, removal and installation, 3-13

Temperature (ECT) sensor(s), replacement, 6-13

temperature sending unit, check and replacement, 3-14

type, 1-1

Cooling system

check, 1-16

servicing (draining, flushing and refilling), 1-24

**Cooling, heating and air conditioning systems,
troubleshooting, 3-5**

**Countershaft (output shaft) speed sensor,
replacement, 6-16**

Cowl cover, removal and installation, 11-10

Crankshaft front oil seal, replacement

DOHC engines, 2B-6

SOHC engines, 2A-15

Crankshaft Position (CKP) sensor, replacement, 6-12

Crankshaft pulley, replacement

DOHC engines, 2B-6

SOHC engines, 2A-15

Crankshaft, removal and installation, 2C-14

Cruise control system, general information, 12-22

Cylinder compression check, 2C-4

Cylinder head, removal and installation

DOHC engines, 2B-9

SOHC engines, 2A-17

D

Dashboard trim panels, removal and installation, 11-18

Defogger, rear window, check and repair, 12-12

Diagnosis, 0-23

**Diagnostic Trouble Codes (DTCs), obtaining
and clearing, 6-5**
Differential, rear (CR-V)
lubricant
change, 1-25
level check, 1-12
type, 1-1
oil seals, replacement, 8-11
removal and installation, 8-12
Disc brake
caliper, removal and installation, 9-9
disc, inspection, removal and installation, 9-10
pads, replacement, 9-7
Disconnecting quick-connect fuel line fittings, 4-5
Door
latch, lock cylinder and handles, removal and
installation, 11-15
removal, installation and adjustment, 11-14
trim panels, removal and installation, 11-12
window glass regulator, removal and installation, 11-16
window glass, removal and installation, 11-16
Double overhead camshaft (DOHC) engines
balance shaft assembly and balance shafts, removal,
inspection and installation, 2B-10
camshafts and rocker arms, removal, inspection
and installation, 2B-7
crankshaft pulley and front oil seal, removal and
installation, 2B-6
cylinder head, removal and installation, 2B-9
exhaust manifold, removal and installation, 2B-4
flywheel/driveplate, removal and installation, 2B-11
intake manifold, removal and installation, 2B-4
i-VTEC system, description and component checks, 2B-7
mounts, check and replacement, 2B-11
oil pan, removal and installation, 2B-9
oil pump, removal, inspection and installation, 2B-10
rear main oil seal, replacement, 2B-11
repair operations possible with the engine in
the vehicle, 2B-3
timing chain and sprockets, removal, inspection and
installation, 2B-5
timing chain cover, removal and installation, 2B-5
Top Dead Center (TDC) for number 1 piston,
locating, 2B-4
valve cover, removal and installation, 2B-4
Driveaxle
boot check, 1-19
boot, replacement, 8-7
oil seals (manual transaxle), replacement, 7A-1
removal and installation, 8-6
Drivebelt
check, adjustment and replacement, 1-22
tensioner, replacement, 1-24
Driveplate, removal and installation
DOHC engines, 2B-11
SOHC engines, 2A-21

**Driveshaft (4WD CR-V models), removal and
installation, 8-10**
Drum/parking brake shoes, replacement, 9-11

E

Electrical connectors, general information, 12-4
Electrical troubleshooting, general information, 12-1
**Electronic throttle components (2005 and 2006 CR-V),
replacement, 4-18**
Emissions and engine control systems, 6-1
**Engine Coolant Temperature (ECT) sensor(s),
replacement, 6-13**
Engine coolant, level check, 1-10
**Engine cooling fans and switch, removal and
installation, 3-11**
Engine electrical systems
general information and precautions, 5-1
troubleshooting, 5-3
Engine mounts, check and replacement
DOHC engines, 2B-11
SOHC engines, 2A-21
Engine oil
and oil filter change, 1-13
life indicator, resetting, 1-14
level check, 1-9
type and viscosity, 1-1
Engine overhaul
disassembly sequence, 2C-8
reassembly sequence, 2C-16
Engine rebuilding alternatives, 2C-6
Engine removal, methods and precautions, 2C-6
Engine, general overhaul procedures
crankshaft, removal and installation, 2C-14
cylinder compression check, 2C-4
engine overhaul
disassembly sequence, 2C-8
reassembly sequence, 2C-16
engine rebuilding alternatives, 2C-6
engine removal, methods and precautions, 2C-6
engine, removal and installation, 2C-7
initial start-up and break-in after overhaul, 2C-16
oil pressure check, 2C-4
pistons and connecting rods, removal and
installation, 2C-9
vacuum gauge diagnostic checks, 2C-5
Engine, in-vehicle repair procedures
Double overhead camshaft (DOHC) engines
balance shaft assembly and balance shafts,
removal, inspection and installation, 2B-10
camshafts and rocker arms, removal, inspection
and installation, 2B-7
crankshaft pulley and front oil seal, removal and
installation, 2B-6
cylinder head, removal and installation, 2B-9

exhaust manifold, removal and installation, 2B-4
flywheel/driveplate, removal and installation, 2B-11
intake manifold, removal and installation, 2B-4
i-VTEC system, description and component
    checks, 2B-7
mounts, check and replacement, 2B-11
oil pan, removal and installation, 2B-9
oil pump, removal, inspection and installation, 2B-10
rear main oil seal, replacement, 2B-11
repair operations possible with the engine in the
    vehicle, 2B-3
timing chain and sprockets, removal, inspection
    and installation, 2B-5
timing chain cover, removal and installation, 2B-5
Top Dead Center (TDC) for number 1 piston,
    locating, 2B-4
valve cover, removal and installation, 2B-4
Single overhead camshaft (SOHC) engines
camshaft, removal, inspection and installation, 2A-16
crankshaft pulley and front oil seal,
    replacement, 2A-15
cylinder head, removal and installation, 2A-17
exhaust manifold, removal and installation, 2A-7
flywheel/driveplate, removal and installation, 2A-21
intake manifold, removal and installation, 2A-5
mounts, check and replacement, 2A-21
oil pan, removal and installation, 2A-18
oil pump, removal, inspection and
    installation, 2A-20
rear main oil seal, replacement, 2A-21
repair operations possible with the engine in
    the vehicle, 2A-4
rocker arm assembly, removal, inspection and
    installation, 2A-9
timing belt and sprockets (1.7L engines), removal,
    inspection and installation, 2A-12
timing chain and sprockets (1.8L engines),
    removal, inspection and installation, 2A-14
timing chain cover/oil pump housing (1.8L engine),
    removal and installation, 2A-13
Top Dead Center (TDC) for number 1 piston,
    locating, 2A-4
valve cover, removal and installation, 2A-4
VTEC system, description and component
    checks, 2A-8
Engine, removal and installation, 2C-7
**Evaporative emissions control (EVAP) system,
    component replacement, 6-21**
**Exhaust Gas Recirculation (EGR) valve,
    replacement, 6-23**
Exhaust manifold, removal and installation
DOHC engines, 2B-4
SOHC engines, 2A-7
Exhaust system
check, 1-22
servicing, general information, 4-4

F

Fans, engine cooling, removal and installation, 3-11
Fastener and trim removal, 11-5
Fault finding, 0-23
Fender, front, removal and installation, 11-8
Filter replacement
engine air, 1-20
engine oil, 1-13
interior ventilation, 1-21
Firing order, 1-2
Fluid level checks, 1-9
automatic transaxle, 1-11
brake fluid, 1-10
clutch fluid, 1-10
engine coolant, 1-10
engine oil, 1-9
manual transaxle, 1-12
power steering, 1-11
rear differential (CR-V), 1-12
windshield washer, 1-10
Fluids and lubricants
capacities, 1-2
recommended, 1-1
Flywheel/driveplate, removal and installation
DOHC engines, 2B-11
SOHC engines, 2A-21
Fraction/decimal/millimeter equivalents, 0-19
Front hub and bearing assembly, replacement, 10-8
Fuel
fittings, disconnecting, 4-5
general information and precautions, 4-2
lines and fittings, general information and
    disconnection, 4-3
pressure regulator, replacement, 4-6
pressure relief procedure, 4-3
pressure, check, 4-3
pulsation damper, removal and installation, 4-15
pump/fuel filter/fuel gauge sending unit module,
    replacement, 4-8
pump/fuel gauge sending unit module, removal
    and installation, 4-4
rail and injectors, removal and installation, 4-16
system check, 1-21
tank, removal and installation, 4-9
troubleshooting, 4-2
Fuel and exhaust systems, 4-1
Fuses, general information, 12-3
Fusible links, general information, 12-3

G

General engine overhaul procedures
crankshaft, removal and installation, 2C-14
cylinder compression check, 2C-4

engine overhaul
   disassembly sequence, 2C-8
   reassembly sequence, 2C-16
engine rebuilding alternatives, 2C-6
engine removal, methods and precautions, 2C-6
engine, removal and installation, 2C-7
initial start-up and break-in after overhaul, 2C-16
oil pressure check, 2C-4
pistons and connecting rods, removal and
   installation, 2C-9
vacuum gauge diagnostic checks, 2C-5
Grille, radiator, removal and installation, 11-7

H

Headlight
   adjustment, 12-15
   bulb, replacement, 12-14
   housing, replacement, 12-13
Heater core, replacement, 3-17
**Heater/air conditioning control assembly, removal
   and installation, 3-15**
**Heating and air conditioning system, check and
   maintenance, 3-7**
Hood latch and cable, removal and installation, 11-7
Hood, removal, installation and adjustment, 11-6
Horn, replacement, 12-20
Hub and bearing assembly, replacement
   front, 10-8
   rear, 10-11

I

**Idle Air Control (IAC) valve (2005 and earlier Civics,
   2004 and earlier CR-Vs), replacement, 6-20**
Ignition coil(s), replacement, 5-6
Ignition switch and key lock cylinder, replacement, 12-5
Information sensors, 6-4
Initial start-up and break-in after overhaul, 2C-16
Injectors, fuel, removal and installation, 4-16
Input shaft (mainshaft) speed sensor, replacement, 6-14
Instrument
   cluster, removal and installation, 12-9
   panel switches, replacement, 12-6
   panel, removal and installation, 11-22
Intake Air Temperature (IAT) sensor, replacement, 6-13
**Intake Manifold Runner Control (IMRC) system,
   component replacement, 6-20**
**Intake Manifold Tuning (IMT) system, component
   replacement, 6-20**
Intake manifold, removal and installation
   DOHC engines, 2B-4
   SOHC engines, 2A-5

Interior ventilation filter replacement, 1-21
**Interlock system (automatic transaxle), description
   and solenoid replacement, 7B-5**
Introduction, 0-5
**i-VTEC system, description and component checks
   (DOHC engines), 2B-7**

J

Jacking and towing, 0-18
Jump starting, 0-17

K

Key fob, battery replacement, 12-5
Key lock cylinder and latch, removal and installation
   door, 11-15
   liftgate, 11-10
   tailgate, 11-24
   trunk lid, 11-11
Key lock cylinder, ignition, replacement, 12-5
Knock sensor, replacement, 6-14

L

Liftgate
   and assist strut (CR-V models), removal, installation
      and adjustment, 11-24
   handle, latch and lock cylinder, removal and
      installation, 11-10
   removal, installation and adjustment, 11-10
Lubricants and chemicals, 0-22
Lubricants and fluids
   capacities, 1-2
   recommended, 1-1

M

Maintenance
   schedule, 1-4
   techniques, tools and working facilities, 0-11
**Manifold Absolute Pressure (MAP) sensor,
   replacement, 6-15**
Manual transaxle
   back-up light switch, replacement, 7A-2
   driveaxle oil seals, replacement, 7A-1
   lubricant
      change, 1-28
      level check, 1-12
      type, 1-1

mount, check and replacement, 7A-2
overhaul, general information, 7A-3
removal and installation, 7A-2
shift cables, removal and installation, 7A-2
**Mass Air Flow (MAF)/Intake Air Temperature (IAT)
sensor, replacement, 6-13**
Master cylinder, removal and installation
brake, 9-15
clutch, 8-2
Mirrors, removal and installation, 11-16

O

**Obtaining and clearing Diagnostic Trouble Codes
(DTCs), 6-5**
Oil pan, removal and installation
DOHC engines, 2B-9
SOHC engines, 2A-18
Oil pressure check, 2C-4
Oil pump, removal, inspection and installation
DOHC engines, 2B-10
SOHC engines, 2A-20
Oil, engine
level check, 1-9
type and viscosity, 1-1
On-Board Diagnosis (OBD) system
general description, 6-5
scan tool information, 6-5
**Output shaft (countershaft) speed sensor,
replacement, 6-16**
Oxygen sensors, replacement, 6-16

P

Pads, disc brake, replacement, 9-7
Paint scratches, repairing, 11-2
Parking brake, adjustment, 9-18
Parts, replacement, buying, 0-11
**Pistons and connecting rods, removal and
installation, 2C-9**
**Positive Crankcase Ventilation (PCV) valve,
replacement, 6-24**
Power brake booster, removal and installation, 9-17
Power door lock system, general information, 12-22
Power steering
fluid level check, 1-11
fluid type, 1-1
pump, removal and installation, 10-16
system, bleeding, 10-16
**Power Steering Pressure (PSP) switch,
replacement, 6-17**
Power window control unit, resetting, 5-5
Power window system, general information, 12-22

Powertrain Control Module (PCM)
idle learn procedure, 5-5
removal and installation, 6-18
Pressure regulator, fuel, replacement, 4-6
Pressure switch, air conditioning, replacement, 3-20

Q

Quick-connect fuel line fittings, disconnecting, 4-5

R

Radiator
grille, removal and installation, 11-7
removal and installation, 3-13
Radio and speakers, removal and installation, 12-9
**Rear hub and bearing assembly, removal and
installation, 10-11**
Rear main oil seal, replacement
DOHC engines, 2B-11
SOHC engines, 2A-21
Rear shelf trim panel, removal and installation, 11-25
**Rear tailgate glass and support struts (CR-V models),
removal, installation and adjustment, 11-25**
Rear window defogger, check and repair, 12-12
Recall information, 0-7
**Receiver-drier, air conditioning, removal and
installation, 3-19**
Recommended lubricants and fluids, 1-1
Relays, general information and testing, 12-3
**Release bearing and lever, clutch, removal,
inspection and installation, 8-5**
Release cylinder, clutch, removal and installation, 8-2
Repair of minor paint scratches, 11-2
**Repair operations possible with the engine in
the vehicle**
DOHC engines, 2B-3
SOHC engines, 2A-4
Replacement parts, buying, 0-11
**Rocker arm assembly, removal, inspection and
installation**
DOHC engines, 2B-7
SOHC engines, 2A-9
Rotating the tires, 1-17
Rotor, brake, inspection, removal and installation, 9-10
Routine maintenance schedule, 1-4

S

Safety first!, 0-21
Safety recall information, 0-7
Scan tool information, 6-5
Scheduled maintenance, 1-1
Seat belt check, 1-17

Seats, removal and installation, 11-23
Shift cable, replacement
    automatic transaxle, 7B-2
    manual transaxle, 7A-2
Shift lever (automatic transaxle), removal and installation, 7B-4
Shock absorber (rear, 2006 and later Civics), removal and installation, 10-9
Shock absorber/coil spring assembly (rear), removal, component replacement and installation, 10-8
Shoes, drum/parking brake, replacement, 9-11
Single overhead camshaft (SOHC) engines
    camshaft, removal, inspection and installation, 2A-16
    crankshaft pulley and front oil seal, replacement, 2A-15
    cylinder head, removal and installation, 2A-17
    exhaust manifold, removal and installation, 2A-7
    flywheel/driveplate, removal and installation, 2A-21
    intake manifold, removal and installation, 2A-5
    mounts, check and replacement, 2A-21
    oil pan, removal and installation, 2A-18
    oil pump, removal, inspection and installation, 2A-20
    rear main oil seal, replacement, 2A-21
    repair operations possible with the engine in the vehicle, 2A-4
    rocker arm assembly, removal, inspection and installation, 2A-9
    timing belt and sprockets (1.7L engines), removal, inspection and installation, 2A-12
    timing chain and sprockets (1.8L engines), removal, inspection and installation, 2A-14
    timing chain cover/oil pump housing (1.8L engine), removal and installation, 2A-13
    Top Dead Center (TDC) for number 1 piston, locating, 2A-4
    valve cover, removal and installation, 2A-4
    VTEC system, description and component checks, 2A-8
Slave cylinder, clutch, removal and installation, 8-2
Spare tire, installing, 0-18
Spark plug
    check and replacement, 1-26
    torque, 1-3
    type and gap, 1-2
Speakers, removal and installation, 12-9
Speed sensors, replacement
    input shaft (mainshaft), 6-14
    output shaft (countershaft), 6-16
Stabilizer bar and bushings, removal, inspection and installation
    front, 10-5
    rear, 10-12
Starter motor, removal and installation, 5-8
Steering column
    covers, removal and installation, 11-22
    switches, replacement, 12-5
    removal and installation, 10-14
Steering gear, removal and installation, 10-15

Steering knuckle and hub, removal and installation, 10-8
Steering wheel, removal and installation, 10-12
Steering, suspension and driveaxle boot check, 1-19
Stop light switch, replacement, 9-19
Strut assembly (front), removal, inspection and installation, 10-5
Strut/spring assembly, replacement, 10-6
Subframe, removal and installation, 10-16
Suspension and steering systems, general information, 10-3
Suspension arms (rear) and rear knuckle, removal and installation, 10-10

T

Tailgate
    and assist strut (CR-V models), removal, installation and adjustment, 11-24
    latch, lock cylinder and handle, removal and installation, 11-24
    rear glass and support struts (CR-V models), removal, installation and adjustment, 11-25
Tensioner, drivebelt, replacement, 1-24
Thermostat, check and replacement, 3-10
Throttle body, removal and installation, 4-14
Throttle Position (TP) sensor, replacement, 6-18
Tie-rod ends, removal and installation, 10-14
Timing belt and sprockets (1.7L SOHC engines), removal, inspection and installation, 2A-12
Timing chain and sprockets, removal, inspection and installation
    1.8L SOHC engine, 2A-14
    DOHC engines, 2B-5
Timing chain cover (DOHC engines), removal and installation, 2B-5
Timing chain cover/oil pump housing (1.8L SOHC engine), removal and installation, 2A-13
Tire and tire pressure checks, 1-12
Tire rotation, 1-17
Tire, spare, installing, 0-18
Tools and working facilities, 0-11
Top Dead Center (TDC) for number 1 piston, locating
    DOHC engines, 2B-4
    SOHC engines, 2A-4
Torque specifications
    cylinder head bolts
        Double overhead camshaft (DOHC) engines, 2B-2
        SOHC) engines, 2A-3
    spark plugs, 1-3
    thermostat housing cover bolts, 3-1
    water pump bolts, 3-1
    wheel lug nuts, 1-3
    Other torque specifications can be found in the Chapter that deals with the component being serviced.

Towing, 0-18
Transaxle, automatic
  Continuously Variable Transaxle (CVT), removal and
    installation, 7B-6
  diagnosis, general, 7B-1
  fluid
    change, 1-28
    level check, 1-11
    type, 1-1
  interlock system, description and solenoid
    replacment, 7B-5
  overhaul, general information, 7B-7
  removal and installation, 7B-6
  shift
    cable, check, replacement and adjustment, 7B-2
    lever, removal and installation, 7B-4
Transaxle, manual
  back-up light switch, replacement, 7A-2
  driveaxle oil seals, replacement, 7A-1
  lubricant
    change, 1-28
    level check, 1-12
    type, 1-1
  mount, check and replacement, 7A-2
  overhaul, general information, 7A-3
  removal and installation, 7A-2
  shift cables, removal and installation, 7A-2
Transfer case (4WD CR-V models), removal and
  installation, 8-12
Transmission range switch, replacement and
  adjustment, 6-18
Trim panels, removal and installation
  dashboard, 11-18
  door, 11-12
  rear shelf, 11-25
Trouble codes, obtaining and clearing, 6-5
Troubleshooting, 0-23
  brakes, 9-3
  cooling, heating and air conditioning systems, 3-5
  engine electrical systems, 5-3
  fuel and exhaust systems, 4-2
Trunk lid
  latch and lock cylinder, removal and installation, 11-11
  removal, installation and adjustment, 11-11
Trunk release lever and fuel door cables, removal
  and installation, 11-12
Tune-up and routine maintenance, 1-1
Tune-up general information, 1-5

U
Underhood hose check and replacement, 1-20
Upholstery, maintenance, 11-5

V
Vacuum gauge diagnostic checks, 2C-5
Valve clearance check and adjustment, 1-25
Valve cover, removal and installation
  DOHC engines, 2B-4
  SOHC engines, 2A-4
Variable Valve Timing and Lift Electronic Control
  (VTEC) system, description and component
  replacement, 6-24
Vehicle identification numbers, 0-6
Vehicle Stability Assist (VSA) system, general
  information, 9-20
Vinyl trim, maintenance, 11-5
VTEC system, description and component checks
  (SOHC engines), 2A-8

W
Water pump, replacement, 3-14
Wheel alignment, general information, 10-18
Wheel cylinder, removal and installation, 9-14
Wheels and tires, general information, 10-17
Window glass regulator, removal and
  installation, 11-16
Window glass, door, removal and installation, 11-16
Windshield
  washer fluid, level check, 1-10
  wiper blade inspection and replacement, 1-15
  wiper motor, check and replacement, 12-20
Wiring diagrams, general information, 12-24
Working facilities, 0-11

Haynes Automotive Manuals

NOTE: If you do not see a listing for your vehicle, consult your local Haynes dealer for the latest product information.

ACURA
- **12020** Integra '86 thru '89 & Legend '86 thru '90
- **12021** Integra '90 thru '93 & Legend '91 thru '95
  Integra '94 thru '00 - see HONDA Civic (42025)
  MDX '01 thru '07 - see HONDA Pilot (42037)
- **12050** Acura TL all models '99 thru '08

AMC
  Jeep CJ - see JEEP (50020)
- **14020** Mid-size models '70 thru '83
- **14025** (Renault) Alliance & Encore '83 thru '87

AUDI
- **15020** 4000 all models '80 thru '87
- **15025** 5000 all models '77 thru '83
- **15026** 5000 all models '84 thru '88
  Audi A4 '96 thru '01 - see VW Passat (96023)
- **15030** Audi A4 '02 thru '08

AUSTIN-HEALEY
  Sprite - see MG Midget (66015)

BMW
- **18020** 3/5 Series '82 thru '92
- **18021** 3-Series incl. Z3 models '92 thru '98
- **18022** 3-Series incl. Z4 models '99 thru '05
- **18023** 3-Series '06 thru '10
- **18025** 320i all 4 cyl models '75 thru '83
- **18050** 1500 thru 2002 except Turbo '59 thru '77

BUICK
- **19010** Buick Century '97 thru '05
  Century (front-wheel drive) - see GM (38005)
- **19020** Buick, Oldsmobile & Pontiac Full-size
  (Front-wheel drive) '85 thru '05
  Buick Electra, LeSabre and Park Avenue;
  Oldsmobile Delta 88 Royale, Ninety Eight
  and Regency; Pontiac Bonneville
- **19025** Buick, Oldsmobile & Pontiac Full-size
  (Rear wheel drive) '70 thru '90
  Buick Estate, Electra, LeSabre, Limited,
  Oldsmobile Custom Cruiser, Delta 88,
  Ninety-eight, Pontiac Bonneville,
  Catalina, Grandville, Parisienne
- **19030** Mid-size Regal & Century all rear-drive
  models with V6, V8 and Turbo '74 thru '87
  Regal - see GENERAL MOTORS (38010)
  Riviera - see GENERAL MOTORS (38030)
  Roadmaster - see CHEVROLET (24046)
  Skyhawk - see GENERAL MOTORS (38015)
  Skylark - see GM (38020, 38025)
  Somerset - see GENERAL MOTORS (38025)

CADILLAC
- **21015** CTS & CTS-V '03 thru '12
- **21030** Cadillac Rear Wheel Drive '70 thru '93
  Cimarron - see GENERAL MOTORS (38015)
  DeVille - see GM (38031 & 38032)
  Eldorado - see GM (38030 & 38031)
  Fleetwood - see GM (38031)
  Seville - see GM (38030, 38031 & 38032)

CHEVROLET
- **10305** Chevrolet Engine Overhaul Manual
- **24010** Astro & GMC Safari Mini-vans '85 thru '05
- **24015** Camaro V8 all models '70 thru '81
- **24016** Camaro all models '82 thru '92
- **24017** Camaro & Firebird '93 thru '02
  Cavalier - see GENERAL MOTORS (38016)
  Celebrity - see GENERAL MOTORS (38005)
- **24020** Chevelle, Malibu & El Camino '69 thru '87
- **24024** Chevette & Pontiac T1000 '76 thru '87
  Citation - see GENERAL MOTORS (38020)
- **24027** Colorado & GMC Canyon '04 thru '10
- **24032** Corsica/Beretta all models '87 thru '96
- **24040** Corvette all V8 models '68 thru '82
- **24041** Corvette all models '84 thru '96
- **24045** Full-size Sedans Caprice, Impala, Biscayne,
  Bel Air & Wagons '69 thru '90
- **24046** Impala SS & Caprice and Buick Roadmaster
  '91 thru '96
  Impala '00 thru '05 - see LUMINA (24048)
- **24047** Impala & Monte Carlo all models '06 thru '11
  Lumina '90 thru '94 - see GM (38010)
- **24048** Lumina & Monte Carlo '95 thru '05
  Lumina APV - see GM (38035)
- **24050** Luv Pick-up all 2WD & 4WD '72 thru '82
  Malibu '97 thru '03 - see GM (38026)
- **24055** Monte Carlo all models '70 thru '88
  Monte Carlo '95 thru '01 - see LUMINA (24048)
- **24059** Nova all V8 models '69 thru '79
- **24060** Nova and Geo Prizm '85 thru '92
- **24064** Pick-ups '67 thru '87 - Chevrolet & GMC
- **24065** Pick-ups '88 thru '98 - Chevrolet & GMC
- **24066** Pick-ups '99 thru '06 - Chevrolet & GMC
- **24067** Chevrolet Silverado & GMC Sierra '07 thru '12
- **24070** S-10 & S-15 Pick-ups '82 thru '93,
  Blazer & Jimmy '83 thru '94,
- **24071** S-10 & Sonoma Pick-ups '94 thru '04, includ-
  ing Blazer, Jimmy & Hombre
- **24072** Chevrolet TrailBlazer, GMC Envoy &
  Oldsmobile Bravada '02 thru '09
- **24075** Sprint '85 thru '88 & Geo Metro '89 thru '01
- **24080** Vans - Chevrolet & GMC '68 thru '96
- **24081** Chevrolet Express & GMC Savana
  Full-size Vans '96 thru '10

CHRYSLER
- **10310** Chrysler Engine Overhaul Manual
- **25015** Chrysler Cirrus, Dodge Stratus,
  Plymouth Breeze '95 thru '00
- **25020** Full-size Front-Wheel Drive '88 thru '93
  K-Cars - see DODGE Aries (30008)
  Laser - see DODGE Daytona (30030)
- **25025** Chrysler LHS, Concorde, New Yorker,
  Dodge Intrepid, Eagle Vision, '93 thru '97
- **25026** Chrysler LHS, Concorde, 300M,
  Dodge Intrepid, '98 thru '04
- **25027** Chrysler 300, Dodge Charger &
  Magnum '05 thru '09
- **25030** Chrysler & Plymouth Mid-size
  front wheel drive '82 thru '95
  Rear-wheel Drive - see Dodge (30050)
- **25035** PT Cruiser all models '01 thru '10
- **25040** Chrysler Sebring '95 thru '06, Dodge Stratus
  '01 thru '06, Dodge Avenger '95 thru '00

DATSUN
- **28005** 200SX all models '80 thru '83
- **28007** B-210 all models '73 thru '78
- **28009** 210 all models '79 thru '82
- **28012** 240Z, 260Z & 280Z Coupe '70 thru '78
- **28014** 280ZX Coupe & 2+2 '79 thru '83
  300ZX - see NISSAN (72010)
- **28018** 510 & PL521 Pick-up '68 thru '73
- **28020** 510 all models '78 thru '81
- **28022** 620 Series Pick-up all models '73 thru '79
  720 Series Pick-up - see NISSAN (72030)
- **28025** 810/Maxima all gasoline models '77 thru '84

DODGE
  400 & 600 - see CHRYSLER (25030)
- **30008** Aries & Plymouth Reliant '81 thru '89
- **30010** Caravan & Plymouth Voyager '84 thru '95
- **30011** Caravan & Plymouth Voyager '96 thru '02
- **30012** Challenger/Plymouth Saporro '78 thru '83
- **30013** Caravan, Chrysler Voyager, Town &
  Country '03 thru '07
- **30016** Colt & Plymouth Champ '78 thru '87
- **30020** Dakota Pick-ups all models '87 thru '96
- **30021** Durango '98 & '99, Dakota '97 thru '99
- **30022** Durango '00 thru '03 Dakota '00 thru '04
- **30023** Durango '04 thru '09, Dakota '05 thru '11
- **30025** Dart, Demon, Plymouth Barracuda,
  Duster & Valiant 6 cyl models '67 thru '76
- **30030** Daytona & Chrysler Laser '84 thru '89
  Intrepid - see CHRYSLER (25025, 25026)
- **30034** Neon all models '95 thru '99
- **30035** Omni & Plymouth Horizon '78 thru '90
- **30036** Dodge and Plymouth Neon '00 thru '05
- **30040** Pick-ups all full-size models '74 thru '93
- **30041** Pick-ups all full-size models '94 thru '01
- **30042** Pick-ups full-size models '02 thru '08
- **30045** Ram 50/D50 Pick-ups & Raider and
  Plymouth Arrow Pick-ups '79 thru '93
- **30050** Dodge/Plymouth/Chrysler RWD '71 thru '89
- **30055** Shadow & Plymouth Sundance '87 thru '94
- **30060** Spirit & Plymouth Acclaim '89 thru '95
- **30065** Vans - Dodge & Plymouth '71 thru '03

EAGLE
  Talon - see MITSUBISHI (68030, 68031)
  Vision - see CHRYSLER (25025)

FIAT
- **34010** 124 Sport Coupe & Spider '68 thru '78
- **34025** X1/9 all models '74 thru '80

FORD
- **10320** Ford Engine Overhaul Manual
- **10355** Ford Automatic Transmission Overhaul
- **11500** Mustang '64-1/2 thru '70 Restoration Guide
- **36004** Aerostar Mini-vans all models '86 thru '97
- **36006** Contour & Mercury Mystique '95 thru '00
- **36008** Courier Pick-up all models '72 thru '82
- **36012** Crown Victoria & Mercury Grand
  Marquis '88 thru '10
- **36016** Escort/Mercury Lynx all models '81 thru '90
- **36020** Escort/Mercury Tracer '91 thru '02
- **36022** Escape & Mazda Tribute '01 thru '11
- **36024** Explorer & Mazda Navajo '91 thru '01
- **36025** Explorer/Mercury Mountaineer '02 thru '10
- **36028** Fairmont & Mercury Zephyr '78 thru '83
- **36030** Festiva & Aspire '88 thru '97
- **36032** Fiesta all models '77 thru '80
- **36034** Focus all models '00 thru '11
- **36036** Ford & Mercury Full-size '75 thru '87
- **36044** Ford & Mercury Mid-size '75 thru '86
- **36045** Fusion & Mercury Milan '06 thru '10
- **36048** Mustang V8 all models '64-1/2 thru '73
- **36049** Mustang II 4 cyl, V6 & V8 models '74 thru '78
- **36050** Mustang & Mercury Capri '79 thru '93
- **36051** Mustang all models '94 thru '04
- **36052** Mustang '05 thru '10
- **36054** Pick-ups & Bronco '73 thru '79
- **36058** Pick-ups & Bronco '80 thru '96
- **36059** F-150 & Expedition '97 thru '09, F-250 '97
  thru '99 & Lincoln Navigator '98 thru '09
- **36060** Super Duty Pick-ups, Excursion '99 thru '10
- **36061** F-150 full-size '04 thru '10
- **36062** Pinto & Mercury Bobcat '75 thru '80
- **36066** Probe all models '89 thru '92
  Probe '93 thru '97 - see MAZDA 626 (61042)
- **36070** Ranger/Bronco II gasoline models '83 thru '92
- **36071** Ranger '93 thru '10 & Mazda Pick-ups '94 thru '09
- **36074** Taurus & Mercury Sable '86 thru '95
- **36075** Taurus & Mercury Sable '96 thru '05
- **36078** Tempo & Mercury Topaz '84 thru '94
- **36082** Thunderbird/Mercury Cougar '83 thru '88
- **36086** Thunderbird/Mercury Cougar '89 thru '97
- **36090** Vans all V8 Econoline models '69 thru '91
- **36094** Vans full size '92 thru '10
- **36097** Windstar Mini-van '95 thru '07

GENERAL MOTORS
- **10360** GM Automatic Transmission Overhaul
- **38005** Buick Century, Chevrolet Celebrity,
  Oldsmobile Cutlass Ciera & Pontiac 6000
  all models '82 thru '96
- **38010** Buick Regal, Chevrolet Lumina,
  Oldsmobile Cutlass Supreme &
  Pontiac Grand Prix (FWD) '88 thru '07
- **38015** Buick Skyhawk, Cadillac Cimarron,
  Chevrolet Cavalier, Oldsmobile Firenza &
  Pontiac J-2000 & Sunbird '82 thru '94
- **38016** Chevrolet Cavalier &
  Pontiac Sunfire '95 thru '05
- **38017** Chevrolet Cobalt & Pontiac G5 '05 thru '11
- **38020** Buick Skylark, Chevrolet Citation,
  Olds Omega, Pontiac Phoenix '80 thru '85
- **38025** Buick Skylark & Somerset,
  Oldsmobile Achieva & Calais and
  Pontiac Grand Am all models '85 thru '98
- **38026** Chevrolet Malibu, Olds Alero & Cutlass,
  Pontiac Grand Am '97 thru '03
- **38027** Chevrolet Malibu '04 thru '10
- **38030** Cadillac Eldorado, Seville, Oldsmobile
  Toronado, Buick Riviera '71 thru '85
- **38031** Cadillac Eldorado & Seville, DeVille, Fleetwood
  & Olds Toronado, Buick Riviera '86 thru '93
- **38032** Cadillac DeVille '94 thru '05 & Seville '92 thru '04
  Cadillac DTS '06 thru '10
- **38035** Chevrolet Lumina APV, Olds Silhouette
  & Pontiac Trans Sport all models '90 thru '96
- **38036** Chevrolet Venture, Olds Silhouette,
  Pontiac Trans Sport & Montana '97 thru '05
  General Motors Full-size
  Rear-wheel drive - see BUICK (19025)
- **38040** Chevrolet Equinox '05 thru '09 Pontiac
  Torrent '06 thru '09
- **38070** Chevrolet HHR '06 thru '11

GEO
  Metro - see CHEVROLET Sprint (24075)
  Prizm - '85 thru '92 see CHEVY (24060),
  '93 thru '02 see TOYOTA Corolla (92036)
- **40030** Storm all models '90 thru '93
  Tracker - see SUZUKI Samurai (90010)

GMC
  Vans & Pick-ups - see CHEVROLET

HONDA
- **42010** Accord CVCC all models '76 thru '83
- **42011** Accord all models '84 thru '89
- **42012** Accord all models '90 thru '93
- **42013** Accord all models '94 thru '97
- **42014** Accord all models '98 thru '02
- **42015** Accord '03 thru '07
- **42020** Civic 1200 all models '73 thru '79
- **42021** Civic 1300 & 1500 CVCC '80 thru '83
- **42022** Civic 1500 CVCC all models '75 thru '79

(Continued on other side)

NOTE: If you do not see a listing for your vehicle, consult your local Haynes dealer for the latest product information.

42023 **Civic** all models '84 thru '91
42024 **Civic & del Sol** '92 thru '95
42025 **Civic** '96 thru '00, **CR-V** '97 thru '01,
     Acura Integra '94 thru '00
42026 **Civic** '01 thru '10, **CR-V** '02 thru '09
42035 **Odyssey** all models '99 thru '10
     Passport - see ISUZU Rodeo (47017)
42037 **Honda Pilot** '03 thru '07, **Acura MDX** '01 thru '07
42040 **Prelude CVCC** all models '79 thru '89

HYUNDAI
43010 **Elantra** all models '96 thru '10
43015 **Excel & Accent** all models '86 thru '09
43050 **Santa Fe** all models '01 thru '06
43055 **Sonata** all models '99 thru '08

INFINITI
     G35 '03 thru '08 - see NISSAN 350Z (72011)

ISUZU
     Hombre - see CHEVROLET S-10 (24071)
47017 **Rodeo, Amigo & Honda Passport** '89 thru '02
47020 **Trooper & Pick-up** '81 thru '93

JAGUAR
49010 **XJ6** all 6 cyl models '68 thru '86
49011 **XJ6** all models '88 thru '94
49015 **XJ12 & XJS** all 12 cyl models '72 thru '85

JEEP
50010 **Cherokee, Comanche & Wagoneer Limited**
     all models '84 thru '01
50020 **CJ** all models '49 thru '86
50025 **Grand Cherokee** all models '93 thru '04
50026 **Grand Cherokee** '05 thru '09
50029 **Grand Wagoneer & Pick-up** '72 thru '91
     Grand Wagoneer '84 thru '91, Cherokee &
     Wagoneer '72 thru '83, Pick-up '72 thru '88
50030 **Wrangler** all models '87 thru '11
50035 **Liberty** '02 thru '07

KIA
54050 **Optima** '01 thru '10
54070 **Sephia** '94 thru '01, **Spectra** '00 thru '09,
     Sportage '05 thru '10

LEXUS
     ES 300/330 - see TOYOTA Camry (92007) (92008)
     RX 330 - see TOYOTA Highlander (92095)

LINCOLN
     Navigator - see FORD Pick-up (36059)
59010 **Rear-Wheel Drive** all models '70 thru '10

MAZDA
61010 **GLC Hatchback (rear-wheel drive)** '77 thru '83
61011 **GLC (front-wheel drive)** '81 thru '85
61012 **Mazda3** '04 thru '11
61015 **323 & Protegé** '90 thru '03
61016 **MX-5 Miata** '90 thru '09
61020 **MPV** all models '89 thru '98
     Navajo - see Ford Explorer (36024)
61030 **Pick-ups** '72 thru '93
     Pick-ups '94 thru '00 - see Ford Ranger (36071)
61035 **RX-7** all models '79 thru '85
61036 **RX-7** all models '86 thru '91
61040 **626 (rear-wheel drive)** all models '79 thru '82
61041 **626/MX-6 (front-wheel drive)** '83 thru '92
61042 **626, MX-6/Ford Probe** '93 thru '02
61043 **Mazda6** '03 thru '11

MERCEDES-BENZ
63012 **123 Series Diesel** '76 thru '85
63015 **190 Series** four-cyl gas models, '84 thru '88
63020 **230/250/280** 6 cyl sohc models '68 thru '72
63025 **280 123 Series** gasoline models '77 thru '81
63030 **350 & 450** all models '71 thru '80
63040 **C-Class:** C230/C240/C280/C320/C350 '01 thru '07

MERCURY
64200 **Villager & Nissan Quest** '93 thru '01
     All other titles, see FORD Listing.

MG
66010 **MGB** Roadster & GT Coupe '62 thru '80
66015 **MG Midget, Austin Healey Sprite** '58 thru '80

MINI
67020 **Mini** '02 thru '11

MITSUBISHI
68020 **Cordia, Tredia, Galant, Precis &**
     Mirage '83 thru '93
68030 **Eclipse, Eagle Talon & Ply. Laser** '90 thru '94
68031 **Eclipse** '95 thru '05, **Eagle Talon** '95 thru '98
68035 **Galant** '94 thru '10
68040 **Pick-up** '83 thru '96 & **Montero** '83 thru '93

NISSAN
72010 **300ZX** all models including Turbo '84 thru '89
72011 **350Z & Infiniti G35** all models '03 thru '08
72015 **Altima** all models '93 thru '06
72016 **Altima** '07 thru '10
72020 **Maxima** all models '85 thru '92
72021 **Maxima** all models '93 thru '04
72025 **Murano** '03 thru '10
72030 **Pick-ups** '80 thru '97 **Pathfinder** '87 thru '95
72031 **Frontier Pick-up, Xterra, Pathfinder** '96 thru '04
72032 **Frontier & Xterra** '05 thru '11
72040 **Pulsar** all models '83 thru '86
     Quest - see MERCURY Villager (64200)
72050 **Sentra** all models '82 thru '94
72051 **Sentra & 200SX** all models '95 thru '06
72060 **Stanza** all models '82 thru '90
72070 **Titan pick-ups** '04 thru '10 **Armada** '05 thru '10

OLDSMOBILE
73015 **Cutlass** V6 & V8 gas models '74 thru '88
     For other OLDSMOBILE titles, see BUICK,
     CHEVROLET or GENERAL MOTORS listing.

PLYMOUTH
     For PLYMOUTH titles, see DODGE listing.

PONTIAC
79008 **Fiero** all models '84 thru '88
79018 **Firebird** V8 models except Turbo '70 thru '81
79019 **Firebird** all models '82 thru '92
79025 **G6** all models '05 thru '09
79040 **Mid-size Rear-wheel Drive** '70 thru '87
     Vibe '03 thru '11 - see TOYOTA Matrix (92060)
     For other PONTIAC titles, see BUICK,
     CHEVROLET or GENERAL MOTORS listing.

PORSCHE
80020 **911** except Turbo & Carrera 4 '65 thru '89
80025 **914** all 4 cyl models '69 thru '76
80030 **924** all models including Turbo '76 thru '82
80035 **944** all models including Turbo '83 thru '89

RENAULT
     Alliance & Encore - see AMC (14020)

SAAB
84010 **900** all models including Turbo '79 thru '88

SATURN
87010 **Saturn** all S-series models '91 thru '02
87011 **Saturn Ion** '03 thru '07
87020 **Saturn** all L-series models '00 thru '04
87040 **Saturn VUE** '02 thru '07

SUBARU
89002 **1100, 1300, 1400 & 1600** '71 thru '79
89003 **1600 & 1800** 2WD & 4WD '80 thru '94
89100 **Legacy** all models '90 thru '99
89101 **Legacy & Forester** '00 thru '06

SUZUKI
90010 **Samurai/Sidekick & Geo Tracker** '86 thru '01

TOYOTA
92005 **Camry** all models '83 thru '91
92006 **Camry** all models '92 thru '96
92007 **Camry, Avalon, Solara, Lexus ES 300** '97 thru '01
92008 **Toyota Camry, Avalon and Solara and**
     Lexus ES 300/330 all models '02 thru '06
92009 **Camry** '07 thru '11
92015 **Celica Rear Wheel Drive** '71 thru '85
92020 **Celica Front Wheel Drive** '86 thru '99
92025 **Celica Supra** all models '79 thru '92
92030 **Corolla** all models '75 thru '79
92032 **Corolla** all rear wheel drive models '80 thru '87
92035 **Corolla** all front wheel drive models '84 thru '92
92036 **Corolla & Geo Prizm** '93 thru '02
92037 **Corolla** models '03 thru '11
92040 **Corolla Tercel** all models '80 thru '82
92045 **Corona** all models '74 thru '82
92050 **Cressida** all models '78 thru '82
92055 **Land Cruiser FJ40, 43, 45, 55** '68 thru '82
92056 **Land Cruiser FJ60, 62, 80, FZJ80** '80 thru '96
92060 **Matrix & Pontiac Vibe** '03 thru '11
92065 **MR2** all models '85 thru '87
92070 **Pick-up** all models '69 thru '78
92075 **Pick-up** all models '79 thru '95
92076 **Tacoma, 4Runner, & T100** '93 thru '04
92077 **Tacoma** all models '05 thru '09
92078 **Tundra** '00 thru '06 & **Sequoia** '01 thru '07
92079 **4Runner** all models '03 thru '09
92080 **Previa** all models '91 thru '95
92081 **Prius** all models '01 thru '08
92082 **RAV4** all models '96 thru '10
92085 **Tercel** all models '87 thru '94
92090 **Sienna** all models '98 thru '09
92095 **Highlander & Lexus RX-330** '99 thru '07

TRIUMPH
94007 **Spitfire** all models '62 thru '81
94010 **TR7** all models '75 thru '81

VW
96008 **Beetle & Karmann Ghia** '54 thru '79
96009 **New Beetle** '98 thru '11
96016 **Rabbit, Jetta, Scirocco & Pick-up** gas
     models '75 thru '92 & Convertible '80 thru '92
96017 **Golf, GTI & Jetta** '93 thru '98, **Cabrio** '95 thru '02
96018 **Golf, GTI, Jetta** '99 thru '05
96019 **Jetta, Rabbit, GTI & Golf** '05 thru '11
96020 **Rabbit, Jetta & Pick-up** diesel '77 thru '84
96023 **Passat** '98 thru '05, **Audi A4** '96 thru '01
96030 **Transporter 1600** all models '68 thru '79
96035 **Transporter 1700, 1800 & 2000** '72 thru '79
96040 **Type 3 1500 & 1600** all models '63 thru '73
96045 **Vanagon** all air-cooled models '80 thru '83

VOLVO
97010 **120, 130 Series & 1800 Sports** '61 thru '73
97015 **140 Series** all models '66 thru '74
97020 **240 Series** all models '76 thru '93
97040 **740 & 760 Series** all models '82 thru '88
97050 **850 Series** all models '93 thru '97

TECHBOOK MANUALS
10205 **Automotive Computer Codes**
10206 **OBD-II & Electronic Engine Management**
10210 **Automotive Emissions Control Manual**
10215 **Fuel Injection Manual** '78 thru '85
10220 **Fuel Injection Manual** '86 thru '99
10225 **Holley Carburetor Manual**
10230 **Rochester Carburetor Manual**
10240 **Weber/Zenith/Stromberg/SU Carburetors**
10305 **Chevrolet Engine Overhaul Manual**
10310 **Chrysler Engine Overhaul Manual**
10320 **Ford Engine Overhaul Manual**
10330 **GM and Ford Diesel Engine Repair Manual**
10333 **Engine Performance Manual**
10340 **Small Engine Repair Manual,** 5 HP & Less
10341 **Small Engine Repair Manual,** 5.5 - 20 HP
10345 **Suspension, Steering & Driveline Manual**
10355 **Ford Automatic Transmission Overhaul**
10360 **GM Automatic Transmission Overhaul**
10405 **Automotive Body Repair & Painting**
10410 **Automotive Brake Manual**
10411 **Automotive Anti-lock Brake (ABS) Systems**
10415 **Automotive Detailing Manual**
10420 **Automotive Electrical Manual**
10425 **Automotive Heating & Air Conditioning**
10430 **Automotive Reference Manual & Dictionary**
10435 **Automotive Tools Manual**
10440 **Used Car Buying Guide**
10445 **Welding Manual**
10450 **ATV Basics**
10452 **Scooters** 50cc to 250cc

SPANISH MANUALS
98903 **Reparación de Carrocería & Pintura**
98904 **Manual de Carburador Modelos**
     Holley & Rochester
98905 **Códigos Automotrices de la Computadora**
98906 **OBD-II & Sistemas de Control Electrónico**
     del Motor
98910 **Frenos Automotriz**
98913 **Electricidad Automotriz**
98915 **Inyección de Combustible** '86 al '99
99040 **Chevrolet & GMC Camionetas** '67 al '87
99041 **Chevrolet & GMC Camionetas** '88 al '98
99042 **Chevrolet & GMC Camionetas**
     Cerradas '68 al '95
99043 **Chevrolet/GMC Camionetas** '94 al '04
99048 **Chevrolet/GMC Camionetas** '99 al '06
99055 **Dodge Caravan & Plymouth Voyager** '84 al '95
99075 **Ford Camionetas y Bronco** '80 al '94
99076 **Ford F-150** '97 al '09
99077 **Ford Camionetas Cerradas** '69 al '91
99088 **Ford Modelos de Tamaño Mediano** '75 al '86
99089 **Ford Camionetas Ranger** '93 al '10
99091 **Ford Taurus & Mercury Sable** '86 al '95
99095 **GM Modelos de Tamaño Grande** '70 al '90
99100 **GM Modelos de Tamaño Mediano** '70 al '88
99106 **Jeep Cherokee, Wagoneer & Comanche**
     '84 al '00
99110 **Nissan Camioneta** '80 al '96, **Pathfinder** '87 al '95
99118 **Nissan Sentra** '82 al '94
99125 **Toyota Camionetas y 4Runner** '79 al '95

Over 100 Haynes
motorcycle manuals
also available

7-12

Haynes North America, Inc., 861 Lawrence Drive, Newbury Park, CA 91320-1514 • (805) 498-6703 • http://www.haynes.com